Freedom's Ferment

PHASES OF AMERICAN SOCIAL HISTORY TO 1860

ALICE FELT TYLER

Freedom's Ferment

PHASES OF AMERICAN SOCIAL HISTORY TO 1860

Essay Index Reprint Series

 BOOKS FOR LIBRARIES PRESS
FREEPORT, NEW YORK

INTERNATIONAL STANDARD BOOK NUMBER:
0-8369-1898-3

LIBRARY OF CONGRESS CATALOG CARD NUMBER:
78-128324

PRINTED IN THE UNITED STATES OF AMERICA

Foreword

Any period of history, any era of man's endeavor to make this world a better place for himself and his children, has a right to be known for its highest aspirations, its loftiest moments, as well as for its futilities, its fads, and its crackpots. The exuberance and optimism of the young American republic and its willingness to listen to every new idea — to believe that because it was new it might be better — made it susceptible to imposture and charlatanry. Holding fast to certain truths, it could not refuse a hearing to half-truths. When science, too, was young and its methods and disciplines were little understood, much that was pseudo-scientific or not scientific at all became glamorous if embellished with the terms of science.

For too long we have paid amused attention to the fads and fancies of the early nineteenth century. Phrenology, hydropathy, mesmerism, health and diet notions, free love, spiritual affinities, and all the other eccentricities of the era have had more than their due share of the limelight. Alongside them were fundamentals of faith, crusades, reforms, and reformers whose effect on American civilization was profound and permanent. The bases of our social history were well laid and deep; there is more than froth in our heritage from the past. The religious movements and the adventures in reform of the early years of the republic were the truly significant activities of the men and women of the age, and they contributed much to the way of life of twentieth-century America.

It is with gratitude that I acknowledge my debt to the friends who have borne with me in my enthusiasm for a past century. The kindest and most long-suffering among them have been the graduate students who have investigated with me the highways and byways of that period, whose findings have supplemented mine, and whose conclusions have confirmed or corrected my own. My gratitude goes, also, to the staff of the University of Minnesota Library, whose cooperation and courtesy have never failed me. And, finally, it is impossible to overestimate, and difficult to express, my sense of indebtedness to Zephyra Shepherd, whose aid in typing, proofreading, and indexing have made such unpleasant necessities endurable.

A. F. T.

v

Table of Contents

List of Illustrations

PART ONE

The Faith of the Young Republic

The time has come when the experiment is to be made whether the world is to be emancipated and rendered happy, or whether the whole creation shall groan and travail together in pain. . . . If it had been the design of Heaven to establish a powerful nation in the full enjoyment of civil and religious liberty, where all the energies of man might find full scope and excitement, on purpose to show the world by one great successful experiment of what man is capable . . . where should such an experiment have been made but in this country! . . . The light of such a hemisphere shall go up to Heaven, it will throw its beams beyond the waves; it will shine into the darkness there, and be comprehended — it will awaken desire, and hope, and effort, and produce revolutions and overturnings until the world is free. . . . Floods have been poured upon the rising flame, but they can no more extinguish it than they can extinguish the flames of Aetna. Still it burns, and still the mountain murmurs; and soon it will explode with voices and thunderings, and great earthquakes. . . . Then will the trumpet of jubilee sound, and earth's debased millions will leap from the dust, and shake off their chains, and cry, "Hosanna to the Son of David!" [1]

With this vision of the future as a new and glorious epoch Lyman Beecher a hundred years ago voiced the exuberant optimism of the young American republic in which he lived. In that time, if ever in American history, the spirit of man seemed free and the individual could assert his independence of choice in matters of faith and theory. The militant democracy of the period was a declaration of faith in man and in the perfectibility of his institutions. The idea of progress so inherent in the American way of life and so much a part of the philosophy of the age was at the same time a challenge to traditional beliefs and institutions and an impetus to experimentation with new theories and humanitarian reforms.

The period was one of restless ferment. An expanding West was beckoning the hungry and dissatisfied to an endless search for the pot of gold. Growing industrialization and urbanization in the East, new means of communication and transportation, new marvels of

I

invention and science, and advance in the mechanization of industry, all were dislocating influences of mounting importance. And increasing immigration was bringing into the country thousands of Europeans who were dissatisfied with the difficult conditions of life in their native lands. Nor did religion place any restraint on the unrest; recurring revivals, emphasis on individual conversion and personal salvation, and the multiplicity of sects, all made religion responsive to the restlessness of the time rather than a calming influence upon it. The pious editors of the writings of a Shaker seeress asserted in their preface to her revelations:

Let any candid people, endowed with a common share of discernment seriously examine the signs of the times, and view the many wonderful events and extraordinary changes that are constantly taking place in the moral religious and political world, as well as in the natural elements, through the operations of Providence, and they cannot but consider the present age as commencing the most extraordinary and momentous era that ever took place on earth.[2]

Each in his own way the citizens of the young republic recognized the ferment of the era and made answer to its challenge. Itinerant revivalists and the most orthodox of clergymen alike responded with missionary zeal. For an influential few transcendentalism proved to be a satisfying reconciliation between the rationalism of their training and the romanticism of the age, while among the less intellectual, adventism, spiritualism, Mormonism, and perfectionism each won adherents who founded churches and preached their creeds with fervor. To these sects were added the cults and communities transplanted from abroad. The combination of religious toleration, overflowing optimism, and cheap lands caused Europeans of unorthodox faith or unusual social ideas to seek asylum in America. Each such sect, each isolated religious community, each social utopia, was an evidence of the tolerant, eclectic spirit of the young republic, and each made its contribution to the culture of the land that gave it sanctuary.

The desire to perfect human institutions was the basic cause for each sect and community, and this same desire lay at the roots of all the many social reform movements of the period. The American reformer was the product of evangelical religion, which presented to every person the necessity for positive action to save his own soul, and dynamic frontier democracy, which was rooted deep in a belief in the worth of the individual. Born of this combination, the reformer considered reform at once his duty and his right, and he did not limit his activities to one phase of social betterment. Education, temperance, universal peace, prison reform, the rights of women, the evils of slavery, the dangers of Catholicism, all were legitimate fields for his efforts.

The American reformer knew that he did not work alone. He recognized that each cause he espoused was a part of a world of progress and aspiration, but peculiarly his was the freedom to experiment, for in his homeland there was room and hospitality for adventure. Happy in his privilege, he acknowledged his duty and accepted for his age the sign of his crusade. It is with him, his quest for perfection, and his faith in his right to be free that this story deals.

The sources for the story are many and varied. Such was the volume of contemporary material on the American scene that one hardy author introduced his own book with these verses:

> O books! books! books! it makes me sick
> To think how ye are multiplied,
> Like Egypt's frogs, ye poke up thick
> Your ugly heads on every side.
>
> If a new thought but shakes its ear
> Or wags its tail, tho' starved it look,
> The world the precious news must hear
> The presses groan, and lo! a book.[3]

In its first half century the United States was visited by scores of curious European travelers who came to investigate the strange new world that was being created in the Western Hemisphere. In their accounts of the experience they praised, or condemned, the institutions and national characteristics spread out before them, seized avidly upon all differences from the European norm, and worried each peculiarity beyond recognition and beyond any just limit of its importance. Americans themselves, with the keen sensitiveness of the young and the boasting enthusiasm natural to vigorous creators of new ideas and institutions, examined the work of their hands and, believing it good, reassured themselves and answered their calumniators in a flood of aggressive replies. Every American interested in a reform movement, a new cult, or a utopian scheme burst into print, adding another to the rapidly growing list of polemic books and pamphlets. From this variety of sources it is possible to recapture something of the inward spirit that gave rise to the more familiar and more tangible events of America's youth.*

* A general bibliography and the bibliographical notes for each chapter are given in a separate section, beginning on page 551.

CHAPTER 1

Dynamic Democracy

It was a long process of democratization, begun before the signing of the Declaration of Independence, accelerated by the Revolution, and continued through the influence of the frontier, that made American society, in the words of the French traveler, Michel Chevalier, in 1834, "essentially and radically a democracy, not in name merely but in deed."[1] At least a brief review of this vigorous, dynamic democracy must precede the story of the manifold movements, theories, and crusades of the early nineteenth century, for which it provided the fundamental background.

COLONIAL BEGINNINGS

It is perhaps doubtful whether the self-exiled Europeans who peopled the American colonies had chosen the braver course in attempting to solve their problems by escape to a new world, but it is impossible to doubt their independence of thought, their vigor of action, and their willingness to work hard to translate their dreams into the reality of new wealth and new institutions. For them the rights of the individual were axiomatic, and self-government was a natural assumption as well as a geographical necessity. Their philosophy was based upon the Calvinistic ideas of the Puritans and the teachings of the great English theorists of the Parliamentarian revolt of the seventeenth century, who had emphasized the importance of the individual and his union with other individuals in organizations based upon mutual consent.

The Calvinism of many of the early settlers tended toward republicanism and was democratic in its implications.[2] The Separatist movement that resulted in the Congregationalism of New England placed further emphasis upon the local church units and the individual members, and Congregationalism found its political counterpart in the New England town meeting, where democracy reached a high level. The followers of Roger Williams, who established both the colony of Rhode Island and the American Baptist church, added an element of great importance to American thinking in their insistence upon the complete separation of church and state and the absolute freedom of the individual to choose for himself in matters of religion. The Quakers of Pennsylvania contributed the pacifism characteristic of their faith and a deep-seated hatred of slavery that was to bear fruit in a later day.

Three thousand miles of sea, to be traversed in colonial days only with the danger and discomfort of a long and tedious voyage, caused the European individual transplanted in America to feel himself separated from his old world. He found it easy to accept the idea of a natural, "absolute, unrelated man" who existed and had acquired property before governments were developed to make demands upon his liberty and property. Since he must combine with other colonists to meet common problems and make use of common opportunities, he accepted without question the idea that government sprang from the people and is the agent of the people. It was natural, therefore, for American political leaders to accept John Locke, the great exponent of English constitutional development, as their spokesman, the interpreter of their ideas of natural laws, individual liberties, and the right of revolution when they were oppressed by an illegitimate use of authority.

The presence of the frontier was of tremendous importance in the development of American ideas of government. Each colony had "back-country" districts that were thinly populated, subject to Indian attacks, and far removed from the political and cultural institutions of the tidewater areas. The individualism of the frontier early came into conflict with the growing authoritarianism of colonial governments, and out of that friction came a continual pressure for further democratization and for greater representation for the newer and poorer districts. At the same time these frontier areas felt little need for formal governmental control and came gradually to believe that, beyond protection from Indian attack or foreign invasion and the securing of the liberties of the individual, there was no reason for elaborate government.

Without benefit of Darwin, survival of the fittest was the law of the frontier, and individual initiative, fortitude, and ability were more important than governmental forms. Owing to the very nature of his life, the frontiersman was a believer in laissez faire doctrines and in the limitation of government to the barest necessities for individual freedom. Neither tidewater aristocracy nor absentee imperial dictation was acceptable to the Westerners of any of the colonies. Although few frontiersmen had ever heard of John Locke, his philosophy was suited to the conditions of frontier life. The gradual development of political and cultural institutions in the tidewater areas served as a bridge between English ideas and forms and the isolation and independence of the frontier, but these institutions were subjected constantly to the leveling influence of frontier equalitarianism.

In the mid-eighteenth century the teachings of the French philosophes were added to this colonial heritage. The doctrines of Rousseau, in so far as they were known, fell upon well-prepared ground, for men closely in contact with nature could have found nothing incongruous in Rousseau's arguments for liberty and equality. Montesquieu's theories of the separation of powers were quite in accord with colonial ideas, for sharp divisions already existed between executive, legislative, and judicial functions, and the colonials delighted in imposing checks upon the authority of their royal governors. The doctrines of the physiocrats, too, seemed logical to a people whose livelihood was dependent upon the soil or the sea, and later the theory of laissez faire struck a sympathetic cord in those who were irritated by the mercantilistic restrictions of an absentee imperialistic government. In short, American conditions made possible and natural the creation of institutions more nearly in accord with the doctrines of Locke and the philosophes than Europe — or America — realized.

The mounting crisis in the relations between England and her colonies called forth these political ideas that had been latent in the minds of Americans, and their formulation in the Declaration of Independence was of vital importance to the new nation. The theory of the Declaration can be stated briefly: The individual existed before government and was endowed with natural rights, a part of which he delegated to government in order to protect the rest; therefore, when governments prove unsatisfactory, the people have a right to alter or amend them. The natural rights that are the basis of all political rights were explicitly stated: All men are created equal; all have been endowed by God with certain inalienable rights, of which they cannot be deprived by themselves or by any other power; among these rights are life, liberty, and the pursuit of happiness.

Looking about him at a world in which such rights were denied, Jefferson wished to have as the foundation stone of the democratic system he saw for the future the broadest possible statement of the rights of men as individuals and citizens. The Declaration impels acceptance of the idea that governmental power is derived from the consent of the governed and has no authority save that delegated to it by the people.

IN THE NEW STATES

The state constitutions drawn up to supplant the old colonial governments did not evidence a full acceptance of the "self-evident truths" of the Declaration. The very patriots who heartily applauded the sweeping equalitarianism of the Declaration proceeded to draw up constitutions in which political equality was denied. The principles to which they subscribed in theory were too advanced to be put into operation at once, and, after paying respect to them in well-turned phrases, the new state constitutions embodied many of the old distinctions between rich and poor, educated and ignorant, religious conformists and nonconformists, that had marked the colonial governments. Each state constitution contained some reiteration of the idea of government by consent and of the right to life, liberty, and property. Each stated that political power was "vested in and derived from" the people. Public officials were declared to be responsible to the people, and the civil liberties of the citizens were protected in bills of rights embodying the principles of cherished liberties won by countless struggles throughout English history. Both from desire and from necessity great steps were taken in the liberalization of institutions. Many members of the old governing class had been Tories and had no part in making the new constitutions. It was necessary to make concessions to the masses of citizens in order to win allegiance to the new governments and support for the Revolution.

It was inevitable that everywhere the suffrage should be broadened to include all members of the middle class, which was bearing the brunt of the war. Nowhere was immediate manhood suffrage or the universal right to hold office introduced, but more men voted than ever before, and popular consent was widespread enough to root the new constitutions deep in the lives of the people. Further liberalization could be obtained by legal processes of amendment when the demand grew irresistible. In some states the suffrage requirement was on the basis of taxpaying, in others a specified income from freehold estates was required, in still others religious requirements were added. Since most citizens paid some taxes and land was cheap, probably few men were permanently deprived of the right to vote. But the right to hold office was much more carefully safeguarded, with the intent to keep government in the control of the well-educated and well-to-do. Religious and property requirements together were increased, so that thousands were deprived of the privilege of seeking public office. Only well-to-do Christians were permitted to be legislators, and in most states none but the rich might hope to be governor. Although the theory was accepted that all government rested upon the consent of the governed, only the taxpaying, property-owning governed could give that consent or participate in that government; although liberty of conscience was another accepted principle, often only a Protestant was permitted to hold office under a government guaranteeing such liberty.

So far as the form of government was concerned there was little of radical change in the transition from colony to state, and there was as great a uniformity in the structure of government in all the states as there had been in the colonial period. There was a general distrust of the executive — a relic of the resentment against the colonial governors — and the legislature was looked upon as the guardian of popular rights, but even the legislature was hemmed in by the operation of the widely accepted principles of the separation of powers and the need for checks and balances. Government was considered a potential danger and of dubious benefit. James Truslow Adams quotes a New England farmer of the period who asserted that the country did not need "any goviner but the guviner of the univarse and under him a States General to Consult with the wrest of the united states for the good of the whole."[3]

Although a free people did not require powerful or elaborate organs of government, there were some negative activities that might be undertaken to achieve the equality of opportunity that was the dream of free men. The Anglican church was disestablished in the South before 1800, and even in New England, where the Congregationalism created by the Puritan theocracy was strong, the dissenter was permitted to offer a certificate of allegiance to another faith in order to free himself from the church tax. In the early years of the nineteenth century Calvinism was forced to give up its last vestige of state support, and religious restriction in suffrage, officeholding, and taxpaying disappeared from the land.

The new state legislatures turned also to an attack upon that other stronghold of privilege—the laws of primogeniture and entail. By 1785 Virginia led the way by making real as well as personal property subject to ordinary laws of inheritance. More or less promptly other states followed Virginia's example until by the end of Washington's first administration these special privileges of a landed aristocracy had disappeared.

Another blow was struck at the "aristocracy of birth and rank" in the confiscation of the estates of many Loyalist landowners. In the course of the Revolution, the supporters of which at no time constituted a majority of the population, thousands of the most substantial citizens had left the country voluntarily or had been forced into exile, and their estates were sold by the states in small parcels to enterprising farmers. New men appeared in the commercial world, too, to rebuild the business enterprises of the exiled Loyalists. From Maine to Georgia the Revolution meant a shift in the class structure and the emergence of new men into positions of power. The sense of social change that everywhere prevailed was well expressed in the words of a contemporary South Carolina writer: "There is nothing more common than to confound the terms of the American Revolution with those of the late American war. The American war is over, but this is far from being the case with the American Revolution. On the contrary, nothing but the first act of that great drama is closed."

Although the theory of the Revolution was undoubtedly more democratic than its practice, the social and intellectual revolution was as evident as the political, and the Revolutionary years established an American tradition and American faith different from those of the European countries from which the colonists had come. By the end of the Revolution it was apparent that the new nation was to endure without an established church, without a feudal aristocracy or a military caste, and without an elaborate bureaucracy extending a controlling influence over every phase of its development. On the positive side this American tradition emphasized the necessity for education and for humanitarian reforms of many kinds, but it showed preference for the greatest diversity in achieving these ends.

THE CONSERVATIVE REACTION

For some the war against England had been only the first act in the real revolution; for others it had already carried social change too far. The economic distress of the years 1785–86 increased the dissatisfaction of those who felt that the revolution had stopped in mid-course, and the leftist movement reached its climax in Massachusetts in an armed revolt of debtor farmers led by Daniel Shays, a veteran of the War of Independence. Shays's rebellion attracted wide attention and called forth expressions of opinion from startled leaders who rose to defend the well-ordered control of society that had, they felt, been challenged from below.[4]

Unsuccessful in its main objectives, Shays's rebellion was not only an impetus to the movement for a stronger national government but also a warning to the entrenched wellborn, a class already dubious of the value of democratic institutions. If the years from the Revolution to the safe establishment of the Constitution may be called "the critical period," it is partly in the sense that further democratization seemed blocked by the privileged classes. Even in the Revolutionary period few of the leaders had been genuine believers in democracy; the implications of the theory of the rule of the majority were frightening to them. The chaotic conditions of the succeeding years cooled what little ardor they still had and convinced them that a strong government was necessary, a government that could secure property from assault and protect the established order. The aristocracy looked to the Constitutional Convention that assembled in May 1787 to provide a governmental structure that could be relied upon to maintain the ascendancy of men of wealth and education.

In their correspondence, in the debates of the Constitutional Convention, and in their public addresses many of the conservative leaders stated frankly their distrust of the common people. Elbridge Gerry of Massachusetts, an erstwhile liberal, admitted regretfully that he had been too republican in the past but had been "taught by experience the danger of the levelling spirit," so that he now believed the troubles of the country were the result of "an excess of democracy." [5] Edmund Randolph agreed that the evils of the times had "originated in the turbulence and follies of democracy," and the eminent Pennsylvanian, Gouveneur Morris, announced that there was no more justification for giving the vote to the "ignorant and dependent" than for giving it to children. [6]

The classic expressions of this distrust of democracy are in the writings of the despairing Federalists, Fisher Ames of Massachusetts and Timothy Dwight of Connecticut. Convinced that submission to democratic institutions would spell the doom of the nation, these pessimists never ceased predicting the ultimate fate of the country they professed to love but for which they saw no hope. Ames lamented that "our country is too big for union, too sordid for patriotism, too democratic for liberty," and Dwight, the college president and divine, believed that the great object of democracy was to destroy every trace of civilization in the world and force mankind back into a savage state. [7] All this fear of democracy was summed up in the gross but unequivocal statement of Hamilton: "Your people, sir — your people is a great *beast!*"

THE CONSTITUTION

With apprehension and hatred thick in the air, it was remarkable that the delegates who assembled in Philadelphia in 1787 to make "a more perfect union" were as statesmanlike and farsighted as they proved to be. They were men who had been concerned with public affairs for many years. They represented the army, the bar, the diplomatic corps, and various other branches of government service. None of the Revolutionary radicals were present. It was inevitable in these circumstances that the Constitution should be a conservative document. Wherever necessary the makers of the Constitution made such adjustments and compromises as were required to produce a strong, workable federal government, but they did not intend to establish a democratic government, and their rejection of the right of the masses to rule is inherent in the document they drew up. They were "elite conscious," and they identified the interests of their own class with the interests of the general public, their devotion to their group with solicitude for the public welfare.

Among other matters the debate on the political future of the lands recently opened for settlement in the West showed clearly the aristocratic sentiment of the convention. The members had no illusions as to the independent spirit of the "Settlements," and they felt the class prejudice that had been created by earlier disputes with the back country. Gouveneur Morris declared that the "busy haunts of men, not the remote wilderness, is the proper school of political talents." He believed that "the rule of representation ought to be so fixed as to secure to the Atlantic states a prevalence in the National Councils." Only when James Wilson of Pennsylvania stated, with common sense and cool logic, that discrimination against the West would but duplicate the errors whereby Great Britain had caused the American Revolution, did the agitated members decide to admit the Western territories on an equal basis with the original states whenever their population should make such action necessary. Wilson's calm statement that when the West should acquire a majority it would control "whether we will or no" was unanswerable.

As soon as the Constitution was published and its terms became known, opposition appeared. Excitement was intense among those informed and interested, and every available agency of publicity and propaganda was used in influencing voters and delegates. It is difficult to estimate the actual public support of the Constitution, since only about one third of the male adults could vote in the elections and many qualified voters abstained through indifference or ignorance.[8] But from analyses of the debates of the ratification conventions it is possible to make some general statements. The aristocracy was fairly well satisfied with the new Constitution; the democrats fought against it. Small farmers and the back-country men, especially in areas where the burden of debt was heavy, were generally opposed to ratification, whereas creditors and holders of public securities favored it. The advocates of paper money and of stay laws for debtors were against it, and only the desire for protection from the Indians could bring the frontiersmen into line in favor of a strong government. But however close the margin, the Constitution was ratified, and with its acceptance the American way of life entered upon a new phase; the democratization begun in the colonial period and advanced by the Revolution found new channels under the Constitution along which to proceed.

THE JEFFERSONIAN REVOLUTION

The debates over ratification had shown a dynamic democracy among the people that could not be denied. A national bill of rights guaranteeing civil liberties was formulated by the first Congress under the Constitution, while legislation within the states and amendments to state constitutions, or in several cases entirely new constitutions, gave evidence of the force of these democratic tendencies.

In the East, as one conservative said, good citizens trembled and awaited the catastrophe, while the more vigorous among them fought energetically to halt the advance of democracy and its demands for more elective offices, shorter tenures, speedier justice, and manhood suffrage. Democratic forces proved too strong, however, and one by one the constitutions of the Eastern states were liberalized, until Virginia, the Carolinas, and Rhode Island remained the sole strongholds of aristocratic control. In those states the predominance of the aristocracy was maintained until the Civil War or shortly before. But all in all, the constitutional changes within the states in the first half century of the republic made possible the development of democratic political institutions and furnished the basic foundation for the wide range of social and economic reform movements of the period.

The new national government under the Constitution was administered for a decade by conservatives who based their actions on the principle of the superiority of a ruling class. They believed sincerely that government could be safely entrusted only to the "well-born, well-educated, and well-to-do," and that the masses of the people should be filled with gratitude to receive the benefits of the wise administration of public affairs by these few. This system of "overhead management" was apparent in the work of Hamilton and became the general tone of the Federalist administrations. But the domination of the wellborn was destined to be brief. As soon as the first party of the common man was organized under the leadership of Jefferson, a bitter campaign against the wealthy and wellborn was instituted. The Jeffersonian Revolution of 1800 ended all hope of establishing on American soil any party or group that openly upheld the rights of the few over the many.

Jeffersonian democracy did not mean any fundamental alteration in the Constitution or any immediate changes in the structure of government. It meant that control shifted from the commercial Northeast led by Hamilton and the Federalists to the agrarian masses dominated by the landowning aristocracy of Southern planters. It condemned the granting of special privileges to bankers, merchants, and manufacturers and appealed to the agriculturalists who made up the bulk of the population in 1800.[9] In a country where land was plentiful and cheap, Jeffersonian agrarianism, thus defined and expounded, spread rapidly. Every new state added to the Union increased the opponents of Federalism in national politics. The way for a triumphant democracy was being prepared even though Jeffersonianism was deep-rooted in the interests of a planter aristocracy.

THE ROLE OF THE FRONTIER

That triumph was the work of the Western frontier. Frederick Jackson Turner, the historian whose name is identified with the frontier, has wisely said that the West is at bottom a form of society, rather than an area. From the beginning each colony had its frontier, its West: areas in which men of courage and vigor won new opportunities, where land was cheap or free and the struggle for existence, although severe, brought rewards commensurate with the effort expended. There the "cake of custom" was broken, old standards were discarded, new ideals and new institutions were set up. The back country was relatively near the Atlantic Coast in the early days, but it was pushed farther west, north, or south decade by decade. In 1790 one hundred thousand had reached the Mississippi Valley. The census of 1810 showed a Western population of a million, that of 1830 gave the West more than three and a half millions, and that of 1840 made the total six millions.

Those who went to the West were poor, but they could not have been destitute. The cost of transportation was not insignificant, the price of land, although low, made some capital necessary, and the settler and his family must have support until the new land could be brought under cultivation. During years of prosperity when money was plentiful, thousands of substantial settlers sought homes in the West. Single men might brave the wilderness without resources, but only in case of general economic depression and dire distress did men with families attempt to do so. In the hard times after 1815 the westward routes were jammed, as the East and the older West poured their poor and discontented onto the newer lands.

The East was alarmed at the loss of population, and understandably so. The creation of a democratic farming population in the new territories would endanger the control of the older states in national affairs and weaken the influence of the commercial and manufacturing interests. Cheap lands in the West would decrease land values at home, while the migration of Eastern farmers and immigrants would reduce the supply of cheap labor for Eastern industries and break down the well-ordered structure of Eastern economic and social life. President Timothy Dwight of Yale College wrote thus about the emigrants:

In a political view, their emigration is of very serious utility to the ancient settlements. All countries contain restless inhabitants; men impatient of labour; men, who will contract debts without intending to pay them; who had rather talk than work; whose vanity persuades them that they are wise, and prevents them from knowing that they are fools; who are delighted with innovation; who think places of power and profit due to their peculiar merits; who feel, that every change from good order and established society will be beneficial to themselves; who have nothing to lose, and therefore expect to be gainers by every scramble; and who, of course, spend life in disturbing others, with the hope of gaining something for themselves. Under despotic governments they are awed into quiet; but in every free community they create, to a greater or less extent, continual turmoil; and have often overturned the peace, liberty, and happiness, of their fellow-citizens.[10]

This contemptuous view of the qualities of the pioneer was doubtless coupled with, if not caused by, a certain reluctance to part with a heretofore subservient lower class, but it was not reflected in the Westerners' hard-learned estimate of the qualities necessary for a successful frontiersman. One of them wrote,

If you value ease more than money or prosperity, don't come. . . . Hands are too few for the work, houses for the inhabitants, and days for the day's work to be done. . . . Next if you can't stand seeing your old New England ideas, ways of doing, and living, and in fact, all of the good old Yankee fashions knocked out of shape or altered, or thrown by as unsuited to the climate, don't be caught out here. But if you can bear grief with a smile, can put up with a scale of accommodations ranging from the soft side of a plank before the fire . . . down through the middling and inferior grades, if you are never at a loss for ways to do the most impracticable things without tools; if you can do all this and some more come on. . . . It is a universal rule here to help one another, each one keeping an eye single to his own business.[11]

The frontiersman from foreign lands wrote with gusto about the rewards that awaited his efforts:

This is the country for a man to enjoy himself . . . where you may see prairies 60 miles long and ten broad, not a stone or a stick in them, at two dollars an acre, that will produce from seventy to one hundred bushels of Indian corn per acre: too rich for wheat or any other kind of grain. . . . I believe I saw more peaches and apples rotting on the ground, than would sink the British fleet. I was at many plantations in Ohio where they no more knew the number of their hogs than myself. . . . And they have such flocks of turkies, geese, ducks, and hams, as would surprise you. . . . The poorest family has a cow or two and some sheep: and in fall can gather as many apples and peaches as serves the year round. Good rye whiskey; apple and peach brandy, at forty cents per gallon, which I think equal to rum. . . . The poorest families adorn the table three times a day like a wedding dinner — tea, coffee, beef, fowls, pies, eggs, pickles, good bread; and their favorite beverage is whiskey or peach brandy. Say, is it so in England? [12]

Such accounts of the plenty of the New World spread the "America fever" abroad, where the people were already made restive by the rapid progress of the industrial revolution.[13] Consolation and inspiration both, the American dream was shared by the immigrant with his friends, relatives, and fellow countrymen at home. Gross and practical as some of its aspects were, the basis of that dream was the satisfaction of the age-old hunger for land and for the security that possession of fertile acres could bring. This sense of satisfaction has probably never been better expressed than by a French immigrant of the pre-Revolutionary period, Crèvecoeur, the author of the *Letters From an American Farmer*, who wrote in almost lyric tones:

Precious soil, I say to myself, by what singular custom of law is it that thou wast made to constitute the riches of the freeholder? What should we American farmers be without the distinct possession of that soil? It feeds, it clothes us, from it we draw in ever greater exuberancy, our best meat, our richest drink, the very honey of our bees comes from this privileged spot. No wonder we should thus cherish its possessions, no wonder that so many Europeans who have never been able to say that such portion of land was theirs, cross the Atlantic to realize that happiness.[14]

A similar appreciation, coupled with realization of the political advantages offered, may be found in the reasons for migration given by George Flower, an Englishman who helped to settle the English Prairie of Illinois in 1817.

A real liberty is found in the country, apart from all its political theories. The practical liberty of America is found in its great space and small population. Good land, dog-cheap everywhere, and for nothing, if you will go for it, gives as much elbow room to every man as he chooses to take. Poor laborers, from every country in Europe, hear of this cheap land, are attracted to it, perhaps without any political opinions. They come, they toil, they prosper. This is the real liberty of America.[15]

From whatever background they came, no matter how diverse their motives or their equipment, the frontier shaped these settlers into its own pattern. And the type of American developed under frontier conditions set his mark upon the life of his nation so unmistakably that the philosophy of the frontier came to color the activities of the entire United States. Equality of condition was a fact, not a theory, on the frontier; station, education, refinement, and even wealth mattered little. All must face the same perils and hardships, the same grueling labor in clearing the land, the same isolation, the same lack of the refinements of civilization. The weaklings moved on, dropped back, or died of their failures, while the vigorous and self-reliant remained to become the leaders and the models of frontier achievement. The successful settler produced by the frontier was a self-made, self-confident man, like his neighbors but standing out among them because of his strength as an individual.

The same conditions produced the paradox of the frontier — a belief in equality so profound that the American almost confounded equality of opportunity with equality of ability, together with an intense, militant individualism that resented all restrictions and was restless, buoyant, self-assertive, and optimistic. The frontiersman had the utmost confidence in himself, his region, and his country, and he both craved and resented comparisons and criticisms.[16] Acknowledging no debt to the past, he believed in progress and accepted change as the natural order. Hopeful and idealistic, he yet could not forget the necessity for common sense and a realistic attitude, for the conquest of the wilderness was an arduous task, exacting, monotonous, and burdensome. It was wasteful of human life, especially of women and children, and it was destructive of culture and neglectful of social relationships.

The lawlessness of the frontier was doubtless partly legendary; certainly the bandits and renegades have had their day in Western literature. But with due allowance for exaggeration, there is still much justice in the emphasis upon the coarseness and violence of frontier life. All the travelers speak of the constant fighting, the gouging, ear-biting, and rough and tumble of Western personal dispute, and the vocabulary and anecdotes of the West vividly illustrate the crudeness of its life. The frontiersman was repelled by pretension, preferring his acquaintances to be no better than himself. An educated Englishman, residing in Illinois in the 1820's, commented bitterly on this trait:

A man to be popular in our new Western towns and with the country people around, should be acquainted with everybody, shake hands with everybody, and wear an old coat, with at least one good hole in it. A little whiskey and a few squirts of tobacco juice are indispensable. From much of the former you may be excused if you treat liberally to others. If there is one fool bigger than another, defer to him, make much of him. If there is one fellow a little more greasy and dirty than another, be sure to *hug* him. Do all this and you have done much toward being a popular man. At least you could scarcely have a jury-case carried against you.[17]

The frontier's faith in democracy and freedom soon took on an element of crusading zeal as Americans became convinced of the glorious future ahead of them and came to consider themselves entrusted with the mission of portraying democracy to less favored nations. A magazine article in 1821, perhaps with some sense of humor, illustrated this confidence in the future with the statement:

Other nations boast of what they are or have been, but the true citizen of the United States exalts his head to the skies in the contemplation of what the grandeur of his country is going to be. Others claim respect and honor because of the things done by a long line of ancestors; an American appeals to prophecy, and with Malthus in one hand and a map of the back country in the other he defies us to a comparison with America as she is to be, and chuckles his delight over the splendors the geometrical ratio is to shed over her story. This appeal to the future is his never-failing resource. If an English traveller complains of their inns and hints his dislike of sleeping four in a bed, he is denounced as a calumniator and then told to wait a hundred years and see the superiority of American inns to British. If Shakespeare, Milton, Newton are named, he is again told to wait until we have cleared our land, till we have idle time to attend to other things; wait until 1900, and then see how much nobler our poets and profounder our astronomers and longer our telescopes than any that decrepit old hemisphere of yours will produce.[18]

Francis Grund, writing in 1836 for an English public, made the same sort of comment in his statement that Americans loved their country not for what it then was, but for what it was to be — not the land of their fathers, but the land their children were destined to inherit.[19] The Scotsman, Alexander Mackay, heard the same idea from a South Carolina farmer in response to a question about genealogy: "We don't vally those things in this country. It's what's above ground, not what's under, that we think on." [20] Whether or not the visiting Europeans approved of American democracy, and many did not,[21] they all were agreed that Americans themselves were content with their institutions and believed them better than those of Europe.

This American solidarity was noted by the most famous foreign visitor of the period, Alexis de Tocqueville, in a letter from the United States in June 1831.[22] After stating that he envied Americans the comfort of their common opinions, he went on to enumerate them: All the people believe that a republic is the best possible government and do not question that the people have a right to govern themselves. This belief is almost a *faith*, which is at basis a faith in the good sense of human beings and in the perfectibility of human institutions. In order that those institutions may constantly improve, education and enlightenment must become as universal as suffrage. De Tocqueville found no evidence of ancient traditions and little effect of old customs or memories. Americans were a new people. He felt that the reason there was so great a respect for law was that the people made it themselves and could change it themselves. "It is really an incredible thing . . . to see how this people keeps itself in order through the single conviction that its only safeguard against itself lies in itself." Somewhat reluctantly, apparently, the young Frenchman admitted that on the whole the country presented "an admirable spectacle!" His great work published some years later, *Democracy in America*, reaffirmed this first impression, saying,

In America, the principle of the sovereignty of the people is not either barren or concealed . . . it is recognized by the customs and proclaimed by the laws. . . . If there be a country in the world where the doctrine of the sovereignty of the people can be fairly appreciated, where it can be studied in its application to the affairs of society, and where its dangers and its advantages may be foreseen, that country is assuredly America.[23]

The American's own view of his achievement in democracy was usually optimistic, sometimes complacent, but occasionally tempered by analysis and criticism. The novelist, James Fenimore Cooper, although professing belief in democracy, was a caustic critic of American life, attacking what he thought were its abuses and faults with a vehemence that won him many enemies. In his *America and the Americans: Notions Picked up by a Travelling Bachelor*, published in 1836, he endeavored to explain his country to the outside world and to express his own faith. But in *The American Democrat*, designed for his own countrymen, he warned of the danger of the rise of a "vulgar tyrant" and repeatedly asserted that the leading principle of a republic must be that political power is a trust to be guarded with "ceaseless vigilance." Feeling that imperfect as popular government was, it was less dangerous than any other, Cooper came to the conclusion that men of intelligence and wealth, of education and station, must take their proper place in democratic society and aid in directing national policies.

JACKSONIAN DEMOCRACY

The self-conscious democracy of the West, in conjunction with the laboring classes of the seaboard states, exercised its newly acquired manhood suffrage in 1828 to bring about the Jacksonian Revolution and install "Old Hickory," the hero of the land-speculating, Indian-fighting West, in the White House. The Westerners did not regard government as a difficult matter, nor did they consider special qualifications necessary for election to office. A man who could conquer the wilderness, bring his land under cultivation, and win the respect of his fellows might be expected to succeed in any office to which he was elected. Rotation in office, many elective offices, and frequent elections were a part of Western practice and were considered "salutary principles which disjoint the schemes of usurpation, and frustrate the systematic continuance of power." [24]

Interest in politics was widespread in the West, and election day — or days, for many Western states kept the polls open for several days — was a memorable occasion. Campaigning was rough and ready, speeches were forceful if not grammatical, voting was viva voce, and on election days candidates sat with the election clerks, thanked their supporters personally, and provided limitless quantities of liquor for the thirsty voters. Adolphus Frederick Hubbard, running for governor of Illinois against Ninian Edwards, gave to his audience the creed of the frontier candidate:

Fellow citizens, I offer myself as a candidate before you, for the office of governor. I do not pretend to be a man of extraordinary talents, nor do I claim to be equal to Julius Caesar or Napoleon Bonaparte, nor yet to be as great a man as my opponent, Governor Edwards. Nevertheless, I think I can govern you pretty well. I do not think it will take an extraordinary smart man to govern you; for to tell the truth, Fellow citizens, I do not think you will be very hard to govern no how. [25]

With the election of Andrew Jackson the creed of the frontier won its victory in the arena of national affairs, and the Western interest in politics became national with the rise of the common man to political importance. While officeholders trembled and Washington official and social circles paled with anticipatory anguish, [26] the President-elect prepared to act in accordance with a creed that summarizes well the essential faith of the young republic:

I believe man can be elevated; man can become more and more endowed with divinity; and as he does he becomes more God-like in his character and capable of governing himself. Let us go on elevating our people, perfecting our institutions, until democracy shall reach such a point of perfection that we can acclaim with truth that the voice of the people is the voice of God. [27]

CHAPTER 2

Evangelical Religion

The religious heritage of the young republic was as important in the development of nineteenth-century ideas as were the liberties won in the struggle with civil authorities. "When the common man has freed himself from political absolutism, he will become dissatisfied with theological absolutism."[1] The cold and repressive doctrines of Calvinism could not win the hearts of those who escaped from its control when its dictatorial governmental power came to an end. Moreover, the rationalism of John Locke and the French philosophes had the same dislocating effect on religious thinking as on political ideas. Calvin's doctrine of total depravity might have sufficed an older generation as an explanation of the presence of evil in human society, but man's reason found other causes, and his common sense rejected the idea that he and his neighbor were utterly depraved. The idea of progress and of the importance of the individual undermined the old doctrines of election and predestination. The consequent dissatisfaction with Genevan dogma, coupled with the aridity and dullness of New England cultural life, caused the people to turn with eagerness to evangelical Protestantism. Rebellion against Calvinism forced into the open field of battle a question that was fundamental both in theology and in political and cultural life: Is the will of man completely free or is it wholly subject to the "stable" will of God?

JONATHAN EDWARDS AND THE GREAT AWAKENING

Puritanism thus assailed found in Jonathan Edwards a formidable defender. But the Calvinist doctrine that survived the struggle was so modified by the work of its defender that it has ever since been called Edwardian. Related by birth or marriage to many of the dominant families of the Puritan hierarchy and descended from four generations of men interested in religious questions, Edwards was conditioned in every way for the task he was to assume. Had he lived in New England in the greater intellectual freedom of the next century or in London or Paris in his own time, he might well have been one of the greatest philosophical thinkers of all ages.

Gifted and scholarly, deeply emotional, and yet analytical, he was carried by his metaphysical and philosophical studies beyond the old controversies of nominalism and realism toward a mysticism and transcendentalism that was far from the Calvinistic creed.

This keen interest in philosophy, however, did not lead Edwards away from theology and the defense of New England Puritanism, for his conversion was followed by entry into the ministry and active championship of the old faith. Yet he could never give up his vision of man freely willing good instead of evil, of right triumphant over wrong, and of a new world order representing the victory of divine sovereignty. So the doctrine of depravity was softened into the idea that man left to himself is lost, but that conversion and regeneration are possible for every contrite soul. Predestination lost its horror as Edwardian theology drew close to the teaching of John Wesley that salvation is free to all who are converted.

After some years as pastor in the quiet little town of Northampton, Massachusetts, Edwards led his flock through the first revival of the century. Small as it was in comparison with the later "outpourings of God's spirit," this Edwardian revival had all their characteristics. During a sermon on the wrath of God the gallery of the church fell on the pews below, the occupants of which were saved only by the grace of God and the high backs of the pews. This shock was followed by an increase of interest in religion. The first conversion came in December 1734, when a young woman who had been the "greatest company-keeper" in town professed her penitence. She was followed by many young people, the contagion spread to their elders, and soon salvation became the sole topic of interest. Regular business was almost suspended, and the meetinghouse and parsonage became the center of the town. It was a happy time for Edwards, for the millennium seemed at hand.

But suddenly the spell was broken when one of those "under conviction," but to whom no joyful experience had been vouchsafed, committed suicide. A "dead time in religion" followed, and Edwards felt that God's favor had been withdrawn. His constant efforts to revive the former enthusiasm confirmed both himself and his envious clerical followers in the type of preaching and doctrine that might arouse fear and repentance. The imprecatory sermons that frightened his hearers furnished models for the generations that followed. It is hard even yet to forgive the author of "The Eternity of Hell Torments," "The Evil of the Wicked Contemplated by the Righteous," and, most famous of all, "Sinners in the Hands of an Angry God."

The soil so arduously cultivated by Edwards and other preachers using similar methods was ready to produce an abundant harvest for George Whitefield when he came from England a few years later. He was received as an angel of God, and his progress through the countryside was marked by greater and greater crowds and more and more emotionalism. Queues of people were waiting outside the churches at three in the morning in order to obtain seats for the early service, men gave up all business to attend session after session, and many left their homes to follow him from town to town. He preached sermons of a kind America had never known. There was no emphasis upon doctrine or logic; theology was discarded for drama. Entirely without notes but with gestures, laughter, songs, and tears he carried his audience with him into the realm of pure emotion.

This Great Awakening led to schism and disruption in the old churches. Many ministers were shocked by the new methods of preaching and by the hysterical emotionalism engendered in the audiences of revivalist preachers. They called attention to the excesses and to the dead time that seemed to follow the tumult of the revival. They asserted that whatever gains were made in church membership were counteracted by the backsliding of the new converts when the excitement subsided. Above all they disapproved the doctrinal changes implied in the teaching of salvation for all through the process of conversion. Even the Edwardian compromises were too much of an innovation for the orthodox Presbyterian and Congregational churchmen. The followers of Edwards came to be called New Lights, and the orthodox Genevans were called the Old Light clergy. Wasting their energies in attacks upon each other, the various factions of the old churches lost their hold on the allegiance of the people.

RATIONALISM AND RELIGION

The second half of the eighteenth century, the period of the American and French revolutions, saw the acceptance of rationalism and a further lessening of the hold of Calvinistic theology. The Puritan conception of a just but angry Jehovah threatening with hell-fire and damnation a generation foreordained to salvation or destruction had no validity in the light of reason. Progress, perfectibility, individual worth, and the goodness of the natural man were substituted for the old ideas of abased man saved from eternal punishment only by the interposition of an arbitrary Providence.

The attacks of the philosophers upon the evils and the reactionary and arbitrary nature of the established churches led many to turn away from religion altogether and, accepting reason as their sole guide, to become agnostic or frankly atheistic. Others repudiated only organized and dogmatic religious forms, keeping their belief in the existence of a divine Creator to whom man owed allegiance. And for many rationalistic thinkers agnosticism and deism merely paved the way to complete indifference toward religion and to concentration on man's inherent ability to perfect his own institutions.

Such ideas were cold satisfaction to others. Their revulsion from the evils of organized religion in their day was matched by their dislike for rationalistic philosophy. Their solution for the dilemma was a frank escape to supernaturalism and a return to the pietism and emotionalism of the early Reformation period and of many pre-Reformation heretical sects.

The deists of the late colonial period and of the infant republic were usually political radicals as well. They advocated independence, fought in the Revolution, and ended their careers supporting the French Revolution and Jeffersonian democracy. Indeed, Jefferson himself was the arch-deist, and for that reason was all the more detested by the New England orthodox Federalist of the Fisher Ames sort.

The stronghold of Federalism and Calvinism was not without its own rebels, however, for General Ethan Allen of Green Mountain fame was a doughty rationalist and agnostic. In 1785 appeared the first copies of his *Reason the Only Oracle of Man, or a Compendious System of Natural Religion* . . . which the freethinkers called "Ethan Allen's Bible." The blunt old warrior stated in his preface that it was an impertinence for authors to apologize for their works, for "if a book cannot stand on its two hind legs, it should have been

stifled in the birth." Desire for knowledge, the greatest attribute of
man, said Allen, had led him to explore nature's laws, with the
result that science now gave him explanations for many things that
had previously seemed to be mysteries. God was the First Cause,
the Creator of the universe, far too remote and impersonal a force
to manifest interest in sect or individual. Prayer and belief in miracles alike were, to Allen, impertinent, and he thought man would
do well to seek only to make his life conform with the laws of nature, attempting neither to dictate to God nor to demand miraculous aberration of law. Personal or revealed religion was an impossibility for the rational man.

Unitarianism was even more destructive of orthodoxy than
was deism. In New England it cut across both Episcopal and
Congregational-Presbyterian churches, taking over many whole congregations complete with clergy and church property. In a series
of suits in Massachusetts courts it was established that when a majority of any congregation became Unitarian the property of the
church belonged to the new organization and not to the old, which
had come to represent a minority of the congregation. In 1785 the
Episcopalian King's Chapel in Boston turned Unitarian under its
pastor, James Freeman, and when Freeman was refused ordination
by the Episcopal church he received it from his own congregation
acting as an independent religious organization.

The classic expression of Unitarian doctrine was William Ellery
Channing's sermon at the ordination of Jared Sparkes in Baltimore
in 1819. From French revolutionary philosophy and New England
idealism, from English Arian thought and Jeffersonian democracy,
Channing brought together the three dominant ideas of the American Unitarian faith: the loving kindness of God, the nobility of
man, and the joy of a religious life. All Channing's lofty and pervasive ethical teaching was compressed into his statement, "The adoration of goodness — this is religion." The English traveler, Thomas
Hamilton, summarized the usual British estimate of Unitarianism:

Unitarianism is the democracy of religion. Its creed makes fewer demands on the faith or the imagination, than that of any other Christian
sect. It appeals to known reason in every step of its progress, and while
it narrows the compass of miracle, enlarges that of demonstration. Its
followers have less bigotry than other religionists, because they have

less enthusiasm. They refuse credence to the doctrine of one grand universal atonement, and appeal to none of those sudden and preternatural impulses which have given assurance to the pious of other sects. A Unitarian will take nothing for granted but the absolute and plenary efficacy of his own reason in matters of religion. He is not a fanatic, but a dogmatist; one who will admit of no distinction between the incomprehensible and the false. With such views of the Bostonians and their prevailing religion, I can not help believing that there exists a curious felicity of adaptation in both. . . . Jonathan chose his religion, as one does a hat, because it fitted him.[2]

Since Unitarians had the simplest of all creeds, fundamentally just an agreement on the tenets they did not subscribe to in other faiths, they had few doctrinal quarrels. Because they had little missionary zeal and appealed to reason rather than to emotion, they gained relatively few adherents. Their importance and leadership, however, were out of all proportion to their numbers, for they were largely of the middle and upper classes, representing both wealth and learning. They were strong in the literary and cultural centers of New England.

If Unitarianism was the faith of the well-to-do, well-educated dissenters from the doctrines of Calvin, the poorer New Englanders with liberal ideas adopted the Universalism brought to America by John Murray in 1770. There was little difference in theology between the two sects; the Universalists merely placed their emphasis upon the denial of hell and the doctrine of universal salvation. There were few Universalist churches in the Eastern cities, but they were numerous in the country districts. On the frontier their doctrine of free salvation made them the bugbear of the hell-fire–preaching Methodists, who, together with a group of Free-Will Baptists, invaded New England after 1790 and struggled against the orthodox, the Universalists, and the unchurched of the back country, using the circuit-rider and revivalist tactics that they were to find so effective in the West.

On the New England frontier the itinerant Methodist or Baptist found a people used to high seasoning in their religious diet and able to appreciate the imprecations and threats of damnation that were designed to strike terror into the hearts of the unconverted. The revivalists had little use for the hair-splitting controversies of the New England churches and gave short shrift to the Edwardian attempt to reconcile free will and predestination, quoting the contemptuous limerick of the circuit-riding Lorenzo Dow:

> You can and you can't
> You will and you won't
> You'll be damned if you do,
> You'll be damned if you don't.

But among well-read Unitarians revivalistic tactics met with little success, as the following excerpt from the manuscript diary of a New Hampshire girl of seventeen will show:

We went this evening to hear Lorenzo Dow, a famous Methodist preacher, his appearance was enough to frighten one and his preaching disgusted all — the meeting house was crowded full. Think we should have been as wise if we had staid at home.

RELIGION IN NEW ENGLAND COLLEGES

For a time rationalism and secularism penetrated deep into the New England colleges that had served as a training ground for orthodox clergy. Yale College became a hotbed of radicalism — at least in the eyes of conservative divines. Students called each other by the names of French radicals and met to discuss progress, perfection, and the rights of man. In the words of the author of a history of a neighboring college, "the dams and dykes seemed to be swept away, and irreligion, immorality, scepticism, and infidelity came in like a flood." [3] In 1799 only four or five Yale undergraduates professed religion, and in 1800 there was but one church member in the graduating class. "A young man who belonged to the church in that day was a phenomenon — almost a miracle." [4] At Harvard the situation was much the same, except that Unitarianism had crept into the faculty. By the end of the century, with the appointment of Henry Ware to the Hollis professorship of theology, Unitarianism was fairly entrenched in the old training school for Puritan divines.

Both Old and New Light Calvinists were then awakened to the danger that threatened them in the very institutions that had been their strongholds. When Timothy Dwight, a grandson of Jonathan Edwards, was called to be president of Yale, he felt that the mantle of his grandfather had descended upon him and that it was both his duty and his opportunity to purify the college that had so fallen from grace. He preached the Edwardian doctrine of a "race dead in sin" and condemned pleasure, idleness, and devotion to the arts. The ethics he taught was a mass of prohibitions, but he taught with such forcefulness that the result was a religious revival. The young men he guided into the ministry carried his teaching far afield and brought evangelical zeal and missionary spirit into the old churches of New England. There were fifteen periods of revival at Yale in the first forty years of the nineteenth century, and at the end of that time more than half the students were again affiliated with some church. Their deepened interest in religion must have been, at least in part, responsible for their interest in a wide variety of reform movements. In writing of the revival of 1802 a participant recorded:

Wheresoever students were found – in their rooms, in the chapel, in the hall, in the college-yard, in their walks about the city – the reigning impression was, "surely God is in this place!" The salvation of the soul was the great subject of conversation, of absorbing interest.[5]

A conservative like Dwight, Jedidiah Morse endeavored first to combat Unitarianism in the Harvard faculty and then, failing in that, to establish a new theological school devoted to orthodox teaching. Andover Theological Seminary was the result. Andover carried forward the work of developing an evangelical spirit that could combat the wiles of heretical doctrine. The advice of Jedidiah Morse was, "Let us guard against the insidious encroachments of *innovation* – that evil and beguiling spirit which is now stalking to and fro in the earth, seeking whom it may devour." And by *innovation* Morse meant anything in the way of religious doctrine that had been evolved since Jonathan Edwards.[6]

So forceful were the sermons and the imprecations of the faculties of both Andover Academy and Andover Seminary that the hill on which the two schools stood was long called Brimstone Hill. Religion was the main theme in and out of classes. One day the headmaster of the academy dismissed classes with the remark, "There will now be a prayer meeting; those who wish to lie down in everlasting burning may go, the rest will stay." Only two hardy – or hardened – boys departed. An academy senior, after listening to a sermon on the text, "And ye shall see them sit down with Abraham and Isaac and Jacob in the Kingdom of Heaven and ye yourselves cast out," wrote in his diary that it was evident that some will be finally rejected from the Kingdom of Heaven and it is probable that it will be a part of their punishment to see those who were their former companions enjoying that blessed state from which they are excluded by their own folly and sin. The punishment and tortures of condemned spirits will be increasing to all eternity. How tremendous and overwhelming is the thought that the suffering of one soul will be greater than the united suffering of all in the universe for millions of ages.[7]

Constant pressure upon the young student to choose a life of devotion to religion was characteristic of most American colleges in the first half of the nineteenth century — especially of those in New England and those founded by New Englanders. College revivals lacked much of the excitement of Methodist exhortation and the Western camp meeting, but they were very effective. There was a period of gradual preparation: Pious students conducted prayer meetings in each dormitory every evening; inquiry meetings were held by the college officials; often the president's house was opened for religious discussion; and the entire faculty, many of whom were preachers, cooperated in directing meetings.

Out on the frontier the colleges founded by New Englanders carried on the same sort of work. Oberlin was long famous for its advocacy of evangelical religion and all manner of reform movements, and Knox College in Illinois, also founded by men from New England, produced a revival every winter as a part of the regular course. This was accompanied by "prayer meetings before breakfast, at noon, after school, and sermons served hot to us every night, everybody on hand, everybody expected to stand up and give testimony," for there were "those vital questions . . . of temperance, abolitionism and conversion of lost souls, this last, first and foremost."[8]

MISSIONARY SOCIETIES

Before long this increase of interest was reflected in movements designed to spread religious enterprise over the entire world. In 1789 the General Assembly of the Presbyterian Church authorized a Home Missionary Society, and soon the churches of Connecticut and Massachusetts were organizing similar societies with the objective of "propagating the gospel in the new settlements." The missionaries sent by these societies joined with the itinerant Methodist preachers in bringing about the great revival in the West in the years following 1800.

But America was too small a field for the ebullient religious enthusiasm of the day. A Board of Commissioners for Foreign Missions was founded in 1810 as a joint Presbyterian and Congregational enterprise, and two years later the first two American missionaries were sent to India. Judson and Rice became Baptists on the voyage to their new field and thus established Baptist foreign missionary work. The Methodists founded their first foreign mission society in 1819 and kept pace with the Baptists in annual expenditures. By 1850 the foreign missionary work of all denominations called for an expenditure of about $650,000 annually.[9]

When young Samuel John Mills, a Williams College student, was sent to the frontier to preach, he found huge areas with no churches, a few itinerant preachers, but little visible evidence of any religious influence. Appalled by the magnitude of the work and the distances to be traveled, Mills organized Bible societies and distributed hundreds of Bibles from Pittsburgh to New Orleans. At his urging the American Bible Society was organized in 1816. Cooperating with missionaries and local preachers throughout the West, the society formed over two hundred local groups, which by 1821 had distributed 140,000 Bibles.

The work of the missionary and Bible societies was supplemented by that of tract societies founded to publish religious works. The largest and most important was the American Tract Society founded in 1825; by 1850 it was expending more than $300,000 annually.

There were other societies for all sorts of purposes. Some were denominational, some interdenominational; all seemed desirable to enough people so that support was provided for them. Societies were established for the aid of seamen, for the Christianization of Jews, and for the publication of anti-Catholic literature. Churches founded orphanages and carried on work for the poor and the defective. Humanitarianism and religion were closely allied, and it was a far cry from the "dead time in religion" of the eighteenth century to the social application of evangelical fervor in the mid-nineteenth.

RELIGION ON THE FRONTIER

So much were the Western revivals and the religious awakening in the older sections of the country parts of the same movement that it is difficult to be sure whether the lines of influence extended from the East westward or whether the movement beginning in the West about 1800 was the spark that set off the Eastern quickening of interest. Perhaps it is better to think of the two as spontaneous movements occurring at nearly the same time, with the same fundamental causes, each having great effect upon the other, and both combining to exert a tremendous influence upon the social history of the nation throughout the following century.

The settlers who made their way across the mountains during and immediately after the Revolution cut themselves off from the churches of the Eastern states, and for a time the isolation of the families lost in the little forest clearings was one of the greatest hardships of Western life. But settlement rapidly increased, and the frontiersmen, eager to take advantage of every opportunity for community life, welcomed the missionary and flocked to revival meetings. The Presbyterians were in a good position to assume responsibility for missionary work, for they were already entrenched in the Allegheny region in the Scotch-Irish settlements that stretched from Pennsylvania to Georgia. The Congregational church, too, might well have been expected to flourish wherever emigrants from New England settled extensively. Both the Congregational and the Presbyterian churches insisted upon an educated clergy and endeavored to bring culture to the Western communities as rapidly as possible, and both considered missionary activity in the West a patriotic as well as a religious duty. Their appeal to the frontiersman, however, was decidedly less than that of the Baptist and Methodist churches.

The Baptist church, which had spread rapidly after the Great Awakening, went over the mountains with the pioneers, and its simplicity of doctrine and organization fitted into the frontier atmosphere. The Baptist preachers were indigenous — from the ranks of the frontier farmers themselves — and were, at least at first, self-supporting, tilling their own soil five or six days a week. The Baptist insistence on immersion was a tangible issue that appealed to the frontier, and it figured large in frontier theological discussions, serving to distinguish the Baptists from sects very similar to them in other respects.

The Methodist church was the most vigorous in Western enterprise, and Methodist churches were soon the most numerous. Their organization was autocratic and centralized, and their first American bishop, Francis Asbury, was an aggressive, restless, incredibly active and vigorous person, well fitted to direct a flock of circuit-riding evangelists. Methodist doctrine, however, was exceedingly democratic, emphasizing the gospel of free will and free grace, the belief that men are equal before the Lord, and the tenet that each must obtain his own salvation through conversion. The ideal of Methodism was the "creedless religion of the heart."

In the West the Methodist church made wide use of the circuit rider—a practice that was copied by other churches. The circuits were long and the life arduous. Preferably unmarried, practically without a home, the circuit rider and his horse traversed the back country. Not awaiting the arrival of Methodist settlers, he organized Methodist "classes" wherever he found settlers interested in any religious service. Each rider supervised twenty to thirty such local units, preaching almost every day in the week. The riders themselves came up from the ranks. Vigorous young lay preachers were encouraged to "exercise their gifts" and were given exhorting licenses by the presiding elders. Some of them became circuit riders and rendered long years of hard service. Western elders, too, and even bishops were for all practical purposes circuit riders, for they found it necessary to travel extensively to keep in touch with their far-flung districts.

The few Catholics in the West were served by itinerant priests except in the French settlements. John Carroll of Maryland was made the first American Catholic bishop in 1789, but his communicants numbered only about thirty thousand at that time. The Catholic church looked to immigration from Catholic countries for recruits and was not of much significance in the West until the purchase of Louisiana added French Catholics and the following years saw the beginning of Irish and German immigration. The early Western travelers noted that there were almost no Episcopalians on the frontier. It was not until after 1815 that Bishop

Chase established both churches and schools in the Ohio-Illinois country.

CAMP-MEETING REVIVALISM

When the godlessness of the backwoodsmen began to be a matter of concern to the missionaries and the circuit riders, drastic measures were used to bring conviction of sin, repentance, and conversion. Upon men accustomed to the terrors of the wilderness — loneliness, wild animals, Indian raids — mild homilies had no effect, but vivid pictures of hell-fire and damnation contrasted with the happiness and peace of salvation, if used with sufficient dramatic force, would bring the strong man to his knees. As Ralph Leslie Rusk says, the Protestant sects succeeded in the West in inverse ratio to their intellectual attainments and in direct ratio to their emotional appeal.[10]

Frontier religion was an intensely individual experience. Its major tenets were these: Before conversion man's soul is shackled by sin; acceptance of religion means freedom from bondage; salvation must come through conversion consciously experienced at a definite time and place. This revivalistic type of Christianity was not created by the frontier, but there it found its natural habitat and ran riot in every extreme of emotion and in primitive abandon. A militant evangelical Protestantism preached by itinerant ministers often as illiterate as those who listened to them was the force that exhilarated, united, and at the same time tamed the frontier. Such a West was ripe for the excitement of the camp meeting and the efforts of the revivalist. So much alone, the frontiersman was peculiarly susceptible to crowd psychology; leading a violent life, he reacted violently to the vigorous preaching of the frontier evangelists. The revival was to him both a social event and an intense religious experience.

The revival movement began soon after the Revolution in the back country of North Carolina, Virginia, and Maryland. In 1787 a revival at the Jones' Hole church in Virginia was accompanied by the violence and physical manifestations later characteristic of the Western camp meetings. In the midst of the screaming, groaning, and dancing a part of the church wall collapsed. Impervious to the falling bricks and mortar, the frenzied people continued their excitement until exhausted, and later one man proudly proclaimed that just before he experienced conversion the Lord himself hit him with a brick. Thirty-five hundred converts were claimed for this and other revivals of the period. In Maryland the Methodists gained so many adherents that other sects were alarmed lest "at this rate the Methodists will get all the people."

Coincident with the revival movement just starting in the New England churches, this Methodist and Baptist expansion in the South greatly increased the desire of all churches to carry religion and salvation to the "Godless West." On the frontier missionaries from the Northeast met the representatives of the Allegheny Presbyterian synods and the circuit-riding Methodist preachers. They were, for the most part, eager young men; afraid of the worldliness of the seaboard states and convinced of the wickedness and desperate need of the West, they wished to dedicate their lives to the preaching of salvation.

Such a frontier preacher was James McGready, who came over the mountains from the Carolinas into southwest Kentucky in 1796. Logan County had long been known as "Rogue's Harbor," and its collection of horse thieves, murderers, highway robbers, counterfeiters, fugitive bond-servants, and runaway debtors were not easily won. Meetings were well attended, but no conversions were made. Then in the summer of 1799 McGready held a sacramental meeting at the Red River from which he hoped to secure better results. Two young preachers, brothers by the name of McGee, one a Methodist and one a Presbyterian, happened by and came to assist in the preaching. And there, much to the astonishment of congregation and preachers alike, began a revival that was to develop into one of the greatest religious excitements of all time. A letter from John McGee to a presiding elder of the Methodist church describes the scene — soon to be typical of Western revivals:

William felt such a power come over him that he quit his seat and sat down on the floor of the pulpit. I suppose not knowing what he did. A power which caused me to tremble was upon me. There was a solemn weeping all over the house. At length I rose up and exhorted them to let the Lord God Omnipotent reign in their hearts, and submit to Him, and their souls would live. Many broke silence. The woman [sic] in the east end of the house shouted tremendously. I left the pulpit and went through the audience shouting and exhorting with all possible ecstasy and energy, and the floor was soon covered with the slain.[11]

This time the excitement did not collapse after the meeting ended but spread like wildfire through Kentucky and Tennessee. The next summer so many people flocked to the Gasper River sacramental meeting that it was necessary to hold the services outdoors. This first camp meeting, for the services were held from Friday to Tuesday, was the scene of violent preaching and much shouting and weeping. Preaching, praying, and singing went on all through the day and night except for the hours from midnight to dawn. Little attention was paid to food and still less to rest. When Saturday morning broke, the "slain" — those struggling with conviction of sin — were lying in anguish all about the camp, and by the end of the session the conversions were many.

Ten such camp meetings were held in southwest Kentucky during that season and still more the next summer. One of them was attended by Barton Stone, the pastor of the Cane Ridge church in Bourbon County, who then went home and vividly described the camp-meeting revival he had witnessed. Catching his excitement, the members of the Cane Ridge church made arrangements for a camp meeting of their own. It was a union meeting of Presbyterians and Methodists and lasted from Friday to Wednesday. More than twenty thousand people attended, and the excitement was intense. The diary of the Reverend Mr. Lyle, who was present, described the crowd as rushing hysterically from preacher to preacher and swarming about those who were "fallen" in the agonies of their conviction of sin.

Two young men, Peter Cartwright and James Finley, later the most famous of all the backwoods preachers, were present at the Cane Ridge meeting. Finley was converted on this occasion and wrote of it in his *Autobiography* in vivid terms:

The noise was like the roar of Niagara. The vast sea of human beings seemed to be agitated as if by a storm. I counted seven ministers all preaching at once, some on stumps, others in wagons, and one . . . was standing on a tree trunk which had, in falling, lodged against another. Some of the people were singing, others praying, some crying for mercy in the most piteous accents, while others were shouting most vociferously. . . . At one time I saw at least five hundred swept down in a moment, as if a battery of a thousand guns had been opened upon them, and then immediately followed shrieks and shouts that rent the very heavens.[12]

After the Cane Ridge meeting the contagion spread rapidly. Through the summers of 1802 and 1803 the frontiersmen flocked to meetings held in dozens of forest clearings. By 1805 the fever had greatly diminished, and as the years went by it became intermittent, although there were annual camp meetings in many districts throughout the century.

There is only occasional mention in contemporary accounts of camp meetings in the East — one even of a meeting on Long Island — but it is obvious that the evangelical, romantic type of religiosity was carried back from the frontier to the Eastern states. Yet methods and manifestations differed greatly in the East. Where churches were more numerous and population less scattered, revivals were usually held indoors in the form of protracted meetings conducted either by the resident ministers or by an imported evangelist. Western camp-meeting methods and measures were used to some extent — bolder preaching, praying for individuals by name, insistence upon public evidence of conversion, and a pledge that the penitent would "serve the Lord." There were interdenominational meetings, mass conversions, and mass admissions to the church. But there was less "shouting" in the East and fewer physical manifestations of religious excitement.

These physical extremes of religious enthusiasm were peculiarly a camp-meeting phenomenon. A special terminology was quickly evolved. All such manifestations of excitement were called "exercises." The falling exercise has been mentioned, the shouting exercise is obvious, the jerking exercise came a little later but was perhaps the most prevalent. All observers give detailed descriptions of the "jerks." Peter Cartwright's *Autobiography* includes a full account of this form of religious hysteria, concluding with the story of the unrepentant sinner who swore he would "drink the damned jerks to death." His arms jerked so violently that he dropped his whisky bottle and could not pick it up again. His curses filled the air until his head jerked with such force that he broke his neck. Cartwright piously comments, "I always looked upon the jerks as a judgment sent from God." [13]

The barking exercise seems to have been common, too. As the name indicates, the afflicted often dropped on all fours and barked like dogs. In packs they would dash at a tree as they had seen dogs do when treeing an opossum. This was called "treeing the devil." The running, rolling, and laughing exercises need no description; the last became so prevalent that the "Holy Laugh" seems to have been almost a part of the services. Often the preachers encouraged dancing to relieve the tension, and the solemn prancing about reminded observers of the services of the Shaker communities. Some accounts mention local variations that indicate the vivid imaginations of certain of those under conviction. At one camp meeting several men dropped on their knees in the aisles and played marbles in literal obedience to the admonition, "Except ye be converted, and become as little children, ye shall not enter into the kingdom of heaven." An Irish preacher named McNemar crawled on the ground saying, "I am the serpent that tempted Eve." A canny Scot, unaffected by the hysteria, thereupon stepped on his head with the quotation, "The seed of woman shall bruise the serpent's head."[14] Along with this wide variety of physical phenomena came genuine trances and visions.

The attitude of the preachers usually determined the quantity and the variety of the extravagances. The better educated preachers, especially the Presbyterians, opposed the most intense excitement. Where the preachers themselves were calm and controlled there were few excesses; a period of quiet prayer was a sure cure for an incipient epidemic of jerks. The Methodist and Baptist itinerant preachers used the physical exercises to procure conversions. Hysterical preachers had a hypnotic effect upon the people, and their ranting was often the signal for mass hysteria. Those with a sense of humor, even though the humor may have been crude and coarse, held their audiences in control and relieved the intensity of emotion with gibes and apt stories. Forceful and competent evangelists like Finis Ewing and Peter Cartwright used much practical psychology in managing their huge audiences. They were utterly fearless, sturdy, honest, and self-controlled.

Taking stock after the initial wave of revival had swept across the Middle West, the churches found that, even with some allowance for backsliding, they had gained many new members, the Methodists and Baptists having reaped the largest harvest. With the same tendency to emotionalism that had characterized the revivals, the frontiersman turned to a survey of religious doctrine. His militant individualism made him the ardent champion of whatever dogma he found interesting. The results were schism within the churches and a galaxy of new sects. The Methodists with their auto-cratic church government and relatively uncomplicated creed had the least difficulty, whereas the Baptists with their independent local church organization and the absence of real control in their associa-tions split into numerous groups. There were Hard- and Soft-Shell Baptists, United Baptists, Particular and General Baptists, Primitive and Free-Will Baptists, while the Disciples of Christ, the Christian church, and the Campbellites (followers of Thomas and Alexander Campbell) were offshoots of the Western Baptist church. Usually the differences were upon minor points — immersion versus sprin-kling, infant versus adult baptism — but the quarrels were hot. Even such minor issues as the use of the psalms in the church services led to disputes and schism. Many of the new sects were short-lived; some were permanent.

The Presbyterians, too, had serious doctrinal difficulties in the West. One schism that occurred in the Cumberland region was occasioned by a dispute over the ordination of preachers who had not met the usual Presbyterian standard of training and over the whole matter of revivalistic methods. Those who advocated adopt-ing Methodist doctrines and methods seceded and formed the Cum-berland Presbyterian church, which grew rapidly in the West because of its circuit-riding and camp-meeting methods. Another Presbyterian schism came because of the promulgation of New Light doctrines in the West. A group of ministers who, in direct contravention of all Calvinist doctrine, placed their emphasis upon God's love for the whole world and the possibility of salvation for all sinners, were forced out of the church and formed a sect called simply the Christians, which later was merged with the Campbellite Disciples.

The close union between American political and religious faith is shown in the infinite tolerance accorded this apparently endless multiplication of sects. James Fenimore Cooper wrote that it was a mistake to think that America's liberality on religious subjects was due to the lack of an established church. "On the contrary," he said, "the fact that there is no establishment is owing . . . to the sentiment of the people." [15] Even more explicitly, Emerson

Davis, in a book published in 1851, said: "Men are free, and claim the right to think for themselves in religious as well as in political matters." [16]

During the excitement over the affairs of war-torn Europe there was a temporary subsidence of religious enthusiasm, but with the return of peace in 1815 came a renewal of interest in camp meetings, and the resulting revivals had an effect upon the Eastern states, too. Western New York was visited by so many waves of religious emotion that it acquired the name of a "burnt" district where it was difficult to create any excitement. But it was in western New York that Charles Grandison Finney in the mid-1820's began the evangelical work that was to continue throughout his life. His published memoirs are one long chronicle of revival meetings conducted in most of the Eastern cities and throughout the upper Middle West — a chronicle of the successes of the eloquent preacher whose hypnotic eye and terroristic imagery swept hundreds of converts into the fold in an upsurge of religious excitement that came to be known as the Great Revival.

Although he was not a camp-meeting evangelist, Finney used many of the tactics of the Western itinerant preacher. He preached not only salvation but reform, and many who came under his influence turned to the abolition and temperance societies and made of them crusades as vigorous as Finney's own. Indeed, the Great Revival was the fountain of energy from which came much of the impetus for the various reform movements. The whole-souled young reformers of this period disregarded the doctrinal disputes of earlier days and threw their energies into social reform.

This religious fervor may itself have been in part responsible for the development in the same period of free-thought and atheistic agencies to voice the opinions of its opponents. Frances Wright and Robert Dale Owen led the way with their *Free Enquirer*, the German rationalistic groups in their Turnvereins followed, and in the 1840's there was even some attempt at national organization with scantily attended conventions in 1845 and 1847. This movement made little appeal except in the cities, where it was militant and where it allied itself with the socialism that was being adopted by some of the workingmen. It scarcely threatened the grip of the clergy, but they swept at once into an attack upon "infidelity," closing their ranks against the common enemy with public meetings and sermons and with attempts to stifle the atheist press.[17]

OBSERVERS AND CRITICS

The frank and open adoption of emotionalism in religion and the sensational methods of revivalists did not go unnoticed by American and European contemporary commentators. Margaret Bayard Smith in describing a revival in Washington in 1822 stated that the preachers were

introducing all the habits and hymns of the Methodists into our Presbyterian churches . . . that they were going through the highways and hedges, to invite guests . . . into every house exhorting the people, particularly into all the taverns, grog-shops, and other resorts of dissipation and vice. Whether all these excessive efforts will produce a permanent reformation I know not; but there is something very repugnant to my feelings in the public way in which they discuss the conversions and convictions of people and in which young ladies and children display their feelings and talk of their convictions and experiences. Dr. May calls the peculiar fever, the *night* fever, and he says almost all cases were produced by night meetings, crowded rooms, excited feelings, and exposure to night air.[18]

A somewhat less naïve explanation of revivalistic phenomena was made by Bishop Hopkins of Vermont, who stated that revivalists secured conversions solely because of the terror induced by their exhortations. Disapproval of such tactics seems to have been prevalent among the Episcopalian clergy, one of whom Captain Marryat quoted as saying that revivals were

those startling and astounding shocks which are constantly invented, artfully and habitually applied, under all the power of sympathy, and of a studied and enthusiastic elocution, by a large class of preachers among us. To startle and to shock is their great secret power.[19]

But the American clergy in general probably felt that the revival had come to stay and could be made a valuable part of the religious program of the Protestant churches.

European travelers almost invariably were taken to camp meetings, especially in the West, and reacted to the experience in accord with their own temperaments. Captain Marryat drew back in disgust from the preacher who began his prayer with the words "Almighty and diabolical God," and deprecated all the excesses and extravagances of evangelical religion. Frances Trollope made many caustic comments about both revivals and preachers. Always suspecting the worst, she felt sure that such sessions must turn at times into sex orgies, although the only ocular evidence she had was the sight of a preacher whispering consolation into the ear of a sobbing and distraught young feminine convert.

James Stuart was much impressed by the perfect decorum of the audience, the "faultless" sermons, and the magnificent singing. The revival he attended, however, was on Long Island; he was not exposed to the crudities of a genuine frontier camp meeting. It is more surprising to find the usually censorious Thomas Hamilton commending the camp meeting as an agency of civilization.

In a free community [he wrote] the follies of the fanatic are harmless. The points on which he differs from those around him are rarely of a nature to produce injurious effects on his conduct as a citizen. But the man without religion acknowledges no restraint but human laws; and the dungeon and the gibbet are necessary to secure the rights and interests of his fellow-citizens from violation. There can be no doubt, therefore, that in a newly settled country the strong effect produced by these camp-meetings and revivals is on the whole beneficial. The restraints of public opinion and penal legislation are little felt in the wilderness; and, in such circumstances, the higher principle of action, communicated by religion, is a new and additional security to society.[20]

Two of the most detailed descriptions of camp-meeting revivals are those of Francis Lieber and Fredrika Bremer, written nearly twenty years apart and published in 1835 and 1853. Lieber was repelled by the emotionalism of the camp meeting he attended and was shocked by the "scenes of unrestrained excitement," but the Swedish traveler, Fredrika Bremer, was much impressed by the immense crowd of both white and colored people at the Georgia camp meeting she witnessed in the early 1850's. The grandeur of the night meeting in the forest, the eight fine altars, the campfires of resinous wood, the superb singing of the thousands of Negroes, the wails of the penitent, the thunder and lightning of an approaching storm — all, she said, combined to make the night one never to be forgotten.

The effects of the absence of state control and the consequent multiplicity of sects seemed to interest all foreign observers. Many of them mention the lack of religious intolerance in the United

States and the easy "live and let live" philosophy apparent in the attitude of most men. Alexander Mackay, who traveled extensively in America in the 1840's, was so impressed that he wrote:

It is true that the insulting term "toleration" is but seldom heard in America in connexion with the religious system of the country. To say that one tolerates another's creed, implies some right to disallow it, a right that happens to be suspended or in abeyance for the time being. The only mode in which the American manifests any intolerance in reference to religion is that they will not tolerate that the independence of the individual should in any degree, be called in question in connexion with it.[21]

On the more fundamental question of the connection between the American democratic faith and the emotional perfectionistic religion that had swept over the United States the observers seemed in agreement. Again and again missionaries and patriots identified democratic with religious faith and asserted that neither could stand alone, that combined they furnished an invincible bulwark for American freedom. Timothy Flint, writer and missionary preacher of the first decade of the century, emphasized always that missionary enterprise in the West was for the good of the whole country; the West must not fall into Godless anarchy, for the representative institutions of the East would then also perish. As the Western missionary told De Tocqueville, "It is, therefore, our interest that the New States should be religious, in order that they may permit us to remain free."

In an essay published in 1851, Mark Hopkins, president of Williams College, expressed the same feeling that democracy must be linked with Christianity:

Man himself is the highest product of this lower world, those institutions would seem to be the best which show, not the most imposing results of aggregated labor, but humanity itself, in its most general cultivation and highest forms. This idea finds its origin and support in the value which Christianity places upon the individual, and, fully carried out, must overthrow all systems of darkness and mere authority. Individual liberty and responsibility involve the right of private judgment; this involves the right to all the light necessary to form a correct judgment; and this again must involve the education of the people, and the overthrow of everything, civil and religious, which will not stand the ordeal of the most scrutinizing examination and of the freest discussion.[22]

Regardless of their differences as to details, European and American observers alike were insistent upon the prominence of the part played by religion in the Western World. They saw that the same intensity of faith vivified both the democracy and the religious experience of many Americans, and they realized the potentialities of that combination. The mind and heart quickened by the "lively joy" of a vital religious experience were easily turned toward social reforms, and the spirit of inquiry and soul-searching that animated the revival had a dynamic social significance. The American faith in democratic institutions found its alter ego in the romantic evangelical spirit of American religious life. Together they gave to the Americans of the first half century of the republic their conviction that their institutions could be perfected and their national destiny be fulfilled.

PART TWO
Cults and Utopias

The only limits to the diversity of new faiths in the first half of the nineteenth century were the limits of men's own differences and of their aspirations and imaginations. Every new prophet or group of philosophers might expect to find a following among men of like ideas and ideals, and each new reform or doctrine found advocates among those stirred by the general ferment of the period. Individualism bred diversity and multiplicity both in religious sects and in reform movements. Every aspect of society and every phase of life were subject to the eager scrutiny of inquiring minds, and the optimistic liberalism of the day caused men to believe in the possibility of creating a new heaven and a new earth by the intensity of their efforts and the efficacy of their faith.

In 1840 a convention in Boston of the Friends of Universal Reform (usually referred to as the Charndon Street Convention) was attended by a motley crowd representing many shades of radical thinking. Emerson somewhat critically and yet humorously described them thus:

If the assembly was disorderly, it was picturesque. Madmen, madwomen, men with beards, Dunkers, Muggletonians, Come-outers, Groaners, Agrarians, Seventh-Day Baptists, Quakers, Abolitionists, Calvinists, Unitarians, and Philosophers — all came successively to the top, and seized their moment, if not their hour, wherein to chide, or pray, or preach, or protest.[1]

The existence of such an assemblage and the elements of which it was composed are evidence of the complexity and diversity of the ebullient faith of the mid-nineteenth century. The idea of progress carried to the extreme of belief in the possibility of perfection was a heady wine, causing in many men an emotional intoxication that led to a confused view of the world about them. From this very confusion came numerous new religious cults and social experiments in communal living.

46

CHAPTER 3

Transcendentalism

Part of this movement and yet not of it, unleashed from the practical but not running a "mad chase" — unless it was touched with the divine madness of creative genius — the Transcendentalism of New England had a vital share in the vivification of the American spirit in the second quarter of the nineteenth century. Through their sublime mysticism the Transcendentalists made the direct contact between the individual soul and its Creator that was demanded by every Western itinerant evangelist. For them perfection was an objective to be reached in God's infinite time by a long road marked by milestones of educational and social achievement, and their millennium was a vision of a day when man should at last bring to a glorious fruition the capacities with which he was endowed. Transcendentalism is difficult to define, and the Transcendentalists defy precise description, but the importance of both the movement and its members is unquestioned. Without a definite creed, Transcendentalism was at once a faith, a philosophy, a mystical religion, and an ethical way of life. A list of those connected with the movement is a roster of the creative minds of New England in the period of its belated but charming cultural flowering.*

THE TRANSCENDENTAL FAITH

Just as New England Unitarianism stemmed from orthodox Calvinistic Congregationalism in the eighteenth century, so Transcendentalism was an offshoot of Unitarianism when it too had grown orthodox and conservative. The typical Unitarian was tolerant, kindly, with cultivated tastes and high moral standards; he accepted civic responsibility, was markedly philanthropic, and considered himself the champion of intellectual causes and of New England idealism. The liberalness of Unitarian dogma — or rather the lack of dogma — appealed to the "best people" of New England, but

* In the history of American literature and philosophic thought the subject of Transcendentalism looms large. In an account of social history in the period of the Transcendentalists it is necessary to give only a brief summary of their ideas and their careers in order to bring out their share in the religious diversity of the day. The part of each great Transcendentalist in other fields is discussed in the subsequent accounts of the various cults, communities, and reforms.

these same "best people" were conservative in everything except religion. Economically they were prosperous, and their main interests lay in commerce and in property rights. Politically they were Federalists, and later Whigs, rather than Democrats. It was a common expression in New England that "Unitarianism was the cult of the arrived," but no one could assert that it was either emotionally spiritual or deeply philosophical. It was negative even in its individualism and coldly reasoning in its acceptance of the privileged position of its select membership.

Transcendentalism brought, for a decade, a spiritual vigor into the formalism of Unitarianism that made it a creative force. This dynamic element was, in the words of one of the Transcendentalists, "an assertion of the inalienable integrity of man, of the immanence of Divinity in instinct. . . . Amidst materialists, zealots and sceptics, the Transcendentalist believed in perpetual inspiration, the miraculous power of will, and a birthright to universal good." [1] O. B. Frothingham, the historian of Transcendentalism and an heir to its tradition and ideals, spoke of it as a transference of supernatural attributes to the natural constitution of mankind. Through this transference man had the power to go beyond the realm of his senses and to perceive that which lay beyond all physical phenomena. Transcendentalism meant, as one of its adherents whimsically said, "a little beyond." It was based on the fundamental belief that the individual soul is identified with God and that instinct, insight, and intuition are the tests and methods of realizing that union. In his first series of essays Emerson endeavored to give the essence of the faith of the Transcendentalist:

He believes in miracles, in the perpetual openness of the human mind to the new influx of light and power, he believes in inspiration and ecstasy. He wishes that the spiritual principle should be suffered to demonstrate itself to the end, in all possible applications to the state of man, without the admission of anything unspiritual; that is anything positive, dogmatic, personal.[2]

The mysticism of Transcendentalism is obvious, and the theory of the oversoul with its mystical union with God may present difficulties to the comprehension of those not of the elect, but its idealism and its critical impatience with any achievement short of the ideal made it a force to be reckoned with.

The Transcendentalist rejected the cold spirit and the compromises of the Unitarian, but, since he too was of the intellectual few, he retained the critical, rational methods. He accepted the maxims listed by William Henry Channing: * "Trust, dare and be; infinite good is ready for your asking; seek and find. All that your fellows claim or need is that you should become, in fact, your highest self; fulfill, then, your ideal." [3] These maxims placed the emphasis upon individualism and a dignified self-reliance. The mind and soul of man, self-purified and self-taught, might transcend reason and intuitively reach the spiritual absolutes through which man could find the reality behind the outer shell of life. Transcendentalism emphasized man "as a solitary independent being, striving for sublime knowledge." [4]

Mystical and metaphysical though these abstractions may seem, the Transcendentalists were in many respects very practical men. Their philosophy was always tinged with Yankee coolness and shrewdness, and their feet were always solidly upon the ground even though they might use the stars as hitching posts for their thoughts. Their main concern was truth, unchangeable and eternal, and their constant objective was reality — in religion, in government, in economics, and in the social order. Their courage was on a par with their vision, for they were willing to put their grasp of these realities to the test of making them a part of their daily life. They translated the romantic spirit into action and used its vitality in humanitarian reform and in the furtherance of human liberty.

The origin of the Transcendental faith was complex. Its American heritage was readily apparent: New England Calvinism freed from dogma by the negative principles of Unitarianism was its theological background; Yankee shrewdness, practical sense, and self-reliance, coupled with a large portion of traditional New England conscience, provided the psychological setting. The spark that set it off and the force that gave it motion were in the spirit of the age, a spirit made up of individualism and dynamic religious revivalism. From Europe the movement gathered strength from three sources: French revolutionary thought, the German philosophical idealism of Kant and his disciples, and English literary romanticism.

* William Henry Channing was the nephew of the more famous Unitarian minister, William Ellery Channing, who was the beloved "Dr. Channing."

Transcendentalism owed much to the teachings of Plato, Pytha-
goras, and Plotinus. Not for nothing had the intellectual class of
New England been subjected to a classical education. Indeed, the
philosophical transcendentalism from which the American group
drew much of their inspiration has at times been called Neo-
Platonism. They found food for thought, also, in the works of
Oriental philosophers and in those of the medieval mystics. The
language of mysticism is the same in every age and among all
peoples, and the American movement was a genuine renaissance of
mystical and transcendental thought.

The authors most constantly read and discussed by the Concord
philosophers included Rousseau, Coleridge, Wordsworth, Carlyle,
Cousin, Constant, Kant, Richter, Schiller, Goethe, Swedenborg,
and Pestalozzi, with a varying admixture of Greek and Oriental
names. The movement was bound up with the growth of the scientific spirit, and regardless of the fact that its philosophy was
based on the ideas that all religious absolutes are nonempirical and
that nonempirical sources or principles of knowledge are transcendental — that is, transcend experience and reason — the American
Transcendentalist was an eager experimenter. To him no institution of his day was sacrosanct; slavery, education, property rights,
the position of women, and the relations of labor and capital were
all under fire. The search for truth and reality carried on in a period
of social unrest was an incentive to radicalism of the first magnitude.

THE TRANSCENDENTAL CLUB

Although the fire lighted by the Transcendentalists warmed and
inspired many who never laid claim to the name or acknowledged
the cult, the actual group of Transcendentalists was very small. In
Boston in 1836 about a dozen New England writers, many of them
Unitarian clergymen, began to meet in what soon was called the
Transcendental Club. The group had little or no organization; its
purpose was to discuss German philosophy and all the emotional
ferment of the day. There was little cohesion in the group and no
unanimity of opinion. Its members were, as Emerson said, "only
agreed in having fallen upon Coleridge and Wordsworth, and
Goethe, then on Carlyle, with pleasure and sympathy."

The nucleus of the group was the select few who came together in the home of George Ripley on the night of September 19, 1836: Ralph Waldo Emerson, Frederick Henry Hedge, Bronson Alcott, James Freeman Clarke, and Convers Francis. It is impossible to make any complete list of those who joined the group in later meetings or to be sure which of those who were present occasionally should be considered members. Among these were Theodore Parker, Margaret Fuller, Orestes Brownson, William Henry Channing, Elizabeth and Sophia Peabody, Thoreau, Hawthorne, Jones Very, C. P. Cranch, Cyrus Bartol, and Charles Follen. George Bancroft, the historian, and Dr. Channing, to whom many of the members owed so much, seem to have been present once or twice. Topics for discussion were informally decided upon, and the members of the club came together with such guests as they cared to invite and held a symposium that lasted well into the night.

After some years of these informal meetings it was decided that the group should sponsor a literary review, and the *Dial* was the result. The editor of the magazine for the first years of its short existence was Margaret Fuller. She was followed by Emerson, who continued the publication for two years more. Its articles, poems, and reviews were drawn from almost all the members of the Transcendental Club and from a select few of like interests. Never a financial success, the publication of the *Dial* was made possible only by the devotion of its editors and the cooperation of its contributors, but in the four years of its existence (1840–44) it made its mark upon American literary history. As compared with other periodicals of its day its breadth of scope, vitality of expression, and intensity of emotional appeal are striking. From its pages emanate the religious impulse, crusading zeal, ethical philosophy, and critical spirit of the Transcendentalist movement.

From the "Orphic Sayings" of Bronson Alcott and the poetry of Jones Very to the "Thoughts on Theology" of Theodore Parker and the articles on Oriental philosophy by Thoreau, the *Dial* published the essence of the thinking of the group that dominated the New England literary world. Its translations of the works of German authors and its reviews of a wide range of English and American writers popularized modern philosophic and literary thought and created new standards for American work. One of the greatest services of the *Dial* to American letters and to American life was the opportunity it gladly offered to all young writers for the publication of their poems, essays, and critical articles. Coming as it did when American democratic thought was ready for its most complete expression and when romanticism was combining with the scientific spirit to create a new world in which reform and progress seemed inevitable, the new journal offered a medium for the expression of ideas other than those of the Transcendentalists.

Although the *Dial* was discontinued in 1844, it was followed by other reviews of a similar nature under different sponsorship but with much the same clientele and the same group of contributors. At no time in the twenty-year period during which Transcendentalism was a vital factor in American life were its members without some means for the satisfaction of their passion for self-expression.[5]

BRONSON ALCOTT AND THE CONVERSATIONS

That passion could be satisfied for some of the Transcendentalists by the publication of their critical or creative literary work, but there were others who found their medium of expression in talk. All America in the mid-nineteenth century seemed willing to spend the evenings, and often many daytime hours as well, in listening to lectures on every variety of subject by almost any speaker who felt he had a message to impart. The lyceum flourished, rivaling the pulpit and the public library in popularity. The pros and cons of every project of reform were heard throughout the length and breadth of the land. No prophet failed of a hearing, and the advocates of all new movements, no matter how wild-eyed they might be, found eager audiences.

The offering of the Transcendentalists for the cultivated ears of Boston society was of a slightly different and more refined form. The elite flocked to the "Conversations" of Bronson Alcott and of Margaret Fuller and found much to approve in the erudite and lofty discussions of the philosophical, historical, or literary subjects presented for their edification. These Conversations seem to have been of the nature of a carefully planned series of informal lectures on related subjects. Twenty-five to thirty people seemed the most responsive audience, and usually ten or twelve besides the leader or lecturer participated in the discussion.

Alcott began his lecture-conversations in 1839 after the failure of his Temple School and continued them for many years, even going on long tours through the country holding these symposiums at every stop — often on such abstract subjects as "Self-culture" or "Human Life." Talking was his forte. In the Conversations he was both effective and charming; his voice was pleasing and expressive; every sentence seemed to flow forth extemporaneously in a stream of beauty and order. Emerson, who like many writers was a hesitant and fumbling talker, was charmed with the splendor of Alcott's talk and confided to his journal that Alcott

delights in speculation, in nothing so much, and is very well endowed and weaponed for that work with a copious, accurate and elegant vocabulary. . . . He speaks truth truly, for the expression is adequate. Yet he knows only this one language. He hardly needs an antagonist — he needs only an intelligent ear. When he is greeted by loving and intelligent persons, his discourse soars to a wonderful height, so regular, so lucid, so playful, so new and disdainful of all boundaries of tradition and experience, that the hearers seem no longer to have bodies of material gravity but almost they can mount into the air at pleasure, or leap at one bound out of this poor solar system.[6]

For nearly four decades Alcott attracted his audiences of thirty to sixty persons for evenings of soliloquy and discussions. Most at home in Boston, he yet found congenial souls when the talks were given elsewhere. O. B. Frothingham, who often attended the Boston Conversations, wrote of them with warm approval. The topics, he said, were of general interest, and if the group was

awake and sympathetic . . . the season was delightful. The unfailing serenity of the leader, his wealth of mental resource, his hospitality of thought, his wit, his extraordinary felicity of language, his delicacy of touch, ready appreciation of different views, and singular grace in turning opinions toward the light, made it clear to all present that to this especial calling he was chosen.[7]

His adverse critics, however, were many. Fredrika Bremer heard him twice and commented dryly, "Alcott drank water, and we drank fog."[8] The contemptuous attitude of some of his American contemporaries is well expressed in a bit of verse by J. T. Trowbridge, which, strangely enough, seems to condemn its author more than the mystical genius of whom it was written:

> Do you care to meet Alcott? His mind is a mirror
> Reflecting the unspoken thought of his hearer.

To the great, he is great; to the fool he's a fool —
In the world's dreary desert a crystalline pool
Where a lion looks in and a lion appears,
But an ass will see only his own ass's ears.[9]

MARGARET FULLER

The Conversations of Margaret Fuller, similar to those of Alcott, were first held in Boston in 1839 and were continued through five winters, until she went to New York at the invitation of Horace Greeley to write literary criticism for the *Tribune*. She was one of the most striking members of the Transcendentalist group, although Frothingham states that, strictly speaking, she cannot be classed as a Transcendentalist. She was, he says, enthusiastic and magnetic rather than philosophical and far more poetic than systematic. Her life was dramatic and in many ways tragic. Her indomitable spirit, sweeping interests, and ceaseless activity were characteristic of the age and the group with which she was identified, and her capacity for friendship is evidenced in every contemporary account of her life and work.

An intelligent and precocious child, she early became the constant care of a doctrinaire father. She was taught Latin and English grammar simultaneously and began to read Latin at the mature age of six. She was taught never to speak until she was sure her meaning would be crystal clear and never to make a statement for which she could not give a meaning. Her father believed the old Roman writers furnished the best evidence of the virtues he wished to inculcate, and Margaret was given Virgil and Horace to read before she was ten. The days were not long enough for the tasks set for the brilliant child, so she was kept up late and denied playtime and the companionship of children. When she was at last sent away to school she was in every way a misfit — too advanced mentally, badly adjusted socially. Sensitive and neurotic, she derived her greatest satisfaction from being startlingly different from her schoolmates and found little happiness until she was mature enough to form friendships in the Boston and Concord group of literary philosophers.

Her life in Boston was full and satisfying. She taught in Bronson Alcott's Temple School, was editor of the *Dial* for two years, and was a member of the Transcendental Club and the friend of its greatest figures. Later, in New York, she was interested in a wide variety of practical reforms and, through the publication of her *Woman in the Nineteenth Century*, became known as one of the leading feminists of the period. In 1846 she went abroad, where she was secretly married to the Marquis Ossoli, an Italian deeply involved in the Revolution of 1848. Passionately devoted to Italy and its struggle for liberalism and unity, Margaret threw herself into the cause and suffered acutely in its failure. In 1850 she returned to America with her husband and infant son, only to have her life end with theirs in a shipwreck off the Long Island coast.

The intellectual arrogance of her childhood never completely left her. It was with sincerity and conviction that she said, "I now know all the people worth knowing in America, and I find no intellect comparable to my own." Her friend and biographer was no more than just in speaking of her "mountainous *me*." [10] Much of her inspiration came from the great thinkers and writers of history, but to Emerson she always gladly acknowledged a debt of gratitude. "His influence," she wrote, "has been more beneficial to me than that of any American, and from him I first learned what is meant by an inward life. Many other springs have since fed the stream of living waters, but he first opened the fountain." [11]

Her peculiar power of intellect and flashing brilliance of mind were recognized by the Transcendentalists, who paid her the tribute of believing that she might under more favorable circumstances have become one of the greatest critics and poets of modern times. This frustration of genius, which she as well as they recognized, W. H. Channing considered one of the tragedies of Miss Fuller's life.

But [he went on] the tragedy of Margaret's history was deeper yet. Behind the poet was the woman — the fond and relying, the heroic and disinterested woman. The very glow of her poetic enthusiasm was but an outflush of trustful affection; the very restlessness of her intellect was the confession that her heart had found no home. [12]

Horace Greeley used this quotation in the chapter on Margaret Fuller in his *Recollections of a Busy Life*, concluding in agreement, "If *I* had attempted to say this, I should have somehow blundered out that, noble and great as she was, a good husband and two or three bouncing babies would have emancipated her from a deal of cant and nonsense." [13]

No achievement of the mind could completely satisfy the woman, and her belated romance, wifehood, and motherhood came to her only as a stormy prelude to the storm in which her life was lost. Her great aim in life was self-culture, and her chief contribution to the Transcendentalist movement and to the cultural life of her time was her keen appreciation of the possibilities of the development of the mind. Her genius was recognized, and her interest in the problems of the day and in the advancement of women stimulated the interest of others. Her influence was out of proportion to her actual contributions to either American thought or American letters.

RALPH WALDO EMERSON

Margaret Fuller was only one among many young American writers of the mid-nineteenth century who acknowledged their debts of gratitude to Emerson. The secret of his influence must be sought in his philosophy, his critical faculty, and his personality. The strength of that influence cannot be estimated with any degree of accuracy, but it is probable that the danger would be of under- rather than overstatement. For countless people the liberating effect of the Transcendentalist movement came through the medium of Emerson's words. From early maturity he devoted his life to the expression of a noble and idealistic philosophy and to the critical measurement of the ideas and institutions of the world about him by the standards of such a creed. In an entry in his journal shortly before 1840 Emerson expressed the purpose which was to guide him throughout his life:

I am to fire with what skill I can the artillery of sympathy and emotion. I am to indicate constantly, though all unworthy, the Ideal and Holy Life, the life within life, the Forgotten Good, the Unknown Cause in which we sprawl and sin. I am to try the magic of sincerity, that luxury permitted only to kings and poets. I am to celebrate the spiritual powers in their infinite contrast to the mechanical powers and the mechanical philosophy of this time.[14]

This challenging assertion of purpose came at a time when Americans were beginning to recognize that "mechanical powers" were destined to master their national life unless the "mechanical philosophy" could be countered by an increasing devotion to spiritual values.

A Unitarian minister and the son of a minister, Emerson quietly gave up his pastorate in his early thirties to devote himself to a life of study and to the development of his own philosophy of life. His contacts with, and his influence upon, his contemporaries came through his occasional addresses, his essays, translations, poems, and critical reviews. Accepting the Transcendentalist's faith that there is a divinity in man, he sought to find the place of man in nature and turned to the woods and fields of New England for his answer. He was a bookish man with little previous experience in the world out of doors, and this first acquaintance with the realities of nature resulted in 1836 in an essay, "Nature," that was saturated with idealism, optimism, and joy in life itself. In the next few years a succession of addresses placed before the world the quintessence of his developing philosophy. In "The American Scholar," first given as an address before a meeting of the Phi Beta Kappa Society in August 1837, Emerson sounded a note of independence for American letters, bidding the American scholar to cast off his subserviency to European tradition. He stated in the broadest terms the office and duties of the scholar and issued a challenge to all creative genius in his statement, "If a single man plant himself indomitably on his instincts, and there abide, the huge world will come round to him." Again and again, in the "Divinity School Address," in addresses on "Man the Reformer" and on "Literary Ethics," and in the first series of essays, which contained the famous "Self Reliance" and "Compensation" treatises, he reiterated the same ideas: that man's powers are sufficient for his needs, that the universe is a divine whole — man, his fellows, nature, God — and that this divinity must rule. Such a world is full of opportunities, and Emerson called upon all creative minds to grasp them and to change the institutions under which men lived to fit this revolutionary, idealistic conception. In short, the essence of his teaching was individualism, the primacy of the mind, and the connection of the individual intelligence with the divine.

Emerson thus became the spokesman of Transcendentalism and the prophet of the new age. Frothingham entitled the chapter devoted to Emerson "The Seer," and Van Wyck Brooks calls him the "New England Prophet," [15] but he was a prophet whose honor was secure in his own time and his own country because he was, as his German admirer, Herman Grimm, stated, "a perfect swimmer on the ocean of modern existence." The secret of his power was the fact that he was expressing in its highest idealistic form the spirit of his own age. The doctrine he preached was that of Luther, Rousseau, and Jefferson — revivalistic, romantic, and democratic.

The government of the republic was much in Emerson's mind, nor did he overlook the economic aspects of modern life. Both his belief in individualism and his feeling that the state must be freed from the control of those who would use it to further their own economic interests led him to the Jeffersonian democratic philosophy of a state whose functions were limited, and he feared the tyranny of a strong government with power to coerce the individual. Again and again he recorded in his journal his belief in democracy, a democracy that "has its root in the sacred truth that every man hath in him the divine Reason" and is based upon a "spirit of love for the general good."

With an acute sensitiveness to all that violated the rights of the individual, Emerson deplored the materialism of the day, condemned Negro slavery and every other variety of bondage, and sympathized with the reformers who worked to benefit society, even though his serenity and his individualism kept him from taking an active part in reform movements. Although he comprehended the dangers inherent in the increasing power of industrial capitalism, his agrarian and physiocratic views made it impossible for him to advocate socialism. Indeed, as his ideas slowly developed, he more nearly approached philosophical anarchism, which was little understood by most of his disciples. In his "Essay on Politics" appears this statement:

. . . the less government we have the better — the fewer laws, and the less confided power. The antidote to this abuse of formal government is . . . the appearance of the wise man; of whom the existing government is, it must be owned, but a shabby imitation. . . . To educate the wise man the State exists, and with the appearance of the wise man the State expires. The appearance of character makes the state unnecessary. The wise man is the State.[16]

And with that final conclusion he swung around to a view somewhat like that of Carlyle and won the approval of Nietzsche. To the American of his own day, Emerson was the realization of his own highest ideal — the completely free and untrammeled individual, serene, civilized, and benevolent.

HENRY DAVID THOREAU

The sole purpose of Thoreau's life was to find a basis for ideal living. Where a larger group of Transcendentalists founded Brook Farm, and Bronson Alcott with his family and a few friends built a communistic home at Fruitlands, Thoreau retired for two years to Walden Pond in an intensely individualistic experiment in living all his own. Little understood in his own day, Thoreau has increased in stature as the years have passed until the twentieth century acclaims him as possibly the greatest of the Transcendentalists. To his friends — Emerson, Hawthorne, Ellery Channing, Alcott — he was a genius, rugged, often acid or thorny, always stimulating. Outside of that small circle he was little known. He has been called the "Poet-Naturalist," but he was not solely poet or naturalist; he was one of the most profound scholars of his day. Greek was his second language, and Oriental philosophers and religious leaders were known to him through French and German versions. His contributions to the *Dial* were largely his translations into English of Far Eastern writings.

His great book *Walden* has been acclaimed by a later generation as a portrayal of a philosophy and way of life that repudiates the whole middle class philosophy of exploitation of both nature and man upon which the world about him was based. Stating calmly at the beginning of *Walden*, "I have travelled a good deal in Concord; and everywhere . . . the inhabitants have appeared to me to be doing penance in a thousand remarkable ways," Thoreau went on to criticize the wealth-getting, competitive, exploiting life of his day:

I see young men . . . whose misfortune it is to have inherited farms, houses, barns, cattle and farming tools. . . . Who made them serfs of the soil? Why should they eat their sixty acres, when man is condemned to eat only his peck of dirt? Why should they begin digging their graves as soon as they are born? . . . Men labor under a mistake. The better part of the man is soon plowed into the soil for compost. . . . Most men . . . through mere ignorance or mistake, are so occupied with the factitious cares and superfluously hard labors of life, that its finer fruits cannot be plucked by them . . . the laboring man has not leisure for a true integrity day by day. . . . He has no time for anything but a machine.[17]

Trade, he wrote, curses everything it touches, but apart from the world of trade it could be a joyous experience to earn one's bread. Life could be a glorious and satisfying thing.

I have learned this, at least, by my experiment: that if one advances confidently in the direction of his dreams, and endeavors to live the life which he has imagined, he will meet with a success unexpected in common hours. . . . It is a ridiculous demand which England and America make, that you shall speak so that they can understand you. . . . I fear chiefly lest my expression may not be *extra-vagant* enough, may not wander far enough beyond the narrow limits of my daily experience, so as to be adequate to the truth of which I am convinced. . . . Why level downward to our dullest perception always, and praise that as common sense? The commonest sense is the sense of men asleep, which they express by snoring. . . . Why should we be in such desperate haste to succeed and in such desperate enterprises? If a man does not keep pace with his companion, perhaps it is because he hears a different drummer. . . . The light which puts out our eyes is darkness to us. Only that day dawns to which we are awake. There is more day to dawn. The sun is but a morning star.[18]

Emerging from the serenity of Walden to a Concord village disturbed by the Mexican War, Thoreau refused his support to a state that tolerated such abuses as slavery and warfare. His passive resistance was expressed by refusal to pay his taxes. The result was twofold: a short stay in jail for the philosopher and, more important for posterity, an essay called "Civil Disobedience," a credo of philosophical anarchism that is believed to have been an inspiration to Mahatma Gandhi.

I believe . . . that government is best which governs not at all; and when men are ready for it, that will be the kind of government which they will have. . . . A government in which the majority rules in all cases cannot be based on justice. . . . There is but little virtue in the action of masses of men. . . . If the law is of such a nature that it requires you to be an agent of injustice to another, then, I say, break the law. Let your life be a counter friction to stop the machine.[19]

Slavery and the Fugitive Slave Law aroused him to break forth once more, with a stern essay, "Slavery in Massachusetts." The execution of John Brown caused his bitter "Last Days of John Brown" and the "Plea for Captain John Brown," in which he rejoiced that he lived in the age of John Brown and condemned in scathing words the laws that made him a felon: ". . . in cases of the highest importance, it is of no consequence whether a man breaks a human law or not. . . . A counterfeiting law-factory, standing half in a slave land and half in a free! What kind of laws for free men can you expect from that!"[20] Thoreau was to the day of his death the romantic rebel, the complete disciple of laissez faire. He carried to its logical conclusion the philosophy inherent in the liberalism of the early nineteenth century.

THEODORE PARKER

No man could present a greater contrast to Thoreau than did Theodore Parker, and the fact that two men so different in all but a few characteristics should be thus placed together is evidence both of the diversity within that group and of the fundamental vitality of those few common factors. Parker was first and foremost a preacher, one of the greatest of a long line of New England preachers. Parrington says that his nature was two-sided, a perfect and harmonious blending of the practical, logical, and lucid on the one hand, and of emotional, mystical idealistic, and religious characteristics on the other. Of all the Transcendentalists he best understood the social and political trends of the day. He was a born fighter: brave, energetic, uncompromising, and yet intensely practical. He was no fanatic, and for all his philosophical mysticism, he neither underestimated the adversary nor gave too much weight to the force of moral suasion alone. The antislavery movement was the reform closest to his heart, and in a Boston that frowned upon such agitation, he repudiated the Fugitive Slave Law and worked for the cause of abolition.

Parker's learning was prodigious. At the age of eight he had read Homer and Plutarch. He began his study of metaphysics at twelve and read enormously throughout his schooldays — history, politics, and philosophy. His linguistic ability was remarkable. Thomas Wentworth Higginson says he was the master of nineteen or twenty languages; it is certain that he knew Greek and Latin thoroughly as well as French, Spanish, German, and Italian, and that he read Arabic, Hebrew, Persian, and Coptic. His memory was astonishingly plastic. As a schoolboy he could memorize a poem of five hundred to a thousand words with one reading. In his later years he had a library of thirteen thousand volumes, which skeptics maintained he could not have read. His friend, James Freeman Clarke, approached him one day with the question, "Do you read all of your books, and do you know what is in them?" "I read them all," was Parker's reply, "and can give you a table of contents for each." [21] This erudition was not stored lumber, for his energy was not that of a recluse. He read and studied in order to enrich his preaching and to replenish constantly his philosophical and religious resources by drawing upon all that men had accomplished in the past. Frothingham says:

All that Parker had went into his preaching, the wealth of his library, the treasures of his heart, the sweetness of his closet meditation, the solemnity of his lonely musings. But it was not this that gave him his great power as a preacher. That, we are persuaded, was due in chief part to the earnestness of his faith in the transcendental philosophy.[22]

Parker's religious belief can be summarized briefly. He was the heir to New England Calvinism and Unitarianism with the addition of transcendental optimism and perfectionism. He believed in the infinite perfection of God, the adequacy of man, and the sufficiency of natural religion. He identified God with nature and with man and believed that God was infinite and perfect love. His wide reading as well as his belief in the perfectibility of man led him to accept, even before their Darwinian exposition, the theories of evolution and the progressive development of the human animal as well as other forms of life.

Parker was surprisingly modern in his view of the economic basis of politics and sharply critical of the emphasis upon money-getting in both the political parties of the day. In a period when feminism was new and, in the minds of most Bostonians, somewhat disreputable, the earliest women preachers were welcomed in his pulpit, and he was willing to concede to women every equality in law and society. In dealing with the "woman question," as it was called, he was, however, always somewhat handicapped by the fact that he idealized women. His own marriage was a happy one, and he had a thoroughly wholesome attitude toward the question of sex. Marriage and divorce laws, suffrage and property laws should, he thought, be changed to give women the place due them. In many other respects Parker's form of Christianity was a socialized religion. Prison reform, prevention of vice and crime, labor problems, the peace movement, education reforms, temperance, abolition — all such social problems were parts of a common whole, and a real reform could be accomplished only by a study of society as a whole. Every phase of life was of interest to Parker, and his learning and wisdom were respected by the leaders of all the reform movements.

In 1860, after years of incredible energy and exertion, Parker's life came to an end — burned out at fifty. In his last letter to his church he was able to express his tremendous joy in life and his optimism for the future:

Several times in my life I have met with what seemed worse than death . . . yet my griefs all turned into blessings; the joyous seed I planted came up discipline and I wished to tear it from the ground, but it flowered fair and bore a sweeter, sounder fruit than I expected from what I set in earth. As I look over my life I find no disappointment I could afford to lose; the cloudy morning has turned out the fairer day; the wounds of my enemies have done me good. So wondrous is this human life, not ruled by fate but Providence, which is Wisdom married unto Love, each infinite. . . . This progressive development does not end with us; we have seen only the beginning, the future triumphs of the race must be vastly greater than all accomplished yet. In the primal instincts and automatic desires of man, I have found a prophecy that what he wants is possible, and shall one day be actual. It is a glorious future on earth which I have set before your eyes and hopes. What good is not with us is before, to be attained by toil and thought and religious life.[23]

ORESTES BROWNSON

Parker's life, his preaching, and his philosophy were entirely harmonized and unified. Orestes Brownson, on the other hand, found in Transcendentalism only a way-station on a long and often disappointing journey toward religious peace. From earliest childhood, religion was important to him, and he seems to have been, as Frothingham says, completely at the mercy of every novelty in speculation. He was a poor boy, reared in upstate Vermont, badly educated, but intensely and restlessly intellectual. When he was nineteen years of age, his constant alarm over his soul's salvation sent him into the Presbyterian church. The doctrines of total depravity and predestination were too horrible for acceptance, however, and after two years he turned from Presbyterianism to its antithesis, Universalism. In 1826, when he was twenty-three, he became a preacher and, shortly, the editor of a church paper. But theological doubts still perplexed him, and he filled the journal with his own speculations, to the distress of its readers.

In 1829 he heard an address by Frances Wright, the prominent English socialist and feminist, and turned his attention to the ideas of Robert Owen and the utopian socialists. Cutting himself loose from the Universalist church, he spent some years in developing radical political and social theories and in attempting to organize a workingmen's party. In this period he seems to have rejected all religion and gone over to agnosticism, but by 1831 his own restless searching for truth drove him back, and he became a follower of Dr. Channing. From Unitarianism it was but a step to Transcendentalism, and from a working class movement it was easy to go over into the social reforms of the day.

Brownson had too much respect for education to be a Jacksonian Democrat and too much of reforming individualism to subscribe to the tenets of the Whigs. The panic of 1837 crushed his hopes for labor organization and for the education of laborers in special schools, and he came to the conclusion that the whole social order was at fault, that "the issue is now between the privileged and the under-privileged." Like most of the Transcendentalists, he was distressed by the evidences of increasing government activity and as the years went by went over more and more to the agrarian political philosophy of Calhoun, especially where Calhoun advocated the protection of the rights of a minority against the will of the majority.

In the meantime religion continued to occupy his mind, and Unitarianism soon failed to satisfy him. The natural religion of Channing and Parker was not enough; Brownson turned back to the divinity of Christ. His essay, "The Mediatorial Life of Christ," showed that he had abandoned Channing and the Transcendentalists, for he had come to feel that "the tendency to resolve God into nature is unscriptural and fatal to religion." [24] In 1844 he at last found the peace and security he craved in the Catholic church, where his restless questioning came to an end in the acceptance of authority and discipline.

Gloomy and analytical, restless and willful, Brownson was not a pleasant companion for the Transcendentalists, with whom he associated for a decade, although for the moment his philosophy was that of the group. His service to Transcendentalism and to American letters lay in his editorship of the *Boston Quarterly Review* from 1838 to 1842. He undertook the *Review*, he said, "not because I am certain that the public wants it, but because I want it." Whatever its opinions were to be, he declared, they would probably be heretical, for he was willing to publish the views of any group that wished to place its ideas before the public. The journal was designed to support democratic principles and measures; its great idea was to be "freedom." As Brownson became more and more interested in the laboring classes, his review tended to discuss problems of the day to the exclusion of other topics, and in 1842 he merged it with the *Democratic Review*, which was devoted largely to social questions. When he became a Catholic he began the publication of an even more personal journal entitled *Brownson's Quarterly Review*.

The *Boston Quarterly Review* dealt with many subjects, but all of them were treated from a Transcendentalist point of view. Every problem discussed by intellectual New England was mirrored in the *Review*. George Bancroft, George Ripley, Bronson Alcott, Margaret Fuller, Elizabeth Peabody, Theodore Parker, W. H. Channing, and Albert Brisbane wrote for it, and in it Emerson's addresses and essays received their most searching reviews. When its last number appeared, William Ellery Channing gave it its accolade in the statement, "Take it all in all, it was the best journal this country has ever produced, at once the most American, practical and awakening; the more so because its editor was a learner and shared his studies with his readers." [25]

WILLIAM ELLERY CHANNING

Any account of the Transcendentalists must pay tribute to the new life breathed into the Unitarian faith by William Ellery Channing, who died in 1842, when the Transcendentalist movement was at its height. Scarcely a member of the movement had reached maturity without coming closely under the beneficent influence of his deep spirituality and his beautiful optimistic nature. Channing, the Unitarian preacher, was at the same time the first of the Transcendentalists. As early as 1819 he announced his belief in God's beneficence; later he added the idea of man's excellence and then gradually fused the two into the feeling that religion itself is but the "adoration of goodness."

Harriet Martineau, the English traveler, wrote of Channing:

The one remarkable thing about him is his spirituality; and this is shown in a way which must strike the most careless observer, but of which he is himself unconscious. . . . Everyone who converses with him is struck with his natural, supreme regard to the true and the right; with the absence of all suspicion that anything can stand the competition with these. . . . His charity towards frailty is as singular as his reprobation of spiritual vices is indignant. The genial side of his nature is turned toward the weak, and the sorely tempted and the fallen best know the real softness and meekness of his character.[26]

And a voice from another world confirmed Miss Martineau when the eccentric exiled Bonapartist, Achille Murat, who was, strangely enough, a friend of Emerson, wrote from frontier Florida that the Unitarians "have at their head at the present time a man of the rarest merit and of exemplary virtue, a genuine Plato — Dr. Channing." [27]

With his interest in his fellow men and his keen sense of justice, it was inevitable that Dr. Channing should take an interest in the reforms that were occupying the attention of so many of his younger friends. He disliked controversy and was distressed at the acrimoniousness and violence of controversialists. He hated slavery but could not condone the extreme and incendiary statements of the abolitionists. He appealed to Henry Clay against the annexation of Texas and published several essays on the slavery controversy. The passions of his life were two, a respect for human nature and a reverence for human liberty; slavery was compatible with neither. In politics his philosophy was Jeffersonian, for he believed that "man is too ignorant to govern much, to form vast plans for states and empires. Human policy has almost always been in conflict with the great laws of social well-being; and the less we rely on it the better. The less of power given to man over man the better." [28]

With Jefferson and with the earlier French philosophers Channing was the champion of civil liberties. One of his most important contributions to the antislavery controversy is at the same time a part of his great legacy to posterity. The conspiracy of silence that the slave-owners were attempting to fasten upon the country called for his defense of the freedom of discussion. That defense might at the same time serve as the apologia of the Transcendentalists, for with their individualism and their diversity there was little to hold them together except their common belief in the eternal Godlikeness of man and in the wide range of reform movements they so freely and publicly discussed. The American democratic and evangelical faith could not have existed if the right of man to think, to speak, and to choose as he wished had been denied. Channing wrote:

Of all powers, the last to be entrusted to the multitude of men, is that of determining what questions shall be discussed. The greatest truths are often the most unpopular and exasperating; and were they to be denied discussion, till the many should be ready to accept them, they would never establish themselves in the general mind. The progress of society depends on nothing more than on the exposure of time-honored abuses, which cannot be touched without offending multitudes, than on the promulgation of principles, which are in advance of public sentiment and practice, and which are constantly at war with the habits, prejudices, and immediate interests of large classes of the community. Of consequence, the multitude, if once allowed to dictate or proscribe the subjects of discussion, would strike society with spiritual blindness, and death. . . . The right of free discussion is therefore to be guarded by the friends of mankind, with peculiar jealousy. It is at once the most sacred, and the most endangered of all our rights. He who would rob his neighbor of it, should have a mark set on him as the worst enemy of freedom.[29]

CHAPTER 4

Millennialism and Spiritualism

Through the western part of upstate Vermont and westward across New York from Albany to Buffalo ran one of the main routes from New England to the Great Lakes and the Middle West, and over it poured thousands of settlers from the hill towns of the East toward the new lands beyond the horizon. Untouched by foreign immigration in the first half of the nineteenth century, this strip was entirely American. It was without large cities except for Albany, the capital of New York, and Buffalo, the entrepôt of the Great Lakes trade. Few factory towns had sprung up in the region, and its population was largely made up of small farmers.

This was the area that was sometimes called the "burnt" district because it had been swept by so many fires of religious excitement. Anything new in the way of religious belief seemed attractive to the jaded appetites of its inhabitants, and no new sect lacked some following. As early as 1790, when Vermont was just entering the Union as the fourteenth state, the Dorrilites ran their brief course. Their leader, Dorril, professed to be a prophet, basing his organization upon the communism thought to have been a tenet of the early Christian church. Vegetarianism and a prohibition on all clothing made at the expense of animal life were among his dictates. When his proud boast that "no arm can hurt my flesh" was proved untrue and he was felled by the blow of an unbeliever, the little group of a few score Dorrilites broke up and the sect disappeared.

A decade later near Rutland, Vermont, a man named Winchell claimed to be able to discover buried treasure by the use of a divining rod. He fell in with a certain Nathaniel Wood, whose heterodoxy had previously caused his expulsion from the Congregational church. They combined forces, and the divining rod became the instrument of revelation. Opposition increased the fanaticism of the little cult, and the end of the world was prophesied with dire results for their opponents. When the prophecies failed, the "Wood Scrape," as it was called, disappeared in its turn, and most of the leaders moved on into western New York, where the son of one of them was among the early converts of Joseph Smith.

In the period of revivals after 1815 the Green Mountain region saw yet another strange sect. A man named Bullard was the leader of the Pilgrims, a little group of about a hundred deluded souls who sought to discard the evidences of civilization and live in accord with primitive religious teaching. To communism, theocracy, and dictatorship, the sect added such peculiarities as refusal to wash, to shave, or to wear any clothing save bearskin tunics with leather girdles. The Pilgrims, too, moved westward across New York and settled first in Ohio and then in Missouri, where for some reason the leadership of Bullard disintegrated and his flock dispersed. Perhaps bearskin apparel and the absence of bathing were not such distinguishing characteristics on the Western frontier.

From northern Vermont also came the strange beliefs of William Miller; in the western part of the "burnt" district were heard the spirit-rappings of the Fox sisters; and from the same area came, later, the Perfectionism of John Humphrey Noyes and the first essays of Joseph Smith toward the establishment of a new religion.

Here the primitive Christianity of the revivalists encouraged a literal acceptance of biblical teaching and a pietism similar to that of the most extreme seventeenth-century English Puritans. Such a literal reading of the Bible led to interpretations of the contemporary scene that were full of danger for those whose piety exceeded their balance of judgment. Thoreau well understood the social dynamite in the teachings of Christ and, in surveying his New England, regretted that "Christianity only hopes. It has hung its harp in the willows, and cannot sing a song in a strange land. It has dreamed a sad dream and does not yet welcome the morning with joy." [1] And again, under "Sunday" in *The Week*, he wrote that he knew of no book that had so few readers as the Bible.

To Christians [he ironically commented] no less than Greeks and Jews, it is foolishness and a stumbling block. There are, indeed, severe things in it which no man should read aloud more than once. "Seek first the kingdom of heaven." — "Lay not up for yourselves treasures on earth." — "For what is a man profited, if he shall gain the whole world, and lose his own soul? or what shall a man give in exchange for his soul?" . . . Who, without cant, can read them aloud? Who, without cant, can hear them, and not go out of the meeting-house? They never *were* read, they never *were* heard. Let but one of these sentences be rightly read from any pulpit in the land, and there would not be left one stone of that meeting-house upon another.[2]

Without the wisdom of a Thoreau to guide them, many nine-teenth-century religious natures were led by their reading of the Bible to accept a millennialism that announced the second coming of Christ and the establishment of the kingdom of God on earth. The prophecies of the New Testament taken as divine promises to be literally fulfilled in God's good time made a heady wine for Americans of primitive faith and literal minds. The less the world about them seemed to conform to the teachings of the Bible, the more true appeared the prophecies of millennial glory.

THE MILLERITE MILLENNIAL FAITH

William Miller, the chief exponent of Millennialism in America, was born near Pittsfield, Massachusetts, in 1782, the eldest of six-teen children in an old New England family. His father was a Revolutionary War veteran and his mother the daughter of a Bap-tist preacher. When he was four years old, the family migrated northward to the frontier country of upper Vermont, where a log cabin was their first home. Young William could have had very little formal schooling, but he read all the books that came his way, providing light for his studies during long winter evenings by stor-ing carefully the choice pine knots found in the family wood lot. He had access to the library of the Vermont radical, Matthew Lyon, famed for his trial under the Sedition Act of 1798, and accumulated a large fund of historical information, which he used later in bol-stering his own theories. He married early and settled in the near-by village of Poultney, where he made full use of the village library, became known as the author of a patriotic song and other doggerel verse, joined the Masonic order, and was elected to local office, first as constable and then as sheriff. He was a Jeffersonian Democrat in politics and drifted with the current radical trend away from Cal-vinism to the careless deism of the young democrats. His worldli-ness was confirmed by army service in the War of 1812.

Miller's attention was caught by a local revival soon after the war, however, and he devoted himself from that time forward to a consideration of the state of his soul. Month after month he studied the Bible and attended church services, growing more and more de-spondent. Finally, and in the end suddenly, he experienced conver-sion in the approved manner, joined the Calvinistic Baptist church, and there found comfort and happiness. His was a sincere and lasting piety. His days were filled with the labors of tending his two-hundred-acre farm, but the long evenings and quiet Sundays were spent in constant perusal of the Bible. He came to believe that the Scriptures should be accepted in entirety and literally and that every biblical prophecy would be fulfilled in the exact way and time it specified. The possibility of Christ's second coming soon became the most fascinating of all ideas for him, and he filled his leisure with intricate calculations to determine the time for such an advent. On the basis of Daniel's vision of the ram, the he-goat, and the little horn, in which there is mention of twenty-three hundred days, Miller made an elaborate calculation which, he thought, proved that the Second Advent would occur about the year 1843.

Year after year Miller went over his calculations, puzzled over the meaning of obscure biblical references, and grew stronger in his own convictions. He was a quiet, mild-mannered man and a poor speaker, but he longed for the conversion of his friends and was convinced of his duty to prepare for the dread advent all those whom he could reach. In 1822 he prepared a long creed of twenty-two articles setting forth the reasons for his beliefs, but many years elapsed before he made public announcement of his faith. In 1828, at a revival in Low Hampton, Miller felt a "call" to tell the world of his discovery, but he was afraid of being criticized and misunderstood.

I tried to excuse myself [he said] for not going out and proclaiming it to the world. I told the Lord that I was not used to speaking; that I had not the necessary qualifications for gaining the attention of an audience; that I was very diffident, and feard to go before the world; that I was slow of speech and of a slow tongue. But I could get no relief.[3]

His ideas became known, however, through conversation with his family and with neighbors, and in 1832 he was asked to discuss them in a near-by church, where for some reason there was no preacher for the Sunday services. The emergency, the long-repressed desire to share his vision, the curiosity of his friendly listeners, all contributed to give him confidence, and he suddenly found himself eloquent with eager, vivid speech depicting the glory of the advent, the joy of those who were saved, the suffering of the wicked. His fascinated audience asked him to stay on for a week's revival service, at the end of which he joyfully recorded that thirteen families had been converted.

After that his invitations to preach were numerous; Baptist, Methodist, and occasionally Congregational churches were thrown open to him, and he became known as a lecturer with a message on the second coming of Christ. In 1833 he became a Baptist minister and a revivalist, winning converts here and there to the Christian faith if not to his belief in the nearness of the second coming and of judgment day.

Although Miller's popularity as a revivalist grew rapidly in up-state Vermont, New York, and New Hampshire, he might easily have had nothing but a local reputation had he not made an excursion far afield in a series of lectures in Massachusetts in 1840. For he then first met the Reverend Joshua V. Himes, the pastor of the Charndon Street Baptist Chapel in Boston, who became publicity agent, manager, and promoter for the quiet, middle-aged preacher from Vermont. Himes loved crowds, revivalism, emotional religion, camp meetings, and their attendant exhibitions of fear and penitence, and the opportunity to stage one of the most stupendous revival movements of all time was irresistible.

It was Himes who arranged Miller's later speaking tours, advertised his movements, arranged the huge camp meetings, edited the Millennialist newspapers, the *Signs of the Times* in Boston and the New York *Midnight Cry*, and promoted the building of the great Millennial Tabernacle in Boston. Something of Himes's enthusiasm was infused into the diffident prophet of the second coming, and Miller's preaching was constantly more successful as the dread year 1843 approached. In six months he delivered more than three hundred lectures, the constant theme of which was, Are you ready to meet your Saviour? Thousands were turned away from meetings, tents were put up on the outskirts of towns, tabernacles were built, and popular excitement was intense.

Only the Middle West, remembering the camp meetings in the Kentucky forests a generation earlier, could have found anything familiar in the intense emotionalism of the Adventists' meetings by the summer of 1842 — the last whole year they felt sure would be vouchsafed them. Miller himself was not a violent or ranting speaker. The tremendous effect of his preaching lay in its deadly sincerity and its biblical imagery. It is obvious that upon a receptive audience the following plea must have had a dramatic effect:

I am satisfied that the end of the world is at hand. The evidence flows in from every quarter. . . . Soon, very soon God will arise in his anger and the vine of the earth will be reaped. *See! See!* — the angel with his sharp sickle is about to take the field! See yonder trembling victims fall before his pestilential breath! High and low, rich and poor, trembling and falling before the appalling grave, the dreadful cholera. . . . Behold, the heavens grow black with clouds; the sun has veiled himself; the moon, pale and forsaken, hangs in middle air; the hail descends; the seven thunders utter loud their voices; the lightnings send their vivid gleams and sulphurous flames abroad; and the great city of the nations falls to rise no more forever and forever! At this dread moment, look! The clouds have burst asunder; the heavens appear; the great white throne is in sight! Amazement fills the Universe with awe! He comes! — He comes! — Behold the Saviour comes! — Lift up your heads, ye saints — He comes! He comes! He comes! [4]

The dramatic effect of poetry was not forgotten, and full use was made of music in increasing the intensity of feeling in revival meetings. In 1843 a hymn book, *The Millennial Harp,* was published by the Reverend Joshua Himes and was used thereafter in all meetings. The revivalistic worth of its contents seems more apparent than its literary merit, for the following is a fair example:

The Alarm

We are living, we are dwelling
In a grand and awful time;
In an age on ages telling ·
To be living is sublime.
Hark the waking up of nations,
Gog and Magog to the fray;
Hark! What soundeth? Is Creation
Groaning for its latter day?
Hark the onset! Will you fold your
Faith-dead arms in lazy lock?
Up, O, up! thou drowsy soldier —
Worlds are charging to the shock!

Books and pamphlets on the subject of the Second Advent, pro and con, poured from the press "as profusely as autumn leaves, and, to most minds, about as devoid of nutriment." [5] The Bishop of Vermont published a brochure condemning the error of attempting to fix a date for the second coming. Ministers of all sects throughout New England and the near-by states were active in print and in the pulpit in condemning the whole movement. Mobs of angry citizens tried to break up some of the Millerite meetings; even the prophet himself was assailed with eggs and decayed vegetables. But the crowds grew more dense, and the number of converts mounted.

Miller himself, no longer young, worn out with both labor and emotion, was ill through most of 1843 and took little part in the preaching of that year. But his pen was active, and his lieutenants carried on the work — in some instances with too great a zeal. Himes constantly increased the workers in the field until there were several hundred itinerant speakers and a million converts were claimed. There were huge meetings in New York and Philadelphia, and the Middle West was invaded. In the absence of the prophet, Himes expended all his advertising ability and his great energy in advancing the cause. Dates for future meetings were announced with the proviso "if time continues," and the immediacy of all measures was stressed. Sunday schools were organized, children's books and catechisms were published, and the Millennialist newspapers printed children's stories that ended with the words, "And that's the way the world is coming to an end."

THE MILLENNIAL YEAR

As the excitement mounted, men began to demand a date — a definite day for the great event of the Lord's coming. Miller was reluctant to make any such statement. The year 1843 was to him the last sure "year of time"; whether the advent would occur during 1843 or shortly thereafter, he could not say. Even if his estimate should prove slightly inaccurate, he pleaded, his followers should have faith that their deliverance would come soon, in God's appointed time. Many of the Millerite preachers, however, were far less cautious. Their radicalism distressed Miller, and even Himes, more and more as 1843 wore on. A certain John Starkweather encouraged the most violent physical manifestations of conversion among his followers, and hallucinations and catalyptic and epileptic attacks were considered evidences of extreme piety. Mesmerism was one of his accomplishments, and his camp meetings were orgies of exhibitionism that were heartily condemned by the leaders of the

movement. Miller himself was always opposed to fanaticism, per-
version of his ideas, and all "excess of zeal" — little realizing that the
dynamite of his original thesis was far too dangerous a weapon to
place in the hands of his followers.

As 1843 drew to its close, the dangers of such religious excitement and delusion became apparent. Suicides were attributed to
despair over the necessity of facing the day of judgment. The state
insane asylums reported the admission of several who had been
crazed by fear of the end of the world. In Portsmouth, New Hampshire, a Millerite in voluminous white robes climbed a tree, tried to
fly when he thought the fatal hour was near, fell, and broke his
neck. A Massachusetts farmer cut his wife's throat because she refused to be·converted to Millerism, and a despairing mother poi-
soned herself and all her children. The editor of a New Bedford
paper described the somewhat amusing anguish of a mechanic whom
he had seen kneeling in the snow with a Millerite pamphlet in each
hand, praying and blaspheming alternately in a "most piteous manner." In Wilkesbarre, Pennsylvania, a storekeeper requested the
sheriff to give all his goods to anyone who would take them away,
and in New York another merchant offered to give a pair of shoes
to anyone who needed them, since "he had no further use for
them." [6]

With the passing of the year 1843 — the Last Year — the month
of the spring equinox in 1844 was accepted as the appointed time,
although the prophet still claimed no knowledge of an exact date.
Worn out by strain and illness, William Miller eagerly awaited the
end. "The time," he wrote on March 25, "as I have calculated it is
now filled up, and I expect every moment to see the Saviour
descend from heaven. I have now nothing to look for but this glorious hope." [7]

But the month of March passed, and "time" still continued. The
doubtful departed from Millennialist ranks, and the scoffers were
heard in taunts of renewed vigor. The workers in the field and the
leaders made great efforts to keep interest alive and to refute the
accusations of fraud and delusion. The great tabernacle in Boston
was opened in May 1844, workers scurried from city to city, and
camp meetings were held even in faraway Kentucky and Iowa.
The tired, discouraged old prophet was persuaded to write a "Let-

ter to Second Advent Believers" for publication in the various newspapers of the sect. There is profound pathos in his frank confession of his error in calculation and in his disappointment in the continuance of his own stay on earth, and there is quiet self-respect in his statement,

Were I to live my life over again, with the same evidence that I then had, to be honest with God and man I should have to do as I have done. Although opposers said it would not come, they produced no weighty arguments. It was evidently guess work with them; and I then thought, and do now, that their denial was based more on an unwillingness for the Lord to come than on any arguments leading to such a conclusion.[8]

Under pressure of popular demand for a new Advent Day, the Millerite leaders chose October 22, 1844, on the basis that the Jewish method of calculation made that the much heralded "tenth day of the seventh month." Such definite assertions did not have Miller's approval, and it was only after a delegation of his field workers had reasoned with him long that his hopes were stirred and he, too, came to believe that the end of the world would surely come in October. Thus stimulated, the excitement was revived and soon exceeded the proportions of the preceding season. Preparations for the end were made by countless hundreds of joyous or desperate souls. White cloth was purchased and made into ascension robes. Nearly all secular business was neglected after the first of October. Honest debtors sold all they had in order to meet their end with a clean slate, while many men of wealth realized upon their assets in order to help coreligionists whose debts were heavy. Voting was light in some districts in the fall elections, because men were concerned with eternal verities and had no time for such mundane things. Some, however, taking literally the biblical admonition to "occupy until I come," continued their normal enterprises as though time would continue indefinitely.

Close observers noted that almost all those making conspicuous preparation for the end of the world and, indeed, the largest part of all Millennialist audiences were relatively poor and uneducated people. They were, for the most part, converts from the Methodist and Calvinistic Baptist sects; very few Unitarians, Presbyterians, or Episcopalians were found among them. It was the farmers, storekeepers, and laborers who flocked to the standard of the Second Advent preachers — as they had to that of the itinerant evangelists — and accepted the doctrine of immediate translation to a blissful heaven.

There was much popular opposition to the Millerites as their chosen day approached. Fear or derision caused mobs to assemble, and there was serious rioting. The police closed several meeting places on the pretext that the streets were being blocked. In Boston crowds of curious boys crowded the fences and the roofs of low buildings near the Millennial Tabernacle in the belief that at the appointed hour the roof would sail away and the triumphant worshipers would ascend to heaven. Much to their disappointment the mayor closed the building, saying the noise was a nuisance. In the country districts chores were left undone and crops unharvested, until town selectmen notified farmers that their work must be attended to or they would be treated as idlers and vagrants.

Plans were made among the Millerites to meet the long-awaited day in groups. Tents were put up outside cities, preferably on hilltops, and hundreds of people assembled on the night of October 21 to keep their vigil together. No provision was made for food or rest, and as the night passed and then the day, and the next night wore on, the tension was intolerable. In some sections severe storms and heavy rainfall added to the alarm and suffering. The plight of the children in these camps was piteous, but many of their elders succumbed more completely to the nervous strain. There were several suicides, and as the dawn of October 23 served notice that "time continued" regardless of prophecy, some heart-broken Millennialists were led away insane.

This final disappointment marked the end of the Millerite movement. Most of the prophet's devoted followers admitted their delusion and went about the process of renewing the normal routine of their lives. Some, feeling that the Lord as well as the prophet had cheated them, became frankly irreligious, while others, emotionally unhinged, remained in the Millerite association and led the sect into radical fanaticism, much to the distress of Miller and his devoted adherents, who admitted the errors of their mathematics but continued to uphold the truth of their major premise — that the Second Advent was near.

The last years of Miller's life were spent in despondency and ill-health and in a struggle to encourage a few followers to keep the Adventist faith alive. Read out of the Baptist church, Miller and the loyal members of his congregation formed a little Adventist church of their own, and the former prophet went up and down the Lake Champlain country in a vain effort to win enough support to re-establish Millennialism. He died in 1849, discredited and almost forgotten. Joshua Himes lived on until 1895 — for many years as an Episcopalian clergyman in faraway South Dakota. He must have kept some vestige of his belief in the millennium to the day of his death, for he arranged to be buried on a hilltop in order to be as near as possible when Gabriel should blow his horn.

Adventism as a religious sect did not completely disappear with the debacle of 1844. Here and there in Europe and America later in the century small Adventist churches appeared, but instead of the excited thousands — some said millions — of the day of the Great Delusion there were then only a few scattered hundreds who accepted the doctrine of the second coming.

SPIRITUALISM AS A PHASE OF AMERICA'S FAITH

Adventism was only one manifestation of the desire to break down all barriers between this world and the next — between man and the Creator and between living aspirants after perfection and the elect who had preceded them in the quest for salvation. No question has been more persistent in the human mind than that of immortality, and some form of spiritualism, or attempt at contact with the spirit world, has appeared in many countries and among people in all stages of civilization. The Spiritualism that swept over the United States in the mid nineteenth century was remarkable only for its vigor and for the large numbers of men and women who became deeply interested in it. How thoroughly it was a legitimate offspring of the age, an expression of the young republic's faith, is well shown by the words of Andrew Jackson Davis, Spiritualist himself and precursor of the American medium:

. . . the era of mythology and superstition is fast decaying. Ignorance, bigotry, skepticism, fanaticism, intolerance, spiritual depression, and all slavery — the great evils which now beset mankind — are rapidly dispersing; they shall recede entirely from the earth, never again to enslave and degrade humanity. This world of thought and affection, and of social relations, shall be progressively purified, until there shall be unfolded a new heaven and a new earth wherein dwelleth righteousness. And the evils which *now* exist, shall be known only to those who will trace the history of our race; which they will do with mingling feelings of pity and regret. By spiritual intercourse we learn that all men shall ultimately be joined into one Brotherhood, their interests shall be pure and reciprocal; their customs shall be just and harmonious; they shall be as one Body, animated by Universal Love and governed by pure Wisdom. Man's future is glowing with a beautiful radiance. The mental sky is fast becoming clear and serene; the scene is one of grandeur and sublimity. Truth *will* consume all error and artificial theology, whose power is weakened; and whose corruptions are revealed, by the divine light of Nature's manifestations. Yea *all evil and error* will be finally subdued, and banished by the triumph of the principles that are *good*, *divine*, and *unchangeable*, and unrighteousness shall be no more! Streams of good and healthy inspirations will spring up, and flow down to cleanse and refresh the moral world, on whose advancing tide the whole race will ascend to intellectual and social harmony, and to a high state of spiritual elevation and intercourse.[9]

This optimism was truly American, and its vision of a glorious future was little different from that of Lyman Beecher or of many other American writers of the period. The only unusual note was the mention of spiritual intercourse, and that idea had become familiar to Americans through acquaintance with the life and teachings of the Swedish savant, Emanuel Swedenborg, whose works had been brought to this country with those of other eighteenth-century philosophers. In the great renewal of interest in all such ideas in the early nineteenth century, Swedenborg's philosophy was widely discussed, Swedenborgian societies were formed, and his New Church attracted many small groups of adherents. In regard to life after death, Swedenborgianism provided for a very real and tangible spirit world, where men could continue to grow toward perfection, where all children were received alike, whether baptized or not, and grew to maturity under the care of older and wiser spirits, and where there was no eternal punishment, but only provision for the improvement of imperfect souls.

If Swedenborgianism predisposed the educated to an interest in the spirit world, there were other agencies more effective upon minds less well trained. Emma Hardinge, an ardent Spiritualist and early historian of the movement, names many somewhat incongruous "adventists of Spiritualism": mesmerism, electro-biology, clairvoyance, chemistry, physiology, phrenology, and magnetism. In other words, she believed that all the new ideas of science and pseudo science led men to the point where there seemed no barrier between their minds and the solution of the ultimate mysteries of death and immortality. Spiritualism, she said, was the "coronal glory of the capital" of the column of all the sciences.[10]

With a similar feeling that there were no limits set for the minds and spirits of men and no obstacle in the way of new divine revelations, Paulina Bates, a Shaker seeress of the early nineteenth century, wrote in defense of her mediumistic powers:

Whence arises the opinion that there is no further revelation from God ever to be looked for? Surely not from the sacred scriptures, nor from sound reason; for these declare that the works of the Great Cause are continually increasing. Do not all the elements of nature, with all their powers, and the faculties of man, continue to be more and more developed and brought to light? And shall the spiritual powers and light of divine truth remain stationary, and no further increase of knowledge be given on these subjects, in comparison of which all natural and earthly things sink into insignificance? [11]

ANDREW JACKSON DAVIS

Andrew Jackson Davis, the "Poughkeepsie Seer," a later clairvoyant of somewhat the same kind as Paulina Bates, was born in 1826. His father was a shoemaker and a weaver, reputed to be "honest but shiftless" and often out of a job. The boy was undersized, probably poorly nourished, delicate, and sensitive. He had little schooling and at the age of fifteen was apprenticed to a shoemaker. In 1843 a lecturer on animal magnetism, a Professor Grimes, came to Poughkeepsie, and it was discovered that young Davis was easily hypnotized. After that a village tailor named Levington continually hypnotized the boy and made of him a professional medium whose chief occupation was clairvoyant diagnosis and prescription for disease.

After a year of this life Davis wandered off in a self-induced trance and came back after some days with a tale of long conversations with Galen and Swedenborg, in which he had been given instruction as to the use to be made of his contact with the supernatural. Soon he met a doctor and a minister who took upon themselves the work of guiding — or exploiting — his peculiar gifts. The doctor acted as professional collaborator in his medical work and as his "magnetizer," while the minister became the scribe who took down the words that flowed through him in his trances. Thus were prepared the many lectures and books that bear his name.

Among them only two need be mentioned. *The Magic Staff* was Davis' autobiography up to 1857. It was followed by a supplement for his later years. The book reveals him as a sincere, earnest, but confused reformer, interested in every sort of radical idea and convinced of his mission and of the reality of his contact with the spirit world. He founded no church and sought no mass conversions, but held himself to be a link between this world and a greater, eternal realm. His first contribution in the field of philosophy and probably his best known work was a series of lectures made in a state of trance, entitled *The Principles of Nature, Her Divine Revelations, and A Voice to Mankind*, but sometimes called *The Harmonial Philosophy*. The work is, as the title indicates, in three parts. The first two form a long and vague description of the evolution of the universe from a primal fire mist. The scientific part of the description is a hodgepodge of half-digested fact and theory, a mixture of all ideas current in that day. The philosophy is involved, wordy, and often scarcely intelligible, owing much to Swedenborgianism and other types of mystical symbolism. The central idea seems to be that the universe is one great whole. The "Voice to Mankind" is another hodgepodge, this time of social reforms and crude socialistic theory, with a mixture of phalanxes and cooperatives.

Clairvoyance aside, there is nothing in the book that could not have been produced by a man with a retentive memory who had had access to books or had heard lectures upon such subjects. Continual hypnotism might conceivably have released Davis' subconscious mind and permitted the outpouring of everything stored in his memory. There seems to have been no conscious plagiarism and no intent of fraud. In fact, there is far too much confusion and too little accuracy for a charge of plagiarism to hold water. *The Harmonial Philosophy* went through thirty-four editions in thirty years. Somehow Davis had managed to express the aspirations and social needs of the inarticulate and to voice their protest against the waste, the injustice, and the futilities of modern industrial society. Andrew Jackson Davis deserves a place among the names both of American reformers and of American Spiritualists.

THE FOX SISTERS OF HYDESVILLE, NEW YORK

A series of occurrences in a little village in northern New York in 1848 set off a Spiritualist excitement that was soon to become almost a mania. In that village lived a farmer, John D. Fox, with his wife and two young daughters, Maggie and Katie. An elder sister, Leah Fish, a young widow, lived in the near-by city of Rochester and made her living teaching music. In February trouble began for the Fox family. Mysterious rappings sounded on the floor, walls, and furniture of whatever room the children happened to be occupying. The mother was frightened, the father scoffed, and the little girls seemed to enjoy the excitement.

One night the younger child, Katie, called out, "Here Mr. Split-foot, do as I do!" and the mysterious influence, whatever its nature, responded with the same number of raps the child gave. The mother's long testimony, taken in the first investigation of the phenomena, is the best account of how from that small beginning she and the children worked out a system of communication by which the "spirits" answered with raps any questions they were asked. In this way various local mysteries were solved, and much excitement was created. Neighbors flocked in to see and to hear the communications with the spirit world. The elder sister came home to act as manager for the exhibitions. She always insisted that the public meetings were held only at the urgent insistence of the spirits, who had a great revelation to make to the world through the Fox sisters. At any rate, with the collaboration of an E. W. Capron of Auburn, New York, who became a Spiritualist and a medium himself, the sisters became professional mediums, holding public meetings and charging fees. At once investigations were conducted by indignant unbelievers, and in the ensuing publicity hundreds of eager converts were made. Other mediums sprang up all over the country, although the Fox sisters remained very much the vogue, and Spiritualist circles were formed in every town and nearly every village.[12]

Techniques were developed rapidly. The spirits, through Mrs. Fish, demanded darkness, and, indeed, the manifestations were far more numerous when the darkness was absolute. Table moving,

A Western camp meeting

The Fox sisters, spirit rappers

Orestes Brownson,
Transcendentalist editor

William Miller,
evangelist of the Great Delusion

"Last Day Tokens" of the Millerite Millennialists

spirit writing, and cold ghostly hands were soon added to the mystic raps, and within a few years almost all the phenomena of twentieth-century Spiritualism were in evidence. Prominent people became interested in the Fox girls and in the subject of spirit contacts. Horace Greeley took the sisters into his home when they were in New York and said in the *Tribune* that "it would be the basest cowardice not to say that we are convinced beyond a doubt of their perfect integrity and good faith." [13] In his *Recollections* Greeley states that he never felt the rappings were a fraud, but, he adds, he was disinclined to go deeply into the matter, because "to sit for two dreary, mortal hours, in a darkened room, in a mixed company, waiting for someone's disembodied grandfather or aunt to tip a table or rap on a door, is dull music at best." [14]

Judge Edmonds of the New York supreme court came to investigate and was completely won over by the Fox sisters. The fact that he had for some time been in a state of great depression and had given up all religious faith may have contributed to his conversion. In 1853 he published, jointly with a Dr. Dexter, a lengthy treatise on Spiritualism that greatly increased its popularity. Ex-Governor Tallmadge of Wisconsin, a wealthy New Yorker named Partridge, and an elderly scientist, Professor Hare, lent respectability to the movement, and soon a group of ministerial converts gave it a religious significance and made of it a cult.

Some years later the Fox sisters, as the result of a family quarrel, recanted and exposed their whole career as one great fraud, admitting that the rappings had from the first been produced by the joints of their toes — hence the "Mr. Splitfoot." But their confession had very little effect on the Spiritualists, who insisted that the recantation, not the career, was the fraud, and that the unfortunate Katie, who made the confession, had yielded to the pressure of evil advisers. Harvard professors attended séances and argued gravely over the possibility of deception, even as other competent observers were proving fraud on the part of many mediums.

In the period from the first popular interest in the 1840's to the Civil War, American Spiritualism was not a separate church; it remained a movement in a chaotic state. There were hundreds of mediums and Spiritualist circles, but little or no coherence or organization. If an analysis were made of those who were most concerned in the movement, most of the leaders would probably be found among those who had, through rationalism or indifference, lost all interest in any organized religion. Some, however, came from the Universalist ministry, whether or not because there was any particular connection between their Universalism and their interest in Spiritualism it is impossible to state. Séances were attended by men and women from all classes and professions. A judge, a state governor, several legislators, a scientist, and a sprinkling of university professors and newspaper editors were mentioned with pride by the Spiritualist writers, but the rank and file of those interested were the same sort of people who went over to many of the other religious extravagances of the period.

From the beginning there seemed to be a connection between Spiritualism and social reform. The Shakers were Christian communists, Brook Farm was interested in Swedenborgianism, the Hopedale Community had as its head the Reverend Adin Ballou, who became a Spiritualist. The Wisconsin Phalanx was founded by Warren Chase of Spiritualist renown, and the North American Phalanx was the work of Horace Greeley. In 1851 the Spiritualists founded a very short-lived communistic society of their own at Mountain Cove, Virginia, and a settlement founded in the same year at Modern Times, Long Island, had Spiritualist leanings. Spiritualism also played its part in the movements for the reform of the institution of marriage. *Spiritual affinities* and *spiritual wives* were phrases used by certain radical theorists, and violent opposers of Spiritualism hurled the dread accusation of "free love" at even the slightest relaxing of standards in matters of sex. Andrew Jackson Davis and many other mediums were reformers along several lines, although the biographer of Katie Fox insists that "Katie was as ignorant as a vegetable of the social tendencies which surrounded her mediumship. No social theory of any kind either progressive or alarmist even entered her head." [15]

All who believed in the authenticity of Spiritualist phenomena were not convinced of the wisdom of tampering with the spirit world. Not yet aware of the complexities of man's mental structure, they felt there was dire danger in too much knowledge of the mysteries of life and death. That religious experimenter, Orestes Brownson, wrote a book, partly autobiographical, partly fiction, called *The Spirit Rapper*. In it he accepted the work of the mediums as done in good faith and their communications as valid, but he maintained that their spirits were demoniac and dangerous agencies. He deplored the fact that the movement had grown to such an extent without a serious effort to arrest it. "It is," he said, "making sad havoc with religion, breaking up churches, taking its victims from all denominations, with stern impartiality; and yet the great body of those not under its influence merely deny, laugh, or cry out 'humbug!' 'delusion!' Delusion it is. I know it now, but not in their sense." [16] And Thomas Low Nichols, a New Englander who espoused many a reform movement of the period from 1830 to 1860 and who was a somewhat unwilling believer in Spiritualist phenomena, ended with these words a long description of séances he had attended:

Without wishing to give an uncharitable judgment, I think it may be conceded that spiritualism has been revolutionary, chaotic, disorderly, tending, for the present at least, in many cases, to produce moral and social evils. That it may be providential, and tend to good in the future, few will be rash enough to deny.[17]

With all its crudities and all its extravagances, the Spiritualist movement of the period after 1848 was an integral part both of the romantic faith of America and of the American reform movements of the time. It was in some respects, as Emma Hardinge claimed, the "coronal glory" of the optimism and faith in the individual that characterized American thought. The Transcendentalist, the Millerite, and the Spiritualist, each in his own way, typified the eagerness with which the New World grasped at things of the spirit.

CHAPTER 5

The Stake in Zion

Neither so dramatic in its appeal as Spiritualism nor so immediate in pledge of a more glorious day as Millerism, but yet filled with millennialism and utopian prophecy, was the religious faith of Joseph Smith and his Latter Day Saints. The founder and almost all the early leaders of this new church were born on American soil and were, to a marked degree, men from the same old New England stock. Through the first decade its membership came almost entirely from the same class of people: the poor, restless, and dissatisfied, those who succumbed eagerly to religious emotionalism and those whose fortunes were at low ebb. Something new in the way of faith, anything new in the way of economic status, new homes, new lands, new masters – all were enticing since nothing could fail to be better than the old. Where life as it was promised little satisfaction, change might be expected to bring improvement.

THE EARLY LIFE OF JOSEPH SMITH

Born in Vermont in 1808, Joseph Smith was the fourth child of wandering, ne'er-do-well parents. His father and mother were both from old New England families that seem to have been poor and totally undistinguished for generations. Sometimes farming, sometimes keeping a village store, Joseph Smith, the father, moved his growing family nineteen times in ten years, succeeding no better in each new habitat. In 1816 he finally decided to try a new state and moved to the village of Palmyra, New York, where he ran a small "Cake and Beer Shop" and did odd jobs on the side. The family had little success in the new venture, the shop was given up, and farming was tried again. This time the Smiths squatted on the land of some nonresident minors and built a four-room log cabin. There they stayed until Joseph Jr. started his new religion and swept the whole family into a sort of Arabian Nights adventure.

Joseph Sr. seems to have been first a Universalist and later a Methodist, although in neither instance with great conviction. As he grew older he dreamed dreams and had what he called visions, which seem to have made some impression on his own family. His wife, Lucy Mack Smith, was far more interested in religion than he, although she found comfort in none of the current sects and was always on the watch for some new cult. Coming of a family addicted to revelations and a belief in the miraculous, she puzzled over their dreams and visions and believed their claims about their persecutions. What comfort her hard life afforded seems to have been derived from her neurotic religiosity and from the hope that one of her sons might have a messianic career. The strain of epilepsy in her family was transmitted in a mild form to her children, and they were early imbued with her religious emotionalism.

There was nothing in the early life of Joseph Jr. to indicate that he might rise above the level of the family. On the village street he was the butt of practical jokes and seems to have been regarded as "not quite bright." His Mormon biographer, Orson Pratt, could find no evidence that his education extended beyond the most elementary knowledge of the three R's, and many Mormons have claimed that this very paucity of training and background is proof of divine aid and inspiration in his achievement. Early opponents of Mormonism carefully recorded the opinions of "Young Joe" expressed by New York neighbors of the Smith family. "Shiftless," "indolent," "prevaricating," and "cunning" were the adjectives most commonly used. Frequent mention is made of Joseph's imagination and his wild pretensions and claims to power and wealth. Daniel Hendrix, a Palmyra resident who aided Smith in publishing *The Book of Mormon*, has left a description that summarizes the scattered opinions of others:

Joe was the most ragged, lazy fellow in the place, and that is saying a good deal. . . . I can see him now in my mind's eye, with his torn and patched trousers held to his form by a pair of suspenders made out of sheeting, with his calico shirt as dirty and black as the earth, and his uncombed hair sticking through the holes in his old battered hat. In winter I used to pity him, for his shoes were so old and worn out that he must have suffered in the snow and slush; yet Joe had a jovial, easy, don't-care way about him that made him a lot of warm friends. . . . I never knew so ignorant a man as Joe was to have such a fertile imagination. He never could tell a common occurrence in his daily life without embellishing the story with his imagination.[1]

In the years before 1830 the Joseph Smiths, father and son, spent much of their time hunting for buried treasure or lost articles with a forked stick, preferably of witch hazel. Their success with the divining rod was negligible, but such was the gullibility of their neighbors or the plausibility of their excuses that they were often employed. Joe's mother forgot his failures and, remembering only his claims, spread the story of his mystical power. Joseph Sr. seems to have been equally deluded and gravely announced that it was best to dig for treasure in the summer, when the heat of the sun brought the money to the surface of the earth. Among the stones found near Palmyra were certain small, peculiar glasslike objects that the superstitious called "magic stones" or "peek stones." The fortunate owner of such a stone was thought to be able, by gazing intently into it, to find lost or stolen goods. Young Joseph saw his first peek stone in 1818 and yearned for one like it. Some years later, while helping in the digging of a well, he found such a stone and kept it as his most cherished possession, gazing into it until he convinced himself that it conferred upon him powers not often given to men. There was as yet no religious significance in these pretensions; they merely won for the boy a certain prestige with the more superstitious of his fellows and compensated in a measure for his inferior position in all other respects.

SMITH'S CONVERSION AND THE BOOK OF MORMON

In 1820 there was much excitement in Palmyra. A new wave of revivalism was sweeping across New York, and Methodist, Baptist, and Presbyterian evangelists vied with each other in camp meetings and revival services. The elder Smiths succumbed to the fever and joined the Presbyterian church. Young Joseph held aloof but eagerly attended the meetings. With his usual skill at adding imaginative detail to his own stories, he stumbled home one day to relate a marvelous tale of his own solitary conversion. Praying alone in a retired spot, he had been "seized upon by some power which entirely overcame me . . . so that I could not speak." In utter terror he lay expecting destruction, until a brilliant light revealed to him "two personages" whose brightness and glory defied all description. They spoke to him, announcing that they were the Saviour and God the Father, and told him that all existing religious beliefs were false and he should accept none of them. Joseph's mother believed every word of the story and repeated it far and wide, even though the evangelists to whom she had been listening used every argument to persuade her and her son of their error. Apparently from that time on the Smiths expected Joseph to continue his miraculous contacts, for they all left the Presbyterian fold and awaited the establishment of the new faith predicted by the visitants.

From this point in the career of Joseph Smith it is impossible to determine what degree of veracity and sincerity to ascribe to the accounts of the young man and his family and friends. It is equally impossible to make any statement for or against the validity of his whole contention without touching upon a controversy that began with the very inception of the Mormon faith and has continued to this day. For many he was to be the prophet and favored confidant of God, the founder of the only true church, and the father and messiah of his people. To countless thousands of others he has seemed a liar and a deliberate charlatan, a comic figure of deception and crime, whose tragic death was a fitting end to a career that had meant delusion and disaster for his followers. Modern biographers with a leaning toward psychology and psychiatry call him a self-deceived zealot, a man of split personality, afflicted with epilepsy, dementia praecox, and various other ills of unbalanced mind, evolving his new religion in the realm of the subconscious, deceiving others because he first deceived himself. Conscious or unconscious charlatan, self-deceived or flamboyantly triumphant in his ability to take advantage of the gullibility of others, true or false prophet, the crude, uneducated, neurotic farmer and treasure hunter became a man of unusual powers of leadership and of remarkable success as an organizer. Valid or invalid in its fundamental tenets, the Mormon church became a fact, and Joseph Smith was its Prophet.

The circumstances of the finding of the plates from which *The Book of Mormon* was translated are somewhat obscure, because of the conflicting accounts Smith gave. The story he told first was of finding with the aid of his peek stone a book hidden in the ground. It was a tale of ancient secular history, which he was able to read, again with the aid of the magic stone. But in later variations on the story the book became metallic, and then golden, and finally there evolved an elaborate description of engraved golden plates. There was some talk of translation, publication, and sale, and even of exhibiting the plates with an admission fee for the benefit of the Smiths. Indeed, from the beginning the idea of financial return for the "discovery" seems to have been prominent. Gradually the idea of a new Bible, and even of a new church, began to grow in the minds of Joseph and his family. With the hypersensitivity of Lucy Mack Smith for all religious stimuli such a transfer of ideas seems inevitable. Whether there was at this early date any shrewd outside adviser aiding the Smiths it is impossible to state.

The authenticity of the golden plates is of vital importance of course, for if they were part of an elaborate hoax, there is no valid basis for the Mormon church. It can only be said that, aside from Smith's own claims, there is no well-based evidence given by creditable witnesses that the plates ever existed. When the decision was made to call them a new Bible, the arrangements for translation were such as to preserve them from hostile eyes. Allegedly using magic stones or spectacles, called the Urim and Thummim, Smith made the translation orally in a curtained recess while in the outer chamber an assistant copied down his words. Apparently as a necessary preliminary to securing aid for financing publication, Smith finally agreed to permit a few of his eager assistants to look at the plates in the box he had made to contain them.

There are several versions of the exhibition of the plates to the Three Witnesses, as the Mormon church has always called them. They were taken out into the woods with the box which, they were told, held the plates; there were some hours of prayer and exhortation, and then at last they were permitted to look into the box. After renewed prayers, the three men were willing to sign a long affidavit to the effect that they had seen the plates. It contained the following somewhat sweeping statement:

We have seen the engravings which are upon the plates; and they have been shewn unto us by the power of God, and not of man. And we declare with words of soberness, that an angel of God came down from heaven, and he brought and laid before our eyes, that we beheld and saw the plates, and the engravings thereon; and we know that it is by the grace of God, the Father, and our Lord Jesus Christ, that we beheld and bear record that these things are true, and it is marvelous in our eyes, nevertheless the voice of the Lord commanded that we should bear record of it.[2]

Martin Harris, one of the three, later testified that he had not seen the plates as one would an ordinary object, but rather "with the eyes of faith . . . though at the time they were covered with a cloth." The solemnity of the experience in the woods made such an impression upon all three men that they maintained throughout their lives that they had seen the golden plates. Not even later apostasy from the Mormon faith lessened their steadfastness. It must be conceded that they *thought* the vision had been vouchsafed them, although it is obvious that the setting and circumstances were ideal for hallucination or light hypnosis. They did so desperately want to see, and the prayers and exhortations had been so fervent.

After a similar exhibition to eight witnesses, the precious plates were not again exposed to prying eyes. As the last words of the translation were written, an angel appeared and swept away both the plates and the magic aids used in their translation. At least so Joseph Smith declared.[3]

In the meantime the Smith family had continued its normal life of shiftless poverty. Joseph used his peek stone in an effort to win a livelihood with little exertion and found it as successful as the divining rod had been. About this time he met and won the heart of Emma Hale, a farmer's daughter somewhat above him in station. Her father insisted that he settle down and show himself able to earn a decent living before marrying Emma. But work was irksome, and the young people did not want to wait; so there was a romantic elopement, and Joseph took his bride back to live with his family in Palmyra. With another member, and that one who wanted a secure and comfortable life, the shiftless Smith family needed a surer and larger income. Perhaps the translation of the golden plates could be made to provide it.

Martin Harris and the Whitmer family, whose members had been witnesses to the existence of the plates, were prevailed upon to finance the publication of the translation, and in 1830 there appeared for sale in upper New York a book that bore on its title page the inscription: *The Book of Mormon. An Account Written by the Hand of Mormon upon Plates Taken from the Plates of Nephi.* A summary of the contents included the statement that the revelation had been "sealed by the hand of Moroni, and hid up unto the Lord, to come forth in due time, by way of the Gentile — The interpretation thereof by the Gift of God." The first edition contained the damaging admission, "By Joseph Smith, Junior, Author and Proprietor," but later editions omitted any claim to earthly authorship.

In style of writing the book was an imitation of the King James version, and some of its chapters were lifted bodily from the Old and New Testaments. Nearly six hundred pages long and lethally dull, it was ornamented by occasional bits from Shakespeare, and contained sections of pseudo history of ancient America and of religious teaching. It was full of faulty grammar and anachronisms and was apparently not considered a perfect translation by Smith and his successors, since several thousand corrections have been made. But, regardless of its peculiarities, *The Book of Mormon* has been translated into twelve languages, and some twenty thousand copies have been printed each year for a century.

At once the question arose as to where the ignorant Joseph could have obtained both ideas and data for so pretentious a volume. For Mormons the answer is simple: The whole project, plates and translation, was inspired, and Joseph Smith was chosen of God as the medium for establishing His church on earth. For the anti-Mormon or non-Mormon, the solution is not so simple. Biographers and critics, delving into all the known facts of the lives of Smith and his early followers, have worried out of them a variety of explanations. There was, for instance, the famous discovery of an unpublished novel by a man named Spaulding that was in many ways similar to the historical parts of *The Book of Mormon*, and it was proved that Smith might have seen this manuscript or have heard portions of it read. The fact that Sidney Rigdon, Campbellite Baptist minister and later a disciple of Smith's, was in the vicinity of Palmyra at certain critical times has led him to be considered the source of the work.

Modern writers tend to attribute much of the book to Joseph Smith's subconscious mind in some sort of trancelike state. "Every word," says Beardsley, "which the subconscious personality emitted through the vocal chords of Joseph Smith, Jr., is explicable to the psychologist. . . . Every phrase, every sentence, every idea had an origin somewhere in Joe's past mental experience."[4] The dreams of his grandfathers and of his mother, his constant Bible reading, the Indian legends of western New York, the stories of Captain Kidd, the economic, political, and social ideas of his own day, all were worked into the book. Mysterious and abnormal it may be, as were the processes of Joseph's mind, but no supernatural explanation is necessary, nor does one need to find any other human agency. Even in the 1830's Alexander Campbell wrote:

He decides all of the great controversies . . . infant baptism, the Trinity, regeneration, repentance, justification, the fall of man, atonement, transubstantiation, fasting, penance, church government, the call to the ministry, the general resurrection, eternal punishment, who may baptise, and even the questions of Free-masonry, republican government, and the rights of man.[5]

Not for nothing had Joseph Smith been a sermon-taster and a ne'er-do-well loafer around the village store.

THE ESTABLISHMENT OF THE MORMON CHURCH

Whether author or prophet, Joseph Smith was without honor in his own country. The precious book did not sell well. So by special revelation its price was lowered to one dollar and twenty-five cents, and Joseph's father and brothers were commissioned as book agents. They traveled far and wide, advertising it as a history of the Indians when Bibles seemed unmarketable and accepting part payment in such commodities as wood, vegetables, and chickens. In the meantime the project of establishing a new church got under way. Joseph announced that by angelic baptism he had been ordained the First Elder of the church with power to ordain his assistants. A state charter was procured, and in April 1830 "The Church of Jesus Christ" met for the first time in the house of Peter Whitmer. The Smith and Whitmer families and a half-dozen other followers made up the first congregation.

At first the growth was very slow. The Smiths commanded no respect in that district, and Joseph's pretensions were not taken seriously. The new church might easily have died at this juncture had it not been for the promoting activities of two Campbellite ministers from Ohio, Parley Pratt and Sidney Rigdon. Their first contacts with Smith are a little obscure, but it is certain that in the winter of 1830, on their advice, it was decided to move the new church from Palmyra to Ohio. In 1833 a resident of Palmyra wrote,

All the Mormons have left this part of the state, and so palpable is their imposture that nothing is here said or thought of the subject, except when inquiries from abroad are occasionally made concerning them. I know of no one now living in this section of the country that ever gave them credence.[6]

The move to Ohio was a great strategic step, for at Kirtland in the Western Reserve there was a more fertile field, already tilled by such able husbandmen as the revivalist leaders of the older churches. Anything new in religion was assured of a hearing, and no one was familiar with the sordid background of Joseph Smith.

There were many converts during the early years in Kirtland, among them some of the ablest men the Latter Day Saints, as they were then called, were to acquire. The Young brothers, Phineas and Brigham, their father, their sister and her husband, and a family friend, Heber Kimball, all became members of the church between 1830 and 1832. Brigham Young's biographer suggests that that shrewd and skeptical young man early discerned that the new religion might easily be made a paying proposition.[7] Parley Pratt's brother, Orson, later one of the leaders of the church, was baptized at nineteen. He became a mathematician of prominence whose *Quadratic Equations* was used as a textbook in the University of Paris. W. W. Phelps, the ex-editor of an anti-Masonic newspaper in New York, came into the church, bringing his literary and editorial ability to its service. It was he who was responsible for much of the Prophet's literary work; he edited the revelations, wrote the speeches, and acted as press agent.

THE CHURCH OF THE LATTER DAY SAINTS IN OHIO

With these and other able, if self-interested, leaders the new church was provided with priests, missionaries, and administrators. The change of scene and the presence of admiring converts encouraged Joseph Smith to ever more dramatic evidences of leadership and of his messianic character. He attempted miracles of healing, essayed to walk upon the water, tried to raise the dead. He was continually in communion with God, who spoke through him in the revelations by which Smith governed his church and dictated to his lieutenants. At first these revelations may have been the product of self-hypnosis or of the same sort of self-delusion that had produced *The Book of Mormon;* later in their frequency and their trivial character they could have been only the convenient device used to secure mastery by a shrewd but cynical dictator. At first

Smith used the technique of the translation, gazing into his peek stone until the revelation was formed in his mind — or appeared to him. Later he merely deliberated briefly and then uttered each sentence slowly and impressively while a scribe wrote it down. He seldom permitted his subordinates to make revelations and could always end any dispute by producing one of his own.

In the early years of the Church of the Latter Day Saints there was little formal doctrine. Like other sects of the frontier, it was primitive and pentecostal in its teaching, and, like the Millerites, the Mormons had as their chief drawing card the belief that the world was whirling to a speedy destruction in which only the Saints would be saved. The millennium was mentioned over and over again in Joseph Smith's revelations, and the missionaries of the church recounted in their sermons every dire portent of coming disaster, from crop failures and falling stars to biblical prophecies. Early Mormon newspapers appear always to have borne such names as the *Millennial Star* and the *Signs of the Times*. Another major tenet of early Mormonism was that the survivors of the day of judgment — all the Saints — were destined to inherit the earth. For them a very real and material paradise would be prepared. After a careful estimate of the tillable land of the earth and of the probable number to be saved, Orson Pratt in 1852 announced that every Saint would receive for his own more than one hundred and fifty acres of land.

When the early missionaries went out to preach, there were almost as many gospels as there were preachers, and in their eagerness to acquire converts even the church leaders hurried from place to place, with as little organization as they had doctrine. Their tactics were those of the Methodist circuit riders of an earlier day — circuit riders like Lorenzo Dow rather than Peter Cartwright — and the revival meetings were choice examples of religious emotionalism and exhibitionism. Joseph Smith frowned upon the excesses and finally produced a revelation that said they were instigated by the devil; miracles, trances, and special visions were to be reserved for the Prophet and Revelator; they were not for the common herd.

A little later Rigdon and Pratt, using *The Book of Mormon* and the accumulated revelations, got out a *Book of Doctrine and Covenants* that went far toward bringing order out of the doctrinal chaos. Evangelical work was still based on the idea of restoring the apostolic church and on millennialism; miracles, visions, the gift of tongues, and the famous revelations were retained as drawing cards; but a queer hodgepodge of Campbellite dogma, perfectionism, paganism, and Oriental philosophy, with a strong admixture of sex, formed the body of Mormon doctrine. Only the American backwoods in the mid-nineteenth century could have produced such a conglomeration.

The development of the planned and controlled economy of the later Mormon church was very slow. At first Smith seems to have had no ideas on the subject of church finance other than that it should produce a living for himself and his family, but as the work went on, revelation after revelation dealt with tithing, church building, and support for the leaders. Literal interpretation of the Bible and emphasis upon primitive Christianity, as well as knowledge of communistic settlements elsewhere in the West, led to a crude attempt at a similar experiment in Kirtland. These communistic leanings were not suppressed but sublimated. The trustees of the church were to be also the trustees of the funds of the members, and the trustees of both church and funds were but the lieutenants of the Prophet. Newcomers were induced to turn over their assets to the trustees, receiving in return notes and deeds to lands owned by the church upon which they might build their homes.

Smith reserved for himself such potentially lucrative posts as storekeeper and land agent. Later, when followers were many and business was good, the profits accruing to the Seer were large, but in the infancy of Kirtland there was little money in such undertakings. The financial expedients resorted to by the church leaders were of every variety; they borrowed from one firm to pay another, converts who were skilled artisans were put to work on the temple and other building enterprises, and occasionally a new member with wealth was acquired just as a mortgage fell due. But it was a hand-to-mouth existence, and the leaders constantly tightened their control over all visible assets of the faithful.

There were many apostasies among the disillusioned, but the efforts of the missionaries brought in new converts to outnumber the deserters. Soon closer organization was needed. In 1835 an elaborate hierarchy was set up to replace the simple rule by elders and trustees. Joseph Smith was, of course, President. Sidney Rigdon and

Hyrum Smith, brother of Joseph, were Counselors. These three made up the Presidency, which, with a Quorum of Twelve Apostles (including Brigham Young, the Pratt brothers, Heber Kimball, Orson Hyde, and William Smith) and a Quorum of Seventies, formed from the heads of the Seventies into which the entire church was divided, made up the directorate of the church.

Thus within a half-dozen years the church had acquired several thousand members, a body of doctrine, an elaborate hierarchy with the Prophet as its dictator, and a centralized, controlled economic order that might be called state socialism. This close coordination of economic and political organization, permitting the hierarchy to control both the votes and the property of the members of the church, was at the same time one of the reasons for Mormon strength and the cause for the hatred and disaster the church was to meet in Missouri and Illinois.

DIFFICULTIES IN OHIO AND MISSOURI

With due regard for such remarkable achievement it must be admitted that all was not well with the church. Joseph and the Apostles were away much of the time on missionary and money-getting expeditions. There were innumerable jealousies and disputes among the leaders and violent quarrels within the Smith family. Accusations of gross immorality were made against those in high places, and the first breath of the idea of polygamy antagonized many. Apostasy and schism assailed the church from within, while Mormon financial practices and the rumors of low moral standards angered their Gentile neighbors.

Dire difficulties were soon encountered in the colony established in Missouri by Mormon missionaries. As the entrepôt for trade to the West, Independence was a boom town with its full quota of ruffians and renegades from all parts of the Union. There was friction from the beginning between Mormons and Gentiles and constant accusations on both sides of violence and petty thievery. The Mormon colony grew rapidly and acquired more and more land, the Mormons voted as a unit as Joseph Smith ordered, and they made no secret of the Prophet's promise that the whole state of Missouri would ultimately belong to them. Their attitude toward both Indians and Negroes won them the hatred of the Missourians, for they sent missionaries to the former and were thought to incite the latter to flight or insurrection. That Mormon conduct was in large measure the cause for their troubles was admitted by one of their leaders, W. W. Phelps, in 1833: "Our people fare very well, and, when they are discreet, little or no persecution is felt."[8]

Finally the Mormons were presented with an ultimatum demanding that they settle their affairs and leave Jackson County "within a reasonable time." The Missourians for their part offered to pay the Mormons liberally for their land and improvements. Insisting that these demands were religious persecution, the Mormon leaders tried to get satisfaction from the courts, only to find that judges and juries were opposed to them. Strong in their faith, the Mormons continued building, brought in new settlers, and gave no sign of departure. Civil war broke out, and, with loud denunciations of the persecution, the Jackson County Mormons, outnumbered and outfought, moved into Clay County, where there already were Mormon settlers. Here the story was the same, and by 1836 they were forced to move on again, this time to Caldwell County, an almost unsettled area where there seemed little opposition to their coming. They secured large tracts of good land, founded a county seat called Far West, and built houses, a school, and shops. They elected their own town and county officials, began to prosper, and in their contentment had little reason to create any disturbance.

Meanwhile the friction in Ohio was coming to a head over the mismanagement of Mormon business and financial affairs. There were no profits in the various enterprises of the church and little prospect of easy money anywhere in the tightening money market that presaged the panic of 1837. Heavily in debt and without any ready cash, Smith decided to resort to the West's favorite remedy, wildcat banking, choosing the most inauspicious time, the fall of 1836, to launch the new enterprise. He applied to the state legislature for a charter for the Kirtland Safety Bank, for which he expected to declare a capital of $4,000,000, to be made up by selling shares at fifty dollars each to the faithful Saints. When the request for a charter was refused by justly suspicious state authorities, Smith was not balked. It might be necessary to have a charter for a bank, but there was no such requirement for an anti-banking institution!

So the Kirtland Safety Society Anti-Banking Company was established with thirty-two officials, each paid a salary of a dollar per day. Two hundred thousand dollars worth of notes that had been prepared for the bank proper were salvaged for use by stamping *Anti* and *ing* in small letters before and after the word *Bank*, which had been engraved in much larger letters. The signatures of Smith and Rigdon served to give the notes prestige, and, upon church orders, they circulated locally at par. Abroad they were put into circulation by the missionaries, who vied with each other in bringing back better money in exchange. The stock of the Anti-Banking Company was sold to the Saints on easy terms or in exchange for almost worthless town lots. Although the paper value of the stock was supposedly $4,000,000, the actual cash resources of the bank amounted to about $15,000, and yet Smith assured the anxious Saints that "the bank is of God and cannot fail."

More than tricks, however, was needed to convince the business world that the Anti-Bank was solvent. At its managers' flat refusal to redeem its paper in specie, creditors assailed from all sides, the state declared its banking laws had been violated, and Smith and Rigdon were arrested and held on bail. The bank was forced to close its doors, and the angry Saints rebelled against the leaders whose dupes they had been. No Gentile could exceed the violence or match the accusations hurled at the Prophet and the Apostles by the disgruntled citizens of Kirtland. Smith read them out of the church with vituperation equally violent. He said they had "had recourse to the foulest lying to hide their iniquity" and referred to them as "this gang of horse-thieves and drunkards." The church leaders turned on each other with mutual accusations of intemperance, fraud, and polygamy. Smith tried to brazen out all charges, but, faced with trial for mismanagement and peculation, he gave up the fight and fled to the Missouri colony for safety.

Smith's own account and that of the church make much of the "persecutions" he suffered and mention the wild flight from armed pursuers who followed the Prophet for two hundred miles. There seems no evidence of any such pursuit but instead every indication that the non-Mormons and the apostates from the church were quite content to be rid of the discredited leaders. The scandals added to the panic and the bank and business failures made the

Kirtland situation desperate, and much of the Mormon property passed into Gentile hands. Many of the faithful followed Smith; a few others clung to what property there was left in Kirtland and to their Mormon religion, although they were without a prophet. After the death of Joseph Smith they affiliated with the minority group that followed Smith's family rather than Brigham Young. In 1901 the Kirtland district reported a membership of about four hundred.

Disaster did not discourage Joseph Smith but seemed merely to spur him on to greater efforts and more extravagant pretensions. He no longer thought of himself as the humble revelator of God's word; overweening self-confidence led him to declare, "God is my right-hand man." Assuming full leadership as soon as he reached Missouri, he involved the peaceful Mormons there in difficulties that forced them out of the state in a few months. At a great Fourth of July celebration for both Mormons and Gentiles, he announced a revelation that God had ordered the Saints to buy up all the land around Far West. In the chief address of the day Sidney Rigdon bitterly recounted the persecutions the Mormons had suffered and announced their refusal to submit longer to oppression.

[We] will bear it no more. Our rights shall no more be trampled on with impunity. The man, or set of men, who attempt it, does it at the expense of their lives. And that mob that comes on us to disturb us, it shall be between us and them a *war of extermination, for we will follow them till the last drop of their blood is spilled, or else they will have to exterminate us.* . . . Remember it then, all men.[9]

Breathing defiance against attacks that had not yet come, Smith and Rigdon organized their forces in the fall of 1838. A fighting band was formed, depredations were made on the property of Missourians, and retaliation was met by armed combat. Guerilla warfare followed between Mormon bands and state militia, the inevitable result of which was another Mormon disaster. Joseph Smith and the Mormon leaders were arrested, and their followers were driven from the state to take refuge across the Mississippi. With the connivance of the Missouri authorities Smith escaped from custody in April 1839 and joined his flock in Illinois, where a new Stake in Zion was established.

JOSEPH SMITH IN ILLINOIS

The demoralized and poverty-stricken Mormons welcomed their Prophet with unshaken confidence in his ability to solve their difficulties and lead them on to prosperity and security. The rank and file had always been simple, credulous, trusting people, content to let their leaders make all important decisions. The Prophet, now thirty-four years of age, was more than six feet tall, vigorous, and handsome. He was overflowing with self-confidence, energy, and good spirits, and his frequent lapses from virtue made him seem even more a man whom they could love and trust. His amusing pretensions to culture and learning, his vulgarity, his rowdy sense of humor, even his sensuality, were in tune with the rough frontier life they all led, and his shrewdness and organizing ability were respected. The early years in Illinois were the most successful period of Joseph Smith's career.

There were few settlers in the region around the little village of Commerce. The riverbanks were marshy and malarial, and few envied the exiles who began to buy land early in 1839 on both sides of the river. Poor as they were, their arrival brought business to the neighborhood, and the prospect of several thousand new settlers filled both Whigs and Democrats with pleasurable excitement and some anxiety, for the balance between the two parties was close in southern Illinois. As the election year of 1840 drew near both Whigs and Democrats wooed the artful Prophet. His price was a charter for Nauvoo, the city the Mormons were building on the site of the village of Commerce a few miles from Quincy. The Whigs promised the charter, and the Mormons voted solidly for the Whig ticket, but they let it be known that they had made no pledge for the future. The Mormon vote aided in cutting the Democratic majority down to the lowest point it had reached since the establishment of the party. The warning was heeded, and at the next session of the legislature the charter asked by Smith was voted promptly. Stephen A. Douglas and Abraham Lincoln both courted the Mormon vote and helped push the charter through the legislature, and Douglas, as lawyer and judge, was to aid Smith in many ways in the following years.

The Nauvoo charter was a remarkable document. It gave almost

Nauvoo, Illinois, in the 1840's

unlimited powers to the mayor and aldermen, who could pass any law not repugnant to the Constitution of the United States; the mayor's court was given exclusive jurisdiction over all cases arising out of city ordinances; and the town was permitted to have its own militia, which was to be subject only to the command of the mayor. A charter was granted also for Nauvoo University, and the Nauvoo House, designed as a tavern and a home for the mayor, was incorporated. Thus an embryo state within a state was authorized. Joseph Smith, of course, became mayor and head of the mayor's court, and the aldermen were his henchmen. The Nauvoo Legion was equipped with arms, band, and uniforms, but the university remained a paper institution, which, however, gave honorary degrees to politicians and newspaper men who spoke well of the Mormons.

Prosperity followed the liberality of the Illinois government. A pottery, a brickyard, a quarry, and toolworks were established. There was much gayety in the new city: dances, music, athletic events, and a good deal of pageantry connected with the militia, with the church ceremonies, and with those of the newly organized Masonic Lodge. But lawlessness was apparent, also, and the laxity of the municipal court made Nauvoo a happy hunting ground for fugitives from justice elsewhere. The ferry across the river was known as Thieves' Ferry. There was a decidedly rowdy aspect to the little theocratic state—a rowdyism not repugnant to members of its government.

Mormon missionaries sent to England found a vast reservoir of new adherents in the poorer districts of English factory towns, where discontent and superstition combined to make conversion easy, especially when land was promised to all who would migrate. Dr. Charles Mackay states that ten thousand converts were made in the period 1838–43, and that was just a beginning. An emigration agency was set up in Liverpool, and a Mormon representative was appointed for every port. In 1849 a permanent immigrant fund established by the church provided aid for those too poor to pay for their own passage. In 1841 the population of Nauvoo was nine thousand; by 1845 it was estimated at fifteen thousand. The little river town with its unique government and its peculiar people became the mecca for many travelers, and business boomed at the Nauvoo House.

All was not well, however. The state government was dissatisfied, and state authorities were lukewarm to the Prophet, whose
control over an ever increasing number of votes gave him a balance
of power in elections. Again the arrogance and aggressiveness of the
Mormons led to trouble with their neighbors. Feeling the constant
menace to his power and to his people, Joseph Smith alternated between egotistical bombast and protective measures. Perhaps the increasing tension wore on his nerves and made him less cautious and
sensitive to public opinion. At any rate he chose this period to inaugurate polygamy among a chosen few of his flock. In 1843 he
made known a revelation giving divine authorization for the practice. Secrecy was insisted upon but was, of course, impossible to
maintain when the wives of the Prophet increased to twenty-eight
and several of the leaders kept pace with him. The rumor of polygamy roused non-Mormon neighbors to frenzy, and, when polygamy
was accompanied by a complex system of marriage whereby one
woman could be "sealed" to one husband for this life and to another
for eternity, opposition appeared among Mormons as well.

Within four years, therefore, of the Mormon entry into Illinois
trouble was approaching from at least three sources: the state government, the non-Mormon residents of near-by communities, and
the dissatisfied Mormons themselves. In 1843 the Prophet's over-
zealous bargaining with both parties before the state election caused
the Mormons to lose all support in the legislature, and an attempt to
annul the Nauvoo charter was defeated only by the efforts of William Smith, whom the Mormon leaders had put there to safeguard
their interests.

About this time, too, the Mormons petitioned Congress to have a
separate territory made of Nauvoo, and then, to cap the climax,
Joseph Smith decided to run for the position of President of the
United States in 1844. He had written to both Clay and Calhoun
asking their support in collecting from the state of Missouri compensation for the losses suffered by the Mormons there.[10] Receiving
no satisfaction from them, he drew up a platform full of panaceas
for a wide variety of troubles. He wished to curtail the activities of
government and to reduce the number of congressmen and cut their
pay to two dollars a day. The prisoners in penitentiaries would be
freed with a blessing, and deserters from the army would go unpun-

ished if Joseph Smith became president. Slaves were to be freed with ample compensation for their owners. Oregon, Texas, California, Canada, and Mexico were all to be annexed, if they should agree to such action. The platform closed with the signature of the candidate as the "friend of the people and of unadulterated freedom." The Mormon missionaries promptly became campaigners and went through the country preaching its salvation through the election of Joseph Smith. One may doubt that the Prophet expected election in 1844, but his self-confidence and vanity were such that he probably saw no insuperable barrier to his reaching the presidency eventually. In the meantime the campaign would be good advertising, and the missionaries would get converts as well as votes.

Affairs in Illinois, however, had reached such a crisis that only by the greatest circumspection and caution could Smith have avoided disaster. Instead, every flamboyant and reckless act of that last year hastened the catastrophe. All that was needed was some episode, some sign of weakness, to crystallize the antagonism into action. That episode came when Smith attempted to acquire the wife of one of the Nauvoo Mormons. The angry husband and his friends rebelled and established the *Nauvoo Expositor*, the first issue of which was published June 7, 1844. Under the slogan "The Truth, the Whole Truth, and Nothing but the Truth," a complete exposé was made of the new doctrine of polygamy in theory and practice. These accusations were followed by criticism of Joseph Smith's political and economic policies.

Such insubordination was met with violent action. The paper was suppressed, all available copies of the issue were burned, and the municipal council of Nauvoo took action against the proprietors in a trial that was a travesty of all the usual forms of justice. Thomas Ford, the governor of Illinois, observing with benevolent interest the revolt in Nauvoo, called the trial "the most curious and irregular" one ever recorded in a civilized country, "and one finds difficulty in determining whether the proceedings of the council were more the result of insanity or depravity." [11] The *Expositor* presses were destroyed and the Nauvoo Legion was ordered out in readiness for trouble.

And trouble came with great speed. The leaders of the Mormon revolt fled to near-by Carthage, the anti-Mormon counties called out their local militia, and Governor Ford came down from the state capital in an effort to keep within some form of legality the huge mob collecting to storm Nauvoo. With the state militia and its officers as violently anti-Mormon as the civilian mob, justice and order were impossible. Under promise of a fair trial, Joseph and Hyrum Smith were persuaded to surrender, only to be murdered, on June 27, in the feebly defended Carthage jail. The militia and the mob then descended upon Nauvoo, which surrendered after some show of resistance.

For the third time in little more than a decade the hapless Saints were forced to make preparation for departure from their Stake in Zion. Time was given them to settle their affairs, sell their property, and reorganize their shattered government. The Prophet's family broke away from the main body, repudiated polygamy on the grounds that Joseph had neither preached nor practiced it, and led a small minority of the Saints over into Iowa to create the Reorganized Church of Jesus Christ of Latter Day Saints, which has remained small and independent for nearly one hundred years. The main body of the Mormons, after a bitter struggle among the leaders, agreed to accept Brigham Young as the successor to the Prophet and to follow him on the long journey to their permanent Zion beyond the mountains. A third very small faction went first to Wisconsin and then to a group of islands in Lake Michigan with James Jesse Strang, one of the most eccentric of all those who claimed the mantle of Joseph Smith. Ignorant, poor, and credulous, these people conceded complete dictatorship to Strang, accepting polygamy, communism, and eventually even his claim to be their king. The Kingdom of Saint James was short-lived, for again the angry non-Mormon neighbors attacked the Saints, and the twenty-five hundred subjects of a murdered monarch were dispersed.[12]

After much suffering the main body of the Mormons reached the region of the great Salt Lake, where they founded their State of Deseret outside the boundaries of the United States. Within a few years the Mexican War was to bring them back under the government they had hoped to escape, but their isolation was so complete that for many years they were left in peace to develop under the dictation of Brigham Young, the "Old Boss." Their numbers grew from 6,000 to 200,000 in thirty years, and their wealth increased in proportion. Polygamy provided a cheap labor supply well adapted for the patriarchal development of an agrarian community, and their views on the position of women ensured them adequate and docile domestic service. The isolation of Salt Lake made apostasy difficult, and the firm control of Brigham Young kept the rank and file subservient. If there were any dissatisfied they had to remain to share the blessings, or to be exploited for the greater glory, of the new Zion.

CHAPTER 6

Religious Communism in America

Freedom to practice the articles of their faith, no matter how peculiar they might be, coupled with the possibility of economic security in a country where land was cheap and plentiful, turned the leaders of many European cults to America. Believing they had discovered a new, exclusive, and unique pathway to salvation and to the world's redemption, the adherents of many of these sects wished to build new homes away from the contaminating influence of older faiths where there could be no contact with the corrupting and diverting aspects of modern civilization. The frontier offered land, livelihood, and solitude to both European and American religious experiments.

THE REASONS FOR COMMUNISTIC ORGANIZATION

The leaders of these new sects emphasized their separateness and the need for the close association of all members. The more peculiar the tenets of their faith, the more necessary became the intensive instruction, criticism, and supervision that communty living could make possible. Revivalists found themselves constantly faced with the problem of backsliding; apostasy was the bugbear of all new sects. Isolation and segregation into unitary communities were found to be more effective counteragents than the Methodists' protracted meetings.

To this basic reason for religious communism may be added another equally practical in nature. Both in Europe and in America by far the larger number of converts to new pietistic creeds were poor men and women who brought with them only the potential value of their capacity to work. Without capital and without influence, they were defenseless against the antagonism of accepted faiths, established churches, and arbitrary governments. Migration to a new land, or removal from well-settled areas to the frontier, required considerable capital expenditure. The funds of the few well-to-do converts must be used to pay for the transfer of the many whose contributions could be slight. Emigration expenditures and land purchases were, therefore, communal enterprises conducted by the leaders as agents or trustees. The indigent, the aged, and the weak were from the beginning a charge upon those who were more fortunate or more provident. Land once purchased and a new life once established, it was difficult to get rid of that burden and to make any arrangement for the return to individual ownership. Many sects not originally communistic thus had communism thrust upon them for social and economic reasons.

This communism, adopted through necessity, often became an end in itself, for which religious sanctions were found. The leaders of the sect soon discovered that it made more complete the separateness they thought essential and infinitely increased their ability to control the rank and file. There were decided advantages in the planned economy of cooperative enterprise. If well managed and carefully supervised, the religious community soon became a going concern with rapidly increasing assets. For many members security and plenty were prized above independence and the opportunity for individual gain. The few who were irked by rigid economic controls were apt also to resent the spiritual dictation of the leaders, and in the eyes of the governing body of the sect these independent thinkers might well be dispensed with. Whether or not such seceders should receive a share of the joint assets of the community was a difficult problem, solved in various ways by different communities.

Almost all the early sects that adopted a communal way of life were pietistic in faith, basing their belief upon a literal interpretation of biblical teaching. They rejected all existing hierarchies and dogmas and found in the Bible all they needed in the way of theology and guidance. The primitive Christian church became their model, and they rejected all the structures that had been erected upon that foundation since the beginning of the Christian era. Intensive and prolonged reading of the Bible gave to the leaders of each sect support for the religious principles peculiar to it, and it was easy for the close student of primitive Christianity to find authorization for religious communism. When necessity began, and expediency prolonged, community of property rights, dogma soon provided the sanction of religion.

These religious communities were never very numerous, nor was the total number of adherents great. Some of them were short-lived, some lasted a century or more. One of the oldest, the Shaker

Society, still has a few adherents after one hundred and sixty years. They antedate modern socialism but have little in common with even its earlier utopian aspects. Although many of the sects were of European origin and most of their members were immigrants, the communities themselves were peculiarly American and could have operated only in the atmosphere of American freedom and tolerance for experimentation.*

Whatever the country of their origin, finding their common inspiration in the Bible, they developed, as they grew in American soil, many similarities in belief. They were all perfectionist in that they sought to build for themselves an ideal or perfect way of life. They were in large degree millennialists, since they accepted in some form the New Testament teaching in regard to the second coming of Christ. Some of them were avowedly spiritualistic; all of them had periods of confidence in miracles. They were also alike in that they were almost entirely composed of a poor, ill-educated, credulous, and trusting rank and file, obedient to and dependent upon a strict and autocratic leader or leaders. The few notable exceptions to this generalization were communities organized somewhat late in the period and only in the broadest sense religious, since their major objectives were social. Such experiments in living as Noyes's Oneida Community, Alcott's Fruitlands, and the Transcendentalists' Brook Farm defy generalization and classification, but they serve to make the transition from religious communism to nineteenth-century socialistic theory.

Similar in some respects though they were, it is the infinite diversity of the religious sects that makes them interesting. Each was allowed to work out its own destiny almost without interference in an America that had room for many and varied faiths and no great antipathy to eccentricity. During the century of the late colonial

* In his *American Socialisms* John Humphrey Noyes asserts that the communities were the result of revivalism and socialism but makes the error of stating that the revivals were purely American while the socialism was an importation from Europe. He overlooks the fact that many of the sects originated in the pietistic revivals that marked the return of emotional faith in Europe after the French Revolution. He also fails to emphasize that with many sects communism was adopted only through necessity and found a purely biblical justification through leaders who had never heard of Fourier or socialism. It is, however, interesting to note that the four standard texts on the subject of both religious and socialistic communities were all published between 1870 and 1903, when American interest in modern socialism was being aroused.[1]

and early national period many religious sects found in community of goods the solution for their economic and social problems. One or two of them were established in the colonial period, two or three during or after the Revolution, the rest in the early decades of the nineteenth century. Of the sects selected for special analysis here, the settlement of German pietists at Ephrata, Pennsylvania, was the first chronologically, but it was not the first religious community in America. In 1680 a group of Protestant mystics established in northern Maryland the Lobadist Community, which, although short-lived, owned at one time 4,000 acres of land. Also, in 1694 the Community of the Woman in the Wilderness was founded in Pennsylvania.

THE EPHRATA CLOISTER

During the period of great German migration to Pennsylvania, a young man named Conrad Beissel fled from religious persecution in the Palatinate and found his way to Lancaster County, Pennsylvania.[2] He had apparently hoped to join a group of pietists that had established a community on the Wissahickon River a generation earlier, but he found that the community was no longer in existence. In 1724 he joined the Dunkers, a very pious German Mennonite sect, Baptist or Anabaptist in dogma. Living a solitary life devoted to the study of the Bible and the obligation it placed upon the individual Christian, he became convinced that the seventh instead of the first day of the week should be observed as a day of worship and published a book to prove his thesis. The Dunkers repudiated his teaching, but a few followers came to live near his wilderness retreat. In two or three decades the new sect numbered about three hundred.

Simplicity was the keynote of the little settlement that chose the name Ephrata. There was no written constitution and no binding contract, no ritual and no exalted ministry, although the two sacraments of baptism and communion were kept. The New Testament was both the confession of faith and the guide for government. The Ephratists denied the doctrine of original sin as well as that of eternal punishment. They refused to countenance violence of any kind, were opposed to all war, and even refused to be parties to litigation.

Celibacy was considered desirable but was not required. In the earlier years, however, most of the membership was undoubtedly celibate and very ascetic in mode of life. The celibate groups lived apart in almost complete seclusion. A Sister House was built for the women, who were organized into the Sisterhood of the Roses of Sharon or Spiritual Virgins, and a similar Brother House was provided for the tonsured, bearded brotherhood. The life in these celibate orders was rigorous, the day's program leaving no time for levity, gossip, or idleness. The day began at five in the morning. Matins and a song service came before six; then there was work until nine, when breakfast was served. From nine-thirty to five the community labored, meeting again for a simple meal at the end of the day. The hours from seven to nine in the evening were to be spent in reading and study. Retiring at nine, the communities met again at midnight for another service, making in all four periods of worship each day. The two orders dressed alike in white robes of homespun wool or linen. They were vegetarian by principle, and their houses were furnished with a minimum of comfort.

Besides these celibate groups there was the "outdoor" membership, probably larger in number, made up of the married folk who lived as families near the houses of the cloistered orders. Since a period of probation was required of the candidates for the orders, and since no vows were required, there was doubtless some fluctuation in the make-up of cloistered and outdoor groups. If a sister or brother decided to marry and leave the celibate house, a place was made for a new family among the outdoor members, whose lives were less restricted. Nearly all seceders from the celibate groups settled near by and sent their children to be educated by the brothers or sisters of the cloistered orders. After about 1750, when probably a majority of the members were celibate, the two orders gradually decreased in membership and the emphasis upon celibacy declined. Sister Beverly, the last of the Order of the Roses of Sharon, died at the age of eighty in 1852.

In the matter of communal property, too, there seems to have been no hard and fast rule. In the days when the larger number of the society lived in the Brother and Sister houses all land given to or purchased by them was held in common, as were the products of their labor. But no one was required to surrender his individual possessions, and there was no communism for outdoor members.

At the height of the society's prosperity paper, oil, and flour

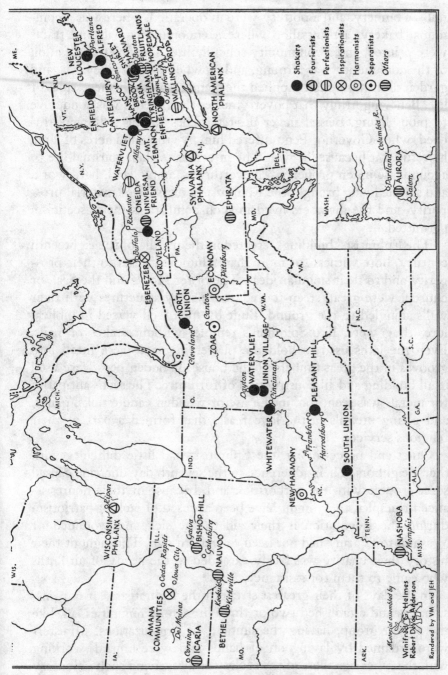

Communal settlements in the United States before 1860, including those discussed in the text but not all those in the United States

Shakers ● Fourierists ⊘ Perfectionists ◐ Inspirationists ⊗ Harmonists ⊙ Separatists ◉ Others ⊖

NEW GLOUCESTER
Portland
ALFRED
SHIRLEY
Harvard
Concord
FRUITLANDS
HOPEDALE
ENFIELD
Boston
CANTERBURY
BROOK FARM
LYRINGHAM
WATERVLIET
Albany
MT. LEBANON
ENFIELD CONN.
Hartford
WALLINGFORD
NORTH AMERICAN PHALANX
Rochester
ONEIDA
UNIVERSAL FRIEND
Buffalo
SYLVANIA PHALANX
N.J.
DEL.
EPHRATA
MD.
GROVELAND
EBENEZER
NORTH UNION
ECONOMY
Pittsburg
Canton
ZOAR
Cleveland
W.VA.
VA.
Dayton
WATERVLIET
UNION VILLAGE
Cincinnati
PLEASANT HILL
WHITEWATER
NEW HARMONY
Frankfort
Harrodsburg
SOUTH UNION
KY.
N.C.
S.C.
GA.
ALA.
TENN.
NASHOBA
Memphis
MISS.
WISCONSIN PHALANX
Ripon
Galva
BISHOP HILL
Galesburg
NAUVOO
Keokuk
Kirksville
Cedar Rapids
Iowa City
AMANA COMMUNITIES
Des Moines
Corning
ICARIA
BETHEL
Portland
AURORA
Salem
Columbia R.
WASH.

Material assembled by
Winifred C. Holmes
Robert Duncan Anderson
Rendered by VM and JEH

113

mills, a tannery, and a pottery were in operation. There was a communal bakery, a print shop where Mennonite hymnals and tracts were printed, and a community schoolhouse. The chief occupation of the community was farming, and its wheat, wool, vineyards, and garden plots more than supplied the members with the necessities of life. Believing firmly that poverty rather than wealth was conducive to pious living, Beissel never desired riches for his followers. Indeed, when Governor Penn offered him five thousand acres of land, he refused it because "it would be injurious to their spiritual life to accumulate much property." Nevertheless, ample land, hard work, and simple living brought the Ephratists a measure of material prosperity, and the members lived in such comfort as their asceticism permitted.

The Ephratists' buildings, erected in the middle of the eighteenth century, bore witness for more than a hundred years to their prosperity and to their singular ideas. The Sister House and the Saal, or church, were great, steep-roofed, three-story structures with their walls shingled to the ground. Built by men well versed in biblical lore, they were, like Solomon's temple, without spikes or nails. Even the laths used to hold the plaster in place were fitted into grooves in the great timbers of the house. Wooden pegs were used in all building and all construction of furniture. The sect's antipathy for metals was seen, too, in the use of wooden candlesticks, plates, and eating utensils in the love feasts that formed a part of their religious services.

Quiet and peace-loving, the Ephratists had little difficulty with their neighbors. Their adherence to the seventh day doctrine caused some trouble with the authorities, and, because of their nonresistance principles, they might have been accused of lack of patriotism during the Revolution if their aid to the sick and wounded of Washington's army had not been so well known. Throughout their history their charity was freely extended to the needy of all faiths who came to them for assistance.

In the days of their greatest strength the Ephratists sent out missionaries and established two or three branch communities, all, like the parent group, having the simplest of organizations. Ministers were ordained by laying on of hands and were unpaid, working with the other members of the society and receiving such voluntary assistance as might be necessary to give them freedom for church work. Sermons were simple and inspirational in character. Although musical instruments were not favored, choir and community singing was highly developed, and the Ephrata hymnals and part singing were famous in their time. Education was considered important. The Sunday school, founded in 1740, was the first of its kind in England or America. The Ephrata Academy was known throughout Pennsylvania and attracted a few pupils from Philadelphia and Baltimore.

When Conrad Beissel died in 1786, the years of growth were over for Ephrata. Its members were long-lived, however, and its property was considerable; decline it might, but its demise was slow in coming. In 1812 the society was incorporated, and its affairs were put in the hands of three elected trustees. In 1900 seventeen members, all elderly people, were the heirs to the traditions of Ephrata and to its greatly diminished property. No new members had been admitted for some time, and there was no prospect of any for the future. The little village was a shadow of its past; the vitality of its religious faith and of its communal life belonged to an era long since forgotten.

JEMIMA WILKINSON, THE UNIVERSAL FRIEND

Jemima Wilkinson and the religious sect she founded differed in almost every respect from the community at Ephrata. Born in 1752, Jemima was the daughter of Jeremiah Wilkinson, a prosperous Rhode Island farmer who was at one time a member of the colony council. The mother, a Quakeress, died when Jemima, the eighth of twelve children, was a small child. Brought up in a motherless household, the girl was willful, headstrong, and romantic. All the contemporary accounts seem to agree as to her beauty and the forcefulness of her personality. As a young girl she seems to have wanted chiefly pretty clothes and a good time. Her father sent her to learn the trade of a tailoress, but she found living under authority uncongenial and soon came back home.

When she was sixteen a revival in the neighborhood turned her attention to religion. She became interested in, although she never openly joined, the New Light Baptists, a pietistic separatist sect with extremely evangelical teachings. In the same period Jemima was probably influenced by the teachings of Mother Ann Lee, the founder of the Shaker church. Jemima became more and more moody and temperamental, spending much time in reading the Bible and in solitary meditation on religious matters. Her health was impaired, and in 1776 she spent some months in bed, suffering frequent bouts of some sort of fever. Ill and unhappy, she had visions, dreams, and visitations, culminating in a trance that lasted for thirty-six hours. This prolonged trance furnished the rather slight basis for the story, given much credence later, that she was at this time pronounced dead and that during the funeral rites she rose from her coffin to assure the assembled friends and relatives that she had died and was now risen from the dead.[3]

Whatever the nature of her illness and of this trance, there was a sharp turn for the better immediately after this experience, and Jemima was soon well and strong. She herself seems to have been convinced that there was something miraculous about her recovery and always maintained that she had died during the trance and that her soul had gone to heaven. Her body, she believed, had been re-animated by a spirit, perhaps that of Christ himself, sent to make God's will known to man once more. From that day she refused to be known as Jemima, claiming instead the title of the Universal Friend.

Since the purpose of this "Spirit of Life" that had occupied her body was to instruct the world in the way to salvation, Jemima, or the Friend, began to hold open-air meetings of a revivalistic nature. The powers she claimed for her new personality were those of prophecy, revelation, and healing. It seems impossible that this was barefaced and deliberate imposture. It is much more probable that Jemima, like other founders of new faiths, had first deluded herself and was quite sincere in the belief that her body was now the "tabernacle," as she called it, of the Holy Spirit. Unless one is willing to grant the sincerity of her belief that she had been chosen as an instrument for the redemption of the world, it is difficult to explain the reception of her claims in the following years. The clue to her appeal must lie in the magnetism and attractiveness of her personality. All accounts mention her beauty, her tall, graceful figure, her excellent manners, and her hypnotic eyes.

The religious doctrines preached by the Friend were a composite of many current in her day. Her sermons were filled with the message of universal love and universal peace – the message of her Quaker ancestors given to a people in the throes of the Revolution. Millennialism came into her teaching, for she believed that the spirit that had reanimated her dead body would remain a thousand years and then "be swept to Heaven in a cloud of glory." She believed that Saturday was the biblical Sabbath, but was willing to calm local prejudice by accepting Sunday as a rest day and holiday – thus recommending a five-day week! The Friend advocated celibacy, but at first there was apparently no mention of communism; her ideas in regard to social and economic matters seem to have developed as specific problems confronted her.

The meetings of the Universal Friend were well attended from the first. When her followers numbered about twenty, she went with them on horseback on a tour through southern New England. Dressed in flowing robes, Jemima rode ahead of the cavalcade, stopping to preach wherever an audience gathered. Converts were many and not all from the poor and oppressed. Many substantial Yankee farmers accepted the teachings of the Friend, and several educated and wealthy citizens of New England and Pennsylvania gave her their allegiance and much of their property. Governor Hopkins of Rhode Island listened to her with favor, and John Babcock, a friend of Washington, became a follower. William Potter, who was twice chief justice of the court of common pleas, was one of her most devoted adherents. She made her home in his household for six years. James Parker, a man of wealth and influence, financed much of her work in its earlier years. In 1782 the Friend went to Philadelphia, where she was favorably received by the Quakers, who placed a meetinghouse at her disposal. She gained a number of followers there, and in Worcester, Pennsylvania, she made enough converts to warrant establishing a sort of branch church.

About this time the idea of removal to the frontier began to appeal to Jemima and her friends. In addition to the usual motives for such a move, there were others more personal. Jemima had got into difficulties in both Rhode Island and Pennsylvania because of her teachings in regard to celibacy and the subordination of family affairs to religious matters. The extravagance of the converts, who claimed that the Friend was Jesus come to earth again, added to the difficulties of the new sect. Repudiated by the Quakers, Jemima lost many of her Pennsylvania converts. New England churches were roused against her, and she was derided in their pulpits. There were also charges of the misuse of funds and of rapacity in demands for contributions. Irate husbands, whose wives followed Jemima's advice and denied them conjugal rights, added to the furor against her.

Faced with these difficulties, Jemima sought a revelation as to the future and announced that she had been commanded to "go into a strange country, and to a people of strange language; but fear not, for lo! the angel of His presence shall go with thee; He shall lead thee, and the Shekirah shall be thy reward." [4] With this project in view, and perhaps with other motives as well, the Friend advocated the pooling of resources in a common stock in the control of men who would act in accordance with her instructions.

Western New York was just opening up to settlement in those days, and it was to Genesee County that twenty-five of the Friend's disciples went in 1788 to secure land and prepare the way for the rest of the faithful. Near Seneca Lake, with the Seneca Indians for neighbors, the New Jerusalem was established. Between two and three hundred settlers followed the Friend to the new home in the wilderness, and the process of clearing and tilling the land was quickly under way. More than fifteen thousand acres of land were purchased, the members of the sect contributing to the price in proportion to their means and making Jemima trustee for the whole society.

In this New Jerusalem a suitable house was built for the Friend, and a large tract of land was set aside for her support. Voluntary contributions of livestock and labor soon brought her land under cultivation so that she and the "sisterhood" of her household could live in comfort. Jemima established good relations with the Indians, and there were no other near neighbors to cause her difficulty. The first decade after the settlement in New York was the most prosperous and peaceful period in the history of the Society of the Universal Friend. Jemima, too, throve; her people were contented, no one disputed her authority, and life was decidedly satisfactory.

There are several contemporary descriptions of the Friend and her colony written by travelers who visited the New Jerusalem. They all mention her peculiar but luxurious dress, the marking *U.F.*

on her furniture, and her handsome carriage with its doors labeled *Universal Friend*. The Duc de la Rochefoucauld Liancourt published in 1799 a travel account that contained a dozen pages telling of his visit to the society.[5] He attended a meeting in Jemima's house, which he found simple but "far from the cell of a nun." The meeting, he said, was made up of about thirty persons — men, women, and children.

Jemima stood at the door of her bed-chamber on a carpet, with an armchair behind her. She had on a white morning gown, and waistcoat, such as men wear, and a petticoat of the same color. Her black hair was cut short, carefully combed, and divided behind into three ringlets; she wore a stock, and a white silk cravat, which was tied about her neck with affected negligence. In point of delivery, she preached with more ease than any other Quaker I have yet heard; but the subject matter of her discourse was an eternal repetition of the same topics, death, sin, and repentance. She is said to be about forty years of age, but she did not appear to be more than thirty. She is of middle stature, well made, of a florid countenance, and has fine teeth, and beautiful eyes. Her action is studied; she aims at simplicity, but there is something pedantic in her manner.

After a bountiful dinner provided by the Friend for the entire assemblage, although she herself retired and ate in solitude, the French traveler departed, evidently far from convinced of the validity of her claims. After repeating, with no attempt at proof, much of the ill-natured gossip he had heard in regard to Jemima's morals, he wound up the account of his visit with the remark:

We had indeed already seen more than enough to estimate the character of this bad actress, whose pretended sanctity only inspired us with contempt and disgust, and who is altogether incapable of imposing upon any person of common understanding, unless those of the most simple minds, or down right enthusiasts. Her speeches are so strongly contradicted by the tenor of her actions; her whole conduct, her expence, compared with that of other families, within a circumference of fifty miles, her way of living and her dress, form such a striking contrast with her harangues on the subject of contemning earthly enjoyments; and the extreme assiduity, with which she is continually endeavouring to induce children, over whom she has any influence, to leave their parents and form a part of her community; all these particulars so strongly militate against the doctrines of peace and universal love, which she is incessantly preaching, that we were actually struck with abhorrence of her duplicity and hypocrisy, as soon as . . . our curiosity subsided.

Other contemporaries were not so harsh in their judgment. A writer in *Tait's Magazine*, after commenting on the impressiveness of Jemima's appearance, wrote, "The *tout ensemble*, or entire person of Jemima Wilkinson, taken with her carriage, manners, and dress, would impress the beholder with strong intellect, decision of character, deep sincerity, and passionate devotion." [6] In his *History of Yates County, New York*, published in 1848, S. C. Cleveland reviewed all the evidence to be found about the Universal Friend. He came to the conclusion that she was sincere and lived an honest and consistent moral life. She was, he said, well-read, a profound student of the Bible, and an advocate of pure and upright living. He denied that she had claimed the power to perform miracles or to be a second Messiah and stated that any such claims made by her followers were not authorized by her.

These differences of opinion on the part of outside observers were reflected in the dissension among the Friend's own followers. Perhaps too many of them were well educated and independent, perhaps Jemima grew too dictatorial in her treatment of the rank and file, perhaps the economic interests of individuals and community clashed. Whatever the reason, there were quarrels, lawsuits, and withdrawals. Both James Parker and William Potter seceded and sued for a share of the property commensurate to their contributions. They had the Friend arrested for blasphemy, and both cases came before the state courts. The society had never been incorporated, and Jemima's trusteeship was questioned by other claimants, so that the affairs of the New Jerusalem were constantly in court. The Friend was acquitted on the blasphemy charge and was upheld in her claim to be the sole trustee of the society, but the litigation over property rights did not end until some years after her death.

Despite the withdrawal of some of its leading members the little community held together until the Friend's death in 1819. Some seventy-five men with their families and more than one hundred women, many of them celibate, constituted the faithful, who had been taught to believe that the spirit which had long ago entered the body of Jemima Wilkinson could not die. The Friend herself seems to have believed this, and there was much alarm when the "tabernacle" grew so seriously ill that the approach of death was recognized. When the life of the Friend came to an end, her body was kept for four days in the hope of a miracle and was then walled into a part of the cellar until it could be secretly buried. Only the descendants of those who participated in that burial know to this day where in that lovely valley the body of the Universal Friend came to its final rest. Her estate was left to two of the "sisterhood," who were charged with the guardianship of the poor. The Friend had no successor; her followers were released by her death from any allegiance to the sect, for there had never been any bond except her personality. All property other than her estate was theirs, to be used as they chose, and a few of their descendants still live within the confines of that New Jerusalem that was built one hundred and fifty years ago.

THE HARMONY SOCIETY OF THE RAPPITES

Toward the end of the eighteenth century a group of German pietists in Württemburg led a revolt against the indifference and rationalism that had crept into the Lutheran church. At first they hoped to carry on a reform movement within the church, and the preaching of their greatest intellectual leader, Michael Hahn, was directed toward that end. They won the hatred of the clergy, however, and found themselves in bad repute with the state. Hahn and the timid gave way in the persecution that followed, but the bolder pietists turned separatist and declared their willingness to follow their leader, George Rapp, a farmer and vine grower, to America.

The doctrines of the group, as developed in the struggle with the state church, were similar to those of the Shakers. They, too, found justification for celibacy in the first chapter of Genesis, although they did not formally adopt it until 1807. They were millennialists, and Rapp often said that he lived only to present his followers to God.[7] Throughout their history the Rappites kept their affairs in order so that they might at any time undertake the journey to the "land of Israel." When it became necessary to pool their assets in order to migrate and to purchase the land for their new homes, they adopted communism and later found scriptural sanction for it. They refused to believe in eternal punishment and were inclined to Universalist doctrines in regard to the life after death.

In 1803 George Rapp and his son came to the United States to prepare for the migration of the group. They purchased five thou-

sand acres of land in western Pennsylvania and sent for their followers, who arrived six hundred strong in the next year. The Rapps
were wise leaders, and the German peasants were industrious and
obedient. They cleared their lands and built their homes with alac-
rity and seem to have prospered from the beginning. In 1805 a
"Community of Equality" was formally established. All cash, land,
and chattels were given to the community to be administered by
the superintendents appointed by Rapp for that purpose. In 1807
the Rappites decided upon formal renunciation of marriage, all married couples separated, and no further marriages were allowed.*
From that time on recruitment was almost entirely by new immigration from Germany. Rapp had no missionary or proselyting zeal,
and the language barrier kept out English-speaking people.

Agriculture was, of course, the main economic basis of the society, although they soon built a tannery, mills, a woolen factory,
and a distillery. By 1810 they had two thousand acres under cultivation. Again cooperation, able direction, and mass production brought
good returns from the fertile soil, so that five years after their arrival in America a visitor said of them:

. . . we were struck with surprise and admiration at the astonishing
progress in improvements and the establishment of manufactories which
this little republic has made in five years. They have done more substantial good in the short period of five years than the same number of
families, scattered about the country could have done in fifty. This
arises from their unity and fraternal love, added to their uniform and
persevering industry.[8]

The colony was, however, twelve miles from navigation, and the
river was the only decent road to markets. The land, too, did not
suit them, for it was not adaptable to vine and fruit culture. So in
1815 the Pennsylvania land was sold for one hundred thousand dollars, and the whole community — now numbering eight hundred —
went down the Ohio in boats to build a new home on a tract of
land just above the mouth of the Wabash River. Here, in a new village called Harmony, they repeated their achievements in clearing
the land and establishing their industries. Again in a five-year period
they brought three thousand acres under cultivation and caused

---

* According to John Duss, *The Harmonists: A Personal History* (1943), the prohibition on marriage was not strictly enforced. Some couples continued to have
children — much to Rapp's disgust.

envy and surprise to their Hoosier neighbors. Many of their buildings are still standing to testify to the excellence of the materials and workmanship that made them.

The Harmonists kept few records; much of what is known about them is taken from the accounts of travelers. John Woods, an Englishman who visited them in this period, wrote enthusiastically of their industrial achievements and said their property was worth a million dollars. He mentioned their terraced vineyards, their beautifully matched teams of horses, and their fat milch cows.[9] George Flower, a resident of the English Prairie across the river in the Illinois territory, said the contrast between the Rappite village and ordinary frontier settlements was great. A poor frontiersman who brought his grain to the Harmony mill to be ground told Flower, "I studies and I studies on it" — as the Englishman himself seems to have done.[10]

Alone among American communities, so far as is known, the Harmony settlement was a subject for poetic comment by a famous Englishman. In Canto XV of *Don Juan* Byron wrote,

> When Rapp the Harmonist embargo'd Marriage
>   In his harmonious settlement which flourishes
> Strangely enough as yet without miscarriage,
>   Because it breeds no more mouths than it nourishes,
> Without those sad expenses which disparage what
>   Nature most encourages —
>   Why call'd he 'Harmony' a state *sans* wedlock?
> Now here I've got the preacher at a dead lock,
>
> Because he either meant to sneer at Harmony
>   Or Marriage, by divorcing them thus oddly.
> But whether reverend Rapp learn'd this in Germany
>   Or not, 'tis said his sect is rich and godly,
> Pious and pure, beyond what I can term any
>   Of ours . . .

Rapp's dictatorship was emphasized by another famous Englishman, Morris Birkbeck, who wrote in his diary in 1817 an account of a visit to the Indiana settlement. Success there, he said, was due to the "association of numbers in application of good capital," but he could not fully approve, for "a slavish acquiescence, under a disgusting superstition, is so remarkable an ingredient in their character that it checks all desire of imitation."[11]

Life at Harmony was similar to that in other religious communities in many ways. The day's routine roused the settlers at five and
put them to bed at nine. In accordance with German custom men
and women both worked in the fields and vineyards, and they
marched to work and home again to the music of their German
band. They had five meals during their long day, and although they
were not vegetarians, they abstained from pork. Flowers they loved,
and they grew them for pleasure rather than for their medicinal
value, placing bouquets even on the machines in their factories. Just
outside the village they built a labyrinth of vines and shrubs around
a summerhouse that was crude and rough outside but beautifully
finished within, as a symbol of their belief that toil and suffering in
this world are preludes to the joy and beauty of the future life.

Rappite church services were simple. George Rapp preached,
and to him confession was made by all who desired admission to the
colony. No quarrel was allowed to go overnight unsettled, and
everyone who had sinned confessed to Rapp before sleeping. It was
a patriarchal church, and its pastor looked the part he had created
for himself. More than six feet tall, he was kindly, cheerful, and
much beloved. Undisputed head of his colony, he worked with and
through a cabinet or committee chosen from the community, dele-
gating to his able son Frederick all business matters of the society.

After ten years in Indiana Rapp again grew restless. He apparently thought better markets could be obtained nearer Pittsburgh
and perhaps was influenced by a feeling that life was too easy on
the Wabash and that his flock was more closely held together and
more completely under his sway when the going was more difficult.
Whatever the reason, he gave Richard Flower, who was leaving the
English Prairie for a visit to England, a commission to sell the entire
property. Flower went to New Lanark in Scotland and laid the
whole project before Robert Owen, who was looking for a site for
the establishment of a socialist community. The famous philanthropist was struck by the advantages of securing a location so ad-
mirably prepared for his experiment and soon closed the bargain,
agreeing to pay one hundred and fifty thousand dollars for all the
Rappite properties — a great loss if Woods's estimate of a million
dollars as their value was at all correct.

Once more the colonists followed Rapp to a new home in the

wilderness; this time to land on the Ohio eighteen miles from Pittsburgh, where they built a village that they called Economy. Again
they went through the process of planting their fields and establishing their industries, and this time Rapp was willing to settle down.

In 1831 the community fell into grave difficulty when a charlatan and troublemaker came to them with high recommendations
from Germany. This man, who called himself Count Maximilian de
Leon but whose real name was Bernhard Müller, sowed dissension
in Rapp's quiet garden. Advocating marriage and the enjoyment
of the pleasures and luxuries to which their means entitled them, he
persuaded a minority of more than two hundred to secede from
Rapp's authority. The seceders won a grant of one hundred thousand dollars as their share of the common funds and withdrew to
build themselves a village ten miles from the mother colony. Under
De Leon's guidance, they brought suit for additional grants and
caused trouble in other ways for several years. The courts decided
in Rapp's favor, however, and after mulcting his dupes of most of
their funds, Müller left them for other fields. Disillusioned, some
drifted back to Economy, others sought land and homes for themselves elsewhere, and a few formed the nucleus for a new community in Missouri under the leadership of a certain William Keil.

After George Rapp died in 1847, his work was carried on by
trustees, but no one could be said to have succeeded him. He had
been too completely "the supreme arbiter in all questions that arose.
His word was law. It was enough to know that 'Father Rapp says
it' to satisfy all the community on any subject whatever." [12] The
community grew steadily smaller; in 1866 there were two hundred
and fifty members left, all growing old. Rappite property was estimated in 1870 to be worth about twenty million dollars. This was
doubtless greatly in excess of its actual value, and it is certain that
decline was rapid as the energy of the colony lessened and it failed
to keep pace with the machine age. In 1900 there were but a half-
dozen members living, and the affairs of the society were wound up
in 1905 by authority of the United States Supreme Court.

BETHEL AND AURORA

The Rappites indirectly contributed to the development of two
other communities somewhat like their own. Born in Prussia in

1812, William Keil, the leader of the two, came to the United States as a young man and set up a tailor shop in New York. Perhaps the panic of 1837 made him feel that he could not make a success of life there. At any rate, the year 1838 found him in Pittsburgh practicing medicine, although without training or license, and listening to revival services in the German Methodist church. He was converted and soon expressed a desire to be a preacher, probably of the frontier circuit-riding variety, for he had had no education or previous training for the ministry. He did acquire a license to act as local or lay preacher, but, irked by the Methodists' slowness in giving him advancement, he left the church altogether, taking with him the congregation of the little Deer Creek church over which he had been placed.

There was no other local sect that Keil wished to join. Either his desire to control his own group or his rapidly developing ideas on doctrine made a new faith the only solution for his problem. In any event, by 1840 he claimed to have reverted to literal Bible teaching, repudiated all religious sects, and sent out some of his faithful followers as missionaries to acquire converts. The reception given them varied. Sometimes they won adherents; occasionally rotten eggs and other missiles were hurled at them.

At this juncture, when the movement might easily have died out, Keil met a group of the Rappite seceders who had just been deserted by the pseudo Count de Leon. They accepted Keil as their leader and brought to him much in the way of doctrine and social and economic ideas. He took over George Rapp's practice of hearing confessions and adopted his theories on the communal life, rejecting, however, the idea of celibacy. He also rejected the sacraments of baptism, confirmation, and communion. The Bible, Keil announced, was the foundation of his faith and the Golden Rule its only motto or creed. Marriage was a civil ceremony performed by a justice of the peace. There were few religious holidays or feast days. The Rappite seceders, although simple German peasants, had been under the tutelage of an able leader for twenty years; nearly all of them knew at least one trade, and they sincerely desired the type of life to which they had been accustomed. Under Keil's direction they were willing to work for a communal society such as they had had under George Rapp.

Penniless as they were, it was obvious that they should move west to cheap lands, and a site was chosen in Shelby County, Missouri, not far from the Mississippi River and very near the area from which the Mormons had so recently been expelled. Land was acquired until the total holding was more than five thousand acres. At Bethel, as the settlement was called, communism was definitely established. All land was held in common, and each member put his assets into the pool. A list was kept, however, of all contributions, and the Bethel community does not seem to have refused some repayment if a member wished to withdraw. In fact, there were several instances of withdrawal from the community attended by an allotment of land, upon which the seceder continued to live, apparently in complete social accord and friendship with his neighbors of the communal group.

Cheap land and the high prices of a boom period caused the colony to prosper, and in the early 1850's its numbers rose to nearly one thousand. Keil was restless, however, and apprehensive of the effect upon his docile followers of the rapid increase of settlement in eastern Missouri. Bethel lay near the route then being traversed by thousands who were seeking new homes in the Oregon country. The industrious Bethelites built covered wagons for the emigrants and sold them provisions for the journey westward. Soon Keil himself became infected with the Oregon fever and began to plan the removal of as many of the community as would go with him.

The saga of that journey over the Oregon trail is as stirring as the Mormon hegira of the preceding decade. Scouts were sent a year ahead of the migration to decide upon the location of the new community; wagons were built and provisions were stored. Dr. Keil's young son, Willie, was one of the most enthusiastic participants in the work of preparation, but just before the expedition was to depart the boy fell ill with malaria. To quiet him as he raved in delirium, the father promised that nothing should prevent his accompanying the wagon train to Oregon. When the expedition was ready to start, the lad was dying. Faithful to his promise the father made arrangements for the son's journey. The wagon the boy had helped to build became a hearse, and the mules he had hoped to drive led the way for the wagons of his friends in the long and wearisome journey to the new home in Oregon. As they left Bethel the men and women of this funeral train sang the song "*Das Grab ist tief und still*," composed by Keil for music written by one of the colony. In fact the Bethelites sang their way across the plains and the mountains, and the story of the cavalcade of singing white men led by a wagon containing the coffin of the son of their leader became a legend among the Indians of the Northwest.

Between 1854 and 1863 about two thirds of the Bethelites went west to establish the new village of Aurora, which was built on the same principle as the one they had left. Aurora, too, prospered in moderation. There was no niggardliness in the lives of the settlers; there was plenty for all, and they lived simply but well. Charles Nordhoff, who visited both Bethel and Aurora about 1870, commented upon the monotony of the communal life and the general lack of comfort and beauty.

The bond that held the two communities together was the dynamic personality of Keil. Under his guidance, even though his control over Bethel was exerted only by deputies, his followers were content to live from 1844 until his death in 1879. Few of the original members of the society left; few of the young people remained for long. The leader endeavored to provide for the continuance of communal life by the appointment of trustees to manage each group, but his death showed the futility of such plans. Both societies dissolved almost at once. All land and property were divided, with an allotment to each man and woman in proportion to his or her years of service. There seems to have been no dispute over this division — the riches were not on a scale to excite great avarice — and the villages drowsed on as before. In 1883 Bethel became an incorporated village with a population of three hundred; Aurora at the same time had about two hundred and fifty inhabitants.

THE SEPARATISTS OF ZOAR

More nearly like the Rappite community in origin was the settlement of German Separatists at Zoar, Ohio. There is a dearth of source material for this society. Almost no records were kept, not even lists of settlers; apparently the written or printed word was of little significance to them, and there is little to relieve the general drabness of their story. In their homeland these German pietists had broken with the established church and adopted beliefs

much like those of the Quakers. They had no ritual and no ordained ministers, they would not take oaths, they were pacifists, and
they would doff their hats to no one. They were constantly in
trouble over the question of military service and of attendance in state
schools. A famine in 1816 crystallized their discontent, and in 1817
three hundred of them from Württemburg, Bavaria, and Baden
gathered in Hamburg preparatory to migration to America. Those
who had funds paid for the passage of those who had none, and
some of the penniless agreed to work out their passage money on
arrival in the United States. They asked only to be allowed to accompany their leader, Joseph Michael Bäumler, later called Bimeler, to whatever new home he might choose.

They settled in northern Ohio, where Bimeler had contracted
for about five thousand acres of land at a price of fifteen thousand
dollars to be paid in installments, the first due after ten years. They
named their community Zoar because it was a refuge from the evils
of this world as the biblical Zoar had been from the wickedness of
Sodom. Cooperative enterprise was necessary for clearing and planting the land and building their homes. Communal ownership was
forced upon them by their poverty, by the problem of the sick and
aged, and by the jealousy of a few for Bimeler, in whose name all
deeds had been entered. In 1819 those who favored communism
succeeded in getting a vote to put all their possessions into a common stock under the direction of trustees. Fifty-three men and one
hundred and four women signed the agreement. These same men
and women agreed to give up marriage, and thus limit the population, until the debt should be paid. Communism and celibacy were
adopted, therefore, for economic and not religious reasons. The
first was permanent, the second purely a temporary arrangement. In
1832 the Society of the Separatists of Zoar was incorporated by action of the state legislature, and from that time on it received state
protection from the claims of dissatisfied seceders.

With the growth of Ohio prosperity came to the industrious settlers of Zoar. Their first great economic progress came in 1833
through a contract to aid in the building of the Ohio Canal, which
crossed their lands. The twenty thousand dollars thus earned
cleared their debts and permitted them to build new industries,
while the canal itself gave them a route to markets. Because of the

language barrier and their lack of missionary zeal there was no appeal to non-German neighbors, but they received a few recruits from Germany. The largest population of the village, attained about 1840, was five hundred. Bimeler was their leader, their preacher, and their business manager. His leadership was quiet, economically sound, farsighted, and benevolent. When he died in 1853 he was lamented by all, and he had no successor. No preacher ever occupied the pulpit designed for him in the new church, completed after his death. A lay reader conducted the services by reading from Bimeler's published discourses.

After Bimeler's death the community declined steadily both in numbers and prosperity. Machine production in the world outside made their milling industries profitless, and they gave up one at a time their brickyard, their ore furnaces, and their tannery. They were poor, ignorant peasants in the beginning, and so they remained, quite placidly content with the comfortable livelihood their fertile lands and their industry assured them; their morality and honesty prevented exploitation by corrupt trustees. Their simple piety survived the loss of their religious leader; no Separatist of Zoar was ever convicted on a criminal charge. Their dress was simple, their houses plain; they traveled little and felt little desire for those things which, never having had, they did not miss. In the later years their greatest trial was the desire of their young people to seek their fortunes in that place designated vaguely as "the World." As in other communities, the breath of life lasted long after the real energy had departed. Communal property rights, inertia, and inbreeding held the group together. Although the days of its strength were all lived out in the pre-Civil War period, the final dissolution did not come until 1898, when a decision was taken to divide the property and dissolve the society.

THE AMANA SOCIETY

The Amana Society, or the Community of True Inspiration, was another pietistic sect, formed in rural Germany under the leadership of Michael Krausent, a tailor of Strasbourg, Christian Metz, carpenter, and Barbara Heinemann, a servant girl. By visions, dreams, revelations, and inner promptings, these three built up their doctrine and won their followers. They called their church the New

Community and accepted the Bible as their sole guide, repudiating the established church. For protection from persecution and for economic and social reasons the leaders gathered their flock about them on estates leased from great landowners or rented from monasteries and convents.[13] However, rents were high and land prices exorbitant, and there was a disastrous drought in 1842. So the leaders decided to emigrate.

Near Buffalo, New York, those sent ahead to buy land founded a community called Ebenezer, and to this community the members of the sect began to come in 1843. There is no mention of communism in the accounts of the sect in Germany. Again it was the circumstances of their New World life that forced communal organization. In the constitution drawn up by the Ebenezer villages in 1843, it was stated that all property, excepting clothing and household goods, should be held in common for a two-year period at least, and that those who advanced money should eventually receive a "proportionate share." All land titles were vested in sixteen trustees. Once established this community in goods could not easily be dissolved. Realizing that their people would disperse and the whole enterprise would fail if the joint-stock system should be given up, the leaders received revelation after revelation on the merits of communism, until the people were educated to accept it as the best form of enterprise.

Between 1843 and 1846 eight hundred emigrants from Germany arrived, and four villages were established, each with its meetinghouse, store, school, and local government. By the early 1850's more land was needed. Doubtful of the advisability of remaining so near the distractions of Buffalo, the trustees sent agents to buy land farther west. They found their new home in the valley of the Iowa River, where they eventually owned holdings of twenty-six thousand acres. Moving the whole settlement to Iowa was a gradual process, but within ten years the last member of the True Inspiration had left New York, and in 1859 the Amana Society was incorporated under the laws of Iowa.

The community prospered in its early years. The rise in the value of its lands and the fertility of the soil soon provided the settlers with capital and adequate income. Divided into seven villages, they lived severely in a simple, democratic regime. They carried on the usual village industries, finding textile weaving, especially blanket making, a profitable sideline. They retained the German language and made little provision for anything beyond an elementary education. Without ever advocating celibacy, they did not look with great approval upon matrimony and prevented hasty unions by requiring a year's separation before those who had proclaimed their intentions were united in marriage. As in the case of other settlements, there was a gradual decline in numbers in the period after the Civil War. Many of the young people left the community, and few recruits were gained from outside its limits. Content, peaceful, and secure, the remainder lived on well into the twentieth century before the communal ties were dissolved and the property was divided.

ERIC JANSON AND BISHOP HILL

Similar in many ways — in pietistic origin, in poverty, and in submission to a forceful leader — to the societies established by German sects, the Swedish colony founded by Eric Janson at Bishop Hill, Illinois, differed greatly from the others in the tempestuous nature of its history and the brevity of its existence. Excitement began for each convert as soon as he turned from his quiet village to follow the standard of the firebrand, Eric Janson; hardship and privation went with him across the ocean to the New World; violence dwelt with him and took the life of his leader; and tension and excitement pursued him until the community dissolved in grief and dissension in 1860.

Part of the inquietude and trouble of the Bishop Hill colony was due to the character and personality of its leader. Bishop, prophet, or Messiah — he called himself all three — Janson was never the paternal leader or the patient teacher of the flock that followed him with blind devotion. He was volatile, talkative, and intolerant of criticism; his ignorance and inexperience were equaled only by his overweening self-confidence and his certainty of his divine mission. A grand fighter, he tackled every adversary without fear and often without judgment. But not all the burden of blame for the failure of the colony lies upon Janson. The men who followed him in leadership were equally lacking in wisdom and equally adventuresome.

In the brief history of the Bishop Hill community may be found

Amana Village in Iowa, a settlement of the Community of True Inspiration

The Brother House at Ephrata, built entirely without nails. It was also used as a hospital.

Father George Rapp　　　　　*William Keil*

From Robert J. Hendricks, *Bethel and Aurora*, 1933, by permission of Paul R. Hendricks

The funeral train of Willie Keil on the way to Oregon

in miniature the rise and fall of fortune of many a man and group of men of the Middle West in the boom years after 1845 and in the crash of the panic of 1857. The enterprising Swedes in charge of the little colony were, unlike their counterparts in the German communities, quick to be infected with the spirit of the times, and they plunged the society into the speculative enterprise that was invading all Western business.

As in the case of many of these smaller sects, the history of the group is in large part the biography of its founder. Janson was born in 1808 of poor parents. As a child he was not strong, played little with other children, was moody and unhappy. During adolescence he became a religious enthusiast of a restless, reforming nature. His real conversion and dedication came at the age of twenty-two, when he is reported to have fallen from his horse because of pain caused by the rheumatism with which he had been long afflicted. As he lay by the side of the road he heard, or thought he heard, a voice saying, "It is written that whatsoever you ask in prayer, believing that it shall be given unto you, and all things are possible to him who believes, and when you call, I will answer you, says the Lord." He thereupon got himself up from the roadside and never again felt a twinge of the rheumatism that had caused his fall.[14] From that day he began to preach to the people near him and to read religious books constantly. For ten turbulent years he taught, preached, and harangued in fulfillment of the mission to which he felt he had been summoned.

Perfectionism and millennialism came to Janson through Methodism and through prolonged study of the Book of Revelation in the New Testament. Soon he claimed to be the "God-sent prophet," "the restorer of true doctrine," "the vicar of Christ on earth." Like other pietists he believed that Christianity had left the church when it became a state religion after Constantine, and he was convinced that he had been sent to restore it. He called upon the Swedish people to accept his leadership and to help found a New Jerusalem in which to await the millennium. He soon had hundreds of followers.

It is not difficult to understand the appeal of this peasant-preacher of a new faith. He was a striking figure, dramatic in his ugliness; he was of middle height, pale, with thin sunken cheeks, long prominent teeth, a scarred forehead, hypnotic blue eyes, and twitching facial muscles. He was a gifted orator, with a prodigious memory and magnificent self-confidence. His voice was harsh but clear, and his sermons were like those of the Methodist revivalists. He spoke dramatically of his visions and of his power to heal disease, drive out devils, and perform other miracles. Even his failures in endeavoring to prove these statements did not lose him adherents, for he could shout down every critic and curse every doubter in a terrifying manner. At one time he closed all argument by exclaiming, "All authority has been given unto me in heaven and on earth. If I so willed, you should at once fall dead at my feet and go to hell."

It is also easy to understand the instant opposition of the Lutheran clergy, whose services he forbade his followers to attend and whom he called "pillars of hell" and "arch purveyors of the devil." Whenever they were opposed the Jansonists "praised the Lord who tried their faith by allowing them to be persecuted. They marched along the public high ways at night and sang spiritual hymns, or gathered in front of the parsonages to pray for the conversion of their unregenerate pastors." [15] When their meetings were broken up, the Jansonists stole secretly out to the woods at midnight to sing and pray, until the ecclesiastical authorities professed to fear a peasants' revolt and called Janson a second Münzer.

In June of 1844 Janson conducted a great burning of religious books on the shore of a lake in Alfta parish, saying gleefully, "Satan had a glorious jubilee when Luther's writings were published; now, when they are burnt, he will have to be in mourning." Thus goaded, the clergy caused the arrest of Janson. Attempts were made to prove him insane, but, since the crown refused to keep a man in prison for religious differences, he was released, only to stage a second holocaust of books in October. Again he was arrested and again freed, meetings were broken up by the police or by mobs of the orthodox, and the Jansonists feared that their property was to be confiscated and their persons imprisoned. They decided to emigrate, and representatives were sent to buy land for them in America.

Upon hearing from their agents that a site had been chosen, those who were ready to migrate went in small groups to various ports and took passage in whatever boats they could find. Janson, disguised as a woman, fled on skis across the Norwegian frontier and joined one party at Oslo. Of this first migration one ship was lost with all on board; two were wrecked, although the passengers' lives were saved; and one of the five ships was so buffeted by storm that it was five months on the way. Cholera appeared on all the vessels, and food and water proved insufficient. Janson consoled the suffering emigrants by claiming that the millennium would soon be theirs, that they would have the gift of tongues so that the strange language would not trouble them, and that soon from their New Jerusalem "should radiate a true Christianity that should convert America and from America spread over all the world."

Janson and the first arrivals in 1846 went by steamboat to Albany and then by the Erie Canal and the Great Lakes to Chicago; from there they walked one hundred miles to the little village of Victoria, near which the land secured by their agents was located. By December four hundred Swedes had arrived, and they faced the Illinois winter with only a few log cabins and four tents for shelter. The first cold sent them underground into sod houses and dugouts — "mud caves" the Swedes called them — where thirty or forty persons were packed into quarters about twenty-five by eighteen feet in size. Worn out by the long journey, underfed, and cold, many of them died in that first winter, while others, thoroughly disillusioned, left to find work and shelter elsewhere. Undiscouraged and defiant, Janson rose at five every morning and urged his flock out of their hovels for prayer and religious service, warming them by his fervent exhortation, promising them riches, and prophesying the rapid growth of their church. Those who were ill were accused of little faith, of which death was a proof, and night guards were stationed to prevent desertion.

Building went on during the winter, and cultivation began with the spring. A tabernacle large enough to house a thousand was built of logs and canvas; a school was opened in a "mud cave"; and Janson made preparations to convert America to his beliefs by appointing twelve apostles who, after learning English, were to become missionaries of Jansonism. The colonists used near-by materials for the construction of adobe or cement houses. Few frame buildings were constructed, because lumber was expensive. Within three years the group had bought ten thousand acres. New immigrants arriving in 1847 spent the severe winter with their compatriots in the completed houses and in the dugouts that it still was necessary to use. All those who came, however, did not remain. In 1848 two hundred withdrew and, joining the Methodist church, settled near by on land they purchased for themselves.

During 1847 the Jansonists grew food crops and many acres of flax, from the manufacture of which they hoped to obtain cash for needed supplies. Each year an increasing amount of cloth and carpeting was made, until the peak was reached in 1857 with the manufacture of about one hundred and fifty thousand yards. After that little was sold, for the completion of the Burlington railroad caused the cheap manufactured goods of the East to flood the Western market. Since there were many more women than men in the colony and men were needed in the industrial plants, women were more frequently seen doing farm labor. Dairy work, cheese-making, gardening, and working with the flax were their special province. As new groups from Sweden arrived — the yearly immigration did not cease until 1854, and in all about fifteen hundred came — the new colonists were fitted into the community economy where they were best adapted or most needed.

One of the community's greatest disasters came with the arrival of one of these Swedish groups in 1849. On the last stages of the journey Asiatic cholera appeared in the party, and several of its members died. Cholera then broke out in Bishop Hill, and nearly one hundred and fifty of the colonists died. In panic many fled to other towns, but the dread disease followed them. Their prophet and healer was powerless and somewhat discredited, for his own wife was one of the victims.

Janson's ideas on marriage, which had not been constant, were shown in an interesting light at this time. Study of the Bible had at first caused him to favor celibacy, and the hard struggle of providing for the settlers had forced restriction of births during the first years. So marriages were forbidden for the time and the married were asked to live apart, but the measure was unpopular and unenforceable. Then Janson veered completely to a new point of view. In 1848 he issued a command: "All to whom God has given a desire to marry should forthwith be joined together or else be condemned to hell!" Mass marriage ceremonies followed; twenty-five couples on one Sunday, fourteen on another. As for the leader himself, a few days after his wife's death it was announced that a new "spiritual mother" for the community was essential, and the Bishop would remarry at once. Several women volunteered for the position, and a Mrs. Pollock, thrice widowed, no longer young but still attractive, was chosen.

Although the community grew more prosperous and life became much easier, trouble was ahead for the Jansonists. The Bishop grew more arrogant with the success of his venture and interfered constantly in the domestic affairs of the colonists. He preached at length on Sundays and reviled all who refused to listen attentively. Even the Deity was treated abruptly, for one day when work on a dam was endangered by rain, Janson prayed loudly, "If You, O God, do not give good weather so that we can finish the work we have at hand, I shall depose You from your seat of omnipotence, and You shall not reign either in heaven or on earth, for You cannot reign without me." [16]

Serious trouble came when Janson endeavored to interfere in the affairs of John Root and his wife, who was a cousin of the Bishop. Root was an adventurer who had joined the colony for reasons of his own, and he seems to have been lazy, rough, and a thoroughly bad lot. When he left the community in 1849, he insisted upon taking his wife with him, but Janson refused to let her go. Then followed a tragicomedy of kidnaping and pursuit, of flight and lawsuit, that ended the next year when Root shot Janson in the courthouse in Cambridge, Illinois.

The Bishop's mantle finally fell upon Jonas Olson, who had been one of the leading men of the sect since its beginnings in Sweden. There seems to be some difference of opinion on the character and ability of Olson, but all authorities agree that he was as tyrannical as Janson had been. In 1853 the colony was incorporated, apparently without the knowledge of the illiterate rank and file, and seven trustees were self-appointed to manage its affairs. From that time on Olson as chief trustee was in charge at Bishop Hill, while Olaf Johnson was the colony's agent in all business transactions. Under the charter there was prosperity at first, for the community shared in the advantages of the boom period of the early 1850's, but, swept away by the business opportunities of the day, Johnson speculated wildly with society funds. Agricultural prices were high, the colony flour mill was working overtime, and there was money to invest. So Johnson bought town lots in Galva and railroad, canal, and bank stock, started a pork-packing business, and built a grain elevator. When the crash came in 1857 the Jansonists' prosperity vanished, and the deluded settlers found themselves saddled with debt.

Olson, too, was having difficulties. Although in general the colony's missionaries had met with little success, a certain Nils Hedin had visited other communistic settlements and had brought back a few converts from the disintegrating Hopedale Community and many ideas gleaned from the Shakers of Kentucky. Among these ideas was celibacy, and he convinced Olson of its merits. For the second time in a decade the settlers of Bishop Hill resisted an attempt to force celibacy upon them, this time with the threat of dissolution. When to this dissatisfaction was added the shock of financial catastrophe, the end of communal life was inevitable. It was some twelve years before the final division of assets was arranged, and then only after expensive and prolonged litigation.

With the end of communal life the Jansonists, whose religion had centered around the personality of their dead leader, wandered off into other churches. Some became Methodists, a few returned to Lutheranism, more became Seventh Day Adventists. One or two made their way to Kentucky and joined the Shaker community of Pleasant Hill, while several of the most completely disillusioned accepted the atheistic opinions of Robert Ingersoll. And so ended one of the most dramatic of the experiments in religious communism.

NORDHOFF'S CONCLUSIONS

Charles Nordhoff, who made a careful study of almost all the communities that lived on into the 1860's, ended his book on the subject with a summary of his observations. He was convinced that the Germans made better communists than any other people. They were contented, docile, and willing to obey their leaders. A commune, he felt, could only succeed when composed of persons who were agreed upon some question of religious belief, although there was no need for fanaticism. Community living had many economic advantages, and American communities showed a great variety of business and mechanical skills as well as excellent agricultural organization — but for the religious communities these, of course, were not the first consideration. Social equality and economic security were, Nordhoff thought, the great boons offered by communal life. The religious communities offered, as well, the congenial companionship of members of a common faith. In the community the persecutions and trials of earlier experiences could be forgotten, and the members of the society could prepare in peace for the eternal reward each sect claimed as the climax of its difficult road to salvation.

CHAPTER 7

The Shaker Communities

In 1774 there landed in New York an unassuming and unprepossessing woman and eight persons who had left England with her to establish their faith in a new and freer world. The woman was Ann Lee Stanley, who as Mother Ann was to build in America a church called officially the Millennial Church or the United Society of Believers but commonly called, by its members as well as the outside world, the Shaker Society. The Shakers were to be the largest, the most permanent, and in many ways the most interesting and significant of the religious communistic settlements in the United States. After the first generation their membership was to be largely native American, and their importance in American religious and social history overshadows that of all the minor sects and communities.

Established before 1800, they were to have within twenty-five years about twenty settlements in seven states, and in their period of maximum growth in the second quarter of the nineteenth century, a total membership of about six thousand.* Long after the Civil War ushered in an era of industrial development and social change the United Society lived on, its doctrines and its way of life unchanged, although its membership steadily declined. In the present day, more than two hundred years after the birth of Mother Ann, there are fewer than one hundred Shakers in the country, distributed in the two or three communities they have contrived to keep in operation. Few converts have been made in recent years, and the shrunken "families" in each community are composed of aged men and women who employ labor to perform the tasks and keep up the lands and buildings they are too feeble and too few to operate.

---

* It is impossible to find two accounts giving the same number of Shaker settlements. The difficulty seems to be that several colonies were not permanent and the total, therefore, varies with the number of such short-lived settlements included. Edward Deming Andrews, probably the greatest living authority on the Shaker movement, lists a relatively small number, including four colonies in Massachusetts, two in Maine, two in New Hampshire, one in Connecticut, and two in New York — all founded before 1800; after 1800 four colonies were established in Ohio and two in Kentucky, one (for a short time) in Indiana, and another in New York. He records no new societies for the period after 1830.

ENGLISH ORIGINS

Ann Lee was the daughter of John Lee, a blacksmith, and was born in Toad Lane, Manchester, England, in 1736. Her parents were poor, and she was one of eight children; so work rather than school was her childhood lot, and she never learned to read or write. First sent to work in a cotton factory, she later was a cutter of hatter's fur, and still later worked as a cook in the Manchester Infirmary. She seems to have been pious from childhood, for the early accounts state that she

was the subject of religious impressions, and was peculiarly favored with heavenly visions. As she advanced in years she was strongly impressed with a sense of the great depravity of human nature and of the odiousness of sin, and especially of the impure nature of sexual coition. She often expressed her feelings to her mother concerning these things, and earnestly desired that she might be kept from the snares of sin, and from those abominations which her soul abhorred.[1]

Regardless of the fears and scruples attributed to her by all Shaker authorities, she was, "through the importunities of her relations," induced at an early age to marry Abraham Stanley, another blacksmith, by whom she had four children who died in infancy or early childhood. There seems to have been no ease or comfort and little happiness in her life. In 1758 she was converted, or rather, as an old chronicle of her life quaintly puts it, "she became the subject of the work that was under the ministration of James and Jane Wardley," and joined the sect already called the Shakers.

The history of this sect goes back to the France of Louis XIV. In the year 1688 a group of Dauphiny peasants, calling themselves Prophets, claimed the inspiration of the Holy Ghost and went about preaching a return to the primitive Christian faith. They grew in numbers and in the violence of their actions. They believed physical manifestations to be the outward sign of religious fervor, and "they had strange fits, which came upon them with tremblings and faintings, as in a swoon, which made them stretch out their arms and legs and stagger several times before they dropped down."[2] In trances they saw visions, and after the "agitations of the body" they received the gift of prophecy.

Persecution was, of course, their lot in France, and the few thousands that embraced the new teaching were soon eliminated or won

back to Catholicism. Three or four of them, however, escaped to
England, where they continued their prophecies and their teachings. They were millennialists, crying warning of Christ's second
coming and predicting famine and pestilence for the wicked. They
claimed the gift of languages and the gift of healing as well as that
of prophecy. They won a few adherents, chiefly from the working
classes, and eventually the little group fell under the leadership of
James and Jane Wardley, who had been Quakers and brought with
them much of Quaker doctrine. The violence of the early physical
manifestations was subdued into a ritualistic dance in which worship could be expressed by the body as well as by the heart and
soul. It was this that gave the sect the name of Shaking Quakers or
just Shakers.

After her acceptance by the Shakers, Ann Lee went through
nine years of trial and religious unrest.

It appears that in watchings, fastings, tears and incessant cries to God,
she labored day and night, for deliverance from the very nature of sin;
and that, under the most severe tribulation of mind, and the most violent
temptations and buffetings of the enemy, the agony of her soul was so
extreme as to occasion a perspiration of blood. Sometimes, for whole
nights together her cries, screeches and groans were such as to fill every
soul around with fear and trembling.[3]

The commentator does not state how much of the poor woman's
anguish of soul was occasioned by her hard work, unhappy married
life, and the loss one after another of her children. Some comfort
came to her from her association with the Shakers, and, when she
felt revelations had come to her in the trances that followed her
greatest suffering, she went about with the Wardleys preaching and
teaching wherever they could get a hearing. Town authorities did
not look with pleasure upon such unorthodox meetings, and the
Shakers were imprisoned for "profaning the Sabbath." In 1770 Ann
spent some time in the Manchester jail, where she meditated upon
religion and received revelations of the "root of human depravity,
and the cause of man's fall." When freed she began to preach with
such new vision and authority that she was soon recognized as the
"visible leader of the Church of God upon earth."

New persecutions followed. Ann was often imprisoned, was
stoned by mobs, and threatened with having her tongue bored with

a hot iron. At one time she was kept in a locked cell for fourteen days in the hope that starvation might rid the town of this woman who would not be silenced, but a faithful disciple fed her by pouring milk through the stem of a pipe inserted through the keyhole, and the designs of her enemies were thwarted. Finally, despairing of peace at home and having acquired a few followers who were able to provide financial assistance, Mother Ann decided to seek asylum in the New World. In the summer of 1774, accompanied by eight of her flock — including her husband, a brother, and a niece — the leader of the Shaker church sailed in the ship *Mariah* for America.

MOTHER ANN IN AMERICA

The three months' voyage was not a season of rest and quiet. The Shakers "went forth, in obedience to their inward feelings, to praise God in songs and dances" and so offended the captain that he threatened to throw them overboard. But in a storm that almost wrecked their leaky ship the Shakers manned the pumps and, praying loudly, did their part to save the vessel from destruction. Restored to the captain's favor, they ended the voyage in good order and set forth in New York almost penniless to seek their fortunes. A few of them went up the Hudson and settled on wooded land northwest of Albany, near a village then called Niskeyuna, later named Watervliet. Mother Ann stayed in New York and worked as a laundress until her husband deserted her for another woman. Then she joined the others at Niskeyuna, aiding them in clearing and planting the land they had settled upon.

For five years the little group labored in the wilderness without molestation and without winning converts from the villages near them. In 1779 the New Light Baptists conducted a religious revival at New Lebanon. It quickly ran its course, but a few who were moved by it but were not satisfied by Baptist doctrine came to visit Mother Ann and her followers and were soon ardent Shakers. This interest spread, and soon Mother Ann was traveling through New England winning converts and gathering them into little congregations similar to that at Niskeyuna. Everywhere the staid Puritans were alarmed at the novel services and doctrines of the new sect, and persecution followed similar to that suffered in England, except that it seems to have been caused by mob violence rather than by government action. Mother Ann was arrested only once in America, and that was on the charge that she and her followers were British and inimical to the American cause.

Between 1780 and 1784 many converts were made, miracles were attributed to Mother Ann and the elders she appointed,[4] and the foundations were laid for colonies in Massachusetts, Maine, Connecticut, and New Hampshire. Their valiant leader, however, was worn out by these exertions and in 1784, "having finished her work on earth she was called to bid adieu to all terrestrial things, and was released from her labors, her sorrows and her sufferings, and calmly resigned her soul to God."[5]

The accounts of the life of this remarkable woman, written within twenty years of her death by members of the sect who had known her or her original followers, all give a picture of a person of great piety and sincerity, unselfish, utterly fearless, and entirely devoted to the cause of winning the world to a way of life she believed essential to salvation. She had the dignity of bearing and the simplicity of speech and manner that befitted her convictions as to her divine calling. She showed no trace of pride or avarice, and her reported sayings are filled with practical common sense and moral teaching. Frugality, charity, industry, honesty, humility, and temperance were the virtues she taught her "children," who she prayed would live together in love and peacefulness. Charity was in her constant admonition, "Remember the cries of those who are in need and trouble; that when you are in trouble, God may hear your prayers." Childless, she loved all children and was always attentive to their care and training. "It needs great wisdom," she said, "to bring up children." She urged her people, old and young, to "be faithful with their hands. Every faithful man will go forth and put up his fences in season, and will plow his ground in season, and put his crops into the ground in season; and such a man may with confidence look for a blessing."[6]

Many new sects have not survived the death of the leader who initiated them. The Shakers were fortunate in having strong men and women from whom new leadership could come. William Lee, the devoted companion of Mother Ann in all her experiences, died a few months before his sister, so her mantle fell upon James Whittaker, who had come from England in the little group of eight. He was followed in 1787 by Elder Joseph Meacham and Eldress Lucy Wright, both American born and of old New England stock. They seem to have been remarkably able. Joseph Meacham had been a Baptist minister; Lucy Wright was a woman of great executive ability. Under their leadership the doctrines of Shakerism were elaborated and systematized, the Shaker way of life was developed, and the close governmental organization of the Shaker church was worked out. When Lucy Wright died in 1821, the church was entering upon the period of its greatest membership and prosperity, and all the major Shaker communities had been established. With the work of Elder Frederick W. Evans, who joined the church in 1830 and was an elder from 1836 to his death in 1892, the Shaker order reached its completed form.*

THE EXPANSION OF SHAKERISM

Although there were about a dozen Shaker communities by 1800, they were small and poor, and there seemed little prospect of great gains. Shortly after that date the entire picture was changed by the news of the great revivals in the West. Remembering that their first success in America had followed the New Light Baptist revival of 1779, the Shakers prepared to take advantage of the new religious agitation. In 1805 John Meacham, Benjamin S. Youngs, and Issachar Bates were sent from Mt. Lebanon across the country on foot to the Ohio Valley to reap the harvest the revivalists had sown in the camp meetings that had shaken the frontier. After winning many converts at Turtle Creek, they moved on to Cane Ridge, Kentucky, where the revival was still in progress and where, much to the anger and distress of the revivalists,[7] the Shakers acquired many adherents.

Issachar Bates went back, again on foot, to Mt. Lebanon and collected funds for the continuance of the work. Land was purchased in the West, and new communities were founded. In all ten sisters and twelve brethren were sent west to assist in the organization of

* Evans was one of the "universal reformers" of the period. In England he was an Owenite and freethinking radical. After he came to America in 1820, he aided his brother, G. H. Evans, a friend of Horace Greeley, in publishing the *Working Man's Advocate* and other working class papers. He maintained his interest in Owen's utopian socialism until the failure of the New Harmony experiment; then, turning elsewhere for communistic living, he gave up his materialistic philosophy and devoted his energies wholeheartedly to the Shaker Society.

the Shaker church on the frontier, where they welcomed all comers, "Indian, pioneer or planter, ignorant Negro or Presbyterian divine." Between 1801 and 1811 Issachar Bates traveled, mostly on foot, some thirty-eight thousand miles and heard the first confessions of more than a thousand applicants for membership. Wherever a revival provided a favorable atmosphere for Shaker teaching, the itinerants of the society vied with those of the evangelical church in gathering in the converts. Four communities were founded in Ohio and two in Kentucky. One of the latter, the colony at Pleasant Hill, was destined to last until well into the twentieth century. In the early days of these settlements there was much opposition and several outbursts of mob violence. The courts of the Western states pretty generally upheld the legality of the Shaker covenant, however, and the essentially peaceful nature of the Shakers themselves soon disarmed the opponents. The Western Shakers were, for the most part, prosperous, and their communities grew in numbers, reaching their maximum size, as in the East, in the years 1830–50, when their combined membership was estimated at six thousand.

THE DOCTRINE OF THE SHAKERS

Mother Ann's contribution to Shaker teaching can be summed up in her belief that God is a dual personality, that in Christ the masculine side of that personality was made manifest, and that in the fullness of time, in her own life, there was a second incarnation of the Holy Spirit whereby the feminine element of God appeared to continue the work begun by Christ. Her church was, therefore, a millennial one, and since she received her inspiration through trance and revelation, it was also, from the beginning, spiritualistic in belief. Aside from these fundamental tenets, Mother Ann added to the usual dogmas of pietistic groups only her insistence upon celibacy. She drew heavily upon Quaker ideas. Implicit in all her statements was the belief in the Bible as the source of all religious faith, and she sought always a literal interpretation of every passage, especially those of prophecy and revelation.

The leaders of the church after the death of Mother Ann enlarged upon her teachings and developed a body of doctrine from which the Shakers have not deviated. Shaker adventism was shown to be spiritual and not physical. "As the substance of the first woman was taken from the body of the first man; so that Divine Spirit with which the second woman was endowed . . . was taken from the Spirit of Christ." [8] Mother Ann thus became the "Second pillar of the Church of God," but the Shakers were careful to state that they did not mean the "human tabernacle" of Ann Lee. That was but the instrument for the expression of divine truth, which could not complete its work until all men had become spiritual. The Shaker church alone, with its demand for strict chastity, could ensure such purity and spirituality. Since the millennium was believed to be at hand, there was no reason for the further continuance of the human race, and continence would prepare the faithful for the perfect state promised them. Perfectionism was an integral part of Shaker doctrine. In the new order that which had been "earthly, sensual, devilish" would be "spiritual, divine, and heavenly." [9]

A life in preparation for such a perfect state must be lived in accord with the twelve virtues: faith, hope, honesty, continence, innocence, simplicity, meekness, humility, prudence, patience, thankfulness, and charity. Constant watchfulness was necessary to maintain a life based upon these virtues; therefore full auricular confession was demanded from everyone entering the church and was required at intervals from members. With their consciences freed by confession the faithful might attain the desired virtues by observance of the seven moral principles upon which the Shaker societies were grounded: duty to God, duty to man, separation from the world, practical peace, simplicity of language, right use of property, and a virgin life. For one who lived in accordance with these principles heaven and resurrection began on this earth — a resurrection from the animal to the spiritual plane — and perfection might be attained through practicing the spiritual and moral virtues taught and exemplified by Jesus Christ. [10]

Shaker doctrines or concepts in regard to the life after death were a complex but important part of their whole theology. They held that there had been four cycles or periods in religious history and that the present or fourth period was the new dispensation after the advent of Mother Ann. The heaven of this cycle was believed to be in the process of formation, for the day of judgment, or "beginning of Christ's kingdom on earth," dated from the establishment of the Shaker church and would be completed by its development. The mission of the church was to gather in the elect who might attain perfection and salvation through lives of purification and a denial of the flesh. In the spirit world the Shakers would continue to win those who had died without accepting Shaker doctrines, until eventually all would be saved. The Shakers believed, therefore, in the punishment of the wicked only for a season, in a probationary state in the spirit world, and in a final salvation for all; that is, they were Universalists. Since the Shaker way of life was too hard for the ordinary, carnal man, the Shakers were willing to admit that on this earth their communities would, in fact should, be few and their total membership small. The world, they said, was an "Outer Order" where property and marriage were not crimes or sinful. The process of redemption would be long and would, of necessity, be largely a purification in the next world.[11]

THE ORGANIZATION AND GOVERNMENT OF THE SHAKER COMMUNITIES

Humble though the individual Shaker was commanded to be, belief in the mission of the Shaker church as the sole true agency of salvation made the society itself both exclusive and arrogant. The difficulty of the life and the restrictions imposed upon the individual were distinctions of which the Shaker was proud. Secure in his position among the chosen few, the Shaker was willing to submit to the semimilitary government that made possible the close communal life demanded by his faith. The desires of the individual were subordinate to the good of the community, and the decision as to what constituted that good was in the hands of a small, carefully selected group. To the outsider the Shaker community seemed a complete and stifling despotism; to the Shaker, who had learned to give up his own will, the good of the society might best be left to those whose authority was derived from Mother Ann.

The "Head of Influence" or final authority in the Shaker Society was the ministry of the church at Mt. Lebanon, one of the oldest and largest of the communities. This ministry was self-perpetuating with one elder or eldress as its head, and it chose, or at least approved, the elders and eldresses composing the ministry in each of the other communities. Equality of the sexes and the duality of life were recognized in the fact that each ministry was composed of an equal number of each sex. At Mt. Lebanon there were two elders and two eldresses. Each community was divided into "families" of from thirty to a hundred members. These families lived and worked separately, for both economic and social reasons. At Mt. Lebanon, where the total membership reached six hundred, the land and industries were sufficient to support eight families; the North Family, the South Family, the Church Family, and so on. The families were ruled over by elders and deacons appointed by the ministry. In each community the ministry lived apart in special quarters designed for them. The deacons, usually two or four for each family, with men and women equally represented, superintended all labor. Trustees appointed by the ministry held all property and made all business contacts with the outside world. The laws and orders of the church were detailed and explicit, and printed copies of them were in the hands of each ministry. They were for the most part made up of the decisions of the various elders and eldresses that had been approved by the central ministry at Mt. Lebanon. All tracts, hymnals, and other publications were also submitted to the "Head of Influence" before publication. The hierarchy, therefore, was absolute in power, and from its dicta there was no redress. Democracy was not a part of the Shaker way of life.[12]

Membership in the Shaker church was purely voluntary, and the elders were careful to give a full explanation of all rules and requirements. There was no fixed creed or any condition laid down for entrance other than the biblical command, "If any man will come after me, let him deny himself, and take up his cross daily, and follow me." There were three classes or orders: a Novitiate Order for new members, who were for the time permitted to keep their property and live with their natural families, although celibacy was required of them; a Junior Order of unmarried people who intended to become full members but who had not as yet given up their property rights; and the Senior Order made up of those who had, after long preparation, been admitted to full membership. Members of any of the three classes were free to leave the community at will and might be expelled for cause by the ministry of their local society. No seceding member was entitled to receive any compensation for labor performed or, in the case of members of the Senior Order, goods turned over to the community. The society could, however, and often did make some compensation to those who withdrew.

It seems to have been the consistent practice of the Shakers to discourage hasty decisions on the part of applicants, and a reasonably long probationary period was insisted upon. No "believing" husband or wife was advised to separate from the "unbelieving" spouse without mutual agreement and satisfactory arrangements for children and property. New members were required "to rectify all wrongs and settle all claims" before admission. In case a member entered the order with his or her minor children, provision was made for granting the children a share of the parent's estate in the event that upon attaining their majority the children did not choose to become members of the order. Orphan children adopted by the Shakers were given the same opportunity of choosing at the age of twenty-one whether or not they wished to become full members.[13]

THE SHAKER WAY OF LIFE

Under the supervision of the central ministry, the Shaker communities East and West worked out a common way of life. Although a large part of each colony was always composed of those who had "in the World" been poor and little educated, there was an admixture of clergymen, lawyers, doctors, students, and even soldiers. There were representatives of all Protestant denominations, but the Baptists, Methodists, Presbyterians, and Adventists furnished the greatest number. An occasional Jew joined the Shakers, but there seems to be no record of a Roman Catholic's having been received. Whatever their previous condition in life, they had a common bond in their conversion and, usually, another in their happiness in the communal life. Those who resented authoritarian control did not long remain in the society, and their departure was a further assurance of peace for those who stayed.

Shaker discipline permeated every phase of daily life. The members of the community from the ministry down to the novices arose early and worked steadily, but without undue pressure, at the tasks appointed for them by the deacons and deaconesses. Men and women did not ordinarily work together, although a brother was often appointed to help the sisters in some strenuous labor such as the work in the family dairy or laundry. Outdoor work, especially field

The Shakers' sacred dance, to shake sin from the body through the finger tips

The wheel dance, another Shaker religious exercise

A Shaker sister

Elder Frederick W. Evans

The simple beauty of Shaker craftsmanship

labor, was always considered men's work. The sisters did all the work inside the house. Occasionally outside labor was employed for field work and in various industrial enterprises, but there was no servant class. There was little idleness in the community, a fact that one Shaker youth with a sense of humor noted in verse:

> I'm overrun with work and chores
> Upon the farm or within doors.
> Whichever way I turn my eyes;
> Enough to fill me with surprise.
> How can I bear with such a plan?
> No time to be a gentleman!
> All work — work — work, still rushing on,
> And *conscience* too, still pushing on,
> When will the working all be done?
> When will this lengthy thread be spun?
> As long as *working* is the cry
> How can I e'er find time to die? [14]

Shaker dress was uniform and simple, resembling that of the Quakers. Shaker architecture was very simple, too, but their buildings were substantial, well constructed, and decidedly utilitarian. The huge family houses at Mt. Lebanon, for instance, resemble barracks or school dormitories, and the immense barns indicate the flourishing state of Shaker agriculture when they were built. Occasionally some builder with an eye for line and proportion produced a structure of stark simplicity but of great beauty — a forerunner of modern functional architecture. The great stone house at Pleasant Hill, Kentucky, erected in 1824, is an example of such building and has made that quiet, almost deserted village a mecca for modern architects.

Shaker churches and most of the family houses had two entrances, one for men, the other for women, and the houses had separate stairways as well, leading to the sleeping quarters, which were also carefully divided between the sexes. Men and women ate in the same dining rooms but not at the same tables — and they ate in silence. All rooms were painfully clean and neat. There were no curtains at the windows, no pictures on the walls, and only small hand-woven rag rugs on the floors. The reason given by the Shakers for this austerity was simply that curtains, pictures, and carpets gathered dust. But Shaker furniture was adequate and comfortable.

*The Church Family House of the Shaker colony at Shakertown,
Pleasant Hill, Kentucky*

Their chairs, desks, and tables are now highly valued antiques and
are models for firms manufacturing copies of old furniture.[15] Or-
derliness was regarded as a domestic virtue next only to cleanliness.
Every room was provided with a row of pegs about four or five
feet from the floor, upon which all coats, hats, and bonnets were
hung. Chairs and other articles of furniture were suspended on
these pegs while the rooms were cleaned.

In household appointments and in laborsaving devices the Yankee
ingenuity of both sexes was given full play. There is scarcely a
room of the North Family House still in use at Mt. Lebanon that
does not contain some evidence of clever adaptation of device to
local necessity. There is, for example, a "cooling room" where re-
frigeration was provided by running spring water through coils of
pipes, and there are radiators for heating the house that were installed before 1860 according to the specifications made by Elder
Frederick Evans himself. In the old stone house at Pleasant Hill
dumb waiters, a huge oven with coils of heating pipes, and apple
parers and corers bear silent witness to the Shakers' ability to make
the task of preparing food for a large number as easy as possible.

Nordhoff mentioned that, although it had been used for thirty years when he first saw it, the floor of the great assembly room at Mt. Lebanon seemed as bright and new as though it had just been laid. He attributed its condition to the fact that whenever they came into the room the Shakers wore a soft leather shoe made without nails or pegs in the sole. He said,

They have invented many such tricks of housekeeping, and I could see that they acted just as a parcel of old bachelors and old maids would, anywhere else, in these particulars — setting such store by personal comfort, neatness and order; and no doubt thinking much of such minor morals.[16]

Regarding charity as one of the cardinal virtues, the Shakers were openhanded in their treatment of all who were in need. Early in their history, long before there were adequate state institutions for orphans or for the children of parents unable to provide their support, the Shakers made a practice of adopting children brought to them for care. This charity was not entirely disinterested, because it was one of the two methods of recruiting members. Many children, in the days of Shaker strength, remained with the society after attaining their majority.

Tramps were never turned away unfed, and curious visitors from the outside world were housed and fed in quarters set aside for them. The consensus of opinion of such travelers was that the accommodations were clean and comfortable and the food plain but well cooked and bountiful. Since many of the Shakers were vegetarians, a special table was set for those who refused meat, but visitors to several of the communities in different periods mention that no pork was ever served. The temperance movement began early in the Shaker communities, and total abstinence was customary. The use of tobacco was permitted but not encouraged, and many Shakers abstained from its use, as they did from eating meat, as a matter of self-discipline. An elder interviewed each visitor and placed at his disposal complete information about the community, asking only his respectful attention and his observance of the ordinary rules of hospitality. Nordhoff quotes an amusing poem that he found on the wall of the visitors' dining room at Mt. Lebanon. "Eat hearty and decent and clean out your plate" is a summary of its advice to visitors! The second of its eight stanzas reads:

We wish to speak plainly
  And use no deceit;
We like to see fragments
  Left wholesome and neat:
To customs and fashions
  We make no pretence;
Yet think we can tell
  What belongs to good sense.[17]

The children of Shaker communities were well cared for. A "care-taker" was appointed for each sex, boys and girls were separated, they were dressed in miniature copies of the Shaker costume, and their lives were carefully supervised. Little time was left for play, but it was not forbidden. Elementary education was provided, with separate schoolrooms for boys and girls. Often boys were taught in the winter months, girls in the summer. These schools were not remarkable in any way but were probably up to the standard of local schools of the same period. Higher education was not provided or encouraged, because it was thought to cause restlessness and dissatisfaction. Boys were taught all branches of farm work and at least one of the trades or vocations in which the society specialized. Girls were early inducted into all the many activities of the women of the community, and a dowry was often provided if a girl left the family to marry in the world outside the Shaker community. Some choice was permitted in the matter of vocation. If a young person decided to leave the society upon attaining his majority, employment was practically assured him, for his vocational education was usually superior to that of others of his social class outside the Shaker community. Usually a small sum was given him in order that he might not enter the outside world penniless.

For children and adults alike few books were permitted, and even Bible reading does not seem to have been customary. At family meetings excerpts from books, periodicals, and newspapers were read by an elder, and some discussion was allowed. Shaker books, hymnals, and pamphlets were provided for all, and there were at different times several Shaker periodicals; Nordhoff mentions also a weekly newspaper. Of cultural life there was little and of the arts less; utility and uniformity seem to have been the desire of the elders and the safeguards of communism. Individualism was constantly held in check.

The Shakers recognized the need for social contacts, however. It was not customary for any individual, even an elder, to room alone; work was always done in pairs or in groups, of the same sex of course, so that there was constant opportunity for exchange of ideas. The working day was nearly twelve hours long, ending with supper at six; bedtime came at nine, leaving the hours between for social affairs — and careful provision was made for those hours. There was some sort of a meeting each night — for worship, for instruction, or for conversation. On one night, usually Monday, there were social gatherings of small groups of men and women, six or eight sisters sitting in a row talking with a similar line of brothers across the room. Conversation was on matters of family or church concern, and careful watch prevented the development of any romance.

Some feminine instinct was probably satisfied by the custom of assigning each brother to a sister who became responsible for the care of his clothes and his laundry and for general oversight of his habits and appearance. Since there were many more women than men in most Shaker communities, this custom may have worked some injustice. Perhaps the women deprived of this privilege were assigned the care of children. No pets were allowed, so the thwarted maternal instinct could not get satisfaction by pampering community dogs or cats.

It was a busy life with little time for contemplation of its barrenness. For many it must have seemed adequate in its peace and security. The few upon whom it palled had always the alternative of secession.

THE ORDER OF SHAKER WORSHIP

Celibacy and communism were the basic principles of the Shaker life,[18] but its unifying, vitalizing center was in its religious service. The Shaker believed that worship should be through every possible medium and with mind, heart, and body. From the days of the French Prophets dancing had been a part of the service. At first there was little singing; in the days of Mother Ann a humming accompaniment gave rhythm to the dance. But with the impact of Western revivalism the part of song in the Shaker service was recognized. Out in the West converts were made from the Methodist and Baptist sects, and to the stirring tunes of those sects were set words acceptable to the Shakers. New life was given to the dancing and marching "labours" when they were accompanied by these hymns. Soon they were an important part of all services.[19] Whether he expressed his fervor through prayer, preaching, song, or dance, every worshiper was expected to participate. Worship was a social act, an integral part of communal life. Shaker services were visited by many European travelers of the early nineteenth century and by innumerable curious Americans, and, since the Shakers themselves rarely wrote of their services, the accounts of these contemporary observers have been drawn upon for details. Many of the accounts were so fully illustrated with sketches and drawings that the services can be reconstructed with some accuracy.

In the early 1830's De Tocqueville and De Beaumont visited the Lebanon colony and attended the Shaker service, which must have been strange indeed to their Catholic eyes. De Beaumont dismissed the whole service with the laconic comment, "They are mad"; De Tocqueville was more descriptive:

They placed themselves two by two in a curving line, so that the men and women made but a single circle. They then held their elbows against the body, stretched out their fore arms and let their hands hang, which gave them the air of trained dogs who are forced to walk on their hind legs. Thus prepared, they intoned an air more lamentable than all the others, and began to turn about the room, an exercise which they continued during a good quarter hour.[20]

The aristocratic Mrs. Basil Hall found the service uninteresting and wrote, "I hardly think they were worth the trouble of a dusty drive of sixteen miles on a hot day,"[21] and a young American of the period observed, "Two more spectacles like that and I become a Catholic!" Captain Marryat, who visited them in 1839, described the dance as a rhythmical advancing and retreating of two rows starting about ten feet apart, singing the while a wordless sort of chant that went "Law, law, de lawdel law." The much-traveled Captain felt the Shaker dance fell far short of any aesthetic ideal.[22]

The ever-critical Thomas Hamilton saw little to praise in Shakerism, but he reported verbatim a brief address by an elder whose complaints he felt were valid. Said the speaker to the visitors in the church:

Strangers, I would address myself to you. What motives brought you to this place of worship, I know not. Some may have come to join in our devotions, but the greater part of you, I fear, have come only to see the peculiarities of our worship. To this we do not object. We court no concealment in anything we do, but we demand of you in return, that you offer no indecent interruption to our religious solemnities. I beseech you to remember that we are Christians like yourselves, that we are engaged in offering adoration to the Great God who fashioned us all as we are. If you do not respect us, respect yourselves, and however ridiculous our forms may seem to you, we entreat you will at least not interrupt our devotional exercises by any demonstration of contempt.[23]

Cooper, on the other hand, who visited the Shakers at about this same time, found little to condemn in the service, which, he said, was fitted to the poor and ignorant who composed the community. The dancing, he thought, was grave and solemn, and without excitement. The singing was in time to the dance though in a "villainous nasal cadency," and the whole service was quiet and inoffensive.[24] In 1838 Horace Greeley spent a Sunday with the Shakers and came home enthusiastic about their sincerity and about the "homeliness" and cooperative enterprise of the service. He called the Watervliet community an Arcadia and a democrat's paradise and found nothing offensive, although much that seemed too idealistic to be practicable, in their teachings.[25]

Two or three years later the accounts changed. Both singing and dancing had become more violent, and a strange excitement had appeared in the service. About 1841 James Silk Buckingham wrote that after a quiet devotional beginning — in which some of the congregational testimonies were in the nature of spiritualistic revelations — the "labour" of dancing began, with hymns set to very lively tunes. Then the injunction in the following verse was literally obeyed:

> Perpetual blessings do demand
> Perpetual praise on every hand;
> Then leap for joy, with dance and song,
> To praise the Lord for ever.

One hymn was set to the tune of "Scots wha' ha'e wi' Wallace bled," sung so rapidly that the dance was a quickstep. Another was to the air of the less respectable old English song, "Nancy Dawson," and "to this lively and merry tune, the whole body, now formed into three abreast . . . literally scampered round the room in a quick gallopade, every individual of both the choir and the dancers, singing with all their might. . . ." After several such dances the participants seemed ungovernable in their ecstasy, and about half a dozen women

whirled themselves round, in what opera dancers call a *pirouette*, performing at least fifty revolutions each — their arms extended horizontally, their clothes being blown out like an air balloon all around their persons — their heads sometimes falling on one side, and sometimes hanging forward on the bosom — till they would at length faint away in hysterical convulsions and be caught in the arms of the surrounding dancers.[26]

Two or three years later when Charles Dickens visited the Shakers and asked to see a church service, his request was refused with the statement that no religious meeting was open to the public, and he departed with his desire unsatisfied, leaving as record of his visit only the disapproving comment, "We walked into a grim room, where several grim hats were hanging on grim pegs, and the time was grimly told by a grim clock which uttered every tick with a kind of struggle, as if it broke the grim silence reluctantly, and under protest." [27] The prohibition on all visitors extended from 1842 to 1845, but they were not again welcome for some time after that. It is not until the 1850's that descriptions of Shaker services were again published, and then the accounts were like those of the early thirties. The service is called "dignified, sincere, and beautiful," and the music "simple and melodious." [28] Throughout the rest of the nineteenth century decorum and solemn ritualism form the keynote of all reports.

Somewhere from the depths of human nature and human needs there had come into the Shaker communities about 1837 a wild burst of the spiritualism that was inherent in Shaker doctrine. For six or seven years it ran its course, affecting every community and revolutionizing its service and its communal life. As in the case of the Rochester rappers a decade later, the movement began among the children. At Watervliet little girls were seized with "shaking and turning exercises." They held conversations with spirits and sang songs taught them by angelic visitants. The contagion spread to all the Shaker communities, and soon it swept like a revival over those of all ages. By 1838 it was in full tide, with trances, visitations, jerks, and revelations the order of every service. It is no wonder that the perplexed and half-disapproving ministry decided to close all services to the public.

The day of the child mediums was soon over. Then adults, mostly women, received written and oral messages from spirits of famous dead and dictated songs and even books revealed or inspired from the other world.[29] These mediums claimed the gift of unknown tongues and were reported to speak in Hebrew, Greek, Latin, Spanish, and Chinese — although doubtless quite unintelligibly to students of the languages.

North American Indians were frequent spirit visitors coming to learn of the Shakers the way to salvation. The songs revealed by them vary from the jargon of

> Quo ve lorezum quuni
> qui quini qure quini que
> Hock a nick a hick nick . . .

to the Indian gift song that appeared at Harvard, Massachusetts, during this spiritual excitement:

> Me hab brat you lub and Wampum
> Me hab brat you cake and wine
> Me hab brat you many presents
> Dat will make de whity shine
> Do receive de pretty presents
> Jest de best dat we can bring
> Modder's pretty shiny children
> O how dood to take us in.[30]

Negro and Chinese visitants contributed their doggerel, while many of the "unknown tongues" resembled no language at all but were just a repetition of syllables strung together in such a way as to furnish a dance rhythm.

Despite its extravagances there was much that was beautiful in the spiritualistic expression of the revival spirit. Those with deep religious feeling and sufficient imagination tried constantly to sublimate all this wild emotion and to keep its outpourings within channels befitting religious experience. In 1842 word went out from Mt. Lebanon that each society should select a site on a hill or mountain top for outdoor festivals. Known as "fountains" or "feast-grounds" these remote plots were the scenes of services made up of dance, song, and séance.[31] At appointed times the whole community would climb the hill to receive the blessings, gifts, and communications brought them by the mediums. Wholly imaginary gifts of food, jewels, and clothing were enjoyed with appropriate gestures and signs of pleasure. At the end of several hours of ecstatic if fantastic communication with the spirit world, the weary assemblage wound its way down the hill to the quiet village below and resumed the routine labors whose dullness had been for the time forgotten.

Communal participation in the spirit-inspired revival was effected through the peculiar "gifts" that were prescribed by the mediums. The "sowing gift" involved a march of all brethren and sisters through the fields sowing imaginary seeds of blessing. The gift of healing was especially active at this time, and numerous accounts of faith healing are extant. "Mother Ann's Sweeping Gift" was a work of spiritual cleansing in which four men and four women went from room to room through every dwelling, praying and singing in each room. The "Midnight Cry" was the effort, repeated each year for a decade, of a band of "instruments" in each community, who went through the buildings at midnight, singing and calling on the society to assemble and worship. All these performances were said to have been ordered by Mother Ann and the first elders as preparation for the reception of higher spiritual truths, and while the fever lasted they probably did keep interest alive.[32]

After 1844 the excitement diminished, almost all the mediums returned to normal life, and the revivalism induced by spirit visitants gradually died out. According to Shaker authorities the withdrawal of the spirits was but temporary. They professed to have work for a ocasion "among the inhabitants of Zion." After that period they promised to return to their earthly labors, when "not a palace nor a hamlet upon earth should remain unvisited by them."[33] When the Rochester manifestations began in 1848, the Shakers hailed them as a fulfillment of that promise.

COMMUNAL LIFE AND ECONOMIC DEVELOPMENT

The spiritualistic fervor of the period from 1837 to 1845 and the period of greatest growth and greatest economic achievement were coincident, but the economic development of Shakerism long outlived the days of spirit visitants. Agriculture was the basis of Shaker economic and social life as it was that of a large part of the "world outside" in the first half century of the republic. The first Shaker societies were established in regions suitable for farming, and the early converts were, for the most part, farming people. Agriculture became for them both a means of livelihood and a sacred calling. The elders of the society firmly believed that "every commune, to prosper, must be founded, as far as industry goes, on agriculture. Only the simple labors and manners of a farming people can hold a community together." [34]

The clearing and cultivation of the soil, the cutting of wood for fuel, and the sowing and harvesting of the crops utilized a large part of the labor of the men in the early days of each society, since the Shaker church moved westward with the frontier. Cooking, cleaning, spinning, weaving, and sewing filled the days of the women, upon whom fell also the work of garden, dairy, and laundry. But many hands, careful management, and the advantages of large-scale production and communal living soon brought agricultural produce more than sufficient to satisfy the needs of the society.

From the first years the Shakers practiced diversified agriculture, intensive farming, and division of labor. The early records show that wheat, oats, rye, barley, corn, flax, and potatoes were the first crops at Mt. Lebanon and that within a decade of the founding of that society three thousand bushels of potatoes a year were being harvested. Corn, apples, and other products were dried, special gardens were set aside for the production of seeds and herbs, and Shaker dairy products were prepared for market. Huge barns were built; breeds of domestic animals were improved by the importation of superior strains of cattle and sheep; poultry and bees were kept. The various branches of agriculture were managed by persons — "farm deacons," "orchard deacons," "herb deacons" — who by calling and long experience became wise in both the production of goods and the vagaries of the markets. [35] At the same time deeply religious and dependent upon the soil, the Shaker came to believe that there was a close connection between his faith and his day's work. As one observer put it, they felt that "if you would have a lovely garden, you should live a lovely life." [36]

Shaker women preparing medicinal herbs

It was not long before the community authorities decided that complete self-sufficiency was not necessary or wise. Instead advantage was taken of demand for certain products, and attention was concentrated on their production even though the society must then purchase from the "world's people" other goods to meet their needs. In many societies these special products were garden seeds, herbs, and drugs. With their passion for doing useful things and for benefiting the world at large by their efforts, the Shakers came to feel a special duty or calling in their medicinal herb industry. At first they used wild herbs mostly; in later years they imported and naturalized many foreign herbs. Before the middle of the nineteenth century the Shaker societies were among the country's greatest producers of seeds and herbs. They made their own bottles, jars, boxes, bags, and labels, and invented and manufactured many devices used in preparing these goods for market.

Another industry based upon agriculture was that of drying vegetables and fruits for winter use. Tanning of leather and cloth-making soon were using far more raw products than Shaker farms furnished, and surpluses were made for sale outside. Broom- and brush-making were common; baskets and many-sized oval wooden boxes were products peculiar to certain communities; the manufacture of palm leaf and straw bonnets was an important Shaker industry, and many a feminine head in the "world outside" was crowned by this demure headgear. Shaker cloaks were popular, also, and blankets, hand-woven carpeting, and woolen cloth were sold. Certain communities won a reputation for special products, which found a market in other societies and outside as well. Mt. Lebanon, for instance, has always been known for the excellence of its cabinet work, and the chairs from the workshops there are things of beauty as well as of utility. Pleasant Hill, Kentucky, grew silk worms and made silk kerchiefs that were highly desired by the sisters of distant communities.

Of Yankee stock, the early Shakers possessed inventive ability, and their workshops and kitchens were filled with evidences of their ingenuity in saving steps and labor. They have claimed many inventions as their own, although the fact that they did not generally acquire patents made it easy for others to obtain the credit and profit resulting from them. The Shaker historians, Anna White and Leila Taylor, gave an impressive list of inventions and ended by stating that if it were extended to "little labor saving contrivances about the dwellings, shops and barns,[it] would seem endless." The important inventions claimed by the Shakers include the buzz saw and cut nails (both invented by a woman), the screw propeller, the rotary harrow, the metallic pen, the threshing machine (1815), the common clothes pin, an apple parer, and a revolving oven.[37]

The Shaker family was the industrial as well as the agricultural unit, and the deacons and trustees watched over all activities. The families were large enough to get whatever advantages accrue from cooperative production and division of labor. Families traded with each other, pooled their knowledge, and cooperated in their efforts. The deacons arranged for agencies outside, sent out peddlers, and even established wholesale houses for their more important goods. The Shakers maintained local stores in the communities and bartered with neighboring farmers for the products they needed. The whole system was amazingly productive, showing, as Andrews says, the advantages of corporate effort in a period when the country at large was in the era of small-scale production and individual enterprise. For many years the central ministry at Mt. Lebanon and many of the community elders were men of great ability with a genius for organization. The rank and file of Shakers were industrious, obedient, and devoted. The result was an increase in the value of their properties and a rise in their living standards to the highest point compatible with their austere way of life.

It is difficult to make any estimate of Shaker wealth. Their production was great and their sales were large, but the margin of profit seems to have been small. Their moral code forbade excessive charges for what seemed to them a service or duty. Sharp practices were foreign to their dealings, and they were forbidden to speculate or to contract debts of any description. It is probable that too much of their capital was invested in land — at least, the elders in a later period felt that the outlying farms were a liability — and with the advent of the machine age much of their equipment became obsolete and their early advantage of large-scale production was lost. The peak of Shaker industry, or enterprise, and wealth came in the period 1830–60, the years in which their numbers also were the greatest.

Two comments by visitors may serve as summary. One was by Harriet Martineau, the distinguished English traveler, who visited the Hancock community in 1837:

There is no question of their entire success as far as wealth is concerned. A very moderate amount of labour has secured to them in perfection all the comforts of life that they know how to enjoy, and as much wealth besides as would command the intellectual luxuries of which they do not dream. The earth does not show more flourishing fields, gardens and orchards, than theirs. . . . If happiness lay in bread and butter, and such things these people have attained the *summum bonum*. . . . If such external provision, with a great amount of accumulated wealth besides, is the result of cooperation and community of property among an ignorant, conceited, inert society like this, what might not the same principles of association achieve among a more intelligent set of people, stimulated by education and exhilarated by the enjoyment of all the blessings which Providence has placed within the reach of man? [38]

With less of the reformer's criticism and perhaps more understanding of the religious aspects of Shakerism, another who visited the community twenty years later wrote:

I am convinced, from observation and from the testimony of their immediate neighbors, that they live in strict accordance with their professions. They are hospitable to strangers, and kind and benevolent

toward the community around them. In morals and citizenship they
are above reproach; and they are loved by those who know them best.
They have been ridiculed and maligned by those who must have been
either ignorant or wicked; for it seems impossible for any candid man,
after becoming acquainted with their character, to regard them otherwise than with the deepest sympathy and respect. Surely the sacrifices
of the dearest interests of earth are sufficient guarantees of their sincerity.[39]

CHAPTER 8

American Utopias of Religious Origin

Alongside the transplanted European cults for which community of property and enterprise was, at least in its inception, only an expedient circumstance, developed a number of utopian experiments in which some form of socialism or communism was voluntarily established as a cardinal article of faith. The chief reason for their existence was the urgent desire of their founders to create for themselves a utopia that might serve as nucleus or model for a new and better social order. These experiments were a protest against the evils found in a world where modern industrialization and mechanization were beginning to have effect; they were at the same time an expression of the optimistic faith in the perfectibility of human institutions that was characteristic of the period. They represent to some extent a desire to escape from certain unpleasant features of the life of the day, but even more they demonstrate the zeal for reform that was the heritage of revivalism. In communal life those of like mind might solve the problems of the day.

These utopian societies fall into two groups, one drawing its inspiration from the teachings of religion, the other from the ideas of two Old World reformers, Robert Owen and Charles Fourier. Although only a few of these experiments can be described in this chapter and the next, there were in all more than fifty of them in nineteenth-century America. As Emerson wrote to Carlyle in the autumn of 1840, "We are all a little wild here with numberless projects of social reform. Not a reading man but has a draft of a new community in his waistcoat pocket."

THE HOPEDALE COMMUNITY

One of the better known of the American ventures in Christian Socialism was the Hopedale Community near Milford, Massachusetts. Its founder and guiding spirit was the Reverend Adin Ballou, a minister of the Universalist church and a relative of one of its founders. More radical than many of his colleagues, he had long been known as a champion of the temperance, antislavery, and peace movements. He was a correspondent of Dr. Channing and a co-worker with Theodore Parker and William Lloyd Garrison.

Sometime before 1840 he became convinced "that it was one of the declared objects of Christ's labors to inaugurate the kingdom of heaven *on the earth;* and that it was the imperative duty of his disciples to pray and to work earnestly for that sublime end, as one of the best preliminaries to immortal blessedness." [1]

Ballou believed New Testament teachings could be "actualized," and he invited others who felt as he did to join him in a settlement where religion and socialism would combine to achieve a utopia that might start a world movement toward a more perfect life. As a means to this end he began the publication of a biweekly paper called the *Practical Christian,* the first number of which appeared in April 1840, and the last just twenty years later. The history of the Hopedale Community falls within those twenty years.

Within a year some thirty men and women responded to Adin Ballou's call, and, after a careful study of previous communistic settlements and of socialistic principles in general, they drew up a constitution for "Fraternal Communism" that is a reformer's document from beginning to end. After a preliminary declaration in favor of temperance, peace, chastity, nonviolence, and various other reforms, the constitution provided for "personal equality irrespective of sex, color, occupation, wealth, rank, or any other natural or adventitious peculiarity." Family life was to be maintained, with separate lodgings for each family if it so desired. Pure communism was rejected in favor of a system called "joint stock proprietorship," by which negotiable shares of fifty dollars each were to be sold to those desiring to join the enterprise. Whenever a stockholder might wish to convert his stock it was to be offered to the other stockholders; failing a purchaser, the community agreed to buy it at par value out of funds set aside for that purpose. If the community prospered dividends were to be paid on the stock. The members were to live and work together; "suitable employment" was to be provided for every individual — man, woman, and child — at a fixed scale of wages based upon (for adults) an eight-hour day and forty-eight hour week. The officers of the community, to be chosen by the stockholding members, were to include, besides the usual president and secretary, six "intendants" to whom the various branches of community life and industry were to be entrusted. [2]

This constitution was sent out to many persons known to be interested in reform movements and was met with mingled sympathy, approval, caution, and admonition. The dean of all New England preachers, Dr. William Ellery Channing, acclaimed the ends for which the community was to be established, saying,

I have for a very long time dreamed of an association, in which the members, instead of preying on one another and seeking to put one another down, after the fashion of this world, should live together as brothers, seeking one another's elevation and spiritual growth. But the materials for such a community I have not seen.

After that rueful comment, Channing went on to list the obstacles in the way of success, the chief being the "difficulty of reconciling so many wills, of bringing so many individuals to such a unity of feeling and judgment as is necessary to the management of an extensive common concern." [3] Many years later, when the Hopedale Community had failed in that effort to reconcile individualism and communal interests, Adin Ballou regretfully acknowledged that Dr. Channing was one of the wisest men he had ever known. The very difficulties that Channing suggested, Ballou wrote, "we were obliged to encounter, spite of all our sanguine hopes and resolves, and they finally proved too much for our virtue and wisdom. Instead of rising above and overcoming them, we were in the end overcome by them." [4]

In 1841 farm land was purchased, and a few families gathered together in the old farm buildings to make a beginning of the new utopia. At first there were many discouragements, the joint stock sold slowly, members were few, the old buildings were uncomfortable and inadequate, and there were many disputes about principles and objectives. But slowly the movement grew; influential friends gave it publicity, and funds and new members came in to ensure its survival. Within a decade the community owned five hundred acres of farm land — not all arable to be sure — and had built thirty new dwellings, three mechanic shops with water power and machinery, a chapel, barns, and other buildings. The number of families had grown to thirty-six, and the total population of the village was nearly two hundred.

In a prospectus written by Mr. Ballou in 1851 the purposes of the society as finally formulated were clearly set forth, and its fundamental differences from the religious communities described in the preceding chapters were evident. No person could be a member of the community who could not "cordially assent" to a "simple declaration of faith in the religion of Jesus Christ" and who would not acknowledge "subjection to all the moral obligations of that religion." Beyond that simple basis for joint effort there were no religious qualifications.

Each individual is left to judge for him or herself, with entire freedom, what abstract doctrines are taught, and also what external religious rights are enjoined in the religion of Christ. . . . In such matters all the members are free, with mutual love and toleration, to follow their own highest convictions of truth and religious duty. . . . But in practical Christianity this Church is precise and direct. There its essentials are specific. It insists on supreme love to God and man.

Then follows a long list of the "practical" reforms advocated — reform movements by no means peculiar to the society and so evidence of the fact that Hopedale was a part of the whole wave of social reform. Profanity, unchastity, intemperance, slaveholding, war, capital punishment, mobocracy, personal violence, military service — in short, "all things known to be sinful against God or human nature" — were condemned as contrary to "obligatory righteousness." Calling Hopedale a "miniature Christian Republic," the prospectus went on to state that it was a "universal religious, moral, philanthropic, and social reform Association" and a Missionary Society, a Temperance Society, an Anti-Slavery Society, a Peace Society, and a Woman's Rights Association. Its socialism was labeled "Christian," and its great aim was stated as the "harmonization of just individual freedom with social co-operation." The liberality and tolerance of the Hopedale Community were expressed in the statement:

Let each class of dissenting socialists stand aloof from our Republic and experiment to their heart's content on their own wiser systems. It is their right to do so uninjured, at their own cost. It is desirable that they should do so in order that it may be demonstrated as soon as possible which the true social system is. When the radically defective have failed there will be a harmonious concentration of all the true and good around the Practical Christianity Standard.

Written in the period of the greatest success of the society, midway between its founding and its end, this statement of creed and policy breathes forth the sincerity, high moral principles, and re-

forming zeal of its authors, but it also expresses the extreme individualism that was the greatest weakness of the experiment. From the
first there were disputes and debates at Hopedale. Those who had
invested in the community stock wanted dividends and privileges
commensurate with their investment. A second group desired a sub-
stitution of communism for the joint-stock socialism and the abolition of all evidences of capitalism. When the dissatisfied seceded —
and there were many seceders — the society's practice of purchasing
their stock and refunding their capital caused financial embarrassment for the community. Under pressure, amendments were made
to the constitution to permit greater economic freedom to the members. Those who wished to invest labor and capital in the joint
enterprise might do so; he who wished to "transact business by
himself, as may please him" was equally free; and between the two
extremes there were some who owned stock but conducted private
enterprises on the side.[5] The same compromises were made all along
the line — in the use and payment of child labor, in education, in
housing, and in community business.

For some years, however, the community made progress toward
economic success. Most members were honest and devoted and did
their best to make the experiment succeed, and the advantages of
cooperative economy and fairly large-scale production brought
profits of a sort. Starting from very little in 1842, the joint-stock
investment in 1856 was $40,000, and the individual property of
members, nearly all produced at Hopedale, was $90,000. When the
community affairs were wound up all debts were paid, and no one
could be said to have lost much financially from the sixteen years
of united effort. If all two hundred members had had sufficient interest at the end to continue the project, there is little reason to
suppose that the same moderate success might not have continued.
It seems safe to say that the failure was at least partly due to lack of
zeal or lack of will to continue. The energetic developed their private ventures; the unambitious seemed satisfied to put in no more
time or labor than was essential to keep the community above
water. There was no growth and little vitality.

The end came unexpectedly. As the joint stock had been offered
for sale, two enterprising brothers, Ebenezer and George Draper,
had bought it up, until they owned three fourths of the entire stock.

Ebenezer Draper became president of the community when Adin Ballou resigned in 1853, confident at last of the success of his experiment in practical Christianity and worn out by his labors in its behalf. But only three years later the brothers Draper decided that the community business was no longer profitable and that their funds would be more productive if transferred to their private enterprises. They proposed, therefore, to close out the community while it was still a going concern, to pay all its debts and wind up all its business. The fact of the matter was that the more dominant brother, George Draper, had made up his mind that the socialistic scheme was impracticable and was determined to withdraw from it at once. That decision sealed the doom of the community. The other members had no alternative except to yield, for they could not command sufficient capital to buy the stock of the Draper brothers.

Others must have felt "the deathlike chill" that Ballou said "settled upon and almost froze my heart" when the aspirations and the labor of their best years thus came to naught. But it is doubtful that they all rose above their mortification and disappointment, as he did, to a philosophic level where they could analyze their failure and come to some conclusions as to the factors that caused it. Ballou always believed that the Hopedale Community had been founded upon fundamental principles that were true for all time. About its defects he said:

It is my deliberate and solemn conviction that the predominating cause of the failure . . . was a moral and spiritual, not a financial one — a deficiency among its members of those graces and powers of character which are requisite to the realization of the Christian ideal of human society.

His statement of secondary causes and his advice to those who might wish to try such an experiment under better auspices were penetrating and wise. His statement, "The work of Social Reform is by no means abandoned; it is only suspended till the world is fitted by intellectual growth and spiritual elevation to take it up again and prosecute it to successful results," [6] may be repeated as an epitaph for this truly American experiment in communal living — a utopia and a failure but a fitting expression of the spirit of the land of the free.

"TRANSCENDENTAL WILD OATS"

Different from the Hopedale Community in almost every way, except that it, too, represented an effort to establish a new way of life, the experiment of Bronson Alcott and Charles Lane at Fruitlands has a place in the story of American utopias. As an episode in the life of the "Transcendental Talker" it loomed large, for in all sincerity he and his few associates endeavored to plant an earthly paradise in which their dreams might be realized. But since the entire history of the undertaking covered only a few months and touched the lives and expressed the aspirations of only a small group, it cannot be considered an important manifestation of the zeal for reform. Even its failure as an attempt at communal life had little significance, since the principles upon which the experiment rested were never fully formulated, apparently, in the somewhat confused minds of those who were responsible for it.[7]

In 1842 Alcott came back from the trip to England that had been planned to bring him out of the despondency occasioned by the failure of his Temple School in Boston. His theories on education and on life in general had had a respectful hearing abroad, where his ideas and his reputation as a Transcendentalist philosopher were better known than his failures. Conversation with English friends who were reformers of a universal if not practical variety had led Alcott to believe, as he wrote in his journal,

Our freer, but yet far from freed, land is the asylum, if asylum there be, for the hope of man; and, there, if anywhere, is the second Eden to be planted in which the divine seed is to bruise the head of Evil and restore Man to his rightful communion with God in the Paradise of Good.

The doubt expressed by the conditional mood in this excerpt disappeared in an engulfing enthusiasm that caused him to throw himself without reservation into an attempt to create a Transcendentalist's Eden. The failure of the attempt left him crushed and exhausted, anxious to die rather than face a world from which hope and dreams had departed.

Among Alcott's English friends was Charles Lane, an enigmatic figure whose personality and ideas were to have effect both upon the Alcott family and the history of utopias. Lane, who came to the United States with Alcott in 1842, was an English mystic and reformer whose life presents such inconsistencies and contrasts that it is difficult to arrive at any explanation of its paradoxes. He urged the celibate life upon the Alcott family and placed his son in the Shaker settlement of Harvard, but soon afterward he remarried and started a new family, which eventually included five more children. He had countless theories on education and the care of children and yet was so coldly forbidding that the Alcott children learned to hate and fear him. While proclaiming the United States a "freer world," he proceeded to advocate, in the cause of reform, the overthrow of the American government. Such was the strange partner Alcott had selected for his venture. And the partner bade fair to become the master, for it was Lane's money that paid Alcott's debts and purchased the land needed for the new Eden.

These utopians bought ninety acres of farm land in a beautiful valley near the village of Harvard about fifty miles from Concord. The house was not a part of the purchase but was given rent-free for a year, and was furnished with the household equipment of the Alcott family supplemented by contributions from others who joined the community. Lane and his son and the Alcotts and their four small daughters moved out to their new home, which Alcott named Fruitlands, in the spring of 1843. There they were joined by a group, always small and never for long exactly the same, that included, among others, the Englishman, H. C. Wright; Isaac Hecker, New York baker and champion of American labor, at that time a Transcendentalist, later a Catholic priest; Anna Page, who sometimes acted as the children's governess; Abram Wood, who persuaded his friends to call him Wood Abram; and Joseph Palmer, Fitchburg farmer and the only practical man of the lot.*

The iron will of Charles Lane was apparent in the asceticism that was inaugurated for the whole household, and the judgment of Lane was accepted in the matter of farm economy, although his

* In a day when beards were unfashionable Palmer became known as "the man with a beard." No amount of ridicule could bring him to dispense with the adornment, which he felt would not have been his if the Lord had not wanted man to wear beards. He was an antislavery man and a total abstainer, and his advocacy of prison reform was based upon firsthand knowledge, for he was in prison more than a year for assaulting those who taunted him about his beard. After the failure of Fruitlands, Palmer bought the property from Lane and lived there the rest of his life. It was his beautiful furniture that made the old house charming in 1843 and that has since been brought back to it in the restoration for which Clara Endicott Sears was responsible.

knowledge of rural life had been gained from a study of market prices in the city of London. Dogmatic, full of the ideas of European social reformers, and, temporarily at least, determined upon the denial of every natural desire, Lane drove the little colony along the path he had mapped out for it. Frivolity and pleasure were to be denied even the children, whose every hour was to be spent in work, study, and the contemplation of higher things. But the Alcotts enjoyed their charming little birthday festivals and the letters and poems that punctuated their family intercourse. And at any hour of the day, long Conversations in the Alcott manner might deal with such topics as friendship, innocence, or fidelity.

Potatoes, apples, and whole wheat bread were the staples of diet at Fruitlands, although there seems to have been no condemnation of other fruits and vegetables. Producing them, however, was difficult, for Lane was as opposed to the use of beasts of burden as he was to human slavery; "spade culture" must suffice. Cotton was the product of slave labor, and the use of wool deprived the sheep of their property; therefore the inhabitants of Fruitlands wore linen smocks and trousers or — in the case of Mrs. Alcott, Miss Page, and the children — the garments later made famous by Amelia Bloomer. Bathing in cold water was considered desirable — if indeed the methods of housekeeping did not make it necessary — and the men used the brook while the children were bathed in a homemade shower that involved sheets draped over a circle of clothesline, a ladder (for their father), a pail of cold water, and a sieve. Contemporary accounts do not mention the methods used by Mrs. Alcott and Miss Page.

Expeditions to carry the new gospel to the outside world — perhaps in the hope that the world might contribute to the cost of the experiment — resulted in the neglect of the one food crop that seemed to offer sustenance for the winter, and had it not been for the labor of Mrs. Alcott and the children even these few precious acres of barley would have gone unharvested. As an economic venture Fruitlands presents little of interest to posterity.

The relations between the Alcotts and Charles Lane grew steadily worse, until Mrs. Alcott and the children came to regard him as the author of all their woes. The lack of any prospect of success, or indeed of food, led all the others — except the faithful Joseph

Palmer — to disappear one at a time in the autumn of 1843. Mr. Lane and his son became more and more interested in the Shaker settlement near by and spent much of their time there. It became obvious, even to Alcott, that the experiment, so hopefully if unrealistically begun, must end in failure. In November the diary of little Louisa Alcott records, "Father and Mr. Lane had a talk, and Father asked us if *we* saw any reason for us to separate. Mother wanted to, she is so tired. I like it, but not the school part, nor Mr. Lane." [8]

A few weeks later, in January 1844, Charles Lane and his son went to live with the Shakers. Their departure, which signified the failure of the Fruitlands venture, came at a time when Alcott was desperately ill. It is difficult to fill in the story of those bleak December and January days when the little family was alone in the old house, but Louisa's romantic account, *The Transcendental Wild Oats*, may be taken as worthy of trust in its main outline and general sentiment if not in its detail. After long days through which Alcott lay with his face to the wall, wanting only to die with the utopia for which he had had such glorious dreams, the weary wife who had watched over his anguish heard his voice again in the one word, "Hope." When his strength returned, the family made plans to leave Fruitlands and late in January piled their household goods on an oxcart and set out for a new home. The conclusion of Louisa's semifictionalized account sums up Alcott's aspirations and disappointment in this Transcendentalist project:

"Ah, me! my happy dream. How much I leave behind that never can be mine again," said Abel [Alcott], looking back at the lost Paradise, lying white and chill in its shroud of snow. . . . "Poor Fruitlands! The name was as great a failure as the rest," continued Abel, with a sigh, as a frost-bitten apple fell from a leafless bough at his feet.[9]

BROOK FARM

In a lighter vein, a happy idyll instead of a tragicomedy, is the story of the Brook Farm experiment in living. Likewise the product of Transcendentalism, Brook Farm is even more difficult than Fruitlands to define and classify. It was socialistic rather than communistic, and its joint-stock system was similar to that of Hopedale. Deeply religious in feeling and idealistic in aspiration, its founders were Unitarians and Transcendentalists, nonsectarian and tolerant of all creeds and faiths. They were men of culture as well, highly educated, cognizant of all the movements for reform, full of humanitarianism, and convinced that a society could be developed whose institutions would be the realization of their ideals.

Life at Brook Farm was simple in all things material, as democratic as the New England town meeting in its organization, but delightfully varied in its cultural and social aspects. It is no wonder that all those who in later years wrote about their experiences at Brook Farm concluded that these were the pleasantest, the happiest, the most memorable years of their lives. Even Hawthorne, whose *Blithedale Romance* was the not too complimentary product of his brief stay at Brook Farm, alluded in afteryears to his "having had the good fortune, for a time to be personally connected with it," and hid away in the last chapter of his novel this revealing passage:

Often in these years that are darkening around me, I remember our beautiful scheme of a noble and unselfish life, and how fair in that first summer appeared the prospect that it might endure for generations, and be perfected, as the ages rolled by, into the system of a people and a world. Were my former associates now there — were there only three or four of those true-hearted men still laboring in the sun — I sometimes fancy that I should direct my world-weary footsteps thitherward, and entreat them to receive me for old friendship's sake. More and more I feel we struck upon what ought to be a truth. Posterity may dig it up and profit by it.

Brook Farm was, in a sense, a Transcendentalist missionary and educational enterprise. Its work was propaganda and example; its objective was the creation, in miniature, of a world in which the latent possibilities of each member might be realized and the lives of all might be complete, fully developed, satisfactory to themselves and to society. This was the first and Transcendentalist phase of the experiment. Its idealism lasted on into the later years when the leaders were persuaded to transform Brook Farm into a Fourierist phalanx, so that to the end the society was more Transcendentalist than socialistic. It was, as one author stated, "the most brilliant and fascinating page in the otherwise rather monotonous and prosaic history of Fourierist experiments in America." Since it was not the outgrowth of poverty or oppression, there was no cankering fear at Brook Farm, nor were there memories of past wrongs and apprehensions as to a dubious future to hold the society to-gether. It was always psychologically as well as legally a voluntary association, and its members remained to the end men of many in-terests and intellectual resources who could not be made bankrupt in spirit or in mind by the failure of the enterprise.

The founder of Brook Farm and its mainstay for the six years of its existence was George Ripley, Boston Unitarian minister and member of the Transcendental Club, but the project seems to have been almost as much the joint interest of the entire group as was the *Dial*, its literary review. Not that all of them were entirely certain about it. Emerson wrote in his journal, "I wished to be con-vinced, to be thawed, to be made nobly mad by the kindlings be-fore my eye of a new dawn of human piety. But this scheme was arithmetic and comfort. . . . a rage in our poverty and politics to live rich and gentlemanlike, an anchor to leeward against a change of weather; a prudent forecast on the probable issue of the great questions of Pauperism and Poverty." Margaret Fuller, too, had reservations. "I will not throw any cold water," she wrote, "yet I wish him [Ripley] the aid of some equal and faithful friend in the beginning, the rather that his own mind, though that of a captain, is not that of a conqueror." In the end, although she frequently visited Brook Farm and was so identified with it that she is sup-posed to have been the Zenobia of Hawthorne's novel, she decided to "look on and see the coral insects at work." [10]

Ripley's objectives, as given in his own words, were:

. . . to insure a more natural union between intellectual and manual labor than now exists; to combine the thinker and the worker, as far as possible in the same individual; to guarantee the highest mental free-dom, by providing all with labor adapted to their tastes and talents, and securing to them the fruits of their industry; to do away with the necessity of menial services by opening the benefits of education and the profits of labor to all; and thus to prepare a society of liberal, in-telligent, and cultivated persons, whose relations with each other would permit a more wholesome and simple life than can be led amidst the pressure of our competitive institutions. [11]

The decision to form such a society was made in 1841, and the site chosen was the Ellis farm some nine miles from Boston, where Rip-ley and his wife had often spent the summer months. The officers of the association were to be elected by the shareholders — every person holding one or more shares to have one vote — and were to be unpaid except at the rate of one dollar for a ten-hour day when they were actually employed in official duties. Every subscriber to the joint stock was entitled to the tuition of one child in the community school; all labor, manual or otherwise, was to be paid for at the same rate per hour; and the work week was to be forty-eight hours for the winter months and sixty hours for the summer. Board was to be charged against the labor of all adults, with a lower rate for children over ten years of age. Children under ten and all persons over seventy were to receive board without charge, while those who came to Brook Farm to attend the school were to be charged for board and tuition. It was expected that five per cent interest could be paid on each share of stock.

Whether or not the association thus planned was socialistic is a moot question. Some of those most interested in the venture disclaimed any desire for socialism. However, when it was decided, in 1845, to turn it into a Fourierist phalanx little change in the original constitution was deemed necessary. It is certain, moreover, that the ideas of its originators envisaged a new attitude toward labor and the creation of a society that might be called utopian.

At Brook Farm domestic service was abolished as degrading to the servitor, and menial labor, both within the household and on the farm, was divided among all the members of the society. Hawthorne mentions the fact that a pitchfork was placed in his hands on the first day of his residence at Brook Farm and that the manure pile was the scene of his first labors.[12] Students in the school were required to work with their hands for a part of every day so that they, too, might share in the "true relation between labor and the people." Whether socialist or not, Brook Farm was certainly a cooperative enterprise, utopian and visionary only in its confidence in the constancy and zeal of its members.

Provided thus with a constitution and a country home, and given favorable publicity by the *Dial* and the words of leading New England writers and clergymen, Brook Farm began its career under good auspices. At no time did it lack eager applicants for membership,[13] and the Brook Farm school was a success from the beginning. It was not long before the old farmhouse was inadequate, and new living quarters were built. A day nursery, the school, several workshops, and other buildings were constructed. The Nest, the Eyrie, Pilgrim House, and the Cottage were built, none of them luxurious dwellings, but all comfortable and pleasant enough. When the number of residents reached seventy there was again some overcrowding, but as one youth said, he never went to his tiny room except to sleep, and there was always a jolly crowd in the family living rooms. This enlargement of physical plant was quite a substantial achievement for the first four years of a new venture, and the fact that money had to be borrowed to make this possible was immaterial, since the debt was owed to those interested in the society.

At first the farm absorbed the attention of the men of the community, but they soon found that the land was not productive and that their hay and food crops were inadequate and of poor quality. When they endeavored to establish a nursery and greenhouse, they were confronted with the necessity for expensive fertilizers. As an agricultural or horticultural enterprise Brook Farm could not be made profitable without tools, equipment, and special skills that they could not easily acquire. The community established a printing press and had its own carpenters and shoemakers, and Isaac Hecker, who spent some time also at Fruitlands, plied his trade of baker for some months. The advent of a few skilled workmen made the manufacture of sashes, doors, and blinds profitable. Some Britannia ware also was made but with very little cash result. Industrially neither as a society nor as a phalanx was Brook Farm a great success, and when it was sold in 1849 the proceeds — $19,150 — little more than sufficed to pay its debts.

The schools of Brook Farm present a much brighter picture, and there is every reason to suppose that, had all energies been concentrated on education, permanent achievements of a progressive nature might well have been made. The whole educational project has a twentieth-century aspect. There was an infant school for children under six years of age, a primary school for those between six and ten, and a six-year preparatory course designed to fit students for college. In addition, an agricultural course was offered, and every effort was made to arrange classes or tutoring for young people who wanted special courses or advanced work under certain of the instructors. Each student was expected to work two or more hours a day at some sort of manual labor, several worked for their board, and all were called upon occasionally to assist in waiting on table or in the kitchen.

It was, however, in curriculum and methods of instruction rather than in organization that really radical departures from the practice of contemporary schools were made. The whole Brook Farm system was based upon complete freedom of intercourse between students and faculty. They lived and worked together. Advanced classes were held informally at any convenient hour, and the contacts of student and instructor were many and varied. Education, in short, might continue effectively in study, barn, parlor, or workshop. As for the curriculum, there was of course the customary emphasis upon the classics and upon mathematics, but history, modern languages, literature, philosophy, and botany were offered as well, and they were taught by masters in those fields. Drawing, dancing, and music were not neglected; probably for the first time in the history of education in America the works of Mozart, Haydn, and Beethoven were a part of daily life. Literary and debating societies, play production, dramatic readings, and concerts added to the educational fare. The faculty was almost uniformly good, including Ripley himself, Charles Dana, John Dwight, and others of high reputation.

Since the Brook Farm school was especially recommended by the Harvard faculty as an excellent place to prepare for college and since many of the New England intelligentsia were interested in it, the list of its thirty or more pupils contained names well known in American letters. George Bancroft sent his two sons, Margaret Fuller her young brother; Horace Sumner, brother of the famous Charles, was there, and also Sarah Stearns, Caroline Kittredge, and a son of Orestes Brownson. But George William and Burrill Curtis were the best loved leaders of the school, and their active minds and wide cultural interests set its tone.

The visitors to Brook Farm offered another opportunity for liberal education. Their names make up a list of the cream of American letters and thought: Margaret Fuller, Emerson, Parker, Robert Owen, Brownson, Greeley, Brisbane, Elizabeth Peabody, Alcott, and Channing. Informal talk, formal Conversations, and every sort of lecture made the dinner and evening hours occasions to remember. Since almost all the older people at Brook Farm were interested in some sort of reform movement, groups went into Boston frequently for meetings where questions of the day were discussed. Other excursions were planned for concerts and the theater, and Elizabeth Peabody's bookshop in Boston was the meeting place for all Brook Farm residents when they went to the city.

The informality and spontaneity that characterized the educational program were carried over into the social life of Brook Farm and made it altogether delightful. In his *Historic Notes of Life and Letters in New England*, Emerson wrote a commendation that was blended with good-humored criticism:

The founders of Brook Farm should have this praise, that they made what all people try to make, an agreeable place to live in. All comers, even the most fastidious, found it the pleasantest of residences. It is certain that freedom from household routine, variety of character and talent, variety of work, variety of means of thought and instruction, art, music, poetry, reading, masquerade, did not permit sluggishness or despondency; broke up routine. There is agreement that it was to most of the associates, education; to many the most important period of their life, the birth of valued friendships, their first acquaintance with the riches of conversation, their training in behavior. The art of letter writing, it is said, was immensely cultivated. Letters were always flying, not only from house to house, but from room to room. It was a perpetual picnic, a French Revolution in small, an Age of Reason in a patty-pan.[14]

Orestes Brownson, who liked Brook Farm and approved its educational theories, said that it was "half a charming adventure, half a solemn experiment," and added that it was fun to live there, even better to visit.

As might be expected, there is every evidence that the students loved the regime. Every record of their life at Brook Farm pays tribute to its charm and to its glorious opportunities for a rich social experience. A young English governess, Georgiana Bruce, came to Brook Farm to study and worked in the household and the infant school for her board and tuition. Her account of her years there breathes her delight in the cultural and social life of the society.

What a royal time we had. The days were full of affection and sunshine. . . . The very air seemed to hold more exhilarating qualities than any I had breathed before. Democracy and culture made the animus of the association. Had the world denied you opportunity for education? Here your highest needs should be satisfied. . . . What a heavenly world this was getting to be![15]

The optimism of the whole community is reflected in her remark that "no Adventist ever believed more absolutely in the second coming of Christ than we in the reorganization of society on a fraternal basis."

The unconventionality of Brook Farm social life was commented upon by most observers — and condemned by a few. The constant and friendly visitor, Margaret Fuller, for example, found it hard to get used to the fact that in the crowded parlor the young people sat on the floor during her Conversations. Thomas Wentworth Higginson, who never lived at Brook Farm but visited his cousin there, left a record of the gay costume parties, at one of which his cousin Barbara appeared in "a pretty Creole dress made of handkerchiefs from the West Indies," and he spoke with apparent envy of the unconventional but gay clothes worn on everyday occasions by the Brook Farm boys — blouses of gay-colored chintz and "little round visorless caps with tassels." [16] He does not mention the fact that the workaday costume of Brook Farm girls included short skirts or knickers. In his *American Notebooks, 1841–1852* Hawthorne described in charming detail one of the gay picnics at the Farm where, in honor of Frank Dana's birthday, a rural masquerade brought into the woods Indian squaws, a fortuneteller, gypsies, Diana, foresters, and children of all ages.[17]

It is George William Curtis, however, who, in one of his Easy Chair essays in *Harper's Monthly*, left the most charming picture of Brook Farm life:

The society of Brook Farm was composed of every kind of person. There were the ripest scholars, men and women of the most aesthetic culture and accomplishment, young farmers, seamstresses, mechanics and preachers — the lazy, the conceited, the sentimental. But they were associated in such a spirit and under such conditions that, with some extravagance, the best of everybody appeared, and there was a kind of high *esprit de corps*. . . . There was plenty of steady, essential, hard work, for the founding of an earthly paradise upon a rough New England farm is no pastime. But with the best intention, and much practical knowledge and industry, and devotion, there was in the nature of the case an inevitable lack of method, and the economical failure was almost a foregone conclusion. But there were never such witty potato-patches and such sparkling cornfields before or since. The weeds were scratched out of the ground to the music of Tennyson and Browning,

Brook Farm, the Transcendentalist utopia

The dining room at Fruitlands

From Pierrepont Noyes, *My Father's House,* 1937, by permission of Farrar and Rinehart

John Humphrey Noyes, Perfectionist

and the nooning was an hour as gay and bright as any brilliant midnight at Ambrose's.[18]

It is interesting to speculate upon the possible success of Brook Farm if the school had been permitted to remain the major interest of the association. But the guiding spirits of the Farm were not men with only one interest; indeed their minds seem to have been open to the call for universal reform. In the beginning there was little of socialist theory at the Farm; fraternal association or cooperation was the keynote. But Ripley as a Boston clergyman interested in the cause of labor had been shocked by the suffering of the people in the panic of 1837, and when the works of the French socialist Fourier were published in the United States and discussed at Brook Farm, Ripley brought some of the New York Fourierists to the Farm for lectures and discussion meetings. Albert Brisbane, leading American Fourierist, and Horace Greeley, whom he had converted to socialism, were most interested and appreciative visitors, and through their efforts the Brook Farm trustees were won over to the cause in 1844. In her *Letters from Brook Farm* Marianne Dwight told of the anxious days when the fateful decision was being made and of the care with which the new constitution for a Brook Farm Phalanx was worked out.[19]

Under the new constitution Brook Farm was for the first time legally incorporated in 1845 and proceeded to borrow money in order to establish industries and set up the series or labor groups demanded by Fourierist theories. The new government was complicated. The Farming Series was divided into the Cattle Group, the Milking Group, the Planting Group, and so on; the Mechanical Series and the Domestic Series were similarly divided; each Group elected a chief, and the Group chiefs elected a Series chief. The chiefs of all the Series formed a controlling body for the Phalanx. This was in effect, and in miniature, a sort of guild socialism, and upon it the residents of Brook Farm staked their fortune.

Given the personnel and the influential friends of Brook Farm, it is easy to see what a feather its conversion to formal socialism was in the cap of the American Fourierist movement. It was intended from the beginning to utilize the intellects and literary abilities of the Farm in the propaganda crusade for the larger movement. John Allen, the editor of a periodical called *Social Reform*, came into the society to help in the project, and in June 1845 there appeared the first number of the *Harbinger*, which was for four years the most important socialist paper of the day.

The new publication seemed to be a success — in everything except paying its way — and there was a ready hearing everywhere for the distinguished lecturers sent out from Brook Farm to act as missionaries for the cause of socialism. The school was neglected in order to give more attention to the magazine and the struggling industries, and there was a plaintive undertone of worry over the lack of funds and the increasing indebtedness. In order to attract new members and to house the paraphernalia of the Phalanx activities, it was deemed advisable to put up a new building much larger than anything they had as yet constructed. Begun in 1845, the new phalanstery was almost completed in March 1846, and the association was ready to celebrate the beginning of a new and more prosperous era, when all their hopes were dashed by a fire that entirely consumed the new building. The seven thousand dollars collected, or borrowed, with such great effort were gone; there was no insurance and little chance of further gifts. Brisbane and Greeley, interested in newer experiments,[20] found no time or energy for the problems of the Brook Farm Phalanx, and bankruptcy seemed inevitable. Membership, too, was falling off, and several cases of smallpox added to the difficulties. The year 1846–47 was filled with discussion and ended in a sad acceptance of the fact that the end must be faced. At a joint meeting of the stockholders and the friendly creditors it was decided to dispose of all assets, pay all debts, and close the books of what had been the brightest and happiest of American utopias.

JOHN HUMPHREY NOYES AND THE ONEIDA COMMUNITY

The belief in the possibility of human perfection appeared in the teaching of all the faiths that preached the importance of conversion and of direct contact of the individual soul with an omnipotent and omniscient God, but it was the fundamental creed of but one of the groups that sought to establish a new Eden. Perfectionists, individually and in tiny groups, had throughout the days of revivalism often expressed their joy in their new freedom from a sense of sin. Some of them had drifted into the radical sects; the rest had remained isolated extremists in the more orthodox churches of their own communities. There was no sect with perfectionism as its major tenet until the appearance of John Humphrey Noyes, in whom these scattered perfectionists found their leader. Under his direction and inspired by his zeal, they set forth, with numbers augmented by his teaching, to create for themselves a community in which the perfection they desired might be attained.

There was nothing in the heritage or early life of John Humphrey Noyes to indicate that he might someday lead one of the most radical movements of an era of experimentation and make it succeed over a period of fifty years to such an extent as to confound those who were horrified by his doctrines. This "greatest of the Vermont prophets" was born in 1811, the son of John and Polly (Hayes) Noyes and the descendant of generations of sturdy, well-to-do, eminently respectable New Englanders. There was no hardship or privation in John Humphrey's childhood. His father was successful in business and prominent in state politics; his mother was capable and devoted; they had eight or nine lively, normal children. No picture could present a sharper contrast to the youth of Joseph Smith or Mother Ann Lee, and yet the Vermont lad was to found a movement in which were combined some of the characteristics of Mormonism and Shakerism.

Noyes graduated from Dartmouth in 1830 and came home to Putney, Vermont, to study law. A year later the great revivalist, Charles Finney, swept through New England on one of his preaching tours, and the young law student was one of his converts. The ministry then became Noyes's goal. A year at Andover was followed by two at Yale, and the young man was licensed to preach. Until that point there had been little that was unusual in his progress, but with his first preaching he exposed beliefs that were at once to cut him off from serving any orthodox church or sect. Perfectionism may have been implicit in the promises of the revivalists, but proclaimed from the pulpit as a reality for the individual, it was a most unorthodox doctrine, and the young divinity student was examined by his teachers. When he calmly asserted that with conversion came a complete release from sin, his license to preach was revoked, in spite of his adding that freedom from sin did not mean one was incapable of improvement. "I do not pretend," he said, "to perfection in externals, I only claim purity of heart and the answer of a good conscience toward God." [21]

Had young Noyes not been expelled from the ministry, his zeal might have been diverted into the temperance and antislavery movements, in which his interest was strong. But refused ordination and all opportunity to pursue his chosen profession, he devoted himself to elaborating his perfectionism into a creed. Keen, logical, interested in many types of reform, and utterly fearless, Noyes found himself moving gradually far to the left in his religious and social ideas. Neither his doctrine nor his social theories came to him quickly or in complete form. For twelve years he wandered about, preaching to those of perfectionist ideas, talking with other iconoclasts, studying what he called "the Sin system, the Marriage system, the Work system, and the Death system." Always he sought solutions for these problems, and when he had arrived at some conclusion as to cause and remedy, he had courage and independence enough to put his ideas into practice.

Opposition and ostracism stimulated Noyes's thinking and served to precipitate his ideas. After studying the history of many radical sects and many reform movements, he became convinced that both orthodox religious doctrine and the existing social order were wrong and should be replaced by a new system, for "the next phase of national history will be that of Revivalism and Socialism harmonized and working together for the Kingdom of Heaven." [22]

Noyes's sympathy for the laboring people was aroused by their hardships in the period of depression following 1837. He studied the teachings of Robert Owen and of Fourier and was keenly interested in the religious and economic bases of the Shakers and of Brook Farm. He became convinced that socialism without religion was impossible, but that combined with perfectionism it would become invincible. The family, he believed, must always be the central unit of society, but the ordinary family relationship was full of injustice and bred competition and dissension among men. The necessary reconciliation of family life and Christian socialism could only be achieved through a new type of "marriage system." This reasoning led young Noyes to investigate the social aspects of the sexual relationship. Here he was blazing a new path and one fraught with grave dangers.

Like Mother Ann and the leaders of other sects, Noyes drew upon his own experience for material for his social theories. An unhappy love affair, after which the woman of his choice married another man, led him to write to a friend:

When the will of God is done on earth as it is in heaven there will be no marriage. Exclusiveness, jealousy, quarreling have no place at the marriage supper of the Lamb. . . . I call a certain woman my wife. She is yours, she is Christ's, and in him she is the bride of all saints. She is now in the hands of a stranger, and according to my promise to her I rejoice. My claim upon her cuts directly across the marriage covenant of this world, and God knows the end.[23]

Noyes recovered from this misadventure in a few years and married Harriet Holton, but their happiness was marred by the fact that four of the five children that came in rapid succession were stillborn. Harriet's suffering, borne so uncomplainingly as a part of woman's lot, made Noyes question both the justice of man's domination over woman and the nature of sexual intercourse. Out of these two experiences grew the doctrines of complex marriage and male continence that were to be the center of the social order established at Oneida.

After Noyes's marriage he settled down in Putney, Vermont, his childhood home, and began to gather about him a few people who subscribed to his teachings. His first converts were his brother George, two sisters, and their husbands. A few others, mostly people with means, came to live with them, and in the early 1840's "communism of property" was decided upon. In 1845 an elaborate constitution was drawn up, and officers were selected. The little group kept its ideas before those interested in perfectionism by the publication of periodicals — first the *Witness*, then the *Perfectionist*, and in 1846 the *Spiritual Magazine*. Thus a new sect, the Perfectionists, was formed.

The life of the little community was very simple; several of its members lived in the Noyes household, others in dwellings near by. They built a little store and a chapel and paid their way from a common purse in charge of a community treasurer. The women of the group did all the housework and cooking, but were freed from part of what they all regarded as "kitchen slavery" by the elimination of formal meals. After an early and substantial breakfast the cooking for the rest of the day was done, all the dishes for the preceding twenty-four hours were washed, food and dishes were conveniently arranged on the pantry shelves, and the women walked out of the kitchen, free from household cares until the next morning.

In work out of doors, also, prolonged and exhausting labor was discouraged. Noyes had studied diet fads and problems of medicine and health. Although not completely vegetarian, the colony ate little meat, avoided drugs, and lived very simply. For a time faith healing was attempted and seeming miracles appeared to justify faith in Noyes's gifts. A kind of lofty spiritualism was preached, for Noyes believed in direct revelation of God's will and did not close his mind to the possibility of spirit intercourse.

The non-Perfectionist members of the Noyes clan and interested friends and neighbors might look with alarm upon the spectacle of John Noyes wasting his inheritance in such a fashion, but there was no great stir of disapproval until rumors began to circulate that the communism of the group had been extended to other things than property. Noyes had made no secret of his antagonism to the institution of marriage and in his lecture trips through New England had openly advocated its abolition or modification. He had himself been legally married, however, as had those who came to live with him at Putney, and there was before 1846 no evidence that the group had disregarded the marriage ties. In that year, after much consultation with his followers, Noyes decided that the last steps should be taken to complete his new social order, and "complex marriage" was instituted with the union of Noyes and Mary Cragin, the wife of another member of the community.

Briefly defined, complex marriage meant that each woman in the group was the wife of every man and that every man was the husband of each woman. No sexual intercourse was permitted, however, without the complete willingness of both parties and without careful regulation. Male continence was practiced, and propagation was regarded as a matter for group discussion. The widest selection for sexual experiences was encouraged, but the Perfectionists resented the charge of "free love," for they held that all matters of sex were more carefully regulated among them than in the "world outside" and that their sex relationships were governed by "sanctions rooted deep in the community religion." Those who fell victims to "special love" were carefully separated, for permanent unions based upon the exclusive love of one man for one woman were regarded as unsocial and as dangerous to communal interests.

These doctrines were not worked out all at once, nor was there any immediate publication of the complex marriage theory, but the little town of Putney was horrified by the mere rumor that it had been put into practice. Fathers sent their daughters away to escape possible contagion, clergymen rose in their wrath and preached anti-Perfectionist sermons, and angry neighbors met to take steps to rid the town of such social rebels. Noyes was arrested, and, although he and his community laughed at the alarm of the orthodox, it was deemed wise to avoid mob action by leaving Putney for regions less conservative — and less inhabited.

Over in New York Perfectionism had been preached by Charles Dutton, a Yale associate of Noyes, and a few persons who had been attracted to the new faith had kept in touch with the Putney group. After visiting with them for some time, Noyes decided that the Oneida Creek region would suit his own purposes, and he arranged for the removal thither of his Vermont followers.

The exodus from Vermont began in 1848, and soon the few buildings in the Oneida wilderness were overcrowded. Building must be done at once, and necessity as well as conviction led Noyes to decide upon a single large communal dwelling. Before their first winter in New York the Perfectionists constructed a four-story barnlike building sixty feet long by thirty-five in width. Into its building went every energy; women worked with the men even in excavating, and Noyes himself worked as mason. For practical reasons the Oneida women in that very summer adopted the simplified dress known as the Bloomer costume and went about in trousers and short-skirted tunics. They cut their hair, also, so as to contribute the time saved to the common cause. After the emergency was over they refused to give up their comfort, and the reformed dress was a part of community practice from 1848 onward.

There was always more work to be done. In 1848 the community numbered fifty-one, in 1849 eighty-seven, and in 1851 two hundred and five. Each year additions had to be made to the "Mansion House";[24] stables, shops, and other buildings had to be erected.

In a local joke the community folks were reported to hang their partitions on hinges, and to set their buildings on castors so they could be moved about more easily.

At first farming and logging were the main industries of the Oneida Community. The Perfectionists endeavored to produce what they consumed, but they had little success and were forced to use part of their original capital of one hundred thousand dollars. Noyes, whose restless energies were not satisfied in rural life, went off to Brooklyn, where he lost a great deal of money in a publishing venture. In 1854 he returned to Oneida to find his colony in serious straits and turned his keen mind to the task of restoring it to solvency. Expenses were cut to the bone, peddlers were sent out to earn a little money by the sale of notions, and Noyes searched for some industrial enterprise that might prove profitable. He found it when a man who had invented a new variety of steel traps joined the community, and all available workmen were used in the manufacture of traps. The enterprise was almost immediately successful; soon Oneida traps were considered the best in the land and were sold as far away as the Hudson's Bay Company. The men of the community were all Americans — nearly all Yankees — and inventive. They utilized water power, invented new machines, practiced until they became skilled laborers, and reaped a huge profit from the manufacture of traps.

Noyes became convinced that the success of the community depended upon industry rather than upon agriculture, and new lines of activity were developed. When peddlers brought back word of the need for sewing and embroidery silks, Noyes sent girls to a Connecticut factory to learn the trade, bought machinery, and started the manufacture of sewing silk. When a group of community women canned more fruit than the household could eat, they sought a market for their surplus outside. Soon they were beset with orders and were forced to purchase fruits from all the neighboring farms to meet the demand. Somewhat later a member of the community began to make silver spoons. When the market proved good, knives and forks were added, and the Perfectionists soon discovered that they had chanced upon their most profitable enterprise. The height of their success in business came after the Civil War and is not a part of this account. It is enough to say that Noyes proved at the

Oneida Community that there was no inherent reason why a communistic settlement could not become a thriving industrial establishment.

The progress of the community toward economic success was accompanied by the development of business administration. In matters of doctrine and social structure the dictate of Noyes was usually sufficient, but for business affairs there was a remarkably modern and efficient organization and careful accounting. Socialism and group enterprise were made effective through the activities of standing committees, twenty-one of them, overseeing finance, amusements, patents, printing, water power, and the like. The business of the community was divided into forty-eight departments, ranging from the silk factory to the day nursery and the preparation of musical programs. The work assignments were in charge of an employment committee, whose policy it was to change the occupation of each individual frequently in order to prevent monotony, class distinction, regimentation, and other evils of industrial work. Special training and special abilities or desires were recognized wherever it seemed best for both the individual and the community. Competitive enterprise was discouraged, and excessive zeal or labor was frowned upon. Wherever the work was of a kind that women could do there was no sex discrimination, and complete equality prevailed.

Community life was designed to be satisfying, well rounded, and not too difficult. The Oneida leaders were not ascetic or overly self-denying. They intended that the members of the community should all be happy, industrious, and contented. The working day was long, but the work itself was not very hard, and food and housing, though simple, were adequate. Economic security and pleasant living conditions were accepted as basic necessities. As the community prospered, labor was hired for the sort of work that was regarded as mere drudgery — and it is notable that household service was one of the first to receive such assistance. Children remained with their mothers until they could walk and were then placed in a general nursery in the care of those who had both training and vocation for the work. They were well supplied with toys and with playtime and were, one author stated, permitted to sleep each morning until they woke of their own accord. Many Oneida practices in child training anticipated those of the so-called progressive schools of a later day.[25] For both children and adults there was a program of amusement and recreation that was varied and interesting: plays, concerts, games, sports, tableaux, lectures, readings — reminiscent of Brook Farm although not perhaps on quite such a lofty intellectual level. Whenever young people of ability desired advanced education, provision was made for sending them to schools or universities in the "outside world," provided the good of the community was advanced thereby. Medicine, law, engineering, and teaching were recognized as special skills of great social value, and the community usually had students "abroad" for such training.

Harmony in community life was recognized as an absolute necessity. Every effort was made to remove the competitive spirit; "special love" was forbidden, the rearing of children was regarded as a communal responsibility, no one type of mind or one variety of labor was given favor over another, and in every case the individual was expected to subordinate his interests to those of the group. All these measures might, however, have failed to produce harmony if there had not existed throughout the history of the community an institution known as "mutual criticism," by which all discord and complaint were forced into the open and both the subject of criticism and his criticizers were put through a moral and emotional purge of great psychological value.

In the early days the whole community attended the criticism, and there was a general discussion and dissection of the victim's motives and shortcomings. As numbers grew, such sessions were usually held before committees over which "Father" Noyes was accustomed to preside; only a *cause célèbre* was heard in full assembly. Allan Estlake, a member of the community, reported one young probationer's account of his first terrifying criticism:

Here was I who had been doing my utmost to lead the right kind of life, had been a laborer in churches, in religious meetings, in Sunday and Ragged Schools; had always stood ready to empty my pockets to the needy — I, who for months had been shaping my conduct and ideas into form . . . to match the requirements of the Oneida Community, was shaken from center to circumference. Every trait of my character that I took any pride or comfort in seemed to be cruelly discounted; and after, as it were, being turned inside out and thoroughly inspected, I was, metaphorically, stood upon my head, and allowed to drain till all the self-righteousness had dripped out of me. . . . For days and weeks after I found myself recalling various passages of my criticism and reviewing them in a new light; the more I pondered, the more convinced I became of the justice of what at first my spirit had so violently rebelled against. In my subsequent experience with criticism, I have invariably found that, in points wherein I thought myself the most abused, I have, on mature reflection, found the deepest truth. *Today I feel that I would gladly give many years of my life if I could have just one more criticism from John H. Noyes.*[26]

All this consideration of the economic and cultural life of the community must not be allowed to obscure the fact that it was deeply rooted in religion and in social theory. John Humphrey Noyes firmly believed that no community could be successful whose basis was not religious, and only a communal home could provide the means for putting into practice the sort of religious doctrine he had developed. Socialism and Perfectionism were inseparable — if Noyes's ideas as to the bases of Perfectionism were accepted. What those views were on the interrelation of religion, communism, and sex, Noyes made clear in a long letter to the English traveler, William Hepworth Dixon, in 1867:

It is evident from what we have seen that Revivals breed social revolutions. All the social irregularities reported in the papers followed in the train of revivals; and, so far as I know, all revivals have developed tendencies to such irregularities. The philosophy of the matter seems to be this: Revivals are theocratic in their very nature; they introduce God into human affairs. . . . In the conservative theory of Revivals, this power is restricted to the conversion of souls; but in actual experience it goes, or tends to go, into all the affairs of life. . . . And the theocratic tendency, if it goes beyond religion, naturally runs first into some form of Socialism. Religious love is very near neighbor to sexual love, and they always get mixed in the intimacies and social excitements of Revivals. The next thing a man wants, after he has found the salvation of his soul, is to find his Eve and his Paradise. . . . A worldly wise man might say, they [these facts] show that Revivals are damnable delusions, leading to immorality and disorganization of society. I should say, they show that Revivals, because they are divine, require for their complement, a divine organization of society, which all who love Revivals and the good of mankind should fearlessly seek to discover and inaugurate. . . . The course of things may be restated thus: Revivals lead to religious love; religious love excites the passions; the converts, finding themselves in theocratic liberty, begin to look about for their mates and their paradise. Here begins divergence. If women have the lead, the feminine idea that ordinary wedded love is carnal and unholy rises and becomes a ruling principle. Mating on the Spiritual plane with all the heights and depths of sentimental love, becomes the order of the day. Then, if a prudent Mother Ann is at the head of affairs, the sexes are fenced off from each other and carry on their Platonic intercourse through the grating. . . . On the other hand, if the leaders are men, the theocratic impulse takes the opposite direction, and polygamy in some form is the result. Thus Mormonism is the masculine form, as Shakerism is the feminine form, of the more morbid products of Revivals. Our Oneida Socialism, too, is a masculine product of the Great Revivals. . . . I made ready for the realization of it by clearing the field in which I worked of all libertinism, and by educating our Putney family in male continence and criticism. When all was ready in 1846, I launched the theory into practice. . . . It is notable that all the socialisms that have sprung from revivals have prospered. They are utterly opposed to each other . . . [yet] however false and mutually repugnant the religious socialisms may be in their details, they are all based on the theocratic principle — they all recognize the right of religious inspiration to shape society and dictate the form of family life. In this Mormons, Shakers, and Bible-Communists agree. I believe this to be a true principle and one that is dear to the heavens . . . and I expect that this principle and not Republicanism, (the mere power of human Law), will at last triumph in some form here and throughout the world.[27]

Since, as one of the Oneida women expressed it, "It was never, in our minds an experiment, we believed we were living under a system which the whole world would sooner or later adopt,"[28] the leaders at Oneida were constantly alert to get their views before the world and to counteract misrepresentation. Visitors were cordially received, the utmost frankness characterized Noyes's discussion of even the most controversial tenets of Perfectionism, and the printing and editorial departments of community business were highly developed. In 1847 Noyes published *The Berean*, a book composed in the main of articles written in the past decade. In the next year appeared the famous *Bible Communism*, which was, as its author said, "the frankest possible disclosure of the theory of entire communism."[29] In this work Noyes's theories of complex marriage and male continence were carefully worked out. The community also published a paper called the *Circular*, which contained not only news but editorials and articles on questions of doctrine and policies. There was never any effort to disguise the social theories of the community, and when Noyes was haled before the courts in

Vermont and New York, he was completely frank and outspoken on the question of his views on sex.

The theories first expounded at Putney remained with very little change until 1879, when, owing to pressure from without, Noyes advised that the whole practice of complex marriage be given up.[30] Almost at once the socialistic basis for community industries came into question, and in 1880 a majority of the group decided upon the incorporation of Oneida Community Ltd., as a joint-stock company, the shares of which should be divided among the erstwhile communists. So ended, in prosperity and amity, one of the most successful and interesting of the social and economic experiments of the period.

CHAPTER 9

Utopian Socialism in America

Often the ideas and aspirations out of which American utopias developed were of foreign origin, and many of them owed little or nothing to religious emotionalism or religious creeds. The rapid advance in mechanization that was altering every aspect of economic life was also causing profound dislocation in the social structure. Complicated and expensive machinery made the factory the industrial unit, and the factory system necessitated concentrations of population to satisfy the demands of the machines for labor. Old towns became larger and new towns were built, and men, women, and children were crowded into them without regard for comfort, sanitation, or adequate living standards. With no asset save the work his hands might do, the laborer was at first without defense against the excessive demands of the captain of industry, and industrial capitalism grew at the expense of the helpless poor. For many years there was a shocking lag between industrial progress and social reorganization. In an appreciation of that lag lay the origin of much of nineteenth-century humanitarianism and utopian socialism, in both Europe and America.

ROBERT OWEN AND NEW HARMONY

Robert Owen was one of the first to recognize the problem and to seek some solution for it. He belonged to the laboring class himself, for he was born in North Wales in 1771 into a poor but self-respecting and independent family. His father was a saddler and ironmonger, and the boy, the sixth of seven children, was given only an elementary education, but he read everything that came his way. Leaving for London to seek his fortune at the mature age of ten, he found employment in a drapery shop owned by a Scotsman named McGuffog, who grew fond of the boy and permitted him to read whatever he chose from his own library. Religion seems to have been the lad's chief preoccupation, perhaps because most of the books in the library were on religious subjects or because McGuffog belonged to the Church of Scotland and his wife to the Church of England and they took the boy with them first to one

church and then to the other. Whatever the reason for his early interest, before he was fourteen he had abandoned all religious belief.
"But my religious feelings," he wrote, "were immediately replaced
by the spirit of universal charity — not for a sect or a party, or for a
country or a colour — but for the human race, and with a real and
ardent desire to do them good." [1]

That desire was never forgotten as the young man climbed to
the top of British industrial society. In a day when other captains
of industry were forgetting or ignoring all the tragedies of the industrial revolution, Robert Owen kept constantly before him the
problem he considered the greatest of the age, the problem that

connects itself with the unexampled increase of productive power,
which human beings in civilized life have acquired in little more than a
single century, and with the momentous question whether this vast gift
of labor-saving inventions is to result in mitigation of the toil and melioration of the condition of the millions who have acquired it. [2]

At New Lanark in Scotland Owen built what was, for his day, a
model factory town, and there he tackled the problems of child
labor, sanitation, education, and other aspects of the machine age
that have since become the concern of social and governmental
agencies. He early recognized the necessity for legislation for the
benefit of the working classes and was an ardent supporter of acts
limiting child labor and providing for factory inspection. After the
close of the Napoleonic conflict in 1815, he espoused the cause of
the unemployed and did everything in his power to persuade his
contemporaries that provision must be made for society's unfortunates.

By 1820 Owen was determined to found some sort of settlement
in which his fundamental social principles could be worked out.
Why did he choose the United States as the field for his first experiment? Chance probably played a part. George Rapp was willing to
sell his establishment in Indiana, and Richard Flower on a visit to
England got in touch with Owen in Rapp's behalf. But there were
other reasons. Owen's imagination had been touched by the glamor
of the unknown. America, with its lack of class rigidity, its ac-
knowledgment of the worth of the common man, and its willingness
to accept the novel and the untried, lured him on. On the frontier,
where vested interests would be weak and distractions and obstruc-

tions would be of little moment, a new social order might have a chance to grow, and a utopia might be created to serve as a model for all mankind.[3]

Before leaving for America Owen himself, in a pamphlet called *Discourses on a New System of Society,* announced his plan to establish at New Harmony, Indiana, an experiment in socialism. In appealing to Americans of liberal ideas he said, "By a hard struggle you have attained political liberty, but you have yet to acquire real mental liberty, and, if you cannot possess yourselves of it, your political liberty will be precarious and of much less value."[4]

The publication of the *Discourses* immediately attracted attention in America, and the arrival of the great philanthropist was eagerly awaited. Late in 1824 Owen and his son William crossed the ocean and went at once to Indiana to inspect the New Harmony site and close the deal with the Rappites. William Owen was left to prepare for the coming of the "industrious and well-disposed," while his father traveled eastward to announce the initiation of the project.

On February 25 and March 7, 1825, Robert Owen spoke in the hall of the House of Representatives in Washington to huge audiences of governmental officials, including President Monroe. These speeches, giving both a statement of his plans and a manifesto of his principles, ended with an invitation to all in sympathy with his ideas to join in the work. Margaret Bayard Smith, who never missed a celebrity or failed to make shrewd comment on an event, recorded in her notebook her understanding of Owen's intentions:

Mr. Owen cares not how degraded, vicious or ignorant his new colonists may be, as he feels the power of his system to be such, that they can soon be rendered virtuous and educated. At Lanark, he said, he had commenced with the dregs of society. In a population of 2400 criminals and ignorant persons, he had never made any punishments or rewards, beyond a small fine, to restrain vice and encourage happiness which resulted from good conduct and to encourage virtue. . . . "They want nothing [he said] and therefore are without temptation — make a man happy and you make him virtuous — this is the whole of my system, to make him happy, I enlighten his mind and occupy his hands, and I have so managed the art of instruction that individuals seek it as an amusement. Two of the most powerful moral agents I use are musick and dancing. Relaxation after labour, and amusement are both physically and morally necessary. Dancing combines both exer-

From a contemporary drawing

Robert Owen

cise and amusement, and of all pleasures musick is the most innocent and exhilarates the spirits while it soothes the passions. I require my people to labour only eight hours out of the twenty-four. Instruction and amusement diversify the intermediate hours." [5]

The response to Owen's invitation was immediate and beyond both expectation and preparation. In the spring and summer of 1825 nine hundred eager colonists arrived on the banks of the Wabash. Although there were few of the "degraded, vicious or ignorant" among them, they were, as Robert Dale Owen wrote, "a heterogeneous collection of radicals, enthusiastic devotees to principle, honest latitudinarians, and lazy theorists, with a sprinkling of unprincipled sharpers thrown in." [6] More than "musick and dancing" would be necessary to weld together the denizens of New Harmony.

Owen himself admitted that the transition from an individualistic to a socialistic system would require time and education — to change the selfish habits of the old order and to prepare for the community of interests of the new. In an address to the first arrivals at New Harmony in April 1825, he called the village a halfway house,

. . . the best half-way house I could procure for those who are going to travel this extraordinary journey with me; and although it is not intended to be our permanent residence, I hope it will be found not a bad traveller's tavern, in which we shall remain only until we can change our old garments, and fully prepare ourselves for the new state of existence into which we hope to enter. [7]

For this probationary period he proposed a temporary constitution recognizing him as sole proprietor of the enterprise, working through a committee that would eventually be entirely elective. Each family was to provide itself with its own furniture and equipment; each able-bodied person was to work, under the guidance of the administrative committee, at some trade or occupation, and for this labor credit would be entered at the public store, from which food and other goods might be drawn. Any member of the association might, during the first year, withdraw upon a week's notice, with the promise of payment in cash for all unexpended credits. In other words, New Harmony started out as a cooperative but not a communistic society. The plant was owned by Owen, and he took all the risk; the others had at stake only what it had cost to transport them to Indiana and the value of such labor as they might perform. At the same time Owen and his agents were in control; all community projects and activities were subject to their dictation, and the whole scheme might be dropped if they so desired.

During the months that Owen remained in America he attracted a goodly number of radical-minded intelligentsia to his project, but they were mostly men of European birth and training. Eminent in this group was William Maclure, sometimes called "the Father of American Geology," a man intensely interested in the new Pestalozzian education. Thomas Say, a zoologist, Charles Alexander Lesueur, naturalist and painter, Constantine Raffinesque, an ichthyologist, and Dr. Gerard Troost, a Dutch scientist, all came to New Harmony to work for the creation of a new order. Joseph Neef, Madame Fretageot, and Phiquepol d'Arusmont, Pestalozzians all, came to aid in the education of a young generation that would be free from all the restrictions and inhibitions of contemporary society and receptive of new ideas. Frances Wright, English reformer and writer, was an enthusiastic visitor. Robert Owen's four sons, all educated in Swiss schools, devoted their energies to various phases of the project, and all contemporary accounts mention the presence of "cultured ladies" and "reformers" whose ideas would today earn them the name of crackpot.

One thing bound these leaders together; they were all freethinkers who had, for one reason or another, discarded religious creeds. Alexander Campbell called New Harmony a "focus of enlightened atheism"; certainly it was the home of scientific materialists intent upon creating a utopia according to their theories of society. The rank and file of community residents were neither atheists nor fanatic theorists; their motives for following Robert Owen to Indiana were a mixture in which desire for land, economic security, and interesting society were predominant. Although the group had so few characteristics in common that generalizations are difficult, it is clear that they were, one and all, individualistic and unfitted by temperament or any previous experience for community discipline.

In the first year the great lack was skilled workmen. The executive committee hoped to operate all the Rappite industries and to make some progress with Owen's elaborate plans for community buildings. These were to form a hollow square one thousand feet long, and were to house an academy and a university as well as all departments of community life. Actually it was possible to accomplish relatively little. The saw and grist mills were operated with profit; the hat- and boot-making shops were successful; soap, candles, and glue were made in excess of the needs of the community. But the dyeworks, the pottery, and the cotton and woolen mills were idle. The village was so overcrowded that housing conditions were bad, and there was little room for social and recreational activities. William Owen anxiously wrote his father that there was no room for more, and that all applicants must be refused admission except those who were masons, carpenters, bricklayers, cooks, or laundresses. Equipment was as deficient as were laborers; shingles, bricks, lime, boards, and all sorts of supplies must be produced by the community before they could be used in building.

But in spite of all these initial difficulties, life at New Harmony was not without its compensations. There was great energy, ceaseless activity, and much good fellowship. The schools were quickly established and were run on Pestalozzian principles, which must have necessitated novel and amusing adjustments when applied on the Western frontier. A newspaper, the *New Harmony Gazette*, was printed with William and Robert Dale Owen as editors, a Philanthropic Lodge of Masons was installed, and a Female Social Society was organized. There were social gatherings almost nightly at which the "musick and dancing" upon which Owen depended were encouraged. Lectures on the social system and on cooperative principles were frequent. There were no community religious services, and no religious instruction in the schools, but permission was given to ministers of any faith to preach in the old Rappite church if they so desired. On Sunday mornings, however, the church was reserved for lectures on the social order.

Robert Owen spent a part of 1825 in England, but he returned to the Indiana village in January 1826 and at once threw himself into the work of organizing and directing the enterprise. Whatever success it had seems to have been due to his administrative ability. Because New Harmony residents believed that his business experience would bring order out of chaos and ensure success, they worked with greater energy under his direction. Encouraged by their efforts and eager to put his principles to the test of experience,

Owen declared the probationary period at an end, although it had lasted only nine months instead of the two or more years of his original plan. A constitution for a Community of Equality was drawn up.[8] Provision was made for complete communism, lawmaking power was vested in an assembly composed of all adult residents, and executive power was given to a council composed of the community officers and the superintendents of the departments of community enterprise. These departments were six: agriculture, manufacture, literature, science, education, domestic economy, general economy, and commerce.

For a time Owen's ability as a manager seemed to make the plan work, but dissension soon appeared, and one constitutional amendment followed another in rapid succession. The community seemed to fluctuate between a desire for the town-meeting type of democratic control and an acceptance of the imported theory of guild, or occupational, socialism. Then on July 4, 1826, Owen made public his Declaration of Mental Independence, in which he condemned the institution of private property, the control of organized religion, and the bondage of the marriage ties. These ideas were acceptable to very few Americans, and they greatly weakened the popular appeal of the New Harmony movement.

When the new constitution had been put into effect, Owen made another long visit to England, leaving New Harmony in the hands of his sons and his scientific friends. That their difficulties were many was evidenced by the pleas of the *Gazette* for concord and unanimity among the residents of the village seemingly misnamed Harmony. Some of the specific admonitions are revealing indeed. Community members were urged, among other things, to abstain from abuse, "growling," and loud talking; to give up "grumbling, carping, and murmuring" against those who shirked work; to be tolerant toward the intemperate and those who had the "disease of laziness"; to keep children under control, and out of the dining room at mealtime; to feel no anger against "female members upon their aversion to the work of cooperation, or when they brawl, quarrel, or indulge in loud talk."

Dissension, due either to conflicting theories or to dissatisfaction with the lack of religious organization, had led to the founding of several offshoots of New Harmony — Yellow Springs, Macluria,

Feiba Peveli, and half a dozen others, all near the village of New Harmony.* These communities were also in a precarious state.

When Owen returned in 1827 and surveyed the results of two years of education in cooperative living, he was ready to admit his failure. Perhaps Owen the businessman, faced with an insolvent concern, was ready to write the undertaking off and acknowledge his losses; perhaps Owen the paternalistic reformer, recognizing that here he had material quite different from his docile Scottish laborers, could see no solution to the problem and wished to drop the whole embarrassing puzzle. In any case, he proposed that the whole project be returned to him for settlement and dissolution.

The New Harmony settlers were to be given lands on long lease or through sale at low prices, and each settler or group was to have every accommodation Owen could grant. As for himself, he wished to withdraw at once and permanently, writing off as lost about four fifths of his personal fortune. Many of the New Harmony residents took advantage of his terms and remained in the neighborhood as small farmers or artisans long after their efforts at utopianism were forgotten. The subsidiary communities broke up on similar terms, and their villages were deserted. Robert Owen returned to his career as reformer and philanthropist in Great Britain, handing over to his sons, who remained to become valuable American citizens, all that remained of his holdings on the Wabash.

Many reasons have been given for the fate of this, the first creation in the New World of utopian socialism on a European model. Its failure was inevitable, says the eminent British guild socialist, G. D. H. Cole, because the whole project was the work of a small group of idealists each trying to put his own ideals into practice.[9] And Robert Owen himself said with sorrow:

I tried here a new course for which I was induced to hope that fifty years of political liberty had prepared the American population . . . but experience proved that the attempt was premature to unite a number of strangers not previously educated for that purpose, who should carry on extensive operations for their common interest, and live together as a common family.[10]

The merits and defects of the colony during its brief existence

* There were a number of Owenite groups elsewhere, not financially connected with New Harmony: twelve in Indiana, three in New York, two in Ohio, and one each in Pennsylvania and Tennessee. They all disappeared before 1830.

were subjects for comment by various European and American travelers. One of the shrewdest of them was Bernhard, Duke of Saxe-Weimar Eisenach, whose *Travels Through North America during the Years 1825 and 1826* contained a long description of life at New Harmony. The duke believed the project appeared to succeed only when Owen was present and dictated policy, that it relapsed into anarchy when he was absent. He thought that Owen, for all his practical abilities, was a theorist who looked "for nothing less than to remodel the world entirely; to root out all crime; to abolish all punishment; to create similar views and similar wants, and in this manner to avoid all dissension and war-fare." In place of this concord the duke found an obstinate adherence to self-interest and social distinctions that prevented happy relationships, for the "young ladies and gentlemen of quality will not mix with the common sort, and I believe that all well brought up members are disgusted and will soon abandon the society." [11]

In a pamphlet entitled *Twelve Months in New Harmony*, Paul Brown expressed the discontent of the commoner at New Harmony. He accused Owen of lack of generosity, of insincerity, and of lack of integrity and magnanimity. There was, he felt, too much music and dancing, too much education, too much red tape, and too little food. "The place was full of clamor, disaffections, and calumny." While the "aristocrats" quarreled with the commoners the cabbage fields went to ruin. The plebeian Brown confirmed the German aristocrat's opinion of irreconcilable social differences, stating that "the people of the town continued strangers to each other, in spite of all their meetings, their balls, their frequent occasions of congregating in the hall, and all their pretense of cooperation."

Unjust as Brown's pamphlet undoubtedly was, it was evidence of the discontent at New Harmony. "Owenism" was sweeping and iconoclastic in theory but without any consistent and considered plan. The failure to regulate either the number or the type of members and the lack of economic self-sufficiency doomed the colony from the beginning. [12] William and Robert Dale Owen, who lived more closely in touch with the people of New Harmony than did their father and who came to know American conditions far better than he could know them, gave their estimate of the experiment in a valedictory editorial in the *Gazette*:

Our opinion is that Robert Owen ascribed too little influence to the early anti-social circumstances that had surrounded many of the quickly collected inhabitants of New Harmony before their arrival there, and too much to those circumstances which his experience might enable them to create around themselves in the future.

And some years later Robert Dale Owen shrewdly remarked that the United States was a poor place, after all, for a communistic experiment, because wages were too high and land was too cheap to foster any feeling of the necessity for cooperative action. Certainly Robert Owen, the European theorist, despite his expenditure of energy and funds and his enthusiasm and sincerity, could not find a common ground upon which a thousand ill-assorted Americans could work for a new social order.

FRANCES WRIGHT AND NASHOBA

The name of Frances Wright will always be associated with that of Robert Owen, and her activities in the United States were an expression of the same humanitarian and socialistic thinking that motivated him. Frances Wright was the daughter of a Scottish tradesman who had won the suspicion of his fellow townsmen by subsidizing a cheap edition of Thomas Paine's *Rights of Man*. Born shortly before 1800, she came into a world full of revolutionary ideas, and her life was one of devotion to the many causes that appealed to her ready sympathy. Even in her orphaned childhood she espoused the cause of the poor and upbraided her wealthy relatives for injustice in the distribution of riches. Her interest in the United States was aroused at an early age when she heard a Tory aunt speak of the wickedness of the colonials who had rebelled against their king. Upon attaining her majority and some control over her slender fortune, she set sail for the United States with her younger sister, writing to a disapproving uncle that she chose America for her travels rather than Italy because "a new country inhabited by free men was . . . more worthy to attract curiosity than countries in ruins inhabited by slaves." [13]

With the keenest interest the young women traveled extensively through the Northern states. In New York they made acquaintances in literary and dramatic circles, for Frances hoped to be a poet and a playwright; indeed her play *Altorf* was produced in New York City but it had little success. Upon returning to England in 1820 she set herself to write the usual travel book, and in *Views of Society and Manners in America in a Series of Letters from that Country during the Years 1818, 1819, and 1820 by an Englishwoman* she described American democratic institutions in terms so glowing as to win the disapproval of all British aristocrats and the plaudits of European liberals.

Thereafter Frances traveled widely and met numerous celebrities — the most important being General Lafayette, of whom she became a great admirer and the almost constant companion, much to the embarrassment of the gentleman's family. When Lafayette sailed for America in 1824 for his triumphal journey through the country that claimed him as citizen and savior, the Wright sisters followed him, expecting to travel as near the entourage of their "adopted father" as the proprieties would allow. The ardent Frances had at that time no other idea than those of keeping near her idol and of renewing her acquaintance with the land she had learned to love some years before. But events in America changed her plans and involved her for many years in New World reforms.

Frances Wright undoubtedly met and talked with Robert Owen in Washington and found herself much intrigued by his schemes for a Western utopia. Owen, however, was completely cold to a cause that Frances had embraced. Some years before, through conversations with Jefferson, she had become interested in the problem of Negro slavery and had often thought of the necessity for giving the slave education enough to protect him when he should acquire his freedom. Could not Owen's idea of a cooperative settlement in the West be successfully combined with an experiment in the education of the Negro?

Frances Wright had long been interested also in the English colony in Illinois founded by George Flower and Morris Birkbeck for the benefit of English immigrants driven across the sea by the depression at the close of the Napoleonic Wars. The resistance of the English Prairie to the attempt to legalize slavery in Illinois increased Miss Wright's interest, and in the early spring of 1825 she set out for Illinois to discuss her ideas with George Flower, who had rented lands to free Negroes and had already purchased twenty-five slaves, freed them, and sent them to Haiti. En route the Wright sisters stopped at New Harmony, where the Rappites were packing their goods and William Owen was preparing for the eager hundreds that were soon to arrive.

In George Flower Frances found a friend and ally with whom to work out her nebulous plans for the Negro race; he seemed to find nothing chimerical in her scheme for introducing Owenite theories on a slave plantation in the South. Together they created, on paper, a model community with farms, schools, and workshops where grateful slaves would work eagerly in a common effort to win their freedom and to acquire skills that would earn them a livelihood when they were free.

Giving up all thought of returning to Europe, Miss Wright went on to New Orleans, searching along the way for a site for the projected experiment. Land near Memphis, Tennessee, won her favor, and she went back to New England to enlist the support of Northern abolitionists. In the summer of 1825 she published a pamphlet, *A Plan for the Gradual Abolition of Slavery in the United States without Danger of Loss to the Citizens of the South*, which was a direct bid for government participation. Her proposal was for a donation of public lands in various sections of the South where experimental farms might be established similar to the one she was about to open in Tennessee. Initial expenses, she felt, might be met by the subscriptions of philanthropists, and she optimistically predicted that, although each of these farms would require an investment of $41,000, the first year's profits, after deducting interest, would be about $10,000! Upon each farm fifty to one hundred Negroes would labor for freedom. Five to ten years was considered the time it would take an able-bodied slave to repay the price paid for him and to acquire the industrial education necessary for him in a free life. Eventual colonization outside the United States was planned for all Negroes thus trained and emancipated.

Fantastic as this scheme seems today, Frances Wright worked wholeheartedly to put it into effect. She bought the Tennessee plantation, already called Nashoba, and on it, with the aid of George Flower, she soon established nine adult slaves and a few children. A record of the short-lived colony was kept in the "Journal of the Plantation," which still exists to bear pathetic witness to the difficulties that beset the courageous Scotswoman. The slaves once installed and an overseer, Richesson Whitbey, secured to manage the

estate, Frances spent much of her time in the more congenial society of New Harmony, where she became a leader in the discussion of all sorts of radical theories. In 1826 she drew up a deed of
trust that stated her dual objective for Nashoba: a model training
plantation where blacks might buy their freedom and a white cooperative community on the Owenite plan. Ten trustees were designated, and among them Frances, with characteristic optimism,
named several famous men who did not learn of their selection until
Nashoba became notorious.

With the decline of New Harmony, Miss Wright's ideas of the
future of Nashoba grew more grandiose. Her dreams transmuted
the little group of log huts in the wilderness into a beautiful community where kindred souls might commune while every bodily
need was cared for by devoted Negroes whom she had started on
their road to freedom. In the spring of 1827, however, when she
revisited Nashoba with Robert Dale Owen, she found that her
dream and the reality were far apart. As Owen wrote many years
later,

. . . even sanguine I had to admit that the outlook was unpromising.
The land was all second rate only, and scarce a hundred acres of it cleared.
Three or four squared log houses and a few small cabins for the slaves
the only buildings. Slaves released from the fear of the lash worked in-
dolently under the management of Whitby, whose education in an easy-
going Shaker village had not at all fitted him for the post of plantation
overseer. . . . Discouraging enough, certainly! [14]

Leaving poor fever-ridden Camilla Wright, an eccentric named
Richardson, and the hapless Whitbey in charge, Frances and Robert Dale Owen went abroad in search of "congenial associates" and
new inspiration. When Miss Wright returned in the late winter,
Frances Trollope traveled with her and stopped for a few days at
Nashoba. Her keen eyes were not blinded by her friend's rosy
dreams, and her comment was a clear prediction of the crash that
was soon to come:

The forest [as they approached Nashoba] became thicker and more
dreary looking every mile we advanced; but our ever grinning negro
declared it was a right good road, and that we should be sure to get to
Nashoba, and so we did . . . and one glance sufficed to convince me,
that every idea I had formed of the place was as far as possible from the
truth. Desolation was the only feeling — the only word that presented

itself; but it was not spoken. I think, however, that Miss Wright was aware of the effect her forest-home produced on me; and I doubt not that the conviction reached us both at the same moment, that we had erred in thinking that a few months passed together at this spot could be productive of pleasure to either, but to do her justice, I believe her mind was so exclusively occupied by the object she had then in view, that all things else were worthless or indifferent to her, I never heard or read of any enthusiasm approaching hers, except in a few instances, in ages past, of religious fanaticism.[15]

This quality of enthusiasm or fanaticism Mrs. Trollope might have discovered some weeks before if she had been permitted to read a dissertation that Miss Wright wrote on shipboard. It was entitled, "Explanatory Notes Respecting the Nature and Object of the Institution at Nashoba and the Principles upon Which It Is Founded: Addressed to the Friends of Human Improvement in All Countries and of All Nations." The appearance of this tract in the *Memphis Advocate* was the death knell of Nashoba and of Frances Wright's influence in much of America, for in it she stated her iconoclastic views on social problems. She commended Owen's cooperative principles, except that in her village manual labor was to be done by slaves. She tacitly approved miscegenation and openly advocated the abolition of the institution of marriage, adding a bit of dynamite with the remark,

Let us not teach, that virtue consists in the crucifying of the affections and appetites, but in their judicious government! Let us not attach ideas of purity to monastic chastity, impossible to man or woman without consequences fraught with evil, nor ideas of vice to connexions formed under auspices of kind feeling.

The furor of criticism that met this announcement did not greatly disturb Miss Wright, but the monotony and desolation of Nashoba finally conquered her. In April 1828 she left the plantation and went to New Harmony, where she lived a far more congenial life of giving lectures and assisting in editing the *New Harmony Gazette*. She found a new interest in the denunciation of the Christian religion and conducted a campaign in opposition to revivals. The clergy named her the Priestess of Beelzebub, for they feared the keen analytical mind and the dramatic oratory of this opponent whose audiences were always large if not always approving.

Later in the year the indefatigable Fanny appointed Whitbey, now the husband of her sister Camilla, as attorney to settle the affairs of bankrupt Nashoba and departed for a broader field in New York. Arrangements were finally made to free all the Nashoba Negroes and take them to Haiti, where they were established in homes of their own.

Miss Wright's reputation as a radical speaker had preceded her to New York, and the Masonic Hall — hired with her private funds — was filled to capacity with those who were determined to hear her lectures, interrupted though they were by heckling, by smoke-producing devices, and by sudden darkness when her adversaries turned off the gas. Her enemies found fresh ammunition against her when Lewis and Arthur Tappan, strict Presbyterians and owners of the *Journal of Commerce*, began to publish excerpts from her "Explanatory Notes." Assailed as a "woman impervious to the voice of virtue and case-hardened against shame" and as "a female monster whom all decent people ought to avoid," Fanny felt the need of a press of her own and decided to print in New York a second issue of the *Free Enquirer*, the new name of the *New Harmony Gazette*, of which she was still an editor. This new enterprise brought her into contact with New York labor leaders, who awakened her interest in what was to be her last great cause in America — the cause of the workingman.

THE STATUS OF AMERICAN LABOR

The years since the beginning of the nineteenth century had witnessed a rapid mechanization of industry in the seaboard states, and factory towns had sprung up like mushrooms wherever water power ensured success for enterprise. The old period of domestic handicraft seemed nearing its end in America as in Europe. At first few persons recognized the trend of the time or the social consequences of industrialization. Men had always worked long hours, and women and children in the village and on the farm had borne their full share of work from dawn to dusk. To some the factory offered opportunity for labor pleasanter and more remunerative than any they had yet known. Many craftsmen, however, feared the machine as an impersonal and implacable rival but saw no way of blocking its progress. Some communities eagerly sought the profits and benefits of the new order; others resented the changes made by steam and **water power.**

On the surface at least the United States seemed able to escape the direst consequences of rapid industrialization, for scarcity of labor and high living standards prevented the abject poverty and misery of the early factory towns in England. Nearly every British traveler in the 1830's was taken to Lowell and Waltham, Massachusetts, to view what were considered model factory towns. Almost without exception their accounts paid tribute to the cleanliness, the healthfulness, and the generally high standards of town, textile factory, and workers. In his *American Notes* Dickens called attention to the independence and self-respect of the well-dressed, well-mannered working girls of Lowell. He mentioned good working conditions, good boardinghouses provided with "joint stock" pianos, the fewness of children in the factory, the factory library, and the newspaper entirely managed by the girls, whose own articles, poems, and stories appeared in its pages.[16] Harriet Martineau "rejoiced" as she watched a procession of well-dressed mechanics, and although she thought American working people labored harder than those of their class in England, she believed they were better paid, better fed, and healthier.[17]

Michel Chevalier also visited Lowell and observed the conditions carefully. He stated that most of the five thousand girls operating the mills were daughters of New England farmers who expected to work in the factory four or five years in order to save two or three hundred dollars for themselves or their parents. A seventy-hour week was not too strenuous for these healthy farm girls, and their five years' residence did not menace their future welfare. They were housed in company boardinghouses, and from one third to one half of their three-dollar weekly wage was deducted in payment for food and lodging. Church attendance was required, neither card games nor "ardent spirits" were permitted, and any "dissolute" worker was assured dismissal. Chevalier believed that scarcity of labor, as well as Puritan standards, led the factory owners to safeguard the welfare of their employees.[18]

None of the travelers seem to have asked the girls what they thought of the life they must lead in the factory towns. The girls came in willingly at first, but by 1846 conditions had changed. We read that "a long, low, black wagon, termed a 'slaver,' makes trips to the north of the state [Massachusetts] cruising around Vermont and New Hampshire, with a commander who is paid one dollar a head for all [the girls] he brings to market and more in proportion to the distance — if they bring them from a distance they cannot easily get back." [19]

Nearly every traveler mentions in this connection that cheap land in the West was one reason for labor scarcity and high wage scales.* And, indeed, as New England girls left the hill farms to work in the village mill, or went even farther afield to find work in the new factory towns, many of New England's young men were turning from the stone-choked fields of their home states to the more productive lands of the Ohio country. Both movements were a part of the transformation of the Northeast from an agrarian to an industrial economy. When a small textile factory was built somewhere on almost every little stream on which water power could be developed, the transition from domestic to factory production was made without much difficulty. The growth of factory towns on the larger streams came more slowly, and it was not until after 1830 that American labor faced all the problems of the new industrial order. Even then the wide expanse of free land and the workingman's possession of the franchise were factors that distinguished the problems of the American laborer from those of the European worker.

Labor solidarity, or self-consciousness, was slow in coming under such conditions. Before 1825 there were only a few local "associations" and those in but a few trades. These societies were often of a benevolent or mutual insurance nature and bore little resemblance to modern labor organizations. The cordwainers (shoemakers) of Philadelphia and New York seem to have been the first workingmen's group to organize to raise wages, and in the first great legal decision on a labor issue the Philadelphia shoemakers in 1815 were penalized for conspiracy. Labor organization in itself was never declared illegal in American courts, and no laws against such combinations were passed, but for a twenty-year period union activities were blocked by a conservative judiciary acting on proof of con-

---

* This is the so-called safety-valve theory that was made much of throughout the nineteenth century. Whether or not mechanics actually went West was never ascertained. Modern scholarship has attacked the theory, but the substance of the articles on the subject leaves the basic facts of the effect of the West unchallenged. If mechanics cannot be shown to have gone West, cheap land did drain off immigrants and the farm boys of the East, and labor scarcity remained a factor in American life.[20]

spiracy. It was not until 1840 in the case of *Commonwealth* v. *Hunt* that a chief justice of the Massachusetts supreme court, in a stirring decision, held the action of workingmen in combining to raise wages to be legal.[21]

And so the first steps were taken on the long road toward the participation of labor in determining the conditions under which it must work. The depression of 1819 acted as a temporary deterrent, but with the return of prosperity in the early twenties progress was rapid. From 1825 to 1837 hundreds of local trade societies were formed, city federations of these societies were organized, and, as the boom of the early thirties brought rising commodity prices, national associations arose in various crafts which in 1834 combined in a National Trades' Union. In this period a New York newspaper asserted that two thirds of the workers of that city were organized. Alarmed employers combined in associations of their own to combat this hothouse growth of labor organizations, and there were repeated conflicts showing many of the aspects of modern industrial strife — strikes, picketing, ostracism of scabs, black-listing, boycotts, and so on.

Realization of his own needs and of the position of his class in the young republic led the American workingman to make political action one of his first concerns. With other Americans he had accepted the doctrines of the Declaration of Independence without question; he now began to feel that the only equality he possessed was the equality of manhood suffrage, and he wished to use that franchise to procure the changes he desired. The candidacy of Andrew Jackson and the platform of the new Democratic party gave workingmen a focus in national politics; for local issues they created their own party — or parties, for each large city had its own. The first labor party in world history was organized in Philadelphia in July 1828.[22] The new party had as its organ the *Mechanics' Free Press*, and in New York a similar local party had the benefit of Frances Wright's *Free Enquirer* and of a new paper, the *Working Man's Advocate*, with which she was so closely affiliated that its platform was nicknamed "the Fanny Wright ticket."

The demands of labor were much the same everywhere. Labor party platforms proposed (1) equal universal education, (2) the abolition of imprisonment for debt, (3) the abolition of licensed monopolies, (4) the revision of the militia system, (5) a less expensive legal system, (6) equal property taxes, (7) an effective lien law for laborers on buildings, (8) a district system of election, and (9) no legislation on religion and the removal of all religion restrictions. This formal program was augmented by an eager espousal of almost every variety of reform. The workingmen championed the cause of temperance, the abolition of capital punishment, the abolition of child labor, and a ten-hour day, and they condemned lotteries, the "conspiracy" decisions, and competition with prison labor. Encouraged by some slight success in city elections the labor press in 1830 announced triumphantly: "From Maine to Georgia, within a few months past, we discern symptoms of a revolution which will be second to none save that of '76." And again, "Throughout this vast republic, the farmers, mechanics, and working men are assembling . . . to impart to its laws and administration those principles of liberty and equality unfolded in the Declaration of our Independence." [23]

The year 1830 marked the peak of the activities of the workingmen's parties. There was a decline in the next year, and in 1832 separate political organization of labor was ended as the workingmen flocked to the polls to re-elect Andrew Jackson, who was as much their idol as he was the hero of the new West. Then, as throughout the century since 1830, the American federal system was a barrier to the creation of a national labor party and a contributing cause for the abandonment of local political organizations. With the increase in prosperity after 1832 the workingmen turned to direct action for their own betterment, and the union movement grew at the expense of political combination. The climax came in 1834 with the organization of the New England Association of Farmers, Mechanics and other Workingmen. This union of all kinds of workers showed great promise until the panic of 1837 put an end to its brief career.

The depression that followed this panic was one of the worst the nation has ever experienced, and not until 1843 could any return of prosperity be noted. In September 1837 *Niles' Register* reported that nine tenths of the country's factories were closed and that there was unemployment everywhere. During the late thirties there were in all cities voluntary societies for relief of the poor. Many gave money; among those without money but with quickened sympathy was young Horace Greeley, who spent his days visiting New York's destitute. Years later he wrote:

I saw two families, including six or eight children burrowing in one cellar under a stable, — a prey to famine on the one hand and to vermin and cutaneous maladies on the other, with sickness adding its horrors to those of a polluted atmosphere and a wintry temperature. I saw some men who each, somehow, managed to support his family on an income of five dollars per week or less, yet who cheerfully gave something to mitigate the sufferings of those who were *really* poor. I saw three widows, with as many children, living in an attic on the profits of an apple stand which yielded less than three dollars per week, and the landlord came in for a full third of that. But worst to bear of all was the pitiful plea of stout, resolute, single young men and young women: "We do not want alms; we are not beggars; we hate to sit here day by day idle and useless; help us to work, — we want no other help; why is it that we have nothing to do?" [24]

In those dark years labor lost all its gains, and labor unions were abandoned. Whereas the demand for workers during the preceding boom had given labor a basis for collective bargaining, unemployment produced docility and gave employers an advantage they were not to lose until the Civil War period. Meanwhile the cause of the workingman was furthered more through the efforts of sympathetic humanitarians than through those of the workingmen themselves.

Frances Wright was not the only person of importance to champion the cause of labor. Robert Dale Owen and his fellow worker at New Harmony, Phiquepol d'Arusmont, whom Miss Wright later married, were with her from the first. In 1829 Orestes Brownson, then a Universalist minister, heard her lecture and became interested in the Owen-Wright theories. He contributed various articles to the *Free Enquirer*, was associated with the Working Man's party in New York, and was for many years a Democrat. Brownson became a consistent defender of the rights of minorities, and in his editorials in the *Democratic Review* and in his many lectures he advocated free schools, industrial education, and social justice. Others sought a solution, in the fashion characteristic of the time, by establishing socialist utopias for the working classes.

Robert Owen's dream phalanstery

New Harmony as it was

*Frances Wright,
courageous dreamer*

Nashoba — the desolate reality of Frances Wright's dream

FOURIERIST PHALANXES

Through a series of articles entitled "What Shall Be Done about Labor?" which he wrote for the *New Yorker*, Horace Greeley came in touch with Albert Brisbane, who had studied in Paris the theories of the French socialists, Saint-Simon and Charles Fourier. Greeley accepted many of Brisbane's ideas, and together they wrote for the *Future*, the *Tribune*, and also occasionally for the *Plebeian*, the *Democrat*, and the *Dial*. Brisbane was already the author of *The Social Destiny of Man*, an exposition of the doctrines of Fourier, and in 1843 he published *A Concise Exposition of the Doctrine of Association*, which became the Bible of American Fourierism. These two crusaders for social reorganization were joined by Parke Godwin, whose *Popular View of the Doctrines of Charles Fourier* brought those doctrines nearer the level of the common man.

Brisbane's philosophy was most clearly expressed in a quotation given in his wife's *Albert Brisbane: A Mental Biography:*

Far away in the distant future I saw a globe resplendent, cultivated and embellished, transformed into the grandest and most beautiful work of art by the combined efforts of humanity. I saw upon it a race developed, perfected by the continued influence, generation after generation, of true social institutions; a humanity worthy of that Cosmic Soul of which I instinctively felt it to be a part.[25]

Horace Greeley summarized his own social creed in the following terms: There should be no paupers and no surplus labor; unemployment indicates sheer lack of brains, and inefficiency in production and waste in consumption of the product of a national industry that has never worked to half its capacity have resulted in social anarchy; isolation is the curse of the laboring classes, and only in unity can a solution be found for the problems of labor; therefore, education is the great desideratum, and in association the future may be assured.[26]

These views were in accord with Brisbane's somewhat loftier statement, but the two men in action were poor team-mates. Brisbane was nonplused at the rapid spread of the idea of association in response to Greeley's newspaper campaign. He had expected years of hard work and a slow accumulation of capital before the first Fourierist phalanx could be established. He felt that no association could succeed until all "the faculties of the soul found adequate expression" within the community. Life within the phalanx must be more attractive in every way than that in the world outside. But Greeley was eager to try the associative idea in miniature as an immediate palliative for the hardships of depression.

As we have seen, the Brook Farm experiment in Fourierism was disappointing for Greeley and Brisbane and disastrous for the Farm. Many other short-lived phalanxes were formed — between forty and fifty in all: six each in New York and Pennsylvania, eight in Ohio, three in Massachusetts, two in New Jersey, and others in Illinois, Michigan, Wisconsin, Indiana, and Iowa.[27] Their average duration was two years — and that only because one of them lasted twelve years.

Only two of these attempts merit further mention. The Sylvania Phalanx, established in 1842, was the first and had Greeley for its treasurer. Its site, selected by a landscape painter, a doctor, and a cooper, was some twenty-three hundred acres of land in northern Pennsylvania, where land was cheap because of barren soil and lack of access to markets. On the land were an old gristmill and three frame houses, which were expected to accommodate more than a hundred settlers from the New York and Albany working classes. Only four acres of the land were tillable, and the return on it in the one year of the settlement was eleven bushels of grain. The experiment cost Greeley five thousand dollars, which his heirs eventually recovered from the increased value of the timber growing on the original tract.

The North American Phalanx, founded in 1843, was the Fourierist colony that lasted for twelve years. Brisbane, Godwin, Greeley, Ripley, and Channing were all interested in it and much was written about it. Noyes called it the "test-experiment on which Fourierism practically staked its all in this country."

The site chosen was near Red Bank, New Jersey, where good farm land and easy access to markets were available. In September 1843 a few families took possession and began the construction of community buildings. Within a year the number of residents rose to ninety, and it was never much larger. Agriculture was expected to be the chief occupation of the association, but a gristmill was built and a few small industries were carried on under the Fourier system of groups and series. The original investment was eight thousand dollars; in 1852 the value of the property was estimated at eighty thousand dollars with an outstanding debt of less than twenty thousand. Greeley was probably correct in stating, when the colony disbanded in 1854, that financial failure was not the cause, for when all books were closed the stockholders were paid two thirds of the face value of their shares.

Each member was given the choice of the work he should perform, and each worked as much or as little as he chose. The wage scale varied, the highest rate, about ten cents an hour, going to "necessary but repulsive" labor and the lowest to agreeable work. Each worker was credited with the amount and kind of his or her labor each day and paid in full every month, any profits being divided annually. Rent was charged for lodging, and meals were served à la carte, with a small monthly dining room service charge. The earnings of phalanx members were low, but so were all living costs. The members were somewhat on the Brook Farm order and were for the most part congenial and happy. Many of them said in later years that the experience in the phalanx was the happiest part of their lives. But realization of Brisbane's ideal of a socially complete community was as distant in 1854 as in 1843.

All the many visitors to the North American Phalanx mention the pleasant friendly atmosphere, but they do not fail to state that plain living, no luxuries, and few comforts were the accompaniment of high thinking. Fredrika Bremer included a careful description of Red Bank in her *Homes of the New World*. She mentioned all the attractive features of cooperative housekeeping, economic security, and simple but comfortable living, but she concluded with the wail of the true individualist, that she would rather live "on the bleakest granite mountain of Sweden, alone by myself, and live on bread, and water, and potatoes . . . than in a Phalanstery on the most fertile soil, in the midst of associate brethren and sisters!" [28]

The members of the phalanx must have at heart agreed with her. When their mill burned in 1854 and they met to consider Greeley's offer of a loan to finance rebuilding, some intrepid soul unexpectedly moved that they make no effort to rebuild but instead dissolve the phalanx, and much to their own surprise, the motion carried by a large majority. What a free people might choose to create in the way of association, they were equally free to undo, and the rejection of the principle was as voluntary as its adoption.

ETIENNE CABET AND ICARIA

Only one other American utopia need be described. It, too, was European in origin, but, unlike the Owen and Fourier settlements, it was European in personnel as well. Etienne Cabet was born in Dijon, France, in 1788, the son of a cooper. Becoming interested in democracy in a day when democracy was criminal radicalism, he joined the French Carbonari, was imprisoned and exiled for his political beliefs, and became recognized as a socialist leader. In 1840 he published a book entitled *Le Voyage en Icarie*, which elaborated his idea of a communistic society. This treatise was widely read and was followed by the publication of other tracts and a periodical, *Populaire*, further describing the sort of social order he wished to create. Groups of urban artisans were formed all over France to study his theories. They adopted the name Icarian and subscribed with enthusiasm to all his writings.

In May 1847, when his followers were said to number four million, Cabet suggested that they found their Icaria in the new American state of Texas, a site selected apparently on the advice of Robert Owen, with whom Cabet was in correspondence. Soon Cabet was visited by agents of the ever-alert land companies, and he selected for the settlement a vast tract of a million acres in the valley of the Red River, "a beautiful stream," *Populaire* declared, "navigable up to our very settlement, and we will be able to extend our territory indefinitely." [29] Early in February 1848, without waiting for the report of agents sent to inspect the lands in Texas, more than three hundred men embarked for Icaria, after agreeing to accept Cabet as dictator for a period of ten years.

This advance guard reached New Orleans on the 27th of March, only to be met with disillusionment. Shreveport, Louisiana, could be reached by boat, but Icaria lay two hundred and fifty miles beyond, across a trackless wilderness of prairies, swamps, trees, and unbridged streams. They could acquire but one wagon and three ox teams; all their bulky equipment had to be left in Shreveport. On the long march scores fell ill, food was scarce, and their hardships were almost unbearable. And when they reached the Red River lands the chimera of a million fertile acres vanished. Each settler was to have a half section provided he built a house on it by July 1; after that date he would have to buy his land at the rate of a dollar an acre. But worse than that, the half sections were not contiguous but were separated by other half sections retained by the company, whose own grant from Texas had been in the form of alternate sections.

The valiant settlers did manage by July 1 to secure more than ten thousand acres scattered in two townships — but how could they found a commune with unitary dining halls and cooperative agriculture? Unused to farming and totally ignorant of prairie conditions, they broke the plow instead of the prairie, and the season ended in complete discouragement. Letters to Cabet stated that the Texas project must be abandoned, that heat and fever had sapped their strength and famine faced them if they remained.

The effect on Cabet of this apparent failure of his Texas utopia is illuminating. He charged his people with imprudence and carelessness; they had attempted too much and had wasted their resources and sapped their energies in the process. He seems never to have considered that he was in any way to blame or to have admitted that a leader should have made investigations before trusting his people to the vicissitudes of a distant and unknown country. This same inability to face realities and the same reliance on some sort of special providence was shown when Cabet said that he lacked funds and might consider his course hopeless if the whole Icarian project were not based upon such grand truths that it must win universal sympathy and open universal purse strings.[30] With this touching confidence in miracles, Cabet set forth himself to lead his flock to whatever haven they might find outside the cruel state of Texas.

It is interesting to speculate upon the possible course of events if a revolution had not occurred in France in 1848, if Cabet had been able — as he had, of course, intended — to capitalize upon the widespread discontent with the Bourgeois Monarchy, and if he had been able to lead to America the two thousand colonists whom he had confidently expected, supported by the money of the million who would stay at home. Would Icaria have been a success? Would rational, democratic communism have survived its contact with the Western frontier? On the other hand, it is interesting to consider whether after the revolution Cabet might not have recalled the first expedition and have thrown in his lot with the leftist groups in the Second Republic, if he had been on good terms with Ledru-Rollin and Louis Blanc, the French socialist leaders.

As it was, February 1849 found Cabet and four hundred and eighty Icarians in New Orleans with no homes and a capital of less than fifty dollars apiece. Many of the less sanguine soon decided to sever their connections with the movement. Some returned to France; others found employment in New Orleans. Exploring parties sent out to select a home for the rest found one made to order in the town of Nauvoo, Illinois, from which the Mormons had recently departed. On the 15th of March two hundred and sixty French Icarians reached Nauvoo, twenty having died of fever on the river journey from New Orleans. After Texas, conditions in Nauvoo must have seemed ideal to these urban workingmen. Houses were to be had for a song, and the Icarians bought fifteen acres in the town, including a compact group of houses, the Mormon mill and distillery, and the buildings around "Temple Square."

For five years the Icarians were happy and prosperous. They constructed community buildings and used the old Mormon arsenal as a workshop for their various crafts. They operated a sawmill, a flour mill, and a distillery — and all the whisky was offered for sale, since the Icarians used neither alcohol nor tobacco. They rented a thousand acres of land, which they cultivated with great care. Their school, newspaper, print shop, and library were notable. Much of Icarian propaganda literature was published at Nauvoo and sent back to Paris for distribution. The Icarian musical and theatrical performances were regarded as village assets and attracted many visitors. The French were quiet and industrious and were looked upon with favor by their neighbors, who still vividly remembered the turbulent Mormons. To be sure, their communism was an eccentricity and their irreligion might be condemned, but their morals were good and their manners excellent.

Within five years the number of Icarians doubled. The collapse of the Second Republic caused many French radicals to renew their interest in their comrades overseas, and Cabet hoped Nauvoo would be but one colony among many. Land was purchased in his name in Iowa, and a small group of men was sent there to bring it under cultivation and to build homes for a new settlement. The increasing business activity of the community and his own increased responsibilities led Cabet in 1850 to seek incorporation under the laws of Illinois. The state legislature, however, was still smarting from the struggle with Joseph Smith and was reluctant to incorporate any peculiar society without assurance of its democratic, or at least republican, organization. It was necessary, therefore, for Cabet to relinquish his position as dictator and to provide Icaria with a constitution. The document he drew up was long, extremely democratic, and replete with assertions of its conformity with the sentiments of the Declaration of Independence.[31]

But the creator of Icaria did not thereby surrender his desire to exercise power. Icaria was his lifework and dearest interest; only he could presume to direct its policies and oversee its daily life. For five years the people dutifully elected men of his choice for the board of directors, and the directors in turn elected Cabet their president. But he was nearing seventy and growing more arbitrary and more visionary; opposition to his rule was inevitable. In the August election of 1856 the anti-Cabet faction secured a majority of the directors, but on Cabet's advice the retiring members of the board refused to surrender their offices, and the Nauvoo police had to intervene to prevent bloodshed while the majority party forcibly seated the men of its choice.

Personal success now came to mean more to Cabet than the welfare of his colony. He discredited the majority with the French society and stopped all flow of money from France, he refused to surrender title to the Iowa lands or to the Nauvoo holdings, and he sought to undermine the confidence of the creditors of the community. His minority party refused to cooperate, and the controversy spread so that there were miniature wars in all departments, including the kindergarten. Even in the dining room the two factions glowered at each other from separate tables. After an unsuccessful attempt to wreck the settlement by having the legislature repeal its charter, Cabet admitted his defeat by withdrawing from Nauvoo to St. Louis with one hundred and eighty faithful followers. Much to their sorrow, this move was almost immediately followed by Cabet's death. In November 1856 a stroke of apoplexy ended the life of the doughty old fighter.

The panic of 1857 and the ensuing depression presented both factions with problems difficult to solve. The St. Louis group bought, largely on credit, a small estate six miles from St. Louis, where they endeavored to build the "true Icaria." They were beset with further dissension and secession and finally, in 1864, turned their property over to their creditors and disbanded. The Nauvoo group found it impossible in the depression to sell enough goods to keep up the payments on the colony's debts, and they, too, abandoned their homes to their creditors. The majority party had, however, retained possession of the Iowa lands, although the Cabet heirs refused to surrender title, and the colonists therefore packed their goods and moved to what was then almost a wilderness. They sold enough of their land to complete the payments on the rest, and there, poor and hard-working but relatively content, they lived until 1895, when they voted to distribute their property and dissolve the communal ties.

Once more the hospitable American frontier had received a peculiar people whose desire it was to live apart and according to its own theories and ideals, and once more it had slowly added its pressures of individualism and opportunity to the stresses of internal friction to bring about the end of the experiment. Icaria sank, as had other bright hopes, into the main stream of American life, its ideals not fully realized but contributing their share to the democratic philosophy of the New World.

PART THREE

Humanitarian Crusades

William Lloyd Garrison was expressing the spirit of his day when he exclaimed, "I shall assume, as self-evident truths, that the liberty of a people is a gift of God and nature . . . that the right to be free is a truth planted in the hearts of men, and acknowledged so to be by all that have hearkened to the voice of nature." [1] This right to be free, rooted deep in democracy and evangelical religion, needed only to be coupled to nineteenth-century faith in progress to produce a crusading zeal that swept men into all sorts of reform movements designed to perfect the institutions of contemporary society.

Human freedom came to have many aspects for the reformer, who was so fundamentally a perfectionist. His vision was of an America whose government, based on popular consent, should function to prevent the denial of the liberties of the individual, to protect the rights of the unfortunate, and to prohibit the mistreatment of the delinquent. And he saw that upon his shoulders rested the burden of educating the youth of the republic to recognize its civic obligations and to strive for the betterment of society.

From the first these humanitarian reformers were outspoken in favor of revising the penal codes and liberalizing all legislation dealing with debtors. They also recognized society's responsibility toward the orphan, the impoverished, and the defective, and aware of the effect of environment upon the individual, they became advocates of temperance and of universal peace. Convinced, too, that it was the destiny of his country to lead mankind toward a better life, the nineteenth-century crusader easily became antiforeign when he felt American institutions to be menaced by ideas from abroad, and his evangelical Protestantism was quick to alarm when foreign Catholics flocked to the shores of his homeland.

American women worked zealously for each of these reforms until they reached the limits set for them by men, whose liberalism and willingness to experiment stopped short at certain barriers of custom and prejudice. Then women turned a part of their attention to acquiring for themselves, in the name of their common humanity, some of that freedom of opportunity they had sought for others.

Men and women both realized that the equalitarianism of American democracy made the presence of Negro slavery incongruous and anachronistic in a free and humane society. Entangled with every phase of American life in that period, a background for every crusade, the slavery question became the central issue for all reformers, and eventually the antislavery cause absorbed all the enterprise of those who sought to perfect the institutions of the young republic.

CHAPTER 10

Education and the American Faith

The very close connection between education and religious faith in early America, and one important reason for it, are well expressed in the phrases inscribed on the west gateway of Harvard Yard:

AFTER GOD HAD CARRIED US SAFE TO NEW ENGLAND
AND WE HAD BUILDED OUR HOUSES
PROVIDED NECESSARIES FOR OUR LIVELIHOOD
REARED CONVENIENT PLACES FOR GOD'S WORSHIP
AND SETTLED THE CIVILL GOVERNMENT
ONE OF THE NEXT THINGS WE LONGED FOR
AND LOOKED AFTER WAS TO ADVANCE LEARNING
AND PERPETUATE IT TO POSTERITY
DREADING TO LEAVE AN ILLITERATE MINISTRY
TO THE CHURCHES WHEN OUR PRESENT MINISTERS
SHALL LIE IN DUST.

Institutions of higher learning were established and maintained to educate young men for the ministry, and the piety prescribed by the theocracy permeated elementary education as well. From the first primer, which taught the alphabet in religious couplets beginning,

A   In Adam's fall
We sinned all

through the Dilworth reader (1740), whose first lesson began,

No Man may put off the Law of God.
The Way of God is no ill Way.
My Joy is in God all the Day.
A bad Man is a Foe to God.

to the weighty tomes on the desk of the theologian, all education was impregnated with religious teaching. This indoctrination was most pronounced in Puritan New England but was inevitable everywhere in the colonies, whether children were taught in schools, by private tutors, or in the homes, for the same texts were used, and the final authority on all matters of education was the clergy. Colonial teachers were more often than not lads whose principal interest was training for the ministry.

In colonial New England, where the democracy of the town

227

In Adam's Fall
We finned all.

Thy Life to mend,
God's Book attend.

The Cat doth play,
And after flay.

A Dog will bite
A Thief at Night.

The Eagle's Flight
Is out of Sight.

The idle Fool
Is whipt at School

As runs the Glafs,
Man's life doth pafs.

My Book and Heart
Shall never part.

Job feels the Rod,
Yet blefses God.

Proud Korah'stroop
Was fwallow'd up.

The Lion bold
The Lamb doth
hold.

The Moon gives light
In Time of Night.

Nightingales fing
In Time of Spring.

The royal Oak, it
was the Tree
That fav'd his roy-
al Majefty.

Peter denies
His Lord, and cries.

Queen Efther comes
in royal State,
To fave the Jews
from difmal Fate.

Rachael doth mourn
For her firft born.

Samuel anoints
Whom God ap-
points.

Time cuts down all,
Both great and fmall.

Uriah's beauteous
Wife
Made David feek
his life.

Whales in the Sea
God's Voice obey.

Xerxes the Great
did die,
And fo muft you
and I.

Youth forward flips,
Death fooneft nips.

Zaccheus, he
Did climb the Tree,
His Lord to fee.

An alphabet of jingles from a primer printed in Boston about 1800 meeting early made common schools possible, it is probable that a large majority of the children were properly instructed in the consequences of "Adam's fall" and that they were taught to write, to "cipher," and to spell — after a fashion.[1] Elsewhere elementary instruction was less universal and the common school less well known. In all back-country areas illiteracy was widespread, and the man who made his X on a legal document represented a majority of the community. And even in New England there was little concern over the education of girls. In 1782 the Reverend John Eliot wrote to his friend and fellow minister, Jeremy Belknap of Dover, New Hampshire:

We don't pretend to teach yᵉ female part of yᵉ town anything more than dancing, or a little music perhaps . . . except yᵉ private schools for writing, which enables them to write a copy, sign their name &c, which they might not be able to do without such a privilege.[2]

But neither in New England nor in the other colonies were men of enlightenment satisfied with the condition of American schools. In 1749 Benjamin Franklin, who was himself largely self-educated, published a pamphlet entitled *Proposals Relating to the Education of Youth in Pensilvania*, which reads like the prospectus of a progressive school of the twentieth century. It was based upon a psychology of learning that must have been the product of Franklin's own experience, for he stated that "learning comes by doing" and advocated using concrete examples and illustrations first, proceeding to abstract ideas only after the concrete evidence was well in mind. He recommended that modern languages be taught before ancient and that the student be led from a study of history to the consideration of customs, political institutions, and legal and economic theories.

There is no evidence that Franklin's program was adopted by any contemporary school or that it made even a stir of comment among schoolmen, but the Junto of young men the sage was instrumental in founding in Philadelphia put some of his ideas into effect in their efforts at self-education. These eighteenth-century youths met as a discussion group, and in their cooperative library they furnished a precedent for later school and public libraries.

Franklin was instrumental, also, in founding a nonsectarian school that was later to be the University of Pennsylvania and in establishing in 1765 the first school of medicine in the colonies. He was also interested in industrial and mechanical education and left money to both Boston and Philadelphia to provide loan funds for poor students. It was in his *Poor Richard's Almanack,* however, that Franklin showed himself to be the inveterate schoolteacher. Utilitarian and pragmatic, the homely wit of Poor Richard's maxims carried Franklin's teachings to thousands of loyal Americans.

During the period of the American Revolution statesmen turned their attention to the problem of educating those upon whose shoulders would fall the burden of making a success of the new republican form of government. The instruction of the people, wrote John Adams, in the practice of "their political and civil duties, as members of society and freemen, ought to be the care of the public, and of all who have any share in the conduct of its affairs in a manner that never yet has been practised in any age or nation." And in 1779 Thomas Jefferson wrote:

Even under the best forms [of government], those entrusted with power have, in time, and by slow operations, perverted it into tyranny; and it is believed that the most effectual means of preventing this would be to illuminate, as far as practicable, the minds of the people at large . . . whence it becomes expedient for promoting the publick happiness that those persons, whom nature hath endowed with genius and virtue, should be rendered by liberal education worthy to receive, and able to guard the sacred deposit of the rights and liberties of their fellow citizens, and that they should be called to that charge without regard to wealth, birth or other accidental condition or circumstance.[3]

Jefferson advocated for Virginia state-supported elementary schools in each locality from which promising boys should be chosen for further education at state expense. The parents of other children were, of course, to be free to send them to private schools. The capstone of this structure of public and private schools was to be the University of Virginia, which he designed to be free, secular, and state-supported. In writing to George Wythe in support of his views Jefferson urged,

Preach, my dear Sir, a crusade against ignorance; establish and improve the law for educating the common people. . . . The tax which will be paid for this purpose, is not more than the thousandth part of what will be paid to kings, priests, and nobles, who will rise up among us if we leave the people in ignorance.[4]

The Old Dominion failed to follow Jefferson's advice in regard to elementary and secondary education but did establish the university, and to the building of this Jefferson devoted the last years of his life. His interest in science and government was reflected in the university's curriculum. No provision was made for a professor of divinity, nor was there to be the rigid discipline prescribed in contemporary colleges. The university administration was to be democratic, vocational training was to be encouraged, and students were to be free to elect such courses as might best serve their needs.

Although less interested in educational theory and curriculums than his fellow Virginian, George Washington again and again expressed his conviction that the new republic must have a literate citizenry. In his will he stated his reasons for desiring a national university:

It has always been a source of serious regret with me to see the youth of these United States sent to foreign countries for the purpose of education, often before their minds were formed, or they had imbibed any adequate ideas of the happiness of their own, contracting too frequently, not only habits of dissipation and *extravagance*, but principles unfriendly to Republican Government, and to the true and genuine liberties of mankind, which thereafter are rarely overcome. For these reasons it has been my ardent wish to see a plan devised on a liberal scale which would have a tendency to spread systematic ideas through all parts of this rising Empire, thereby to do away with local attachments and state prejudices, as far as the nature of things would, or indeed ought to admit, from our national councils. Looking anxiously forward to the accomplishment of so desirable an object as this is . . . my mind has not been able to contemplate any plan more likely to effect the measure than a University in a central part of the United States, to which the youths of fortune and talents from all parts thereof might be sent for the completion of their education, in all the branches of polite literature, in arts and sciences, in acquiring knowledge in the principles of Politics and good Government.[5]

Washington's noble plan for a great national university that might eliminate sectionalism among the country's leaders was not accepted by his or later generations, but less prominent men continued to approach the problem of education in a republic from other angles. A young man of New England, Noah Webster, became aware shortly after the Revolution that all the appurtenances of education were still British, and in studying the textbook situation he developed a philosophy of education that he published under the title,

On the Education of Youth. American education, he said, must be freed from ecclesiastical tyranny and from dependence upon Europe. As a part of his effort toward that end he issued in 1783 his first speller. In this "old blue-backed Spelling Book" and in his later *American Reader* and *American Grammar* [6] Webster earned the title of "the Schoolmaster of America."

Webster's teaching was pragmatic, and his recommendations were utilitarian. He maintained that in a country that did not support a leisure class too much attention to dead languages was unwise. English translations of the classics would bring the wisdom of the ages home to young Americans, and the time saved by the elimination of Greek and Latin might well be spent on the study of history and government and on training in the use of the vernacular. His textbooks were immediately and permanently popular. Within a decade fifty impressions of twenty-five thousand copies each had been made of the *American Spelling Book*, and the grand total published in the nineteenth century is said to have been one hundred million copies. The *Reader* and the *Grammar* were almost as widely used, and the three together determined American usage for generations. In the decade before 1800 Webster published also *An American Selection*, containing patriotic speeches and brief sections on history and geography, a *New England Primer*, which substituted "*A* was an Apple Pie made by the Cook" for the traditional remark about Adam, and the *Little Reader's Assistant*, a collection of short stories with a "Farmer's Catechism" added for good measure.

It is difficult to overestimate the importance of Webster's work as a writer of textbooks. He provided, as he had intended, a framework for education that was free from ecclesiastical tyranny and European dictation. With the publication of his great *American Dictionary of the English Language* in 1828 he completed his work as a scholar and established his principle that English is "a living language and admits of no fixed state." But it was in the statement of his philosophy as an author that he left his best legacy to the American student: "The basis of all excellence in writing and conversation is truth — truth is intellectual gold, which is as durable as it is splendid and valuable." [7]

From the beginning, therefore, American leaders were interested in the spread of education and the reform of its techniques as a necessity for the success of republican institutions. For many years, however, there was little response to the call for reform. It was not until the common man became conscious of the privileges of which he had been deprived and used the suffrage he had acquired to demand education for his children that the state turned to a consideration of the common school. This movement was in accord with the humanitarianism of the time, and the reformers joined the workingmen in seeking remedies for the defects in the educational system. No reform of the 1830's and 1840's aroused greater interest than did that of education, and the champions of its cause were prolific in schemes and methods of curing its ills. Some of the best phrased appeals for reform were enunciated in the Southern states, where there was little legislation on the matter of education. The *Southern Literary Messenger* for May 1, 1836, stated:

Heretofore, and at present to a certain extent, learning has ever belonged to a few, constituting a single class of society which was, of course, the repository of all moral and intellectual power; and these few, having the power in their own group, moulded and wielded the destinies of society. Thus, the elevation of society has ever been characterized by the moral and intellectual education of a single class, and as this class has been cultivated communities have risen or fallen. Thus, the history of society has ever been, like the waves of a rolling sea, a series of fluctuations. . . . Now this principle of universal mental cultivation destroys this usurping, tyrannizing system. It takes from the few the power of holding and disposing of the rights of the many, giving to the many the same mental superiority and knowledge. The promotion and the general well-being of society by a cultivation of the heart and intellect is impliedly required of Americans, from the nature and structure of our government.[8]

And from Ohio in the Old Northwest came similar sentiments expressed even more forcibly:

Other nations have hereditary sovereigns, and one of the most important duties of their governments is to take care of the education of the heir to the throne; *these children all about your streets, who cannot even speak your language, are your future sovereigns.* Is it not important that they be well educated? [9]

The work of propaganda went on unabated for more than a quarter of a century. The Pennsylvania Society for the Promotion of Public Schools did valiant service; the American Lyceum, founded by Josiah Holbrook in 1826, had as one of its major purposes the improvement of schools; and the Western Academic Institute, organized in Cincinnati in 1826, brought Lyman Beecher, Calvin Stowe, and Samuel Lewis into the fight. Articles in the new educational journals, reports of investigators sent abroad, prize essay contests, and annual public conventions increased the enthusiasm. Slowly in many states public pressure forced the enaction of laws providing for new school systems or for the modernization of old ones. That such effort was conscious and effective was evidenced by the comments of many European travelers and was, perhaps, best expressed by the careful and sympathetic Francis Grund.

The most remarkable characteristic of Americans [he wrote] is the uncommon degree of intelligence which pervades all classes. I do not here speak of the higher branches of learning which, in the language of Europe, constitute scholarship; but of the great mass of useful knowledge calculated to benefit and improve the conditions of mankind. It is this latter knowledge for which the Americans are distinguished, and for the attainment of which they have, perhaps, made better provision than any other nation in the world. . . . It is certainly not to be expected that republicans should tax themselves in order to gratify certain elegant tastes which are of no immediate benefit to the public. . . . But let any one cast his eye on the sums annually expended for the establishment and support of common schools and colleges, and he will, at once, be convinced of the liberality of Americans in the cause of education. . . . Who upon entering an American school-room and witnessing the continual exercise in reading and speaking, or listening to the subject of their discourses, and watching the behavior of the pupils toward each other and their teachers, could, for a moment, doubt his being amongst a congregation of young republicans? . . . it would only be necessary to conduct some doubting European politician to an American school-room to convince him at once that there is no immediate prospect of transferring royalty to the shores of the New World.[10]

IMPROVEMENT OF THE COMMON SCHOOL

When the attention of public-spirited men was turned toward education, they soon saw that there was little connection between existing institutions and the ideal of universal education as the necessary accompaniment of democratic government. In the Middle Atlantic states education at public expense was available only to those who were willing to admit to a state of pauperism, and in the South there was little more than lip service to the ideas of Jefferson. The frontier West had always asserted the democratic principle of free schools and had united with the federal government in granting land for school purposes, but thinness of settlement, lack of local interest, lack of teachers, and general poverty had prevented much accomplishment.

Even in the New England states, where the common school had been provided for since the seventeenth century and where secondary school education at public expense had been accepted in theory, the state of affairs was found to be shocking, especially in the rural or district schools. Surveys showed that the once praised common school had been grossly neglected and offered if anything less in the way of education than it had a century before. In rural New England the district schools were ill-ventilated hovels located without thought of beauty or comfort by the roadside somewhere near the center of the school district. The town paid for their construction and upkeep and for the salaries of the teachers, and the main objective of local school boards seemed to be to keep costs as low as possible. In his *Fireside Education* (1838) the popular author, Samuel G. Goodrich, better known under his pen name of Peter Parley, wrote:

The site for a school house is generally in the most neglected, because the cheapest, spot in the town; whereas it should be chosen with special reference to pleasantness of aspect. Its interior, too, should be cheerful and attractive. It ought to be a place loved by the pupils, associated with ideas of comfort, and not with recollections of despotism without and gloom within. . . . Is it not a reproach to human nature that school committees, teachers and fathers, often select a site for a seminary for children with less regard to comfort of position than if they were mere animals? For the sheepfold and the cow-house, sheltered situations are carefully selected; but a bleak hill-top, swept by the winter blast, or a sandy plain, scorched by the dog-day sun, will do for a school-house, especially if it is so useless for everything else as to be given gratis to the district.[11]

Unpainted and desolate without, the district schools were equally unattractive within. The only furniture was a row of desks with backless benches of varying height, placed against the four bare walls. Near the center of the room was a desk for the teacher and a few benches for classes "called up" for recitation. All the furniture was crudely knocked together from rough lumber; there were few windows, no blackboards, and no provision for ventilation or sanitation. Heat was usually furnished by a fireplace, sometimes by a stove, but in either case the children near the source of heat were nicely toasted, while the drinking water in a pail in the corner was covered with a film of ice.

The teachers in these common schools were poorly paid and often little educated. The summer term, attended largely by little children and girls, was usually taught by a woman, whose salary was five or six dollars a month. A man teacher was provided for the winter term, which extended from December to March. His salary was higher, from seven to twelve dollars a month. These sums were not, however, the sole remuneration of teachers, for both men and women had the inestimable privilege of "boarding around" with the families of their pupils. The best teachers were undoubtedly the many young men and women who were procuring funds for their own education by teaching one or more terms each year; the worst were those failures from other professions who sought in teaching the livelihood their own incompetency, bad moral reputation, or constant inebriation had denied them elsewhere. In any case social standing and influence in the community were commensurate with the low salary.

The miserable buildings were overcrowded, for the schools were few and American families were large. Amos Kendall, a Dartmouth student who earned a part of his college expenses by teaching, was in full charge, in 1810, of a one-room rural school attended by eighty-five pupils. It was ungraded, but he made an effort to separate the unwieldy mass into classes and noted in his diary that sixty-three were learning to write, while twenty-one studied arithmetic, nineteen English grammar, nine geography, two Latin, and one Greek.[12] Although young Kendall headed his class at Dartmouth, it is problematical how much he taught the children of Weston, Massachusetts. In the 1820's young Bronson Alcott taught eighty students in a school in Cheshire, Connecticut, and was paid the truly magnificent sum of one hundred and thirty-five dollars for four months' work. His opulence was lessened, however, by the fact that he used more than half his salary to buy blackboards and more comfortable desks for the children.

Most teachers solved the many problems of discipline by constant recourse to the rod or ferule. Texts were few and dull, and the curriculum was restricted to the three R's, with whatever addition of geography, history, and civics the teacher might find time for. Innovations in subject or method were not desired by either parents or school boards, nor were they possible with existing equipment and the heavy teaching loads. For most pupils the deadly monotonous reiteration of a few facts and repeated drill in certain elementary skills made up the educational process. Teacher training, better school plants, and state supervision were the urgent reforms demanded by all public-spirited citizens.

The work of teacher training was begun by Samuel Read Hall in Concord, New Hampshire, in 1823. Hall was a minister who was at the same time profoundly interested in education. He was the entire faculty of the little normal school he started in his own home because he had become aware of the great need for trained teachers while he was earning his college funds by teaching in elementary schools. During the three years he remained in charge of the school more than two hundred students registered for one or more terms. Since it was an entirely new venture, Hall had to devise his own methods and write his own texts. He used blackboards and illustrative material and introduced geography, United States history, "natural philosophy," and classes in science for older pupils. In 1829 his lectures were published — the first book on education to be printed in the United States in the English language. There were thirteen lectures in all, covering the reasons for the current indifference to common schools, the obstacles to their usefulness, the proper training of teachers, practical directions on discipline, management, curriculum, and methods, and one final chapter entitled "For Female Instructors."

So great was the fame of Hall's school that he was called down to Andover, Massachusetts, to head a new school connected with Phillips Academy. This, too, became a teacher training school with a "model school" for practice teaching. It provided a three-year course and maintained a bureau of appointments. Teachers' conventions were held, circulars were distributed, and itinerant teachers were sent out to furnish model classroom instruction. Between 1830 and 1840 Hall published textbooks in geography, arithmetic, history, and grammar, all based on the latest methods and approach. In 1841 he went back to the ministry but continued to teach in the schools of the parishes to which he ministered. He died in 1877, a decade after the publication of his last text, an *Alphabet of Geology*.

In Massachusetts Hall worked with James Carter and Horace Mann for the establishment of normal schools and for legislative provision for a state superintendent of education. In 1837 the office of state superintendent was created with Horace Mann as its first incumbent, and in 1839 the first state normal school in the United States was opened in the town hall of Lexington, Massachusetts. Nor was this just a Massachusetts reform. In 1832 James Wadsworth, New York state commissioner of education, ordered ten thousand copies of Hall's *Lectures* for the instruction of New York teachers, and two years later the state legislature provided for professional education for teachers by allotting funds for the purpose to private academies. Progress came in other states more slowly, but interest was heightened everywhere by the reports of Horace Mann and of Henry Barnard, who was named state superintendent of schools in Connecticut in 1838.

When Mann accepted the post of state superintendent of education in Massachusetts, he was reproached for having given up a promising career as lawyer and legislator to promote a movement in which there would be no chance for honor or fame. His calm reply was, "If the title is not sufficiently honorable now, then it is clearly left for me to elevate it; and I had rather be creditor than debtor to the title." [13] In that spirit he worked indefatigably, fifteen hours a day, for twelve years. Even his vacations were busman's holidays, for he used them to tour other states and foreign countries investigating educational conditions. He was determined to make each annual report a battle in the campaign for better school buildings, textbooks, libraries, and equipment. Through the *Common School Journal*, through teachers' conventions and institutes, and through the establishment of normal schools, he endeavored to raise the standards of teaching. At the same time he worked constantly to secure higher salaries for teachers through state support and increased local taxation. There was no phase of school management, discipline, or curriculum in which he was not interested. His twelve long reports took up everything from corporal punishment to substituting the word method of teaching children to read for the old alphabet type of instruction.

Much of Mann's educational and social theory and many of his specific recommendations were too radical for the conservatives of the Massachusetts legislature as well as for Boston teachers, but during his years in office the state appropriations for education were doubled and millions were spent in the improvement of school buildings. Teachers' salaries were increased, a month was added to the school year, and three normal schools were opened. These concrete achievements may have seemed slight to the man who had devoted twelve years to the cause of education, but as the inauguration of a campaign and as the formulation of a platform for the future Mann's activity was of vital importance. The old lethargy in regard to education disappeared from Massachusetts and from the country at large with the publication of his reports, and social reform along many lines was stimulated by his efforts.

Mann's great reports assert his faith in democracy and his feeling that education was the only hope for the preservation of democratic institutions. "In a republic," he wrote, "ignorance is a crime; and private immorality is not less an opprobrium to the state than it is guilt to the perpetrator." [14] The social responsibility of the state and the duty of its citizens to assume that obligation received classic expression in the concluding sentences of his eighth report:

If we do not prepare children to become good citizens — if we do not develop their capacities, if we do not enrich their minds with knowledge, imbue their hearts with the love of truth and duty, and a reverence for all things sacred and holy, then our republic must go down to destruction, as others have gone before it; and mankind must sweep through another vast cycle of sin and suffering, before the dawn of a better era can arise upon the world. It is for our government, and for that public opinion which, in a republic, governs the government to choose between these alternatives of weal or woe.[15]

This was the clarion cry of democratic humanitarianism. Other men — lesser men perhaps — answered it and carried on the work. Henry Barnard in Connecticut and in Rhode Island promoted programs similar to those of Mann. In Pennsylvania the fight for educational reforms turned on the question of whether state support should be given to all schools and all children or should provide only for the elementary education of the children of the poor. Few communities took advantage of the offer of state aid, made in the laws of 1802, 1804, and 1809, nor did indigent parents come forward to register themselves as paupers in order to claim the benefits of the laws. Some municipal public schools were established, and many religious sects — Mennonites, Lutherans, Friends, German Reformed — opened schools of their own, but there was no new public school law until 1834, and then Thaddeus Stevens was its champion. In his first speeches on education in the state legislature, Stevens asserted the rights of the common people and the necessity for free schools in terms that resemble those of the reports of Horace Mann. As a result of Stevens' efforts the bill became a law, and Pennsylvania joined the states engaged in increasing their facilities for education.

In New Jersey, where a law of 1820 had made provision for pauper schools, a similar battle was fought. The supporters of free public schools for all children watched the debate in Pennsylvania eagerly and used the speeches of Thaddeus Stevens to good effect in their own campaign. In 1838 the fight was won, and the New Jersey system, worked out in the next decade, provided for the education of children of all classes at public expense.

In the state of New York, also, there was a struggle over the removal of the distinction between pay and free pupils. The questions of state aid and of state supervision were equally troublesome, and it was long before New York was able to take the position of leadership commensurate with its wealth and political importance. In 1812 a law was passed that established a system of public schools to be supported in part by state aid, in part by a local tax, and in part by "rate bills" on parents. The urban centers found the rate bill intolerable as workingmen came to have more voice in city affairs. By special legislation city school systems were organized under local boards of education, and local taxes for school purposes were permitted. Before 1850 a large number of cities maintained public schools that were entirely free.

In New York City this was accomplished through the work of the Free School Society, a private corporation of which De Witt Clinton was the first president and largest subscriber. Established in 1805, it opened its first free school in 1809 and thereafter gradually assumed charge of all the public schools in the city. Under the man-

agement of a board of trustees it administered the funds subscribed
by private philanthropy and those obtained from state and local
governments, and for most of the thirty-five and more years of its
history it made no distinction between the children of the well-to-do
and those of the poor.

The rural districts of New York were more conservative, more
conscious of the rights of property, and less willing to assume civic
responsibility. They maintained district schools for the minimum
four-month terms necessary to secure state aid, but were unwilling
to go farther. A statewide campaign in the 1840's brought enough
appeals for free state-supported schools to result in a referendum at
the fall elections. The campaign was one of much propaganda and
many speeches, slogans, and songs, one of the best of which included the following stanza:

> Then free as air should knowledge be —
> And open Wisdom's portal,
> To every thirsty, earnest soul,
> Who longs to be immortal.
> Here rich and poor stand side by side,
> To quaff life's purest chalice,
> And never dream that deathless names
> Belong to cot or palace.[16]

Forced by public opinion to some sort of action, the legislature
compromised by increasing state aid and providing for "union districts" that might establish free schools by local taxation. The rate
bill was retained but for a rapidly decreasing area. In 1867 it was
finally abolished. In the following year it was eliminated in Connecticut as well. Hard as it had been to win the battle with the reluctant taxpayer, victory was at last assured in the Northern states.

The newer Western states soon fell into line, and their school
systems were built on the basis of equal opportunity for all children
at public expense. Gradually special charges upon parents were
abolished, normal schools were established, and the pay and social
standing of teachers were bettered. In the 1850's the South, too,
made rapid progress toward abolishing pauper schools and establishing free public school systems. The total effect of the changes
all over the country was revolutionary in nature. There was a great
increase in the number of schools and in the number of pupils, sec-

ondary schools were built, state and local governments increased their support, and the necessity for state supervision was recognized.

Although the need for the secularization of schools and texts had been admitted from the beginning, American mid-century ideals still demanded that the schools be Christian and highly moral. Educators were often first of all clergymen, and many teachers were, as always before, youths preparing for the ministry. Education in frontier areas continued to be a missionary enterprise. Everywhere private academies and small colleges were founded with the major purpose of combining religious indoctrination and higher education, and denominational theological schools were still, for many educators, the summit of the process.[17]

THE VOICE OF THE OPPOSITION

The stubbornness of the opposition to free schools and the reluctance of many teachers to admit the wisdom of innovation were as remarkable as was the devotion of the reformers, who felt they had put on the cross for a holy crusade. The rights of property were said to be challenged when the state levied taxes to educate "other people's children," and the howls of the taxpayer were heard throughout the land. It was argued that parents had the right to provide for the education of their own children and that the privilege to pay for their attendance at private schools should not be curtailed by the necessity for paying again to the tax collector. Taxation for the benefit of others was called tyranny by those who had no children; public benefits were said to lessen "sturdy independence" and "individual initiative"; man, it was asserted, could receive full benefit only from that to which he had contributed. Those who supported parochial schools spoke darkly of double taxation, and religious denominations maintaining such schools sought a share of state aid. Immigrant groups protested that they preferred to send their children to schools where the language, religion, and traditions of their homelands might be taught, and they objected to a tax for public schools. Compulsory attendance, it was believed, robbed parents of full control over their children and deprived them of their right to the proceeds of the labor such children might perform. Pitiful word pictures were painted of ill and starving parents suffering at home while strapping boys of twelve or fourteen went merrily off to school.

Protests came also from those who doubted the wisdom of universal education. An appeal to the North Carolina legislature in 1829 stated frankly:

Gentlemen, I hope you do not conceive it at all necessary that *everybody* should be able to read, write, and cipher. If one is to keep a store or a school, or to be a lawyer or physician, such branches may, *perhaps*, be taught him; though I do not look upon them as by any means indispensable; but if he is to be a plain farmer, or a mechanic, they are of no manner of use, but rather a detriment.[18]

And the farmer himself objected to expensive innovation in no uncertain terms. In New York one rural district adopted resolutions stating that it was in favor of "a simple and plain system of popular education, without normal schools, teachers' institutes, district school journals, supported by the State, or hordes of state officials." But conservatism was not the property of farmers alone. There were many in the teaching profession who frowned upon the reform movement. A professor at Yale, about 1830, expressed his objections in frank and not disinterested terms:

We find no advantage in pursuing a different course of instruction from what has hitherto been practised. That has stood the test of experience. It was surely an outrage to alter it. The world talks about improvement in instruction . . . and about a thousand never-tested notions. They are good for nothing. I would not give a straw for all of them. . . . The money ought to be appropriated to better purposes — to the support of colleges. What good can be done in common schools? Our dependence must rest upon colleges chiefly. Cannot some means be devised to get a part, or the whole, of the School Funds applied to the use of Colleges, and save it . . . instead of its being thrown away? [19]

Other teachers feared that the path of progress would be filled with stones or thorns and entered it with reluctance. A veteran instructor of youth, Jacob Abbott, published *The Teacher* in 1833 to warn the profession against innovation. He approved the older methods of instruction, even the most condemned system of oral simultaneous rote-answers to set questions, and advocated strict discipline and increased moral and religious instruction. In a chapter entitled "Scheming," he warned young teachers against new methods, especially those that might be opposed by school boards or parents. Teachers should "confine themselves to their proper sphere"; the schoolroom was not the teacher's empire; he was hired by employers to whom belonged the right to determine policy, and even "if they wish to have a course pursued which is manifestly inexpedient or wrong, *they still* have a right to decide." [20]

Seldom did any member of the opposition use the term "the rights of the child." The recognition of these rights came as a victory of the humanitarian liberals, after a struggle that justified the statement of one of its historians: "The fight for free schools was one of the great landmarks of American democracy." [21]

PRIVATE SCHOOLS

In the years when the battle for reform was concentrated on elementary education, and when the public high school was no more than a reference, under the name of "seminary," in the constitutions or statutes of a few states, secondary education was carried on by the academies founded in countless towns with the bequests of civic-minded citizens and the contributions of parents and subscribers. There were one hundred and twelve academies in Massachusetts alone in 1840. In these schools most of the leaders of the Northern states in the early years of the century were prepared for college, and to them the states looked for models when the responsibility of the state for secondary education was recognized. Many of them went out of existence when public high schools were established. Some were converted into public schools by the purchase of their physical plants by the towns in which they were located; others have survived into the twentieth century and are among the best of the private schools of today. Although these town academies were the peculiar institution of New England, the name was given also to Southern private schools, and in the prewar South such schools furnished practically the only means of acquiring secondary education and college preparatory work.

Slowly these academies began to respond to the demand for reform. Some of them opened their doors to girls and thus played a part in the movement for the education of women. This step was taken with some reluctance and with many safeguards. At Deerfield, in Massachusetts, for instance, girls and boys were taught in separate classes and had separate playgrounds and separate entrances to all buildings. Girls were not admitted to Phillips Academy at Andover, but a separate school, Abbot Academy, was opened for them in the same town in 1838.

The need for secondary education for young people who could not attend college was recognized in the creation of special schools where the emphasis was upon instruction in English. In Boston, where the old Latin Grammar School had for two centuries fitted boys for college, an English Classical School was opened in 1821.[22] At Andover an English School was established under the auspices of Phillips Academy for the dual purpose of training boys and girls in the use of the vernacular and of serving as a teacher training institute.

Willing as were those who controlled the academies and other private schools to enlarge their curriculums and modernize their methods of teaching, they were in general a conservative group that looked upon the free high schools with the suspicion accorded an intruder. There was a long process of attrition in which many of the Northern academies disappeared or were turned into state-supported free schools. In the South they survived, for even after the Civil War, when public schools were established, the tradition endured that a gentleman's son should be privately educated.

PROGRESSIVE SCHOOLS

There was in this period of social ferment a group of new schools—some very short-lived—that attempted to put into effect all that was most modern and progressive in educational theory and practice. Americans who had read Rousseau's *Emile* were ready to accept the educational theories of the famous Swiss pedagogue, Pestalozzi, who had established a school in his native land where Rousseau's ideas could be put into practice and modified in the light of actual experience with children. Pestalozzi believed that the development of man proceeded according to natural laws and that the teacher's function was to assist nature in achieving the harmonious development of all the faculties. Education should be moral and religious, natural and not mechanical, and based upon the needs of the individual. Intuition and reasoning should be developed, and mere memory work should be discouraged. It was the work of the school to fit the child for his place in society. The Pestalozzian schools became the mecca for educators of all countries, and through travelers and men trained by the Swiss master — Froebel, Fellenberg, Neef, and others — his ideas were carried far afield. Pestalozzian schools were established in many lands, and Pestalozzian ideas were slowly worked into the methods and curriculums of public schools everywhere.

In America one of the earliest reflections of Pestalozzian teaching was in the school established by Joseph Neef and William Maclure at New Harmony, Indiana, in the regime of Robert Owen, who had himself used the ideas of the Swiss educator in his schools at New Lanark. The end of the New Harmony community terminated this experiment in education, but the work of adapting the new ideas to American conditions was carried on by others. In many ways the school at Brook Farm, which has already been discussed in another connection, was the epitome of all that was idealistic and idyllic in American educational reform.

Another charming experiment was the Temple School of Bronson Alcott, the Transcendentalist. Convinced of the importance of teaching and sure of his own love for children, Alcott early decided to devote himself to education. Traditional procedures seemed inadequate to him, and he read everything that came his way in which educational problems were discussed: Robert Owen's *New View of Society;* William Russell's *American Journal of Education;* Joseph Neef's *Sketch of a Plan and Method in Education;* and the *Hints to Parents . . . in the Spirit of Pestalozzi.* His brother William knew a man who had visited Fellenberg's school in Hofwyl, and Alcott himself corresponded with William Maclure of New Harmony and with a Dr. Keagy who had opened a Pestalozzian school in Pennsylvania. By 1830 Alcott had determined that teaching the young was to be his work in life.

In the district schools of Connecticut, where he did his first teaching, he endeavored to put his Pestalozzian theories into practice, but he received little encouragement for his innovations. It was not until he went to Boston in 1834 that he found his intellectual and spiritual home. There the sort of idealism that was the core of his thinking found a hearing, and on Tremont Street in the Masonic Temple Alcott opened the school upon which his reputation as a teacher was to stand. To it were sent about forty children from many of Boston's most cultured and liberal families.

At Alcott's own expense the big classroom of Temple School was charmingly furnished. There were carpets, pictures, busts, a bas-relief of Jesus, and a statue of a symbolic figure, Silence. Each child had his own chair, desk, and blackboard. Elizabeth Peabody, one of the ablest and best informed women of Boston, was Alcott's assistant in the school, and it is her *Record of a School* that provides its history. There all Alcott's theories were applied. Children were taught as individuals, each making progress at his own rate of speed. Discipline, on the other hand, was considered a social matter, and problems of that kind were referred to the whole school for consideration. There was no corporal punishment; a quiet, harmonious atmosphere and an interesting round of activities were usually effective in maintaining order.

The curriculum of Temple School was much richer in content than that of the usual school of the day and was designed to develop the "three-fold nature of childhood." The subjects taught were divided as follows: under "The Spiritual Faculty" were listed Listening to Sacred Readings, Conversations on the Gospels, Writing Journals, Self-Analysis and Self-Discipline, Listening to Readings from Works of Genius, Motives to Study and Action, and Government of the School; under "The Imaginative Faculty" were Spelling and Reading, Writing and Sketching from Nature, Picturesque Geography, Writing Journals and Epistles, Illustrating Words, Listening to Readings, and Conversation; under "The Rational Faculty" came Defining Words, Analyzing Speech, Self-Analysis, Arithmetic, Study of the Human Body, Reasonings on Conduct, and Discipline.[23]

From the obvious emphasis on self-analysis in that curriculum a modern parent or teacher might infer that Temple School produced a class of introspective, self-conscious little prigs. Alcott was a philosopher, not a psychologist, and his delight in contemplating the unfolding mind of the child may have led him to aid too much in the process. Indeed, Alcott's supporters were not unaware of the danger. Wise old Dr. Channing wrote him anxiously:

I want light as to the degree to which the mind of the child should be turned inward. The free development of the spiritual nature may be impeded by too much analysis of it. The soul is somewhat jealous of being watched and it is no small part of wisdom to know when to leave it to its impulses and when to restrain it. The strong passion of the young for the outward is an indication of Nature to be respected. Spirituality may be too exclusive for its own good.[24]

To this letter Alcott returned a characteristic reply: "This I have done reverently and in faith, not in doubt, nor with profane curiosity" — the inference being that, acting in good faith, a Transcendentalist could not act wrongly.

In 1836, however, this Transcendentalist was inexpedient if not wrong, and he wrecked the school and his career as a teacher by too searching an examination of the ideas of the children in a series of Conversations on the Gospels. With the utmost humility and reverence and with as complete a lack of sophistication as the children could have had, Alcott approached the Conversations, which were conducted on Socratic lines. "All truth is written," he explained. "My business is to lead you to find it in your own Souls." In an era when mention of sex was unthinkable in cultivated society, Alcott began the Conversations with the mystery of the birth of Christ. Sex to him was holy and purely spiritual, transcendental and sublimated. Delicacy and vagueness permeated his every remark, but the damage was done. Irate parents entered complaints; Miss Peabody resigned in alarm for her own reputation; and the trusting philosopher decided to publish, at his own expense, the records of the Conversations, in order that the public might realize the purity of his motives and the sincerity of his religious faith. The publication was ill-advised, however, for it gave the controversy a wider hearing, and the book received very unfavorable comment from the shocked ministers and teachers who wrote reviews of it.

Within six months the enrollment of Temple School dropped from forty to ten. The panic of 1837 added its deterring influence, and in 1838 Alcott was forced to give up the rooms in the temple and transfer his three pupils to his own home. Soon, ill and discouraged, he gave up teaching altogether and left for England on a tour for which Emerson provided the funds.

No one of Alcott's contemporaries set higher standards for teaching or for teachers. His dominant motive had been the loving guidance of children, from whom he hoped to learn of the human soul and its relation to God. The incredibly high level he wished teachers to attain demanded a pure heart, an unsophisticated conscience, elevated principles, an amiable temper, religious faith, and a devotion to work which would make of it a happiness rather than a duty.[25]

A school as progressive but of an entirely different character was established on Round Hill, Northampton, Massachusetts, in the autumn of 1823 by George Bancroft and Joseph Cogswell. Bancroft had recently returned from student years in Germany, where he had grown familiar with schools that seemed far in advance of those in the United States. In Joseph Cogswell he found an able associate who was both a scholar and an administrator and more devoted to the cause of education than was Bancroft himself. Round Hill School was designed to be a college preparatory school, taking boys from the age of nine to sixteen. Its prospectus stated that its discipline was to be "precautionary rather than punitive"; that English, mathematics, and modern languages were to be taught as well as the classics; and that gymnastics, games, and outdoor exercise were to be a regular part of the school life, which was to be simple, quiet, and wholesome.

For a few years Round Hill prospered. Life there was anything but soft. The boys rose at six; prayers, study, breakfast, and exercises filled the time until nine, when the school day began. Classes ran from nine to twelve and from two to four; the hours between were devoted to dinner and exercise. From four to five there were organized sports, then supper, "declamations," study, "devotions," and bed — at eight-thirty.[26] The program was undeniably pleasant and varied. There were sketching and riding lessons, long tramps through the woods and along the river, a country camping site called "crony village," an annual journey to some point of interest, . and — an innovation that may or may not have seemed pleasant to the boys — foreign language tables in the dining room.

The highest standards were maintained at Round Hill. Every boy was put upon his mettle, and every effort was made to develop in him a desire for what Cogswell called "absolute excellence." Discipline seems to have been no great problem in that hive of constant activity.

We derive no aid [wrote Cogswell] from the fear of the lash. . . . Although we inflict no punishments . . . you must not think we allow a boy to suppose that there is no evil to result from disobedience, or idleness, or misconduct. We endeavor to ascertain what every one can do, and then we secure the performance of the task by cutting off all hopes of being allowed to play until it is performed. . . . The method of instruction which we adopt furnishes as delicate a test for the presence of brains, as prussic acid does for that of iron.[27]

Each boy was taught individually and was advanced on his merits, a plan most unusual for that day and one putting great demands on his instructors. The teaching staff was excellent, including as modern language teachers a German, a Frenchman, and an Italian. Supervised play in all sorts of weather added to the burden on the staff, and only really devoted teachers could long qualify, for, wrote Cogswell: "So satisfied am I that the capacity for improvement is the characteristic of man . . . that I am willing to risk the opinion that when none is made, the fault must lie as much in the teacher as in the one to be taught." [28]

Although the reputation of Round Hill was deservedly high and its standards were praised by all who visited the school, it was not destined to take a permanent place among American preparatory schools. Bancroft was not happy in teaching and withdrew after a few years to carry on his literary work. The staff was as high-priced as it was excellent, and the financial burden became too heavy for Cogswell to support. There was no endowment, and it was impossible to stretch the tuition fees of the forty or more students to cover the expenses of maintenance; so in 1834 Cogswell decided to close it, although it had been a great success in every way other than that of making both ends meet. The only conclusions to be drawn from its history are that excellence was expensive, and that private schools offering all that was provided at Round Hill required either an endowment or a clientele that would pay fees higher than were then customary.

THE EDUCATION OF WOMEN

Recognition of the duty of the community in respect to the education of women was slow in coming. In the colonial period there were a few private schools for "young ladies" in which attention was generally devoted to the more graceful handicrafts. The town academies established in the early nineteenth century were usually open to girls as well as to boys, and there girls obtained enough knowledge of elementary school subjects to offer themselves as teachers in the district schools, where they earned less than half the salaries paid their brothers for the same work.

The pioneer in the field of higher education for women was Emma Hart Willard, who published her *Plan for Improving Female Education* in 1819. Her restless mind was not content with the educational opportunities offered her, and she continued her own studies while she taught and after her marriage. Geometry, the principles of John Locke, and Paley's *Moral Philosophy* carried her on to subjects taught young men only after entrance to college. In 1814 she opened a school of her own in Philadelphia, where seventy girls were instructed in subjects new to women by teachers using the most modern methods.

Mrs. Willard felt that the state should aid in establishing schools for women, but when she failed to secure state funds for her school, she accepted the invitation of a group of citizens of Troy, New York, to open a school for which they would erect an adequate building. Troy Female Seminary was opened in 1821 and was an immediate success. To the surprise of those who doubted the mental capacity of girls, the ninety students at the Troy Seminary seemed quite able to assimilate the doses of mathematics, history, geography, and physics administered to them. Mrs. Willard believed that school life should approximate that of the community, so the seminary had a student self-government association. Teacher training was her great objective, and in the decade before the first normal schools, she prepared two hundred girls for the teaching profession. So devoted was she to the cause that during the seventeen years of her principalship she loaned nearly seventy-five thousand dollars to girls who were earning their own way through school.

Another pioneer was Catherine Beecher, eldest daughter of Lyman Beecher, who opened a little school in Hartford, Connecticut, about the time that Mrs. Willard was building Troy Seminary. When her family moved to Cincinnati, Catherine opened a girls' school there which was a failure because of lack of funds, although it was overcrowded with eager students. Miss Beecher was another devotee of courses for the training of teachers — especially of what she called "missionary teachers" for the schools of the South and the West.[29] She was anxious, also, to provide preparation for young women in their careers as wives and mothers. Physical training and domestic science seemed more important to her than courses duplicating the work given the young men of the day. She wrote books on domestic science and even a recipe book in behalf of the cause — the profits from which went into her work.

Miss Beecher's life was that of a propagandist, one of constant travel, lectures, organization, and writing. Aided by the clergy, by mothers, and by schoolteachers, she endeavored to break down resistance to her ideas and to obtain money for her projects. Her pamphlet *American Women, Will You Save Your Country?* and the more important *Essay on the Education of the Female Teacher* were regarded as classics in their fields. Her belief that woman's place was in the home was expressed in the prospectus of Milwaukee College for Women, founded as a result of her efforts "to train women to be healthful, intelligent, and successful wives, mothers, and housekeepers."

Perhaps the best known of this group of women educators was Mary Lyon, the founder of Mount Holyoke College. Like Emma Willard she was educated in an academy near her Massachusetts home. As a young district schoolteacher she earned one dollar a week and "boarded around," but curiosity and ambition drove her to continual study, and she early conceived the idea that later came to life in South Hadley. It was her desire to found a school of college rank and standards for the training of teachers and missionaries, one that should be attended by those in the "middle walks of life." For several years she taught with Zilpha Grant in New Ipswich Academy, and there she began her campaign for funds for a girls' college, obtaining her first thousand dollars from the housewives of the town in a house-to-house canvass. She was an inveterate beggar; the twenty-seven thousand dollars that went into the building of Mount Holyoke came from eighteen hundred people in ninety towns. Befriended by Professor Edward Hitchcock and Professor William Seymour Tyler of Amherst College, she decided to found her school in the near-by village of South Hadley, and there in 1837 the new seminary was opened with one hundred and sixteen students and four teachers.

The entrance requirements and, aside from the fact that at first no foreign languages were taught, the instruction were on the same level as those of the men's colleges. As the school grew and more teachers were added, the curriculum was expanded, but it was not until 1888, almost forty years after the death of Miss Lyon, that Mount Holyoke was granted a charter as a full-fledged college for women.

At some time before the founding of the school, Miss Lyon visited a manual labor institution in New York state, where she picked up, if she had not already acquired it, the idea that the girls in her school should aid in the housework of the establishment. With the lack of household conveniences in that day, this requirement meant a Spartan life for the "young ladies" during the New England winters. One of them wrote that on Thanksgiving day "we all had the privilege of sleeping as long as we wished in the morning, provided we were ready for breakfast by 8 o'clock. I rose at five, an hour later than usual and worked two hours and a half before breakfast." [30]

Miss Lyon was pious as well as energetic, and the atmosphere of Mount Holyoke was quite as revivalist as that of the neighboring institution in Amherst. The constant round of prayers and fast days was accepted without protest by most of the docile maidens but found a rebel in the young Emily Dickinson, who attended the school in Miss Lyon's later years. When the announcement was made that Christmas Day would be observed as a day of fasting and meditation, each girl remaining secluded in her own room all day, Emily alone refused to rise in approval — and she took the next stage for Amherst to celebrate Christmas with her family. In dealing with the individualistic Emily, Miss Lyon found use, apparently, for her own favorite maxim: "It is one of the nicest of mental operations to distinguish between what is very difficult and what is utterly impossible." [31]

These were the pioneers in the field of education for women. Other schools of the day were less progressive and followed the older pattern of teaching the "principles of Morality, Humility, and the Love of Virtue" by a smattering of religious teaching and a modicum of needlework and other feminine graces. When even Emma Willard and Catherine Beecher taught that women should be educated to take a woman's place in life, it was little wonder that there was slow progress toward equal educational opportunities for women. The only professions outside the home that were open to them were those of teacher or missionary, and for the latter it was better that they be married. The few eccentric women who tried to obtain medical or theological training were socially ostracized, and even Catherine Beecher found it wise to ask men to lecture in her cause while she worked outside the public eye. It is probable that most public-spirited American citizens of that day would have been content to subscribe to the views of the well-known teacher, Alonzo Potter, who recorded in his *School and the School Master* in 1842 that the education of a girl was designed to fit her for the work of a Christian matron, and

. . . to fit her for such a noble ministry she needs a training quite different from that given to the other sex. Her delicacy and purity must remain untarnished. Her diffidence and even bashfulness, at once a grace and a protection should be cherished as a peculiar treasure. She is to have all accomplishments which lend a charm to her person and manners; but these must be held as insignificant, when compared with those which qualify her for the duties of a wife and mother, and which inspire a taste for the privacy of domestic life, for its pleasures and privileges. . . . But she cannot too studiously shun the gaze of the multitude. The strife and tumults of the senate-house and the platform are too much even for her eye to rest upon, much more for her voice to mingle in. Her chastity is her tower of strength, her modesty and gentleness are her charm, and her ability to meet the high claims of her family and dependents, the noblest power she can exhibit to the admiration of the world.[32]

THE PROGRESS OF HIGHER EDUCATION

There was a corresponding development, if not so dramatic a one, in the American college in the same period. The changes may be illustrated from the stories of a few colleges and universities that seem to be typical.

In 1817 boys entered Harvard at twelve to fifteen years, prepared only in the classics and in them but poorly. The curriculum was narrow and the standards of scholarship low. College clubs were mostly drinking bouts, and college holidays might easily turn into brawls.[33] But in the 1820's and 1830's, when a group of young men who had studied abroad joined the Harvard faculty, modern languages, literature, history, political science and economy, and the sciences were added to the program, and the whole of college life was altered. The improvement of preparatory schools permitted the stepping up of entrance age and requirements so that the college began to assume the appearance of an institution of higher learning.

The change came slowly, however; even when Emerson made his famous Phi Beta Kappa address, Harvard was just a small college of about three hundred students in a sleepy little town of less than ten thousand population. Commencement was a state holiday with booths, fairs, horse races, and other attractions at which students and alumni disported themselves with gaiety. The students were rough and ready and rebellious. Young John Marsh, who graduated from Harvard in 1823, was involved in the turbulent activities of his class to such an extent that he was suspended twice and came near ending his college career in disgrace. In his junior year he participated in a riot during which a number of valuable books and papers were filched from the college library and burned in front of University Hall. One protesting professor had a bucket of ink emptied on his head, and another was almost killed by a falling cannon ball. The windows of the president's house were broken and other damage was done to college property.[34]

Sobriety was more prevalent in New Haven, for Yale was a center for Congregational orthodoxy and, after the beginning of the religious revivals at the turn of the century, was sought out by those who intended to become ministers or missionaries. Innovations in curriculum and methods came even more slowly at Yale than at Harvard, since orthodoxy in religion was accompanied by conservatism in educational lines. It was from Yale, however, that many students went west in the 1820's and 1830's to play a great part in the establishment of educational institutions on the frontier. And it was to Yale and Princeton that students went from the schools of the South for advanced study.

Dartmouth College, founded in colonial days, was still almost a frontier school in the early nineteenth century. The *Autobiography of Amos Kendall*, by a man who entered Dartmouth in 1807, records "student customs" that showed little piety but much disorderliness. Boys who boarded themselves took pride in robbing the hen roosts of the village and obtained their fuel from the wood piles of their neighbors. Literary society meetings often ended in drunken riots that shattered the stillness of the winter nights. It is difficult to be quite sure whether the annual revivals of Amherst or the wild pranks of the boys of Hanover and Cambridge were more characteristic of American college life in that period.

In the first half of the nineteenth century many new colleges were founded, especially in the West and the South, and most of them were in the beginning missionary enterprises and extremely religious, if not always denominational. Probably the most famous of the Presbyterian schools of the South was Transylvania College, founded in 1780, in the region later to be called Kentucky, by an act of the Virginia legislature, which set aside eight thousand acres of land for the college. A few years later the grant was increased to twenty thousand acres, all college property was declared exempt from taxation, and both students and faculty were freed from the obligation of military service. It was carefully decreed by the Episcopalian or freethinking legislators that there should be no religious tests and no special privilege for any sect, but the Presbyterian domination of the frontier is evident in the fact that the board of trustees was consistently of that faith until 1818.

During those years Transylvania was little more than a small grammar school or academy. The citizens of Lexington came to feel that the conservative trustees were blocking the growth of both town and college. Political liberals were in control of the legislature after 1816, however, and a plan was devised to liberalize and popularize the college. Victorious in securing a new board of trustees free from Calvinistic domination, the liberals installed Horace Holley, a well-known Unitarian, as president. His regime was notable for new texts, extended curriculum, and increased enrollment. A law department and a medical school were founded, the faculty was enlarged, and the creation of a real state university seemed imminent. But the Presbyterians kept up the fight, determined to wreck Holley and his "ungodly" administration even if at the same time they wrecked the college. After a weary decade Holley gave up the struggle and resigned in 1827. During the next fifteen years four Presbyterian ministers were successively president of Transylvania, and the institution steadily declined. Niels Sonne, the author of a recent monograph, *Liberal Kentucky, 1780–1828*, concludes a discussion of Transylvania with the statement:

The ideal of a great central state university open to all religious denominations, and conducted on liberal principles, had been effectively quashed. With it went the possibility of the domination of liberal religious opinion in the state. Collegiate education now became the function of the small denominational college.[35]

This victory of denominationalism was equally apparent in other Southern states and was, perhaps, inevitable in view of the intense emotional revivalism of the Protestant churches of the region. The Methodists established Randolph-Macon College in Virginia and La Grange College in Alabama in 1829. In Georgia there was an early Baptist college, and the state university was strongly Presbyterian. In 1837 the Methodists entered the field with Emory College, which was to be not only sectarian but at the same time a manual labor school. Under the guidance of Augustus Baldwin Longstreet, better known today as the author of charming tales of the South than as minister or educator, the new institution was almost immediately successful, and it soon rivaled the University of Georgia as an educational center.

North of the Ohio, too, most of the colleges were affiliated with some religious body, usually the Congregational or, more often, the Presbyterian church. There the founding of a college was often an experiment in town planting as well, for hardy pioneers built homes and colleges in the wilderness with the same economic enterprise and religious zeal that had marked the establishment of Puritan towns in the colonial era. These small sectarian colleges of the West and the South were the very essence of American civilization, for in their founding was combined the westward movement, the religious diversity and passionate faith of American individualism and Protestantism, and a devotion to the ideal that every aspiring youth should find available the means of acquiring whatever measure of education he desired.

The name of these colleges was legion. Many of them were, in fact, no more than mere academies and some were very short-lived, but an astonishing number survived into the twentieth century, living symbols of the frontier's religiosity and its tolerance of diversity. Two of the most interesting and influential were linked from the time of their founding in the 1830's, and for more than a hundred years there have been marked parallels in their history. Oberlin College in Ohio and Knox College in Illinois were both colonies as well as colleges, for their founders were groups of settlers carefully picked by pious leaders to establish both a town and a college on the frontier. They were alike, too, in that almost every influence of their early years came from New England or from a section of New York that had been settled from New England. Both colleges had some connection with the family of Lyman Beecher, and with that stormy evangelist, Charles Grandison Finney; both were deeply involved in the slavery controversy and were stations of the Underground Railroad; both were pioneers in the education of women; and both were founded upon the principle of student self-help through manual labor.

The idea of the state university was older than the Union itself, but its rapid growth and great importance were not to come until after the Civil War. Provision was made for a state university in the first constitution of Pennsylvania, and North Carolina and Vermont each passed a law creating one, on paper, during the Revolution. The University of Georgia was founded in 1785, that of Tennessee in 1794, while the University of Virginia was the last great enterprise of Thomas Jefferson. New England (except for Vermont), already provided with old and respected colleges, was little interested in the movement; it was in the West that it was to find its most congenial setting, and there the new states were more than generous with grants of land and encouragement of every sort.

In 1821 the infant Territory of Michigan envisaged the establishment of a complete educational system like the Napoleonic University of France, to be called "The Catholepistemiad of Michigania," apparently in agreement with Huxley that "no system of public education is worth the name of national unless it creates a great educational ladder, with one end in the gutter and the other in the university." It was not until 1835, however, that the present University of Michigan was founded. Its first president was Henry Tappan, and its first catalogue contained a statement that might well be the credo of those building institutions of higher education in a democratic state:

An institution cannot deserve the name of a university which does not aim in all the material of learning, in the professorships it establishes, and in the whole scope of its provisions, to make it possible for every student to study what he pleases and to any extent he pleases. Nor can it be regarded as consistent with the spirit of a free country to deny to its citizens the possibilities of the highest knowledge.[36]

In the years before the establishment of the public school system pious Americans endeavored to instill religion and dispel illiteracy through Sunday schools. The earliest such school to achieve success was founded in Philadelphia in 1790 and was conducted under the patronage of Bishop White, Dr. Benjamin Rush, Mathew Carey the economist, and other prominent citizens. Reading, writing, and arithmetic were taught by paid teachers to such children of the poor as desired admission. The number of these schools grew rapidly, and textbooks and catechisms were printed especially for them — books which were, if possible, still more pious than those used in contemporary public schools. In 1824 the American Sunday School Union, a nondenominational society, was formed with the dual purpose of extending the work of such schools and of publishing books for Sunday school libraries. In the work of this society many theological students found vacation work. Between 1824 and 1850 more than eight hundred volumes were published — manuals, biographies, texts, maps, and the like. In 1855 the receipts from book sales were nearly two hundred thousand dollars.

These Sunday schools often used the Bell-Lancaster system of student teaching, which was used also in the free schools for poor children in parts of Pennsylvania, New Jersey, and other states. Lancastrian methods were quite simple, although there were a great many variations on the main theme; basically they meant the training of a small group of older children, or monitors, who were then entrusted with passing on the skills they had acquired to groups of younger children. One paid teacher could thus "educate" a very large number through the lips of the parrot monitors. The teaching was made as simple and mechanical as possible, with a great deal of group recitation and oral repetition of information imparted by the monitor. The system was fairly effective for cultivating basic skills in the three R's, and it certainly was a cheap method of reducing illiteracy. It flourished between 1800 and 1830, but fell into disrepute under the hearty condemnation of such educators as Horace Mann and Henry Barnard when the era of real reform began.

The disapproval of American workers was fully as emphatic, and it was as much their objection to class distinction as it was the educators' censure of techniques that eventually caused the rejection of the Lancastrian system. The assertion of American democratic ideals is implicit in every sentence of this statement by Walter R. Johnson of Pennsylvania in 1825:

Only allow the rich (no matter under what pretext, whether of philanthropy, or patriotism, or interest) to prescribe the education of the poor, and they prescribe their condition and relative importance. If anything be anti-republican, it certainly is so, directly or indirectly, to maintain that, although a hundred dollars a year is not too much to expend for the mental improvement of the son of a wealthy merchant, lawyer and physician, a two dollar education is quite sufficient for the children of the poor, or in other words, the mass of our fellow citizens.[37]

The libraries established by the Sunday schools were a permanent institution of much value and the forerunner of the school and public libraries of a much later date. One of the first recommendations of educational reformers was the creation of a library system for public schools, or at least the purchase of books in each district for use in the schools. Subscription libraries dated back to colonial days. Benjamin Franklin's Philadelphia Junto had bought books for a little circulating library of their own in the mid-eighteenth century. The Boston Athenaeum was incorporated in 1807 and was maintained by private subscription, as was the much later Boston Public Library (1852). There were similar institutions in other large cities, and even in quite small towns subscribers could be found for library societies.

The Harvard College library of twenty thousand volumes led the list of college libraries, and every little academy had a store of books. One other variety of semipublic library must have been peculiar to the New England of the 1830's. Occasionally in travelers' accounts and in diaries appears a reference to the "factory library." Whether this was maintained by a benevolent proprietor or by the subscriptions of workers, it is difficult to ascertain. In the diary of one New England maiden, not herself a factory worker, there is frequent mention of stopping at the factory in the village "to change my book." Similar small libraries were sometimes provided by workingmen's associations, and in the rural districts farmers' library societies organized by subscription seem to have been common. Some of their collections of books are still in existence and show a wide variety of titles.

In 1859 Rhee's *Manual of Public Libraries* listed over fifty thousand libraries in the United States — thirty thousand in Sunday schools, eighteen thousand in other schools, and nearly three thousand in cities and towns — with an estimated aggregate of nearly thirteen million volumes. The period of the endowed library began just shortly before the Civil War, too late to have had much effect on Rhee's list. John Jacob Astor left a large sum of money to establish a library in New York City, and under the guidance of Joseph Cogswell the funds were expended for a great reference collection that was later incorporated in the New York Public Library. The philanthropist and antislavery leader, Gerrit Smith, provided funds for the Oswego library in 1853, and Seth Grosvenor founded the Buffalo library in 1857. Thus the library slowly came into its own as an agent in the education of the great American public.

The movement for agricultural and mechanical education also began in this period, although little was accomplished before the Civil War. The state of New York, in 1819, appropriated twenty thousand dollars for a two-year program for the promotion of agriculture and manufacture. The fund was to be distributed among the counties for the use of agricultural societies and for the "diffusion of correct agricultural information." At about the same time an agricultural school was opened in Maine, and throughout the period many persons advocated the idea of instruction in agriculture in the district schools.

In 1822 the New York legislature passed an act incorporating the Mechanic and Scientific Institute, the purpose of which was the "instituting and maintaining of scientific and practical lectures applicable to the arts, and for collecting and forming a repository of machinery, tools, and generally for enlarging the knowledge and improving the condition of mechanics, artisans and manufacturers." A few years later the Rensselaer School of Troy, New York, was incorporated to teach scientific methods of agriculture as well as various branches of what we would today call vocational training. Through these and similar schools a beginning was made in the development of technical training.

With its goal "the advancement of education — especially in common schools — and the general diffusion of knowledge," the American Lyceum was organized in 1826. The chief complaint of those who were seeking educational reform was the indifference and apathy of the public. The lyceum movement was designed to do away with that lack of interest by stimulating discussion of subjects relating to education, and by teaching the average man to desire and to demand the privileges for his children that had long been advocated by philanthropists and reformers. In short, the American Lyceum was an instrument of public education and of propaganda.[38]

The object of the lyceum seems to have been the promotion of education in every way for every person; it was a sort of universal self-and-community-improvement association. As announced in 1829 the purposes were to improve the mind, and social intercourse, by the study of worthwhile subjects, to use old library facilities and create new ones, to encourage and assist academies, to raise the character of public schools, to compile materials for local history, and to make agricultural and geological surveys. Town lyceums were to be formed wherever the public could be made to desire them, they were to send representatives to county and state lyceums, and a national organization was to coordinate and direct the whole program.

Always strongest in New England, the movement spread into more than half the states of the Union and was carried by the lecture tours of its zealous founder, Josiah Holbrook, as far south as Georgia. The scope of the movement is suggested, perhaps, by the figures for its peak in the state where it was most popular: in 1839 there were one hundred and thirty-seven local lyceums in Massachusetts with a total average attendance of nearly thirty-three thousand. The life of the national lyceum was short, perhaps because education was recognized to be, in large part, a matter of local and state interest, but the local lyceums lived on for many years and played a great part in public education. The meetings served as forums on such practical questions as school textbooks, circulating libraries, taxes for educational purposes, and the creation of local and state boards of education.

The success of the lyceum in stimulating public interest in a variety of subjects was recorded in the comments of travelers. A member of the British Parliament visiting the United States in 1838 reported his surprise at the diffusion of knowledge in the United States:

Thousands of children, of not more than eight or ten years old, know more of geology, mineralogy, botany, statistical facts, etc. in fine, of what concerns their daily and national interests and occupations than was probably known thirty years ago by any five individuals in the United States.[39]

But it is to those who attended the weekly lyceum meetings that one must go for homely evidence of the educational effect of these local forums. A New Hampshire girl of eighteen described in her diary the meetings she attended through the winter of 1829–30. In February there were talks on anatomy delivered by the local Unitarian minister. In March a visiting scientist gave a series of lectures on chemical subjects, beginning with the "general properties of matter, with an illustration of the difference between attraction and chemical affinity," and going on through "Light, Heat and Electricity" to a grand climax, in a "hall crowded with spectators," of experiments on the combustion of phosphorus and hydrogen gas. And "the last and most interesting experiment was breathing the exhilarating gas, it affected some much more than others, the sensations appeared to be very pleasing generally except in one instance a man was so violent as to endanger his life." [40]

Libraries and lyceums thus contributed to the continual process of self-education to which Americans with active minds devoted so much time and energy in this period. Their ancestors had been sermon-tasters, accustomed to the long dissertations and disputations of Protestant theologians; now through these village forums they became lecture addicts and listened with unparalleled patience for the next forty years to the lectures of itinerant scholars, who, beginning their careers in the service of the American Lyceum, continued to make annual lecture tours long after the lyceum was no more. Emerson and Thoreau, Holmes and Lowell, Agassiz, Beecher, Wendell Phillips, and Horace Greeley were veterans of the lyceum platforms who might with justice be called perennial and peripatetic schoolmasters of America.

In every New England hamlet and far away on the Illinois prairie earnest seekers after knowledge taught themselves, spending their long winter evenings reading weighty tomes on history, philosophy, and science. The same New England girl who attended the lyceum so regularly devoted the intervals between — when household duties did not prevent — to a carefully planned course of reading. In one winter she read European history, physiology, Paley's *Moral Philosophy*, a treatise on American trees, and the newest novel by Scott, imported from England. It was a sad night when she had to say in her diary, "I have read nothing today, a wasted day." And many years later she wrote to her sons, who were pioneering in Minnesota, that she was sending them a box containing their winter underwear, some warm mittens, and the back numbers of the *Living Age* and the *Atlantic Monthly;* they might as well "improve your minds when the farm work is slack." Where but in pre-Civil War America could one find such devotion to education? Where and in what other period have so many followed so literally the advice of Noah Webster:

In selecting books for reading, be careful to choose such as furnish the best helps to improvement in morals, literature, arts and sciences, preferring profit to pleasure, and instruction to amusement. A small portion of time may be devoted to such reading as tends to relax the mind, and to such bodily amusements as serve to invigorate muscular strength and the vital functions. But the greatest part of life is to be employed in useful labors, and in various indispensable duties, private, social, and public. Man has but little time to spare for the gratification of the senses and the imagination. . . . Let it then be the first study of your early years to learn in what consists *real worth* or *dignity of character*.[41]

CHAPTER 11

Reform for the Criminal

With the revolutions that marked the end of the eighteenth century the old manner of treating the delinquent and the defective was rejected as an anachronism in a world that had recognized the importance of the individual. Beccaria's *Crime and Punishment* had been as widely read as Rousseau's *Emile,* and Montesquieu was known for his doctrines on the reform of criminal law and procedure as well as for his theories of government. It was early recognized that there was a fundamental incompatibility between the social forces of the American Revolution and the criminal codes of the colonial era. If the equality proclaimed in the Declaration of Independence meant anything at all, it meant equality before the law. If American statesmen were to give more than lip service to the humane and optimistic idea of man's improvability, they must remove the barbarism and vindictiveness from their penal codes and admit that one great objective of punishment for crime must be the reformation of the criminal.

Already men were groping toward the conception that man is in part the product of his environment and that society itself is responsible for many nonsocial actions. Science was soon to suggest that heredity, health, and other physical and psychological factors might play their part in delinquency and deficiency, making the criminal the victim as well as the villain in the social drama that ended in the prisoner's dock, and marking the defective as the unfortunate result of conditions for which he could not be held responsible. "An eye for an eye and a tooth for a tooth" seemed a barbaric principle of social revenge, and the righteous desire of the Puritan to cut off the wicked from the face of the earth gave way to a gentler doctrine of regeneration.

The change was not peculiar to the United States but was a part of the worldwide humanitarianism of the period. As in other lines of social progress, reform crossed national boundaries, and any list of those interested in the improvement of institutions for criminals or defectives must be international in scope. But the part played by the United States was far from ignoble. Indeed, so marked was the American advance in the treatment of society's unfortunates that European travelers made special efforts to visit American prisons and asylums, and European governments commissioned agents to study and report upon American progress.

Always these visitors sought to note such features of American plans as might with profit be copied in their own lands. In their turn, American humanitarians traveling abroad made contact with the managers of European institutions and brought home ideas for further changes in the American system. These humanitarians gave of their time and money to societies organized to work for reform, wrote letters and reports, and left for posterity the record of the movement that had been of such importance to them.

The European visitors differed in their ideas as to why American progress was more marked than that of Europe. Harriet Martineau found the cause for American progress in the democratic faith:

The fundamental democratic principles on which American Society is organized, are those "principles of justice and mercy" by which the guilty, the ignorant, the needy, and the infirm, are saved and blessed. The charity of a democratic society is heart-reviving to witness; for there is a security that no wholesale oppression is bearing down the million in one direction, while charity is lifting up the hundred in another. Generally speaking, the misery that is seen is all that exists: there is no paralysing sense of the hopelessness of setting up individual benevolence against social injustice. If the community has not yet arrived at the point at which all communities are destined to arrive, of perceiving guilt to be infirmity, of obviating punishment, ignorance, and want, still the Americans are more blessed than others, in the certainty that they have far less superinduced misery than society abroad, and are using wiser methods than others for its alleviation.[1]

Other visitors found the explanation in the profound interest of the American people in matters of religion. De Tocqueville called attention to the fact that prison reform in America stemmed from religious concern for the reformation of the criminal and the salvation of his soul. Again and again he discussed prison reform with members of the clergy and noted the fact that the heads of many of the best penal institutions, reform schools, and asylums were ex-ministers of Protestant faiths. But this linking of humanitarianism with religion which was so peculiarly American received its best description, perhaps, in the words of Francis Grund:

Religion has been the basis of the most important American settlements; religion kept their little community together — religion assisted them in their revolutionary struggle; it was religion to which they appealed in defending their rights, and it was religion, in fine, which taught them to prize their liberties. It is with the solemnities of religion that the declaration of independence is yet annually read to the people from the pulpit, or that Americans celebrate the anniversaries of the most important events in their history. It is to religion they have recourse whenever they wish to impress the popular feeling with anything relative to their own country; and it is religion which assists them in all their national undertakings. The Americans look upon religion as a promoter of civil and political liberty; and have, therefore, transferred to it a large portion of the affection which they cherish for the institutions of their country. . . . Religion presides over their councils, aids in the execution of the laws, and adds to the dignity of the judges. Whatever is calculated to diminish its influence and practice, has a tendency to weaken the government, and is, consequently, opposed to the peace and welfare of the United States.[2]

Americans themselves were quite willing to attribute to Christianity the origin of the movement for the relief of the distressed and the reformation of the perverse. The preamble to the constitution of the Philadelphia society formed in 1787 for "Alleviating the Miseries of Public Prisons" began with the biblical text, "I was in prison and ye came unto me," and continued with the announcement:

When we consider that the obligations of benevolence, which are founded on the precepts and example of the Author of Christianity, are not canceled by the follies or crimes of our fellow creatures; and when we reflect upon the miseries which penury, hunger, cold, unnecessary severity, unwholesome apartments, and guilt . . . involve upon them: it becomes us to extend our compassion to that part of mankind, who are subjects of these miseries. By the aid of humanity, their undue and illegal sufferings may be prevented . . . and such degrees and modes of punishment may be discovered and suggested, as may, instead of continuing habits of vice, become the means of restoring our fellow creatures to virtue and happiness.[3]

About forty years later the continuation of this religious zeal was evident in the work of Louis Dwight, the secretary and guiding spirit of the Boston Prison Discipline Society, whose interest in prison reform had been roused to white heat by his experiences as a traveling agent of the American Bible Society commissioned to carry Bibles to the inmates of prisons throughout the United States. For thirty years Dwight devoted himself to the improvement of prison conditions, because he was convinced that

There is but one sufficient excuse for Christians in suffering such evils to exist in prisons in this country, and that is, that they are not acquainted with the real state of things. . . . When I bring before the Church of Christ a statement of what my eyes have seen, there will be a united and powerful effort to alleviate the miseries of prisons.[4]

Thus the work begun in the Age of Reason became a crusade in the years when democracy and religion combined to speed the progress of social reform.

PENAL CODES BEFORE 1815

Criminal law in the American colonies was similar to that of the countries from which the colonists had come. Punishment was almost exclusively corporal — the death penalty for serious crimes and some form of publicly inflicted pain or humiliation for minor offenses. Whipping, mutilation, confinement in stocks, "ducking," and branding were the lesser punishments usually provided in the sentences of colonial courts. Puritanism and Quaker asceticism alike condemned every form of sensuality, and blasphemy and impiety were regarded as crimes against the state. Gambling, drunkenness, dueling, lying, breaking the peace, and conspicuous idleness were considered offenses meriting severe punishment, and the "common scold" was publicly ducked in an attempt to rid the community of the nuisance of her virulence. Local codes meticulously prescribed the number of lashes or the number of hours in the stocks to be imposed for some minor offenses and for others fixed the spot on the offender's body where a designated letter should be burned.

But in a period when there were more than two hundred capital offenses under English law, colonial codes were thought to be extremely mild. In Pennsylvania in the days of the mild Quaker code murder was the only offense punishable by death. The adoption of the English criminal code in 1718 added a dozen others to the list, however, and when the colonial period ended there were twenty capital crimes in Pennsylvania, and the death penalty might be imposed for a second offense in the case of various others. The famous Connecticut Blue Laws provided the death penalty for fourteen crimes, the Duke of York's code for New York listed twelve capital offenses, and Virginia's colonial code, later copied by Kentucky, made provision for twenty-seven. As late as 1789 death was the legal penalty for ten crimes in Massachusetts, Rhode Island, and Connecticut. Obviously there was little need for prisons in colonial America; the "common gaol" for temporary detention was all that was necessary.

Slowly the barbarism of these early codes disappeared. Pennsylvania led the way with the provisions of the constitution of 1776 and the acts of succeeding legislatures. Murder became again the only crime punishable by death, and imprisonment at hard labor was substituted for the cruel forms of corporal punishment — although as late as 1817 a sailor was bound to the iron rings outside the wall of the Walnut Street jail in Philadelphia and was publicly flogged. In the same period other states rewrote their criminal codes and began the slow process of putting into effect their constitutional provisions banning "cruel and unusual" punishments. There was no abrupt transition, nor was the procedure of the various states uniform or simultaneous. In Salem, Massachusetts, in 1801 a forger was made to stand in the pillory for an hour and had his ears cropped, and in Boston two years later two criminals were publicly pilloried before being imprisoned for a year. As late as 1822 a felon was publicly flogged on the Yale campus in view of the college students.

The fate of the "common scold" long remained precarious; apparently imprisonment did not seem an effective remedy. The Philadelphia court of sessions of 1824 sentenced one such neighborhood pest to be ducked, but the sentence was declared obsolete and was not enforced. Georgia scolds were not thus rescued, however, for one was ducked in 1811 and another in 1817. Later still the famous editorial critic, Mrs. Anne Royall, was sentenced by a court in Washington, D. C., to be ducked in the Potomac — a sentence that was quickly commuted to a fine.

With these occasional exceptions it may be stated that in the early years of the century fines or imprisonment or both had replaced the old forms of corporal punishment in the United States. The death penalty was reserved for one or two crimes, and pillory, branding iron, and whipping post had disappeared from public view.

THE EARLY MOVEMENT FOR PRISON REFORM

Offenders against the law were temporarily confined in jail while awaiting trial or punishment. They were not considered to have rights it was necessary to respect, and their comfort in confinement was not a matter of public concern. When imprisonment came to take the place of corporal punishment, the jails became the first prisons and provision was necessary for making them more than temporary abodes. Public-spirited men of the Revolutionary period were quick to see that reforms were necessary before imprisonment could carry with it the possibility of reformation. Anticipating the action of government, such men, exercising the civil liberties granted them in the new constitutions, organized societies to investigate, make reports, and work to alleviate conditions in the public prisons. The Philadelphia Society for Alleviating the Miseries of Public Prisons was the first, and for a long time the most effective, of such organizations, and its work was copied by philanthropists in other communities.[5]

Among the prominent Philadelphians who were willing to share in the work of reform were: Benjamin Franklin, Benjamin Rush, William Bradford, the author of the state's new criminal code, William White, bishop of the Episcopal church and president of the prison society for forty-nine years, Caleb Lownes, head of the Walnut Street jail in its best days, and the Quaker Roberts Vaux and his son Richard, who were the authors of many of the reports of the Philadelphia society. Some of these men were active members of the society, others cooperated with it in its efforts to accomplish its twofold purpose: ameliorating conditions in the Walnut Street and High Street jails in the City of Brotherly Love, and formulating plans for a modern prison to be constructed by the state as a part of its duty to those whom its laws condemned to confinement.

In the year of its organization the society introduced religious services in the Walnut Street jail, an action opposed by the keeper of the jail and made possible only by the written command of the sheriff of the county. This is said to have been the first religious service ever conducted in an American penal institution.[6] Whether that is true or not, the act set the tone for much of the work of this and other similar societies. Sunday services for the assembled prisoners and Sunday schools for religious instruction and for teaching elementary subjects to illiterate prisoners soon came to be major planks in the platform of prison reform groups. Bibles were provided for every cell, and special visitors listened to the stories of the prisoners and gave such counsel as their hearts might dictate.

Prison discipline societies always numbered clergymen among their members and strove to provide the institutions they served with resident chaplains whose entire time could be given to the spiritual regeneration of the prisoners. Missionaries sent out by the prison societies and itinerant evangelists of various faiths conducted revivals within prison walls and rejoiced over the salvation of souls that to the revivalist must have seemed only a shade blacker than those of his usual congregations. Between religious services prisoners were encouraged to commit to memory passages from the Bibles to which they had constant access. One prison visitor reported that in eighteen weeks several prisoners had memorized forty-two entire books of the Bible.[7] Early nineteenth-century religious faith could deny to no one the possibility of spiritual regeneration and conversion. Perfection was not beyond the grasp of even the most degraded soul, and assurance of rebirth and new life for the contrite sinner made the reformation of the criminal seem far from improbable.

Actual conditions in the old jails, now serving as catchalls for all varieties of offenders, the reformers found to be far from conducive to the regeneration of the prisoners. They were instead a school for crime and a breeding place for both physical and mental disease. The early reports of the Philadelphia society may be taken as portrayals of conditions typical throughout the country. Rural jails may have been less crowded and therefore less of a menace to the health and morals of those thrown into them, but wherever illustrative material for them can be found the same black picture appears.

In 1788 Roberts Vaux reported to the Philadelphia society the results of his careful investigation of prison conditions. He had found that the clothing of the prisoners was scanty, because the inmates customarily confiscated the outer garments of incoming prisoners to pay for rum for the whole group. There was no separation of sexes, nor was there any segregation of young offenders; all prisoners were confined in large groups in small rooms with little furniture and less heat. They were charged for food and lodging, poor though both might be, and those judged innocent when their cases came to trial might be detained as debtors for the nonpayment of jail fees. Debtors were confined with criminals and received practically the same treatment. Food was, for the most part, bad, and it seemed to Vaux unnecessarily hard that mothers with babies should be given the same food, both in quality and quantity, as single persons. Rum was sold by the jailers, who expected to profit from the miseries of the wretches in their charge. Vaux's report ended with the recommendation that all prisoners be confined in separate cells and provided with labor — "more private or even solitary labor would more successfully tend to redeem the unhappy objects." Vaux urged that the sexes be separated at all times and that hardened criminals be kept away from first offenders, and he strongly recommended the "prohibition of spirituous liquor among the criminals." [8]

This report, sent in the form of a memorial to the state legislature, produced an immediate and pronounced effect. Its chief recommendations were enacted into laws that provided for the separation of witnesses and debtors from convicts, for the proper segregation of the sexes, for the erection of a block of cells for the solitary confinement of "the more hardened and atrocious offenders," and for the labor of all those convicted of crime. Before 1800, however, conditions were again almost as bad as before; public interest subsided, as the population grew the jails were overcrowded, and the society despaired of any improvement until the state had built an adequate prison. The work of the Pennsylvania reformers was directed, therefore, toward creating a public demand for new prison buildings.

Conditions in other states in the years after the Revolution were similar to those in Pennsylvania. No one knew those conditions better than the notorious Stephen Burroughs, and his memoirs are a mine of information about the jails and prisons of his day as well as about the life of the underworld — and the demiworld — of the period.[9] Burroughs' autobiography, in the form of a series of letters, begins with the 1780's and extends into the early years of the nineteenth century. He admitted that when he was a boy everyone said he would be hanged before he was forty, and the reader of his memoirs is surprised that this fate had not yet overtaken him. After many youthful pranks, Burroughs spent some time at Dartmouth, studied for the ministry, taught a district school, tried the life of a sailor, and wandered about New England, living, apparently, by his wits. He became involved in counterfeiting and was sentenced to three years in jail in Northampton, Massachusetts, thus beginning a career that was to be spent, to a considerable extent, in various houses of detention.

In Northampton he was confined in a small cell with two other men. The food was scanty, the cell was cold, and the men were given no work to do. Their entire time was occupied with efforts to escape, and their failures resulted in repeated floggings and in confinement in a dungeon, where Burroughs was chained to a staple in the floor by ten feet of chain fastened to a six-inch band about his leg. When he attempted to commit suicide by burning the jail, he was again flogged and thrown back into the dungeon, to be chained this time with two leg rings, handcuffs, and an iron around his waist. After a month of solitary confinement, almost without food, in this cold, dark dungeon, Burroughs was transferred to Castle Island in the Boston harbor, where the state maintained a prison managed by the state militia. Again he tried to escape, and again he was whipped and mistreated. Finally his term ended, and he was released, only to fall into further difficulties and to be returned to jail for other offenses. Burroughs' memoirs, even allowing for his undoubted exaggeration, depict the conditions against which the philanthropists were protesting and indicate that pious New England was no more humane than the Quaker capital.

Massachusetts and other states were being roused, however, to build the new prisons necessary to take care of those for whom the new criminal codes prescribed prison sentences. In Virginia in 1800 Thomas Jefferson, using a European plan, designed the Richmond penitentiary to provide solitary confinement for each prisoner. The reforms being instituted in the Walnut Street jail led to similar efforts in new prisons at Newgate, New York, Charlestown, Massachusetts, Baltimore, Maryland, and Windsor, Vermont, in the period 1795–1810. Unfortunately, however, none of these new buildings used the separate cell system, and they were soon so overcrowded that conditions reverted to the old evils. Prisons built in the new Western states were crude efforts to confine the prisoner in security, Connecticut continued to use its copper mine for a prison, and other states relied on their old county jails. The United States could not be said to have evolved a prison system in the first forty years of the republic.

THE RIVAL SYSTEMS

After 1815, in the renewed wave of revivalism and humanitarianism that swept the country, the cause of prison reform gained more adherents and new urgency. The Philadelphia society petitioned the legislature again and again for new buildings, constantly reiterating its plea that prisoners be confined in a solitude upon which religious and reformatory influence might be brought to bear and in which constant salutary labor might inculcate habits of industry that would persist when the prisoner returned to life outside prison walls.

In the state of New York, where the rapid increase of population made action a necessity, two new prisons were provided by law in 1816. The first to be built — the Auburn Penitentiary — was originally designed for the old congregate system, but a group of reformers who were in touch with the Philadelphia society and with movements abroad secured additional legislation instituting the cell system. An economical contractor built the cell block in such a fashion that each man was allotted a space just seven feet long, three and a half feet wide, and seven feet high. These cells were ventilated from the roof and had no outside windows.

The effect of solitary confinement in such close quarters was appalling. The health of the men deteriorated, and several became insane. The men in control of prison policy — Elam Lynds, John Cray, and Gersham Powers — therefore altered the system in 1823 by providing congregate labor in the daytime and the use of the cells only at night. All sorts of workshops were built in the open space between the rectangular cell block and the prison walls, and the men left their cubicles in the early morning for a hard day's labor outside. The discipline was severe. The convicts marched to work in lock step, were never placed face to face, and were strictly forbidden to speak to each other. Every infraction of the rules was instantly and harshly punished. Flogging was selected as the most desirable form of punishment, for, unless extremely severe, it did not long interrupt the prisoner's labor. Working under such a re-

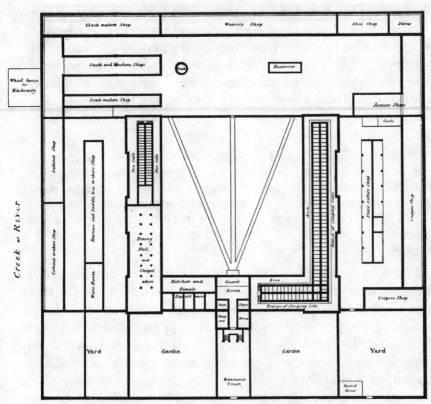

From William Crawford's report on the penitentiaries of the United States, 1834

The Auburn system of cell blocks with common dining quarters, chapel, and workshops

gime, the convicts were relatively easy to control, and one sentinel was sufficient for more than a hundred prisoners. This became known as the Auburn system.

The second of New York's new prisons was constructed, under the supervision of Elam Lynds, at Sing Sing on the Hudson River. Built on the Auburn system, it contained one thousand cells. When De Tocqueville and De Beaumont came to America in 1831 with a commission from the French government to study penal institutions, they made a thorough investigation of this prison, remaining there for nine days, and went away filled with wonder at the success of the system. De Tocqueville commented upon the health of the inmates, the productiveness of their labor, the excess of income

over expenditures, and the encouragement given to moral reform —
although his Gallic realism made him doubt the effectiveness of the
religious influences with men "hardened in crime and inveterately
corrupt." [10] The young Frenchmen were much impressed by the
sight of the prisoners working in the stone quarries in absolute silence, watched by a mere handful of guards, but they felt the prison
was a volcano that might at any moment erupt in violent action.
De Tocqueville wrote:

One cannot see the prison of Sing-Sing and the system of labour which
is there established without being struck by astonishment and fear. Although the discipline is perfect, one feels that it rests on a fragile foundation; it is due to a *tour de force* which is reborn unceasingly and which
has to be reproduced each day, under penalty of compromising the
whole system of discipline. . . . it seems to us impossible not to fear
some sort of catastrophe in the future.[11]

Prison labor was performed under contract, representatives of
the contractor being present to supervise the work done for them.
The English visitor, James Stuart, recorded that in 1829 the expenses of the prison at Auburn were approximately thirty-four
thousand dollars while the receipts from convict labor were nearly
forty thousand.[12] Another Englishman of the period, Henry Tudor,
praised the Auburn system highly, stating that a great many of the
convicts had become honest and industrious citizens when their
prison terms ended, because the combination of solitary confinement and congregate labor had fitted them for better lives.

One of the highly beneficial effects of this excellent system [he
wrote] and a proof of its superior and economical organization is, that
the earnings of the prisoners, in their daily convocations, exceed very
considerably the expenses attendant on their confinement; and which
surplus is, I understand, very wisely and humanely given to the felons,
on their discharge, in order to set them up in some honest calling.[13]

Since their report was designed for the guidance of the French
government in reorganizing its prison system, De Tocqueville and
De Beaumont broke down the figures for expenditures and receipts
and carefully examined statistics as to costs and as to the terms of
contract labor. They found that where the Auburn system was in
effect nearly everything used in the prison was made within its
walls by convict labor and that almost one third of the prisoners

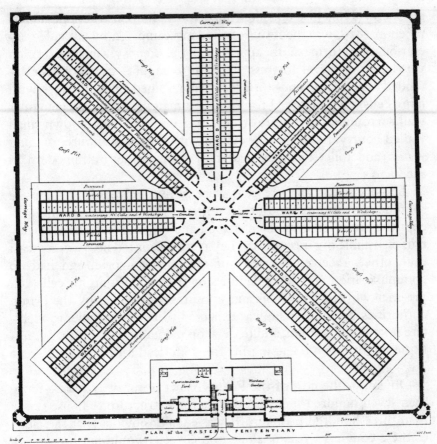

From William Crawford's report on the penitentiaries of the United States, 1834

The Pennsylvania system for solitary confinement, in which each prisoner was provided with a cell and small exercise yard

were occupied in prison economy. Contract labor was leased at about half the rate for free labor, and the receipts made it possible to administer the prisons at no cost, perhaps even at a profit, to the state. Such a system might, they thought, work more profitably in America, where the labor supply was inadequate and the demand for manufactured goods was great, than it would in France, but they agreed that its effects upon French prisoners would be equally beneficial.[14]

Sooner or later all who visited one of the prisons designed on the Auburn system went on to examine the Eastern State Penitentiary at Cherry Hill, just outside Philadelphia. Its construction, undertaken in 1829, was the result of the long campaign by a whole generation of reformers. In appearance the Pennsylvania institution was like a medieval fortress. From an octagonal central tower extended seven long one-storied corridors, lined on both sides with large cells, each designed for a single inmate. A massive rectangular wall surrounded the entire structure. Every cell had its own small walled courtyard and was provided with decent furniture, running water, and toilet facilities that must have seemed ultramodern in the 1830's.

The occupants of these cells were to live and work in complete solitude for the duration of their sentences, receiving no visitors except the prison officers, the chaplain, and the representatives of certain charitable organizations. They were permitted no contacts with each other, received no news of the outside world, and had no communication with their families or friends. Within his cell each prisoner worked with tools and upon tasks provided by the prison authorities. In solitude he was expected to read the Bible, to meditate upon his condition, and to develop mentally and spiritually, until he might, upon obtaining his freedom, lead a new and different life.

Obviously the cost of the Pennsylvania prison was great—more than seven hundred thousand dollars for a structure to house fewer than three hundred prisoners. It was equally obvious that the labor of these convicts working alone in their cells would not be as profitable as the workshops of the Auburn system.[15] The merit of the Pennsylvania plan was claimed to be a greater effectiveness in the reformation of the inmates. Advocates of the Auburn plan countered with the assertion that congregate labor was better for the health of the prisoner, and they quoted figures to show that the death rate was three or four times higher in the Pennsylvania prison than in prisons of the New York type. They claimed that solitary confinement was conducive to insanity, too, and said the New Jersey prison authorities had admitted as much when they reported that upon the first evidence of insanity in a prisoner they placed a second man in his cell—a treatment that "invariably restores the patient."

While the Pennsylvania prison was being built, Louis Dwight, the crusading head of the Boston Prison Discipline Society, was stirring the public conscience of New England to build new prisons and reform the management of older institutions. The Auburn system appealed to Dwight as a program that could be sold both to legislative bodies and to religious organizations interested in the salvation of sinners.

In the Massachusetts prison at Charlestown Dwight found the evils that had been condemned by the prison societies for many years. Not only could he call it a school for crime, but its discipline seemed to him inhumane and indifferent to the moral needs of the prisoners. In 1815 the directors of the prison had issued a declaration that prison "discipline should be as severe as the law of humanity will by any means tolerate" and that the mind of the prisoner "requires to be reduced to a state of humiliation." [16] Perhaps in recognition of this avowed necessity for "conquering the minds" of the prisoners, the old practice of tattooing on each convict the words *Massachusetts State Prison* was not abolished until 1829.

The Boston Prison Discipline Society devoted its energies to changing the public attitude toward prison discipline and to persuading the legislature to appropriate funds for erecting a cell block in the Charlestown prison, so that the Auburn system might be instituted. After that had been done, the Massachusetts prison took its place with Auburn and Sing Sing in attracting American and European visitors interested in prison reform. The changes effected by the religious work of Dwight and the Boston society led most of the visitors to commend the Charlestown prison especially for its reformatory possibilities. The whip, for instance, so often in evidence at Auburn and Sing Sing, was much more sparingly used at Charlestown. Punishment — usually for infraction of the rules for silence — was ordinarily confinement in the cell or a temporary bread-and-water diet.

Dwight was responsible, in part at least, for the establishment of the model prison at Wethersfield, Connecticut, for it was his scathing invective against the continued use of the old copper mine that shamed the legislators into appropriating funds for a new prison. Wethersfield, too, attracted a constant stream of visitors from other states and from foreign countries, and furnished the example used by Dwight as he toured the country in the cause of reform. The low cost of construction, the large returns from prison labor, the educational and religious activities maintained within the prison — all were ammunition for the enthusiastic Mr. Dwight. Connecticut was fortunate in securing as warden the able administrator and supporter of reform measures, Moses Pillsbury,[17] who served in that capacity for twenty years and was followed in office by his equally efficient son, Amos Pillsbury. De Beaumont and De Tocqueville found conditions at Wethersfield excellent and reported that, under the mildest discipline of any prison they had visited, the inmates earned twice their cost to the state. Within a few months of the visit of the laudatory Frenchmen, however, all Connecticut was shaken by the disclosure that this great profit had been secured at the expense of food, fuel, and other comforts to which the prisoners had been entitled. There was need for constant vigilance on the part of prison societies and inspectors.

New Hampshire, Vermont, Kentucky, Ohio, Maryland, and Tennessee fell into line before 1840 and constructed new prisons, using some modification of the Auburn system as their model. In the meantime the Eastern State Penitentiary had been completed, and the controversy over the two systems had got under way. The Philadelphia plan was extolled to Louis Dwight, but his mind was already made up, and for thirty years his vigorous and positive support was given to the Auburn system. Partly because of Dwight's missionary enterprise, but probably still more because of the economic advantages of the Auburn system, most of the prison building of the mid-nineteenth century was on that model. New Jersey, in 1833, built a prison much like the Eastern State Penitentiary, but was never able to provide the combination of large cells, outdoor exercise yards, and full labor for each prisoner that had been the most praised features of that institution. Before 1860 New Jersey went over to the Auburn system. Virginia and Rhode Island also attempted to follow the Pennsylvania system but found administration too difficult and costs too great.

Abroad, however, prisons were built on the Pennsylvania model in several countries at the recommendation of investigators who had been sent to the United States. Nonetheless, European visitors were as divided as Americans about the merits of the rival systems.

De Tocqueville and De Beaumont, qualified investigators, were less outspokenly partisan than certain traveling philanthropists, but they were perhaps better informed and more careful in their estimates. Their considered verdict was this:

The Philadelphia system being also that which produces the deepest impression on the soul of the convict, must effect more reformation than that of Auburn. The latter, however, is perhaps the more conformable to the habits of man in society, and on this account effects a greater number of reformations, which might be called "legal," inasmuch as they produce the external fulfillment of social obligations. If it be so, the Philadelphia system produces more honest men, and that of New York more obedient citizens.[18]

Having thus confounded the Reverend Louis Dwight and all revivalistic prison reformers, the Frenchmen went on to assert that in all American prisons discipline was severe, whether with the objective to punish or to reform. At Auburn they could find little humanitarianism, for order depended upon the whip, and in the Philadelphia prison man's greatest stricture upon man — solitude — was the method used to the same end.

To sum up the whole on this point [they wrote] it must be acknowledged that the penitentiary system in America is severe. Whilst society in the United States gives the example of the most extended liberty, the prisons of the same country offer the spectacle of the most complete despotism. The citizens subject to the law are protected by it; they only cease to be free when they become wicked.[19]

No one among prison authorities or among the ubiquitous European visitors seems to have considered the wishes of the prisoners in regard to these persistent official and unofficial visitations. Harriet Martineau and Charles Dickens repeated at length their private conversations with the prisoners in the eastern Pennsylvania prison — men who were not allowed visits from their friends or relatives but who were presumed to welcome the curiosity of distinguished foreigners. De Tocqueville remained for weeks within prison walls and questioned wardens and prisoners at will, apparently received with as much courtesy by the latter as by the former. In the years when the authorities at Auburn charged twenty-five cents per visitor, one English traveler, and only one, appeared aware of the indignity inflicted upon the prisoner, who even in solitary confinement could find no privacy. Captain Marryat happened on a little book, *The Rat-Trap, or Cogitations of a Convict in the House of Correction*, written by a scholarly American brought low by "intemperance, the prevalent vice of America." This prisoner-author impressed Marryat with the fervor of his protest against public inspection:

Among the annoyances, which others as well as myself felt most galling, was the frequent intrusion of visitors, who had no object but the gratification of a morbid curiosity. Know all persons, that the most debased convict has human feelings, and does not like to be seen in a parti-coloured jacket. . . . Let the throng of uninvited fools who swarmed about us, accept the following sally of the House of Correction muse, from the pen, or rather the fork of a fellow convict.

To Our Visitors
By gazing at us, sirs, pray what do you mean?
Are we the first rascals that ever were seen?
Look into your mirrors — perhaps you may find
All villains are not in South Boston confined.

I'm not a wild beast, to be seen for a penny;
But a man, as well made and as proper as any;
And what we must differ in is, well I wot,
That I have my merits, and you have them not.
. . . .
And now that by staring with mouth and eyes open,
Ye have bruised the reeds that already were broken;
Go home and, by dint of strict mental inspection,
Let each make his own house a House of Correction.[20]

Through all the agitation by enthusiastic and devoted humanitarian reformers much was done. By 1840 twelve Auburn type prisons had been constructed with a total cell capacity of nearly five thousand. All these prisons were operating prosperous industrial departments; four of them had fairly good women's departments; four had permanent chaplains; and several ran Sunday schools for the instruction of illiterates. About one half of them had abolished the use of the lash, and a few — most notably Richmond — were experimenting with the merit system. The Philadelphia system was in operation in two prisons in Pennsylvania and in the New Jersey penitentiary. Maine and Rhode Island had adopted the solitary system in the crudest possible manner; in the Maine prison there were a few underground pits, so crowded that there were always two or more in a cell; in Rhode Island provision had been made for tiny inside cells in the Providence jail. After 1840 improvements were made in old prisons and new building continued, especially in the West. Michigan, Wisconsin, and Iowa built on the Auburn plan, and Alabama and Louisiana copied the cell block system and developed prison industries as a part of the South's attempt to foster industrial advancement.[21] But much remained to be done. As Francis Lieber summarized the state of affairs:

Prisons have been called hospitals for patients laboring under moral diseases, but until recently, they have been in all countries where any existed, and unfortunately continue still to be in most countries, of a kind that they ought to be compared rather to the plague-houses of the East, in which every person afflicted with that mortal disorder is sure to perish, and he who is sent there without yet being attacked, is sure to have it.[22]

IMPRISONMENT FOR DEBT

In the days when corporal punishment was the fate of those who transgressed the laws of the state, the jails were occupied largely by debtors, who were more the victims of certain conditions of society than offenders against its dictates. And when new laws provided imprisonment for offenses that had formerly been punished by lash or executioner, the unfortunate inhabitants of the county jails received as fellow inmates the criminals with whom they had little in common except their helplessness.

The lot of the debtor received little attention in the period of reform after the Revolution. The new states retained the statutes of the colonial period in all their harshness and prescribed imprisonment for the debtor until such time as his debts might be paid. In the period of depression after 1819, the plight of the debtor came up for review, and, once called to the attention of the awakening humanitarian sentiment of the day — and to the attention of the workingmen who were beginning to exercise their newly won suffrage — that plight did not go without remedy.

In 1816 there were nearly two thousand debtors confined in the jails of New York City, the average at any given time being about six hundred. More than a thousand of these unfortunates were confined for debts of less than fifty dollars, and seven hundred of them for debts below twenty-five dollars. The state made no provision for food, furniture, or fuel in the quarters allotted to debtors, and these miserable men would have starved except for the kindness of the Humane Society. In the winter of 1816 the sheriff of the county protested that, since he could not endure to permit his hapless charges to freeze, he had been compelled to pay for fuel from his own purse. One prisoner was held in jail for three years, and another for six years, for a debt under fifty dollars and both were supported during that time entirely by charity.

The futility of such a practice, from the point of view of both debtor and society, was clear. Debtors might be, and often were, imprisoned by unscrupulous competitors for spite, and, while in confinement, it was entirely impossible for them to earn the money to repay the debts for which they had been thrown into jail. In a Vermont case that was given great publicity a man owed a firm of two a debt of fifty-four cents. Each creditor by court action had his debtor imprisoned for twenty-seven cents. The costs in both cases were charged to the debtor, thus increasing his obligation by nearly fifteen dollars. How he could, from the county jail, pay the latter sum when the former had been beyond his resources was not stated in court. The creditors' vindictiveness, which had been the cause of the suit, had been satisfied, however, and the fate of the debtor was considered his just due. The Puritan moral code that considered thrift a major virtue and wealth an evidence of God's favor offered no comfort for those whose poverty or shiftlessness were adjudged indications of probable depravity.

The Boston Society for the Relief of the Distressed reported that about thirty-five hundred persons had been imprisoned for debt in that city from January 1820 to April 1822. Two thousand had been confined for less than twenty dollars each, and nearly five hundred of the whole number were women. The agents of the society estimated that more than ten thousand people were helpless subjects of charity because of the imprisonment of those who might have provided for their care. The society reported the case of a woman who had been taken from her home and little children because of a debt of three dollars, and the even more dramatic case of a man who had been held in jail for thirty years for a trifling debt that had grown to three thousand dollars because of the jail fees, interest, and costs that had accumulated as the years crept by.

In Philadelphia in 1828 the keeper of the debtors' prison reported that he had held more than a thousand men for debts totaling twenty-five thousand dollars, at a cost to the community of nearly twelve times that sum. In the Philadelphia jail seven men were confined for a total of one hundred and seventy-two days for a joint indebtedness of less than three dollars; one was in for two cents. There were nearly a thousand debtors in the Baltimore jail in 1831; more than one half of them owed less than ten dollars, and only about thirty owed as much as one hundred. Examples could be multiplied ad infinitum; the plight of the debtor was the same everywhere.

When sufficient publicity was given to these conditions, changes were made, although progress was slow and there was little uniformity in the way the problem was approached in the various states. It was argued that imprisonment for debt was not democratic and was "obviously intended to increase and confirm the power of a wealthy aristocracy by rendering poverty a crime, and subjecting the liberty of the poor to the capricious will of the rich." [28] One of the first reforms sought was the elimination of the crowd of prisoners whose debts were trivial and whose imprisonment was an expense to society out of all proportion to the total of their debts. In 1817 the New York legislature passed a law making twenty-five dollars the minimum debt for which a man could be imprisoned. Other states quickly followed suit, some of them adding clauses that no women could be jailed for debt. In 1821 Kentucky abolished all imprisonment for debt. A similar law was adopted in Ohio in 1828; Vermont and New Jersey added their approval in 1830; New York did the same two years later; Connecticut followed in 1837, Louisiana in 1840, Missouri in 1845, and Alabama in 1848. So the states fell into line, and the debtors' prison gradually became a thing of the past.

CHAPTER 12

Wards of the State

As soon as men began to consider prison reform, they recognized a fundamental inconsistency in professing concern for the reformation of the criminal and ignoring the condition of those who had been placed in jail because of misdemeanors. Incarcerated in common rooms with hardened criminals, young boys, and older misdemeanants as well, were inevitably schooled in crime and were discharged only to appear again on more serious charges. And the removal of the criminal to the new prisons provided by the states did not solve the problem, for the jails remained a sordid and squalid catchall for the dregs of society. Out of the realization of this situation came two new institutions, correctional rather than penal — the juvenile reform school, or house of refuge, and the house of correction for misdemeanants.

CORRECTIONAL INSTITUTIONS

Even those who doubted the possibility of reforming the hardened criminal were convinced that the child, whose offense had been due more to the environment in which he lived than to his own depravity, might be educated to desire a better life and to play a useful part in the community. The adult, too, who had been arrested for vagrancy, drunkenness, or petty thievery — all due, in large part, to poverty and lack of adequate training — might be turned into a useful member of the society whose previous neglect had placed him in custody.

Charitable and religious organizations had for generations made partial provision for the care of the fatherless. The humanitarianism of the nineteenth century led to a marked increase in the number of orphan asylums and an improvement in the care they provided. Supported by local charity and by religious denominations, orphanages and orphan schools were maintained in all large cities, but even these reached the needs of only a few of the nation's unfortunate children. The offspring of the destitute poor in both urban and rural areas were offered little in the way of education, encouragement, or support. Living largely by their wits, they early fell into the bad graces of the law, and, thrown into jail, they began their careers of crime under good auspices.

The first reform schools were maintained by private charity in connection with urban orphanages. Several European cities were having considerable success with this kind of organization when a group of public-spirited men in New York City worked out a plan for the first institution entirely devoted to the reformation of the juvenile offender. Exercised about the growing number of waifs in their developing commercial center, in 1816 they formed the Society for the Prevention of Pauperism and instituted an investigation of juvenile delinquency. They found that many juries refused to convict children because there was no provision for their care other than in the common gaol, but that, despite this forbearance, an average of seventy-five boys had been sent to prison in each of the years from 1819 to 1821. The problem of the delinquent girl was even more serious, for little provision had as yet been made for the separate care of the woman prisoner. The report of this early society led to the formation of a new group whose objective was to make adequate provision for juvenile offenders of both sexes. With Professor John Griscom as its head, this new society, by means of funds privately contributed, built the New York House of Refuge in 1825. In typical American fashion, the state and the city then came to the aid of the society and appropriated funds to maintain the institution for five years. After 1830 it became entirely a public institution, drawing all its support from public funds.

In 1826 Boston, and in 1828 Philadelphia, followed the example set by New York. A farm school for juvenile delinquents was established in 1835 on Thompson's Island near Boston; a decade later the state of Massachusetts built a large reform school at Westborough, and in 1847 it constructed the first reform school exclusively for girls. Similar institutions were established in other states, so that by 1850 the principle that the delinquent child is a ward of the state had been well established.

In many ways the house of refuge was a part of the prison reform movement, and the separate cell system, the regimentation, and the strict discipline of Auburn Penitentiary were reflected in the regime set up for juvenile offenders. Not until the late 1850's did the cottage type of institutional building make any headway.

At the same time the discipline was modified, and institutional life was profoundly altered by recognition of the fact that the house of refuge was a school as well as a place of confinement. This hybrid nature was indicated in the name "reform school." Since placing the line of demarcation between correction and education was the work of the superintendent, there was wide variation in emphasis in different institutions. Most contemporary observers bore witness to the dual nature of the institutions they visited and appraised the work of those in charge on the basis of their own predilections as to where the emphasis should lie.

Foreign visitors were uniformly enthusiastic about the work done by these "child-saving" institutions and nearly always called special attention to the fact that the men in charge of them were of the highest caliber, educators as well as disciplinarians. One of the first European travelers to inspect the New York House of Refuge was the Duke of Saxe-Weimar Eisenach, who visited it in its first year. He spoke highly of its cleanliness, food, and discipline and commended its educational work for the children within its walls. When he visited it, there were more than a hundred inmates, about three fourths of them boys. They were taught elementary subjects and were given some sort of mechanical training — shoemaking, weaving, carpentry. When the young inmate showed evidence of reform and had acquired the elements of a trade, he or she was apprenticed or "bound out" to a farmer or artisan. Girls were usually placed as household servants, and the visitor naïvely reported that the most difficult of the boys were "disposed of as sailors." [1]

Thomas Hamilton, who visited the New York institution a few years later, described it as a hive of activity where young people were taught "the habits of industry and the principles of religion." It was the practice of the institution, he said, to send young offenders out to the country to work as early as possible, in order to remove them from the temptations of the city and permit them to start a normal life where their previous conduct was not generally known. Hamilton commended the trade schools and ended his account with, for him, the most unusual statement that he "found no fault in any department." [2]

James Silk Buckingham, an indefatigable visitor of institutions, found about two hundred and fifty children in the New York

House of Refuge in 1840, and he was struck by the evidences of bad heritage shown in their faces. One of the fads of the day was evidenced in his closing comment:

They exhibited . . . the worst collection of countenances we had ever seen; and in their heads and faces, the phrenologist and physiognomist would both have found abundant proofs of the general truth of their theories, that the shape of the cranium and the expression of the features are often faithful indexes of the minds within.[3]

Buckingham also visited the Dutch Farm on Long Island, where boy vagrants who had committed no crimes maintained themselves by their own industry, were taught a trade, and were given discipline, moral training, and an elementary education. This farm-school was, he thought, to be especially recommended.

William Crawford, a professional investigator sent over by the English government, visited each state in the Union and reported fully in 1834 on all the institutions he had inspected. His brief statement concerning the New York reform school included a complete schedule of its daily activities. The inmates rose at sunrise (before sunrise in the winter) and went directly to morning prayers; they attended school from five-thirty to seven, then had breakfast and worked until noon. After dinner they spent four hours in the workshops; supper came at five-thirty; after supper there was another hour or two of schoolwork, followed by evening prayers. Such a program, Crawford thought, left no time for mischief and seemed efficacious in producing reformation.[4]

Again it was the two French investigators who provided the most complete information. Their report on the penitentiary system in the United States contained an appendix loaded with detail on the reform schools, and their letters were full of comments on an institution they felt to be very modern, peculiarly American, and a real hope for the future. They were deeply interested in the house of refuge in Boston and in its superintendent, the Reverend E. M. P. Wells, whose influence permeated the entire institution. This refuge was, they felt, half prison, half school, and wholly reformatory. The children associated and conversed freely during the day but were confined in separate rooms or cells at night. They spent four hours in schoolwork, five hours in the workshops, and one hour in religious instruction each day.

But it was the method of discipline that astounded De Tocqueville. Wells had worked out a system of self-government in which children were permitted to participate by consent of a majority of the inmates. Those whose conduct was good were given the right to vote, to hold office, and to elect their own magistrates and monitors. If discipline trouble occurred, twelve jurors were selected from among the boys themselves, and each case was tried with careful procedure to secure justice. A register of moral conduct was kept, to which each child contributed the material for his own dossier. The boys were not allowed to denounce each other's faults and were not punished for their own if they had freely and sincerely confessed. No corporal punishment was inflicted, and the worst of the various deprivations was exclusion from religious services. Bad boys lost their vote, their right to hold office, and the privilege of entering the superintendent's house or consulting with him in any way. For boys whose records were exceptionally good wide liberties were permitted; a few were even given keys and were allowed to come and go as their special activities demanded.

De Tocqueville and De Beaumont both were incredulous, even alarmed, over the Boston system and went away convinced that it worked — as they were forced to admit it did — only because of the dynamic personality of Mr. Wells. They found the New York and Philadelphia systems less "noble," but probably more practicable under ordinary circumstances. In them the hours of shopwork were longer and of schoolwork shorter. Discipline was more comparable to that of the penitentiary and punishments included loss of recreation, solitary confinement, bread-and-water diet, and whipping as a last resort. Nathaniel C. Hart, who headed the New York school, seemed to the young Frenchmen a high type of practical administrator, less idealistic than Wells but more realistic. They approved his practice of apprenticing the young offenders when their time for release came and accepted his estimate that almost fifty-five per cent of the boys released had been genuinely reformed. De Beaumont, who had been extremely dubious about the possibility of reform for the adult criminal, was enthusiastic about the house of refuge. It was, he said, "of all the prisons the only one whose advantages are not balanced by some disadvantages."

The separation of misdemeanants from the hardened criminal

was recommended early in the move for reform, and it was recognized that the vagrant, the inebriated, and the shiftless ne'er-do-well represented a charge on the community that was sure to increase unless they were taught, "reformed," and put to work. As early as 1803 Edward Livingston, then mayor of New York, proposed a city workhouse. Some years later such an institution was built at Bellevue, and in 1826 it was relocated on Blackwells Island. By that time the Auburn cell system was popular, so the new building was equipped with individual cells. About the same time the Arch Street prison in Philadelphia, built in 1816, was turned into a house of correction, but its congregate system made all efforts at reform fruitless. Both institutions were long-lived; neither was a solution of the problem of the misdemeanant. In 1822 Josiah Quincy, then the judge of Essex County, Massachusetts, recommended the establishment of a house of reform for minor offenders where the teaching of handicrafts and other reformatory practices could be inaugurated. His plan was first worked out in a wing of the local jail, but ten years later the Boston House of Correction was constructed with provisions for both labor and discipline. For many years this Boston institution was unique, and it long served as a model for others of the same nature.

There was no widespread adoption of the reform school or the house of correction in the pre-Civil War period. Such correctional work was largely neglected while reformers devoted their attention to the penitentiaries, and its alternative, the local jail, was for many years a blot upon the American social structure. There were at this time probably less than a half-dozen local jails that could be considered good and only one, that at Hartford, Connecticut, that was especially to be commended. The most that can be said is that a few significant contributions were made by institutions and superintendents who were distinctly ahead of their times.

POOR RELIEF

Reformers of the day recognized the care of the indigent poor as another field for humanitarian effort. The problem of poor relief had received little real attention since the days of Queen Elizabeth. To the Puritan idleness was a sin and pauperism was akin to crime, and the fact that in America labor was scarce and land was cheap tended to substantiate the idea that abject poverty was evidence of improvidence, shiftlessness, or criminal waste. So well on into the nineteenth century the poor were treated with infinite variations on the theme of man's inhumanity to man.

In the days when America was largely rural, there was little effort to provide for anything except outdoor relief; there were few almshouses. Such aid as was furnished for the indigent poor was given in their own homes, if they had any; if not, provision was made in the abodes of others. Orphan children and the children of parents who could not support them were bound out. "Going on the town" was a calamity to be avoided at all hazards. The principle was accepted throughout the colonies that support of a poor family devolved upon the locality in which it resided, and no locality accepted any obligation it could possibly evade.

In the larger towns, where there was a greater number of poor people, and in some of the counties of central and southern states it proved economically advantageous to provide almshouses for the unfortunate aged, the orphans, and the maimed or otherwise helpless poor. Often the insane and the imbecile who became charges of the community were housed with them. Where there were no almshouses these irrational unfortunates might be confined in the jail or placed in the custody of someone hired by the town.

Occasionally an almshouse was a well-kept and pleasant place; more often it bore witness to the complete indifference and the parsimony of the community. The Duke of Saxe-Weimar, who assiduously visited every variety of American institution, described in detail one commendable almshouse, the one in Baltimore. Built after the humanitarians had aired the cause of the indigent, it was four years old in 1825 when the noble visitor saw it. There was a wing for men and one for women, an infirmary with separate rooms for the insane, a school for children, and gardens and shops where able-bodied inmates produced articles for the use of the institution.[5]

The Baltimore almshouse was an exception in this period, however. More often children, prostitutes, vagrants, drunkards, idiots, and maniacs were herded together at the least possible cost to the community. Sometimes the almshouses were privately owned and run for profit, taking the poor on contract from the local authorities. Only occasionally was there any attempt to make them workhouses providing salutary employment for their inmates. In 1834, for example, the Boston House of Industry (built in 1821) was so overcrowded that there could be little separation of different classes of inmates. It housed sixty insane or idiotic persons, about one hundred and thirty ill and infirm, more than one hundred children and infants, and two hundred others listed as "unclassified." Its name was a misnomer, for little constructive labor was done.

It was the constant effort of each locality to fulfill the minimum requirements of its obligation at the lowest cost. Children were often bid off at auction for the labor they might perform, and the town paid the amount of the lowest bid for the support of the child "sold." Very illuminating in this connection is an excerpt from the town records of Fitchburg, Massachusetts, an item of 1813 inquiring "what method the town will take to get rid of the support of Ephraim Farnsworth's family." In the selectmen's report of 1820 appears a summary of the conditions on which the poor of the town were farmed out for the year:

. . . the undertaker to Board, Clothe and Comfortably provide for, in sickness and health the persons hereafter named. . . . and if any of the above named persons should decease within the course of the year, the town to be at the expense of burying, and the doctor's bill if any of them are sick. . . . The undertaker to have the benefit of the labor of said Paupers, and receive his pay quarterly.[6]

Whenever possible the town endeavored to escape the burden of caring for those from whom no labor could be expected, and wily selectmen often tried to dump undesirables upon neighboring authorities. One especially unpleasant story tells of the midnight trip of such a "guardian of the poor" who bundled up two imbeciles — they would be unable to name their point of departure — and transported them to a district miles away from the one he served.

Since all towns refused responsibility for vagrants, it became customary for the state to pay for the support of persons without legal residence. As population grew and industries developed, this problem grew more difficult. Increased immigration added to the number of vagrants, especially in the winter months. While the Shakers complained of the number of "winter Shakers," the Northeastern states wailed that the vagrants used their almshouses as inns, wandering from one to another and collecting from each the state aid that could not be denied them. They rendered ineffective the local provisions for relief, increased the hardships of the local poor, and were passed on as quickly as possible by the authorities — often with bribes of liquor.

The pre-Civil War period saw the recognition of these problems and honest humanitarian attempts at their solution. Orphanages, houses of correction, and insane asylums drew great numbers from the jails into institutions more adequate for their needs. Public sentiment was gradually aroused against the "sale" of the indigent poor and against the old practice of binding out unfortunate children. Attempts were made to exclude indigent aliens from the country, and increasing numbers of almshouses were built by town and state funds for institutional relief of cases not otherwise provided for. But these measures were little more than a beginning. As old as the problem of poverty, the question of public relief, so valiantly attacked in the first half of the nineteenth century, still awaits the solution of the parent problem.

THE EDUCATION OF DEAF-MUTES AND THE BLIND

In the era of humanitarian reform the mere rumor of the possibility of alleviating the lot of defective children brought eager queries and pledges of support from hundreds whose lives had been saddened by contact with children thus tragically handicapped. Wherever account is given of American progress in educating those who from birth or, more commonly, through illness have been deprived of the use of one or more of their senses, honor is given to the names of Thomas Hopkins Gallaudet and Samuel Gridley Howe, whose lives were devoted to this cause.

Gallaudet, of French Huguenot extraction, was born in Philadelphia in 1787. He graduated from Yale, studied law for a time, taught for a year or two, traveled a bit, and worked as a clerk in a New York countinghouse. After these varied attempts to find a satisfying profession, he turned in 1811 to the ministry and entered Andover Theological Seminary. Ordained at the age of twenty-seven, he might have been expected to settle down at last as the minister of one of the churches offered to him in recognition of his unquestioned ability. But his attention had been attracted by the plight of little Alice Cogswell, the daughter of a physician in Hartford, Connecticut, who had been a deaf-mute since an illness in her infancy. Gallaudet's family had lived for some time in Hartford, and little Alice was a playmate of his younger sisters. Meeting her often in his father's garden, the serious, philanthropic young man became interested in finding some means of educating her so that her life would be less empty.

Dr. Cogswell himself had been making an investigation of European schools for the deaf, since there were none in America, but the idea of sending the child abroad was distasteful to him. Gallaudet's success in teaching her the connection between a few written words and the objects they represented so encouraged the anxious father that he conceived the idea of sending the young man abroad to study the best European methods of teaching deaf-mutes, so that he might found a school in Hartford where Alice and others similarly afflicted could be taught. A group of philanthropic citizens was interested, subscriptions were raised, and Gallaudet sailed for Europe in May 1813.

In his absence the voluntary committee continued its work. A survey made under the auspices of the Congregational clergy showed that there were at least eighty deaf-mutes in Connecticut and probably four hundred in New England. And in the whole area there was not a single institution for their care and education. The United States of that day could not resist an appeal for help in so humane a cause. Subscriptions poured in, and the state incorporated the "Connecticut Asylum for the education of deaf and dumb persons" with a gift of five thousand dollars — the first such appropriation in the country. When the Congress of the United States, at the urging of the representatives from Connecticut, granted a township of public land for the support of the project, it at once assumed the name of the American Asylum.

In the meantime, in London and in Paris, Gallaudet pursued his quest for knowledge of methods for the instruction of the children who were to be placed in his charge. In Paris he was able to arrange to take back to America with him a young Frenchman, Laurent Clerc, a deaf-mute taught by the Abbé Sicard, dean of European educators of deaf-mutes. With the help of Clerc the success of the American institution seemed assured, and those interested in it turned with renewed efforts to acquiring funds for a building in which it could be housed. Opened in 1817 in temporary quarters, the little experimental school grew from seven to thirty-one pupils within a year.

Its success in teaching deaf-mutes to read and write, to read lips, and to talk by manual signs attracted attention throughout the country, and visitors flocked to Hartford. Gallaudet's interest was not confined to his own institution but encompassed the welfare of all deaf-mutes, and he took his most accomplished pupils on tours, visiting state legislatures and giving exhibitions in churches. Soon other states followed the example of Connecticut, and, with the usual combination of private charity and public appropriation, numerous schools for the deaf and dumb were founded. Between 1816 and 1851, the year of Gallaudet's death, New York, Pennsylvania, Kentucky, Ohio, Virginia, Indiana, Tennessee, Illinois, North Carolina, Georgia, South Carolina, Missouri, and Michigan opened institutions for the deaf.

Gallaudet himself married a deaf-mute, and their son, Edward M. Gallaudet, followed in his father's footsteps and became in 1864 the president of the Columbian Institute (founded in 1857) in Washington. One of the Institute's departments was the National Deaf Mute College, the first institution to offer college work and degrees for the deaf. Ill-health forced the elder Gallaudet to retire from the management of the American Asylum at Hartford in 1830, but retirement did not end his labors as an educator or as a humanitarian. During the next twenty years he wrote textbooks, books for Sunday school libraries, religious tracts, and articles for many educational publications. He was actively interested in a variety of educational reforms, in the lyceum movement, and in the growth of labor unions. The care of the insane became a major interest of his later years, when he served as chaplain of the Worcester Insane Asylum.

Samuel Gridley Howe espoused the cause of the blind with a religious and humanitarian fervor equal to that of Gallaudet. Howe was a somewhat more romantic figure, with such decided charm that his contemporaries wrote of him and his work with an enthusiasm even greater than they accorded the equally pioneer efforts of Gallaudet. Howe was the son of Boston parents, a graduate of the Boston Latin School, of Brown University, and of Harvard Medical School (1824). He spent the next half-dozen years fighting with the revolutionary forces of Greece in their struggle for independence. After the success of that endeavor, Howe traveled in Europe several years, visiting England, France, and Germany in search of material on the education of the blind, in which his interest had been kindled by his friend, Dr. Fisher of Boston.

His first school for the blind was in his own home and numbered six pupils. Elizabeth Peabody, herself an educator as well as a Transcendentalist, wrote of this school:

He had then been about six months at work, and had invented and laboriously executed some books with raised letters, to teach them to read, some geographical maps, and the geometrical diagrams necessary for instruction in mathematics. He had gummed twine, I think, upon cardboard, an enormous labor, to form the letters of the alphabet. I shall not, in all time, forget the impression made upon me by seeing the hero of the Greek Revolution, who had narrowly missed being that of the Polish Revolution also; to see this hero, I say, wholly absorbed, and applying all the energies of his genius to this apparently humble work, and doing it as Christ did, without money and without price.[7]

As soon as his pupils were ready for the experience, Howe took them around the state, giving exhibitions of their achievement to arouse interest in their behalf. Colonel Perkins of Boston was moved to offer his spacious house for a school for the blind if the city would raise fifty thousand dollars for its support. The women of Boston, determined that this should be done, held in Faneuil Hall one of the first great municipal fairs for the cause of charity. More money was obtained by private subscription, and within six weeks the entire amount had been raised so that Perkins Institute could be established.

As the head of this institution for many years, Howe was interested in all the techniques and equipment for teaching the blind. No detail was too trivial to engage his attention — the size of type, the thickness of paper, the height of letters — for his great objective was to make books for the blind more numerous, cheaper, and more easily handled. Devoutly religious, although with a simple and beautiful faith that was far from orthodox, Howe placed his first and greatest emphasis upon bringing the Bible within the reach of the blind. With the aid of the American Bible Society he produced a vast amount of printing in raised type. His school became a teacher training institute, and his pupils were the advance guard in establishing more schools for the blind.

Although best known for his work with the blind, Howe was not indifferent to the cause of other defectives. Deaf-mutes had a special claim on his interest, for one of his greatest triumphs, and probably his greatest delight, was the education of Laura Bridgman, a girl deaf, dumb, and blind who was brought to him for instruction. In 1844 and 1845 he joined Horace Mann in a fight to introduce in schools for deaf-mutes a new method of instruction by which these afflicted children were taught to speak rather than to use the manual language. Gallaudet clung to the older methods, and it was with great difficulty that Howe and Mann won approval for their reform.

When the state legislature was persuaded to consider the plight of the idiot, Howe was put upon the commission of investigation. He visited sixty-three towns and examined nearly six hundred of these pitiable children. His report to the legislature in 1846 was an appeal for the amelioration of their condition and an offer of aid in their education. The work was begun in Perkins Institute in 1848 with a state appropriation of twenty-five hundred dollars a year for three years. At the end of that time the appropriation was increased and a separate building was provided. This work, continued under the inspiration of Howe's enthusiasm, was copied extensively by other states.

When Dorothea Dix began her work for the insane, Howe was the rock upon which she depended; he also gave assistance and encouragement to Father Taylor in his work for American seamen; and he was one of the greatest leaders of the antislavery movement in Massachusetts. The Boston Prison Discipline Society was another of his interests. He could not bring himself to advocate the segregation and punishment of juvenile offenders, for he always held that they should be taught the way to a useful life by being placed in Christian families.

In 1863 Howe was made a member of the Massachusetts Board of State Charities (the first to be established in the United States), and he served on that board, part of the time as its president, until the last year of his life. There is a strong flavor of modern social service, as well as some reflection of early nineteenth-century reluctance to invoke the aid of the government, in the statement made in the first year of his presidency:

General Principles of Public Charity

In considering what measures ought to be taken for the care and treatment of the dependent and vicious classes, we are to bear in mind several principles.

First. That if, by investing one dollar, we prevent an evil the correction of which would cost ten cents a year, we save four per cent.

Second. That it is better to separate and diffuse the dependent classes than to congregate them.

Third. That we ought to avail ourselves as much as possible of those remedial agencies which exist in society — The family, social influences, industrial occupations, and the like.

Fourth. That we should enlist not only the greatest possible amount of popular sympathy, but the greatest number of individuals and of families, in the care and treatment of the dependent.

Fifth. That we should avail ourselves of responsible societies and organizations which aim to reform, support or help any class of dependents; thus lessening the direct agency of the State, and enlarging that of the people themselves.

Sixth. That we should build up public institutions only in the last resort.

Seventh. That these should be kept as small as is consistent with wise economy, and arranged so as to turn the strength and the faculties of the inmates to the best account.

Eighth. That we should not retain the inmates any longer than is manifestly for their good, irrespective of their usefulness in the institution.[8]

THE CARE OF THE INSANE

The attention of humane citizens of Europe and America was turned toward the condition and treatment of the insane early in the nineteenth century. Rationalism sought the cause for the state of the demented person and tests of the effectiveness of treatment, while those who believed in the worth of the individual, no matter how lowly his estate, could not be satisfied with the theory that the insane had lost their humanity and had reverted to the status of animals. Indeed, the humanitarian rejected even cruelty to animals. To this new attitude toward the mentally afflicted the early nineteenth century added the cult of curability that was a part of the current perfectionism.

The insane, therefore, were men and women, not animals; they retained that spark of divinity that was the distinguishing characteristic of noble manhood; their condition was their misfortune and not their fault; society owed them kindness, comfortable environment, and every advantage of scientific treatment; religion demanded the effort to redeem them from madness and to save their immortal souls; optimism and perfectionism encouraged the belief that improving their condition would bring the cure of their insanity. To broadcast and implement these new ideas was the reformer's task.

One of the first hospitals in America was opened in Philadelphia in 1752 with a commission from the colonial legislature to provide care for "lunaticks." Three of its first four patients were insane, and throughout the rest of the century a half dozen or more of such unfortunates were confined in cells in the basement. The first American hospital or asylum exclusively for the insane was established in 1773 in Williamsburg, Virginia. In New York and in Maryland general hospitals opened in the 1790's made some arrangement for insane patients. That seems to have been the extent of institutional care of the insane in the United States before 1800.

In one or two of these hospitals constructive efforts were made to alleviate the condition or promote the cure of insane patients, but in most cases secure confinement was the chief consideration. And only a small minority of the country's insane came into contact with any of these institutions. The rest were cared for, or neglected, in their homes, in the custody of hired keepers, or in jails and almshouses as charges on the community.

The first impetus toward a different attitude came from revolutionary France. An unassuming physician and classical scholar by the name of Philippe Pinel was appointed head of the hospital for the insane connected with L'Hôpital Général of Paris. He found that the chronic insane were treated like animals, confined in boxlike, dark, ill-ventilated cells, allowed few visitors, little clothing, no furniture, and given the coarsest of food. At the slightest evidence of violence they were shackled to the walls of their cells with iron collars that permitted them little movement, and they were fortunate indeed if an especially humane keeper substituted wrist and ankle irons for the iron collars at night so that they might lie down upon their filthy pallets. Pinel and his head keeper, Pussin, determined to see what a more humane treatment would accomplish.

They selected a group of patients for whom they felt there was some possibility of cure, struck off their chains, cleaned and fed them properly, and gradually brought them back to some semblance of humanity. Encouraged by a number of real cures, Pinel published a book describing his work and announcing the results of his experimentation. His conclusion was startling for the day in which it was published:

The insane are, after all, human. They are not animals. No matter what the church or the ignorant may say, they have not been cursed by the good Lord, and part of their bad behavior is due to the fact that they are not given a chance to develop as decent humans should.[9]

The insane man is not an inexplicable monster. He is but one of ourselves, only a little more so. Underneath his wildest paroxysms there is a germ, at least, of rationality and of personal accountability. To believe in this, to seek for it, stimulate it, build it up — here lies the only way of delivering him out of the fatal bondage in which he is held.[10]

An English Quaker, William Tuke, who apparently had never heard of Pinel, in 1796 built in York a private asylum called the Retreat, where he carried on experiments similar to those of the Frenchman. Early in the nineteenth century Tuke published his findings in a book entitled *A Description of the Retreat near York*, and his work became widely known. A few years later two other English physicians established the Lincoln Asylum for the treatment of the insane on humane principles. In these institutions physical restraint was a last resort, and means of therapy were the subject of constant experiment. When in the United States the newly awakened social conscience undertook to improve the status of the insane, the new republic was but copying this movement initiated abroad.

Dr. Benjamin Rush has been called the father of American psychiatry, for in the years after 1783 he tried out in the Philadelphia Hospital many of the new theories coming into vogue in France and England and added methods of his own in the treatment of insane patients. Rush rejected punishment, cruelty, and most forms of restraint and insisted that the keepers, or nurses, should be kind, that they should have adequate training, and that they should put forth every effort to improve the condition of the patients. Many of his ideas concerning treatment have not been accepted by modern medical practice, but no one can deny that he had a scientific approach to the problem, or that his main objective was the betterment of those in his care. He worked with problems of diet, with the relative value of bleeding and emetics, with various methods of water therapy, and with the effectiveness of physical shock in the treatment of violent or hysterical patients. He published in 1812 the first treatise in America on the subject of mental diseases.[11] As much a pioneer as were Pinel and Tuke, Rush carried on his observations and experiments over a long period of years and, more than any other man, aroused public opinion in America to the needs of the mentally afflicted.

There was, however, an exchange of ideas across the seas, and internationalism in regard to experimentation ensured a hearing in America for the results of European efforts. An abridged edition of Tuke's *Description of the Retreat near York* was brought out in the United States, and in the years after 1815, when American humanitarianism had got well under way, several similar hospitals were built: the Quaker Retreat near Philadelphia, founded as a private hospital in 1817, nonsectarian after 1834; the Bloomingdale Hospital in New York City in 1821 with a Quaker, Thomas Eddy, as its guiding spirit and one of America's greatest students of mental diseases, Dr. Pliny Earle, as its chief physician; the McLean Asylum in Massachusetts in 1818, where Dr. Luther Bell instituted the Tuke system; the Retreat in Hartford, Connecticut, in 1824, soon to be recognized as a model institution; and a state asylum in Kentucky in the same year. Virginia built her second state hospital for the insane and South Carolina her first in 1828, and an asylum for the "furiously mad" was opened in Worcester, Massachusetts, in 1836. Vermont, Ohio, Maine, and Pennsylvania had joined the group by 1840.

Much of this activity in the care of the insane resulted from interest in the general problem of poor relief. It was also connected with the movement for reform of penal institutions. In 1807 a law was passed in the state of New York authorizing state care for the insane poor "formerly lodged in jails and poor houses," and in 1836 the state lunatic asylum was built in Utica to house the patients taken over from county almshouses and jails. In the next decade New York made provision, also, for the care of the criminal insane. The same situation led to similar action in other states, although quite naturally changes were made first in states where increasing density of population intensified social problems and caused a growing interest in them.

The joy of the philanthropist and his optimistic view of the new institutions was reflected in the literature of the day. In an article entitled "What Shall We Do with the Insane?" one enthusiastic observer described the miracle he had witnessed in the hospital for the insane:

Its patients were wholly of the pauper class. Its inmates are the worst and most hopeless class of cases; they are the raving madmen and the gibbering idiot, whom, in the language of the inspectors, we had formerly seen "tearing their clothes amid cold, lacerating their bodies, contracting most filthy habits, without self-control, unable to restrain the worst feelings, endeavoring to injure those that approached them, giving vent to their irritation in the most passionate, profane, and filthy language, fearing and feared, hating and almost hated." Now they are all neatly clad by day, and comfortably lodged in separate rooms by night. They walk quietly, with self respect, along their spacious and airy halls, or sit in listening groups around the daily paper, or they dig in the garden, or handle edged tools, or stroll around the neighborhood with kind and careful attendants. They attend soberly and reverently upon religious exercises, and make glad music with their united voices.[12]

Foreign travelers wrote with equal enthusiasm about American success in curing the insane — some of them even to the extent of asserting that more than ninety per cent of those treated were cured.[13] Only slowly did more scientific observation of a larger number of cases over a longer period of years dim this first bright optimism. Later statistics failed to substantiate the claim of a committee reporting in 1832 to the Massachusetts legislature that "it is now abundantly demonstrated that with appropriate medical and moral treatment, insanity yields with more readiness than ordinary diseases." And disillusioned American medical men thirty years later were inclined to agree with Dr. Luther Bell that "when a man becomes insane, he is about used up for this world."[14] It was doubtless an excellent thing that the work of the reformers was done mostly while the earlier optimism was prevalent and while visitors to American institutions could write with so much assurance about the success of the new methods.

It must not be forgotten, however, that the writers and travelers of the 1830's and 1840's were, whether they praised or condemned, describing the show spots of American institutional development. Great progress had been made and the era of neglect was over so far as the humanitarian, the scientist, and the enlightened citizen were concerned; but only a beginning had been made. There were many states as yet untouched by the reform movement.[15] Most of the hospitals built were small and they were soon overcrowded, some of them were private institutions with fees that excluded the poor, and few of them reached out for the insane who lived in rural areas. As late as 1840 a majority of the victims of insanity were still confined in private care, in locked rooms, cages, or outhouses, or in cells in jails and poorhouses — neglected and mistreated as they had been for centuries. It was left for the passionate and crusading pity of one feeble but militant woman to force upon every state of the Union a recognition of its responsibility to its demented and mentally ill citizens.

Dorothea Dix had her roots in the same soil that produced William Lloyd Garrison, John Brown, Susan B. Anthony, and the other fighters of her day. Her cultural growth had begun in the stern Calvinism of her grandmother's home but had flowered in the benign atmosphere of the friendship of Dr. Channing and the group that surrounded him. Her youthful days were filled with work and study and the constant annoyance of ill-health. A private school carried on in her own home provided her with a livelihood while she indefatigably pursued her avocation, the study of the natural sciences. She early displayed an interest in charitable work, opening an additional school in the barn for the poor children of the town. The attention of Dr. Channing was called to the courageous and brilliant young teacher, and for some years she spent much of her time in his home as governess for his children. The incipient tuberculosis that compelled her to give up her school was benefited by long months in his country home and still more by a season spent with his family in the Danish West Indies. Later the death of a relative provided her with a legacy that assured her support and made it unnecessary for her to teach again. But her inflexible conscience refused to permit her the ease of an inactive life.

In 1841 she was asked by a shy young theological student to take a Sunday school class in the women's department of the House of Correction in East Cambridge. There among the prisoners she found a few insane persons confined in a dreary room that was not provided with heat although the March day was terribly cold. Her sympathy aroused, Miss Dix began a campaign to improve the lot of these unfortunates she had seen, and she began to think about the plight of the thousands whose miserable existence she could imagine. Her search for aid led her to Samuel Gridley Howe and Charles Sumner. After they had made a careful investigation, Howe wrote articles demanding reform. The indignant denials of Massachusetts citizens brought the publication of a long letter from Sumner stating that Dr. Howe's reports presented a true picture of the conditions they had seen. Further aroused by this controversy, Miss Dix embarked upon a two-year investigation of all the jails and almshouses of the state, in order to draw up a complete report of the plight of the indigent insane.

In 1843 she presented to the state legislature a memorial summarizing the conditions she had found. Beginning with the famous pledge, "I tell what I have seen," she proceeded to call attention "to the *present* state of insane persons confined within the Commonwealth, in *cages, closets, cellars, stalls, pens! Chained, naked, beaten with rods, and lashed into obedience!*" [16] The facts were irrefutable, and they brought an instant reaction from the people of the state. The keepers of the institutions and the frugal representatives of the rural districts hurled charges of "sensational and slanderous lies." Dorothea Dix was accused of being a sentimental idealist and a snooping, interfering woman, but if her opponents expected to silence her they misjudged their adversary. Backed by Dr. Howe, Horace Mann, and Dr. Luther Bell of the McLean Asylum, she stuck by her guns, providing the legislative committee, of which Dr. Howe was the chairman, with additional information, until the legislature appropriated funds to build a large addition to the Worcester hospital for the insane.

The success of her efforts in Massachusetts was the beginning of a nationwide campaign for state-supported hospitals for the insane, for Miss Dix realized that the same conditions must be prevalent throughout the United States. Rhode Island was the scene for her next efforts. She used the same tactics of careful investigation, accumulation of data, and concise, forceful report, and with the same result; a hospital for the insane was built in Providence. From Rhode

Island she moved on to New Jersey, where in 1845 the public-spirited men she had roused to action forced a bill through the legislature providing the hospital she had demanded. From New Jersey Miss Dix went on to Pennsylvania, and then west and south. Everywhere her tactics were the same. Always she maintained the "womanly dignity" demanded by mid–nineteenth-century canons; she never went before the legislature herself, and she always prepared the ground for her memorials by winning the support of a picked group of leaders, preferably men of all parties. Occasionally she was so bold as to consult with a dozen or more of these men in her boardinghouse. Her letters and conversation provided them with ammunition for the fight; indeed, she all but wrote their speeches.

Between 1844 and 1854 this frail middle-aged woman traveled more than thirty thousand miles, visiting hundreds of prisons, almshouses, jails, and hospitals, collecting data, preparing memorials, and arousing public opinion in behalf of her cause. "They say nothing can be done here," she wrote from North Carolina. "I reply, 'I know no such word in the vocabulary I adopt!'" And the same spirit was evident in a letter to the Massachusetts educator, George Emerson: "I encounter nothing which a determined will created by the necessities of the cause does not enable me to vanquish." So she drove herself onward; Indiana, Illinois, Louisiana, Tennessee, Mississippi, Missouri, North Carolina, the District of Columbia, Michigan, and Wisconsin, all responded to her appeal before 1860; others joined the ranks during or shortly after the Civil War.

Oppressed by the magnitude of her task and convinced, as she told the North Carolina legislature, that she was "the Hope of the poor crazed beings. . . . I am the Revelation of hundreds of wailing, suffering creatures," Miss Dix came to believe that she should solicit the aid of the national government. Since land grants had been given for educational purposes and were talked of for railroad building, she felt that Congress might well provide in the same way for national hospitals. Introduced in 1848, her bill won few supporters at first, because the Northern states were beginning the agitation for free homesteads and were averse to a policy of land grants and reserved sales. But Miss Dix returned to the fray again and again. In 1850 the bill passed the Senate but not the House; in 1854 it passed both houses, only to receive the veto of President Pierce on the grounds that it was unwise for the national government to assume the support of the nation's poor and unconstitutional to make land grants for such a purpose.

Crushed by this defeat and worn out by her ten years of hard work, Miss Dix went abroad for a rest in 1854. Even there she could not forget her cause but joined in the work for the insane in each country she visited. Returning home just as the United States was moving into the Civil War, she was at once involved in hospital work for the Union armies. After the war was over, she again turned to her own crusade until age and weakness forced her retirement. A sentence from a letter by Dr. Charles Nichols of the Bloomingdale Hospital to an English friend may well serve as her epitaph: "There has died and been laid to rest in the most quiet, unostentatious way the most useful and distinguished woman America has yet produced." [17]

CHAPTER 13

The Temperance Crusade

The men and women who were interested in prison reform and in the problem of poverty sought to find the causes of the conditions that had aroused their humanitarian zeal. They came to believe that man was often the victim of circumstances, that his mistakes and misfortunes were in part, at least, the result of his environment, and that the removal of the causes for his antisocial conduct was the best protection for both individual and society. Many who thus analyzed the social conditions of their day came to consider excessive drinking an important factor in the problems of delinquency and dependency.

With characteristic optimism they set out to attack intemperance as well as to ease the conditions resulting from it. If these conditions could be improved, if poverty, crime, and insanity were curable, surely the fundamental stumbling block might be removed, and all society might benefit thereby. This optimism was, perhaps, accompanied by the Puritan's interest in the personal life of his neighbor, an interest never long inactive in American history, even in those periods that seemed most tolerant. If excessive drinking appeared to be an evil that needed elimination, there were many who were willing to accept that elimination as a duty devolving upon all good citizens. Intemperance became not only a sin of the individual but a crime against society, the toleration of which made every citizen a party to it.

THE DRINKING HABITS OF THE EARLY REPUBLIC

Colonial literature and the accounts of travelers are full of references to the many varieties of beverages to be had and of the public's addiction to them. Nature was generous in the New World, and surplus grains and fruits could be turned into drinks to satisfy the palates and warm the hearts of those who could not afford the imported wines and brandies that graced the tables of wealthy merchants and planters. Cider was universally evident; wines and cordials were made from blackberries, grapes, peaches, and cherries; and malt and brewed beverages were made from various grains. Substitutes were soon found for the commodities used in the manufacture of the liquid refreshment of the colonist's hard-drinking English forebears, and he found comfort in the concoctions thus produced.

> If barley be wanting to make into malt,
> We must be content and think it no fault,
> For we can make liquor to sweeten our lips,
> Of pumpkins, and parsnips, and walnut-tree chips.[1]

In the eighteenth century the doughty Puritans began to distill West Indian molasses, producing the rum that was soon the most popular of the more intoxicating beverages. So dependent were New Englanders upon their rum that one wag wrote of them,

> Their only wish and only prayer
> From the present world to the world to come
> Was a string of eels and a jug of rum.[2]

In other colonies whisky, made from surplus grains, took the place of rum or vied with it. Flip, made of beer, sugar, and rum, was given its distinctive flavor by the insertion of a hot poker. Mead, made from wild honey and water, mulled wine, cherry bounce, sling, mum, perry, punch, and toddy varied the liquid diet. Hops grew wild, and malt houses were soon provided, so that breweries were as common as distilleries.

Taverns and public houses saved the traveler from the dire fate of drinking water. It was in the taproom of the tavern that local gossip was exchanged, affairs of state were discussed, views of men from different sections were aired, and policies of importance were formulated. Grog of one sort or another was as powerful an aid to the communication of ideas as was printer's ink. Those who were not travelers drank not only in the taproom but at their own tables and wherever groups congregated for work or social intercourse, their beverages varying with their tastes and the condition of their pocketbooks.

When the colonies became states there was little change in drinking habits. In his witty and racy but moral tale, *The Drunkard's Looking Glass*, "Parson" Mason Weems left for posterity a sample tavern bill of 1812:

> 3 Mint-slings before breakfast, .25 75
> 1 Breakfast 50

9 Tumblers of grog before dinner, 12 1/2..... 1.12 1/2
3 Glasses wine and bitters, 12 1/2............ .37 1/2
Dinner and club........................ 1.25
2 Ticklers of French brandy, .25............ .50
Segars .... .25
Supper and wine........................ 1.25
$$\overline{\qquad\qquad}$$
$6.00 [3]

In the rural districts men did not run up such long accounts, and the fare was not so varied or so expensive, but the quantities of intoxicants imbibed were apparently as great. Horace Greeley reported that

In my childhood [in rural Vermont] there was no merry-making, there was no entertainment of relatives or friends, there was scarcely a casual gathering of two or three neighbors for an evening's social chat, without strong drink. Cider always, while it remained drinkable without severe contortion of visage; rum at seasons and on all occasions, were required and provided. No house or barn was raised without a bountiful supply of the latter, and generally of both. A wedding without "toddy," "flip," "sling," or "punch," with rum undisguised in abundance, would have been deemed a poor, mean affair, even among the penniless; while the more thrifty of course dispensed wine, brandy, and gin in profusion. Dancing — almost the only pastime wherein the sexes jointly participated — was always enlivened and stimulated by liquor. Militia training — then rigidly enforced at least twice a year — usually wound up with a drinking frolic at the village tavern. Election days were drinking days . . . and even funerals were regarded as inadequately celebrated without the dispensing of spirituous consolation.[4]

A barrel of cider per family per week was the average allotment for upstate Vermont, according to Greeley, who ended his description with the dry remark, "The pious probably drank more discreetly than the ungodly; but they all drank to their own satisfaction" — determined by the toleration gained through years of consumption.

The rum of New England was replaced by corn whisky on the frontier, and cider was produced wherever the apple tree grew. The famous Methodist revivalist, James Finley, struggled with the evils of drunkenness as he rode his circuit in the Ohio country in the first decades of the century. He found that "ardent spirits were used as a preventive of disease. It was also regarded as a necessary beverage. A house could not be raised, a field of wheat cut down, nor could there be a log rolling, a husking, a quilting, a wedding, or a funeral without the aid of alcohol." [5]

Whisky was commodity money in the West. In Lexington, Kentucky, even church subscriptions were payable in whisky. In the hill districts, where roads were lacking and distances were great, corn went to market in a jug, and whisky was the only cash or barter crop. The horrors of the drunken brawls in the crude and filthy taverns of the frontier were described with vivid detail by early travelers, and they made a profound impression on the hardy Methodist preacher, Peter Cartwright, who found it difficult to obtain accommodations where he could have rest and comfort without the din of drinking bouts. These roused his ire and led to an intervention that usually terminated his stay.

In the South conditions were the same. The seaboard planters imported vast quantities of wine and brandy; the men of the back country drank corn whisky or, as in Georgia, locally made peach brandy. The author of a quaint old book on the early citizens of Georgia, saying that brandy making and selling were the most profitable of all employments, tells of a man named Micajah McGehee who was the first settler on the Broad River to plant a peach orchard, and it netted him sixteen hundred dollars a year for many years. A considerable part of his product was for home use, but

His constitution was so strong, that he battled with death, taking brandy until he was upwards of eighty years old. When he was young it took drinking all day to make him drunk. He became a member of the Methodist Church during the great religious excitement of 1809–11. He still contrived to get drunk. When he was spoken to about it, he said that the habit was so confirmed that he could not live without the free use of brandy. He was requested to say what quantity was necessary for his health. He agreed to try to *limit himself* to a quart a day, but the allowance failed to keep him alive. [6]

The clergy of the day were not, in Georgia or elsewhere, free from tastes similar to those of the aged Micajah. Frank comments on the amount of liquor consumed at the ordinations of ministers have preserved for us a complete picture of those solemn occasions. One especially good beer was known as Ordination Brew. Tavern bills and church records all bear witness to the cost of the liquid refreshment for such ceremonies, but it was long before there was any comment that the expenditure was anything other than an ordinary and necessary one. In 1729 the Reverend Edwin Jackson was ordained in Pennsylvania at an expense to the parish of twenty-three pounds sterling for "6 barrels and one half of Cyder, 28 gallons of wine, 2 gallons of Brandy and 4 of Rum, Loaf Sugar, Lime Juice and Pipes." The ball after the ceremonies was one "of much expense." [7]

The persistence of these customs is apparent in the fact that nearly one hundred years later the Reverend Leonard Bacon was installed in the First Congregational Church of New Haven, Connecticut, in an impressive service after which free drinks were furnished at a near-by bar to all who chose to order them and were "settled for" by the church. [8]

EARLY PROTESTS AGAINST INTEMPERANCE

In the midst of this general acceptance of hard drinking the cause of temperance began to gain adherents. Colonial courts had condemned drunkards to the stocks or had placarded them with the letter *D* to be worn publicly for a stated period. The colonial and early state legislatures passed innumerable laws to regulate the granting of licenses for the sale of intoxicants, in an effort to keep the traffic in the hands of "responsible and respectable persons." And the Continental Congress, during the Revolution, issued a manifesto against the increasing evil of strong drink:

Resolved, that it be recommended to the several Legislatures of the United States immediately to pass laws the most effectual for putting an immediate stop to the pernicious practice of distilling grain, by which the most extensive evils are likely to be derived, if not quickly prevented.

To this plea only New Hampshire replied, however, and she with only a general condemnation of intemperance.

After the Revolution the interest in temperance increased, and the figures of the early census reports on the importation and manufacture of intoxicants were widely quoted. It was estimated that the consumption of spirits in 1792 was two and a half gallons per person; in 1810, four and a half gallons; and in 1823, seven and a half gallons. Those who had confidently asserted that the excessive drinking was due to the long periods of war in the eighteenth century were confounded by the fact that the consumption of intoxicants increased even more rapidly in the years of peace after the Revolution. The excise tax of 1791 was commended as a move in the direction of limiting consumption, and its removal a decade later was loudly deplored on moral grounds. Petitions were sent to Congress requesting high tariffs on imported liquors. It was noted with disapproval that there were more wet than dry goods in country stores and that all grocers had a barrel on tap, both for sale and for treating those who made purchases.

Protest groups were many but scattered. The philanthropist and propagandist, Anthony Benezet, with some success exhorted the Quakers of Pennsylvania to put their stamp of disapproval upon the use of intoxicants. In 1780 the General Conference of the Methodist Church in America disapproved both the making and the drinking of distilled liquors, and the Methodists carried the torch of temperance reform wherever their preachers rode circuit. Everywhere he went, the itinerant Bishop Asbury spoke emphatically against intemperance and the "Demon Rum." James Finley asserted that in the West all who refused to drink were called, by way of reproach, Methodist fanatics, and that many of his congregations shouted him down when he broached the subject of temperance. In Massachusetts the Reverend Ebenezer Sparhawk deplored the waste of money involved in drinking, the deleterious effect upon the health of the consumer, and the ruin of his immortal soul. His description of the effects of rum was vivid if not accurate:

[It] puts the blood and juices into a most terrible ferment, and disturbs the whole animal economy. It vitiates the humor, relaxes the solids, spoils the constitution, fills the body with diseases, brings on meager looks, a ghastly countenance, and very bad tremblings; yea, when the abuse of it is persisted in, it quite ruins the health, destroys the strength, introduces decay of nature, and hastens death faster than hard labour.[9]

At Yale College at the turn of the century, Timothy Dwight exhorted his students to sobriety as well as to Federalism and godliness as attributes of useful and praiseworthy lives.

Occasionally the laity joined in the move for reform. In 1789 a group of two hundred "respectable farmers" in Litchfield, Connecticut, formed a temporary association "to encourage the disuse of spirituous liquors" and agreed not to use distilled spirits during the ensuing season. Isolated adherents of reform took personal or family pledges to abstain from intoxicants. Micajah Pendleton of Virginia took such a pledge in 1800, and thus started this peculiarly individualist movement.[10]

Occasionally groups of men interested in temperance banded together to further the cause. A physician in the little town of Moreau in upstate New York became alarmed at the effects of drunkenness on the health and morals of the families of the lumberjacks who made up a large part of the town's population. He persuaded the local minister to act with him, and together they won over a group of their fellow townsmen and organized a little temperance society pledged to use no distilled liquors and to work for restrictions on their use among the laboring classes. This Moreau society, founded in 1808, had the distinction of being the first in America, but it was premature, and its appeal to the public through the speeches and pamphlets of its members brought little response. Its form of organization, however, and its pledge and propaganda tactics were to be characteristic of the crusade that began more than a decade later.

THE WORK OF BENJAMIN RUSH AND HIS ASSOCIATES

Through the whole period from the Revolution to 1815, Dr. Benjamin Rush was the center of the agitation for temperance. His *Inquiry into the Effect of Ardent Spirits upon the Human Mind and Body* went through eight editions in those years, and the American Tract Society alone printed one hundred and seventy-two thousand copies before 1850. The first part of the brochure dealt with the effects of ardent spirits on the novice drinker and on the habitual user. Rush described their effect on the mind, the property, and the social status of the excessive user, analyzed the arguments in favor of their use, and listed the few cases where he thought they might be taken in safety. The second part of the book reviewed the substitutes for harmful spirits, recommending cider, beer, wines, tobacco, and coffee. Part three went more deeply into the reasons for excessive drinking and into alternatives and remedies, and ended in alarming statistics of mortality and an appeal for temperance.

The language of the pamphlet was forceful, its illustrative material dramatic, and its descriptions vivid. There is no doubt that it made many converts. In 1790 the College of Physicians and Surgeons of Philadelphia, of which Rush was a member, sent a memorial to Congress stating that

. . . the habitual use of distilled spirits, in any case whatever, is wholly unnecessary; that they neither fortify the body against the morbid effects of heat or cold, nor render labour more easy or productive; and that there are many articles of diet which are not only safe and perfectly salutary, but preferable to distilled spirits, for the above mentioned purposes.[11]

Later temperance leaders often acknowledged their indebtedness to Dr. Rush and reprinted his *Inquiry* as a part of their propaganda. Rush himself regarded this tract as only a part of his work for the cause. He spoke before religious conventions, wrote memorials to the legislature of Pennsylvania, and sought to enlist other philanthropists in the work of reform.

Jeremy Belknap of New England and David Ramsay of South Carolina worked with Rush in the cause of temperance and corresponded with him for many years on conditions in their respective areas. The pictures they drew were pessimistic in the extreme and serve to counterbalance the optimism of the energetic doctor.[12]

Parson Weems joined this moderate work of reform in 1812 with his *Drunkard's Looking Glass*. This urbane if slightly ribald treatise was full of benevolent advice as to how to compromise between appetite and self-interest. Weems's "Golden Receipts against Drunkenness" run as follows:

1. Drink no longer water, but use a *little* wine for thy stomach's sake. Also cyder, ale, beer, etc.
2. Never fight *duels*. Nine times in ten memory of the murdered drives the murderer to the bottle.
3. Never marry but for love. Hatred is repellent; and the husband saunters to the tavern.
4. Provide against *old Bachelorism*. Age wants comfort, and a good wife is the second best in the universe.
5. Never stand surety for a sum that would embarrass you. And if you want, suffer a little rather than borrow, and starve than not pay; for debts and duns have filled the world with sots.
6. Hot coffee in the morning is a good cure for *dram-craving*. And a civic crown to him who will set the fashion of Coffee at dinner.[13]

Temperance and not abstinence, self-control and not self-denial, was the objective of those who were initiating the movement. Spirituous liquors were condemned as misused and harmful, but beverages of smaller alcoholic content were tolerated and, indeed, were recommended as substitutes. The economic and social results of excessive drinking were emphasized, and men were urged to consult their own interests in controlling their drinking habits. It was only among the clergy that the cause of temperance had assumed any of the aspects of a crusade. And it is difficult to discover much of organization or fanaticism even with them. Certainly there was nothing of the crusader in Parson Weems. Before 1810 only the Methodists and the Society of Friends had put the mark of disapproval upon ardent spirits, and the action of these sects had been in the nature of recommendations and pastoral urging rather than direct command or threat of purge.

THE ORIGINS OF THE TEMPERANCE CRUSADE

The origins of the real crusade for temperance were connected with the spread of revivalism in religion and with the advance of humanitarian reform in general. The crusade itself was to be inseparable from the religious motif of the first half of the century, was to be fostered by the clergy, and was a part of the fundamental concern of those of revivalistic faith with the welfare of the souls of their fellow men. The idea of intemperance as a sin that must weigh upon the conscience of the temperate as well as upon the immortal soul of the drunkard is clearly apparent in a speech made by the Reverend John Pierpont before a temperance convention in Boston. He was urging the passage of a law to stop the liquor traffic:

If I be willingly accessory to my brother's death, by a pistol or cord, the law holds me guilty; but guiltless if I mix his death drink in a cup. The halter is my reward if I bring him his death in a bowl of hemlock; if in a glass of spirits, I am rewarded with his purse. Yet who would not rather see his child die, by hemlock than by rum? The law raises me a gallows if I set fire to my neighbor's house, though not a soul perish in the flames. But I may throw a torch into his household — I may lead his children through a fire more consuming than Moloch's — I may make his whole family a burnt offering upon the altar of Mammon, and the same law holds its shield between me and harm.[14]

The interest in temperance was also stimulated by the spread of manhood suffrage and the growth of democratic ideas. If all men were to be allowed to vote, obviously they should be able to cast their ballots wisely. Like Noah Webster's interest in education, the concern of Rush and his associates about the temperance question was increased by a sense of the necessity for an enlightened electorate. In 1811 Rush appeared before the General Association of the Presbyterian Church in Philadelphia and delivered a plea for temperance because of its political effect. Rush spoke without partisanship.[15] Other men were concerned with the wisdom of the voter because they felt that sobriety would make him more willing to listen to the counsel of his betters. The early temperance advocates of New England, for example, were so strongly Federalist in their political affiliations that Federalism and temperance became entangled in public thinking.

Economic difficulties, too, played a part in spreading the interest in temperance. Beginning with the years of the Jeffersonian Embargo Act, times were hard and all classes dependent in any way upon foreign commerce suffered. After the War of 1812 there were years of difficult readjustment, ending in a sharp panic in 1819 with the unemployment, foreclosures, and misery usually attendant upon depression periods. In 1818 the New York Society for the Prevention of Pauperism noted that there were sixteen hundred licensed grocery stores in the city dispensing liquor in small quantities and that the poor purchased grog as readily as groceries. Temperance men everywhere emphasized the connection between excessive drinking and pauperism. They urged stricter licensing laws, the regulation of sale to known drunkards, and the refusal of employers to give grog as part pay for work.

Studies were made of the amount of spirits distilled and consumed and of the cost to the community of caring for the victims of excessive drinking. The report for the city of Albany, for example, gave the population as twenty thousand; the ardent spirits consumed, two hundred thousand gallons; the cost of such spirits, one hundred thousand dollars; the number of habitual drunkards, five hundred, and of "tipplers," four thousand.[16] The 1810 census showed that fourteen thousand distilleries were producing twenty-five million gallons of spirits each year, ninety per cent of which was being consumed in the United States. If the price of such liquors is roughly estimated at fifty cents a gallon, a total of more than twelve million dollars was, in the view of the temperance advocates, wasted annually. And in the early nineteenth century that was more than the total annual expenditure of the national government. It may have been overoptimistic to assume that, if a man could be persuaded to give up intoxicants, he would spend his money for food and clothing for his family, but it was obvious that abstinence would have a marked effect upon pauperism — and doubtless upon the burden borne by the taxpayer.

It was apparent, also, that the success of other reform movements depended to some extent upon the reduction of intemperance. Those who were working for the reformation of the criminal were struck by the correlation between drunkenness and crime. In 1833 a survey of the six hundred and seventeen inmates of Auburn prison showed that two hundred had been grossly intemperate, more than two hundred and fifty moderately intemperate, one hundred and thirty-two temperate, and nineteen total abstainers. Three hundred and fifty had been under the influence of liquor when their crimes were committed.[17] Poorhouses, houses of refuge, workhouses, and reform schools were filled with the intemperate. When scientific study of insanity began, much, perhaps too much, emphasis was laid on the connection between intoxicants and mental derangement. Those who wished to achieve reforms in the field of education sought to protect the child from the evil consequences of the intemperance of his parents. Juvenile delinquency was traced directly to surroundings whose sordidness was due to drink.

The religious aspect was stressed more and more. It was asserted that the revival spirit was easier to arouse in regions where temperance advocates had been active; not only did the "new sobriety" help revivalism, but it also prevented backsliding. A Vermont revivalist noted that the number of conversions "differed little from the number that broke away from the iron bondage of custom and adopted the principle of abstinence,"[18] and out on the frontier James Finley urged upon his converts the temperance pledge, at one time proudly reporting that a thousand people had signed the pledge during one revival. As the years went on, temperance came to be tied up with the millennial concept and with perfectionism. Surely Christ's second coming must be preceded by the elimination of the curse of drunkenness. William Miller himself urged abstinence upon his followers: "Behold the Bridegroom cometh! For your soul's sake drink not another draught, lest he come and find you drunken." [19]

In this general atmosphere of revivalism and reform it was inevitable that the temperance movement, fathered by such men as Benezet and Rush, should become, as did other humane causes of the period, a crusade to be promulgated at all costs. It was equally inevitable that its furtherance should fall, at first, into the hands of the clergy who were responsible for many of the other reforms and, in part, for the revivalism that lay behind them all. In a letter to Jeremy Belknap Dr. Rush said:

From the influence of the Quakers and Methodists in checking this evil, I am disposed to believe that the business must be effected finally by religion alone. Human reason has been employed in vain. . . . we have nothing to hope from the influence of *law* in making men wise and sober. Let these considerations lead us to address the heads of the governing bodies of all the Churches in America. [20]

He did not call on the churches in vain. In 1811, after an address by Rush in person, the General Association of Presbyterian Churches officially deplored the prevalence of the "sin of drunkenness." State associations in Massachusetts, Connecticut, and Vermont and the synods of New York and New Jersey took the same action. The fight for further reform was led by Lyman Beecher, whose interest in temperance had been aroused by reading Dr. Benjamin Rush's *Inquiry into the Effects of Ardent Spirits*. Beecher was particularly disturbed by the customary drinking among the clergy. After attending an ordination in Plymouth, Connecticut, he noted with disapproval that the

. . . preparation for our creature comforts in the sitting room of Mr. Heart's house, besides food, was a broad sideboard covered with decanters and bottles, and sugar and pitchers of water. There we found all the various kinds of liquors then in vogue. The drinking was apparently universal. This preparation was made by the society as a matter of course. When the Consociation arrived, they always took something to drink round; also before public services, and always on their return. As they could not all drink at once, they were obliged to stand and wait as people do when they go to mill.

There was a decanter of spirits also on the dinner-table, to help digestion, and the gentlemen partook of it through the afternoon and evening as they felt the need, some more and some less; and the sideboard, with the spillings of water, and sugar, and liquor, looked and smelled like the bar of a very active grog-shop. None of the Consociation were drunk; but that there was not, at times, a considerable amount of exhilaration, I can not affirm.[21]

Evidently Beecher was not the only one to disapprove, for shortly after this ordination a committee was appointed by the General Association to investigate the drinking habits of the clergy and to suggest remedies. The committee's report in 1812 was extremely cautious, declaring only that intemperance had for some time been increasing but that "after the most faithful and prayerful inquiry, they were obliged to confess they did not perceive that anything could be done." This defeatist attitude roused the dynamic Beecher to action, and he demanded a new committee of inquiry.

The report of this second committee, of which Beecher was chairman, may be considered the inauguration of the temperance movement in New England. In brief, it recommended that all ministers preach temperance sermons; that the clergy refrain from drinking at ecclesiastical meetings; that church members abstain from illegal sale or purchase of spirituous liquors and discipline themselves in their consumption; that parents cease the use of ardent spirits in their homes; that additional compensation be given to workmen, if necessary, in place of the usual rations of cider or rum; that the church undertake the circulation of temperance literature; and that the ministry foster voluntary associations to work for temperance. Above all, adjured Beecher, they must not assume that nothing could be done:

Is it impossible for God to reform and save us? Has He made known His purpose to give us over to destruction? Has He been accustomed to withhold His blessing from humble efforts made to rescue men from the dominion of sin? . . . Immense evils, we are persuaded, afflict communities, not because they are incurable, but because they are tolerated, and great good remains often unaccomplished merely because it is not attempted.[22]

In 1816 the General Conference of the Methodist Church swung that denomination somewhat into line with Beecher's committee by passing a resolution first introduced four years before: "Resolved, that no stationed or local preacher shall retail spirituous or malt liquors without forfeiting his ministerial character among us."

The New England clergy responded to the summons. Ordinations were no longer disgraced by the effects of ardent spirits, and many ministers gave up drinking entirely and began preaching the virtues of temperance. The Reverend Heman Humphrey, later to be the president of Amherst College, began his career as a temperance orator with a series of sermons in 1813. Dr. Justin Edwards of Andover Theological Seminary followed suit in 1814 and came out in favor of total abstinence a few years later.

The results of such sermons were varied; some congregations organized local temperance groups, others protested against the radicalism of their ministers. After a fervent temperance sermon, one Massachusetts pastor, for example, found that a barrel of rum had been deposited on the steps of his church as a silent expression of the disapproval of some of his flock. Out on the Western frontier Peter Cartwright, in endeavoring to get rid of the hard-drinking preachers on his circuit, had difficulty in securing non-"dram-drinkers" for the committees to vote their expulsion. He told of one case in which a popular but inebriated preacher was followed out of the church by thirteen of his loyal friends. The church was hopelessly split on the issue until the day was saved by a glorious revival in which the recalcitrant thirteen and at least forty more sinners came into the fold. The poor preacher, alas, was unregenerate and "lived and died a drunkard." [23]

Out of the interest of the Congregational and Presbyterian churches in Massachusetts came a call for a state convention, which was held in Boston in 1813. The result was the creation of the Massachusetts Society for the Suppression of Intemperance, which had as its guiding spirits such leading Calvinistic preachers as Jedidiah Morse and Eliphalet Porter. Similar societies were established elsewhere, and committees of correspondence were appointed to maintain contacts between them.

There was not as yet much emphasis upon abstinence. Wine was used freely at the meetings of the Massachusetts society, and a brewery was built in Boston to aid in the battle on rum when it was discovered that the city had one licensed grogshop for every twenty-one males sixteen years of age or older. Some societies required no pledge, others asked only abstinence from "too free" or immoderate use, while one Maine society bound the members who so far forgot their commitments to temperance as to get drunk, to "treat all round." [24]

Advocating only halfway measures, never enlisting many to their standard, these early temperance societies were not very effective. Those who were most earnest in the cause were the first to admit their failure and to acknowledge that more and more spirituous liquors were being consumed each year. They sadly agreed with Lyman Beecher: "Intemperance is the sin of our land and with our boundless prosperity is coming in upon us like a flood."

It was not only American observers who were alarmed. Travelers of various nations commented upon the prevalence of drunkenness in all sections of the country and marveled at the amount of hard liquor Americans could consume. Harriet Martineau was puzzled by the question, never satisfactorily answered, of how the vice ever reached the proportions it did

. . . in a country where there is no excuse of want on the one hand, or of habits of conviviality on the other. . . . Certain it is [however] that the vice threatened to poison society. It was as remarkable as licentiousness of other kinds ever was in Paris, or at Vienna. Men who doubted the goodness of the principle of Association in opposition to moral evil, were yet carried away to countenance it by seeing nothing else that was to be done. [25]

It must be admitted, however, that there was an occasional dissenting voice. James Stuart, for example, who spent three years in America, asserted that, although there was a great consumption of spirits, he had seen few drunken persons — fewer than a dozen in all three years. [26] But certainly Stuart saw nothing in the late 1820's to indicate that the early temperance movement had produced results worth noting.

A DECADE OF RAPID PROGRESS

From these humble beginnings came the temperance crusade that swept over the country in the years after 1825, attracting more than a million followers organized in a movement that was to furnish a model for pressure groups. The battle cry of this new phase of the movement was total abstinence, not just moderation, and this abstinence was to be secured by close organization, constant propaganda, and definite pledges. The methods were to be those of the revivalists, and the organization was to devolve upon workers closely connected with the churches.

The campaign began with a series of sermons and articles whose definite purpose was to state the case for abstinence. Dr. Justin Edwards of Andover led the way. In 1816 and again in 1822 his sermons on the subject attracted attention, and in 1825 he published a tract called *The Well-Conducted Farm* which urged abstinence upon farm laborers on both moral and economic grounds. Calvin Chapin, who visited the Western Reserve in Ohio in 1825, came back oppressed by the evils of intemperance in that region and published an article to prove that "abstinence from ardent spirits is the only certain preventive of intemperance." And in the autumn of 1825 Lyman Beecher preached a series of six sermons advocating total abstinence.

Once more Beecher's action was decisive, and his arguments were quoted wherever men of like opinion got together. He put the responsibility squarely upon the moderate and temperate and placed his reliance on moral principles and moral suasion:

What then [said he] is this universal, natural, and national remedy for intemperance? It is the banishment of ardent spirits from the list of lawful objects of commerce by a correct and efficient public sentiment, such as has turned slavery out of half of our land and will yet expel it from the world.

It is the buyers who have created the demand for ardent spirits and made distillation and importation a gainful traffic; and it is the custom of the temperate, too, which inundates the land with the occasion of so much and such unmanageable temptation. Let the temperate cease to buy, and the demand for ardent spirits will fall in the market three-fourths, and ultimately will fail wholly, as the generation of drunkards shall hasten out of time. . . . Let the consumer do his duty, and the capitalist, finding his employment unproductive, will quickly discover other channels of useful enterprise. . . . This, however, can not be done effectually so long as the traffic in ardent spirits is regarded as lawful, and is patronized by men of reputation and moral worth in the land. Like slavery, it must be regarded as sinful, impolitic, and dishonorable. That no measures will avail short of rendering ardent spirits a contraband of trade is nearly self-evident.[27]

Beecher's position was supported by clergy and laymen in all parts of the country, and the publication in 1826 of his *Six Sermons* was followed by a number of pamphlets carrying his arguments still further. In 1828 Dr. Heman Humphrey, president of Amherst College, delivered a Fourth of July address which he called "A Parallel Between Intemperance and the Slave Trade." Slavery and not independence was his theme, he said, for "after the lapse of nearly fifty years of undisputed political freedom, the blood-freezing clank of a cruel bondage is still heard amid our loudest rejoicing"; and that bondage was the thralldom of intemperance. After a lurid description of the African slave trade and its infamous Middle Passage, Humphrey concluded with a still more unpleasant picture of the poverty, insanity, and other horrors attendant upon drunkenness.

As the movement gained ground, other college presidents came to its aid. The Reverend Eliphalet Nott of Union College was a doughty adherent of the cause and his *Lectures on Bible Temperance,* published in 1847, were a notable addition to its literature. President Appleton of Bowdoin College was a leader of the movement in Maine; Presidents Lord of Dartmouth, Mark Hopkins of Williams, Wayland of Brown, and Day of Yale all added their influence. Dr. William Ellery Channing and Dr. Theodore Parker both came over to the cause and preached temperance sermons, although it was with reluctance that they accepted the coercive measures of the later phases of the movement.[28]

In February 1826, at the call of Dr. Justin Edwards, a group of men working with him both on the foreign mission board and in the American Tract Society came together in Boston and drew up a constitution for a new organization to be called the American Society for the Promotion of Temperance. Seven of the sixteen men who signed the document were clergymen, and the society it set up was modeled on the American Board of Commissioners for Foreign Missions. It was a militant organization, the clergy and laymen who sponsored it were able and determined men, and they were skilled in all the arts of argument, emotional appeal, and propaganda. They used revivalistic methods, maintained paid secretaries or campaign managers, sent lecturers throughout the country, kept up a lively press campaign, and published countless pamphlets and a series of temperance periodicals, of which the *Journal of Humanity* was one of the more important.[29] Prize essay contests were conducted with much publicity, and the winning manuscripts were printed and circulated as propaganda literature. The campaign was educational as well as emotional; men were to be convinced not only that drinking was a sin, but also that it was deleterious to the individual and society.

The society held frequent meetings, with each annual meeting in February a gala event. The reports of the society, published annually during its ten years of vigor, were a mine of information to the worker in the field and a source of inspiration and material for argument for temperance advocates everywhere. They included letters, personal experiences, treatises on the ill effects of intemperance, reports on the progress of the movement, and tables and illustrative material of various sorts.[30]

All the propaganda was directed toward the signing of a pledge promising total abstinence from spirituous liquors, and preachers and lecturers urged the pledge upon everyone in their audiences — whether or not the individual was a consumer of such beverages. It was proudly asserted in 1835 that three thousand ministers had signed the pledge, and, doubtless, there were many more women signers. Sunday schools were impressed into service, schoolteachers were encouraged to extol the merits of temperance, and children were warned of the dangers of drink. Medical societies were urged to endorse the campaign, and hundreds of doctors were persuaded to sign statements condemning distilled liquors.

The effectiveness of the campaign was soon evidenced by the increase in the number of temperance societies, and the generalship of the leaders was shown in their methods and forms of organization. These local groups were not sporadic, isolated phenomena; they were units or cells in a well-regulated system. Local societies were grouped into state units, delegates were sent from local meetings to state conventions, and from there to the annual meetings of the parent society. Agents and missionaries were the advance guard in regions where organization had not yet been effected, and older societies fostered the movement in near-by areas. By 1829 there were one thousand local units with a membership of one hundred thousand; two years later the numbers had doubled, and there were nineteen state societies; by 1833 the national society announced four thousand locals and a total membership of half a million, and a year later five thousand societies with a million members. The movement was strongest in New England, New York, and Pennsylvania, with a large membership in the Old Northwest. South of Mason and Dixon's line there were societies in every state, the strongest in Virginia and Georgia, but the number of members was small and only fifteen thousand in the whole South pledged total abstinence from distilled liquors.

From the beginning there were attempts in the several states to organize legislative temperance societies — more, it seems, for purposes of prestige than to procure legislation favoring temperance.[31] In 1832 the movement spread to Congress, where it was backed by Felix Grundy of Tennessee, Lewis Cass of Michigan, and Theodore Frelinghuysen of New Jersey. The objective of the Congressional society formed in February 1833, was to discountenance the use of, and the traffic in, spirituous liquor "by example and by kind moral influence."[32] There is little evidence that legislators were induced to join these societies or to sign the pledge by threats of loss of votes, but compliance with the wishes of a strong and very vocal group of voters was undoubtedly a matter of policy with some candidates for office. They were urged to put themselves on record as supporting this crusade on the grounds that it would be a national disgrace if the United States should falter in maintaining its high standards and its moral leadership. The nations of the world, it was said, were watching the temperance movement in the United States and were ready to imitate the example it set.

From 1826 to 1833 progress was steady, and the success of the movement seemed assured. Local societies pointed with pride to the way housewives boycotted grocery stores that sold intoxicants, to the lessening number of grogshops, and to the business failures of distillery owners.[33] Temperance hotels were built to accommodate a traveling public that disapproved of drink, and college commencements came to be solemn rather than hilarious occasions. Horace Mann in the North and Thomas S. Grimké in the South interested themselves in young men's temperance societies. College men were prevailed upon to organize; Amherst was enthusiastically "dry" from the first with three fourths of the students enrolled. Dartmouth had a society in 1828, and out in Ohio Oberlin boasted a strong coeducational temperance organization.

With so much accomplished, it was, perhaps, inevitable that the enthusiasts should presume too far and ask too much. If abstinence from distilled liquors was a prerequisite for temperance, why should the use of fermented drinks be tolerated when they, too, were intoxicant, though only slightly so, and were, besides, conducive to heavier drinking? And again, if those whose moral and civic sense was acute joined societies and signed pledges voluntarily, there were still countless thousands whose temperance could be guaranteed only by coercive means. Should they be permitted to block the moral crusade and render the successes already obtained mere halfway measures? At the height of the movement's success it foundered on these rocks of thoroughness and immediatism — issues that were also troubling the peace and abolition societies in the same period.

ULTRAISM VERSUS TEMPERANCE

The American Temperance Society was the strongest of the temperance organizations and, through its many branches, the one most closely in contact with the rank and file of workers in the cause. Many societies, however, did not owe their existence to it, and its influence in some states was negligible. It seemed to many temperance advocates that the common cause could best be furthered by uniting the various groups and coordinating their programs and objectives. The executive committee of the American Temperance Society, therefore, took the initiative and issued a call for a convention of delegates from all county and state groups to meet in Philadelphia in May 1833.

It was with the greatest optimism that the leaders faced the four hundred and more representatives of organizations in twenty-one states, but the first general discussion revealed the fundamental differences of opinion and temperament represented at the convention.

One of the first questions to be settled was the type of pledge to be required of members of the new united society. A conservative minority was opposed to any pledge of abstinence and advocated permitting a temperate use of intoxicants. A radical minority wished to broaden the abstinence clause of the customary pledge to include malt and fermented liquors as well as ardent spirits. Both groups had considerable backing, and both could quote authorities and precedents. In the Massachusetts state society, for example, no definite pledge had been required up to 1833, and total abstinence had not been advocated. In the New York society, on the other hand, there were strong leaders who were ready to demand abstinence from "all that intoxicates," regardless of the amount of alcohol in the beverage or of the process by which it was made. Gerrit Smith, member of the wealthy landed gentry and owner of the Peterboro Temperance Hotel, E. C. Delavan, an upstate merchant who had already been sued for libel by the Albany brewers for his assertion that contaminated river water was used in their product, and Arthur Tappan, New York City merchant, publisher, and philanthropist, who even advocated the use of unfermented grape juice for sacramental purposes, were all immediatists and believers in total abstinence — and Gerrit Smith was a leading member of the steering committee of the convention.

Nonetheless it was soon apparent that the majority of the convention would accept nothing more stringent than a pledge to abstain from the consumption of ardent spirits, and the New York ultras were silenced temporarily on that phase of the agenda. They came back into the fray in a bitter wrangle over the attitude of the new society toward the liquor traffic. With advocates of prohibition on the steering committee, it was inevitable that this matter should be discussed, and it was Gerrit Smith who introduced the resolution that started the debate:

Resolved, that in the opinion of this Convention, the traffic in ardent spirits, as a drink, is *morally wrong;* and that the inhabitants of cities, towns, and other local communities, should be permitted by law to prohibit the said traffic within their respective jurisdictions.

This resolution was evidence that the temperance crusade had reached a dividing of the ways. Up to its introduction the emphasis had been upon the persuasion of the consumer; now the *sin* of the producer and retailer was to be stressed and legislative remedies were to be sought. The adoption of the resolution did not mean the end of the argument but merely transferred it to the state and local societies, and the words *morally wrong* became a slogan for the extremists.

These acrimonious debates were ominous for future harmony, but in the main work of the convention — the perfecting of a national society — there was little difficulty. It was decided that the Temperance Union should be a federation composed of the officers of the American Temperance Society, the officers of the state societies, and representatives of various local organizations. The wealthy New York aristocrat, Stephen van Rensselaer, was chosen president, and an executive committee was named to direct propaganda, with a paid executive secretary to coordinate all activities.[34]

The first national convention of the new society was held in 1836, when its name was changed to the American Temperance Union and its acceptance of the radical program was secured by a group of ultras led by Lyman Beecher, Justin Edwards, and Edward Delavan. When the delegates went back to their state and local groups to fight for the acceptance of this program and a new ultra pledge, the temperance movement of the 1830's broke up into warring factions. The New York society refused to follow Delavan's lead, and he resigned. Two thousand of the New York locals did not adopt the new pledge. Ohio also split over the issue, with the temperance group losing ground to the "teetotal" advocates. When the ultras repudiated moral suasion and began a campaign for legislation, the dissension became still more acrimonious. The result was a vast decline in the whole movement. In New York, for instance, a membership of two hundred and twenty-nine thousand in 1836 dropped to one hundred and thirty-one thousand in 1839. In Georgia the struggle was fatal to the state organization, for an ardent ultra, Josiah Flournoy, led a campaign for state prohibition that so involved the state society in local politics that it could not recover from Flournoy's defeat.

Other factors contributed to the decline of the movement in the late 1830's. Many of the temperance leaders — William Lloyd Garrison, Gerrit Smith, and Arthur Tappan, for example — were at the same time ardent abolitionists. Southern advocates of temperance came to identify the two reforms and to repudiate them both.[35] In the North, where abolitionism was frowned on in influential circles, the temperance movement suffered because of the common leadership. A public that did not condemn the antiabolitionists' destruction of Arthur Tappan's library and furniture could scarcely subscribe to his leadership of other reforms. The panic of 1837 and the long years of depression that followed it probably contributed to a decline in interest and support of this as well as of other reform movements — although the arguments that excessive drinking was a major cause for poverty and that its diminution would ease the burden on the taxpayer may have been especially effective in a period of economic stringency. All in all, the years just before 1840 were in marked contrast to the hopeful days of the early 1830's, and the temperance movement seemed destined to failure.

THE ARGUMENTS FOR ABSTINENCE

Through twenty years of agitation by the advocates of temperance, every argument for it was aired, and every measure save national prohibition was tried; when the crusade was again an issue in the early twentieth century the only new line of attack was the constitutional amendment. The evolution of argument and attitude from the reasoned moderation of Benjamin Rush to the Puritanic intolerance of Gerrit Smith was apparent in the pamphlet literature of the day.

Arguing that moderate use precedes excessive consumption, an early pamphleteer followed Rush in condemning ardent spirits and offered figures on the amount and cost of drinking in support of his demands for the repeal of the licensing laws and for prohibitive duties on the importation of spirituous liquors.[36] A few years later Jonathan Kittredge of Lynne, New Hampshire, wrote an *Address on the Effects of Ardent Spirits* that gave a typical picture of the economic ruin and social degradation of the drunkard:

[He] is useless, and worse than useless; he is a pest to all around him. All the feelings of his nature are blunted; he has lost all shame; he procures his accustomed supply of the poison that consumes him; he staggers through the mud, and through filth to his hut; he meets a weeping wife and starving children — he abuses them, he tumbles into the straw, and he rolls and foams like a mad brute, till he is able to go again. He calls for more rum — he repeats the scene from time to time, and from day to day, till soon his nature faints, and he becomes sober in death.

And to this Kittredge added lurid word pictures of the death scenes of such victims:

Some are killed instantly; some die a lingering, gradual death; some commit suicide in fits of intoxication; and some are actually burnt up. I read of an intemperate man, a few years since, whose breath caught fire by coming in contact with a lighted candle, and he was consumed. At the time I disbelieved this story, but my reading has furnished me with well authenticated cases of a combustion of the human body from the use of ardent spirits. . . . They are attended with all the proof one re-

Illustration for the temperance tract, The True History of Deacon Giles' Distillery, *by George Barrell Cheever. The tract was in the form of a dream in which devils acted as workmen in the distillery and played a joke on the deacon by labeling the kegs of liquor with the effects of their contents. The labels became visible only upon the sale of the kegs, thus frightening off the purchasers. The tract caused a famous lawsuit in which a local deacon who owned a distillery was the complainant.*

quires to believe any event. I will state one of them, and from this an idea can be formed of the rest. It is the case of a woman eighty years of age, exceedingly meagre, who had drunk nothing but ardent spirits for several years. She was sitting in her elbow chair, while her waiting maid went out of the room for a few moments. On her return, seeing her mistress on fire, she immediately gave an alarm, and some people came to her assistance, one of them endeavored to extinguish the flames with his hands, but they adhered to them as if they had been dipped in brandy or oil on fire. Water was brought and thrown on the body in abundance, *yet the flame appeared more violent, and was not extinguished until the whole body was consumed.*

The idea that excessive use of ardent spirits made the body combustible was constantly reiterated, and the cases cited were always said to be "well authenticated" and were often accompanied by medical evidence. The *American Temperance Magazine* in 1851

Deacon Giles's distillery with the demons in possession

stated that cases "of the death of inebriates by internal flames kindled spontaneously" were so numerous and incontrovertible that "no person of information will question" them, and then proceeded to describe the last agonies of a man who was "literally roasted from the crown of his head to the soles of his feet," bathed in a flame that made him appear like the "wick of a candle in the midst of its own flame." From the pages of such temperance tracts this idea of spontaneous combustion was lifted to contemporary fiction, and both English and American novelists described in detail deaths due to "internal fires." [37]

All arguments were not so lurid, however, and many pamphleteers used medical evidence of a milder nature, accompanying it by appeals to civic and religious responsibility.[38] A certain Dr. Springwater, "the Cold-Water Man," wrote on *The Evils of Intemperance* in 1832 with much rhetoric and much feeling. Intemperance, he said, wasted property, destroyed health, produced crime, led to poverty, murdered time, destroyed respectability, deteriorated moral feeling, and was a public evil. It was death to religious feeling, the destroyer of domestic happiness, and the murderer of the soul. Moderate drinking was worse than drunkenness, for it deceived the victim, supported the grogshop, set a bad example, weakened the human system so that disease might prey upon it, and eventually "whirled [the soul] to destruction." Dr. Springwater placed equal responsibility upon those who furnished the raw products, those who manufactured the spirits, those who sold them, and those who consumed them. The only cure was total abstinence and the use of cold water.

A novel sort of argument for total abstinence was offered by one Charles T. Woodman. He had been a restless, intemperate youth, in and out of jail, more often drunk than sober, but in 1842 he was won over to temperance and signed the pledge. His *Narrative of a Reformed Inebriate* is full of excellent descriptions of the almshouses and workhouses in which he was often lodged, and the descriptions of his escapades alternate with doggerel verse on various subjects, the evils of drink predominating. Although a baker by trade, he worked in his sober intervals at whatever employment was offered him, and one of his temporary jobs was in a store where medicines and beverages were sold. As an argument against the use of all forms of intoxicants, he gave a long list of recipes for adulterating them and for producing any beverage ordered from those already in stock.[39]

Edward C. Delavan, president of the New York society, was interested in exposing the adulteration of wines and the bad practices of manufacturers. He was the editor of a collection of twenty-four tracts entitled *Temperance Essays and Selections from Different Authors,* which ran into many editions. The matter of communion wine was of great concern to him and to Gerrit Smith and others of his friends, and he published various letters he had received on the subject. He quoted excerpts from the *Lectures on Temperance* of Dr. Eliphalet Nott of Union College, who was regarded as an authority on Scriptural drinking. Nott maintained that nine words in the Hebrew of the Old Testament had been translated into English by the single word *wine* but that their various meanings in the text could not be the same. Some meant a harmless drink, while others made wine a "mocker," or a "serpent's bite," or an "adder's sting." Therefore, he inferred, the Bible approved only unfermented fruit juices, and he answered the troublesome questions about Christ's first miracle by insisting that the wine served at the marriage feast in Cana was unfermented. Delavan's collection also included reprints of Dr. Thomas Sewall's seven plates portraying the effects of alcohol on the human stomach. These colored plates seem to have been the first of a long series of such illustrations designed to convince the healthy of the dangers of intemperance.

Delavan also reprinted an essay by Bishop Alonzo Potter of Pennsylvania on the *Drinking Usages of Society.* This essay was widely circulated and may be found in many pamphlet editions. Bishop Potter's appeal was to those who set the standards of custom and fashion, for, said he, "Fashion propagates itself downward," and the lower classes "take their tone from the upper."

There, in the abodes of all the rich and admired; there, amidst all the enchantments of luxury and elegance; where friend pledges friend; where wine is invoked to lend new animation to gaiety, and impart new brilliancy to wit; in the sparkling glass, which is raised even by the hand of beautiful and lovely woman — there is the most dangerous decay. . . . We do not regulate our watches more carefully or more universally by the town-clock, than do nine tenths of mankind take their tone from the residue, who occupy places towards which all are struggling. . . . Let the responsibility of these drinking usages be put, then, where it justly belongs. . . . Neither the power of law aimed at the traffic in liquors, nor the force of argument addressed to the understandings and the consciences of the many, will ever prevail to cast out the fiend drunkenness, so long as they who are esteemed the favored few uphold with unyielding hand the practice of drinking.[40]

All told, the literature of the temperance advocates was extensive both in the number of tracts and in the total copies of each that were printed. The American Tract Society, the American Sunday School Union, and the American Temperance Union were the chief agencies for printing and distributing propaganda material, the Tract Society alone circulating about five million tracts and more than one hundred and fifty thousand volumes of greater length. Among these Dr. Rush's *Inquiry*, Edwards' *Well-Conducted Farm*, Kittredge's *Address*, and Humphrey's *Dialogue on Ardent Spirits* seem to have been the most popular, for from one to three hundred thousand copies were printed of each.[41] Throughout the period the periodicals devoted to the temperance cause were numerous, and their circulation was extensive.

THE OPPONENTS OF ULTRAISM AND COERCION

The opposition literature is less extensive but fully as varied. Harriet Martineau, writing at the time when ultraism was just beginning to prevail among temperance leaders, seems to have been the first to sound a note of warning. She said she had been told that the people of New England "did good by mania," and this phrase continually recurred to her as she studied the temperance movement. Man must, she felt, be virtuous in and by himself, and the principle of temperance was incommunicable, since no two men's temptations were alike. This was especially true in the case of drinking, she said, because the temptations of the advocates of temperance were immeasurably weaker than those of the masses to be wrought upon. There was, therefore, a "vast quantity of perjury, of false and hasty promising, of lapses, and of secret, solitary drinking." Hypocrisy was added to intemperance; schism developed out of the ignorance of bigots; and new and fatal perils arose to assail freedom of conscience. As a result, "the example of those who have not pledged themselves is the only one morally regarded; all other persons being known to be bound. Virtue under a vow has no spiritual force." The temperance fanatic demanded a complete giving up of self-control and self-defense and the "subservience of conscience to control." The temperance societies were, Miss Martineau thought, created for weak minds and developed "spiritual subservience" in their members.[42]

Bishop John Henry Hopkins of the Episcopal church in Vermont resented the claim that temperance had a religious aspect, and his *The Primitive Church*, published in 1836, contained many arguments against the alliance of religion and the temperance movement. The temperance societies, he said, were based on worldly principles; they opposed vice and attempted to establish virtue by methods that were not in accord with the Word of God, and they gave false prominence to one particular vice, contrary to the doctrines of the Bible. To call temperance a prerequisite or preparation for church membership was "at war with the principles of the Gospel," and to assert that temperance could be relied upon as a remedy against vice was a denial of the religion of Christ. Nor was abstinence to be considered a measure of piety.

Hopkins had the heartiest contempt for those advocates of the cold-water pledge who quibbled over the question of Scriptural drinking, and he noted with sarcasm the arguments about the meaning of the word *wine* in the Bible. It was strange, he said, that the apostles did not know of the distinction between the words meaning fermented and unfermented drinks, and that "they falsely represented Christ as changing the water into wine, when they should have said that he changed it into a sort of grape jelly." [43] Such statements were trivial, he affirmed; the vital question was the loyalty of man to the church and to the teachings of Christ. "The outward reformation of a single vice is nothing, when the heart remains unsanctified and the curse of God still hangs upon the soul." [44]

Published in the same year as *The Primitive Church*, Calvin Colton's *Protestant Jesuitism* censured, not the combination of religion and temperance as advocated in the *Revival Lectures* of Charles G. Finney, but the attempts of nonpolitical voluntary associations to secure political power to effect their moral reforms. He condemned the attempt of a dominant minority to coerce a majority and asserted that the trend of the temperance crusade and the abolition movement alike was toward the destruction of American liberties.

Such movements were inquisitorial and hypocritical and were in the hands of bigots and fanatics, not reformers.

Bishop Hopkins and Calvin Colton were both clergymen. David M. Reese brought science to their aid. In 1838 he published a gem of a book entitled *The Humbugs of New York, being a Remonstrance against Popular Delusion, whether in Science, Philosophy or Religion.* It was a protest against all ultraism. Reese said that medical science could go no further with temperance reformers than to advocate moderation in the use of ardent spirits. He had seen no evidence that wine, beer, and cider were harmful, and he felt that to call total abstinence a moral obligation was utterly unjustifiable. He called teetotalism a "senseless cognomen" and "ultra-temperance" a "reigning humbug." For those who included tobacco, tea, and coffee in their list of the causes for intemperance, Reese had only the heartiest contempt. Their ideas were delusions and impostures — in short, humbugs! [45]

The most complete and carefully reasoned refutation of radical methods was the *Review of the Late Temperance Movements in Massachusetts* by the Reverend Leonard Withington, published in 1840. He protested against all use of what he called "the absolute shall." He did not believe in the efficacy of pledges or of coercive societies and feared the American tendency to follow emotional appeals.

We love excitement; the appetite is increasing upon us; we are a peculiar nation. Some people, I have no doubt, have such a craving for *anti-ism*, for some party to follow, or some object to oppose; that if you could translate them into the bowers of Paradise, beneath the very shadow of the tree of life, their gloomy imagination would conjure up some phantom of evil, some giant of corruption, whom they must oppose with the zeal of holy hatred, and conquer by the arms of party strife. They could not sing the songs of Sion but in the chorus of a faction.[46]

It was impossible, Withington said, to draw a prohibition law that would not be full of inconsistencies and would not divide communities and call forth spies and lawbreakers. And laws that could not be executed were worse than useless, for they would cause a lessening of respect for the government and a disregard for all law.

Withington insisted that sumptuary laws were of no avail, for they were "straws to the whirlwinds," and that reformers had never been effective in stopping other sins by coercive measures. Lying, cheating, fraud, and perjury "still stalk through the land," "delusion still infests our politics," and "pleasure and licentiousness still reign over our cities." Drunkenness cannot be exterminated any more than other sins until "God blesses his Gospel, and a better day dawns on the world." Withington did not despair, however.

The way to promote temperance is very obvious [he wrote]. The child may find it. In the first place, be consistent in your precept and example; be a temperate man yourself; and rely for your influence on the evangelical weapons of light and love. Trace the evil to its cause and endeavor to remove it. Remember that some are drunkards because they are poor; some because they are idle; some because they are disappointed; some because they are ignorant; some from an unhappy nervous system; and all because they are not Christians. Reflect that there are *indirect* as well as *direct* efforts to oppose this evil; and that sometimes the indirect efforts are the most effectual. Is a man idle, endeavor to employ him; is he ignorant, instruct him; is he disappointed, point him to the true source of consolation; and above all things beware how you lord it over his faults, or play the Pharisee over his vices. Recollect that intemperance is seldom an insulated vice; it grows up in wide combinations; and you are never fitted to engage in the subject of reforming it until you have sounded the depths from which it springs. . . . Very little good has ever been done by the *absolute shall*.[47]

THE WASHINGTONIAN MOVEMENT

Whether or not the counsel of such men as Withington would have prevailed if there had been no sudden upsurge of interest in the cause, it is impossible to state. The subsidence of crusading zeal was of short duration, and the year that saw the publication of his plea for moderation was also the year of a revival of interest in the movement — a revival that was extremely emotional and dramatic.

Until 1840 temperance propaganda had been directed toward educating the public in the evils resulting from the use of intoxicants and toward arousing a feeling that the manufacture, sale, or use of such beverages was morally wrong. The temperance societies had been mainly concerned with the future of moderate drinkers and of those who had not yet become drinkers. They had, apparently, been willing to accept the current theory that there was no hope for the confirmed inebriate and had been concerned with him only as a hideous example. His social degradation and his horrible death were used as a warning against drink, but his fate was determined by his fall from grace, and his drunkard's grave was his just desert.

With the organization of the Washington Temperance Society the cause of temperance went into a different phase — so different that the Washingtonians might almost be said to have initiated a new crusade. And this time the leadership came, not from the superior, the untempted, and the incorruptible, but from the condemned and neglected sots who rose from their gutters to conduct the assault upon the enemy that had laid them low.

This new crusade was born in Chase's Tavern in Baltimore on the night of April 2, 1840. A group of six convivial souls, who met there frequently to drink and gamble, had their attention called to a temperance lecture being held in a near-by church. More as an idle joke than with any serious intent, they decided to send a few of their number to listen to the arguments of the reformer. The committee returned convinced of the logic of the speaker, and the whole group spent the night debating the subject of intoxication and their own relation to it. They decided to accept the challenge and pledge themselves to total abstinence from all intoxicants. Having drawn up and signed a comprehensive pledge, they proceeded to organize a society, elect officers, and plan their program. They named their society for the first president of the republic and, proudly calling themselves reformed drunkards, set out to attract others to join in their campaign.

They were immediately successful. With an initiation fee of twenty-five cents and monthly dues of half that sum, the new society recruited its members largely from men whose careers and social standing had been similar to those of its founders. Within a few weeks the numbers attending each meeting were so great that the Washingtonians had to have a hall of their own. They called in no outside speakers; each program was the narration of the life history and regeneration of one or more members of the group, and opportunity was offered for other victims of drink to sign the pledge and in their turn carry on the work. The main objective of the society was the salvation of drunkards by reformed drunkards. Although there was no trace of religion either in the organization or in its appeal, it is impossible to write of it without using the words

The original Washingtonians

340

employed in describing camp meetings and revivals: "experience meetings," "personal testimony," "salvation," "regeneration," "missionaries." And the fact that many of the most ardent Washingtonians became deeply religious men increased the resemblance between the movement and a genuine religious revival.

Before the end of 1840 there were more than a thousand Washingtonians in Baltimore, and the leaders were ready to carry the crusade to other cities. A New York Washingtonian Society was organized with nearly two thousand members, and a month later meetings in Boston ended in the formation of another society there. Missionaries were then sent through every state, and the movement swept across the country like a religious revival. There had been, in the earlier history of the movement, nothing comparable to the intense emotional appeal of the denunciation, by a reformed drunkard, of the cause of his degradation. Temperance lectures became dramatic experience recitals that ended in saving other souls from a fate that had been all too vividly described.

With singing and shouting the Washingtonian pledge was signed by thousands of eager converts. By the end of 1841 in New York, New Jersey, and Pennsylvania alone, twenty-three thousand members had been added to the movement. Two years later the Washingtonians claimed that half a million intemperate drinkers and a hundred thousand drunkards had signed their pledge, and that societies had been formed in every city and town. Such figures should be taken with caution, however, for, as J. A. Krout has pointed out, these societies were mushroom growths and left few permanent records. No one could know how many pledge-signers returned to their cups when the excitement was over.

Conspicuous in the Washingtonian parades were throngs of children wearing white satin badges and carrying banners on which appeared pictures of fountains and processions of people wending their way through leafy groves. These were divisions of the Cold Water Army, founded by the Reverend Thomas Hunt in 1839 just before the Washingtonian crusade began. Greatly augmented by the current enthusiasm, the Cold Water Army became the medium for organizing children for temperance work. Its periodical, the *Cold Water Army*, appeared regularly for twenty years and was a part of the equipment of every Sunday school library. Both the

magazine and the book of the same name by the founder of the organization were filled with short stories and verses designed to cause
fear of "Demon Rum" and joy in persuading other children to sign
the cold-water pledge, which appeared in poor verse:

> We do not think,
> We'll ever drink,
> Whiskey or Gin,
> Brandy or Rum,
>   or anything,
> That'll make drunk come.[48]

The popular and democratic character of the new movement was
apparent in its literature, and the songs, poetry, and fiction offered
for the delectation of adults was of much the same caliber as that
appearing in the children's magazines. To the tune of Yankee Doo-
dle was set the song of "Jonathan's Independence," which began,

> Says Jonathan, says he, today
>   I will be independent,
> And so my grog I'll throw away,
>   And that shall be the end on't.
> Clean the house, the tarnal stuff
>   Sha'n't be here so handy,
> Wife has given the winds her snuff
>   So now here goes my brandy.[49]

This popular ditty was matched by many from the pen of a man
who wrote under the pseudonym of Henry Smith, "the Celebrated
Razor-Strop Man." The author was an English-born, itinerant ped-
dler who had been saved by the Washingtonians and contributed
his verses, anecdotes, and stories to their cause.

The sentimental touch was provided by such poetic collections
as *The Silver Cup of Sparkling Drops* edited by Miss C. B. Porter,
which offered all the old arguments in such effusions as this:

> I gazed upon the tattered garb
>   Of one who stood a listener by;
> The hand of misery pressed him hard,
>   And tears of sorrow swelled his eye.
>
> I gazed upon his pallid cheek,
>   And asked him how his cares begun —
> He sighed, and thus essayed to speak,
>   "The cause of all my grief is *rum*."

I watched a maniac through the gate
  Whose raving shook me to the soul.
I asked what sealed his wretched fate,
  The answer was — "the *cursed bowl.*"

I asked a convict in his chains
  While tears along his cheek did roll;
What devil urged him on to crime —
  His answer was — "the *cursed bowl.*"

I asked the murderer when the rope
  Hung round his neck in death's hard roll;
Bereft of pardon, and of hope —
  His answer was — "the *cursed bowl.*" [50]

Since the Washingtonians made great use of songs in their mass meetings and processions, the volume of musical and poetic propaganda increased rapidly. In 1845 they published *The Washingtonian Teetotaler's Minstrel,* which contained such classics as "The Rum-Seller's Lament," "Dear Father, Drink No More," and "Mother, Dry That Flowing Tear." About the same time appeared the sentimental song "Father, Dear Father, Come Home with Me Now," which has been revived for the amusement of a later generation.

Mrs. Lydia H. Sigourney was a champion of the movement and used her position as associate editor of *Godey's Lady's Book* to open its columns to many writers on temperance. Her own verses and stories had neither distinction nor style, but they were very popular. The *Temperance Tales* of Lucius Manlius Sargent were widely read, although their literary merit was negligible. Their sincerity, missionary zeal, and directness of appeal made them so popular that they ran through more than one hundred editions and were translated into several foreign languages.

The best known writer in the temperance crusade, however, was Timothy Shay Arthur, whose *Ten Nights in a Bar Room* made up in dramatic title for any dullness in the subject matter.[51] There was little of the zealot or the reformer in Arthur. He had happened upon a theme for which there was an excellent market and from which he might derive a good living. His novels and short stories were stereotyped, their themes were highly moral, and their general character was decidedly dull and respectable; but the market was good, and his output was enormous. Besides stories and verse that appeared in *Godey's Lady's Book* and other magazines, he wrote a number of novels and edited several famous collections of tales, poems, and essays. In his *Lights and Shadows of Real Life* and in the *Sons of Temperance Offerings* of 1850 and 1851, Arthur collected a vast amount of temperance material — and published it in de luxe tooled-leather editions for an admiring public.

The backbone of the Washingtonian revival, however, was not the writers who flocked to its support but the evangelists who came from the ranks of the reformed drunkards. The most famous of these traveling workers were John H. W. Hawkins, who was won for the movement in 1840, and John B. Gough, who signed the pledge in Worcester, Massachusetts, in 1842. Hawkins was American born, a hatter by trade, who had early "taken to drink" and who had struggled against his bad habits without avail until he came under the influence of the Washingtonians. He became one of their greatest speakers and, in the eighteen years remaining to him, traveled two hundred thousand miles and delivered five thousand addresses.[52] John B. Gough was a younger man at the time of his "conversion," and his labors lasted for more than forty years. He was born in England but was sent to this country at an early age to seek his fortune. His hardships were incredible, and he sought refuge in drink. After seven years of vagrancy and intemperance, he signed the Washingtonian pledge and devoted himself without faltering to the cause. His *Autobiography and Personal Recollections* and his *Sunlight and Shadow* furnish a complete picture of a very interesting personality and a zealous crusader.

Gough's zeal was like that of William Lloyd Garrison in the cause of abolition, and his statement of purpose resembled Garrison's, for he said, "While I can talk against the drink, I'll talk. When I can only whisper, I'll do that. And when I cannot whisper any longer, faith, I'll make motions — they say I am good at that!"[53] The fervor of his eloquence has been preserved in such excerpts from his addresses as this one:

What fills the almshouses and jails? What brings yon trembling wretch upon the gallows? It is drink. And we might call upon those in the tomb to break forth. Ye mouldering victims! Wipe the grave dust crumbling from your brow; stalk forth in your tattered shrouds and bony whiteness, to testify against the drink! Come, come forth from

From *The Sons of Temperance Offering*, 1851

"*The Temple of Sobriety*"

From *The Sons of Temperance Offering*, 1851

"*Love's Eclipse*"

"*The Drunkard's Progress: From the First Glass to the Grave*"

A Currier and Ives print

the gallows, you spirit-maddened man-slayer! Give up your bloody knife, and stalk forth to testify against it! Crawl from the slimy ooze, ye drowned drunkards, and with suffocation's blue and livid lips speak out against the drink! Unroll the record of the past, and let the recording angel read out the murder indictments written in God's book of remembrance! Ay, let the past be unfolded, and the shrieks of victims wailing be borne down upon the night blast! Snap your burning chains, ye denizens of the pit, and come up sheeted in the fire, dripping with the flames of hell, and with your trumpet tongues testify against the damnation of the drink! [54]

From the point of view of the less dramatic old-line temperance worker, however, there was something unsatisfactory in the work of such men and in the emotionalism and sentimentalism of the writers who carried on the campaign. The intelligentsia wailed that "emotion is supplanting reason," and the clergy were convinced that the Washingtonians were, if not a godless lot, at least a churchless one, making a substitute for religion out of their own doctrine. The new crusaders cared nothing for legislative action and relied entirely upon their ability to persuade the victims of drink to sign the teetotal pledge.[55] Nor were they much concerned about organization or programs of education. Their local societies were never welded into an integrated movement; each group was independent and often short-lived, and when the wave of revivalism had subsided, there was little in the way of permanent organization to continue the work. Since many of the members were reformed inebriates, there was much backsliding, and since they often came from the dregs of society, there was little education or leadership among them. Men of great ability became itinerant lecturers; the rank and file was not of high caliber.

By 1843 many of the Washingtonians had gone over into the older societies; others formed a number of new societies that endeavored to make up for the lack of coordination in their parent Washingtonians. The best known of these new groups, the Order of the Sons of Temperance, was founded in 1842 as a highly centralized, mutual benefit, semisecret organization. It spread rapidly and by 1850 numbered thirty-six grand divisions with nearly six thousand subordinate units and a quarter of a million paying members.[56] The Independent Order of Rechabites, the Temple of Honor, the Cadets of Temperance, the Good Samaritans, and the Good

Templars all claimed numerous members. Some of these societies admitted women; others organized separate branches for women; one at least opened its doors to Negroes. They were all semifraternal in nature, and many of them had mutual aid or insurance features. In the late 1850's a new youth movement, called the Band of Hope, was organized. Some of these organizations were short-lived; others lived long enough to be assimilated into the new temperance movement of a later generation.

THE INTERNATIONAL MOVEMENT

Largely to the clergy was due the international phase of the temperance movement. In 1846 a World's Temperance Convention was held in London to which the United States sent a distinguished delegation including John Marsh, Lyman Beecher, William Lloyd Garrison, Elihu Burritt, the peace advocate, and Frederick Douglass, the famous Negro abolitionist. Seven years later the second world conference was held in New York City under the presidency of Neal Dow, eminent Maine prohibitionist.

Temperance advocates traveled widely, and the United States was visited by several British enthusiasts. Father Mathew, the Irish temperance leader, came in 1849 and was cordially received despite the antiforeign, anti-Catholic sentiment of the period. Catholics listened to him with pride as well as with approval, and they organized numerous Father Mathew societies. Boston abolitionists endeavored to lionize the frail, gentle priest for their own ends, for he had been as outspoken in his condemnation of slavery as of strong drink, but he escaped their toils and went on to the nation's capital, only to find that his antislavery sentiments had caused an acrimonious dispute in the Senate, which desired to honor his achievements in the cause of temperance.[57]

James Silk Buckingham, too, lectured on temperance in many American cities, but perhaps had his most interesting experience in Lexington, Kentucky, where he attended a temperance meeting held out of doors in true camp-meeting style, with exhortations of revivalistic fervor and the singing of the united choirs of the local churches.[58] Buckingham everywhere stressed the universality of the temperance movement and its moral purposes. His arguments were, in general, the same as those of the American crusaders.

THE MAINE LAW AND ITS COUNTERPARTS

Revivified by the Washingtonian movement, the older temperance societies were encouraged to renew their efforts to place on the statute books laws that would regulate or end the traffic in intoxicants. Almost every state had some sort of licensing law designed to ensure sale by recognized and responsible dealers, but the fees were so low that licensing furnished no check upon retailers, and the regulations were so lax that there was little safeguard for the consumer. Between 1830 and 1840 several states experimented with measures providing more drastic regulation and with local option provisions. The most important single piece of such legislation was the Massachusetts law of 1838 prohibiting the retailing of spirituous liquor in any quantity less than fifteen gallons, "and that delivered and carried away all at once." [59] The passage of this bill was followed by a war of petitions and pamphlets, and it was repealed in 1840 and the state once more relied upon local option — with considerable effect, for between 1841 and 1852 no licenses were granted in Boston, and in 1845 no liquor was sold in one hundred towns in the state.

The prohibition idea gained supporters, however, and those states that were winning victories through local option were anxious to complete the process by statewide prohibition while enthusiasm ran high and votes could be secured for such legislation. In Maine the temperance movement had early taken a political turn, and local societies pledged themselves not "to vote for a man for any civil office who is in the habit of using ardent spirits or wine to excess." [60] Under the leadership of Neal Dow of Portland, the state began in 1829 to pass a series of laws tightening up the licensing system. Convinced that there was little hope in this mode of action, the reformers introduced a statewide prohibition bill and inaugurated a battle to get it passed. House-to-house canvasses were made; processions, music, banners, picnics — in fact all the agencies of popular propaganda — were utilized. Prohibition advocates capitalized upon the Washingtonian revival and procured reformed drunkards as speakers. They were defiant of mob action and even hoped for an occasional martyr to keep the excitement at fever pitch. Slowly their legislative supporters grew in numbers, and at last in 1846 they forced through the first comprehensive statewide prohibition act. [61]

Other states were eagerly awaiting the outcome of Maine's action. New York passed a local option bill in 1845, under which five sixths of the towns of the state voted for no license in the next year. Gerrit Smith threw himself into the fight, and, when many communities rescinded their hasty actions a year later, he went over to the idea of complete state prohibition. He labored with such effect that the legislature enacted prohibition in 1854.

In 1852 Vermont adopted by a narrow margin a measure based on the Maine law, and kept it on the statute books for fifty years. Rhode Island and the Territory of Minnesota enacted prohibition laws in 1852, Michigan in 1853, Connecticut in 1854, and New Hampshire, Tennessee, Delaware, Illinois, Indiana, Michigan, Iowa, and Wisconsin by 1855. In the same period the Pennsylvania Assembly passed a prohibition bill, only to have it fail by one vote in the Senate, and a similar measure lost with a tie vote in New Jersey.

Not all these measures were permanent, however, for in a few states they were badly drawn and were declared unconstitutional by the state courts, while in others public support waned and they were amended or repealed. Before 1860 the movement was smothered by the excitement over slavery, and the war years did much damage to prohibition legislation.

There were many people who, although they numbered themselves among the advocates of temperance, were yet uneasy over the adoption of coercive measures. As Harriet Martineau had written many years earlier, the seriousness of the evils of intemperance had caused some men to acquiesce in policies of which they could never wholly approve. In writing of the Maine law, Theodore Parker expressed the feeling of many toward such legislative action:

They have a new law in Maine. It makes the whole state an asylum for the drunkard. . . . The law seems an invasion of private right. It is an invasion, but for the sake of preserving the rights of all. I think wine is a good thing; so is beer, rum, brandy, and the like, when rightly used. I think teetotalers are right in their practice *for these times*, but wrong in their principles. I believe it will be found on examination that, other things being equal, men who use stimulants moderately live longer, and have a sounder old age than teetotalers. But now I think that nine tenths of the alcoholic stimulus that is used is abused. The evil is so monstrous, so patent, so universal, that it becomes the duty of the state to take care of its citizens; the whole of its parts.[62]

In a tract entitled *A Resurrection of the Blue Laws, or Maine Reform in Temperate Doses,* an indignant citizen calling himself a "Primitive Washingtonian" pleaded for a return to the principles of the founding fathers. He held that the Maine law was undoubtedly unconstitutional, was a violation of personal rights, and was an attempt to punish as a crime an act that could not in itself be considered criminal. Human nature, he said, could not be modified by law. Social customs must be changed, popular amusements must be provided at popular prices, and the fundamental causes for intemperance must be remedied before drinking would cease. In Maine, he declared, although the grogshops had been closed, more money was spent for drink than ever before.

This argument was carried a step farther by Edward Payson in another tract called *The Maine Law in the Balance,* in which he declared that many opponents of the Maine law were true temperance men, opposed only to the "despotism of party." He claimed the right of free speech and asserted that there was no reason to suppress investigation. The fundamental error in the theory of the Maine law was, he said,

. . . that a great moral evil, whose cancerous spots have for thousands of years penetrated the body politic through and through, and for hundreds of centuries have clasped it round and round, is susceptible of a radical and nearly instantaneous cure. An ancient philosopher once said, "Give me a lever long enough, and I will move the world." These modern philosophers promise to do the same thing without a lever. "Away," say they, "with your lazy-moving, clumsy contrivance you call moral suasion. No slow coach like that for us. Stand aside, and we will show you a more rapid working.[63]

But it was left for an anonymous author in a tract called *The Ramrod Broken; or The Bible, History, and Common Sense, in Favor of the Moderate Use of Good Spirituous Liquors* to raise the whole argument of legislative coercion to the higher level of political theory:

It may be argued, we very well know, that, as mankind advances in true civilization, they will be more and more disposed to dispense with such an indulgence, even if it be done by the aid of legal provision; but such is in no sense good logic, since the higher the civilization, the more we insist on leaving to individual choice and government; we do not call ourselves free, we do not speak of ourselves as in the enjoyment of any sort of liberty if at some time we are forcibly restrained of what, in even a ruder society, was left to the self-restraining power of the individual.[64]

In the progress of the temperance crusade were apparent all the possibilities of voluntary association and all the practices and methods pertinent to democratic institutions. There were evidenced, as well, all the humanitarian and charitable impulses of the early nineteenth century, given force and driving power by the tremendous upsurge of emotional, revivalistic religion. But back of it all lay the danger, ever present in a democracy, of the infringement by a majority of the rights of a minority and the further dangers inherent in the use of force to settle a moral issue.

CHAPTER 14

Denials of Democratic Principles

Progress toward understanding the full meaning of the democratic faith was not always along the lines of positive assertion. There were in the first half of the nineteenth century some almost hysterical denials of the very foundations of American institutions, occasions when blind prejudice and mass hatred were used in refutation of liberal tenets repeatedly affirmed by statesmen and entrenched in the Constitution itself. And yet, even in their most violent expression, these denials of free speech, of freedom of association, and of freedom of religion were made in the name of the very liberties they attacked — and often by the same men who were fighting hard for liberal reforms in other directions.

It was only through the assertion that Freemasonry was secret, undemocratic, and subversive of American institutions that support could be acquired for the proscription of the Masonic order, and discrimination against the foreign-born was justified by charges that immigrants neither understood the responsibilities of American citizenship nor appreciated its privileges. Religious intolerance could only be roused to fever pitch by linking Catholicism with plots to overthrow the republican form of government and the freedoms guaranteed by the Constitution. There can be no doubt that the sons of the Revolution were loyal to the ideals of their fathers even when, blinded by prejudice and urged on by false teachers, they fought against enemies only in part real or substantial and certainly, to a great extent, created by economic forces far too strong to be subdued or deflected by those who entered into combat with them.

THE ANTIMASONIC MOVEMENT

Social and economic in its origin but largely political in its expression, the attack on the Masonic order in the years after 1827 was an extraordinary manifestation of the combination of principle, prejudice, and hysteria that has often confounded students of American democracy. Perhaps it was no coincidence that this movement began in the "burnt" district of western New York, which had recently been swept by the flames of the Great Revival. From there it spread eastward into Vermont and southern New England and down into western Pennsylvania and northeastern Ohio.

In 1826 there were rumors through western New York that William Morgan, an impoverished stonemason of Batavia, had written a book exposing the secrets of Freemasonry. Morgan was a Virginian by birth, apparently more or less a ne'er-do-well and a wanderer. Somewhere in the course of his travels he had acquired a doubtful claim to membership in the Masonic Order, and he was accepted into the lodge of LeRoy, New York, when he appeared in that neighborhood. In the early 1820's he moved on to Batavia and soon joined in a project to establish a Masonic lodge in that town. Displeased with his lack of standing in the community, the rest of the group discarded the application that Morgan had sponsored and sent in another that did not contain his name. This was thought to be the cause for his decision to publish the secrets of Masonry.

Both Morgan and David Miller, the printer who agreed to get out the book, probably expected to make their fortunes in the venture. Whatever "secrets" Morgan was qualified to disclose pertained only to the lower orders of Masonry, and the two men either were in association with others who would give them information in return for a share of the profits or they had access to previously published, more comprehensive disclosures.

When completed, *Illustrations of Masonry by One of the Fraternity Who Has Devoted Thirty Years to the Subject* was a shoddy piece of work that would probably have attracted very little attention had it not been for the violent attempts to suppress it and the efforts of certain local Masons to silence Morgan. The mere rumor that the work was being prepared had led to protests and warnings. In August 1826 the following notice appeared in the Canandaigua newspaper:

Notice and Caution

If a man calling himself William Morgan should intrude himself upon the community, they should be on their guard, particularly the Masonic fraternity. Any information in relation to Morgan can be obtained by calling at the Masonic Hall in this village. Brethren and companions are particularly requested to observe, mark, and govern themselves accordingly. Morgan is considered a swindler and a dangerous man. There are people in this village who would be glad to see this Captain Morgan.[1]

This notice was followed by various methods of intimidation. Subscriptions to Miller's newspaper were canceled, suits for debt were entered against both Morgan and Miller, and an attempt was made to burn the printing office where the book was being prepared for publication. Morgan was arrested for stealing a shirt and a cravat but was released when he proved that he had borrowed the articles. He was then rearrested and lodged in the Canandaigua jail for non-payment of an old debt of less than three dollars.

On the night of September 12, 1826, men came to the jail and paid the debt, requesting the release of Morgan. When he came out of the building, he was seized by two men, hurried to a carriage, and quickly driven from the town. It was later proved that his abductors were Masons, that relays of horses were furnished by Masons along the route, that he was taken across the Canadian border and then back to old Fort Niagara. After that all trace of him disappeared, and his fate has never been ascertained. Antimasons asserted that he was murdered and that his body was sunk in the Niagara River. A committee of Lewiston citizens opposed to Masonry busied itself for weeks with dredging the river and the south shore of Lake Ontario. When at last a corpse was found, it was called the body of Morgan and was buried at Batavia with great ceremony. Some weeks later proof was offered that one Timothy Munroe had received the honors of the Antimasons, and the fate of Morgan was as obscure as ever. Masons believed he had disappeared voluntarily, one story being that he had been bribed to do so by Masons who had failed in other efforts to silence him, another that he had departed for England to the discomfiture of the Masons, who had hoped to produce him in triumphant refutation of all the calumnies against their order. Rumors galore sprang up about Morgan's fate. He was a hermit in Canada, a merchant in Smyrna, an Indian chief in the Rockies. One report had him hanged as a pirate, and according to another he was a pious convert to Mohammedanism and lived on in peace and comfort in Constantinople.

The excitement was increased by the trials in the following January of four men known to have participated in Morgan's abduction. The charges were conspiracy "to seize, carry off, and hold"; the defendants pleaded guilty and were sentenced to terms of from one month to three years in prison. Masons and their opponents broke into print with equal enthusiasm in the following months. Samuel D. Green, the author of *The Broken Seal; or Personal Reminiscences of the Morgan Abduction and Murder*, was a Batavia Mason who left the ranks and followed Morgan's example in revealing the secrets of Masonic ritual. He testified in the Morgan trials and toured the state of New York lecturing on what were, perhaps, the most exciting events of his life. A committee of Lewiston Antimasons published *The Narrative of the Facts and Circumstances Relating to the Kidnapping and Presumed Murder of William Morgan*, and in faraway Ohio Dyer Burgess wrote *Solomon's Temple Haunted or Free-Masonry, the Man of Sin in the Temple of God*. One Henry Brown wrote *A Narrative of the Anti-Masonick Excitement* for "honest men" who were willing to listen to reason and who refused to succumb to "a popular excitement similar to that of Salem witchcraft." Brown believed there were some honest Antimasons but felt that most of them attacked Masons "with a view to rising on their ruins."

Opponents of the Masons held that the Morgan trials were pure farce and the punishment given the abductors grossly inadequate. They claimed that the whole Masonic order was united in an effort to shield the murderers of Morgan. Two of the Masonic oaths were quoted as evidence of the probable miscarriage of justice. One provided that each initiate swear to assist his fellows whenever they were in difficulty "whether [they] were right or wrong"; the other was a pledge to advance a brother's best interests "by always supporting his military fame and political preferment in opposition to another." These oaths gave weight to the accusations that Masons were obstructing the Morgan investigation and further trials of conspirators. Witnesses were believed to have been spirited away, supposed accomplices disappeared, and men brought before grand juries refused to testify on the ground that they could not be compelled to incriminate themselves. There were loud demands that Masons be excluded from juries and that Masonic judges not be allowed to participate in trials where any party was a member of the order. In the meantime Governor Clinton, himself a Mason, had offered a reward for finding Morgan alive and a larger one for discovering his murderers and proof of his death.

Antimasons summed up all these facts and came to the conclusion that Masonry was inconsistent with American liberties and with the responsibility of citizenship in a democracy. They thereupon set to work in the name of freedom to bring organized social and political pressure to bear against an organization they held to be un-American. Religious denominations turned against the order, preachers who were Masons were forced to resign their lodge membership or their positions, and prominent Masons were refused communion. Women met to resolve that their daughters should not marry Masons and hurried home to persuade or coerce their husbands to withdraw from the order. Business and professional men found it profitable to announce their surrender to popular clamor, and many New York lodges gave up their charters. The Masonic oath was declared to be sacrilegious, and the whole order was called antireligious and undemocratic. A flood of propaganda convinced the uncritical and caused even the conservatives to feel that there must be a measure of truth behind the accusations.

Since much of the criticism was directed toward the political misdemeanors of Masons, it was an easy transition from complaint to political action.[2] In the spring elections of 1827 there was a cry of "No Masons for Office," and opponents of Masonry agreed not to vote for candidates known to belong to the order. In the state elections in the fall of that year the Antimasons polled seventeen thousand votes and elected fifteen members of the lower house of the legislature. All the movement lacked to make it a full-fledged political party was a set of leaders who could whip its chaotic adherents into some sort of unity.

Those leaders were found in two young men of western New York, already friends and already interested in politics. One of them was Thurlow Weed, newspaper editor of Rochester; the other was William Henry Seward, lawyer of Auburn. Both were apparently sincere in their belief that secret societies were harmful and that the Masons had obstructed justice in the Morgan trials,[3] but both, too, were ambitious and were members of a party that was rapidly disintegrating under the onslaught of the Jacksonian Democrats. New blood was necessary for the National Republican party and for the attack upon Jackson, and the Antimasons could furnish that blood and the zeal necessary to make it effective. Under Weed's skillful manipulation the Antimasonic movement was turned from its original purposes and made to serve his ends — much to the distress of such sincere Antimasons as Solomon Southwick and John Crary, who maintained that "true Antimasonry had become subverted to Anti-Jacksonism."

While these two incompatible groups — ambitious would-be political leaders and Antimasonic fanatics — endeavored to present a united front before the world, they quarreled bitterly behind the scenes throughout the brief career of the Antimasonic party. That career, interesting as it is, is political rather than social history. Perhaps its chief accomplishment was inaugurating the brilliant political career of William Henry Seward, whom the Antimasons elected to the state senate in 1830. Long after Antimasonry was forgotten, Seward, as leader of the New York Whigs, governor of the state, and United States senator, continued the work of reform that he began under such peculiar auspices.

In Pennsylvania Antimasonry was identified with the name, and aided in enhancing the fame, of Thaddeus Stevens, whose services for democracy, for education, and for the cause of the Negro were to be freely given for more than forty years. As early as 1820 the Presbyterian Synod of Pittsburgh had pronounced Masonry "unfit for professing Christians." In 1827 "committees of safety" were organized in many western counties, and the Masonic order was condemned as "unrepublican and subversive of the American form of government." When the Antimasons of New York polled thirty thousand votes in 1827 and more than double that number in 1828, Pennsylvania, too, organized an Antimasonic party, and Thaddeus Stevens was its zealot and its prophet.

In 1832 the party in Pennsylvania elected the governor of the state and, with the aid of the Clay group, dominated the legislature. In 1833 Stevens was elected to the legislature, where he kept the Antimasonic party alive for four years in a vigorous but unsuccessful attack upon the right of Masons to serve on juries and act as judges when non-Masons were parties to suits. Nor was he able to get a law suppressing the order. Such was popular pressure, however, that nearly one half of the lodges in Pennsylvania voluntarily surrendered their charters.

In Vermont the clamor of the New York Antimasons fell upon receptive ears. The western slopes of the Green Mountains were conditioned to such waves of hysteria by repeated revivals. The secrecy and oath-taking of the Masonic ritual aroused religious antagonism, and the fact that in Vermont the Masonic order was largely composed of men of wealth and affairs made it easy to stir up the farmers and the poor against it. Led by an ex-Mason of the hill country, General Martin Flint, the Vermont Antimasons marched to victory in 1828 with a platform that included anti-Calvinism and antislavery as well as the cause of the common man against the power of aristocratic secret societies.

The most active Antimasons in Vermont were members of the Baptist, Methodist, or Christian churches. The leaders of the movement were older men once of importance politically, evangelical ministers, and ambitious young men who saw little chance of making names for themselves in the older parties. The Antimasons held the first political convention in Vermont history in 1829 and proceeded to wrest control of state politics from the angry and astonished politicians who had dominated the state for years. William Slade, later an abolition Whig, was sent to Congress, state offices were filled with Antimasons, and the Masonic lodges of the state were deserted. When only a faithful few were left to keep Masonry alive until the days of proscription should pass, the issue over which a political party had been created disappeared. After 1835 the Antimasonic leaders in Vermont, as in New York and Pennsylvania, were taken over into the Whig party.

In Massachusetts and Rhode Island the story was much the same, although the movement showed less strength than in Vermont. In 1833 ex-President John Quincy Adams ran for governor of Massachusetts on the Antimasonic ticket and polled eighteen thousand votes. Davis, the National Republican or Whig candidate, had a plurality of the votes, and the election went to the legislature. Adams withdrew his name and Davis was installed. Two years later the fusion with the Whigs was made permanent, and Antimasonry ceased to be a political issue.

In New Jersey there was some interest among the Quakers. In Connecticut, Maine, and New Hampshire there were state Antimasonic conventions, and in Ohio, Indiana, and Michigan Antimasonry made a brief appeal to groups of New England descent; but in no one of these states was the party of significance.

In national politics the movement made slight impression. National conventions were held in 1830 and in 1831. In the latter year the Antimasonic party, refusing to unite with other anti-Jackson groups in support of Henry Clay, nominated William Wirt, a distinguished Maryland lawyer, for President. Wirt accepted the nomination frankly in the hope that the antiadministration factions that refused to unite on Clay might accept him as their standard-bearer. When the National Republicans nominated Clay, there was nothing to do except permit his name to be used to the end. He made no effort at campaigning but quietly awaited the result of the election, which gave him only the seven electoral college votes of Vermont.

The nomination of Wirt, who refused to condemn all Masons without discrimination, showed the impossibility of reconciling such proscription with the American principles the party professed to defend. At the same time, Wirt's acceptance of such a nomination was evidence of the confusion of party politics in 1832, a confusion that had, in itself, been the chief reason for the growth of political Antimasonry.

The election of 1832 brought to an end the brief career of Antimasonry as a national party. In Pennsylvania the Antimasons of German descent returned to their allegiance to Jackson; elsewhere Antimasonry was absorbed by the Whig party. As Thurlow Weed had hoped from the beginning, out of the confusion a strong new party had arisen, and in the creation of that party the Antimasons played their part. Their fear lest a sinister influence be extended over American law and politics by a favored social group, bound together by solemn oaths in a secret organization, were set at rest by the diminution in numbers and prestige of the Freemasons. It never seemed to occur to Weed, Stevens, or their fellow zealots, when they cried out in condemnation of the lack of democracy of their opponents, that their own proscriptive policies were an equal denial of the rights of free men.

CATHOLICISM IN THE EARLY YEARS OF THE REPUBLIC

The self-appointed guardians of American democratic institutions soon found another cause in which to expend their energies and another set of fears and alarms to arouse them to hysterical action. From the early 1830's until the period of the Civil War anti-

Catholicism was of recurring importance in American social life and politics. It joined with the fears aroused by the rapid increase of immigration, and the two together swept thousands of Americans into highly emotional and violent movements directed against both the foreigner and the Catholic.

The action taken was often simple and direct, but the movement itself was far from simple, and any analysis of it leads deep into the very foundations of the American faith. The American colonies had been born in the travail of the Old World in the era of the Reformation. Protestantism was stamped upon the English settlements with the arrival of the Puritans, whose Calvinism was too close to their hearts to permit the compromises the mother country demanded of them. Quakers, Baptists, and other Nonconformists settled in compact groups. Later German pietists, Scotch-Irish Presbyterians, and French Huguenots added their own fervent anti-Catholic faith to the Protestantism of the English colonies. The enemies of the colonists were the French and the Spanish, whose explorers had been accompanied by black-robed priests and whose Indian allies, presumably converted by those priests, preyed upon the back country. Anti-Catholicism was deep-rooted in the thirteen colonies that in 1776 called themselves the United States. Only in Maryland were Catholics welcomed, and only there did they live in numbers.

Religious toleration, however, was a fundamental tenet of the statesmen who built American institutions. Their charter of religious liberties included the complete separation of church and state. Before the law all religious sects were alike, nor could there be discrimination among citizens on account of religion, or religious qualification for suffrage or for any civil liberty.

American Catholics, on their part, were overjoyed at the manifestations of toleration and were thoroughly in sympathy with the new republic, for which many of them had fought. John Carroll, brother of the Charles Carroll who signed the Declaration, was made the first bishop of Baltimore in 1789 and impressed the deep patriotism of himself and his family upon the American Catholic church. He wanted his clergy and his people to be thoroughly identified with the land in which they lived and to contribute to it, as they received from it, toleration and understanding.

With but thirty thousand Catholics in a population of four million, the most extreme Protestants could have found little cause for fear of Catholic domination. The number that professed that faith grew rapidly, however, in the early years of the republic. Revolutionary uprisings in the French West Indies caused the flight of wealthy and cultured Creoles, many of whom settled in New Orleans or in Atlantic seaboard cities. With each change in the government of France between 1789 and 1815 new groups were forced into exile, and French immigrants crossed the mountains to settle in the Ohio country.

Some of these exiles were Catholic priests, most of them were communicants of that church, and Catholicism gained both in numbers and in strength by their arrival. Some of these refugee priests founded the first Catholic seminary in the United States; six of those who came between 1791 and 1799 became bishops. They were cultured, tactful men, cosmopolitan in background, liberal in outlook, and they did much to build up the church in the land of their adoption. One of these French bishops, Cheverus of Boston, was so respected by the Protestant citizens of Massachusetts that two hundred of them protested against his recall, saying, "We hold him to be a blessing and a treasure in our social community, which we cannot part with, and which, without unjustice to any man, we may affirm, if withdrawn from us, can never be replaced." [4]

In 1803 the United States acquired Louisiana with its old and established French Catholic centers in New Orleans and St. Louis, but even without the Louisiana population the Catholics of the United States numbered nearly ninety thousand by 1815. They were scattered throughout the country, still most numerous in Maryland, but with growing contingents in the cities of the East, where the Irish immigrants were making their homes. A few Catholic Irish came to America in the colonial period, a few more in the first decades of the republic, but the great influx did not begin until after 1815. There were enough New York Irish before 1817 to organize a Shamrock Society, which published *Hints to Emigrants from Europe, Who Intend to Make a Permanent Residence in the United States of America*. The society stated that there were at that date twelve thousand Irish in New York City alone and that other Eastern cities had numbers in similar proportion to their population.

The Catholic church gained little from conversion of native Americans; its great increase came largely from the immigration of European Catholics. In 1810 there were seventy-five thousand Catholics, constituting a little more than one per cent of the total population; in 1840 they numbered a million, or better than five and a half per cent of the population; and in 1860 there were three million of them, about ten per cent of the nation's thirty-one millions.[5]

The church recognized this growth in numbers by multiplying churches and dioceses. In 1820 the diocese of Charleston was organized, and a great statesman of the American church, Bishop John England, was in charge there until 1842. In the early 1820's Catholic organization crossed the mountains, where missionaries had early preached the Catholic way of life. Dioceses were set up for Detroit, Chicago, Pittsburgh, Cleveland, Galveston, and other Western districts in the next decade and a half.

Nor was the Catholic church slow to realize its responsibility to educate those who accepted its spiritual guidance. Georgetown College, first planned in 1786, was finally opened shortly after 1800. After 1805 the resuscitated Jesuit Order was active in the organization of schools and colleges. The first Catholic seminary for the training of priests was opened in Baltimore in 1790, and a college to prepare boys for the seminary was founded a decade later. There was a Catholic college in Pennsylvania shortly after 1800, and Catholic elementary and secondary schools were opened in Kentucky, Indiana, and Michigan in the same decade.

In Detroit the French priest, Father Gabriel Richard, was a pioneer in education and in the preparation of textbooks. It was he who planned the Catholepistemiad or University of Michigania, which was to include a free public school system, libraries, lyceums, museums, a university, and technical schools. The Territory of Michigan accepted the plan in theory at least, pledged fifteen per cent of its taxes to education, and secured Father Richard and a Presbyterian minister as the first faculty, at salaries of twelve dollars and a half a year apiece. One man held seven professorships, the other six. When the University of Michigan was founded on a different plan a few years later, Father Richard was a trustee. He was also a charter member of the Michigan Historical Society and the only Catholic priest ever elected to Congress.

The education of girls was undertaken early. The Order of Sisters of Charity was established about 1805, and the Sacred Heart, the Ursuline, and other teaching orders appeared shortly thereafter. Their convent schools were a great success and were patronized by Protestants and Catholics alike. The nuns were often French, Belgian, German, or Irish ladies of gentle birth and extensive training. Their pupils were carefully guarded and were taught the social graces as well as languages and music. By 1860 there were more than two hundred such schools.

In his *Forty Years of American Life, 1821–1861*, Thomas Low Nichols described several Catholic schools on the frontier in terms that make it easy to understand their popularity. He visited an Ursuline convent in Ohio that he reached after a journey through the forest over a road that was a mere muddy track in the wilderness. The establishment consisted of a large brick building for nuns and pupils and cottages for the farm laborers who cultivated the hundred or more acres of cleared land and did whatever work was needed in the forest lands. Two French priests ministered to the spiritual needs of the convent and the surrounding countryside, and four nuns—one English, one French, one Belgian, and one American—ran the household and taught the thirty pupils. Nichols was royally entertained, with good food and better wine and an evening concert by the girls. He went on to visit a similar establishment in northern Indiana, where a Catholic college, a seminary, a school for boys and one for girls, and an industrial school, all under the excellent management of a French director, had attracted between one and two hundred students.

Nichols asserted that there was little direct proselyting in these Catholic schools, and, perhaps since he was himself a Catholic, he approved the policy because of its results:

. . . everywhere in America, in the best society, the most accomplished and influential ladies have been educated in convents, and though they may never go over to Rome they love and respect their teachers, and defend them from the attacks commonly made against them. All this is favourable to the work of conversion which Catholics hope to accomplish. Education is removing prejudices, and the chaotic condition of the Protestant community, divided into warring sects, increases the power of a Church whose characteristic is unity, and whose claim is infallibility.[6]

These indirect methods of reducing Protestant resistance may not have seemed so innocuous to the frontiersmen who were descendants of Calvinistic New Englanders, and they may have disliked still more some other tactics that Nichols reported:

He [the Father Superior] told me, with a curiously quiet consciousness of power in his tone and manner, how he had put down some bigotry in the neighborhood, which had at one time threatened them, by exercising the political influence given him by the votes of his community. "It is not necessary for us to vote," said he, "we have not that trouble; but the fact that we can do so whenever we choose, and defeat either party, is quite enough to make both treat us with a respectful consideration." [7]

THE INCEPTION OF ANTI-CATHOLICISM

The gains of the Catholics did not go unnoticed in Protestant circles, nor did Americans fail to note how much the growth of the church was due to immigration. Within the hierarchy itself the foreign character of the church was pronounced. The religious orders were an importation from European countries; priests and nuns were more often French, Belgian, or Irish than American; most of the prelates bore foreign names; and large funds were received annually from European missionary organizations for the promotion of the church's work in America.

In the years after the Revolution, America had acquired a faith of its own — a faith composed of emotional revivalism, allegiance to democratic institutions, and belief in the destiny of the United States. A national faith, says Ralph Henry Gabriel in his recent book, *The Course of American Democratic Thought*,[8] needs an adversary; and the adversary was at hand in Catholicism.

It is difficult and doubtless futile to ascertain whether this acceptance of the Catholic church as an opponent of American Protestantism antedated or followed aggressive activities of the Catholics; certainly after the issue was joined both parties were able in offensive and defensive tactics. It is equally purposeless to try to determine whether the Catholic was hated because he was a foreigner or because he was a Catholic. Some of his opponents were most alarmed because of his Catholicism, and the leaders of the nativist movements were from devout and apprehensive Protestant groups, but it is probable that the rank and file in the crises of nativism were actuated by hatred of the ubiquitous foreigner who competed with the native in the labor market and for political control.

Reactions varied, too, in different parts of the country. In Louisiana, for example, where many American-born citizens were Catholic, nativist sentiment was little colored by anti-Catholicism. In New York and New England, on the other hand, the Irishman may have been hated and feared more for his religion than for his foreign birth.

At any rate, suspicion of the naturalized citizen and fear of the sinister designs of the Catholic church have never been entirely absent from the American mind, and outbreaks due to such fears have always accompanied periods of rapid increase in immigration. Between 1830 and 1860 such increase was remarkable, and the outbursts of opposition were frequent and violent.

The news of the passage of the Catholic Emancipation Bill by the British Parliament was received with rejoicing by the Catholic Irish of America and was loudly deprecated by the Orangemen. The removal of the Catholics' civil disabilities in England was regarded by some as a triumph for civil liberties but by others as a victory for Catholicism. The failure of the Revolution of 1830 in Rome and the repressive policies of the pope as a temporal ruler were deplored by American liberals.

These items of foreign news, however, were of concern to relatively few Americans. The words of the famous German scholar, Friedrich von Schlegel, brought the possibility of the expansion of Catholic power much closer home. Schlegel was a friend of Metternich and a counselor of legation in Vienna. In 1828 he gave a series of lectures in which he stressed the connection between monarchy and Catholicism and assailed Protestantism and democracy alike. He called the United States the "nursery of revolution" and stated his belief that Catholic missions in the United States would serve as weapons against republicanism, noxious democratic notions, and heretical doctrines.

Americans considered the Leopold Association, founded in Vienna a year later to promote missions in America, evidence of a plot of European despots against American democracy. In 1832 the Catholic Association for the Propagation of the Faith was founded in Lyons, France, and its funds began to flow into the United States for expenditure in every state but especially on the frontier.

Other evidence of Catholic aggression was found in the provincial councils held in Baltimore at stated intervals beginning in 1829. Catholics were impressed by the ceremony and pomp of the councils, and the press gave them much publicity. One of the chief concerns of the assembled prelates was the matter of counteracting rising anti-Catholic sentiment, and in a series of Pastoral Letters the clergy was instructed in the defense of its Catholic allegiance and was advised to be moderate in speech but watchful and sleepless in upholding the faith. A Catholic Tract Society and a Catholic magazine, the *Metropolitan,* provided further opportunities for the promulgation of Catholic views. Much of this work of organizing Catholic defense was done by the vigorous and able Bishop of Charleston, John England, who made every effort to combat the idea that the church required any allegiance inimical to the civil government.[9]

ANTI-CATHOLIC LITERATURE OF THE 1830's

Despite such efforts, however, the idea of Catholic aggression was quickly and deeply implanted in the receptive minds of Protestant ministers whose emotions had recently been raised to high pitch by the Great Revival. In 1830 a Northern newspaper first made the assertion seen and heard so often in the following years, that the Catholic church was serving as the agent of European governments in an effort to overthrow American democracy. From that time on the idea of a Catholic plot, secret and subversive, permeated all Protestant argument. There were many variations of the supposed plot — ranging from the idea that the West might be overwhelmed by Catholic immigrants to a rumor that the pope himself was to come to set up his domain in the Mississippi Valley.

Of all those who spread this idea none was so explicit and emphatic or more widely read than Lyman Beecher, whose *Plea for the West* was published in 1835. The book was an appeal for funds and for missionaries and preachers to save the West for Protestantism. It emphasized the menace of Catholic domination of the frontier states and portrayed Catholicism as undemocratic and un-American. Beecher held that the activities of a "corps of men acting systematically and perseveringly for its own ends" were especially dangerous in a republic. Working secretly through the "dread confessional" the Catholic powers of Europe could decide elections, influence policy, "inflame and divide the nation, break the bond of our union, and throw down our free institutions." The solution of the problem lay, for Beecher, in schools, preachers, and churches under Protestant control.

Beecher was more than a little irritating to his Catholic opponents in his calm assumption that, in an equal combat between the two faiths, it would be Catholicism that must yield, and in his disclaimer of any desire to restrict or violate the religious and social liberties of the Catholic. All he wanted was to have them "come with their children under the full action of our common schools and republican institutions" so that their allegiance to the faith of their fathers might be weakened and the culture of their homelands forgotten in a complete and unquestioning Americanism. In this desire Beecher saw no parallel to the proselyting endeavors of which he accused the Catholics. He was horrified at the thought of Protestant children being educated by priests and nuns, and, although he piously deplored violence and mob action, his openly expressed fears of religious warfare and Catholic plots were most incendiary. There was little of charity in Calvinism and little of discretion in the religious fervor of the transplanted Puritan.

Soon after the appearance of Beecher's *Plea for the West*, Herman Norton published a little book called *Startling Facts for American Protestants*. Norton repeated the idea of a Catholic plot, asserting that Catholic emigration was being deliberately fostered by foreign powers toward the end of dominating Western settlement — all to increase the desire for British imports in the United States!

Samuel F. B. Morse, inventor of the telegraph, was another eminent anti-Catholic writer. A son of Jedidiah Morse, he had been reared in Calvinism and had early imbibed a hatred of "Popery" that was intensified by his observation of the despotic rule of the pope during a visit to Rome in 1830. For twenty-five years he found time, in the midst of other labors, to write innumerable articles for newspapers, several series of letters intended for publication, and other longer works, all fulminating against the dangers of immigration and Catholicism in combination. In 1835 Morse published *The Imminent Dangers to the Free Institutions of the United States through Foreign Immigration,* in which he asserted that the Jesuits were "papal puppets" who had been instructed to undermine American liberties. The book was a stirring call to action, and its vigorous words provided nativism with its first slogans — "Place your guards," "And first, shut your gates!"

PROPAGANDA PRESS AND DEBATES

As the controversy developed, each side felt the need of a press through which its arguments might reach the public. The Catholics had, to begin with, Bishop England's *United States Catholic Miscellany,* which had been in existence since 1822; the *Metropolitan,* established by the provincial council in 1829; the *Jesuit,* published in Boston after 1829 (later called the *Pilot*); and the *Truth Teller,* a New York paper started in 1825. In the work of answering the often vicious and slanderous attacks of the Protestant press, these were aided from time to time by other Catholic papers set up wherever the controversy happened to be raging. A militant bishop or priest was usually able to provide himself with a paper, and each hot debate was the occasion for founding some partisan sheet.

The Protestants were soon even better supplied with press and propaganda agencies, for not only did they publish newspapers specifically dedicated to exposing the evils of popery, but they were able to enlist the support of innumerable religious and semireligious newspapers and tract societies. The first anti-Catholic weekly was the *Protestant,* which appeared in New York City in 1830. After two years it was followed by the *Reformation Advocate,* which was in turn replaced by the *Protestant Magazine,* a monthly that lasted about a year. The *Native American* was published for the years 1837–40 in Washington, D. C. Other cities harbored for brief periods such sensational journals as *Priestcraft Exposed* (Concord, New Hampshire, 1834), the *Spirit of '76* (New York City, 1835), the *Anti-Romanist* (New York City, 1834), and the *Downfall of Babylon* (Philadelphia and New York, 1834). As interest in the movement fluctuated, these papers were born, made — or failed to make — their appeal, and came to an end, to be followed by others probably under the same editors and the same auspices and with the same clientele.

The panic of 1837 and the subsequent hard times helped to lessen the propaganda barrage, but the early 1840's saw a new flock of nativistic and anti-Catholic sheets. The number of antiforeign newspapers, addresses, pamphlets, and books reached its high point in the years of political nativism and fell off abruptly after the election of 1856.

Public debates on the lecture platform or in print were a favorite polemic device of the 1830's. Certain men became known as doughty defenders on one side or the other, and debates in which they participated were hailed by the public. The attack of the Reverend W. C. Brownlee, pastor of a Dutch Reformed church in New York City and editor of various anti-Catholic publications, was met in 1830 by three Catholic priests whose arguments were printed in the *Truth Teller* or in pamphlet form.[10] In Maryland and Pennsylvania the two Breckinridge brothers, John and Robert, led the Protestant attack and, in the latter state, found a worthy opponent in Father John Hughes, who was soon to be made Bishop of New York. In 1833 it was arranged that John Breckinridge should publish in the *Presbyterian* and Hughes in the *Catholic Herald* articles on various phases of the topic "Is the Protestant Religion the Religion of Christ?" The series dragged on for more than six months without satisfaction to contestants or to readers. During the same months a similar contest was waged in New York between Brownlee and Father Levine, in which Brownlee refused to stick to any subject and supported every argument with vituperation instead of with proof. The Catholics finally announced that they could no longer debate with him, for

To continue polemic discussion with you cannot aid to reputation, for your substitutes for arguments are falsehood, ribald words, gross invective, disgusting calumny, and the recommendation of an obscene tale. Those have been your weapons from your first to your last puerile letter.[11]

In 1835 an oral debate that both sides had long awaited was arranged between Hughes and Breckinridge, the subject to be whether either the Roman Catholic or the Presbyterian teachings were inimical to civil or religious liberty. The debate ran for twelve evenings and was attended by large audiences, made up in part of the lowest elements of the population of Philadelphia. Again a Catholic

logician met a revivalistic Calvinist convinced of the evils of popery, and the contest was without dignity or good result.

In the West the controversy reached its climax in 1837 in a debate in Cincinnati between Bishop Purcell and Alexander Campbell,
the founder of the Campbellite church. Both men were Irish; both
were excellent debaters. There were seven meetings and seven subjects. The debates began at nine-thirty each morning, and the
speeches were long, educational, and historical. Campbell's final argument probably represented local Protestant opinion:

The Roman Catholic religion, if infallible and unsusceptible of reformation, as alleged, is essentially anti-American, being opposed to the genius
of all free institutions, and positively subversive of them, opposing the
general knowledge among the whole community, so essential to liberty
and the permanency of good government.[12]

When a member of a Charleston temperance society likened the
Catholic system of indulgences to the state licensing system, asserting that an indulgence was a sale of permission to sin before the
sinful act was perpetrated, Bishop John England rose to the defense
of the church and engaged Richard Fuller, a Baptist clergyman, in
debate. The argument ran for some months in 1839 in the columns
of the Charleston *Courier,* covering a variety of subjects, from the
morals of the priesthood to the state of affairs in Ireland. This was
the last and one of the most interesting of the discussions. After
nearly a decade of oral and written debates both Catholics and
Protestants came to realize their futility, and after 1840 other methods of propaganda received more attention.

ANTI-CATHOLIC SOCIETIES AND DEMONSTRATIONS

Anti-Catholic proponents added to their own numbers and carried on the attack against their enemy by the method of voluntary
association so beloved by contemporary advocates of reform. The
first Protestant association, organized in New York City in 1831,
was succeeded four years later by the Society for the Diffusion of
Christian Knowledge, with Brownlee as its first president and the
conversion of Catholics to Protestantism as its purpose. A similar
society, headed by a William Hoyt, was intended to operate among
the Catholics in Canada. In 1836 the Protestant Reformation Society was formed to coordinate the work of converting "Papists

to Christianity" and distributing anti-Catholic information. Missionaries were sent out, publication was undertaken, ministers were pledged to give anti-Catholic addresses, and the society spoke through its own organ, the *American Protestant Vindicator*.

The net result of all the agitation was the inculcation of fear and hatred. Public meetings attended by the more violent elements of the urban population and the exhortations of street preachers often ended in rioting or street fights. The Irish of New York and other cities gladly defended themselves and their religion and, indeed, often provoked attack. Riotous crowds were inevitably attracted to the nearest visible evidence of the enemy, and the anger of the mob was wreaked on Catholic institutions. St. Mary's Church in New York City was burned in 1831, in the first of many such fiery substitutes for argument.

One of the best known of Catholic institutions was the Ursuline convent school in Charlestown, a suburb of Boston. The convent had been founded in the early 1820's and by 1834 was patronized by many of the best families of Boston. Of its sixty or more pupils about forty were Protestant girls, many of them the daughters of wealthy Unitarians. Orthodox Congregationalists countered by establishing a rival school, whose lack of success increased their dislike of the Ursulines, and they preached sermons against Catholicism in general and convents in particular. Local antipathy was increased by the friction between Irish Catholic and native laborers, which had resulted in riots half a dozen times before 1834.[13]

Antagonism was intensified by the story of Rebecca Reed, a girl who claimed to have escaped from the convent after terrible experiences. It was quickly shown that Rebecca Reed was not a nun or even a novice, but just a dismissed servant of the convent, but this did little to counteract her dramatic tale. Soon excitement deepened again when a nun, Elizabeth Harrison, fled from the convent while temporarily deranged because of overwork and ill-health. She soon recovered and later voluntarily returned to the convent, but again the damage was done.

On the night of Sunday, August 10, 1834, Lyman Beecher delivered three violently anti-Catholic sermons in different Boston churches. Whether or not any members of the mob that formed the next day had listened to Beecher is unknown, but he was afterward accused of having instigated its action. The mob advanced upon the Ursuline convent, and the police were entirely unable — or unwilling — to control it. The convent was burned and the nuns and their pupils were given barely time enough to escape to near-by refuges.

For a number of days rioting mobs roamed the streets, and only the efforts of Bishop Fenwick prevented the Irish laborers living in railroad camps outside Boston from advancing on the city. Catholic churches were protected by troops, and Irish laborers guarded their homes, while Harvard students patroled the Yard to protect the college from violence. It was an ominous evidence of the effectiveness of the anti-Catholic propaganda that the trial of the leaders of the mob was a farce in which the nuns were insulted and the Catholic church reviled, and that legislators were so intimidated by their constituents that they dared make no reparation.

THE CATHOLIC IMMORALITY MOTIF

The clerical zealots whose natural habitat was the revival sought effective anti-Catholic argument in charges that the priesthood was corrupt and evil, that nuns were immoral, and that through the confessional and the Catholic schools such baseness was carried over to the laity. No story was too obscene, no insinuation too base, and no conclusion too farfetched for Brownlee, Hoyt, and others of their guild. Books so salacious that they would have had no sale in decent circles except for their pseudo-religious character were read in hundreds of pious homes. Ministers, dutifully fulfilling their pledge to preach against popery, went to such tracts for ammunition, and their hearers spread the tales still farther. Such propaganda was difficult to combat and was most incendiary.

Even when the tales of horrors perpetrated in convents were reduced to absurdity by exposure and by their very multiplicity, they were still repeated with gusto by the leaders of the anti-Catholic crusade and accepted by the gullible. The burning of the Ursuline convent was the signal for an outpouring of accounts, true and fabricated, of life in convents in the United States, in Canada, in Cuba, and in Europe. The series began in 1835 with the printing of Rebecca Reed's relatively tame *Six Months in a Convent*. In the case of this, as of other such accounts, a publisher saw the possibility of capitalizing upon a popular issue, and the immediate wide sale of the book was an incentive to other editors to produce stories of convent life and misdeeds.

The most popular and most lurid of such accounts was Maria Monk's *Awful Disclosures of the Hôtel Dieu Nunnery of Montreal*, which appeared in January 1836. The book was apparently dictated by Maria Monk to Theodore Dwight, great-grandson of Jonathan Edwards, was edited by George Bourne and W. C. Brownlee of the anti-Catholic propaganda brotherhood, and was published by men connected with Harper & Brothers publishing house, which did not itself care to handle so controversial a volume. Maria herself seems to have been aided in her "escape" from Canada to New York City by William Hoyt, the head of the bureau devoted to the spread of anti-Catholicism in Canada.

The story was that of a girl of Protestant parentage who was sent to a convent school to be educated. She embraced Catholicism and resolved to become a nun, entering the Hôtel Dieu in Montreal. The obscenities that made up the rest of the book were suggested rather than described. Instructed by the Mother Superior to obey the priests in all things, Maria joined the other novices and the nuns in a prostitute's life. The nunnery was connected with the priests' house by a secret passage, there was a pit in the convent cellar where the bodies of the babies were buried, and the Mother Superior alone kept a record of the births and deaths. Maria herself escaped and reached New York before the birth of her child, whose father, she claimed, was one of the priests in Montreal. And there the first edition ended.

The task of separating truth from fiction in this fantastic tale was immediately undertaken both by outraged Catholics and by disinterested Protestants. Catholic authorities in Montreal quite properly refused to descend into the arena in their own defense, but their champions published a book called *The Awful Exposure of the Atrocious Plot Formed by Certain Individuals against the Clergy and Nuns of Lower Canada, through the Intervention of Maria Monk*. Maria, it was proved by the words of her own mother, had never been a Catholic or an inmate of a convent but had been from childhood both defective and delinquent. Whether or not the *Awful Disclosures* had been the product of her own imagination or of ideas suggested to her by the group of New York anti-Catholics was uncertain. It was intimated that the father of her child was the same William Hoyt under whose auspices she had appeared in New York.

Eventually the Bishop of Montreal permitted an investigation of the convent, and no evidence of a secret passage or a burial pit could be discovered. The investigators declared the institution cleared of blame and asserted that Maria was an impostor, but her New York supporters and the American public refused to be convinced despite all proof. Brownlee angrily exclaimed that those who wished to believe the traducers of Maria Monk could do so; he was satisfied with her unsupported word.

The sale of Maria's book exceeded all expectations, and the public interest was kept up by a second edition in the summer of 1836, carrying the tale through the harrying details of Maria's escape and experiences in New York. In 1837 *Further Disclosures* capitalized on the continued interest in the girl's adventures.

All save those who chose to believe the story because it fitted their own preconceived ideas of Catholic institutions lost faith in the tale of Maria Monk in 1838 when she became the mother of a second illegitimate child. Deserted by her erstwhile defenders, she died in prison in 1849, after her arrest for picking the pocket of her companion in a house of ill fame.

Despite the refutation of the story of Maria Monk, the willingness of the American public to buy, read, and believe such tales excited the cupidity of propagandists and publishers. Anti-Catholic leaders in other cities vied with New York in producing "escaped" nuns, and editors were eager to publish their accounts. Samuel B. Smith of Philadelphia, apostate priest and editor of the *Downfall of Babylon*, backed *The Escape of Sainte Frances Patrick, Another Nun from the Hôtel Dieu Nunnery of Montreal* and also published *Rosamond, or a Narrative of the Captivity and Sufferings of an American Female, under the Papish Priests in the Island of Cuba*. *Rosamond* was full of vile insinuations and included an incredible tale of a plot of Cuban priests to capture young Negroes, kill them, and grind them up for sale as sausage meat. The life story of Edith O'Gorman, *Convent Life Unveiled*, got a wide reading for its cruel and obscene account of the betrayal of the confessional and of the relations between priests and nuns. It seems obvious today that the writers and publishers of most of these pornographic books looked upon the anti-Catholic crusade as a money-making business and exploited their opportunities to the fullest extent. As a Catholic critic of the Maria Monk affair stated, the whole enterprise was the work of "a few needy adventurers, reverend and unreverend." [14] Whatever the cause for their publication, however, there can be no doubt that they conditioned the American mind to violent anti-Catholicism and predisposed it to an intolerance and a persecution that were alien to American ideology.

This outpouring of horror tales did not go unchallenged by the conservative element among the Protestants. Dr. David Reese, who condemned ultraism in all its forms, protested vigorously against those who "go beyond the Bible in their principles." Admitting that the papacy had often been corrupt and accepting many of the charges against Catholic immigrants, he yet deplored intolerance and persecution:

[A] formidable objection to the measures of those who are waging war against Popery in our country, is found in the demoralizing influence of most of their publications. Tales of lust, and blood, and murder, such as those with which the ultra-protestant press is teeming, in all the loathsome and disgusting details in which they are recited; and especially when they are represented as transpiring under the cloak of religion, and the criminals occupying and disgracing the holy office of the ministry, are adapted in the very nature of things to strengthen the hands of infidelity and irreligion. Nor can any virtuous mind of either sex, fail to contract impurity by the perusal of such publications as those we have described. . . . if the deplorable moral influence they are exerting upon the young at present, were justly appreciated, all such works . . . would be burned by the common hangman.[15]

IMMIGRATION AND NATIVISM

European travelers who noticed the growing anti-Catholicism were quick to see its connection with immigration, which they played a part in stimulating. Before 1800 emigrants must have left their homelands with much apprehension as to what lay ahead of them in the unknown world after the weeks or months of ocean voyage. Early emigration had been by groups that had severed their connection with the Old World, and few emigrants had written or returned to report on life overseas. That great opportunities and great wealth awaited their coming was a familiar idea to Europeans, but the way of life to which they must adapt themselves was unknown.

After 1815 all this was changed. Almost innumerable travelers visited the United States and wrote accounts of their observations; the letters of immigrants were read in hundreds of Old World villages; and money was sent to provide for the migration of families and relatives. Industrialization and its attendant shifts in population and occupation set Europeans in motion. Political and economic unrest made countless thousands anxious to emigrate, and news of the labor shortages in the United States led them to New York, Boston, Philadelphia, or New Orleans.

America became the common man's utopia. As one immigrant wrote, in Europe one often heard the expression "a poor man with many children," but in America a man with many children soon ceased to be poor. "Mr. Malthus," he exclaimed, "would not be understood here." [16] There were farms for those who wanted to farm and work for those who had no capital, but the very numbers in which they answered the summons meant that native workers would meet them with antagonism as well as with opportunities. In the decade between 1820 and 1830 about one hundred and fifty thousand immigrants came into the ports of the United States. That number was quadrupled in the next decade. Between 1840 and 1850 more than a million and a half, and in the next ten years nearly two and a half million more, entered the United States.

Of these hundreds of thousands many were Irish Catholics who settled in the industrial cities of the East, and many more were German Catholics who followed the lines of travel westward and settled in the valleys of the Ohio and Mississippi rivers. While their Catholicism made them objects of suspicion for the anti-Catholics, their foreignness and their competition irritated the American-born laborers, and their poverty and illiteracy, their drinking habits, and their improvidence exasperated the taxpayer and alarmed the social reformer. As early as 1819 the Society for the Prevention of Pauperism in the city of New York called attention to the destitution of the immigrant population and to the expense of caring for immigrant paupers.

Soon the charge was heard that Europe was dumping its poor and its criminals upon the United States and that the emigration of these classes was made possible by government subsidies. Studies of the reports of prisons and almshouses showed that in the Eastern cities the foreign-born inmates of such institutions outnumbered the native-born.[17] American consuls reported that from Ireland, from Liverpool and Leeds, and from Hamburg emigrants were departing with the blessing of local authorities expressed in steamship tickets. Other statistics were offered to show the terrible conditions in which many immigrants lived and the devastating effect of epidemic diseases upon the hordes existing in cellars and crowded tenements. The labor troubles of the 1830's were blamed upon the immigrant laborers, and the fact that many of them were living on starvation wages and were being cheated by American contractors into the bargain did not mitigate their offense.

Living in crowded quarters in the city slums, the Irish immigrants easily organized in street gangs whose headquarters were in corner stores or neighborhood saloons. The pursuits of the gangs were sometimes legal and social, sometimes illegal and even criminal, often violent and riotous. In combination these gangs were uncontrollable, and the police were helpless. Election days were often riot days, and anti-Catholic street preachers were lucky if their audiences were not dispersed by a horde of angry Irish. Marching militia and companies of soldiers from the regular army were an everyday sight in the seacoast cities, for calling out the troops was the usual procedure when a riot lasted more than a few hours. As nativism developed, the gangs divided sharply into foreign- and native-born, and the American Guards of the Bowery hated the Irish with a ferocity equaled only by that of the Irish for the Guards. Colorful though they may have been, these gangs were a nightmare for the city fathers and convenient tools for agitators.

American nativism of the period before 1840 was made up, therefore, of diverse elements. Anti-Catholicism was an important factor; economic competition, social problems, and nativist antipathies complicated the picture.

When in some cities from one third to one half of the voters were foreign-born and nearly all the foreign-born voted for one party, the formation of a nativist party or the adoption of nativist principles by the minority party was a step readily taken. In 1837 a nativist party appeared in Germantown, Pennsylvania, and in the same year similar organizations were formed in Washington, D. C., and in New York City. These Native American parties called for a new naturalization law extending the required period of residence to twenty-one years. Their members pledged themselves to vote for no foreign-born candidates, to keep the Bible in the public schools, and to "resist encroachment of foreign civil or spiritual powers upon the institutions of our country." They went into elections with the slogan "No Irish Catholic Ticket" and were at once answered by the angry immigrants with a cry of "Irishmen! to Your Posts!" and by parades of men carrying banners displaying the sign of the cross and the words "In Union Is Our Strength!" The scene was set for trouble when the financial debacle of 1837 put an end, temporarily, to the rising tide of immigration and to the agitation against the Catholic and the foreigner.

ISSUES OF THE 1840'S

One of the questions of importance in the period of the 1840's was that of trusteeship in the control of Catholic church property. The problem was not new; clergy and laity had struggled over it in many parishes since the appointment of the first bishop in the United States. Protestant interest in the question in the 1840's and early 1850's was due in part to the fact that the controversy of that day in New York, the center of the nativistic movement, in part to the fact that lay control of church property seemed more democratic and more American, and in part to the fact that the champion of the rights of the clergy was Bishop Hughes, an antagonist worthy of the steel of any or all of the anti-Catholic protagonists.

When John Hughes became bishop-coadjutor of the New York diocese in 1838, he at once sent a pastoral address to the congregation of his own cathedral acknowledging the legality of the trustees' control over church property but warning them against interference with clergy or sacraments. Several of the Catholic churches of New York City were heavily in debt. Given no aid by the bishop, they were forced into bankruptcy. When their property was put up for sale, the bishop bought it through agents and thus was able to extend his control.[18]

In 1842 Bishop Hughes felt that he was in a position to go farther. He therefore appealed to the churches throughout the diocese to surrender voluntarily all claim to control over church property. With one exception the churches agreed and made arrangements to surrender their property. The exception was the Church of St. Louis in Buffalo, where the recalcitrant trustees created controversy for more than a decade. At no time was the opinion of New York Protestants asked for, but they broke forth in protest and assailed the bishop for denying the rights of the Catholic laity and for acting in contempt of American liberties. The bishop, in his usual caustic vein, published a satirical "apology" in the form of a letter to "David Hale, Esq., who is a Congregationalist in religion; W. L. Stone, Esq., who is some kind of a Presbyterian; M. M. Noah, Esq., who is a Jew; and the editor (whose name I do not know) of a little paper called *The Aurora*." [19]

Another problem that aroused much controversy in New York in this period was that of the distribution of school funds. As the Catholic population grew the Catholic schools were quite inadequate, few immigrant parents could afford to pay school fees, and few parishes could afford to provide free parochial schools. Since the clergy maintained that the public schools were sectarian and anti-Catholic, few Catholic children attended them, and thousands of New York children were not in school at all. In 1838 John A. Dix, secretary of state and ex officio superintendent of schools, opened the question by advocating that religious instruction in the schools be limited to a reading of the Bible "without note or comment." This could not satisfy the Catholics, however, for the Bible used was, of course, the King James version, and, besides, the texts used in the public schools were biased in their treatment of religious history.

Concerned because of the illiteracy of the children of the foreign-born and convinced of the justice of many of the Catholic criticisms, Governor Seward said in his annual message to the legislature in 1840:

The children of foreigners . . . are too often deprived of the advantages of our system of public education, in consequence of prejudices arising from difference of language or religion. It ought never to be forgotten that the public welfare is as deeply concerned in their education as in that of our own children. I do not hesitate, therefore, to recommend the establishment of schools in which they may be instructed by teachers speaking the same language with themselves and professing the same faith.[20]

As Seward's biographer, Frederic Bancroft, says, this proposition was a firebrand. Every anti-Catholic in the state was aroused, and the partisan sectarian press burst into denunciation. The Catholics, on the other hand, considered it a move toward allocating state funds to parochial schools and applied for a share of the grants to the Public School Society on the grounds that attendance in the public schools was a violation of the Catholic conscience and that Catholics must therefore either submit to double taxation or let their children go uneducated.

The Public School Society replied that any such move would be "unconstitutional and inexpedient," that the money could not be spared, and that the charge of sectarianism was unfair, since the society employed six Catholic teachers. When the Catholic application was made public, a Hebrew school and one operated by a Scotch-Presbyterian church also asked for aid. The city fathers held a public hearing at which all Catholic complaints were aired, but the Board of Assistant Aldermen that had been given control of the matter refused the Catholic request. A gesture of conciliation was made, however, in the appointment of a committee to purge the textbooks of references unfair to the Catholics, and there was a great byplay of erasing or blotting out paragraphs and pasting pages together — measures altogether ineffective, because the mutilated volumes soon wore out and were replaced by unexpurgated ones.

After another unsuccessful attempt by Bishop Hughes to secure favorable action by the aldermen, in April 1841 the state superintendent recommended that the Public School Society be replaced by the state system of schools in New York City, and that a school commission be elected in each ward to administer funds and regulate school affairs. In this way Catholic wards could at least be assured of impartial treatment and of religious instruction that conformed to their wishes. The Public School Society opposed this project, the anti-Catholic press rushed into action, and the school question became a political issue. Seward urged the legislature to carry out the superintendent's recommendation, cleverly putting the issue on the broad basis of the need for providing education for the poor.

The Catholics, in the meantime, had become convinced that the plan of the state superintendent was the best they could get, and Hughes sought to convince the Democratic party, to which most of the Irish belonged, of its need of Catholic support. When he failed to secure any pledge of aid from the Democrats, he authorized a Catholic ticket, and in the election the Hughes party polled more than two thousand votes, thus causing a Whig-Nativist victory by a margin of less than three hundred. The disciplined Democrats did not again forget their dependence on the Catholics, but Hughes and his church won the opprobrium of thousands for carrying a religious issue into politics, and the anti-Catholics shouted that the action was proof of the power of the pope to overturn democratic institutions.[21]

The new school law was passed in 1842 despite the furor of the Protestant press, and the public school question ceased to be an issue in the state of New York. The nativists continued to be active, however, and in the next year organized as the American Republican party, with a newspaper of their own, the *American Citizen*.

The contest was then transferred to Philadelphia, where in 1842 Bishop Kenrick wrote a letter to the school authorities complaining about the reading of the Protestant version of the Bible in the schools and asking that Catholic children be allowed to use their own Bibles and be excused from all religious instruction. When the school board complied with his request, the Protestant clergy and the American Protestant Association were up in arms. In pamphlets and newspapers the Catholics were accused of trying "to kick the Bible out of the schools." Mass meetings were held throughout the city, and Protestant speakers aroused the passions of their audiences by intemperate language.

The industrial suburb of Kensington, where many Irish laborers lived, was especially affected. The nativists organized into an American Republican party, and in May 1844 excitement there was at fever pitch. When the Protestants defied the Kensington Catholics by attempting to hold a big nativist mass meeting in their midst, the fight was on. The meeting was broken up by a crowd of militant Irish, but the anti-Catholic forces were convened again for an outdoor rally three days later, with an ominous appeal to the public to "sustain them against the assaults of Aliens and Foreigners."

The nativists came out in full strength, supported by rowdies from the slums of the city who were eager for a fight with the hated Irish. The riot was started — probably by a shot fired from the windows of the near-by headquarters of a fire department unit manned by the militant Irish — and a struggle began that lasted for some days, in the course of which several men were killed and many more wounded. St. Michael's and St. Augustine's churches were burned, Catholic schools were attacked, the militia was called out, and the crew of U.S.S. *Princeton* was landed in an effort to restore order. Many Catholics fled from their homes but later returned to enter a campaign of charges and countercharges in the hearings held after the riot was over.

On the Fourth of July the American Protestant Association staged a huge parade with banners, bands, and floats indicating their anti-Catholic, antiforeign opinions, and more riots followed, necessitating the calling in of five thousand state troops. But in the 1844 election the nativists carried the city.

New York nativists were aroused by the excitement in Philadelphia, and the New York *American Republican* invited violence by heading a description of the riots with the slogan "The Voice of Blood," saying, "A revolution has begun. 'Blood will have Blood.' It cannot sink into the earth and be forgotten. The gory vision will rise like the ghost of the murdered Banquo, and call for revenge." [22] When the anti-Catholic mob started on a campaign of pillage and fire, however, the doughty Bishop Hughes inquired of the authorities whether the city and state were prepared to pay for damage done the property of the Catholic church, and, upon receipt of a negative answer, he stationed between one and two thousand fully armed Irish guards in and about each Catholic church. The American Republicans were furious, but there was nothing to do but call off their mass meetings and calm their more violent members. Bishop Hughes saved New York from riots that might easily have been more disastrous than those in Philadelphia, which, he said, were the result of Catholic weakness.

The Catholic *Freeman's Journal* pointed out that in defending their houses and churches, even with violence, the Catholics were not violating but upholding the law, and that they were justified in repelling aggression at all hazards. In New York as in Philadelphia the American Republican party, through a fusion with the Whigs, carried the city in the 1844 election.

The victories in Philadelphia and New York encouraged the nativists to think the time had come for the creation of a national anti-foreign, anti-Catholic party, and they held a national convention in 1845 at which one hundred and fifty-one delegates represented fourteen states. They estimated their own strength at more than one hundred thousand voters, but either this estimate was exaggerated or the interest in nativism was rapidly waning, for in local elections in 1845 and 1846 the party made a poor showing. Its vote in New York, for example, was but two per cent of the state's total. Texas, the Mexican War, and the slavery issue overshadowed the machinations of the Catholics, and the country was entering upon a new boom period, in which foreign labor and immigrant farmers could be assimilated.

PROPAGANDA TACTICS AFTER 1840

The saga of the escaped nun and the salacious story of clerical corruption declined in popularity after the middle thirties. In order to broaden their movement the Protestant associations found it necessary to reduce the emotional content of their propaganda and to produce genuine argument once more. Mass meetings were condemned as conducive to violence, and anti-Catholic speakers were sent to churches and lyceum or lecture groups instead. Anti-Catholic tracts replaced the tales of clerical wickedness, and new societies were formed to aid in their distribution and to discuss local problems in relation to the Catholic church and the immigrant. The American Protestant Union, with S. F. B. Morse as president, was formed to act as a national society, and local Protestant institutes or unions were organized in large cities to arrange lectures and provide information. New periodicals and newspapers were published, and old ones became more tolerant, or at least changed their type of argument to conform to the new trend. Religious journals and even such secular periodicals as the *New England Magazine* catered to the interest of their readers by publishing arguments against Rome, historical sketches, and stories with an anti-Catholic motif.

In the contest thus put back on a theological basis the Presbyterians were probably the most active and might have led the educational campaign had it not been for the schism within the church.

The attention of the General Assembly of the Methodist Church through the forties was concentrated on the slavery controversy, and the dangers to be feared from Rome were forgotten in the anxiety over the cleavage between North and South. The Congregationalist clergy gave some support to the anti-Catholic cause, and they were joined, strangely enough, by the Episcopalians, who normally stayed rather aloof from reform movements. The Oxford movement in England had brought a branch of the Anglican church very close to Catholicism, some high church Anglicans veered toward the doctrines of auricular confession and clerical celibacy, and a few Anglicans of note crossed over to the Catholic church. Episcopalians viewed these tendencies with alarm and, low church to begin with, emphasized their Protestantism. Baptist, Lutheran, and Dutch Reformed clergy also went on record against the menace of Catholicism.

In 1842 the American Protestant Association was organized to coordinate the efforts of all anti-Catholic groups. It held national meetings, issued reports and addresses, and published its own magazine. It was finally possible, as the association's *Address* of 1843 stated, "to see the Protestant interests of the country *united* in a peaceful, enlightened, and vigorous opposition to the aggressive movements of the Papal Hierarchy against the civil and religious liberties of the United States."

One of the ablest of the new school of protagonists was the Reverend Nicholas Murray, a Presbyterian minister of New Jersey. He was an Irishman by birth and of Catholic parentage. Between 1847 and 1855 he wrote three series of letters to Bishop Hughes that were published in the New York *Observer* under the pseudonym "Kirwan." In the letters every phase of Catholic doctrine and practice was considered — miracles, prayers for those in purgatory, confession, and celibacy. Murray especially deplored the effect of popery on human liberty and besought Americans to defend the land of freedom from an insidious enemy that

. . . has never permitted a spark of liberty to glow for an hour when it could extinguish it. There is not in Europe, at the present hour — perhaps not on earth — a greater civil despot than the Pope. The man that, in Italy, writes a page, or makes a speech in favor of liberty, must fly the kingdom, or be dragged to a dungeon. . . . It is equally the foe of mental liberty. The Bible is without authority, save what your church gives it. And the Bible must teach nothing save what your church allows. And man must believe nothing save what the priest permits. And philosophers must teach nothing save what the church sanctions. . . . And what has been the effect of popery upon the *happiness of our race?* . . . Oh! sir, the pathway of popery through the world is marked by the blood and bones of its victims.[23]

It must have been a relief to the Catholics to face arguments rather than scandals and atrocity tales. For Catholic theologians had had ample training in history and were more skilled in dialectic than their opponents. Bishop Hughes of New York and Bishop Spalding of Louisville wrote several pieces that had a very wide sale. Hughes' *Moral Causes that have Produced the Evil Spirit of the Times* was read by more than a hundred thousand in New York City alone. Bishop Spalding's *Review of D'Aubigne* was an effective refutation of the French author's praise of Luther and Calvin. Catholic writers had long stressed their adherence to American principles of religious toleration; they now advanced to the position that Catholicism was not inimical to American institutions but was, indeed, necessary for their success. In an *Address to the Impartial Public on the Intolerant Spirit of the Times*, Bishop Spalding pointed out that Catholics had originated many of the principles of freedom embodied in the Constitution and that in the periods of Huss and Luther the opponents of Catholicism had been no more tolerant than the Catholics themselves.

In this period several able converts came to the aid of the Catholic apologists. When Orestes Brownson became a Catholic in 1844 the effect on American literary circles was marked. At once he threw his energies into the defense of the church and tried to convince Americans that there was nothing menacing in Catholicism, and Catholics that their church could grow in America only by becoming American and by ridding itself of its distinctively foreign leadership and characteristics. He spoke to his friends in the various reform movements, urging them to cease their attacks on Catholics:

You kill reason, you murder the soul, you assassinate conscience, you sap society, render order impossible, take from law its moral force, from our homes all sanctity, from our lives all security, and leave us a prey to all the low, base, beastly, cruel, violent, wild, and destructive propensities and passions of fallen nature. O, mock us not with the words, Brotherhood, Fraternal Love, Universal Peace.[24]

In his essays and editorials Brownson presented Catholic doctrine to American readers in convincing form, and in two essays on the Philadelphia riots, he pleaded the cause of the immigrant, pointing out that nativists were acting contrary to true Americanism, since America had been built by immigrants and had profited from their services and their cultural contributions.

In the same year that Brownson became a Catholic his friend and fellow Transcendentalist, Isaac Hecker, took the same step. Hecker became a Redemptorist priest and organized the order of Paulist fathers, devoting the rest of his life to the missionary work of the Catholic church in America. Rejecting Protestantism as unreasonable and full of discord, he coupled his Catholic doctrine with the liberal American faith that had developed through his long connection with the reform movements and constantly endeavored to prove that only in the church could true safety for democratic institutions be found. In his books, *The Questions of the Soul* and *Aspirations of Nature*, he presented Catholicism as the real goal of man's religious progress.

NATIVISM OF THE EARLY 1850'S

The violent anti-Catholicism of the years from 1843 to 1845 had no sooner died down and the brief period of political nativism come to its end than events occurred to revive both movements. The terrible famine in Ireland in 1846 and the failure of the Revolutions of 1848 on the Continent were causes for a rapid increase of emigration. Between 1850 and 1860 the number of foreign-born in the United States nearly doubled, the Northwest became the home of German liberals and freethinkers, and the Catholic Irish flocked into the labor camps and the industrial towns. They came in such numbers that they could live in groups retaining their Old World language, culture, and way of life.

American prejudice was again aroused by the very alien lives of the newcomers. A temperance newspaper wailed, "It does not lessen the desire for a Maine law to live near a *Bier Halle* and band of music every Sabbath. Let the Germans respect our customs if they want us to respect theirs." [25] The sight of German bands and of singing and dancing societies in full German costume was only slightly less alarming than that of drilling, semimilitary groups shouting orders in a foreign language. American citizens refused to excuse the violence of the "wild Irish" railroad gangs that enlivened the Saturday nights of so many American towns, even though they could observe their dutiful attendance upon the Catholic church the next morning.

The Irish easily became the tools of city politicians, but it was the radical demands of the Germans that struck alarm into the hearts of Americans. The German-American Association listed as its objectives complete manhood suffrage, the election of *all* officials, the abolition of the President and the Senate, the recall of officers, easier amendment of the Constitution, a department of the national government to protect immigrants, American intervention in behalf of downtrodden liberals abroad, complete religious freedom, and a shorter term of residence for citizenship.[26] The Free Germans of Louisville adopted a platform in 1854 condemning the Fugitive Slave Law, declaring religion to be an absolutely private matter, demanding a homestead law, and advocating free trade, women's suffrage, and an aggressive foreign policy. It was no wonder that Americans felt the world was spinning too rapidly for them!

The first reaction was the formation of secret societies to combat foreign influence, to secure thoroughly American candidates for office, and to advance the interests of American workingmen. The Native Sons of America seems to have been the first of such groups. It was founded in 1844, as was the American Brotherhood, later called the Order of United Americans, which had the United Daughters of America as an auxiliary. Mutual benefit features made the Order of United American Mechanics more than just an anti-foreign organization. The Order of the Star-Spangled Banner was founded in 1850, as was the Order of the Sons of the Sires of '76. By 1852 there were nearly sixty nativistic bodies in New York, and they made some effort to unite upon candidates for local elections. Philadelphia produced the Order of the Sons of America in 1844 and later the Benevolent Order of Bereans.

This revived nativism at once showed its violent side. There were riots all over the country, especially on election days but often begun by some street quarrel. Stones were thrown through the windows of a Catholic church in Boston, a Turnverein hall in Cincinnati was attacked, a Catholic church was blown up in Massachusetts, Catholic church services were rotten-egged in Maine, and a priest was tarred and feathered. Anti-Catholic street speakers were guarded by bands of youthful roughnecks called Wide-Awakes, whose secondary aim was to provoke the Irish to attack them.

In 1852 an ex-priest, Alessandro Gavazzi, traveled about the country to "destroy the Pope," lecturing on all sorts of anti-Catholic subjects. A certain John Orr capitalized on the excitement worked up by Gavazzi and under the name of the Angel Gabriel spoke on street corners in a number of cities. He was arrested in Boston for disturbing the peace with his horn and was finally refused the right to speak anywhere because of the riots that attended his harangues. When a papal legate, Bedini, came to America to participate in a Buffalo trusteeship controversy, his name became the signal for anti-Catholic violence and mobs greeted him everywhere. In New York City the mayor called on good citizens to keep off the streets on Sundays, and Bishop Hughes urged Catholics to stay away from street meetings but to defend themselves if attacked.

There were also riots in Kentucky, and in Nashville, Tennessee, the bishop thought it expedient to cancel a midnight mass on Christmas Eve and to place armed guards around his cathedral. Remote though Knoxville was from ports of entry and from any large immigrant population, Catholics were badly treated there, possibly because of the presence of the picturesque Methodist preacher, Parson Brownlow, who had long been an anti-Catholic. In 1856 he wrote a pamphlet with the alarming title, *Americanism Contrasted with Foreignism, Romanism and Bogus Democracy, in the Light of Reason, History, and Scripture: In Which Certain Demagogues of Tennessee and Elsewhere Are Shown up in Their True Colors.* Among other interesting gleanings from history the Parson included the information that the Catholics had killed sixty-eight million people for the sole offense of being Protestants, and that in so doing they had shed two hundred and seventy-two million gallons of Protestant blood — "enough to overflow the banks of the Mississippi, and destroy all the cotton and sugar plantations in Mississippi and Louisiana." [27]

John P. Sanderson wrote one book called *Republican Landmarks* that was full of statistics on immigration and vague allusions to the "foreign menace," and another, *Startling Facts for Native Americans Called "Know Nothings,"* that was a collection of readings exposing papist plots and the machinations of Bishop Hughes and restating old superstitions and obscenities about the Catholic church. The Wide-Awakes got out an annual collection called *The Wide-Awake Gift* that combined such old stand-bys as "The Star-Spangled Banner," Washington's Farewell Address, and the Constitution with the latest antiforeign articles and editorials. An anonymous writer in 1855 produced *The Sons of the Sires: a History of the Rise, Progress, and Destiny of the American Party,* which played all variations on the theme of Washington's order, "Put none but Americans on guard tonight."

Political nativism was the subject of John Lee Hancock's *Origin and Progress of the American Party in Politics,* which provided a full description, from an entirely native American point of view, of the riots of the early fifties. Thomas R. Whitney detailed the iniquities of the Catholics again in his *Defence of the American Policy,* devoting a whole chapter to "Romish Priests and American Politicians" and others to naturalization, immigration, and the interests of American labor. After the Know-Nothing party appeared, an annual *Know-Nothing Almanac* provided information in very popular and informal style.

Against this barrage conservative Protestants made some effort to defend both the Catholic church and the immigrants. Edward Everett spoke on the "Effects of Immigration," disproving the dangers emphasized by alarmists. Parke Godwin, a New York liberal, wrote an article for *Putnam's Monthly,* January 1855, condemning Know-Nothingism as contrary to American tradition and its principles as unwise and inexpedient. President Lord of Dartmouth got out a *Tract for the Times: National Hospitality,* asserting the mission of the United States as a melting pot and expressing the opinion that "We should open . . . the vast, rich and productive country stretching from sea to sea, and almost wholly lying waste, which the bounty of Providence has conferred on us. Freely we have received, and freely we should give." [28] But the great leader of the attack on the principles of Know-Nothingism was Henry Wise of Virginia, who called the whole movement a humbug, brought statistics to combat statistics, and matched all his opponents' arguments.

The Catholics themselves made less effort to combat this wave of hysteria than they had that of the middle forties. Father Hecker's books appeared in this period but probably were not written because of the attack on the church. Brownson continued his denial of Catholic antagonism to American institutions, going farther, indeed, than the Catholic authorities desired in his effort to Americanize the church. Bishop Spalding published a *Miscellanea* full of ammunition for the defenders of the faith; but Bishop Hughes stayed out of the fight altogether, on the ground that the excitement was temporary, was due to economic and social disorders caused by the increase of immigration, and would die out more quickly if ignored by the Catholic authorities. He ordered Catholics of his diocese to avoid crowds, refuse argument, stay out of fights, and use force only in self-defense.

Out in Kentucky Benedict Webb, under the name "A Kentucky Catholic," wrote a series of letters in answer to attacks on the church by a local editor. Asserting that bigotry was insatiable and would end in depriving Catholics not only of the right to hold office but of all civil liberties, Webb ended his series with the hurt cry that must have been echoed in the hearts of many a Catholic, whether native or foreign-born: "The man who impugns my patriotism on account of my religious opinions, is either an insane bigot who claims my pity, or a foul-mouthed slanderer who has my contempt." [29]

POLITICAL NATIVISM: THE KNOW-NOTHING PARTY

The secret societies from which the Know-Nothing or Native American party sprang were, from their beginning, semipolitical in character. They were provided with elaborate rituals, secret passwords, handclasps, and other accompaniments of fraternal organization. The important Order of the Star-Spangled Banner was typical of many. Its local chapters were represented in state councils, and state councils in a grand council that dictated the policy of the order. Members were admitted only after a careful examination and were required to have had two generations of Protestant and American ancestors and, if married, to have Protestant wives. In the early years of political nativism, candidates were nominated in secret irrespective of party, and no announcement of ticket or platform was

made. On election day mysterious forces seemed to have caused the
election of men heretofore unknown or of candidates whose election had seemed up to that time impossible. Since every member of
the society had been instructed to say, when questioned, that he
knew nothing of the matter, the name "Know-Nothing" was attached to the election phenomenon and to the group or party that
caused it.

In the state elections of 1853 the influence of the new group—
scarcely yet a political party—was felt. Its platform, if one can call
it such, was a queer combination of ideas: public schools were to be
subject to no religious sect, and the Bible was to be kept in the
schools; the period of residence required before naturalization was
to be lengthened to twenty-one years, or a literacy test was to be
administered; a Pacific railroad was to be built; and public lands
were to be sold to actual settlers. In some places additional items were
suggested, such as a denial of full political privileges to foreigners
and to their sons unless they were educated in American schools,
elimination of the names of all foreigners from the ballot, and provisions for the taxing of church property.

In the South nativism was important despite the relatively few
foreigners in that section. New Orleans was a port of entry second
only to New York City, and as the immigrants passed through
to the Upper Mississippi Valley, some of the poor and the weak
stopped off in Louisiana and Mississippi, increasing the cost to those
states for the care of dependents, defectives, and delinquents. Thousands of Germans settled in St. Louis, flocked into the Democratic
party when naturalized, and demanded, among other things, a homestead law to give them easier access to the public lands west of the
river.

Southerners of the 1850's were cruelly conscious of the fact that
they were a minority in the country and that the old balance in
Congress, broken by the entrance of California as a free state, could
not be restored. The advent of hordes of immigrants meant an increase in the numerical majority for the North and a gain for that
section in the House of Representatives. A homestead act would
aggravate the situation by further increasing the number of free
states and therefore of Northern senators. As a Mississippi editor
put it, "settlers on homesteads would be abolitionists. . . . It would

be better for us that the territories should remain a waste, a howling wilderness, trod only by red hunters than be so settled." [30] Since most of the immigrants were openly antislavery men, Southerners had further cause for alarm. Nativism thus became another form of sectionalism.

In the disintegration of old parties that followed the passage of the Kansas-Nebraska Bill in 1854 lay the opportunity for the Native American movement. Some Southern Whigs, keeping their eyes on the major issue, at once took the logical step of going over into the Democratic party, where they increased the pressure for Southern control of the party and set up even stricter tests for Democratic leaders in the North. Many, however, looked with alarm upon the disunionist tendencies of prominent Southern Democrats and, mindful of their long-standing dislike for the party and its principles, found a temporary abiding place in the Native American party. Nativism for them was antiforeignism little tinged with anti-Catholicism. In New Orleans, for example, anti-Catholicism was so little in evidence that French Catholics were admitted to the Native American party. In the other Gulf states, too, mixed Catholic and Protestant tickets were put up by the nativist party. In the border states the important fact was that the Native American party stood for the Union and neither its antiforeign nor its anti-Catholic features were emphasized. In Maryland, where the school bill had roused anti-Catholicism in 1853, sober second thought subordinated the religious issue in later elections in order to attract the Catholic Unionist vote.

Southern Democrats fought back, accusing the Know-Nothing party of being Whiggery in disguise and affirming that its secrecy was a cloak for antislavery doctrines. Augustus Baldwin Longstreet, Southern Methodist, college president, and fire-eater, denied that the Know-Nothing party had any religious basis. He condemned his fellow Methodists for going into it and asserted that they were linking themselves with Northern abolitionists. Henry Wise of Virginia was even more emphatic and conducted his campaign for governor in 1855 on the single plank of exposing and defeating the Know-Nothings. He called "Knownothingism" the "most impious and unprincipled affiliation of bad means, for bad ends, which ever seized upon large masses of men of every opinion and party, and swayed them for a brief period blindly." It was "a proscription of religions, for the demolition of some of the clearest standards of American liberty, and for a fanatical and sectional demolition of slavery."[31]

In the North the antislavery Whigs and the anti-Nebraska Democrats had a choice in 1854 between the Native American party and the newly organized Republican party, which was pledged to the abolition of slavery in the territories and the granting of homesteads to settlers. In the Northwest, where the new party was formed, it won immediate acceptance, and there was little interest in nativism. Those who had lived with the energetic Scandinavians and Germans saw little to fear from their presence or their votes.[32] And the frontier had never been much interested in the alleged Catholic menace. Nativism was condemned by both the Democratic and Republican parties in the Northwest, since the foreign vote was sought by both, and campaigns were fought on personalities rather than principles.

In the Northeast antiforeign and anti-Catholic principles were more deeply rooted, and the Republican party was remote and offered little of local appeal. The disintegration of the Whig party offered an opportunity for the Democrats to exploit the foreign vote, and Whig politicians found the situation intolerable. They were joined by many ambitious young men and by political schemers who saw in the secrecy of the Know-Nothing movement an opportunity for their own advancement. A Massachusetts senator, George Frisbie Hoar, wrote many years later that the party was made up of a few honest anti-Catholics joined by "self-seeking political adventurers and demagogues" who had taken advantage of the political confusion for their own purposes.[33] Many of these men went over to the Republican camp as soon as it was politically advisable to do so.

All this political shifting was apparent in the election of 1854. In the Northwest the Republicans won every state except Illinois, where Douglas' influence kept the Democrats in power. The Republicans won in Maine, and a fusion of Whigs, Democrats, and temperance advocates carried the election in Vermont. In New York the Whigs had Seward's support and managed to hold the state, but as soon as Seward had obtained his re-election to the United States Senate from the Whig legislature, he and his friend, Thurlow

DENIALS OF DEMOCRATIC PRINCIPLES 393

Weed, shifted to the Republican party and carried their supporters with them. In Pennsylvania the Know-Nothings elected several candidates, and in Massachusetts they filled every state office and nearly every legislative seat.

In the spring elections of 1855 Rhode Island, New Hampshire, and Connecticut went into Know-Nothing control, as did Maryland, amid the turbulence of much election rioting. The first real defeat for the party in the East came in Virginia, where Henry Wise's election as governor in 1855 was a deathblow, although the Know-Nothings obtained a majority of the lower house in the state legislature. Kentucky, Texas, and California went over to the nativists in 1855 also, while the Republicans gained votes only in Ohio.

But June of 1855 saw the beginning of the end for the American party. In the meeting of its national council in Philadelphia the cloak of secrecy was thrown off, and the proceedings were reported day by day to the newspapers. This move perhaps won over a few who had balked at the mixing of secret society with political party, but it lost the votes of some of those who had been attracted by the fraternal or lodge features. The council agreed upon the anti-Catholic and antiforeign planks, but it split on the slavery issue, the antislavery men withdrawing when the council accepted a resolution stating that the national government should not legislate upon slavery in the territories or in the District of Columbia and had no power to legislate on slavery in the states.

During 1855 and 1856 the Kansas issue caused thousands to transfer their allegiance to the openly antislavery Republican party, and the nomination of the "Compromiser," Millard Fillmore, by the American party early in 1856 caused further withdrawals from its camp. By the time of the election it was obvious that the party had lost the North and could expect a heavy vote only in the border states. Its platform was a catchall to entice any foot-loose voters, and, as an Indiana member remarked, "if there was anything in it, it was so covered up with verbiage that a President would be elected before the people would find out what it was all about." When the election of 1856 was over, it was found that Fillmore had only the eight electoral college votes contributed by Maryland.

The election of 1856 made very clear the essential weakness of political nativism. In the states where the American party had been in power for two years its record was pitiable and its achievements negligible. The veteran nativist, Samuel Morse, who had jubilantly written in 1854 that he could say "in the spirit of good old Simeon — 'Now let thy servant depart in peace, for mine eyes have seen thy salvation,'" [34] must have been chagrined at the record of the party for which he had had such high hopes. It had shown no leadership and had produced no constructive legislation. In Massachusetts the Know-Nothing legislature was made up of novices — little men, eager for their own advantage, and without a statesman among them. A wag said of them that the preacher of the election sermon should have used a text from Job: "For we are but of yesterday, and know nothing." Their only piece of nativist legislation was an amendment to the constitution that the next legislature killed before it went to the people for ratification.

Know-Nothing legislators were obsessed by the need for investigating nunneries and convent schools, and committees were appointed that went junketing about the state, visiting Catholic institutions and entertaining their friends royally at state expense. Other types of petty graft brought the legislators into disrepute, and few were grieved when the expensive session came to an end. When Henry Wilson, the Know-Nothing Senator from Massachusetts, was asked how he could attempt to overthrow the political organization that had made him, he said testily, "I'll blow the whole thing to hell and damnation" — and the state of Massachusetts seemed quite willing to follow him into the Republican party.

In the other New England states Know-Nothingism seemed but a way-station on the route to Republicanism, a sign of weariness with the old parties and their equivocal position on slavery. In New York Horace Greeley caustically remarked that the American party had about "as many elements of persistence as an anti-cholera or anti-potato-rot party would have." In Maryland the slavery question as well as complex problems in local politics gave the party more strength, but its victories were at the expense of political peace and every election was a brawl. Baltimore was called "mob town," and the Plug-Uglies, Blood Tubs, and Rip Raps kept peaceful citizens from the polls by their violence. It grew more and more obvious that all that held the Border Whigs who had gone into the party was a desire to save the Union, which they felt was being sacrificed to the jingoistic aspirations of the Democrats on the one hand and to the proscriptive tendencies of antislavery men on the other.

The identity between the membership of the old Whig party and that of the Know-Nothing party was pointed out in every state. It was obvious that the Republican party was the new and vigorous organization, and equally obvious that it was a horizontal, exclusively Northern party whose growth presaged secession and civil war. The original anti-Catholic, antiforeign tenets of the American party were lost sight of in the greater issue of slavery.

On the score of the basic principles of nativism, the history of the movement as a whole and of its later political phases makes it clear that the people of the United States did not in great numbers accept those principles; they did not want to "shut the gates" in order to restrict the civil liberties of the Catholics. Allegiance to democratic principles was strong in the hearts of the average citizen, and a majority could never be found to challenge the principles of their fathers.

CHAPTER 15

The Crusade for Peace

So complete were the surveys and so searching the analyses of the early nineteenth-century advocates of peace that, despite the failure of their efforts, their work as a whole was permanent and substantial. They laid the bases for the condemnation of war, explored the arguments in support of peace, and devised systems to provide for the pacific settlement of international disputes. Men of the twentieth century, treading in their footsteps, found use everywhere for the materials they had amassed and often could do no better than to reprint the plans they had evolved.

The peace advocates were few in number; the cause was never popular even with those easily stirred to support reforms. If a zealous reformer had energy enough left for the cause of peace after attending to nearer duties, no one would deny him freedom to work in its behalf, but when the more important cause was in jeopardy all else must be forgotten.

Perhaps, too, there was a fundamental inconsistency between the cause of peace and the tactics of the combative, perfection-seeking Come-Outers of nineteenth-century America. Certainly there was no evidence of pacifism in the practices of the temperance advocates or of the abolitionists. And to the American of the years after 1815 foreign affairs were of little significance in comparison with the crowding events and movements of the domestic scene. Then, if ever, Europe seemed truly remote and the possibility of war far away. The early leaders of the peace movement were men aroused to action by the horrors of the long wars prior to 1815. When their places were taken by younger men, there were few who did not hold the antislavery issue to be more important, and few who did not forget or disregard their peace principles as the days of crisis approached.

EARLY ANTIWAR SENTIMENT

Pacifism was not a new concept. In the middle ages pietistic and heretical sects spread ideas of nonviolence throughout Europe. The Quakers were the great exponents of the doctrine of nonresistance and coupled that tenet with a thoroughgoing humanitarianism that put them in the advance guard of many reform movements. Always they worked for peace, and when in times of war they refused to fight, they won the respect as well as the opprobrium of their contemporaries.

It was the Quaker William Penn who in 1693, in an *Essay Towards the Present and Future Peace of Europe*, developed a scheme for an international tribunal whose decisions on disputes between nations should be binding upon all parties, and it was another Quaker of Pennsylvania, Anthony Benezet, who at the time of the American Revolution worked and wrote in the cause of peace. He endeavored to enlist all "right-minded" persons in his effort to avert war, pleading with one of them:

Friend, I know thou art a man of letters, and a member of the French Academy: the men of letters have written a great many good things of late, they have attacked errors and prejudices, and above all, intolerance; will they not endeavor too, to disgust men with the horrors of war, and to make them live together like friends and brethren? [1]

In 1776 Benezet published a little ten-page pamphlet called *Thoughts on the Nature of War*, in which he declared that the greatest of the evils of war was the damage done to the souls of men who participated. Two years later he sent a little brochure called *Serious Reflections Affectionately Recommended* to all the members of the Continental Congress, imploring that they bend every effort toward securing peace. Throughout the rest of his life Benezet kept up his correspondence advocating peace, always insisting that reason, humanity, and the religion of Jesus Christ all refused to support "that spirit which gives life to war in any of its branches, but apprehend themselves uniformly called to promote to the utmost of their power, the welfare of all men." [2]

The indefatigable Benjamin Rush took time from the other reforms for which he labored to propose a Peace Office for the government of the new republic, arguing cogently that if it was expedient to have a war department, it was far more necessary to equip the state with the machinery for peace. This novel idea was elaborated in an article in Banneker's *Almanack* for 1793. Rush suggested the appointment of a "genuine republican and a sincere Christian" as Secretary of Peace, under whom a system of free schools would teach morals and religion as well as reading and writing. These schools should inculcate the doctrines of peace and stress the sanctity of human life. All laws that might encourage war were to be repealed. Uniforms, titles, and military equipment were to be abolished, for "were there no *uniforms*, there would probably be no armies." Over the door of the Peace Office an emblem should be suspended showing the lamb, the dove, and the olive branch, and bearing in letters of gold the text, "Peace on Earth — Good Will to Men." The building should house, also, a peace museum and an auditorium for concerts and lectures devoted to the cause.

Dr. Rush was convinced that effort should be made to render war and the war office of the government disreputable. He suggested a variety of signs to be placed over the doors of the offices of war departments: "an office for butchering the human species"; "a widow- and orphan-making office"; "an office for making broken bones and wooden legs"; "an office for creating private and public vices"; and others for creating public debts, speculators, stock jobbers and bankrupts, famines, political diseases, poverty, and the destruction of liberty and national happiness.

In the lobby of this office let there be painted the representations of all the common military instruments of death; also human skulls, broken bones, unveined and putrefying dead bodies, hospitals crowded with sick and wounded soldiers, villages on fire, mothers in besieged towns, eating the flesh of their children, ships sinking in the ocean, rivers dyed with blood, and extensive plains without tree or fence, or any other object but the ruins of deserted farm houses. Above all this group of woful figures, let the following words be inserted in red characters, to represent human blood: — "NATIONAL GLORY."

The essay ended with the somewhat satirical comment: "It is to be hoped that no objection will be made to the establishment of such an office while we are engaged in a war with the Indians, for as the *War-Office* of the United States was established in the time of peace, it is equally reasonable that a *Peace Office* should be established in *the time of war*."

Universal in his interests, cosmopolitan in his tastes and his acquaintance, Benjamin Franklin found it necessary to devote his energies to the cause of his country at war, but even during the war he constantly extolled the virtues of peace in his correspondence, and when peace came no one rejoiced more wholeheartedly. In a letter to Sir Joseph Banks in 1783 he expressed his joy that peace had at last been agreed upon: "I hope it will be lasting, and that mankind will at length, as they call themselves reasonable creatures, have reason and sense enough to settle their differences without cutting throats; for, in my opinion, *there never was a good war or a bad peace*." Franklin asserted that war always cost more than either adversary could hope to gain and that the victor would always, in the larger sense, be a loser.[3]

These scattered protests against war did not end with the Revolution, for there was no general peace. A generation grew to manhood in the early nineteenth century without ever having known a year in which wars and rumors of wars had not been the chief subject for concern. The writers of several of the tracts were Quakers, who condemned war on the basis of its inconsistency with Christian principles. Among ministers of other faiths, the Unitarians especially were outspoken in their deprecation of war, perhaps because of their rationalistic principles. With the great revivals shortly after 1800 came a new influence for peace, for the perfectionist carried his faith in God's power to save his creatures on this earth to the point of denying the right of resistance to force.

Some of this literature seems almost painfully familiar today. In a sermon delivered on a day of public fast in 1810 William Ellery Channing commented on the iniquities of the Napoleonic dictatorship:

. . . in addition to his [Napoleon's] lust for power, he is almost compelled by the necessity of his circumstances to carry on the bloody work of conquest. His immense armies, the only foundations of his empire, must be supported. Impoverished France, however, cannot give them support. They must, therefore, live on the spoils of other nations. But the nations which they successively spoil, and whose industry and arts they extinguish, cannot long sustain them. Hence they must pour themselves into new regions. Hence plunder, devastation, and new conquests are not merely the outrages of wanton barbarity; they are essential even to the existence of this tremendous power.

Channing feared for his own country, whose battle he felt England was fighting, although few Americans could be brought to realize their danger:

We seem determined to believe that this storm will spend all its force at a distance. The idea that *we* are marked out as victims of this all destroying despotism, *that our turn is to come and perhaps is near* — this idea strikes our mind as fiction. . . . The history of all ages teaches us, all our knowledge of human nature teaches us, *that a nation of vast and unrivalled power is to be feared by all the world.* . . . Have we nothing to fear because an ocean rolls between us? . . . The *ruin of England* is the first, the most settled purpose of his heart, that nation is the only barrier to his ambition. In the opulence, the energy, the public spirit, the liberty of England he sees the only obstacles to universal dominion. England once fallen and the civilization of the world lies at his feet.

In round terms Channing damned the ideology of France and asserted that Napoleon's conquests began by "corruption, by venality, by bribes," that "the conqueror thinks his work not half finished until the *mind is conquered,* its energy broken, its feeling for the public welfare subdued." [4]

INITIATION OF THE PEACE MOVEMENT

In 1809 a wealthy Presbyterian merchant of New York City, David Low Dodge, published a pamphlet entitled *The Mediator's Kingdom Not of This World.* The antiwar arguments of the brochure were based on the Sermon on the Mount, and its general trend was toward a radical nonresistant position. Several pamphlets were published challenging Dodge's position, and in 1815 he answered all his critics in a little book called *War Inconsistent with the Religion of Jesus Christ.* The economic effects of war were fully apparent in 1815, perhaps for the first time in the world's history, and Dodge emphasized the cost of war expenditures. He seems to have been one of the first to discern that there was little distinction between offensive and defensive wars, and he asserted that every combatant fought in defense of some territory, principle, or ambition. War was, in the mind of Dodge, an unmitigated evil; by it nations were impoverished and liberty was destroyed; from it came despotism, degradation, and economic disaster.

Stirred by news that peace had at last come to a war-weary world, men everywhere were determined that such a cataclysm should never again occur. The czar of Russia combined religion and diplomacy in forming the Holy Alliance, while more realistic statesmen joined in an attempt to control Europe through congresses called by a Quadruple Alliance pledged to defend the status quo. In London the English Friends organized to further the cause of peace, and in the United States peace societies sprang up to spread propaganda for yet another humanitarian movement.

In August 1815 thirty men met with David Low Dodge in New York City and formed what was probably the first peace society in the world. Its constitution condemned all warfare and admitted only members who were in good standing in their respective churches. Although the funds of the little society were very limited, it at once plunged into a propaganda campaign and printed a vast number of peace tracts for distribution in boxes of Dodge's merchandise.[5] This little New York society grew slowly until in 1817 it numbered about sixty devoted members. It later became a branch of another society independently formed in Boston.

Noah Worcester, a Congregational clergyman in New England, was always a liberal, never doctrinaire in his beliefs, and at times accused of heterodoxy. The War of 1812 made him an outspoken advocate of peace, and, during a period when he was without a clerical charge, he found a vehicle for the expression of his antiwar sentiments in the *Christian Disciple,* of which he became editor in 1813. It was with the intention of writing an article on the popular delusions that resulted in war that Worcester began a survey of the wars of the past and of measures that might be used to prevent war in the future. The article grew into a classic in peace literature, *The Solemn Review of the Custom of War, showing that war is the effect of popular delusion, and Proposing a Remedy.* Only by assuming half the expense of publication himself was Worcester able to get his ideas into print in December 1814, but, much to his surprise, the book was immediately successful and was put through five editions in less than two years.

War comes, said Worcester, from the basest passion of human nature; when it is waged for a redress of wrongs, its tendency is to multiply wrongs a hundredfold. The best that can be said for it is that those who wage it may feel that they are "doing evil that good may come." [6] But the originality of *The Solemn Review,* and the reason why it was revived and reread in the early years of the twentieth century, lay in its recommendations for a confederacy of nations and a high court of justice for the settlement of international disputes. Worcester urged the immediate formation of peace societies to begin the education of the public toward those ends and concluded with a stirring denunciation of war as a "heathenish and savage custom, of the most malignant, most desolating and most horrible character. It is the greatest curse, and results from the grossest delusions that ever afflicted a guilty world."

The New England of 1815 could not listen unmoved to a call for societies. In 1815 in the home of William Ellery Channing in Boston a group of those who had been stirred by Worcester's *Solemn Review* met to organize the Massachusetts Peace Society. There were twenty-two charter members, but their energy and prominence soon made up for the smallness of their number. Worcester was the corresponding secretary from the beginning, and also the editor of the society's first periodical, the *Friend of Peace*, whose columns he used to urge the organization of similar societies elsewhere. At the end of its first year the Massachusetts society had almost two hundred members, and in 1818 three hundred more. Wherever *The Solemn Review* and the *Friend of Peace* found their way, peace societies were formed. In 1819 there were seventeen, scattered from Maine to Georgia and from Rhode Island to Indiana. Branch societies were formed in small towns and villages, tracts were distributed, and public meetings were sponsored.

The rosters of these societies contained the names of the intellectual aristocracy of the day. In the Massachusetts society, for example, were gathered Josiah Quincy, the president of Harvard College, and many of its faculty, Francis Parkman, James Russell Lowell, and the Tappan brothers. Many clergymen were members of the peace societies, and the program called upon them for peace sermons at frequent intervals.

At the annual meeting of the Boston ministerial association in 1816 William Ellery Channing placed the responsibility for the peace movement on the shoulders of the clergy, declaring that the miseries and horrors of war could be avoided only by the development of the Christian qualities of nobility, dignity, and moral courage. He thought wars were caused by false patriotism, passion for power, greed, the love of excitement, and the tributes and high position given to warriors. Only education could substitute other qualities and other values and pave the way for peace. Worcester followed Channing's appeal by a circular letter from the society to the "associations, presbyteries, assemblies, and meetings of ministers of religion" appealing for the aid of the clergy.

Statesmen were called upon, also, in the hope that their approval might add to the prestige of the movement. Jefferson expressed his interest in general terms and accepted honorary membership, but blunt old John Adams refused in no uncertain terms:

Universal and perpetual peace appear to me no more or less than ever-lasting passive obedience and non-resistance. The human flock would soon be fleeced and butchered by one or a few. I cannot, therefore, sir, be a subscriber or a member of your society.[7]

These early societies were greatly impressed by the peculiar fitness of the United States to lead in such a crusade. America with its freedom of opportunity, its emphasis upon the worth of the individual, its republican government, and, above all, its isolation from European quarrels might well be the hope of the world. And the responsibility of Americans was great in proportion to the greatness of their privileges. This sense of the mission of the New World was evident in the address of Thomas Dawes at the second annual meeting of the Massachusetts society:

Without intending any invidious comparisons between our own and other nations, it may be observed that they rose by slow degrees from a savage state, and some of its customs grew up with them. The founders of our nation were already civilized. . . . War was not to be a part of their system — it was not to be a profession. . . . We have raised a republican government upon the principles of our ancestors, and let us at least endeavor to ingraft upon it perpetual peace, notwithstanding the incredulity of those who think that nothing which is old can be mended, and nothing which is new can ever succeed.

In the same vein Channing rested his faith in the abolition of war upon his belief in democracy:

War rests upon opinion, and opinion is more and more withdrawing its support. War rests on contempt of human nature, on the long, mournful habit of regarding the mass of human beings as machines, or as animals having no higher use than to be shot at and murdered, for the glory of a chief . . . for the petty interests or selfish rivalries which have inflamed states to conflict. Let the worth of a human being be felt; let the mass of the people be elevated; let it be understood that a man was made to enjoy an unalienable right to improve lofty powers, to secure a vast happiness; and a main pillar of war will fall.[8]

And yet, hopeful as was its beginning, the peace movement made little headway. A few state societies and more that were small and local, an occasional peace sermon by a noted divine, a few thousand tracts published and distributed, a tempest-in-a-teapot campaign against militia training or military chaplainship by the clergy, a spirited but futile advocacy of United States adherence to the Holy Alliance — such was the history of the peace crusade in the first decade of its existence. The truth of the matter was that international peace was not a matter of consuming interest to many Americans in the early nineteenth century, and if some new impetus had not come into the movement, the fire of the peace crusade would have burned itself out before 1830.

WILLIAM LADD AND THE AMERICAN PEACE SOCIETY

The necessary new energy and new spirit came from William Ladd, quite a different sort of man from those who had initiated the earlier societies. Born into a well-to-do New Hampshire family in the days of the Revolution, he had been educated at Harvard, had sailed on his father's ships and been captain of his own vessels, and had been a merchant in Savannah, Georgia, and a cotton planter in Florida. In 1814 he retired with a considerable fortune and settled down on a five-hundred-acre farm in Maine. Interested in his fellow men and absolutely free from malice or hatred, Ladd won many friends through his jollity and good will, and his contemporaries always asserted that he had no enemies. The observant J. S. C. Abbott, who met Ladd in Maine, saw in him nothing of the crusader or the fanatic.

He was the life of the party [he wrote], full of fun and frolic. I was told that his natural temperament was of the most joyous kind. He played with the children as though he were one of them. Some one pleasantly remarked, "when you become a man, you should put away childish things." He promptly replied, "Oh, I fear that I shall never be a *man*, I can never be anything more than a *Ladd*." [9]

The mind and heart of this kindly man were open to any philanthropic cause, and his interest in peace, aroused by President Jesse Appleton of Bowdoin College, was greatly increased by the reading of Worcester's *Solemn Review* and copies of the *Friend of Peace*. As he later confessed, he became convinced that war was an evil which must be banished from civilized society. "I felt it a duty," he said, "which I owe to God and my fellow-creatures to do something to hasten the glorious era when men shall learn war no more." [10] His time and his money were devoted to that end for the rest of his life, and the peace movement became his residuary legatee upon his death. In 1823 he wrote more than thirty articles on peace for the Portland *Christian Mirror* and two years later contributed a second series of even greater length. He joined the Massachusetts Peace Society, established branches for it, and revived the moribund Maine society, organizing branches for it as well. He delivered many addresses in the New England states, and began a correspondence with the London Peace Society and read all its publications.

After a careful study of the American movement, Ladd came to the conclusion that it needed a national organization to unify all the local and state societies, provide a common platform and program, serve as a center for publishing and distributing propaganda, and maintain contacts with the world peace movement. In 1828 he started out on the travels that were to continue through the rest of his life, carrying with him a constitution for a national society drawn up by Noah Worcester, who had eagerly welcomed a new recruit to take the burden from his aging shoulders. Ladd found the New York society very weak but willing to throw in its lot with a new organization, as were Massachusetts, New Hampshire, Philadelphia, and Hartford. After many preliminary meetings and much travel back and forth, in May 1828 Ladd met with a large group of the friends of peace in the home of David Low Dodge in New York City and organized the American Peace Society.

The constitution of the society was brief, providing merely for the necessary details of organization. When it went out to peace groups throughout the country, however, it was accompanied by a circular letter written by Ladd which served as a more detailed prospectus.

We hope [he said] to increase and promote the practice already begun of submitting national differences to amicable discussion and arbitration; and finally of settling all national controversies by an appeal to reason, as becomes rational creatures and not by physical force, as is worthy only of brute beasts; and that this shall be done by a congress of Christian nations whose decrees shall be enforced by public opinion that rules the world.

Ladd's platform was very broad. Any and every method for arousing public opinion in favor of peace was advocated. The old reliance on piety, the ministry, and prayer was stressed, but a new appeal was made to science, economics, humanitarianism, and public service. The controversial issue of whether a peace movement must condemn all war, defensive as well as offensive, had already caused difficulty for more than one society. Ladd faced the issue squarely and declared that the American Peace Society would accept all friends of peace — of whatever religious or political persuasion — for when offensive wars were abolished everyone could work in amity to ban all other varieties of combat.[11]

The eager philanthropists of the day could resist neither Ladd's logic nor his enthusiasm. The optimism of a man who could say, "This is the most auspicious moment that ever occurred in the cause of peace, and I grudge every moment that is not devoted to it," was infectious, and the driving force that made him write, "They might as well throw snowballs into the crater of Vesuvius in the hope of extinguishing it as to expect to cool me," was a good omen for the success of the society. Support came quickly from all the consistent and thoroughgoing reformers.

With the formation of the new society came the retirement of Noah Worcester and the end of the *Friend of Peace*. For three years (1828–31) the *Harbinger of Peace*, edited by Ladd and printed wherever he happened to be, was the official periodical of the society. From 1831 to 1835 the society published the *Calumet*, but the hard-pressed Ladd was glad at that time to combine it with William Watson's *American Advocate of Peace*, and the office of the magazine was moved to Boston, where it was edited by the Reverend George C. Beckwith. Thousands of copies of these papers were distributed as a part of the propaganda work of the society.

PEACE LITERATURE

At Ladd's suggestion, in colleges throughout the country prizes were offered for the best essay on peace, and Ladd himself visited

Benjamin Rush, universal reformer

Elihu Burritt, "the learned blacksmith"

"Jamie and the Bishop," a nativist cartoon showing President James K. Polk attacking the Catholics

many of the schools to stimulate student interest. His success in this work was evidenced by the formation of peace societies at Amherst, Dartmouth, and Oberlin and less organized student activities at Harvard, Union, Knox, and other colleges.

Beginning in 1829, the directors of the American Peace Society periodically offered a prize for the best paper on "A Congress of Nations for the Prevention of War." For some reason the judges repeatedly refused to select a prize winner from among the contestants, but, believing the essays were valuable contributions to peace literature, the officers of the society finally decided to publish the five best papers in a single volume. In editing the essays for publication, Ladd decided to print a summary of the rejected essays with some additions of his own in the form of a sixth essay. The six treatises on a congress of nations appeared in 1840 in a volume of seven hundred pages. It was very well received and sold widely in Europe as well as in the United States. The consensus of opinion was that the Ladd essay had the greatest merit, and it was recognized as a classic contribution to the subject.

The distinctive feature of Ladd's recommendations for a peace structure was his suggestion that there be two separate bodies, a congress of ambassadors for the purpose of "settling the principles of international law . . . and of devising and promoting plans for the preservation of peace," and a court of nations "composed of the most able civilians in the world to arbitrate or judge such cases as should be brought before it, by the mutual consent of two or more contending nations." Ladd paid tribute to democratic institutions and practices in his statement:

Before either the President or the Congress of these United States will act on this subject, the sovereign people must act, and before they will act, they must be acted on by the friends of peace; and the subject must be laid before the people in all parts of our country.[12]

A survey of past wars prepared by a committee of the Massachusetts Peace Society listed nearly three hundred wars of magnitude and classified them in eleven categories, such as wars of ambition, of conquest, of commerce, of religion, and of disputed claims to crowns or territories. The Englishman, Jonathan Dymond, in his *Inquiry into the Accordancy of War with the Principles of Christianity*, stressed the economic factors in war, and Ladd and Beckwith in the *Harbinger* and the *Advocate of Peace* reiterated his arguments. *The Moral Results of War* was another pamphlet by Dymond; Samuel Coues challenged the value of military establishments in a tract entitled *The United States Navy — What Is Its Use?* and Amasa Walker denied the old adage, "In time of peace prepare for war," in a fantasy called *Le Monde*.[13]

In 1838 Emerson came to the aid of the protagonists of peace in an "Address on War" that was often and extensively quoted. He called war an "epidemic insanity" of which all history marked the decline. His optimism led him to say that "universal peace is as sure as is the prevalence of civilization over barbarism, of liberal governments over feudal forms," and his transcendentalism made him believe that "all history teaches wise men to put trust in ideas, and not in circumstances."

But Emerson warned that universal peace could not be achieved by legislation or by manifestoes or even by public opinion, but rather "by private opinion, by private conviction, by private, dear, and earnest love. For the only hope of this cause is in the increased insight, and it is to be accomplished by the spontaneous teaching of the cultivated soul in its secret experience and meditation." Pursuit of peace must, however, be passionate and active, for the "cause of peace is not the cause of cowardice. . . . If peace is to be maintained, it must be by brave men." Emerson ended his address with a ringing challenge to his fellow countrymen:

Where the forest is only now falling, or yet to fall, and the green earth opened to the inundation of emigrant men from all quarters of oppression and guilt; here, where not a family, not a few men, but mankind, shall say what shall be, here, we ask, Shall it be war, or shall it be peace?[14]

Many years later, when the country was torn by civil war, Emerson like Garrison forgot some of the convictions of his earlier years. Coming to feel that there might be occasions when war was morally unavoidable, he wrote:

Though practically nothing is so improbable or perhaps impossible a contingency for me, yet I do not wish to abdicate so extreme a privilege as the use of the sword or the bullet. For the peace of the man who has forsworn the use of the bullet seems to me not quite peace.[15]

William Jay was a constant advocate of arbitration and of a congress of nations. In his *War and Peace: The Evils of the First and a Plan for Preserving the Last*, he urged the insertion in every treaty of some arrangement for the arbitration of any future disputes of the powers signing the treaty. "It is obvious that war might be instantly banished from Europe, would its nations regard themselves as members of one great society, and, by mutual consent, erect a court for the trial and decisions of their respective disputes." [16]

William Jay's support of what was called "stipulated arbitration" brought that device for the advancement of peace before the public. Already local societies had petitioned state legislators to urge some sort of arbitration system upon Congress and the President. In 1837 and 1838 both houses of the Massachusetts legislature had passed resolutions to that effect. The New York society sent a petition direct to Congress, and William Ladd went to Washington in 1837 to urge arbitration upon President Van Buren — neither with any more effect than a similar attempt in the early 1850's produced. The English Quaker and pacifist, Joseph Sturge, visited the United States in 1841 and conferred with Judge William Jay on the question. After his return to London, he urged the policy of "stipulated arbitration" upon the London Peace Society and upon the international peace congresses of the next decade. In 1847 George Beckwith, who had become head of the American Peace Society upon Ladd's death in 1842, published *The Peace Manual — or War and Its Remedies*, a volume listing the physical and moral evils of war and suggesting, among other remedies, arbitration, an international court, and a congress of nations.

In general it may be said that the peace literature of the first half of the nineteenth century was extensive, that it afforded a comprehensive survey of the causes and effects of war, and that it suggested much the same remedies as those tried by later generations of the advocates of peace.

OFFENSIVE AND DEFENSIVE WARS

Just as the temperance movement was disrupted by the controversy over total abstinence and the abolitionists stumbled over the obstacle of immediatism, so the peace crusade split over the denial of the right of defense. The early peace advocates had condemned *all* wars, taking their cue from the Quaker doctrine of nonresistance, but the American Peace Society had sought numbers and support by compromise or by ignoring the issue. All wars were evil, admitted the leaders, but unity and the success of their program demanded a concentration of effort against offensive wars. These abolished, the time might come for a total assault upon war.

Until 1837 the platform of the national society continued to contain the original broad plank inserted by Ladd in 1828, but all was not peace within the organization. Some said that all wars were offensive, others that sophists might justify every war as defensive. Radical speakers roused patriots to frenzy by condemning the American Revolution, and moderates, forced to agree that the line was almost impossible to draw, yet hesitated to assert that all wars were un-Christian. In accordance with the society's liberal principles, its peace periodicals were open to writers on both sides of the controversy, which was carried on also in public debates and innumerable pamphlets.

The most important of the publications condemning all wars was an address by Judge Thomas Grimké of South Carolina before the New Haven Peace Society in 1832. Nothing could be more positive than his statement:

Christians never will bear arms against each other or against them [the heathen]. . . . Christians never shall employ the sword to protect property, character, liberty or life. Let the heathen rule us. . . . Let them insult, persecute, oppress, slay us. Let them confiscate property, slander character . . . separate husband and wife, parent and child . . . poison the comfort and happiness of private and social life; and heap upon us all the enormities and cruelties that malice can suggest and tyranny execute. Still we will bear it all, nor shall the sword ever be employed to deliver, much less to avenge us. . . . Cost what it may, we will return good for evil.[17]

This address was answered by Dr. William Allen, president of Bowdoin College, in a pamphlet entitled *Defensive War Vindicated*, and the fight raged on, much to the edification of the cynical, who found cause for mirth in the spectacle of combat in the ranks of the crusaders for peace. Henry C. Wright, a nonresister, debated with the famous Eliphalet Nott, president of Union College, and turned from that arena to win the support of the Grimké sisters, Garrison, and other radical abolitionists. Garrison agreed in 1837 to give space in the columns of the *Liberator* to the cause of peace and soon became the most valiant advocate of nonresistance.

In the annual meeting of the American Peace Society in 1837 the ultras carried their point and secured a revision of the constitution to state that *all* war was contrary to the spirit of the Gospel and inconsistent with Christianity. This "Gospel decision" divided the society. President Allen of Bowdoin and other members of the society withdrew their support, saying the new measure was but a "dream of weak benevolence," which would mean the annihilation of civil government if carried to its logical conclusion. At the next annual meeting, however, the moderates were in the ascendancy, and George Beckwith persuaded the delegates to accept a compromise measure which condemned all wars but reserved the right of individual self-defense. It urged the support of all persons who desired the "extinction of war, regardless of their convictions on the issue of defensive war." This new declaration brought the policy of the American society into harmony with the English program and established the official position of the society for the rest of its career. But it did not placate the nonresisters, nor did it end their activities.

THE NONRESISTANCE MOVEMENT

As early as 1835, before the issue was forced upon the American Peace Society, William Lloyd Garrison had come to the conclusion that "it is the duty of the followers of Christ to suffer themselves to be defrauded, calumniated and barbarously treated, without resorting either to their own physical energies, or to the force of human law, for restitution or punishment." [18] This nonresistance idea was reinforced and given new direction by association with John Humphrey Noyes, the Perfectionist, who had already signed a declaration severing all connection with the government of the United States. Noyes sent Garrison a long letter in April 1837 which urged Garrison to serve no government save that of Christ and to work for "Universal Emancipation from Sin."

The effect of contact with Noyes's ideas was immediate, and a few weeks later Garrison wrote to Henry Wright that Christians were not authorized "to combine together in order to lacerate, sue, imprison, or hang their enemies, nor even as individuals to resort to physical force to break down the heart of an adversary. . . . Human governments will remain in violent existence as long as men are resolved not to bear the cross of Christ, and be crucified unto the world.[19]

By December 1837 Garrison was ready to lead a new radical peace movement and announced in the *Liberator* that the Quaker doctrine of nonresistance erred only in not going far enough:

If a nation may not redress its wrongs by physical force — if it may not repel or punish a foreign enemy who comes to plunder, enslave or murder its inhabitants — then it may not resort to arms to quell an insurrection, or send to prison or suspend upon a gibbet any transgressors upon its soil. . . . in no case can physical resistance be allowable, either in an individual or collective capacity. . . .

As to the governments of this world, whatever their titles or forms, we shall endeavor to prove that, in their essential elements, and as at present administered, they are Anti-Christ; that they can never, by human 'wisdom, be brought into conformity with the will of God; that they cannot be maintained except by naval and military power; that all their penal enactments, being a dead letter without an army to carry them into effect, are virtually written in human blood; and that the followers of Jesus should instinctively shun their stations of honor, power, and emolument — at the same time "submitting to every ordinance of man for the Lord's sake," and offering no *physical* resistance to any of their mandates, however unjust and tyrannical.[20]

These ideas had already been expressed by the Grimké sisters, whose Quaker background furnished excellent soil for pacifism. They wrote to Gerrit Smith in April 1837 that they were alarmed because the abolitionists were "willing to say at least that the arm of violence should be raised in their behalf," and they asked Smith's support for their nonresistance policy. Angelina's anxiety because her doughty abolitionist friend, Theodore Weld, was not "a peace man" led to the culmination of their romance. Weld's impatience with what he called her "no government" doctrines hurt her tender feelings, and she wrote, pathetically, "We did not understand each other." Weld responded with abject apologies and a declaration of love, which she accepted joyfully — and with a labored explanation of her views on government. Civil government, she wrote,

. . . is based on physical force, physical force is forbidden by the Law of Love. If I have no right to *resist evil* myself, I have no right to call upon another to resist it for me, and if I *must not* call upon the Magistrate to redress my grievances, if I have no right to do so, then he can have no right to render me any such aid. Now the puzzle in my mind is this. If these things *Are So*, then *God has changed* the moral government of his people, and yet *my* favorite theory has been the *unchangeableness* of this government.[21]

That puzzle was as far as the gentle Angelina got with the knotty problem of Christian anarchism, but the more positive Sarah wrote to Gerrit Smith that she subscribed to the "sublime doctrine of acknowledging no government but God's, of loosing myself from all dominion of man both civil and ecclesiastical, the more [that] I am persuaded it is the only doctrine that can bring us that liberty wherewith Christ has made us free." [22] But neither Sarah nor her friend Garrison was able to win over Gerrit Smith or the Tappans.

Committed to this doctrine of nonresistance and no government, Garrison and his friends decided on positive action. At an anniversary gathering of various peace society members on May 29, 1838, Henry Wright moved that a convention be called to discuss principles and methods of securing peace. When the convention assembled, it was apparent that Garrison, Adin Ballou, Henry Wright, Bronson Alcott, Abby Kelly, and Amasa Walker — all prominent radicals — would swing the meeting, made up of nearly two hundred delegates, to the left, or they would secede.

The first issue was the voting rights of women delegates, and the adoption of a resolution recognizing these, supported by all left-wingers, led to the departure of Beckwith and other conservatives. The second and crucial issue was a resolution offered by Wright to the effect that no man and no government has the right to take the life of man on any pretext whatever. The debate was heated, both sides quoting Scripture and every speaker willing to fight for his own interpretation of peace principles. When the resolution was finally passed, it meant in effect the creation of a new organization, a fact that was recognized in the adoption of a new name, the New England Non-Resistance Society.

The Declaration of Principles drawn up by Garrison and adopted as the constitution of the Non-Resistance Society is full of often quoted passages.[23] After a broad denial of allegiance to any human government and a refusal to admit the validity of state, national, or geographical boundaries, or of distinctions of caste, race, or sex, the Declaration went on to assert:

Our country is the world, our countrymen are all mankind. We love the land of our nativity only as we love all other lands. The interests, rights, liberties of American citizens are no more dear to us than are those of the whole human race. Hence we allow no appeal to patriotism, to revenge any national insult or injury. . . .

We conceive, that if a nation has no right to defend itself against foreign enemies, or to punish invaders, no individual possesses that right in his own case. . . .

We register our testimony, not only against all wars, whether offensive or defensive, but all preparations for war; against every naval ship, every arsenal, every fortification; against the militia system and a standing army; against all military chieftains and soldiers; against all monuments commemorative of victory over a fallen foe, all trophies won in battle, all celebrations in honor of military or naval exploits; against all appropriations for the defence of a nation by force of arms, on the part of any legislative body; against every edict of government requiring of its subjects military service.

These beliefs, the Declaration continued, made it impossible for their adherents to hold office, to vote, or to sue or submit to suit. At the same time, being absolutely without malice or thought of violence, they would abstain from plot, treason, or other "evil work" and would have nothing to do with "retaliation, violence, and murder." In no case would they "resist the operation of the law, except by meekly submitting to the penalty of disobedience."

As Parrington says, Garrison's ideas were a somewhat naïve amalgam of French equalitarianism and Yankee perfectionism.[24] These ideas were elaborated in the columns of the *Liberator* and in the *Non-Resistant,* the organ of the new society. They received their most thorough discussion in 1846 in a pamphlet by Adin Ballou called *Christian Non-Resistance in all its Important Bearings, Illustrated and Defended.* Logical consistency was a part of Ballou's religion, and his delight in pushing his "Practical Christianity" to the limit of its communistic and pacifist implications brought him into the ultra camp both in politics and in philosophy. When in the heat of the slavery controversy Garrison forgot all his nonresistance ideas and approved the violence of John Brown, the more consistent Ballou commented sadly upon Garrison's defection. Ballou could understand the position of Thomas Wentworth Higginson, who had always maintained, "I am a Non-Resistant, but not a fool," but he found it hard to forgive Garrison, whose original position had been so unequivocal.

The crisis of 1838 forced upon the American Peace Society a position that grew increasingly difficult as the years went on, and the trend of events swept both parties on the rocks in the days preceding the Civil War. The nonresisters were a minority in the peace cause, which was, in turn, one of the smallest and weakest of the reform movements of the day, but they were men prominent in the abolition and other movements and their ultraism was as disrupting there as in the peace crusade. There is, therefore, considerable significance in their principles, and their radicalism forms an important phase in the development of American political thought — a radicalism based upon religious perfectionism and democratic individualistic philosophy carried to a conclusion that verged upon anarchy.

THE PEACE ADVOCATES AND THE MEXICAN WAR

The questions of the annexation of Texas and the entry of the United States into war with Mexico caused a brief revival of interest in the peace crusade. Since most of the peace advocates were abolitionists, and since the abolitionists were averse to the annexation of more territory into which slavery might go, the cry of imperialism and aggression with which the American Peace Society met the issue was both natural and popular. It would be difficult to prove, however, that the peace society had any effect on the course of events. Certain prominent men who were both abolitionists and members of the peace society were at the same time the leaders of the opposition to the government's action. That is as far as it is safe to go in connecting the peace crusade with the anti-imperialism of the middle forties.

The chief spokesman of the opponents of the Mexican War was Charles Sumner, who rode to fame on the enthusiasm that greeted his oration at the Fourth of July celebration in Boston in 1845. Sumner was a "peace-man" and an abolitionist; he was also an accomplished orator of the flowery and rhetorical school then in vogue; and his Fourth of July speech on "The True Grandeur of Nations" was a significant contribution to peace literature.[25] Sumner analyzed the causes and character of wars, described their horrors, and summarized the prejudices that had kept the custom of war alive. Looking sternly upon the uniformed men in the crowds about him, he questioned the value of standing armies, of the militia, of all fortifications. "War," he concluded, "is utterly and irreconcilably inconsistent with true grandeur," and "the whole earth is the sepulchre of the Lord; nor can any righteous man profane any part thereof." Throughout the crisis Sumner spoke again and again in behalf of peace, and his addresses, reprinted by the peace society, were added to the propaganda literature.

Theodore Parker, too, was drawn into the inner circles of the peace movement by the Texas-Mexican issue. He wrote:

War is an utter violation of Christianity. If war be right, then Christianity is wrong, false, a lie. Every man who understands Christianity knows that war is wrong. . . .

We can refuse to take any part in it; we can encourage others to do the same; we can aid men, if need be, who suffer because they refuse. Men will call us traitors; what then? That hurt nobody in '76. We are a rebellious nation; our whole history is treason; our blood was attainted before we were born; our creeds are infidelity to the mother church; our constitution treason to our fatherland. What of that? Though all the governors of the world bid us commit treason against man, and set the example, let us never submit. Let God only be a master to control our conscience.[26]

The advocates of peace offered five hundred dollars for the best essay on the Mexican War issue, and the prize was won by Abiel Abbott Livermore with his treatise, *The War with Mexico Reviewed*. The essay was long, statistical, dull; but it stated again the bases of the peace movement and, especially, its ideas on an international peace structure.

Much more widely read and effective were the *Biglow Papers* of James Russell Lowell, who, in the poetry and prose of the antiwar Hosea Biglow and the equally outspoken Birdofredom Sawin, gave voice to New England's antislavery and peace ideas. Said Biglow:

> Ez fer war, I call it murder —
>   There you hev it plain an' flat;
> I don't want to go no furder
>   Than my Testyment fer that;
> God hez sed so plump an' fairly,
>   It's ez long ez it is broad,
> An' you've gut to git up airly
>   Ef you want to take in God.

And the stalwart Birdofredom wrote that getting "nimepunce a day for killin' folks comes kind o' low fer murder." [27]

Over the issues of Texas and the Mexican War the great Transcendentalist and individualist, Henry Thoreau, showed himself a forceful defender of the right of civil disobedience and an exponent of many of the tenets of Garrisonian anarchism, though he would not be a member of any organized antiwar movement. In 1846 he was arrested for refusal to pay taxes to a government that tolerated slavery and war, and in 1848 he published an essay entitled "Civil Disobedience" which has long been a classic in that field of political theory. Thoreau was not, in that essay, concerned with tyrants or dictatorship. He presupposed the American democratic system of majority rule, free speech, and popular controls; but even a liberal government, he held, "becomes tyranny when it denies the right of the individual to be responsible for his intellectual and moral integrity."

Government [he wrote] is at best but an expedient; but most governments are usually, and all governments are sometimes, inexpedient. The objections which have been brought against a standing army, and they are many and weighty, and deserve to prevail, may also at last be brought against a standing government. . . . After all, the practical reason why . . . a majority are permitted . . . to rule is not because they are most likely to be right, nor because this seems fairest to the minority, but because they are physically the strongest. . . . the only obligation which I have a right to assume, is to do at any time what I think right.

A common and national result of an undue respect for law is, that you may see a file of soldiers, colonel, captain, corporal, privates, powder-monkeys, and all, marching in admirable order over hill and dale to the wars, against their wills, ay, against their common sense and consciences, which makes it very steep marching indeed, and produces a palpitation of the heart. They have no doubt that it is a damnable business in which they are concerned; they are all peaceably inclined. Now, what are they? Men at all? or small movable forts and magazines, at the service of some unscrupulous man in power? [28]

INTERNATIONAL ASPECTS OF THE PEACE CRUSADE

The peace societies of England and the United States had much in common from the beginning. The leaders were in constant correspondence, periodicals were exchanged, American peace pamphlets were reprinted in London, English tracts were distributed in America, and, with the assistance of the London society, the peace literature in English was translated into various European languages and sent abroad. The Quakers who led the movement in Great Britain seemed to feel that the United States was far enough removed from the scene of European international difficulties to play a prominent part in the cause of peace and were happy to be assured of American support.

Both English and American leaders were interested in the spread of the cause on the Continent, and both had a share in the organization in 1821 of the Société des Amis de la Morale Chrétienne et de la Paix in Paris. This French society was less democratic than the Anglo-Saxon movements, and its leaders were members of the aristocracy and intelligentsia and were often connected with the French government. It did, however, reprint in French the tracts and pamphlets from London and the United States. Countries neighboring on France were interested as well, and a German edition of five thousand copies of Worcester's *Solemn Review* was put on sale in 1820. The famous *Prize Essays on a Congress of Nations* sold heavily abroad, and the movement for "stipulated arbitration" was an international one.

This friendly intercourse was greatly increased by the crises of the period from 1838 to 1854, when, first from one quarter and then from another, international peace was assailed. Anglo-American relations were generally poor in the first part of that period; Canada was restless, and there was international friction over the McLeod affair and over the case of the steamboat *Caroline* — both episodes occurring during an outbreak of Canadian nationalism. After 1840 the dispute over the Maine boundary became acute, and no sooner was that settled by the Webster-Ashburton Treaty than attention was drawn to the heated controversy over the Oregon question. In the same years the British government was involved in wars against China in the Far East and against the Afghans in the wild area north of India. American and British men of peace exchanged commiserations over such involvements of their respective countries.

The years of the greatest international cooperation were also years when prominent Englishmen traveled in the United States, and many Americans made grand tours of European cities in pursuit both of pleasure and information. Henry Barnard from the Connecticut Peace Society and Dr. Heman Humphrey, president of Amherst College, spoke at the annual meeting of the London Peace Society in 1835. In 1841 Joseph Sturge, one of the greatest figures in the British movement, traveled extensively in the United States, everywhere urging that Americans support the project of an international conference of the friends of peace to be held in London at the earliest possible date. The American Peace Society agreed in principle and entered into the plans for holding such a conference immediately after the great antislavery convention in London in June 1843, thus taking advantage of the assemblage there of many men interested in both crusades.

At this first international peace congress, which had an average attendance of about one hundred and fifty, the causes of wars were studied, and their economic aspects were stressed; propaganda methods were analyzed; and many projects were aired for the control of trade in munitions, for arbitration, and for some sort of a congress of nations. The fourteen American delegates agreed with their English friends that the meeting had been a great success, although they could point to no concrete accomplishment.

ELIHU BURRITT AND THE LEAGUE OF UNIVERSAL BROTHERHOOD

Back in the United States once more, the enthusiastic delegates found less unity. The leader of the "reform group" was Elihu Burritt, a new man in peace councils in 1843 but soon to be the leader of the movement, at least in its international aspects. There was probably no more devoted soul in the front ranks of any of the reform movements than Burritt, "the Learned Blacksmith." The old photograph of his lined, ascetic face with its sad, deep-set eyes confirms the fact that here was no dross but only pure spirit; no personal ambition, no narrow fanaticism, only an overwhelming love for humanity and a Christ-like faith in the imperishable nature of man's fundamental desire for good. As the peace movement in its earlier phases had depended upon Dodge and Worcester and Ladd, so in its later days Elihu Burritt was its center of inspiration.

The career of this man had been truly American. He had little formal education but a great capacity for work and an incredible ability at learning languages. He taught himself Latin, Greek, Hebrew, French, German, Spanish, and Italian while plying his trade. He supplemented his meager income by translating foreign books and by an occasional lyceum lecture on natural science. Both philology and science brought him to a sense of the unity and interdependence of men and of their languages. War seemed to him a denial of that fundamental interdependence, and a lecture that he began on "The Anatomy of the Earth" turned into a dissertation on the problem of international peace. In 1843 Burritt lectured in Boston with so much cogency and zeal that he caught the attention of the members of the peace society, who at once enlisted him in their cause.[29]

As a part of his propaganda for peace, Burritt worked out two effective methods of enlisting public support for the prevention of war over Oregon or Texas. Little leaflets bearing the title "Olive Leaf" were prepared and sent to hundreds of American newspapers and to peace groups abroad for republication in any interested papers. Burritt claimed that he sent more than fifteen hundred of these fortnightly circulars to American papers and secured republication in about two hundred. In one "Olive Leaf" Burritt described a plan sent him by an English Quaker, concerned over the Oregon crisis, for an exchange of British and American opinion on that subject. The British press gave the scheme publicity and reprinted the "Olive Leaf."

With enthusiasm aroused in both countries, Burritt's office became the distributing agent for the Friendly Address movement, which was one of the interesting manifestations of international cooperation in the middle forties. British cities paired with American cities, and letters or "addresses" were exchanged, signed by the advocates of peace in each community. Merchants' organizations, free trade societies in England, and laboring men's associations wrote to similar groups across the Atlantic, huge meetings being held to draw up the addresses and obtain an impressive number of signatures. Lucretia Mott, Quaker, abolitionist, and advocate of the rights of women, obtained more than three thousand signatures for a reply from Philadelphia to a letter from the women of Exeter; and four hundred merchants of New York commissioned Lewis Tappan to draw up their response to the merchants of Manchester. In short, while the American Peace Society contented itself with passing resolutions condemning war with either England or Mexico, Burritt was largely responsible for a genuinely popular protest movement.

In 1846 Burritt took over the editorship of the *Advocate of Peace* and expanded its title to the *Advocate of Peace and Universal Broth-*

erhood, which more nearly expressed his own views. In the same year he undertook the publication of a little periodical called the *Bond of Brotherhood*, which he had distributed in railway cars and on canal boats in order to reach a public that did not see the *Advocate* or the *Friendly Addresses*.

All this work in antiwar propaganda led Burritt to feel that the American Peace Society should take a more positive stand in condemning all war, and so in the summer of 1846 he and the radicals forced the issue in the convention of the society. Failing to secure the adoption of their platform, they resigned their offices and left the old society in the control of the conservative group. In the last number of the *Advocate* that he edited Burritt stated the policy of the radical faction and ended an account of his stewardship with the words, "Peace is a spirit, and not an intellectual abstraction; it is a life, not a theory." In his journal for 1846 he dedicated himself to the cause of reform, saying, "The greatest value I attach to life is the capacity and space of laboring for humanity." [30]

Convinced that his usefulness at home was at an end, Burritt went to England, where he was received with joy by the friends made through correspondence. Before leaving the United States, he had planned a new type of peace organization, and in England he at once won adherents to the project. He took over from the temperance societies the idea of a pledge and from his own philosophy the ideal of the brotherhood of man. With the aid of Joseph Sturge, he established the League of Universal Brotherhood as an international association to work for the abolition of war and still more for the promotion of friendly and fraternal relations between nations. The movement spread rapidly in England and Scotland, much more slowly in America. Membership in the League was effected by the signing of a pledge, which began with the statement:

Believing all war to be inconsistent with the spirit of Christianity, and destructive to the best interests of mankind, I do hereby pledge myself never to enlist or enter into any army or navy, or to yield my voluntary support or sanction to the preparation for or prosecution of any war, by whomsoever or for whatsoever proposed, declared, or waged. [31]

Burritt's new movement did not have the official support of the London Peace Society or of the American Peace Society; even the now feeble Non-Resistance Society was divided on the matter, and

Edmund Quincy on the editorial page of the *Liberator* called it a humbug. Among the English people, however, the movement was popular, and within a year thirty thousand had signed the pledge. It spread to the Continent, where societies were formed that sent delegates to annual meetings held in England during the next decade. The Crimean War marked the decline of the movement and its absorption into the stronger London Peace Society.

During his years in England Burritt was also instrumental in bringing about the four international peace conferences that were held between 1848 and 1852. Each conference was well attended and received popular acclaim but produced no visible effect. It was all too apparent to the tireless advocate of peace that the congresses were not of a value commensurate with their cost, and he was content to let the series end with the London conference of 1852. After 1855 Burritt was back in the United States devoting his time to the cause of abolition and to a fruitless effort to prevent the Civil War.

Horace Greeley, who attended a few sessions of the London conference, probably expressed a common sentiment when he wrote that, although he did not see how anyone who did not want to live by injustice, oppression, or murder could disapprove the idea of universal peace, yet he found the atmosphere of the conference intolerable and unreal, for, he said,

. . . suppose there is a portion of the human family who *won't have Peace*, nor let others have it, what then? If you say "Let us have it as soon as we can," I respond with all my heart. I would tolerate war, even against pirates and murderers, no longer than is absolutely necessary to inspire them with a love of Peace, or put them where they can no longer invade the peace of others. But so long as Tyrannies and Aristocracies shall say — as they now practically *do* say all over Europe — "Yes, we too are for Peace, but it must be Peace with absolute submission to our good pleasure — Peace with two thirds of the fruits of Human Labor devoted to the pampering of our luxurious appetites, the maintenance of our pomp, the indulgence of our unbounded desires — it must be a Peace which leaves the Millions in darkness, in hopeless degradation, the slaves of superstition, and the hopeless victims of our lusts." I answer, "No Sirs! On your conditions no Peace is possible, but everlasting War rather, until your unjust pretentions are abandoned or until your power of enforcing them is destroyed." [32]

After about 1850 the peace movements on both sides of the Atlantic gave way before the coming of war. In Europe the Crimean

War, the Polish Revolution, and the wars for the unification of Italy and Germany brought the collapse, and in America peace was laid aside, if not forgotten, in the mounting tension over slavery. Dearer than their pacifism to many of those who protested against the Mexican War was their devotion to the cause of abolition. As we have seen, many former peace advocates turned militant over the "Crime of Kansas" or the execution of John Brown. When the Civil War began, Theodore Parker, in a letter to a friend, epitomized this shift of opinion: "I think we should agree about war. I hate it, deplore it, but yet see its necessity. All the great charters of humanity have been writ in blood, and must continue to be for some centuries." [33]

In Whittier's stirring poem commemorating the international conferences may be found the apologia for the peace advocates of his and a later day, men who fought nobly in accord with their consciences even though their cause seemed lost.

. "What folly, then," the faithless critic cries,
    With sneering lip, and wise world-knowing eyes.
"While fort to fort, and post to post, repeat
    The ceaseless challenge of the war-drum's beat,
    And round the green earth, to the churchbell's chime,
    The morning drum-roll of the camp keeps time,
    To dream of peace amidst a world in arms,
    Of sword and ploughshares changed by Scriptural charms,
    Of nations drunken with the wine of blood,
    Staggering to take the Pledge of Brotherhood.
. . . .
    And Church for State, and State for Church, shall fight,
    And both agree, that Might alone is Right!"
    Despite sneers like these, O faithful few,
    Who dare to hold God's word and witness true,
    Whose clear-eyed faith transcends our evil time,
    And o'er the present wilderness of crime
    Sees the calm future, with its robes of green,
    Its fleece-flecked mountains, and soft streams between —
    Still keep the path which duty bids ye tread,
    Though worldly wisdom shake the cautious head;
    No truth from Heaven descends upon our sphere,
    Without the greeting of the skeptic's sneer;
    Denied and mocked at, till its blessings fall,
    Common as dew and sunshine, over all.

CHAPTER 16

The Rights of Women

In every phase of the American experiment much had depended upon the cooperation of the women. A biography of Mrs. Daniel Boone would be as thrilling an adventure tale as any of the accounts of her intrepid husband, for the frontier woman played no secondary role in the winning of the "dark and bloody ground" of Kentucky and of the newer lands farther West. Each woman who gave up her easier and more sheltered life in the seaboard communities and went with her husband to make a new home beyond the mountains, each woman who packed her household equipment into a covered wagon and ventured out upon the prairies, each emigrant woman who bade farewell to family and friends and crossed the Western ocean to a new life in a new world took on an enhanced value from the frontier.

Something of the equalitarianism of Western philosophy affected woman's status. Although the political equality her menfolk demanded was not accorded her, the omission may have been due, in part at least, to her willingness to consider politics a field outside her interests. In frontier church and camp meeting and school women took their place with scarcely a comment. And the West in general did not forget that on the frontier there had been equality between the sexes, as men and women had faced together the hardships and loneliness of the wilderness, where there had been no pedestal upon which women could be placed and few circumstances in which masculine superiority could be demonstrated.

THE STATUS OF WOMEN IN THE YOUNG REPUBLIC

In the late colonial era and the days of the young republic the American woman lost something of her pioneer equality and independence in becoming a "lady." The new standards for women were a composite of English and European practices with an admixture of Calvinistic teachings in the North and a strong flavor of romanticism in the South. North and South alike expected her to be irreproachable in conduct, tireless in pursuit of domestic virtues, strong in religious faith, spotless in purity, and ignorant of the evils of the world about her.

Of course there was always great disparity between the theory of woman's place and the reality of her actual participation in the life of the family and the community, and occasionally an exceptional woman made her influence so felt that she was accorded recognition far beyond that given her sex in general. Before the Revolution Eliza Lucas came to South Carolina from Antigua and, marrying a member of the Pinckney family, settled there as mistress of a plantation. She introduced indigo culture in the colony and was for many years one of the leaders in the economic development of the lower South. In Massachusetts Mercy Otis Warren, the sister of James Otis, ranked high in the councils of the Revolutionary patriots, and her house was their resort in the stirring days preceding the Declaration of Independence; indeed, she may well have been the first person to urge separation from England upon the Massachusetts delegates to the Continental Congress. Her correspondence with Jefferson and with John Adams continued throughout the Revolution.

John Adams' wife, Abigail, was another feminine adviser to the statesmen, and she early made the connection between the principles for which Americans were contending and the improvement of the legal status of women. In writing to her husband in March 1776, Mrs. Adams expressed quite plainly her feeling that women had a stake in the Revolutionary movement:

. . . in the new code of laws which I suppose it will be necessary for you to make, I desire you would remember the ladies, and be more generous to them than your ancestors. Do not put such unlimited power in the hands of husbands. Remember, all men would be tyrants if they could. If particular care and attention are not paid to the ladies, we are determined to foment a rebellion, and will not hold ourselves bound to obey the laws in which we have no voice or representation.[1]

Hannah Lee Corbin of Virginia in 1778 wrote her brother, Richard Henry Lee, protesting the taxation of women unless they were allowed to vote, and he replied that "women were already possessed of that right." Women did vote for a time in Virginia, and in New Jersey for more than thirty years. But after the Revolution had been won, these tentative concessions were forgotten, and state and national constitutions were drafted without mention of the rights of women. When suffrage was denied to a majority of the men of nearly every state, it was, perhaps, inevitable that none should protest the consignment of women to a legal status similar to that of the Negro.

For more than fifty years women were legally considered perpetual minors: if unmarried, the wards of male relatives; if married, a part of their husbands' chattels. An unmarried woman or a widow was allowed a certain independence in the ownership of property and in earning her own living, although few, indeed, were the occupations she might enter. As late as 1860 the eminent jurist, David Dudley Field, summarized the laws relating to married women thus:

A married woman cannot sue for her services, as all she earns legally belongs to the husband, whereas his earnings belong to himself, and the wife legally has no interest in them. Where children have property and both parents are living, the father is the guardian. In case of the wife's death without a will, the husband is entitled to all her personal property and to a life interest in the whole of her real estate to the entire exclusion of her children, even though this property may have come to her through a former husband and the children of that marriage still be living. If a husband die without a will, the widow is entitled to one-third of the personal property and to a life interest in one-third only of the real estate. In case a wife be personally injured, either in reputation by slander, or in body by accident, compensation must be recovered in the joint name of herself and her husband, and when recovered it belongs to him. . . . The father may by deed or will appoint a guardian for the minor children, who may thus be taken entirely away from the jurisdiction of the mother at his death. . . .[2]

This poor creature was given certain logical and interesting immunities. Her lack of separate legal identity was recognized in laws that held her husband solely responsible for offenses and crimes she might commit in his presence or with his consent. But the value of this recognition is doubtful, for wife beating "with a reasonable instrument" was legal in almost every state as late as 1850. In Massachusetts Judge Buller defined the legal instrument as a "stick no thicker than my thumb," and in New York the courts upheld a worthy Methodist exhorter who beat his wife with a horsewhip every few weeks in order to keep her in proper subjection and prevent her scolding.

In legal status servile and incompetent, by social canon revered and closely guarded, in cold fact a vitally necessary part of a dynamic economic and social system, the American woman of the early nineteenth century, without opportunity of voicing any dissatisfaction outside the domestic circle, was considered by most observers to be content and favored beyond the women of other countries. But Captain Basil Hall, whose own wife accompanied him on all his travels, expressed a note of disapproval that must have surprised American readers. He said the whole level of American society was lowered by the poor position assigned to women. Kindness and politeness were accorded them, but there was no real companionship with men. Social events, therefore, were dull and uninteresting, there was little stimulating conversation, business was discussed interminably, and all the finer social arts were neglected.

The result of all my observations and enquiries [he wrote] is that the women do not enjoy that station in society which has been allotted to them elsewhere; and consequently much of that importance and habitual influence which, from the peculiarity of their nature, they alone can exercise over society in more fortunately arranged communities, seem to be lost.[3]

Serious-minded though they were, the young De Tocqueville and De Beaumont obviously missed the conversation, the gaiety, the possibility for innocent flirtation and light persiflage that European society afforded. Other European visitors commented upon the prudishness and affectation of the "genteel female," as well as upon the general dullness of American social intercourse. Mrs. Trollope thought the life of the American lady most uninteresting, while Harriet Martineau was alarmed by what she called "the political non-existence of women" in America and called attention to its denial of democratic principles. Even Jefferson, she said, had classed women with children and slaves and thus had repudiated the principle of equal rights identified with his name. In the North Miss Martineau found woman's social position better than her legal status, but she had nothing but disapproval for what she astonishingly called "the degradation" of the women of the South:

I have seen, with heart-sorrow, the kind of politeness, the gallantry, so insufficient to the loving heart, with which the wives of the south are treated by their husbands. I have seen the horror of a woman's having to work — to exert the faculties which her Maker gave her; — the eagerness to ensure her unearned ease and rest; the deepest insult which can be offered to an intelligent and conscientious woman. I know the tone of conversation which is adopted toward women; different in its topics and its style from that which any man would dream of offering to any other man. I have heard the boast of the chivalrous consideration in which women are held throughout their woman's paradise; and seen something of the anguish of crushed pride, of the conflict of bitter feelings with which those boasts have been listened to by those whose aspirations teach them the hollowness of the system.[4]

Frances Wright, the brilliant Scotswoman, condemned the married women's property law as "absolute spoilation," permitting "robbery, and all but murder, against the unhappy female who swears away, at one and the same moment, her person and her property."[5] Since marriage imposed such onerous restrictions, she renounced the institution in entirety for her settlement at Nashoba, laying down the rule, "No woman can forfeit her individual rights or independent existence and no man assert over her any rights or power whatsoever beyond what he may exercise over her free and voluntary affections."

These strictures did not go unnoticed by American women themselves. Eliza Farnham wrote a treatise on the subject which she called *Woman and Her Era*, and in 1832 Lydia Maria Child published a two-volume *History of the Condition of Woman in All Ages*. The general trend of the 1820's and 1830's made women conscious of their own lack of opportunities and of their right to develop as persons. Women as well as men experienced the emotions and aspirations of the religious revivals and were imbued with perfectionist ideas. They, too, felt the urge toward humanitarian reform. Made conscious of themselves and their status by the work of such women as Frances Wright and Mrs. Child, and made aware of the needs of other human beings through contact with the humanitarians, American women were ready to advance through participation in many reform movements to an effort to improve their own status as a prerequisite to their real effectiveness in any social work.

Women made up the rank and file of the peace crusade and carried on extensive correspondence with women of other societies in the United States, in England, and in European countries. In the women's temperance societies and auxiliaries and in the women's antislavery societies they became adept at organization and adroit in political manipulation and the direction of public opinion. Their local, state, and national organization was government in miniature.

Auxiliary and subsidiary to the controlling men's organization it was, in origin and in the minds of the masculine leaders; but the women's help was essential for success, and once they were trained to equal effectiveness, the fiction of masculine superiority would be hard to maintain and the barrier of masculine domination might be assailed.

PIONEERS IN THE PROFESSIONS

Women early insisted upon their right to equal opportunities for education. In urging that the new Constitution be distinguished for its encouragement of learning, Abigail Adams wrote, "If you complain of education in sons, what shall I say in regard to daughters, who every day experience the want of it? . . . If we mean to have heroes, statesmen, and philosophers, we should have learned women." And the wise Abigail inculcated her ideas in her son, who rose in the House of Representatives in 1838 to defend the right of women to send petitions to the national legislature:

Why does it follow that women are fitted for nothing but the cares of domestic life . . . for promoting the welfare of their husbands, brothers, sons? . . . I say that the correct principle is that women are not only justified but exhibit the most exalted virtue, when they do depart from the domestic circle, and enter upon the concerns of their country, of humanity, and of their God. . . . Are women to have no opinions or actions on subjects relating to the general welfare? Where did the gentleman get this principle? Did he find it in sacred history — in the language of Miriam the prophetess, in one of the noblest and most sublime songs of triumph that ever met the human eye or ear? Did the gentleman never hear of Deborah, to whom the children of Israel came up for judgment? [6]

For many years Abigail Adams' plea for education for women was unanswered, but early in the nineteenth century, when educational reforms won constant hearing, women came to the fore in advancing the education of their own sex. It is necessary but to mention again the names of Catherine Beecher, Emma Willard, and Mary Lyon. In the Emma Willard school for girls in Troy, New York, and at Mount Holyoke many of the women later well known in the women's rights movement were trained. As assistant matron in the women's prison at Sing Sing, Georgiana Bruce Kirby, the English governess who aided in the school at Brook Farm, taught those in her charge to read and write, read aloud to them as they worked, built up the prison library, and corrected the exercises written on slates and pushed out to her under the doors of the cells after working hours.

It made little difference in what line of interest, business or professional, women of the early nineteenth century became interested, everywhere they met the same prejudice against their participation and the same reluctance to open the way for their proper training. Ministers declaimed about the inferior position of women, made as by an afterthought from Adam's rib and ordained by God as the subordinate and helpmate of man. The sanctity of the home, the purity of womanhood, the delicacy and fragility of feminine charm, were the texts of innumerable exhortations against removing any of the restrictions that hemmed in the cherished creatures. Biblical and biological arguments and illustrations drawn from history were backed by fulsome tributes to contemporary examples of domestic virtues. But little by little women doggedly bored from within, added a slight concession in one field to a gain in another, and finally won a measure of honest consideration on their merits as individuals.

Margaret Fuller, Transcendentalist, author, and editor, was educated by her father as a son would have been and always resented the thought that a woman's mind was different from or inferior to that of a man. In the early 1840's she wrote *The Great Law Suit or Man vs. Woman*, which was republished in 1845 under the more familiar title of *Woman in the Nineteenth Century*, the first logical statement of the position of women to be written by an American.

Miss Fuller condemned the laws that gave men rights over their wives and children and advocated throwing open every occupation to women. "What woman needs," she wrote, "is not as a woman to act or rule, but as a nature to grow, as an intellect to discern, as a soul to live freely and unimpeded, to unfold such powers as were given her when we left our common home." [7] Minds and souls, she said, are neither masculine nor feminine, genius has no sex, and intellectual merit deserves recognition whatever the sex of its possessor. Many a woman of later generations could read with fellow-feeling the Boston bluestocking's plea that women be accepted intellectually and advanced professionally without discrimination because of sex.

Women had long been regarded as the natural teachers of little children, and progress toward a measure of equality in the teaching profession came steadily although slowly. One of the greatest of the advocates of women's rights, Susan B. Anthony, began her career as a teacher. Of Quaker parentage, she always had the Quaker's conception of the equality of the sexes before God and never could understand the ideas current in her youth in regard to the inferiority of women. At seventeen she wrote angrily, "What an absurd notion that women have not intellectual and moral faculties sufficient for anything but domestic concerns." In 1853 she caused consternation in a teachers' convention by a request to enter a debate, which had already lasted for three days, on the question as to why the profession of teacher was less respected than that of lawyer, minister, or doctor. Never before had a woman spoken in such a gathering, and the dignified but determined young Quakeress was kept standing for half an hour while the question of her right to speak was hotly debated. Eventually the president, Professor Davies of West Point, complete in full dress, buff vest, blue coat, and gilt buttons, reluctantly announced, "The lady can speak," and Miss Anthony made this brief and lucid address:

It seems to me, gentlemen, that none of you quite comprehend the cause of the disrespect of which you complain. Do you not see that so long as society says a woman is incompetent to be a lawyer, minister, or doctor, but has ample ability to be a teacher, that every man of you who chooses that profession tacitly acknowledges that he has no more brains than a woman? . . . Would you exalt your profession, exalt those who labor with you. Would you make it more lucrative, increase the salaries of the women engaged in the noble work of educating our future Presidents, Senators, and Congressmen.[8]

In medicine the opposition was much more violent, and intrepid indeed was the young woman of the pre-Civil War period who dared express a desire to be a physician. Those few who were able to break through the barriers raised against them were justly famous in their own day and quite logically became leaders in the feminist crusade; they knew all too well the restrictions and prejudices that hampered their sex.

Dr. Harriot K. Hunt was one of the earliest woman physicians, beginning her practice in 1835. Her training was very sketchy, and her practice seems to have been along lines of general hygiene, hydrotherapy, and psychotherapy rather than medicine, but she was quite successful. She was twice refused admission to Harvard Medical School and was apparently frowned upon by medical men. She lectured on temperance, phrenology, the evils of tobacco, and sex hygiene. She was a woman of wealth and so strongly resented the discrimination against women that she sent an annual protest to the treasurer of Boston against being compelled to pay taxes when she was not represented in the government.

Dr. Hunt was joined in the late 1840's by Elizabeth Blackwell, whose name became of much more significance in the medical world. Miss Blackwell belonged to a large and remarkable Ohio family. Of five sisters two became physicians, one was a musician, one an artist and author of some note, while the fifth — reputed to be the most brilliant — was kept from public life by ill-health. No one of the five married, but they adopted and reared a number of children. One of their brothers married Lucy Stone, a prominent antislavery lecturer and feminist, and another became the husband of Antoinette Brown, one of the earliest woman preachers.

After being refused entry to the medical schools of Philadelphia, Elizabeth Blackwell appeared at Geneva College in western New York, presented evidence of adequate preparation, and asked for admission to the medical school. The authorities were shocked, but, scarcely knowing how to refuse her, they referred the question to the medical students. The young men took the whole matter as a joke and voted her in, fully expecting that after a sad failure she would withdraw, but in 1849 she graduated at the head of her class. Her sister Emily soon acquired a similar degree, and the two went abroad to study. In Paris there was some difficulty over admission to classes and hospitals, and it was suggested that Elizabeth don male dress as a prerequisite to entry. She refused flatly, saying that she would not alter so much as a bonnet string, and the authorities eventually gave way and permitted her to take the work she desired.

In 1857 the sisters opened the New York Infirmary for Women and Children, which they successfully administered for many years. Dr. Emily Blackwell was later dean of the Women's Medical College of New York, and Dr. Elizabeth organized a unit of field nurses during the Civil War. In 1869 she went to England, where she was the first woman to be admitted to the British Medical Registry and where she served for many years as professor of gynecology in the London School of Medicine for Women.

In the middle 1840's a quiet, determined girl appeared before the officials of Oberlin College and demanded that she be allowed to enter the theological course. No woman had ever been admitted to the closed corporation of the clergy, but, adamant against all adverse comment, Antoinette Brown refused to give up her desire to be a minister and finally won the reluctant consent of the college authorities. One kindly professor, aghast at the thought of a woman in the pulpit, told her that, despite his hearty disapproval of her course, he would endeavor to teach her the required subjects, but that he could not surrender the hope that he might persuade her to change her mind. He failed to do so, and Antoinette Brown graduated with the theology class of 1850, although Oberlin tried to hide its shame by omitting her name from the class list. She could obtain neither ordination nor a church to preach in, but in 1853 she acquired renown as the woman delegate refused the right to speak at the World Temperance Convention in New York City and was asked by the indignant supporters of women's rights to preach in Metropolitan Hall. A few days later she was ordained and was called to a church in a little town at the munificent salary of three hundred dollars a year. Miss Brown won the hearts of her liberal parishioners and felt free to invite her college friend, Lucy Stone, to speak in her church. The doughty little clergywoman left the church a little later to become a social worker. Still later she turned minister again, this time as a Unitarian. She married a brother of Dr. Elizabeth Blackwell and lived to the good old age of ninety-six.

Lucy Stone was the eighth of nine children in the family of a New England farmer, and her childhood was filled with work — cooking, cleaning, weaving, sewing, and shoemaking. An extremely observant and sensitive child, she was so horrified at the lot of women that she wanted to die, crying, "Is there anything that will put an end to me?" Finding no answer to that question, she made up her mind to go to college to find out whether the biblical texts quoted to justify woman's degradation were translated correctly and then to devote her life to improving the condition of her sex.

No one encouraged her in this unusual ambition, but her persistence in attempting to vote in church meetings, despite the fact that her vote was never counted, shows that she never lost sight of her objective. At sixteen she taught a district school, saving all that she could of her pittance, but she was twenty-five before she was able to go to college, and then it was Oberlin she chose. Older than most college students, without money, working every available hour, and boarding herself at fifty cents a week, Lucy Stone managed to become a leader in college affairs. She was prominent in the peace society and in the antislavery group; she organized a girl's debating club and taught classes of colored students. When the time of graduation came she was chosen to write a commencement oration, which, by college regulation, must be read for her by a man. Lucy Stone then made her first sacrifice for the cause of women's rights by refusing to accept the honor at all if she could not read the paper she had written.

Her college degree obtained, she alarmed her family by announcing that her chosen profession was that of lecturer in behalf of any good cause she might espouse. Her first public address on women's rights was given in 1847 in a church in Gardner, Massachusetts, where her brother was the minister. A year later she was employed as agent or lecturer for the American Anti-Slavery Society and toured New England with Parker Pillsbury. She was mobbed several times, was stunned by a book hurled by an angry listener, was deluged with cold water, was dropped from her church — in general received the treatment accorded the proponents of an unpopular cause. She never forgot the status of women and was admonished by the officers of the antislavery society for mixing too much women's rights in her discussions of the evils of slavery.

After a time she gave up other reforms and concentrated on the status of women, becoming her own manager and agent, writing her own publicity, and, since she refused to charge admission, passing the hat herself after each lecture. A tiny woman, weighing about one hundred pounds, she had a marvelous voice and was a most effective speaker. Touring the country to lecture on the political, social, and industrial disabilities of women, she spoke to audiences of sufficient size and generosity to yield her seven thousand dollars in three years. Early in her career as a public speaker, she met Henry Blackwell, another brother of the sister physicians, who finally persuaded her to marry him. His pledge to accept the idea of complete equality was sincere and was expressed in the famous Protest, which he wrote and they both signed when, in 1853, they were married by Thomas Wentworth Higginson. After acknowledging their mutual affection, they repudiated the laws of marriage that gave the husband "injurious and unnatural superiority, investing him with legal powers which no honorable man would exercise, and which no man should possess." The Protest ended with a condemnation of "the whole system by which the legal existence of the wife is suspended during marriage." [9]

The *Boston Post* jubilantly hailed the marriage of Lucy Stone in derisive verse, concluding with

> A name like Curtius' shall be his,
> On Fame's loud trumpet blown,
> Who with a wedding kiss shuts up
> The mouth of Lucy Stone! [10]

But the hopes of the *Post* were blasted, for marriage had no such effect. The first American woman to retain her maiden name, "Mrs. Stone" continued to lecture and to attend women's rights conventions. Even in the contentment of a happy marriage, she kept alive her protest against the disabilities of women by permitting her household goods, even her baby's cradle, to be sold for the taxes she refused to pay because she was not represented in the government!

WOMEN WRITERS AND EDITORS

Almost every contemporary commentator on the American scene in the second quarter of the nineteenth century called attention to the tremendous increase in the number of books, magazines, and newspapers being printed in the United States. Every town and hamlet, every church and reform society had its press; pamphlets, tracts, newssheets, and books of all descriptions on every possible subject poured forth to urge support of the innumerable parties and causes to which Americans were devoting their attention.

In this flood of ephemeral publication there was opportunity for women to acquire training in the art of self-expression. Countless little stories and poems were written by women for the annual gift books sponsored by the temperance advocates, and women were largely responsible for the children's periodicals and Sunday school library books devoted to the cause of temperance. An occasional woman among these writers won fame among her contemporaries and some sort of recognition from posterity. Margaret Fuller as editor of the *Dial* was without doubt the most important of the galaxy, but several others had a wide contemporary reputation. Anne Royall of Baltimore was editor of the *Huntress* for twenty-five years. Lydia Maria Child published a paper for children, the *Juvenile Miscellany*, was one of the most prolific writers of antislavery pamphlets, and in 1841 became the editor of the *Anti-Slavery Standard* in New York. Amelia Bloomer, postmistress in a little New York town, was the editor of the *Lily*, a temperance magazine, and achieved immortal fame through her advocacy of a "reform dress" for women, a part of which yet bears her name.

Two of the women who edited newspapers in the period were intensely interested in furthering the claims of their sex. Neither made any one contribution to the cause equal to Margaret Fuller's *Woman in the Nineteenth Century*, but each persistently for many years kept the issue before a wide public.

The fame of *Godey's Lady's Book* as America's first woman's fashion magazine has been revived with the interest in its charming colored illustrations and designs, but the name of its editor, Sarah Josepha Hale, has barely escaped oblivion. And yet Mrs. Hale was an extraordinarily interesting woman with a wide influence upon the thinking of her own day. In all outward things she was Victorian and conservative, intensely feminine and conventional. Her personality and career belong distinctively to the period and the environment in which she lived, and yet her mind and point of view were essentially modern, and her achievements along the lines she serenely marked out for herself are astonishing. Born in 1788, she had the limited formal education of the day but was privately instructed by a devoted Dartmouth brother so that she kept pace with his college studies. She married and had five children, was left a penniless widow when the oldest child was seven years of age, and made a precarious living as a seamstress. She was always writing and eventually had a novel published that won her some renown. When she was forty, she was summoned by Louis Godey, whom she always called the "Prince of Publishers," to be the editor of his *Lady's Book*.

In that editorship, which lasted for nearly fifty years, Mrs. Hale had opportunity to further numerous causes and to reach a wider public in their behalf than could any of the editors of publications devoted to reform measures, for the *Lady's Book* circulation of more than a hundred and fifty thousand put all other subscription lists to shame. Mrs. Hale is said to have "cajoled" the American public into approval of reform measures; she certainly managed to carry on the work of reformer and promoter without shocking her public or diminishing the financial returns of the magazine. She gave Mary Lyon and Mount Holyoke College a vast amount of free publicity, and she was little short of a press agent for Emma Willard. About equal educational and professional opportunities for women, she made statements so radical that only the popularity of *Godey's* other features could have sugar-coated the feminism.

When Elizabeth Blackwell was making her fight for a medical education, Mrs. Hale answered in a series of editorials all the arguments of the opposition. To the query, "What will women doctors do, when it is impossible for them to go out at all times and to all places?" she answered, "Just what male doctors do when they are called for and cannot go. Stay at home!" And when she reached the familiar argument that women would drive men out of employment, she sturdily came back with, "They may as well starve as the women. And if men cannot cope with women in the medical profession let them take an humble occupation in which they can." With unprecedented frankness, Mrs. Hale condemned unlicensed midwifery and advocated the training of women specialists in obstetrics and pediatrics. She helped in establishing the Female Medical College in Philadelphia in 1849 and worked to provide trained nurses for hospitals to which women doctors might take patients.

The editor of the *Lady's Book* advocated public playgrounds for city children as early as 1840, urged education in methods of preventing disease, and, by assuming that all right-minded and well-bred people agreed with her, made effective campaigns against such varied evils as pie for breakfast, airless sleeping rooms, tight corsets, and the Saturday night bath. She made swimming and horseback riding fashionable and established the popularity of the "pic-nic."

Although Mrs. Hale was too conservative, or perhaps too conscious of the subscription list, to advocate suffrage reform, earlier than any of the other feminists she agitated against the restrictions upon married women. But her feminism sometimes took amusing lines. The "reform dress" would not, of course, have been good business, but the word *female* was her pet abomination, and she often campaigned against its use. When her friend Matthew Vassar proposed to found a college for women, her pleasure in the prospect was chilled by word that the institution was to be called Vassar Female College, and she wrote the founder:

Female! What female do you mean? Not a female donkey? Must not your reply be, "I mean a female woman?" Then . . . why degrade the feminine sex to the level of animals? . . . I write thus earnestly because I wish to have Vassar College take the lead in this great improvement in our language.[11]

Whether or not because of Mrs. Hale's demands, the obnoxious word was deleted, and where it had appeared on the original college building the victory was commemorated by a broad blank stone, leaving the inscription, "VASSAR _____ COLLEGE."

Working in an environment far removed from that of the elegant editor of the *Lady's Book,* Jane Grey Swisshelm also made a significant contribution to the cause of women's rights. Born in Pittsburgh, Jane Grey Cannon had only an elementary education. At fourteen she was teaching in a country school, and at twenty-one she married James Swisshelm, with whom she lived most unhappily for twenty years. He was a petty domestic tyrant, ruled by a dominating mother who aided him in making Jane's life miserable. In her autobiography, *Half a Century,* Jane described her sacrifice of literary and artistic tastes, her hard work to help support her household, the constant friction and persecution in a home where not even the pittance she made at dressmaking could be called her own. Bitterly she wrote of her husband:

I knew from the first that his education had been limited, but thought the defect would be easily remedied as he had good abilities, but I discovered he had no love for books. His spiritual guides derided human learning and depended on inspiration. My knowledge stood in the way of my salvation, and I must be that odious thing — a superior wife — or stop my progress, for to be and appear were the same thing. I must be the mate of the man I had chosen; and if he would not come to my level, I must go to his. So I gave up study, and for years did not read one page in any book save the Bible.[12]

Oneida women at work in the business office and the bakery.
Note their Bloomer costume and their short hair.

Elizabeth Cady Stanton

Lucretia Mott

WOMEN CRUSADERS

Susan B. Anthony

Mary Lyon

After many years of subordination, Mrs. Swisshelm's personality and abilities began to assert themselves, partly, perhaps, because it was necessary for her to contribute to the family income. Her mother died, leaving her property in trust for the daughter whose husband she disliked, and that daughter gained firsthand acquaintance with the legal disabilities of married women when her husband sued the estate for the money he said was due him for the time Mrs. Swisshelm had spent nursing her mother in her last illness. It was little wonder that Jane Grey Swisshelm fought for equal legal rights for women. She believed in coeducation, sought the removal of all legal disabilities, and advocated equality of opportunity, but she was surprisingly moderate about political rights. She felt that women should not weaken their cause by impracticable demands. "Take one step at a time," she wrote. "Get a good foothold in it and advance carefully."

Residence for a time in Kentucky made Mrs. Swisshelm an uncompromising abolitionist, and in the 1840's she wrote articles for a succession of antislavery papers in Pittsburgh. When the last of these ceased publication, she started her own newspaper, the *Saturday Visiter*, and thus initiated a career as editor that was to last for many years. In the *Visiter* she attacked the Fugitive Slave Law, condemned Webster's Seventh of March speech, excoriated the slave catchers, and, in general, did all in her power to further the antislavery cause — and, incidentally, to enrage the opposition. When George D. Prentice, a Kentucky editor equally well known for his proslavery and his nativistic opinions, angrily accused Mrs. Swisshelm of being a man, "all but the pantaloons," she pertly retorted,

> Perhaps you have been busy
> Horsewhipping Sal or Lizzie
> Stealing some poor man's baby,
> Selling its mother, maybe.
> You say — and you are witty —
> That I — and, 'tis a pity —
> Of manhood lack but dress;
> But you lack manliness,
> A body clean and new,
> A soul within it, too.
> Nature must change her plan
> Ere you can be a man.[13]

After a legal and permanent separation from her husband, Mrs. Swisshelm went out to the Territory of Minnesota, where she had relatives. In the little town of St. Cloud, she established another newspaper and carried on for many years a constant battle for the reforms in which she was interested.

Of quite a different sort was Anna Ella Carroll of Baltimore. Belonging to one of the first families of Maryland and carefully educated by a devoted father, she early became interested in public affairs. When financial reverses in the family made it advisable for her to earn her own living, she capitalized on her social position in building up an interesting profession as public relations counsel for big business. She maintained a fact-finding service for various shipping and railroad organizations, lobbied for them discreetly in Washington, and wrote legislative reports, propaganda pamphlets, and investment information. Her business interests were with the Whigs, but her social life was based on her connections with Southern Democrats. She was an ardent nationalist, and, although not an antislavery woman, she opposed secession and gave her greatest service and shrewdest advice to the Union cause, winning for herself the title of the "great unrecognized member of Lincoln's cabinet."

Few indeed were the women novelists or poets worthy of note. Catherine Sedgwick, of the well-known Berkshire family, won some recognition as a "lady novelist" and still more as the friend and hostess of other writers, English and American. Mrs. Sigourney, the "Sweet Singer of Hartford," poured out a flood of romantic poems, sentimental sketches, and pious tales of wide vogue in their own day but of no permanent value. The most widely influential woman novelist was, of course, Harriet Beecher Stowe, whose *Uncle Tom's Cabin*, the most popular novel of the period, played a role of inestimable importance in the antislavery movement.

HEALTH AND DRESS

Although deeply concerned with humanitarian reforms and with their own legal and social disabilities, progressive American women found time, as did their brothers, to indulge in the various fads and fancies of their age. They were, perhaps, peculiarly susceptible to new ideas in diet and hygiene, but it would be impossible to show that they were more gullible than their masculine contemporaries in subscribing to the ideas of quacks and charlatans.

Mesmerism, animal magnetism, phrenology, and hydropathy all won women advocates, and countless mothers were grateful for the mild, tasteless homeopathic medicines which their children — and their husbands — would not rebel against. Diet fads and reforms, too, were extremely popular with intelligent women, and many of them became followers of that indefatigable lecturer on matters of health, Sylvester Graham. Abstaining from the use of meat, tea, coffee, and pastries, living mainly upon fruits, vegetables, and bread made from whole wheat flour, they "Grahamized" in concert with Bronson Alcott, Brook Farm, and the Shaker communities.

The dress reform movement belonged peculiarly to women. The so-called Bloomer costume, which seems to have been designed for reasons of health in one of the hydropathic institutes of the period, was introduced to the world of fashion and affairs by Elizabeth Smith, daughter of Gerrit Smith and cousin of Elizabeth Cady Stanton. The costume was neither immodest nor ungainly. It consisted of a loose-fitting dress or coat reaching below the knees and a garment similar to Turkish trousers, gathered at the ankles into walking boots or neatly fitted above house slippers. The wearers of this costume usually cut their hair, too, for comfort's sake, and felt themselves quite emancipated from the bondage of trailing skirts, petticoats, corsets, and festoons of heavy corkscrew curls. Since several of the women prominent in the suffrage movement adopted the reform dress, it was accepted as a badge of radicalism, and its wearers were suspected of "free love" notions and of a desire to be rid of all feminine graces and restrictions.

Mrs. Stanton's reasons for adopting the dress seem the acme of common sense:

To see my cousin [Elizabeth Smith], with a lamp in one hand and a baby in the other, walk upstairs with ease and grace, while, with flowing robes, I pulled myself up with difficulty, lamp and baby out of the question, readily convinced me that there was sore need of a reform in woman's dress and I promptly donned a similar costume.[14]

I have seen galleries of beautiful paintings and statuary in the old world but nowhere is the ideal female form to be found in a huge whaleboned bodice and bedraggled skirt. If the graceful is what you aim at, study the old painters and sculptors, and not Godey's *Book of*

Fashion. But for us, commonplace, everyday, working characters, who wash and iron, bake and brew, carry water and fat babies upstairs and down, bring potatoes, apples, and pans of milk from the cellar, run our own errands, through mud or snow, shovel paths, and work in the garden, why "the drapery" is quite too much — one might as well work with a ball and chain. Is being born a woman so criminal an offense, that we must be doomed to this everlasting bondage? [15]

Despite all ridicule, she wore the Bloomer dress for two years and more, as did Susan B. Anthony, Lucy Stone, Angelina Grimké Weld, and others. The newspapers were full of limericks about them, such as:

> Gibbey, gibbey gab
> The women had a confab
> And demanded the rights
> To wear the tights
> Gibbey, gibbey gab.

> Heigh! ho! the carrion crow
> The bloomer now is all the go.
> Twenty tailors take the stitches
> Twenty women wear the breeches.
> Heigh! ho! in rain or snow,
> The bloomer now is all the go.

It was not criticism or ridicule, however, but dislike of continual nagging attention that caused the feminist leaders to abandon the comfortable garb. After extensive correspondence on the subject, they one by one went back to the long skirts, because, as Lucy Stone said, it was "so much bother to be different." Susan B. Anthony dryly remarked that she found it impossible to obtain a man's attention to her talk when he was completely occupied gazing at her ankles.

WOMEN IN COMMUNISTIC AND RELIGIOUS GROUPS

American radicalism, religious or social, gave those women who adhered to its tenets an equal place in its ranks. Perhaps for that reason, the demand of women for equal legal and political status had for the ordinary man of the period an especially revolutionary connotation. The Shakers led the way in this, but also at New Harmony, at Hopedale, and at Brook Farm, in the Fourier settlements, and especially at Oneida, women encountered no discrimination.

Their cooperation and companionship were a necessary part of community life, and they shared in all affairs and decisions.

This complete democracy had long been a characteristic of some of the more radical religious sects. Among the Quakers and the early Baptists there had been no subordination of women in the councils of the church. In Quaker churches any woman moved by the Divine Spirit might speak as she chose. In the nineteenth century one branch of Quakerism, becoming conservative, frowned upon too much activity by women and upon the participation of either men or women in reform movements. The Hicksite Quakers, however, whose doctrines approached those of the Unitarians, worked vigorously in the camps of the humanitarians and appear to have placed no barriers across the paths of the women belonging to their groups.

Abby Kelly was a Quaker and came to public speaking naturally through her experiences in the church. She attended Mount Holyoke in her youth and later was the first woman to graduate from the regular college division at Oberlin. One of Miss Kelly's first speeches in the antislavery cause was given in Philadelphia Hall in 1838 just before it was burned by a mob. In Massachusetts she was associated with Parker Pillsbury and with Stephen Foster, whom she later married, and was, with them, the target for the stones, eggs, and rotten vegetables of the hooting mobs. A New England minister preached against her from the text, "I have a few things against thee, because thou sufferest that woman Jezebel, which calleth herself a prophetess, to teach, and to seduce my servants to commit fornication," and the orthodox and conventional loudly condemned her as unsexed, bold, and dangerous. Her appointment in 1838 as a member of an important committee of the Massachusetts Anti-Slavery Society split the association in two; eight ministers seceded from the executive group and founded a new society.

WOMEN IN THE ANTISLAVERY MOVEMENT

The Grimké sisters, Sarah and Angelina, became Quakers, too, after they left their South Carolina home and went North to aid in the antislavery cause. They soon found that, although their aid was eagerly accepted, they were criticized and disliked by many abolitionists and were howled down by the riffraff of many audiences solely because they were women venturing into a sphere heretofore reserved for men. The correspondence of the able and spirited sisters throws much light on the difficulties that faced the women who desired to give their support to humanitarian reforms and who were thereby brought face to face with the restrictions on their sex.

Theodore Weld, who later married Angelina, assured the sisters that he had always believed in the equality of the sexes, but he urged them not to let advocacy of the rights of women divert them from the much more important and immediate issue of the sorrows of the Negro slave.

Let us all [he wrote] *first* wake up the nation to lift millions of slaves of both sexes from the dust, and turn them into MEN and then when we all have our hand in, it will be an easy matter to take millions of females from their knees and set them on their feet, or in other words transform them from *babies* into *women*.[16]

And that, with a few exceptions, was the cold comfort women received from the men who sought their aid in the cause of reform. That there was anything incongruous in seeking this aid in the fight for the slaves while women were themselves on their knees seems not to have occurred to Weld or his associates.

The Grimké sisters could not see how women could help in the abolition cause or any other when they were refused the right to speak in its behalf. The orthodox ministers of Massachusetts, in General Association assembled, issued a Pastoral Letter commanding the clergy represented in that association to forbid women to speak from their pulpits. Woman was to be commended for her participation in religious work, said the Letter —

But when she assumes the place and tone of man . . . we put ourselves in self-defense against her; she yields the power which God has given her for her protection, and her character becomes unnatural. If the vine, whose strength and beauty is to lean upon the trellis-work, and half conceal its clusters, thinks to assume the independence and the overshadowing nature of the elm, it will not only cease to bear fruit but fall in shame and dishonor into the dust. We cannot, therefore, but regret the mistaken conduct of those who encourage females to bear an obtrusive and ostentatious part in measures of reform, and countenance any of that sex who so far forget themselves as to itinerate in the character of public lecturers and teachers. We especially deplore the intimate acquaintance and promiscuous conversation of females with regard to things which ought not to be named; by which that modesty and delicacy which is the charm of domestic life, and which constitutes the true influence of woman in society, is consumed, and the way opened, as we apprehend, for degeneracy and ruin.[17]

Sarah Grimké answered this statement in a series of articles called "Letters on the Condition of Women and the Equality of the Sexes." She went to the Bible and the tenets of Quakerism for her arguments and quoted the text, "Thou will be subject unto thy husband and he will rule over thee," and Blackstone's *Commentaries* to show how men had mistreated women.

Whittier, a consistent champion of the rights of women, also answered the Pastoral Letter, in ringing verse commending "Carolina's high-souled daughters." But it was the humorous feminist, Maria Weston Chapman, who reduced the Letter to absurdity in a poem, "The Times That Try Men's Souls," a part of which goes thus:

> Confusion has seized us, and all things go wrong,
>   The women have leaped from "their spheres,"
> And, instead of fixed stars, shoot as comets along,
>   And are setting the world by the ears!
> In courses erratic they're wheeling through space,
> In brainless confusion and meaningless chase.
> . . . .
> Oh! shade of the prophet Mahomet arise!
>   Place woman again in "her sphere,"
> And teach that her soul was not born for the skies,
>   But to flutter a brief moment here.
> This doctrine of Jesus, as preached up by Paul
> If embraced in its spirit, will ruin us all.[18]

In the years after the organization of the American Anti-Slavery Society women formed numerous auxiliary societies to raise money and arouse public opinion. There they learned valuable lessons in the business of organization and propaganda, although, as one of them said, when they first began the work "there was not a woman capable of taking the chair and organizing the meeting in due order, and they had to call in a man to aid them." Once trained, however, they were unexpectedly successful, and the leaders of the parent society wished to use their efforts more extensively. With a little experience in a broader sphere, women of ability began to feel that the "Ladies" societies with their fairs and prayer meetings were childish and that they should participate in all antislavery work on an equal basis. In 1840, however, came two momentous defeats to their ambitions in this direction.

In the convention of the American Anti-Slavery Society in New York, the radical Garrison faction proposed a woman for membership on the executive committee and carried the proposition by a narrow majority. The conservative members at once left the convention and organized a separate national society pledged to distinctly non-Garrisonian principles.* After 1840, therefore, only in the ranks of the Garrisonian abolitionists could women find recognition; and, although that group had had a majority in the convention, it was very apparent that it was a decreasing minority in antislavery ranks as a whole.

The second blow fell in London later in the same year. The British issued a call for a World's Anti-Slavery Convention without specifying that all delegates should be men, and the Pennsylvania and Massachusetts societies sent large delegations that included some eight or nine prominent women. Lucretia Mott and her husband James, Philadelphia Quakers, were both delegates, as were Wendell Phillips and his bride Ann.

Mrs. Mott was a woman of ability and of remarkable character and spirit. Everywhere in her own country men and women had honored and loved her. Her clear, serene eyes, her quiet Quaker dress, and her mild but assured manner had won her the respect even of the mobs that heckled the meetings at which she spoke. Her home was a refuge for fugitive slaves, her advice was sought by Hicksite Quakers everywhere, and her calm judgment was appreciated by the leaders of all the reform movements in which she worked. Her husband adored her, and his chuckle as he once admonished a speaker whose points Lucretia had criticized, saying, "If she thinks thee is wrong, thee had better look it over again," indicated his delight in her wit and wisdom.

Mrs. Mott and her fellow women delegates were uncertain as to their reception in London, but welcomed the opportunity for test-

* For the broader issues involved in this action, see the discussion of its antislavery aspects, pages 497–99.

ing both their status in the reform movements and the strength of the support to be accorded them by the masculine American delegation.

Ann Green Phillips told her husband, "No shilly-shallying, Wendell! Be brave as a lion!" and he prepared to lead the fight for the admission of the women delegates. Many of his fellows from the United States were eager to vote against it and had counseled the English conservatives to stand firm. Phillips opened battle with a motion that a committee be appointed to prepare a list of the members of the convention, with instructions to include in the list "all persons bearing credentials from any Anti-Slavery body." With that the debate was on, and it raged for hours. An English clergyman made a touching appeal to the American women to defer to British prejudice and withdraw their credentials voluntarily, thus permitting the convention to avoid the discourtesy of refusing them. Biblical arguments were hurled at them and ministers of conflicting views quoted texts in a confusing exchange. When eventually the vote was taken, the women were excluded by an overwhelming majority — only to receive the added insult of being asked to attend the meetings in a curtained enclosure and to have "no unpleasant feelings over the outcome." [19]

Garrison was delayed in leaving the United States and did not reach London until the question of the women delegates had been settled, but he expressed his disapproval of their exclusion by refusing to participate in the convention. Sitting with the rejected women or in the gallery, he looked down upon the convention — much to the chagrin of the triumphant men, for, despite the division of opinion in the United States about his leadership, in British antislavery circles he was considered a figure of major importance.

At the London conference, too, were Henry Stanton of New York and his bride, Elizabeth Cady Stanton. The young husband was a Lane Seminary friend of Theodore Weld and a member of the conservative faction of the antislavery society. The bride was the daughter of an eminent lawyer and the cousin of Gerrit Smith. Elizabeth Cady had been interested in the rights of women ever since, as a wide-eyed little girl, she had sat in the office of her adored father and listened to him sadly explaining to women clients that their husbands had legal right to their children and their property. In London Mrs. Stanton began a lifelong friendship with Mrs. Mott and the other women whose credentials had been rejected. These women were left with few illusions as to their position in any organization dominated by men, and they grew steadily more convinced that they must organize in an effort to secure the rights and privileges denied them.

WOMEN IN THE TEMPERANCE MOVEMENT

Women had also long been interested in the cause of temperance, and as the Washingtonian movement had progressed, they had organized Daughters of Temperance societies to work along the same lines as the Sons of Temperance. As in the antislavery movement, the leaders were anxious to utilize their services in propaganda, in children's societies, and in obtaining money for the cause. But again the conservative clergy frowned upon women's participation in meetings and governing bodies.

A convention of all the temperance societies of New York assembled in Albany in January 1852. The Daughters of Temperance had been invited to attend, but when the energetic Susan B. Anthony rose to speak, she was informed that the "ladies" were there to listen, not to take part in the proceedings. Immediately a group of the women present who were not satisfied to be seen and not heard withdrew, and in a meeting of their own organized a Women's State Temperance Association and called a convention to meet later in the year.

Five hundred women answered the call for this Rochester convention. They elected Elizabeth Cady Stanton president of the new society, chose twelve vice-presidents, including Antoinette Brown and Mrs. Gerrit Smith, and made Susan B. Anthony and Amelia Bloomer secretaries. It was obvious that the elite of the women's rights movement had moved in upon the temperance society. In her speech accepting the presidency, Mrs. Stanton threw a bombshell into the ranks of the conservatives by advising women to refuse all conjugal rights to husbands who drank to excess. "Let no drunkard be the father of her children. Let no woman form an alliance with any man who has been suspected even of the vice of intemperance. Be not misled by any pledges, resolves, promises, prayers, or tears." In the state convention of the society the following year Mrs. Stanton endeavored to explain this linking of the issues of temperance and women's rights:

We have been obliged to preach woman's rights, because many, instead of listening to what we had to say on temperance, have questioned the right of a woman to speak on any subject. In courts of justice and legislative assemblies, if the right of the speaker to be there is questioned, all business waits until that point is settled. Now, it is not settled in the mass of minds that woman has any rights on this footstool, and much less a right to stand on an even pedestal with man, look him in the face as an equal, and rebuke the sins of her day and generation. Let it be clearly understood, then, that we are a woman's rights society, that we believe it is woman's duty to speak whenever she feels the impression to do so; that it is her right to be present in all the councils of Church and State.[20]

These were brave words, but they did not meet with the approval of the majority of the convention. When the society was formed, men had been admitted to membership but without the privilege of holding office. The constitution was now altered to give men full membership, and they immediately monopolized the floor, insisting that the society repudiate all connection with women's rights. Miss Anthony made an indignant speech, charging that the men were stealing the association from the women who had founded it, but the mass of delegates, alarmed at Mrs. Stanton's radical ideas on marriage and divorce, listened to the men and voted against her re-election. Miss Anthony and Mrs. Stanton at once severed their connection with the society, and from that day on it declined in importance, maintaining an innocuous existence for a few years and then disappearing altogether. There was not to be another such women's temperance group for twenty years and more.

In 1853, also, women were humiliated in the World's Temperance Convention in New York City. When the American hosts got together to complete arrangements for the gathering, the question arose as to whether representatives of the Women's State Temperance Society should be admitted to this preliminary meeting. Thomas Wentworth Higginson suggested that Lucy Stone be placed on the business committee, and the debate on both questions was furious. Abby Kelly Foster rose to speak, only to have her voice drowned out in the uproar. When a vote was finally taken, the women were again rejected. Mr. Higginson resigned from the committee, calling the proceedings a disgrace, and initiated a move for a "Whole World's Temperance Convention" in which women would be given full recognition. In the *New York Tribune* Horace Greeley arraigned the clergymen who had denied women the right to representation in an assemblage of those who had worked for temperance. He, too, refused to consider any assemblage with such principles a *world* convention and sarcastically called it "An Orthodox White Male Adult Saints' Convention."

When the delegates to the World's Temperance Convention, derisively called the "Half World's Temperance Convention," arrived in New York, the excitement was intense. Meetings were held for several days, with each session dominated by an organized mob. Antoinette Brown had been appointed a delegate by two local societies in assertion of the principle of equal rights. Wendell Phillips accompanied her to the hall to present her credentials, and Neal Dow, presiding as chairman, invited her to speak from the platform. Pandemonium then broke loose. For an hour and a half she stood firm and was yelled at by the assembled delegates, many of them ministers of the Gospel. One Reverend Mr. Chambers shouted constantly, "Shame on the woman, shame on the woman." Later charges that Miss Brown was intruding the subject of women's rights upon a temperance assembly were absurd, for the poor woman said nothing at all. From that opening hour the convention was devoted, as Greeley reported in the *Tribune*, to: "First Day – Crowding a woman off the platform; Second Day – Gagging her; Third Day – Voting that she shall stay gagged."

And so ended the effort of women to obtain equal privileges in the temperance organizations. The schism over "the woman question" was as disastrous for the crusade against liquor as it was for the antislavery association. The great liberal leaders of the reform movements, both men and women, dropped out of the temperance organizations and devoted their energies to activities in which they would not be hampered by conservative advocates of the status quo.

SUPPORT FROM THE LIBERALS

There is no one thing more apparent in the slow progress of American women than the constant and hearty support they received from the men who are still recognized as the embodiment of the American faith and who did most to advance democratic principles and ideals. Always, although the majority was in the camp of the opposition, the best brains and the warmest hearts of the "benevolent empire" of wealthy philanthropic reformers were with the women.

Those who led the crusade found encouragement in their own families. James Mott was scarcely less interested than his wife in the cause of women's rights. Elizabeth Blackwell, Antoinette Brown, and Lucy Stone had the freethinking Blackwell family behind them. Susan B. Anthony owed much to the understanding, sympathy, and support of her Quaker father. Judge Cady, who sent his little daughter to Emma Willard's school and taught her the significance of the laws determining the status of women, contributed much to the career of Elizabeth Cady Stanton. Her cousin, Gerrit Smith, interested her in the temperance and antislavery reforms and advised her early efforts for women's rights. In her husband, Henry Stanton, she found a tower of strength. He did not always approve of her course, but he always recognized her right to choose for herself as to what that course should be, and in the rearing of their seven delightful children they united in common sense and great good humor. The Stanton household was full of fun and gaiety, and Mrs. Stanton's numerous activities got fitted into its full program by dint of much effort and the constant assistance of Miss Anthony.

Angelina and Sarah Grimké found sympathy and understanding among the Quakers of Philadelphia, and the marriage of Angelina and Theodore Weld was a happy one. Ann Green Phillips greatly increased her husband's interest in the antislavery movement, and Wendell Phillips became also a stanch supporter of the women he saw discriminated against in that and other reform movements. Margaret Fuller Ossoli had the friendship and interest of the whole group of Transcendentalists and found love and fulfillment in her Italian marriage. There were few, indeed, of the women active in their own behalf whose life experience was as unhappy as that of Jane Grey Swisshelm.

William Lloyd Garrison, Samuel B. May, and Thomas Wentworth Higginson were constant in their support, and Parker, Emerson, and William Henry Channing added the approval of the

Transcendentalists. Among the editors of metropolitan newspapers, Horace Greeley stood out in approval of the movement, and in commenting upon one of the early conventions for women's rights he made a most unequivocal statement:

I recognize most thoroughly the right of woman to choose her own sphere of activity and usefulness, and to evoke its proper limitations. If she sees fit to navigate vessels, print newspapers, frame laws, select rulers — any or all of these — I know no principle that justifies man in interposing any impediment to her doing so. The only argument entitled to any weight against the fullest concession of the rights you demand, rests in the assumption that woman does not claim any such rights, but chooses to be ruled, guided, impelled, and have her sphere prescribed for her by man.

I think the present state of our laws respecting property and inheritance, as respects married women, show very clearly that woman ought not to be satisfied with her present position; yet it may be that she is so. If all those who have never given this matter a serious thought are to be considered on the side of conservatism, of course that side must preponderate. Be this as it may, woman alone can, in the present state of the controversy, speak effectively for woman, since none others can speak with authority, or from the depths of personal experience.[21]

WOMEN ORGANIZE IN THEIR OWN BEHALF

Realizing at last that they were faced with persistent discrimination along all lines — educational, professional, legal, political, even humanitarian — women began to organize for a campaign in their own behalf. Initiated in one locality by a small group, the movement spread wherever interest could be aroused. A few leaders would issue a call for a state convention, where arrangements were made for closely knit local societies. When sufficient interest was aroused and enough states had been organized, national conventions were held. Speeches, newspaper publicity, letters, platforms, petitions to other organizations and to legislatures — no known agency of propaganda was neglected. Women's rights newspapers were established and women joined in the barrage of pamphlets, printed addresses, and campaign dodgers that had been a part of the tactics of the humanitarians.

This organization of the movement was not of sudden or spectacular origin. In 1840 Mrs. Mott and Mrs. Stanton had talked in London of the possibility of a convention to consider the disabilities of women. But in the following years Mrs. Mott was occupied with the antislavery movement and with the problems of the liberal Quakers, and Mrs. Stanton was busy with household cares and with one baby after another. After all, as Sarah Grimké wrote to an English friend, "it is plainly the duty of woman to nurse her off-spring; it cannot be the duty of man because God has not furnished him with the nourishment necessary for the infant." [22]

In the 1840's, also, Antoinette Brown and Lucy Stone were struggling to obtain professional training against obstacles placed in their way even at liberal Oberlin, and Elizabeth Blackwell and her sister were overcoming obstinate prejudice in the field of medicine. Susan Anthony was running up against discrimination in the teaching profession, and both she and Mrs. Stanton were finding difficulties in their work for temperance. The decision to organize was the result of this long and painful experience.

In the summer of 1848 Lucretia and James Mott went to Waterloo, New York, for a yearly meeting of the Friends. Mrs. Mott went on to visit her sister at Auburn and there met, for the first time since their London experience in 1840, Elizabeth Cady Stanton, who was then living in the near-by town of Seneca Falls. As a result of some cogitation over the teacups, there appeared in the *Seneca Falls County Courier* on July 14 the following announcement:

Seneca Falls Convention

Woman's Rights Convention — a Convention to discuss the social, civil, and religious condition and rights of woman, will be held in the Wesleyan Chapel, at Seneca Falls, N.Y., on Wednesday and Thursday, the 19th and 20th of July, current; commencing at 10 o'clock A.M. During the first day the meeting will be exclusively for women, who are earnestly invited to attend. The public generally are invited to be present on the second day, when Lucretia Mott, of Philadelphia, and other ladies and gentlemen, will address the Convention.[23]

When July 19 arrived, a large number of people, almost as many men as women, appeared at the doors of the Wesleyan Chapel, only to find them locked. A small boy was lifted through an open window, however, and the convention opened according to schedule with James Mott in the chair, an evidence of the inexperience or timidity of the women who had called the convention. With the meeting once opened, the women read their prepared speeches;

Lucretia Mott presented the purpose of the convention, and Mrs. Stanton read the Declaration of Sentiments over which the committee had expended much effort.

The women had used the Declaration of Independence as a model, substituting *Man* for *King George* and listing some eighteen familiar grievances as the basis for their demand for reform. Of these the last was a general arraignment of man's treatment of woman: "He has endeavored, in every way that he could, to destroy her confidence in her own powers, to lessen her self-respect, and to make her willing to lead a dependent and abject life." In view of all these injustices, those "aggrieved, oppressed, and fraudulently deprived of their most sacred rights" asked immediate admission to all the rights and privileges pertaining to citizens of the United States and called upon women everywhere to organize, to petition, to employ agents, to circulate tracts, and to hold conventions.

The Declaration was followed by a series of twelve resolutions in accord with its sentiments. These were all passed unanimously except the ninth, which stated that "it is the duty of the women of this country to secure to themselves their sacred right to the elective franchise." A part of the committee had disapproved this resolution, feeling that in asking too much the women might make their cause ridiculous, but Mrs. Stanton had her way, and with the assistance of Frederick Douglass, the Negro abolitionist, she was able to obtain the acceptance of the resolution by a small majority. Its inclusion was perhaps a mistake, however, for many of the one hundred men and women who signed the Declaration at Seneca Falls withdrew their names when the storm of ridicule broke.

In August 1848 a second women's rights convention was held in Rochester, New York, and with that event the organization of women in their own cause may fairly be said to have begun. Conventions were held in the next two or three years in Massachusetts, Ohio, Pennsylvania, and Indiana, and before the end of a decade the movement had spread through all the Northern states and as far West as Wisconsin and Kansas. Annual national conventions were held beginning in 1850. Nearly every woman who had managed to win recognition in any profession gave aid in the work, and the more liberal masculine leaders of other reform movements all spoke at conventions and kept in touch with the women leaders.

And a fight it was, for it was difficult even to win over the women whom the crusade was designed to benefit. Meetings were often attended by those who desired only to break them up. At the New York convention in 1853, for example, the session had to be closed after hoodlums had filled the air with shouts of "Sit down," "Get out," "Bow-wow," "Go it, Susan," accompanied by hisses and catcalls, while police looked on in apparent approval. And only the *Tribune* and the *Evening Post* condemned the action of the mob.

Lack of funds was another deterrent. Married women had little to call their own, and the salaries of the valiant spinsters left much to be desired. Most of the work was done by voluntary contributions of time and energy. Much of the publicity was free and adverse, but those who could spoke, wrote, and published for the good of the cause. Somehow they managed to get together funds for a few agents to circulate petitions and to hold the local organizations in line. A few women lecturers were well enough known so that admission fees could be charged when they appeared on the program, and some of the country's best known masculine lecturers contributed their services and their fees.

It was uphill work and depended always upon the utter devotion of a few tireless women. In 1849 Richard Henry Dana, a prominent member of literary circles in Brahmin Boston, delivered a lecture throughout the country ridiculing the new demand of American women for greater rights and privileges. He held up Shakespeare's docile, tender, loving women — Desdemona, Juliet, and Ophelia — as examples to be studied and imitated. He did not mention Portia. Lucretia Mott answered his strictures in a "Discourse on Woman" given in the Assembly Hall in Philadelphia and later printed for wide distribution. In remarkably clear, hard-hitting sentences she knocked the props from under Dana's argument, showed its shallowness and sentimentality, and established firmly the bases of the demands made by women. Stating that man-made restrictions had enervated the minds and powers of women, she denied that the sex was willing to be the plaything or the slave of man, and asked that women be allowed to develop as moral, responsible beings. She went into the history of the discrimination against women, analyzed the legal status that women wanted to improve, and demanded

From *Harper's Weekly*, June 11, 1859

An early women's rights convention. Note the friendly gentlemen on the floor and those jeering in the balcony.

equal rights in education, in the professions, in the business world, and before the law. Mrs. Mott's inflexible Quaker principles appeared in the stern statement:

Far be it from me to encourage women to vote, or to take an active part in politics in the present state of our government. Her right to the elective franchise, however, is the same, and should be yielded to her, whether she exercise that right or not. Would that man, too, would have no participation in a government recognizing the life-taking principle; retaliation and the sword. It is unworthy of a Christian nation. But when in the diffusion of light and intelligence a Convention shall be called to make regulations for self-government on Christian principles, I can see no good reason why women should not participate in such an assemblage, taking part equally with man.[24]

Another strong force in defense of women's rights was Ernestine Rose, born Siismund Potoski in Pyeterkow, Poland. Her father had been a Jewish rabbi, and she had been brought up in the strictest observance of their religious faith. As a young woman she rebelled against both religious restrictions and absolutism in government and left Poland, living in France and later in England. In the 1830's she became a friend of Elizabeth Fry and Robert Owen and devoted herself to social reforms. She married a liberal Englishman, William Rose, and came with him to New York, where she at once became interested in the antislavery movement and others. Handsome and cultivated, an able speaker with great dignity and quick wit, she became one of the most valuable of the suffragist lecturers, speaking often and before large audiences in every Northern state. She was chosen to present petitions to legislatures and to give the keynote speeches at conventions, and in general played a large part in the work she had chosen. Cosmopolitan in attitude, she brought a broader vision into the American movement.

Clarina Howard Nichols was another of the same caliber. It was she who organized the women of Vermont, and later, moving west with her family, she worked for the cause in Wisconsin, in Kansas, and in Missouri. She knew every suffrage leader, attended many conventions, and lectured wherever she went. In Massachusetts Paulina Wright Davis, who had shocked the fastidious by her health lectures in an earlier day, called the first national convention, edited the suffrage paper *Una*, and led the local women's rights organization. Out in Ohio Frances D. Gage was a pillar of strength. She had long been a leader in humanitarian and literary circles in Ohio, a correspondent of Harriet Martineau, and a friend of those prominent in the antislavery movement. In 1851 she was made president of the Ohio Women's Convention, which met in Akron, and was joined in leading it by Maria Giddings, daughter of Joshua Giddings, the Congressional defender of the right of petition, and Jane Grey Swisshelm, who was soon to leave Pittsburgh for St. Cloud, Minnesota.

At this Akron convention appeared Sojourner Truth, an old Negress, born a slave in New York, who had long been a worker in the abolition cause. The entry of the tall, gaunt black woman in her gray dress and white turban caused consternation in the convention, for the women were finding it rough going in the storm of protest and criticism raised by members of the clergy who had invaded the meeting and were monopolizing the discussion. But Sojourner delivered them from their adversaries. After listening to the reverend gentlemen patiently for some hours, the old colored woman rose slowly from her seat on the pulpit steps and spoke in deep tones to a suddenly hushed audience:

Wall, chilern, whar dar is so much racket dar must be somethin' out o' kilter. I tink dat 'twixt de niggers of de Souf and de womin at de Norf, all talkin' bout rights, de white men will be in a fix pretty soon. But what's all dis here talkin' 'bout?

Dat man ober dar say dat womin needs to be helped into carriages and lifted ober ditches, and to hab de best place everywhar. Nobody eber helps me into carriages, or ober mud-puddles, or gibs me any best place! And a'n't I a woman? Look at my arm! I have ploughed, and planted and gathered into barns, and no man could head me! And a'n't I a woman? I could work as much and eat as much as a man — when I could get it — and bear de lash as well! And a'n't I a woman? I have borne thirteen chilern, and seen 'em mos' all sold off to slavery, and when I cried out with my mother's grief, none but Jesus heard me! And a'n't I a woman? . . . Den dat little little man in black dar, he say women can't have as much rights as men, 'cause Christ wan't a woman! Whar did your Christ come from? Whar did your Christ come from? From God and a woman! Man had nothin' to do wid Him! [25]

When the deep voice was still and the outstretched arms had fallen and the old Negress sank once more to the pulpit step, the clerical hecklers were silent.

Two names stand out beyond all others in the crusade for women's rights. Elizabeth Cady Stanton and Susan B. Anthony were central figures in its organization period before 1860, and in the next half century they were largely responsible for its continuance to a successful conclusion. Dogged, persistent, capable, and hard-working, the spinster Susan tramped up and down New York in all weathers, organizing, circulating petitions, speaking, and in general fanning the breath of life into a movement that might otherwise have died from opposition or from lack of interest in the rank and file. Mrs. Stanton had a little more of genius and tact, a touch of humor and zest, and an invaluable compound of charm and magnetism.

The friendship between the two women was remarkable. Neither was subordinate to the other; both were vital to the cause. Mrs. Stanton wrote and talked easily and well, and for many years she wrote the speeches for which Miss Anthony collected the material. Henry Stanton once said, "You stir up Susan and she stirs the world," and Mrs. Stanton herself admitted that she "forged the thunder bolts" and Susan fired them. What Susan thought is more difficult to ascertain. There are letters extant that show her rage when matrimony and maternity robbed her of able lieutenants, and other letters urging Mrs. Stanton to put family activities aside and write the call for a convention or the address to accompany a legislative petition. There are plaintive letters from Elizabeth, also, complaining that the demands upon her time are too great, saying that she will not write a single address while nursing the current infant, and once even threatening, "As soon as you all begin to ask too much of me, I shall have a baby! Now, be careful, do not provoke me to that step!"

Susan it was who brought down upon herself the reproaches of many friends of the cause by deliberately assisting a desperate mother to kidnap her child from the husband who had cruelly denied it to her. The woman was the wife of a state senator of Massachusetts and the sister of a United States senator from New York, so the case aroused much comment. Even Phillips and Garrison were horrified and urged that the child be returned to its father. When asked if she did not realize that she was violating the law, Susan calmly replied,

Yes, I do know it, and does not the law of the United States give the slave holder the ownership of the slave? And don't you break the law every time you help a slave to Canada? Well, the law which gives the father the sole ownership of the children is just as wicked, and I'll break it just as quickly. You would die before you would deliver a slave to his master, and I will die before I will give up that child to its father.[26]

In 1848 the legislature of the state of New York, after twelve years of discussion, passed a Married Women's Property Law that gave to women certain limited rights in the control of their own property. From that time women in all the older states where restrictive laws existed worked for their repeal, and in New York petitions were circulated for a law to grant married women full control of their own wages, incomes, and property. One at a time other states followed the example of New York, and in 1860 the New York laws were amended to give women joint guardianship of children, the right to sue and be sued, the right to their own wages, incomes, and real and personal property.

In the matter of more liberal divorce legislation, women made some headway. Even the reformers were horrified at Mrs. Stanton's proposal in 1860 that drunkenness be considered due cause for divorce, and Phillips and Greeley refused to give her their support. But out in Indiana Robert Dale Owen came to her defense, writing letters to the *Tribune* in a published debate with Horace Greeley. As a member of the Indiana legislature, Owen pushed through a bill adding habitual drunkenness to the legal causes for divorce.

In the meantime, men were growing more used to the idea of women in the professions and made many concessions. Women were still a long way from equality there or in the matter of higher education, but the breach had been made and the battle had turned ever so slightly their way. In the matter of suffrage itself there were no gains, nor was success to be achieved for many years. Little could be done as long as the majority of men agreed with the author of an article in *Harper's New Monthly Magazine* in November 1853:

If nothing else, however, should give it [woman suffrage] consequence, it would demand our earnest attention from its intimate connection with all the radical and infidel movements of the day. A strange affinity seems to bind them all together. . . . the claim of woman's rights presents not only the common radical notion which underlies the whole class, but also a peculiar enormity of its own; in some respects more boldly infidel, or defiant both of nature and revelation, than that which characterizes any kindred measure. It is avowedly opposed to the most time-honoured propensities of social life; it is opposed to nature; it is opposed to revelation. . . . This unblushing female Socialism defies alike apostles and prophets. In this respect no kindred movement is so decidedly infidel, so rancorously and avowedly anti-biblical. . . . It is equally opposed to nature and the established order of society founded upon it.[27]

With such opinions accepted in the realm of the "benevolent empire," it was to be expected that in the South, where woman was romantically placed on a pedestal and treated with a sentimentality far removed from the arena of politics, there should be nothing but ridicule for the suffragist. The *Southern Literary Messenger* found welcome amusement in wartime in these verses reprinted from an English magazine:

Short-Skirt-Opathy

Take a pretty girl,
The prettier the better,
Give her naught to read
But novel and love-letter,
Let her go to plays,
Circuses and dances,
Fill her heart with love,
Murder and Romances.

Furnish her with beaux
Too numerous to mention,
Send her to attend
Each "Woman's Rights" Convention,
Humor her to death
When e'er she has the vapors,
Verses let her write
For magazines and papers.

Tell her of her charms
On every occasion,
Make her "talents" rare
The theme of conversation;
Let "affairs of state"
And politics be taught her —
And she'll wear "short skirts and pants,"
Or at least she "orter." [28]

When their most strenuous efforts met with such response, it was no wonder that success did not attend all action. In Mrs. Stanton's words, "no power could have met the prejudice and bigotry of that period more successfully than they did who so bravely and persistently fought and conquered." [29] Fully realizing the justice of their cause and aware of the strength of the forces pitted against them, the women of the early nineteenth century courageously did their share to establish institutions that should be in accord with the American democratic faith.

CHAPTER 17

Like a Fire-bell in the Night

With these words Jefferson expressed his alarm at the bitterness aroused by the question of admitting Missouri as a slave state. Never before had the clangor of that bell seemed so close or so ominous, but the aged statesman had heard it before when its note had merged with the triumphant peals of the Liberty Bell, which he had himself helped to set in motion. To men of the Age of Enlightenment slavery was both an anachronism and a denial of the natural rights they were so eagerly proclaiming. Every truth that Jefferson held to be self-evident was a repudiation of the right of man to hold his fellow human beings in bondage, and no one subscribing to the philosophy of the day could believe life to be tolerable without liberty or the pursuit of happiness possible without freedom. To many the Negro slave may have seemed not quite a man, not entitled to the rights and liberties for which his contemporaries of the white race were contending, but he did not lack defenders.

PRE-REVOLUTIONARY ANTISLAVERY SENTIMENT

Servile labor in America was as old as European settlement in the tidewater area. The lure of the New World drew great numbers of the discontented and dispossessed who were willing to pledge their labor for a period of years to get a start. Negro slaves were introduced to aid in the production of staples in demand abroad, and in New England conquered Indians were forced into servitude. Few voices were raised against any of these methods of increasing the labor supply; economic necessity provided sufficient justification for the exploitation of the unfortunate. An occasional member of some pietistic sect found in his interpretation of primitive Christianity some condemnation for slavery, but in general the hardworking early settlers were untroubled by man's inhumanity to man.

The Anglicans of the plantation colonies accepted slavery, and among the Puritans justification for it was found in the doctrine of election, in which there was no implication of the equality of all men. True, in 1700 Judge Samuel Sewall of Massachusetts published a pamphlet, *The Selling of Joseph, a Memorial,* which condemned the legal recognition of slaves as property, but Sewall was at once answered by John Saffin, a fellow jurist, who defended slavery on the ground that it was specifically sanctioned in both the Old and the New Testament. Later protagonists found their biblical arguments already drawn and illustrated with appropriate texts in this early eighteenth-century tract.

Upon the Quaker lay the burden of keeping alive some sort of argument against slavery. Four Quaker pamphleteers in particular carried the torch. Ralph Sandiford wrote in 1729 a *Brief Exposition of the Practice of the Times,* which was said to have been "packed with Brimstone." The pamphlet was published by Benjamin Franklin and presumably met with his approval. Benjamin Say was an early crusader who traveled throughout the colonies condemning in dramatic and vitriolic terms the institution he so obviously detested. His book, whose long title begins *All Slave Keepers that Keep the Innocent in Bondage, Apostates,* was printed by Franklin in 1737. Methodist revivalists of the next century might well have approved his histrionic talent, for Benjamin Rush thus described one of Say's tricks:

Benjamin Say to show his indignation against the practice of slave-keeping once carried a bladder filled with blood into a meeting; and, in the presence of the whole congregation, thrust a sword, which he had concealed under his coat, into the bladder, exclaiming at the same time, "Thus shall God shed the blood of those persons who enslave their fellow creatures." The terror of this extravagant and unexpected act produced swooning in several of the women of the congregation.[1]

Another Quaker, John Woolman, gentle advocate of all good causes, made the freedom of the slaves a major purpose of his life. His *Journal,* published in 1774, is a classic of humanitarian philosophy and bears witness to his hatred of slavery. In his essay entitled *Some Considerations on the Keeping of Negroes,* published in 1754, he wrote:

Man is born to labour, and experience abundantly sheweth that it is for our good: but where the powerful lay the burthen on the inferior without a Christian education and suitable opportunity of improving the mind, and in treatment which we, in their case, should approve, that they themselves may live at ease and fare sumptuously and lay up riches for their posterity, this . . . I doubt not is sometimes the effect of a perverted mind; for while the life of one is made grievous by the rigour of another it entails misery on both.[2]

With Anthony Benezet, the last of the four, the real crusade may be said to have begun, for Benezet demanded of his fellow Americans some positive action toward the suppression of slavery, and in the slight measure of success he achieved there was omen for the future. In the two decades before the Revolution Benezet published a half-dozen tracts condemning slavery and the slave trade and setting forth a program for emancipation, which he came to regard as a panacea for all the ills of humanity. He spoke first to the Friends, and at their yearly meeting in 1776 he finally won from them the sweeping declaration that members who refused to manumit their slaves should be expelled.

Benezet's longest work, a treatise entitled *Some Historical Account of Guinea*, published in 1772, had a great effect on John Wesley and all Methodism. Wesley's own tract, *Thoughts on Slavery*, was in large part plagiarized from Benezet's work. Together with Rush and Franklin, Benezet entered into long correspondence with European antislavery men, and it was at his request that Rush wrote in 1772 an *Address to the Inhabitants of the British Settlements on the Slavery of Negroes in America*, proposing a plan for levying a high duty upon slaves imported into America. Benezet's whole program included the prohibition of further importation, the freeing of all slaves after a definite term of servitude, and the transport of freedmen to some region beyond the Alleghenies. To him must be given a part, at least, of the credit for the law passed in Pennsylvania in 1780 providing for the gradual emancipation of all slaves in the state.

SLAVERY AND THE DOCTRINE OF NATURAL RIGHTS

As Americans became imbued with the ideas of the French philosophes the cause of the slave was joined with that of the colonist struggling for his natural rights. James Otis in 1762 sarcastically remarked that no government had a right to make hobby horses, asses, and slaves of its subjects, for nature had made enough of the first two "from the harmless peasant in the field to the most refined politician in the Cabinet; but none of the last, which infallibly proves they are unnecessary." And two years later he asserted the fundamental equality of all human beings, white and black, in a pamphlet, *The Rights of the British Colonies Asserted and Proved.*

Southern leaders, too, condemned slavery as a part of the tyranny of the day. Arthur Lee asserted in an essay in 1764 that the mere existence of the institution depraved freemen as well as slaves, for it was "shocking to humanity and abhorrent to the Christian religion." Jefferson included an antislavery clause in his instructions to the Virginia delegates to the Continental Congress, and it was an ill omen for the future that the Virginia Convention refused to approve his proposal — and also that a statement condemning George III for vetoing colonial antislavery acts, written by Jefferson into the first draft of the Declaration of Independence two years later, was struck out because of the objections of Southern members of the Congress. Benezet commented sadly upon the inconsistency of a Declaration that proclaimed the rights of man without condemning the enslavement of the Negro.

If these solemn truths [he said] uttered in such an awful crisis, are *self-evident*: unless we can show that the African race are not *men*, words can hardly express the amazement which naturally arises on reflecting that the very people who make these pompous declarations are slave holders, and, by their legislation, tell us, that these blessings were only meant to be the *rights of white men*, not of all *men;* and would seem to verify the observation of an eminent writer: "When men talk of liberty, they mean their own liberty, and seldom suffer their thoughts on that point to stray to their neighbors." [3]

Benezet's protest was matched by many others in numerous speeches both North and South. In 1785 Jefferson drew up an ordinance for the government of the territories of the United States which provided for the exclusion of slaves after the year 1800, and when this measure failed of passage by one vote, he and other antislavery men felt that a terrible calamity had befallen the country — a calamity not averted by the inclusion of an antislavery clause in the Ordinance of 1787, for that measure covered only the area north of the Ohio River.

State action, too, narrowed the area of slavery. Seven of the thirteen states made provision for emancipation between 1776 and 1804, three of them by postnati laws providing that all children born to slave mothers after a specified date were to be freed at certain ages stated in the law — usually twenty-five to twenty-eight years. Such measures relieved the state of responsibility for the support of children whose parents were slaves, while the masters were presumed to be recompensed for such care by the labor of the young Negroes.

In the same years Maryland, Delaware, and Virginia kept up a lively discussion of emancipation, although there were always enough conservative votes to reject any measure to that end. George Mason of Gunston Hall, master of three hundred slaves, wrote that slavery was a slow poison that undermined the morals of the slave-owners and provided lessons in political tyranny ominous for the future of the republic. "Taught to regard a part of our own Species in the most abject and contemptible Degree below us," he said, "we lose that Idea of the Dignity of Man, which the Hand of Nature had planted in us, for great and useful purposes." [4] Nevertheless, a measure for the gradual emancipation of slaves in Virginia, introduced by St. George Tucker in 1796, was refused consideration, and his antislavery pamphlet explaining the plan met the same fate with the reading public. As the century closed, Bishop Asbury sadly recorded in his diary that slavery would probably exist in Virginia for ages, for "there is not a sufficient sense of religion nor of liberty to destroy it; Methodists, Baptists, Presbyterians, in the highest flights of rapturous piety, still maintain and defend it." [5]

In Maryland the legislature voted down an antislavery measure sponsored by Charles Carroll and William Pinkney in 1789, but two famous antislavery pamphlets — George Buchanan's *Oration upon the Moral and Political Evil of Slavery* (1793), and John Parrish' *Remarks on the Slavery of the Black People* (1806) — were published in the state and had a wide sale. Out on the frontier the question of slavery arose in the debates on a constitution for the new state of Kentucky, and David Rice, the leader of Kentucky Presbyterians, lost a valiant fight for abolition. In the sister state of Tennessee there was no issue; the document that provided the consent of North Carolina for the creation of the new state stipulated that slavery be recognized in Tennessee.

In the lower South, where the black population was denser, few voices were raised in opposition to slavery. Indeed, there seems to have been a direct relation between the number of slaves in a state and its willingness to entertain antislavery measures. One Georgian frankly asserted that domestic slavery was "not a prudent subject of discussion in Georgia whether it be proper or improper," and another announced at the Constitutional Convention in Philadelphia in 1787 that slave importation was one of Georgia's "favorite prerogatives." The idea that slavery was repugnant to democratic ideas found few adherents in Georgia or South Carolina, where great economic interests were dependent upon slave labor. As Washington lamented, "It is not the public but the private interest which influences the generality of mankind; nor can Americans any longer boast an exception."

SLAVERY AND THE CONSTITUTION

Whether from indifference or from a realistic recognition of conditions as they were, the makers of the Constitution did not even debate the subject of domestic slavery. Without openly defending the institution, the slaveholding delegates made it very clear that control over slavery as it already existed was, to them, a matter for the exclusive jurisdiction of the states and that their economic necessities demanded a continuation of importations from Africa for a period of years. Both contentions were tacitly or explicitly granted in the Constitution. The only clauses concerning slaves already in the country were those providing for their enumeration for representation and taxation purposes and for the rendition of fugitives from one state to another, and on these questions there was relatively little debate. The issue of the African slave trade was settled by a compromise providing that the federal government would take no steps to close the trade for a twenty-year period, and the planting states were further placated by a provision prohibiting the levying of export taxes.

In the conventions ratifying the Constitution, especially in the lower South, there were open assertions of the positive merits of slavery and disapproval of any agreement to its limitation. A survey of the expressions of Southern opinion from the last years of the colonial period to the adoption of the Constitution makes it clear that the South as a whole never believed that abolition was expedient, feasible, or in any way desirable. The first attack upon slavery in the national Congress, therefore, would inevitably bring Southern representatives to its defense.

And that attack was not long delayed. In the first year of the first Congress petitions were presented from Quaker antislavery groups that requested immediate action on the matter of the slave trade. The petitions were received and discussed despite the protest of the Southern congressmen, who stated flatly what was to be the Southern position on such discussions until the Civil War ended both discussion and slavery. Slavery, they said, was a matter entirely reserved for state action; it was not a subject for congressional discussion; and, since Congress could not legislate, it was unconstitutional for Congress to consider petitions requesting legislation. From this they proceeded to a defense of the institution on historical and religious grounds. Later proponents of slavery added little except elaboration and illustration to the argument of Jackson of Georgia:

[If my opponent] is guided by that evidence upon which the Christian system is founded, he will find that religion is not against it. He will see, from Genesis to Revelation, the current setting strong that way. There never was a Government on the face of the earth, but what permitted slavery. The purest sons of freedom in the Grecian Republics, the citizens of Athens and Lacedaemon, all held slaves. On this principle the nations of Europe are associated; it is the basis of the feudal system.[6]

And in respect to Southern action if the government should move in opposition to the interests and constitutional rights of the South, the congressmen of 1790 were equally emphatic and prophetic. Tucker of South Carolina asked, "Do these men expect a general emancipation of slaves by law? This would never be submitted to by the South without a civil war."[7]

The result of the debate was inevitable: the African slave trade was not to be interfered with before 1808, nor did Congress have any authority over slavery in the states where it already existed. It was, perhaps, fortunate that the twenty-year abstention on the part of the national government came to an end before the expansion of cotton planting became of great significance. As it was, Southern interests in Congress in 1807 were strong enough to prevent heavy penalties in the statute ending the African slave trade, which went into effect in 1808. Gross violation of the act ended in 1820, when transatlantic slave trading was declared piracy, but smuggling continued to be a problem as the price of slaves rose and the cotton-producing area expanded.

"THE NEGLECTED PERIOD"

The years between 1808 and 1831 have generally been considered years of quiescence in the slavery controversy, years of indifference or of preoccupation with other things. It is equally true that those were years of economic and social change from which later antislavery and proslavery combatants drew their motives and their arguments, and that events in those years gave rise to expressions of opinion identical with those of significance in later years.

From 1808 to 1815 the country was primarily interested in foreign affairs, and slavery for the time was ignored or forgotten. With the coming of peace, however, sectionalism was soon again apparent. The Northeastern states slowly swung over to manufacturing, and the proceeds of merchant capitalism were invested in textile and other industrial establishments that cried for protective tariff legislation. Henry Clay became the father of the American System, by which the West was to be bound to the manufacturing areas through a community of interests in the production and marketing of raw and finished products, alike protected by the tariff. The South, devoted to cotton production by slave labor, saw little gain for itself in the nationalistic policies of tariffs, internal improvements, and more pervasive federal controls and became even more convinced of its agrarian destiny and of its dependence upon the supremacy of state governments.

Both the South and the West were characterized by the individualism of the frontier, but in the Southern states that individualism was intensified by a growing feeling of isolation and of peculiarity in institutions and needs. Slavery and the plantation system tended to prolong the frontier period in even the seaboard states of the South and to keep out immigration and new ideas. There could be in the Old South little of that communal life from which civic responsibility, reform movements, or moral crusades could spring. Although political leadership and policy-making were firmly in the hands of the few with wealth and position, yet there was little insurgency or resentment among the poorer whites, for they shared the common superiority to the Negro laborers and the social mobility of a frontier society.[8]

From the frontier came Southern braggadocio and sensitiveness to criticism, and also the inclination to violence and to the settlement of disputes by personal rather than legal action that resulted in the duel, the feud, and lynch law. Coupled with the frontier spirit was a tendency toward romanticism that colored all the Southerner's attitude toward the world about him. He saw both his community and the world outside as he wished to see them. The "Southern way of life" he so much emphasized was one in which freedom from labor was coupled with economic and social security that no one might challenge with impunity. This gave rise to a complacency and contentment that turned into violent protest when any phase of Southern life was attacked.

In its defense of slavery the South was running counter to the trend of the century. Democracy and liberalism, religious perfectionism and humanitarianism alike, condemned the institution in defense of which the South was forced to repudiate Jefferson, democratic theories, and its own conscience. As William F. Cash says in his *Mind of the South*, the South "in its secret heart always carried a powerful and uneasy sense of the essential rightness of the nineteenth century's position on slavery."[9] During the years before the passionate assault by William Lloyd Garrison and the abolitionist Northerners the defense mechanism of the South was being perfected and its isolation from the trends that were modifying Northern thinking was being established.

As early as 1813 John Taylor of Caroline began in *The Arator* a series of essays on slavery that showed the progress of Southern thinkers to complete justification of the institution. Taylor differed from his friend Jefferson and asserted that the case for emancipation did not rest upon fact. The slaves, he said, were members of a vicious, degraded, and morally inferior race, and their state was capable only of amelioration, not of progress toward freedom. Liberation would be of no value to the Negroes and a disaster for the whites. Diffused through the territories, the burden of slavery on the older states of the South might be lightened, but attack upon the institution could result in nothing but insurrections, murders, and oppression. The controversy over the admission of Missouri as a slave state led Taylor to warn the opponents of slavery:

There remains a right, anterior to every political power whatsoever, and alone, sufficient to put the subject of slavery at rest; the natural right of self-defence. Under this right, societies imprison and put to death. By this right, nations are justified in attacking other nations, which may league with their foes to do them an injury. And by this right, they are justified, if they see danger at a distance, to anticipate it by precautions. It is allowed on all hands, that danger to the slave-holding states lurks in their existing situation, however it has been produced; and it must be admitted, that the right of self-defence applies to that situation, of the necessity for which the parties exposed to the danger are the natural judges: Otherwise this right, the most sacred of all possessed by men, would be no right at all. I leave to the reader the application of these observations.[10]

THE MISSOURI COMPROMISE

When Tallmadge of New York, calling slavery the "monstrous scourge of the human race," proposed that it be prohibited by an amendment to the act admitting Missouri to the Union, he was answered by Southern representatives who sprang to the defense of Missouri with a states' rights and proslavery ideology already full grown. The acrimony of the Southern spokesmen was matched by that of Northern congressmen. Slavery from their point of view was incompatible with natural laws, with divine will, and with the Declaration of Independence. Not the Constitution but the prior pledge to democratic ideals was called upon, and the ultimate recourse of antislavery doctrine was shown to be a higher law than either the Declaration or the Constitution. The fundamental bases for Northern antislavery argument were thus laid by 1820, and upon that foundation abolition crusaders were to build for the next forty years.

The speech of Senator Rufus King of New York was the keystone of Northern argument. His speech was not recorded and must be reconstructed chiefly from the speeches and writings of those who endeavored to refute it, but its essence was an appeal to the laws of nature and of God for a denial of the right of "one man to make a slave of another."

Its effect upon Southerners was electric and immediate. Senator Walker of Alabama, writing a few hours after the speech, declared that "Missouri engulfs everything," and that a tempest had been raised that threatened the existence of the Union itself. King's "impudence astonishes me," wrote Walker. "Every man may draw the inference himself."[11] John Randolph of Roanoke spoke for three hours in an impassioned if somewhat confused defense of slavery.

Others emphasized the constitutional issue, denying the existence of any authority in Congress to legislate on the matter. The merits of a society based upon slavery were described by a group of positivists, while more moderate speakers stressed the value to both North and South of the diffusion of slavery. William Smith of South Carolina made the most militant proslavery speech, and William Pinkney of Maryland appeared as the eloquent defender of the principle of the equality of the states which was the basis of the federal compact.

Eventually Missouri was admitted without restriction — the balance between Northern and Southern states being maintained by the admission of Maine — but the Southern victory was limited by the recognition of the power of Congress to legislate in regard to slavery in the territories.

A few days after the vote on Missouri John Quincy Adams summarized a conversation with Calhoun in which the South Carolinian had expressed a fear of the dissolution of the Union because of the slavery controversy. The sturdy New Englander condemned Calhoun's assumption that manual labor must be performed by slaves, shrewdly, if perhaps unfairly, analyzing Southern thinking in the comment:

It is, in truth, all perverted sentiment — mistaking labor for slavery, and dominion for freedom. The discussion of this Missouri question has betrayed the secret of their souls. In the abstract they admit that slavery is an evil, they disclaim all participation in the introduction of it, and cast all upon the shoulders of our grandam Britain. But when probed to the quick upon it, they show at the bottom of their souls pride and vainglory in their condition of masterdom. They fancy themselves more generous and noble-hearted than the plain freemen who labor for subsistence. They look down upon the simplicity of a Yankee's manners, because he has no habits of overbearing like theirs and cannot treat negroes like dogs. It is among the evils of slavery that it taints the very sources of moral principle. It establishes false estimates of virtue and vice, for what can be more false and heartless than this doctrine which makes the first and holiest rights of humanity to depend upon the color of the skin.[12]

SOUTHERN THEORY FROM THE COMPROMISE TO GARRISON

The years following the Missouri debate were relatively quiet, but there is ample evidence in contemporary material of the hair-trigger temper of the South on the subject of slavery and of the growing antislavery sentiment of the North. Southern pamphleteers sought historical and religious precedents for slavery and began to advocate a caste society as the only true basis for higher civilization. The Greek ideal of a democracy of free men in a society based on slavery was substituted for democracy based on full equality.

Slavery [wrote one advocate] has ever been the stepping ladder by which countries have passed from barbarism to civilization. . . . the division of mankind into grades, and the mutual dependence and relations which result from them, constitutes the very soul of civilization; and the more numerous those grades are, in a country, the more highly civilized may we expect to find it.[13]

The theory that the Negro was of a lower race or order was popular in the South. In 1823 Dr. Thomas Cooper of South Carolina College, who had in earlier days been a champion of democracy, in an article on "Coloured Marriages" frankly said:

. . . people of colour are, in every part of the United States, considered, not merely by the populace, but by the law, as a permanently degraded people; not participating as by right, of the civil privileges belonging to every white man, but enjoying what civil privileges they possess as a right and a grant, as a matter of favour conceded by law, and revocable by law.[14]

Three years later Cooper published his *Essay on the Constitution of the United States and the Questions that Have Arisen under It*, in which he elaborated all the earlier biblical and historical arguments for slavery and asserted that the position of the Southern slave was superior to that of the poor of other regions.

Other pamphleteers accompanied their condemnation of antislavery agitation with threats of disunion. R. J. Turnbull of South Carolina, in commenting on the growth of the British movement for the abolition of slavery in the West Indies, asserted that even a few advocates of abolition in Congress would constitute a menace to the South. The West Indies were approaching ruin, he said, "And so will South Carolina assuredly be ruined, if at this day, there are twenty men in Congress, who are for emancipation, sudden or gradual, and the right of Congress to take *even a vote*, is not RESISTED as an ACT OF WAR, by South Carolina."[15]

This idea that slavery and prosperity were inseparable crops up in many proslavery treatises, and the short step from such a linking to acceptance of slavery as a positive good was made by several writers some years before Garrison had printed the first number of the *Liberator*. This demonstrates fairly conclusively that the full Southern defense of slavery was formulated before, rather than after, the attacks of the abolitionists. Both the complete states' rights theory of Calhoun's *South Carolina Exposition* and the "positive good" theory of the "peculiar institution" were well known among leaders of Southern thought by 1831, and the threat that war would be the result of the infringement of "Southern Rights" had been made before the birth of the American Anti-Slavery Society. The words of Governor Miller to the South Carolina legislature in 1829 are well worth scrutiny as the considered opinion of the executive of the state that was assuming the leadership in Southern thought:

Slavery is not a national evil; on the contrary, it is a national benefit. The agricultural wealth of the country is found in those states owning slaves, and a great portion of the revenue of the Government is derived from the products of slave labor — Slavery exists in some form everywhere, and it is not of much consequence in a philosophical point of view, whether it be voluntary or involuntary. In a political point of view, involuntary slavery has the advantage, since all who enjoy political liberty are then in fact free. Wealth gives no influence at the polls; it does where white men perform the menial services which slaves do here. *Upon this subject it does not become us to speak in a whisper, betray fear, or feign philanthropy.*[16]

Governor Miller the politician obviously saw the advantage of emphasizing the solidarity of the white race and of convincing the nonslaveholding voters of the South of the identity of their interests with those of the planters. The Southern press was quick to grasp the importance of this line of propaganda and was soon claiming as adherents to Miller's views a large majority of the people of the South. In the early 1830's the Charleston *Mercury* asserted that nineteen twentieths of the people of the lower South and "the great mass of the South" as a whole subscribed to the theory that slavery was of genuine benefit to civilization.

This theory was less evident in the border states, where free discussion and frank criticism of slavery continued until there was a reaction against the militant abolitionism of the next decade. It must be admitted, however, that this criticism had to be of border state origin and tactfully presented. At no time after 1820 was there tol-

eration for outside critics. Southern congressmen continued to
maintain that slavery was not a legitimate subject for legislative discussion, and they carefully observed their own taboo by avoiding
the subject until the flood of antislavery petitions began in the
1830's.

After 1820 there was a steady emigration of antislavery Southerners from their homes in slave states to new abodes in the North,
where they often became leaders in the attack on the institution
that caused their exile.[17] The Grimké sisters left Charleston before
1820 and became prominent in the reform movements of the North.
James G. Birney, an Alabama planter, freed his slaves and sought
refuge in Ohio. Levi Coffin, a North Carolina Quaker, found it wise
to transfer to Indiana his efforts to aid hapless Negroes attempting to find their way to sanctuary in the free states or in Canada.
Edward Coles of Virginia took his slaves to Illinois, emancipated
them, purchased land, and built cabins for them; he was later the
governor of that frontier state. By the middle 1820's there was almost no abolition voice in the lower South; those who opposed the
accepted mores had either submitted to the suppression of their beliefs or had left the region.

THE AMERICAN COLONIZATION SOCIETY

There were many slaveowners in the border states who would be
willing or anxious to free their slaves, provided they could be removed from the state in which they were freed. Taunted by the
lower South with the fact that slavery was no longer profitable in
the border states, such owners admitted their poverty but retorted
that their consciences had not been lulled by prosperity. At any
rate, they were willing to enter an organization that would make it
possible both to free and remove their slaves. After considerable
preliminary discussion, in which such prominent national leaders as
Daniel Webster, Theodore Frelinghuysen, John Marshall, James
Monroe, Henry Clay, and Roger Sherman participated, a convention assembled in Washington in January 1817 and organized the
American Colonization Society, with Judge Bushrod Washington
as its first president.

The objectives of the society were the emancipation of the slaves
of those who wished to free them and the transfer of such freedmen

and of other free Negroes to a region procured for them in Africa. The formation of the society was in many ways extremely significant. It was national in scope and represented a willingness on the part of its Northern members to share the guilt for the presence of Negro slaves and to accept part of the responsibility for their manumission. It was most popular in the border states, both free and slave, and never won much support in the lower South, even in the early years of its long history. Furthermore, both Northern and Southern members recognized the race problem and tacitly if not openly subscribed to the "degraded race" theory, which held that it was necessary to remove free Negroes from American society. Indeed, many Northern members were as eager to send the North's free Negroes to Liberia as to manumit the slaves of the South.

Within a few years the organization acquired all the characteristics and techniques of the usual voluntary association. It maintained agents, paid and voluntary, who organized branches, collected funds, and directed propaganda work. It published a newspaper, the *African Repository*, and sought eminent men to head the state societies and local auxiliaries. The normal income of the society came from dues, gifts, and legacies, but it occasionally obtained aid from state governments. National aid was solicited, but there was no congressional appropriation, although the government shared the responsibility for the selection of Liberia as a site for the colony and made some provision for the transport there of Negroes captured in prevention of the illegal slave trade.

Although the local auxiliaries at one time numbered more than two hundred, and although ministers all over the United States preached sermons and took collections in the society's behalf every July for many years, the society was never able to fulfill any considerable part of its expectations. Few Southerners who were willing to free their slaves could afford to pay for transporting them, and the sums contributed in the North were never sufficient to remove a large number of people. At its annual meeting in 1827 Henry Clay said the objective of the society was to send fifty-two thousand Negroes to Africa each year — slightly more than the natural increase of the American Negro population — and that the cost would be more than a million dollars annually with the use of sixty-five thousand tons of shipping. The income of the society never approached the figure Clay set; in 1830 it was about twenty-five thousand dollars, in the peak year of 1832 it was forty-three thousand, in 1838 it dropped to eleven thousand.

The rosy dream of a Negro utopia, which would at the same time block the slave trade at its source and spread the Gospel among the heathen people of all Africa, faded when both white agents and Negro settlers came to realize the long hard struggle that was ahead of them before they could obtain even a livelihood. It was difficult, therefore, to obtain Negroes who were willing to migrate and who would have the initiative, the ability, and the endurance to make successful colonists. Free Negroes in the United States found the prospect unattractive, and many home-loving slaves refused to accept freedom on such terms. In 1817 the free Negroes of Philadelphia drew up an address "to the humane and benevolent inhabitants of the city" stating:

We have no wish to separate from our present homes for any purpose whatever. Contented with our present situation and condition, we are not desirous of increasing their prosperity but by honest efforts, and by the use of those opportunities for their improvement, which the Constitution and the laws allow to all. It is, therefore, with painful solicitude and sorrowing regret, we have seen a plan for colonizing the free people of color of the United States on the coast of Africa.[18]

Between 1820 and 1830 eighteen vessels carried fourteen hundred blacks to Liberia, but most of these were free Negroes. By 1830, after great expenditure of money and effort, two hundred slaves had been freed and sent to Liberia; by 1860 the total had reached nearly four thousand. In the same period probably as many free blacks had been transported. Obviously, colonization offered little to the solution of the problem of three million slaves.[19]

As we have seen, the Colonization Society was from the beginning an attempt at the solution of the problem of the free Negro fully as much as an abolition movement. In neither the North nor the South was the free Negro granted equality politically or economically. He was "a third element in a system planned for two." Poverty, vagabondage, and crime were charged against him and discrimination was his lot everywhere. He was felt to belong to a degraded race, incapable of reaching the standards of American civilization and so not to be permitted participation on an equal basis in the life of the community in which he lived.

In the South the free Negro was considered the potential instigator of slave insurrections, the possible advocate of amalgamation, and a dangerous competitor in fields reserved for the superior race. Henry Clay, an officer of the Colonization Society, apparently forgot the brave words he had uttered twelve years before when he condemned those who wished to end all talk of ultimate emancipation:

They must blow out the moral lights around us, and extinguish that greatest torch of all which America presents to a benighted world, pointing the way to their rights, their liberties, and their happiness. And when they have achieved all these purposes, the work will yet be incomplete. They must penetrate the human soul and eradicate the light of reason, and the love of liberty. Then, and not until then, when universal darkness and despair prevail can you perpetuate slavery and repress all sympathies and all humane and benevolent efforts among freemen, in behalf of the unhappy portion of our race doomed to bondage.[20]

Now, faced with the problem of the free Negro, Clay turned his back on emancipation, saying:

In the slave states the alternative is, that white men must govern the black, or the black the white. In several of these states the number of slaves is greater than that of the white population. An immediate abolition of slavery in them, as these ultra-abolitionists propose, would be followed by a desperate struggle for immediate ascendancy of the black race over the white race, or rather it would be followed by instantaneous collisions between the two races, which would break out into a civil war that would end in the extermination or subjugation of the one race or the other.[21]

The visionary nature of their scheme was not at first apparent to the worthy clergymen who fathered the Colonization Society in the North. Interested in foreign missions, members of educational boards and of prison discipline societies, they felt that the removal of the free Negro would aid in the solution of many problems — would remove from the slums a population sunk in crime and poverty. The Reverend Leonard Bacon of New Haven, Connecticut, long an officer of the Colonization Society, said this very clearly in 1828:

Who are the free people of color in the United States, and what are they? In this city there are from eight hundred to a thousand. Of these a few families are honest, sober, industrious, pious, and in many points respectable. But what are the remainder? Everyone knows their condition to be a condition of deep and dreadful degradation; but few have ever formed any conception of the reality. The fact is that as a class they are branded with ignominy. They are surrounded by every temptation to vice. More than half the incentives to industry, to self-improvement, to frugality, to the common virtues of society, are never addressed to their minds.[22]

Many of Bacon's fellow citizens, however, equally interested in social problems, believed this problem should be met in America, not in Africa. What if the small number of Negroes in Pennsylvania did furnish half the prisoners in the penitentiary? What if the institutions of Connecticut were burdened with the care of Negro unfortunates? Education, secular and religious, could cure this social ill; educate both the Negro and the white man who denied him an equal chance in the world, and the problem of race could be solved in America, the home of the Negro as well as of the white man. These reformers came to feel that the position of the Negro minority was the acid test of American democracy.

In New Haven when Bacon was urging the Negro to go to Africa or to the Western frontier, the Reverend S. S. Jocelyn worked with the black population, teaching, preaching, raising money for schools, even planning a Negro college. In Philadelphia Isaac Hopper, a Quaker, was the overseer of a Negro school and the friend and legal adviser of any of the race who needed help in the local courts. Later, as an inspector of state prisons, he helped black convicts to find means of livelihood and opportunities for honest lives when they were freed from prison. Until his death in 1852 Hopper was known as the champion of the Northern Negro.

To such men as Jocelyn and Hopper the Colonization Society seemed both futile and unjust, and they won increasing support for their views. In 1835 the American Union for Religion and the Improvement of the Colored Race was formed with a program for religious and vocational instruction and for a careful study of all abolition questions. It is significant of the shifting of Northern sentiment that even the Reverend Mr. Bacon backed this new organization and shortly thereafter withdrew from the Colonization Society.

Southern colonizationists, too, became convinced that there was little hope in the movement. W. S. Jenkins says, in his *Pro-Slavery Thought in the Old South*, that the colonization scheme was never "enthusiastically accepted by a preponderance of slave holders," and that those in the society who honestly advocated emancipation were few. Charles Cotesworth Pinckney of South Carolina called the whole project cruel and absurd, and the Charleston *Mercury* stated that the society was "reprobated in the South, and justly stigmatized as murderous in its principles." James G. Birney, an agent for the Colonization Society in the lower South in 1832–33, soon despaired of any concerted action in the slave states toward emancipation. In a letter to R. R. Gurley, the secretary of the Colonization Society, Birney wrote: "Sometimes I fear that the South will do nothing until it is too late, as it will be ten years from this." [23] That same year Birney emancipated his own slaves and moved to Kentucky, where he hoped to publish a newspaper that would lead to emancipation by state action. When he found public opinion there unfavorable even to the establishment of his enterprise, he finally realized the futility of antislavery effort in the South and moved over into Ohio to edit a paper advocating immediate emancipation.

THE GROWTH OF ABOLITIONISM TO 1831

In the years after 1815 an abolition press sprang up both in the North and in the border states. From that period until the Civil War the abolitionists never lacked papers in which to air their views, and the influence of such publications was far in excess of their circulation, for countless newspapers, both North and South, reprinted their articles and editorials. Among the first of the frankly abolition newspapers was the *Philanthropist*, published in Ohio by Charles Osborn, a self-exiled Southern Quaker, from 1817 to 1819. In the latter year Osborn moved to Jonesboro, Tennessee, and began the publication of the *Manumission Intelligencer*. In 1820 Elihu Embree, another Quaker, established the *Emancipator* in Jonesboro and continued its publication until his death a few years later. The *Abolition Intelligencer* was the organ of John Finley Crow of Shelbyville, Kentucky, in the early 1820's, and William Swaim published the Greensboro *Patriot* in North Carolina in the same period. Although the circulation of these border state publications was small, they were evidence of the toleration in this region in the 1820's for antislavery sentiments.

One of the most significant of the antislavery papers was the *Genius of Universal Emancipation*, edited by Benjamin Lundy and founded in Ohio in 1821. Lundy, too, was of Quaker descent. He had assisted Osborn with the *Philanthropist* for a time and had decided to devote himself to the cause of abolition and to publish a paper of his own. During the next fifteen years the *Genius* was published wherever its itinerant editor happened to be and whenever his other activities permitted.

In 1825 Lundy took to Haiti eleven Negroes emancipated and confided to his care by their owners, and there he established them on land obtained from the Haitian government. He was the agent later in the transportation to the same island republic of more than two hundred freedmen from Virginia and North Carolina. His travels were extensive, and his contacts with the friends of abolition were numerous. He visited Boston in the 1820's and commented sadly that he "could hear of no abolitionists resident in that place." Lundy's willingness to settle freedmen outside the borders of the United States led him to Canada and three times to Texas. Everywhere he sought Negroes for his colonization projects and endeavored to unite men of all opinions in the common cause of doing something concrete for freedom.

In 1828 Lundy obtained the aid of a young New Englander, William Lloyd Garrison, who acted as assistant editor of the *Genius* in Baltimore. Garrison's advocacy of immediate and uncompensated emancipation and his vigor in denouncing the domestic slave trade led to his being fined and jailed when a libel suit was brought against him by the owner of a vessel that had transported slaves to New Orleans. This disaster caused the *Genius* to suspend publication and sent Garrison, upon his release, back to Boston to begin his publication of the famous *Liberator*. Lundy went traveling again, returning in the early 1830's to publish his *Genius* in Philadelphia and later in Illinois, where he died in 1839.

Lundy's courage and devotion were characteristic of the early abolitionists, and his lack of fanaticism and yet unwillingness to compromise were shown in all his writings — notably in this reply to a friend who urged him to use milder language:

Every man is entitled to his own opinion, on this as well as on other subjects, but I have always thought that Truth is, or ought to be, so popular, and withal so beautiful, that it stands in no need of decoration. In other words, I have never thought it worthwhile to study to please the advocates of oppression, nor yet those who are so wilfully blind that they cannot see, with the light around them, that it is their duty to exert themselves for the abolition of slavery.[24]

Lundy's lack of equivocation was on principle. On method he was indifferent; emancipation immediate or gradual, the absorption of freedmen into American society or their voluntary colonization overseas, or in Texas or Canada—such matters were of no consequence. The seven-point program announced in the early issues of the *Genius of Universal Emancipation* was eminently practical and yet comprehensive: the national government was to abolish slavery wherever it had sole authority, no new slave states were to be admitted to the Union, the internal slave trade was to be abolished, and the three-fifths compromise of the Constitution was to be repealed. In the free states blacks were to have the same legal status as whites, aid for colonization was to be provided for all who wished to migrate, and gradual emancipation and the repeal of the black codes were to be urged on the slave states.

As abolition societies were formed these seven principles were adopted in whole or in part, and they became familiar to the reading public North and South. The number of such societies is difficult to ascertain. Lundy himself listed more than a hundred and thought there might have been a hundred and fifty. Their work included propaganda, public addresses, petitions to legislatures, the care of free Negroes, investigation of charges of cruelty, protection from kidnaping and illegal sale, Negro schools and Sunday schools, care of the destitute, aid to fugitives, and promotion of the use of plantation products produced by free rather than slave labor.

This last item was a favorite project of Lundy and other Quakers. Levi Coffin of Indiana made many trips south to arrange for the shipping of "free cotton" and later, in Cincinnati, was the manager of an enterprise supported by abolitionists which both manufactured and sold "free" products. The idea was not new. There is frequent mention in Kittredge's *The Old Farmer and His Almanack* of the effort in the first decades of the nineteenth century to develop the New England maple sugar industry in order that sugar produced by slave labor need not be used. "Make your own sugar," went an item in 1805, "and send not to the Indies for it. Feast not on the toil, pain and misery of the wretched." Benjamin Rush seems to have believed that New England could produce maple sugar for export and thus cause the enfranchisement of the slaves of the ruined West Indian cane growers.

Between 1794 and 1829 the abolition societies held twenty-four conventions, usually in Philadelphia. These conventions published reports, made plans for the education of Negroes, drew up petitions for the abolition of slavery in the District of Columbia, and called constant attention to the equality clauses of the Declaration of Independence.

The period from 1808 to 1831 may have been "neglected," but it was certainly not one of stagnation. Interest in abolition was constant, and the effort at cooperation with liberal sentiment in the South was sincere. But for the numerous small abolition groups as for the American Colonization Society there was no significant success. In the latter part of the period Southern abolition societies lost members steadily, and within a decade there were few such organizations active in the South.

DAVID WALKER, THE LIBERATOR, AND NAT TURNER

There lived in Boston a seller of secondhand clothes whose name was David Walker. He had been born in North Carolina in 1785, born free because his mother was a free Negress, and he had found his way North, reaching Boston by 1828. A year later he published at his own expense for distribution among colored people, free and slave, a pamphlet which he called *Walker's Appeal in Four Articles, Together with a Preamble to the Colored Citizens of the World, But in Particular and Very Expressly to Those of the United States.* The pamphlet was incendiary in nature; designedly so, for Walker's solution of the problem of the Negro was insurrection and violence. The articles were expositions of the four causes for the wretchedness of the colored race: slavery, ignorance, religious teaching, and the colonization scheme. Walker sent fifty copies of his *Appeal* to Savannah alone, and free Negroes in other Southern states were known to have copies, although it is doubtful whether it was read by or to the slaves.

Reaction in the South was immediate. The mayor of Savannah wrote to Mayor Harrison Gray Otis of Boston demanding the arrest and punishment of Walker, only to receive an answer that seemed incomprehensible in the South, that Walker had violated no state or national law and could not be interfered with in Massachusetts. The Southern states then endeavored by their own legislation to insulate their slaves from the contamination of such noxious pamphlets. In Georgia a law was passed to place in quarantine Negro sailors on boats coming into Georgia harbors, in order to prevent their having shore leave. If such sailors should be landed for any reason, they were to be put in jail for the duration of the ship's stay in port. In Georgia and elsewhere heavy penalties were provided for the circulation of publications inciting slaves to rebellion. It was made illegal to teach a slave to read; Negroes were not permitted to travel without a white escort, nor could they assemble in large groups unless a white person was present; and roads were patroled to prevent the nocturnal prowlings of blacks unprovided with papers of manumission or written permissions from their owners.

In January 1831 William Lloyd Garrison began the publication of the *Liberator*, announcing in its first issue that he expected to follow the same radical and outspoken policy that had caused his arrest in Baltimore. If Walker's pamphlet had seemed incendiary to the South, the first issue of the *Liberator* was a summons to every agency of self-defense, for it was the cry of the outraged conscience of the white North, and with its passionate assertion there could be no compromise. Unreasoning and unreasonable in its demands, unguarded and unequivocal in its accusations, the *Liberator* broke up the "conspiracy of silence" with which the institution of slavery had been protected. In true American fashion, Garrison invoked the Declaration of Independence and claimed that to the Negro as well as to the white man belonged "life, liberty and the pursuit of happiness." Immediate and unconditional abolition was the burden of his cry —

I *will be* as harsh as truth, and as uncompromising as justice. On this subject, I do not wish to think, to speak, or write, with moderation. . . . I am in earnest — I will not equivocate — I will not excuse — I will not retreat a single inch — AND I WILL BE HEARD.

And the poet, never far below the surface in Garrison, led him to close this first editorial with one of his own verses, ending,

> I swear, while life-blood warms my throbbing veins,
> Still to oppose and thwart, with heart and hand,
> Thy brutalizing sway — till Afric's chains
> Are burst, and Freedom rules the rescued land —
> Trampling Oppression and his iron rod:
> *Such is the vow I take* — SO HELP ME GOD! [25]

The *Liberator* was not widely read in the North, nor did Garrison's position win many supporters there. In its first year it had fifty white subscribers and two years later only four hundred. It was widely read and supported, however, by the free Negroes of the North. It is a rather amusing commentary on the state of opinion of the day that the *Liberator* was made famous by its Southern enemies rather than by Northern adherence to its doctrines. Mailed to the editors of more than a hundred periodicals, it aroused furious comment — coupled with a reprinting of its most radical statements — in the editorial columns of every important Southern paper. Indeed, the educated Southern Negro stood in far greater danger of acquiring noxious ideas from the local press than from the few copies of the *Liberator* circulating in the South.

Whether or not the Southern editors believed Garrison's views were representative of Northern opinion, they did all in their power to arouse the agencies of Southern defense — and to stir a quiescent enemy. Northern editors, who had refused to be moved by Garrison's pleas, began to take notice of the Southern agitation and slowly swung to the defense of the abolitionist's right to be heard. Southern hysteria, out of all proportion to the original cause, expressed itself in the indictment of the absent Garrison by Southern grand juries, in demands for his imprisonment and the suppression of his paper by Southern legislatures and governors, and in additions to the black codes still further restricting the activities of Negroes, free and slave. Garrison became a name of opprobrium, and his doctrines — often misrepresented and misquoted — became symbols of aggression. To the Southerner every antislavery man was a Garrisonian abolitionist. Oversimplification of the nature of the opposition led to a complete and categorical denial of the right to question the Southern position.

By unfortunate coincidence, Southern feeling about the *Liberator* was intensified by a serious uprising among the slaves. Slave insurrections had long been the horror of the South, the dread reason for much Southern defensiveness and emphasis on the race inferiority theory. Twice already in the nineteenth century there had been insurrections of dangerous character. In 1800 the slave Gabriel had led some Virginia Negroes in an uprising that had alarmed all slaveholders. The cherished Southern fiction that the slaves of kind masters did not desire their freedom was dramatically denied in the words of one of the rebels on trial for his life:

I have nothing more to offer than what General Washington would have had to offer, had he been taken by the British officers and put to trial by them. I have ventured my life in endeavouring to obtain the liberty of my countrymen, and am a willing sacrifice to their cause; and I beg as a favour that I may be immediately led to execution. I know that you have pre-determined to shed my blood, why then all this mockery of a trial? [26]

And a generation later, in Charleston, the free Negro, Denmark Vesey, led several thousand of his race in a conspiracy, the betrayal of which brought the arrest of more than a hundred Negroes and the execution of thirty-five.

These were the two major insurrections among many of lesser scope. Over such positive denials of the contentment of the Southern Negro the proponents of slavery threw a mantle of silence and suppression. Slaves must not know of the near success of such attempts, nor must foreigners and Northerners learn of the vulnerability of the Southern position. But the men and women of the South realized their insecurity, and the possibility of insurrection was a nightmare.

Then in August 1831 occurred an insurrection among the slaves of Virginia led by Nat Turner, a mystical, deeply religious man who saw visions and heard voices urging him to action. For two or three days Turner and a handful of followers terrorized the whole of Southampton County and killed more than sixty white men, women, and children. The uprising was planless and had no possible chance of success; quiet was soon restored, and some seventeen slaves and three free Negroes were hanged and twelve were transported. But there was terror throughout the South, for no one could determine whether the Virginia affair was a single sporadic occurrence or part of a well-laid and general plot.

Whether or not the writings of Walker and Garrison contributed to the Nat Turner insurrection, the alarmed South believed they had — or at least that their teachings, if known, would lead to similar uprisings. Walker's *Appeal*, the *Liberator*, and the insurrection were listed as causes for the severity of the additions to the slave codes and for the suppression of antislavery sentiment. The whole matter came up for review in the Virginia legislature in 1831–32, as the members of both houses discussed the whole question of slavery in one of the last great debates on that institution in the pre-Civil War South. The debate was especially significant in that it brought to the defense of slavery a powerful new voice, that of Professor Thomas R. Dew of the College of William and Mary. Dew's work brought out little that was new in Southern theory, but it reinforced and restated ideas that were soon to govern the action and control the thinking of those who spoke for the South.[27]

The Virginia legislature made provision for the protection of slavery after 1832, as did those of the other Southern states. In 1836 Maryland made it a "high offense for a person to write or circulate any publication having a tendency to create discontent among, and stir up to insurrection, the people of color of the state," and provided a prison term of ten to twenty years for any violation of the statute. In 1842 the law was amended to make it a felony for a free Negro to receive abolition newspapers through any post office in the state. Savage penalties were attached to the laws prohibiting the circulation of antislavery literature in the lower South; and the climax was reached when South Carolina made it a crime to subscribe to or receive newspapers, books, or pamphlets "calculated to disaffect any slave or slaves in this state," and when Arkansas prescribed terms in the penitentiary for those who dared to maintain that owners had not the right of property in their slaves.

Then the barrier seemed impenetrable, and the South appeared to have achieved complete success in insulating itself against that progress toward perfection which was so dear to the evangelical faith of the Northern reformers. When the South advanced from this defensive position to demand that the Northern states also limit the expression of opinion, that Congress deny itself the right of discussion, and that all Northern authorities cooperate in the protection of slavery, conflict seemed, if not inevitable, at least "irrepressible."

ANTISLAVERY DOCTRINE AS A PHASE OF THE AMERICAN FAITH

When the third decade of the century opened, the antislavery movement had become an integral part of the larger humanitarian movement that was sweeping through the North. The condition of the free Negro in their midst, the plight of the fugitive slave, and the degradation of the slave in the South were all matters of concern to countless men and women who were filled with the spirit of the time. The humanitarian was preacher as well as social worker, dogmatist as well as pragmatist, and concerned with his own soul's salvation as well as with the well-being of his fellows. Slavery was a sin; from that original premise, progress to the doctrine that this sin must rest upon the consciences of all true Christians was inevitable.

At the same time these religious humanitarians were democrats with a deep conviction of the worth of the individual and of the equality of all men. There could be no greater violation of democracy than the institution of human slavery, no greater degradation for the individual than the auction block. Slavery was a denial, too, of the most elementary human rights, and in defense of slavery the South had attacked the safeguards that had been placed in the Constitution and in every Revolutionary bill of rights to protect the civil liberties which alone could guarantee the democratic way of life. Freedom of discussion was the lifeblood of democracy, and the denial of that freedom in respect to slavery was regarded as an attack upon liberties too vital to be surrendered without a struggle. Slavery thus became a menace to the white citizen and to the non-slavery North as well as to the South.

The abolitionist, when he showed any interest in the economic welfare of the Negro, contented himself with trying to establish his black protégé in a position where he might earn his livelihood and with protecting him from too obvious exploitation. It was not until late in the pre-Civil War period, and then but dimly, that the white laborers of the North began to see that Negro slavery and wage-slavery had something in common and that freeing the Negro would be of significance in the cause of labor. Lincoln seems to have had some idea of this when he wrote in 1863, "The strongest bond of human sympathy, outside the family relation, should be one uniting of all working people, of all nations, and tongues, and kindred"; and yet Lincoln even then was working for the colonization of the freedmen outside the United States. The problem has been directly stated by the Negro historian, Du Bois:

The true significance of slavery in the United States to the whole social development of America lay in the ultimate relation of slaves to democracy. What were to be the limits of democratic control in the United States? If all labor, black as well as white, became free — were given schools and the right to vote — what control could or should be set to the power and action of these laborers? Was the rule of the mass of Americans to be unlimited, and the right to rule extended to all men regardless of race and color, or if not, what power of dictatorship and control; and how would property and privilege be protected? [28]

For much of the period before the Civil War, however, Northern laborers resented black competition, and Western farmers were determined that the territories should be closed to slavery. "Free Soil" meant to them the absence of the Negro farmer and farm laborer.

From whatever sources the antislavery movement came, it was heavily tinged with the Puritan's somewhat sanctimonious concern with the conduct of others. The "holier than thou" attitude of the abolitionist, who insisted that slavery was a sin and the slaveowner a sinner of the deepest dye, was irritating to say the least. The composite picture of the slaveowner to be drawn from the "revelations" of the abolition tracts was that of a cruel and ruthless man, wielding the lash over helpless slaves, indulging his basest passions at the expense of the virtue of his female slaves, and selling his own offspring for profit. The injustice of the portrait and its effect in increasing the antagonism of the South did not deter the grim Puritans who drew it.

Fortunately not all the antislavery crusaders were of that kind. Revivalists coupled a practical interest in social betterment with their concern over the souls of their flocks. Charles G. Finney, greatest of the preachers of the Great Revival, declared that his converts "should set out with determination to aim at being useful in the highest degree possible." [29] It is as difficult to depict a typical abolitionist as it is to picture a typical slaveowner.

THE ORGANIZATION OF THE ANTISLAVERY MOVEMENT

When Garrison was sending out his cry for immediate abolition in the first issues of the *Liberator*, the most promising field for the development of an antislavery crusade was not New England but the Middle West, the region that had furnished the strength of the Great Revival.

The story of the beginnings of the crusade in the West is a romantic tale. The Reverend George Gale converted Charles Finney and started him on his career of revivals and social reforms. Gale then founded Oneida Institute and later Knox College, hotbeds for the antislavery movement, in which many of Finney's converts became interested. Theodore Dwight Weld, a mature, energetic, able student of Hamilton College, was converted by Finney and, choosing the ministry as a career, sought training in Lane Theological Seminary in Cincinnati, a new institution over which Lyman Beecher had just been installed. Weld was the friend and protégé of Charles Stuart, a saintly English abolitionist, and was soon an ardent reformer himself. He and some thirty or forty of Finney's other converts were joined in Cincinnati by a group of young Southerners whose knowledge of slavery was firsthand and who were willing to work with Weld in improving the lot of the colored population of the town. But the activities of these young men in behalf of the Negroes, and especially their ideas of social equality, involved them in trouble with the Lane authorities. Their antislavery society was broken up; their lyceum, schools, and lectures for the Negroes were banned; and President Beecher felt compelled to back the trustees lest the struggling institution lose all public support. The major part of the Lane student body — made up largely of zealous reformers and recent converts, many of them older men — left the institution and began negotiation for transfer to some more hospitable roof.

At this juncture Finney's connection with a group of wealthy New York philanthropists stood his converts in good stead; funds were provided by the Tappan brothers and their associates to establish a theological school in connection with Oberlin College as a refuge for the Lane seceders and such members of the Lane faculty and trustees as had left with them. Oberlin was already a manual labor college and coeducational; it now agreed to admit Negro students and become the center of Western abolitionism. The faculty of near-by Western Reserve College was antislavery also, and Elizur Wright, Jr., and Beriah Green were connected with the antislavery society organized there. From this Western group, whose zeal had been increased and given direction by opposition, came the leaders and agents for the American Anti-Slavery Society, which had been formed two years before the Lane schism.[30]

Garrison's efforts in Boston during 1831 resulted in the formation of the New England Anti-Slavery Society, which he was to dominate throughout his career. Starting with a little group of fifteen, he won their adherence to his doctrine of immediatism and their support for the *Liberator*. This New England group was always radical and vociferous.

In New York the group of philanthropists to which the Tappans belonged formed a committee in 1831 to consider the organization of a national antislavery society, but the violent opposition that greeted Jocelyn's plan for a Negro school in New Haven and the general disapproval of Garrisonian ideas caused the committee to recommend postponement of the project. A central bureau was established in New York, however, with Elizur Wright from Western Reserve in charge, and a newspaper, the *Emancipator*, was founded. This committee adopted the British and Garrisonian slogan of immediate abolition but qualified it for practical purposes by stating that any abolition measure could be called immediate if even the slightest beginning was "immediately prosecuted." The bureau sent out agents to make estimates of the state of public opinion, published antislavery pamphlets, and investigated the attitude of the Colonization Society on emancipation. It was felt that further organization might await the long expected news of British emancipation of West Indian slaves. With such encouragement American opinion might advance sufficiently to make successful organization possible. But the Tappans and others of the New York group grew impatient, and, despite the warning from other antislavery organizations that the American public was not ready to support a national society, they determined to go ahead with plans for a national convention. When news came in 1833 of the passage of the British emancipation law, the New York committee was ready to issue a call for action on a national scale.

In the meantime Garrison had collected funds from his Negro

supporters for a trip to England, the ostensible purpose of which was to solicit money for a Negro school. In England in the summer of 1833 he was the man of the hour, appearing as the representative of a great American movement that was about to follow in the footsteps of the British society. He attacked the colonization movement and pledged American efforts to immediatism. After an experience that must have been thoroughly satisfying to a young man who had had few of the delights of public approval, he came home to urge the immediate formation of a national society to fulfill his grandiose promises.

Under these divided auspices the American Anti-Slavery Society was formed in a convention in Philadelphia in December 1833, and under divided control it operated for the seven years of its troubled existence. It inherited the public dislike of Garrison and the charge of incendiarism that had made Garrison's name opprobrious in the South. "Garrisonianism" meant radicalism, lack of practical planning, and the advocacy of everything ultra in the way of reform. Arthur Tappan, the president selected for the new society, shared Garrison's reputation for ultraism because of his approval of the New Haven Negro College plan and his extreme views on Sabbath observance and other moral issues; but his wealth and generosity made his leadership necessary and inevitable.

The society grew slowly. Its organization was similar to that of the other voluntary societies — national, state, and local units, humanitarian and philanthropic figures as officers, and innumerable devoted agents as field workers, a few paid, the others giving voluntary service. There were at the height of the movement about two thousand societies with two hundred thousand members. Relatively few of the nation's prominent men belonged to the organization, and it never drew in a majority of those who opposed slavery. When John Quincy Adams wrote, "The public mind in my own district and state is convulsed between the slavery and abolition questions, and I walk on the edge of a precipice in every step I take," he was contemplating much more than the activities of the Anti-Slavery Society.

NORTHERN RECEPTION OF ANTISLAVERY AGITATION

Devoted to a constant agitation of the question of slavery in all its aspects, the abolitionists did not, perhaps, need any consistent policy. Garrison and the New England society supported the *Liberator* and continued to revile slaveowners as sinners and the Constitution that protected slavery as a compact with the devil. The New York group carried on a broad publicity program of a much less radical nature. It published four periodicals, one appearing each week of the month: *Human Rights*, the *Anti-Slavery Record*, the *Emancipator*, and the *Slave's Friend*. Tracts of many varieties and authors had a wide distribution, also, and many agents were sent throughout the country to lecture, organize societies, and collect funds for propaganda. The backbone of this part of the work was the Weld-Finney group in the West. Inspired by revivalistic zeal, thoroughly conversant with the problem through connections across the Ohio, these graduates of Oberlin and other antislavery colleges plunged into the work and were responsible for much of whatever measure of success was achieved. They were the link between the new movement and the "benevolent empire" — temperance, peace, and educational reformers and others of like character. Weld was their guide and leader; Birney joined the brigade while still living in Kentucky; Elizur Wright, William Goodell, Beriah Green, and Charles Stuart worked constantly; and in the East they drew support from Gerrit Smith, the Tappans, William Jay, and the Boston reformers, whose benevolent interest was extended to them as well as to Garrison.

The New England poet, John Greenleaf Whittier, had early been won over by Garrison's passionate plea, "The cause is worthy of Gabriel — Yea, the God of Hosts places himself at its head. Whittier, enlist! — Your talent, zeal, influences — all are needed." [31] And Whittier responded by attending the convention that initiated the national society and by the publication of an abolition pamphlet, *Justice and Expediency*, which had a wide circulation. Whittier believed that "the burning, withering concentration of public opinion on the slave system is alone needed for its total annihilation," and his pen was never still in his effort to achieve that end.

Lydia Maria Child wrote in 1833 *An Appeal in Favor of That Class of Americans Called Africans*, a tract that added to the usual description of the horrors of slavery a moving appeal for education and decent treatment for free blacks. It is interesting as one of the earliest protests against race prejudice. The author pleaded,

It merely requires an earnest wish to overcome a prejudice which was "grown with our growth and strengthened with our strength," but which is in fact opposed to the spirit of our religion and contrary to the instinctive good feelings of our nature. When examined in the clear light of reason, it disappears. Prejudices of all kinds have their strongest holds in the minds of the vulgar and the ignorant. In a community as enlightened as our own, they must gradually melt away under the influence of public discussion.[32]

Some pronouncement on slavery by William Ellery Channing had been long awaited by those who revered him, and its preparation caused the author much thought and distress. Channing loved the South, but with all his deeply religious nature he condemned slavery as degrading to both races. Yet, frightened by the bitterness aroused in his own Boston, he was slow to come out into open support of the antislavery movement. He was no fanatic and no immediatist, and his *Slavery*, published in 1835, was not of much satisfaction to the extremists, even though he denied the right to hold property in men, asserted that there was a "higher law, even Virtue, Rectitude, the Voice of Conscience, the Will of God," and declared:

An institution so founded in wrong, so imbued with injustice, cannot be made a good. It cannot, like other institutions, be perpetuated by being improved. To improve it, is to prepare the way for its subversion. Every melioration of the slave's lot is a step toward freedom. Slavery is thus radically, essentially evil.[33]

The essay ended with a section on the abolitionists in which Channing commended them for many things and defended their right to be heard, but condemned their fanaticism, their exaggeration, and their determination to see only one side to the question. He disapproved immediatism and all mob action and pleaded for toleration, for religion, and for union.

In 1839 Theodore Weld made an important contribution to abolition literature in the effective tract, *Slavery as It Is*, compiled largely from Southern newspapers. It contained numerous examples of the cruelty and physical hardships suffered by slaves. Each instance was claimed to be authentic, but there was no pretense that they were typical, nor was there any desire to be fair or impartial. These examples of oppression were accompanied by the personal narratives of abolitionists who had had firsthand acquaintance with slavery. Weld's tract was detested in the South as thoroughly as were the later *Uncle Tom's Cabin* and Helper's *Impending Crisis*.

William Jay, that son of the first Chief Justice who was so concerned with the peace crusade, became a steadfast supporter of the New York society and wrote many essays on slavery. In his *Slavery in America, an Inquiry* he offered elaborate proof that the supporters of colonization had no real desire to see the end of slavery and were chiefly concerned with removing free blacks from the country. The American Anti-Slavery Society was therefore necessary —

When we are asked, what are you doing? Why make a social and political earthquake? Do you wish to ruin the country? we answer, not so. *We* are not making a crisis; *we* are only trying to prevent a catastrophe. A state of things is in progress that must be foreseen, and met with an adequate remedy. The national body is too sick to be cured by quackery: but you will not let us examine it, or talk about it, or discuss the way of cure, or tell the fact of internal alteration. You wish things to take their course; and this is your way, your peace, and your wisdom! As well may impenitence get to heaven by following the *course of this world*, as such a system speed, but certain it is that the malady will be examined and the remedy applied; for God is in it! The cause is His own! [34]

All these pamphlets made relatively little impression on Northern opinion. Their readers were, in large part, men and women already predisposed toward abolition. Revivalistic lectures were far more effective in winning converts to the cause. In one of his reports Theodore Weld described his methods and explained his success as an antislavery agent. He usually lectured at least six times in a town, he said, sometimes as many as thirty times, and made it his object "to inform, indoctrinate, and arm at all points." He did not attempt to organize a society until his principles were fully understood and the community was ready to accept them. He wanted "hearts and heads and tongues — for faith and works," and told his listeners, "If your hearts ache and bleed we want you, you will help us; but if you merely adopt our principles as dry theories, do let us alone, we have millstones enough swinging at our necks already." He presented slavery as a moral issue and found little reason for describing its cruelties or for reviling slaveholders. Political action was not for him; it was the Lord's harvest for which he labored. [35]

In 1836 the number of lecturers for the national society was increased to seventy, to be chosen and instructed by Weld, Whittier, and Henry Stanton, a Finney convert and Lane rebel. The recruits came from the ministry, the theological seminaries, and the colleges, many of them from the Middle West. Warm-hearted, high-spirited youths found satisfaction for both their consciences and their love of adventure in serving as agents or as conductors of the Underground Railroad. Young preachers were as comforted by the thoughts of slaves rescued from their pursuers as by contemplation of souls saved in revivals. Indeed, every convert to religion might be made a worker in the cause. Their spirit was expressed by one of the Oberlin men:

I have walked in a new world. My path has turned with delight. Every foot-tread has touched some spring and revealed fresh treasures of happiness. Life has been *rapture*. I have scarcely felt *trouble;* when it *has* come, it has fallen upon me like the tender snow-flake — so gently. If God should now give me a thorn in the flesh, surely I should not murmur.[36]

The year 1836 marked the height of the success that came from this linking of abolition with the Great Revival. In the next year there was a decline. The panic reduced the funds available for the work; economic unrest caused a lessening of popular interest; and the burden of the extensive program got too heavy even for the tireless leaders. The central office in New York was reorganized with Birney at its head, Weld spent more time in New York, and more attention was devoted to building up the societies already established than to missionary enterprise.

The organization of the national society became decentralized and more difficult to manage. The New England society had always been composed of independent abolitionists, led by Garrison but intent upon self-expression; and Garrison with some of his followers was by this time engaged in supporting nonresistance — a strange bedfellow for their verbal violence — women's rights, and other reforms. He was also bitterly opposed to participation in politics and even repudiated the Constitution and all institutions dependent on it. But in the New York office Birney, who had always urged abolitionists to use every sort of political pressure available to them, slowly veered toward the idea of a separate abolitionist party.

An abolition convention

From Harper's Weekly, May 28, 1859

The crisis in this dissension and disintegration came in 1839–40 when the Garrisonian radicals determined to capture control of the national organization and use it for their own ends. To Garrison everyone who opposed him was an enemy, and, since he was convinced of the validity of his position, all opponents were of necessity wrong. He chose to split the organization on the question of the right of women to share in its administration and packed the 1840 convention with several hundred of his New England followers. Weld, Stanton, and Birney did not oppose the rights of women, but they refused to permit the antislavery movement to become the sounding board for totally unrelated reforms, and they refused to accept the dictation of Garrison. When, by a vote of five hundred and sixty to four hundred and fifty, Garrison won the appointment of a woman to the business committee, the New York group withdrew from the convention and from the society, leaving Garrison and his friends at last in control of the organization which they had long wished to dominate.

The seceders reorganized as the American and Foreign Anti-Slavery Society but never succeeded in carrying either the state societies or any large number of abolition leaders with them. The Garrisonian society kept up its organization for many years but ceased to be of much influence or to represent the growing antislavery feeling of the country. The friends of political action formed the Liberty party, which nominated Birney for president in 1840 and again in 1844, polling barely seven thousand votes in its first election but more than sixty thousand in the second. Progress toward the triumph of the Republican party in 1860 had been started.

OPPOSITION TO THE ABOLITIONISTS IN THE NORTH

Immediatism and Garrisonian radicalism were shocking to those who realized the practical difficulties in the way of any attempt to rid the country of slavery by such means. Large numbers of men who were sincerely opposed to slavery were already enlisted in the Colonization Society and resented having their work ruined by the demand for immediate abolition. Leonard Bacon deplored immediatism in his *Essays on Slavery;* Lyman Beecher advised against violence and pleaded for unity among antislavery men; and David Meredith Reese, who disliked all ultraism, condemned in his *Hum-*

bugs of New York those who held slavery to be a *"sin against God, independent of all* circumstances," and stated that the American Anti-Slavery Society was the "purest of all Humbugs."

In a more temperate vein Francis Wayland, in his popular text, *The Elements of Moral Science*, maintained that slavery could be peacefully eradicated only by "changing the mind of both master and slave, by teaching the one party the love of justice and the fear of God, and by elevating the other to the proper level of individual responsibility."[37] The economist, Mathew Carey, felt that voluntary emancipation with compensation to the owners would be too costly to be practicable and that coercion of the slave states would result in a horrible war. Therefore slavery, although economically undesirable, would remain, and agitation was both futile and unwise. In much the same spirit Horace Greeley, who was later a vigorous opponent of slavery, at this time questioned the methods of the crusaders:

Granted that Slavery ought to be abolished, how was that consummation to be effected by societies and meetings of men, women and children, who owned no slaves, and had no sort of control over, or even intimacy with, those who did? Suppose the people of Vermont all converted to abolition, how was *that* to bring about the overthrow of Slavery in Georgia? I could not say or see, and therefore I was never a member of any distinctly Abolition society and very rarely found time to attend Abolition meetings.[38]

Dr. Daniel Drake of Cincinnati added the protest of those who lived near the slave states against the immigration of free Negroes.[39] And inability to deny that there were two sides to the question led James Russell Lowell, who was certainly no friend of slavery, to write to a friend,

Hath not a slaveholder hands, organs, dimensions, senses, affections, passions? fed with the same food, hurt with the same weapons, subject to the same diseases, healed by the same means, warmed and cooled by the same summer and winter as an abolitionist is? If you prick them do they not bleed? If you tickle them do they not laugh? If you poison them do they not die? If you wrong them shall they not revenge? Nay, I will go a step farther, and ask if all this do not apply to parsons also? Even *they* are human. The longer I live the more I am convinced that the world must be healed by degrees.[40]

Nor were outright defenders of slavery lacking in the North.

Bishop John H. Hopkins of New Hampshire, in a dull tome called *The American Citizen*, maintained that Negroes were better off in slavery than in freedom, and that slaves had less to fear or suffer than the free laborers of the North. He believed that slaves were the happiest of all laborers but that those who desired and merited emancipation should be sent to Liberia. Bishop Hopkins was a well-known conservative, but his views were those of a group probably as numerous if not so vociferous as the early abolitionists.

THE DENIAL OF THE RIGHT OF FREE SPEECH IN THE NORTH

The Northern moderates were not the only opponents the abolitionists had to face. The workingmen's fear of the competition of the free blacks made them resent the idea of further emancipation, and they were easily aroused to mob action against the abolitionists. Thousands of businessmen were disturbed by thoughts of the disruption of trade relationships and by the threat to any species of private property, and wealthy Northerners resented the opprobrium heaped upon Southern friends who attended the same colleges, races, and summer resorts that they did. As the editor of the *Richmond Whig* put it, "Depend upon it, the Northern people will never sacrifice their lucrative trade with the South so long as the hanging of a few thousands will prevent it." [41] In short, organized and aggressive abolitionism was bitterly opposed by many Northern groups. Mobs broke up meetings and attacked antislavery speakers. Lewis Tappan's house in New York City was gutted, Weld and his agents were rotten-egged and even stoned in Ohio, the windows of lecture halls were broken, and audiences were driven away. Fearlessly the agents met their attackers, talked them down, aroused public opinion against them, and sometimes even succeeded in winning them over — always refusing to accept the dictum that they were not to be allowed a hearing.

The antislavery men early recognized that this denial of free speech might be turned to their advantage and that in defense of the fundamental liberties of democracy they might be able to convince men that slavery itself was a repudiation of democratic principles. It was the breaking up of a Utica meeting in 1835 that brought Gerrit Smith into the abolition fold. He summoned the disrupted convention to Peterboro and housed forty of its members under his own roof. From that time on, his time and his money were devoted to the cause. When prevented from establishing his antislavery paper in Danville, Kentucky, Birney wrote to Smith:

It is as much as all the patriotism in our country can do, to keep alive the spirit of liberty in the *free* states. The contest is becoming — has become — one, not alone of freedom for the *black*, but of freedom for the *white*. It has now become absolutely necessary, that Slavery should cease in order that freedom may be preserved to any portion of our land. The antagonist principles of liberty and slavery have been roused into action and one or the other must be victorious. There will be no cessation of the strife, until Slavery shall be exterminated, or liberty destroyed.[42]

Staid Massachusetts was the scene of action for some of the most violent mobs. In 1835 a meeting at which Samuel May spoke was broken up by a shower of brickbats, Whittier was pelted with stones in the same autumn, and the English abolitionist, George Thompson, narrowly escaped with his life from a mob in Concord. When it was announced that Thompson would speak at a meeting of the Massachusetts Female Anti-Slavery Society in Boston, the anti-Garrisonians went into action. Thompson was warned and did not attend the meeting, but the mob found Garrison there. The mayor persuaded the women to leave the meeting and protected them in their departure, but Garrison was dragged through the streets with a rope around his body. Rescued by the mayor, he was deposited in jail for safety. With characteristic ability to utilize every opportunity for propaganda purposes, he inscribed on the walls of his cell this statement:

Wm. Lloyd Garrison was put in this cell on Wednesday afternoon, Oct. 21, 1835, to save him from the violence of a "respectable and influential" mob, who sought to destroy him for preaching the abominable and dangerous doctrine that "all men are created equal," and that all oppression is odious in the sight of God. "Hail Columbia!" Cheers for the Autocrat of Russia and the Sultan of Turkey! [43]

Such episodes won many substantial citizens to the cause of free speech if not of abolition. But the effect of the Boston mob was as nothing compared with that of the murder of Elijah Lovejoy in Alton, Illinois, two years later. Lovejoy was not an abolitionist of the immediatist school but was an advocate of gradual emancipation and the clergyman-editor of a religious paper. In Alton his paper was unpopular, and his printing office was broken into and his press destroyed twice. He was supported by Illinois abolitionists, among them Edward Beecher, and was advised to order a third press and to make a stand on the basis of his constitutional rights. When a committee of Alton citizens tried to persuade Lovejoy to withdraw, he answered them in words that became a classic in the history of the defense of free speech:

Why should I flee from Alton? Is not this a free state? . . . Have I not a right to claim the protection of the laws? What more can I have in any other place? . . . You may hang me up, as the mob hung up the individuals of Vicksburgh! You may burn me at the stake, as they did McIntosh at St. Louis, or you may tar and feather me, or throw me into the Mississippi, as you have threatened to do; but you cannot disgrace me. I, and I alone, can disgrace myself; and the deepest of all disgrace would be, at a time like this to deny my Master by forsaking his cause.[44]

When the new press was installed and Lovejoy and his friends attempted to protect it from assault, the mob turned on them, and Lovejoy was killed. Then through the entire North rang Lovejoy's cry, "Have I not a right to claim the protection of the laws?" and for thousands the cause of the slave and the cause of civil liberty were joined. In the *New Yorker* Horace Greeley said:

Mr. Lovejoy's errors, or those of abolitionists generally, have nothing to do in any shape with the turpitude of this outrage. But for the act of inflexibly maintaining the common rights of every citizen, in defiance of the audacious tyranny of the multitude, he may well be deemed a martyr to public liberty. To talk of resisting what is called public opinion as a crime, is to make Socrates an anarchist and Jesus Christ a felon. . . . We loathe and abhor the miserable cant of those who talk of Mr. Lovejoy as guilty of resisting public opinion. Public opinion forsooth! What right have five hundred or five thousand to interfere with the lawful expression of a freeman's sentiments, because they happen to number more than those who think with him?[45]

Emerson in delivering a lecture on heroism raised his eyes from the pages of his manuscript, and in a voice that is said to have rung out "clear as a rifle shot," interpolated, "It is but the other day that the brave Lovejoy gave his breast to the bullets of a mob for the rights of free speech and opinion and died when it was better not to live." And John Quincy Adams in his introduction to the *Memoir of the*

Rev. Elijah P. Lovejoy, written by the dead man's brothers, summarized a large section of American opinion:

That an American citizen, in a state whose Constitution repudiates all slavery, should die a martyr in defence of the freedom of the press is a phenomenon in the history of this Union. It forms an era in the progress of mankind towards universal emancipation. The incidents which preceded and accompanied, and followed the catastrophe of Mr. Lovejoy's death . . . have given a shock as of an earthquake throughout this continent, which will be felt in the most distant region of the earth.

In Boston Dr. Channing and a hundred others applied for permission to hold a meeting in Faneuil Hall in protest against the Alton affair, and the ancient hall was filled to overflowing on the night of December 8, 1837. Dr. Channing's opening address was moving and impressive, and appropriate resolutions were introduced to obtain the opinion of the meeting on the Alton tragedy. At this point the attorney general of the state spoke from the gallery, blaming Lovejoy for the riot and asserting that he had "died as the fool dieth." Saying the citizens of Alton were doing no more than the Revolutionary rioters of Boston had done, he likened slaves to wild beasts and abolitionists to fools who would turn them loose to prey upon the white people of the South. As the audience sat in shocked silence after the distinguished speaker had ceased, a young man sprang to the platform, and Wendell Phillips made his first antislavery speech. His indignant eloquence brought him instant recognition, and he was a leader of the radical abolitionists from that time onward.[46]

The violence of Alton was repeated, in lesser degree only by chance, in the East a year later. In May 1838 a women's antislavery convention drew a great crowd of famous reformers to Philadelphia, and meetings were scheduled at which Angelina Grimké, Abby Kelly, Lucretia Mott, Maria Chapman, and Garrison were to speak. As Garrison was addressing an audience of three thousand, a mob gathered outside the hall — the famous Pennsylvania Hall built by the abolitionists and dedicated to "Free Discussion, Virtue, Liberty and Independence." Windows were broken, and an attempt was made to drown out the voice of the speaker by howls and shouts of derision, but the mob dispersed without greater violence. On the next day the women were willing to try it again, but the mayor, concerned for their safety, locked the hall and forbade an evening meeting. The mob assembled, however, and finding the building dark and empty broke into it, set fires, and kept off opponents until the hall was destroyed.

In New England the official agents of the antislavery societies were joined by a flock of unofficial, self-appointed itinerant lecturers who visited every village and town expounding abolition doctrine. They were received in the Baptist and Methodist churches but did not meet with much hospitality elsewhere. In Connecticut in 1836 the Reverend Leonard Bacon was the author of a measure adopted by the General Association of Congregational Ministers refusing the use of their pulpits to any itinerant agents or lecturers who came without the consent of the pastors or the regular ecclesiastical bodies. This regulation, called the "Connecticut gag-law," was adopted by other groups in various states and cut the abolition agents off from the use of church buildings in much of New England.

The move was greeted with cries of rage by the radical abolitionists, and the churches were assailed as "Bulwarks of American Slavery." A certain group of itinerant preachers — mostly unordained young men with more zeal than discretion — resolved to test their right to free speech and continued to speak with or without the consent of the clergy. When refused the pulpit, they rose in the midst of regular services and began their diatribes. Sometimes the congregation listened; more often the unwelcome voice was drowned out by the organ or by hymns loudly chanted. Occasionally the invader was thrown out bodily.

The leader of this band of defenders of the "right to be heard" was Stephen S. Foster, a former Dartmouth student and the husband of Abby Kelly, champion of women's rights and almost all other reforms; its historian was Foster's companion in martyrdom, Parker Pillsbury, whose book, *The Acts of the Anti-Slavery Apostles*, is filled with tales of their trials and tribulations. Deadly serious though they were, there is a certain comic relief in their story that is absent from the account of the antislavery riots elsewhere. The Reverend George Storrs, for example, was "jerked" from the pulpit in the midst of a prayer and arraigned before a justice of the peace as a "common brawler." The students of Dartmouth broke up a meeting with hisses, catcalls, and loud applause at the wrong moments. A feminine martyr, Mrs. Almira Scott, who took her knitting to church in protest because the edifice was closed to antislavery agents, was arrested for contempt of worship.

When churches were closed to them, the evangels of freedom attempted to speak from the church steps; they invaded academy halls and town buildings; empty store buildings were hired, boxes and planks were used as seats, and potatoes served for candlesticks. In the larger towns there were riots, and in many country communities the excitement ended in sore heads, damaged property, and jail sentences; but a hearing was demanded, and a hearing of some sort was obtained.

Every such contest won some adherents both to the antislavery cause and to the demand for free speech. The disturbances were the talk of the neighborhood and furnished much free publicity for the abolitionists. The speakers found it very effective to take with them on their travels Negroes and ex-slaves whose accounts of their own sufferings won support for the movement. Frederick Douglass and William Wells Brown, both colored orators, spoke before many a New England audience. And when one farmer rose to say, "It is as bad to enslave black people as white; and if you enslave any it enslaves everybody else; and if you allow slavery in the country you can't keep liberty," the truth expressed could not have been excelled by the most fluent opponent of the gag rule that was then being discussed in Congress.

Another phase of the interference with freedom of speech was the controversy over Prudence Crandall and her school for Negro girls in Canterbury, Connecticut. Miss Crandall was a Quakeress with strong feelings against slavery. Her girls' school in Canterbury seemed a complete success until she admitted a Negro girl, Sarah Harris, the daughter of a Connecticut freedman who was a farmer in the neighborhood. The girl wanted to become a teacher in Negro schools, for her family had been roused by the *Liberator* to desire to aid in the elevation of their own race. White families at once boycotted Miss Crandall's school, but she refused to turn away colored girls and soon determined to make her school into one for Negroes only. New York and Boston abolitionists came to her aid. Samuel May, Garrison, and Arthur Tappan gave both advice and money and were apparently determined to make a test case of the project.

Canterbury thoroughly disapproved of both the project and the notoriety and feared lest it become a haven for free Negroes. Miss Crandall suffered many annoyances; her windows were broken, her well was contaminated, her students were refused seats in the stage-coach and pews in the church, and she was accused of immorality and of seeking white husbands for her colored girls. The hysteria reached a climax in 1833 when the state passed a law providing fine and imprisonment for teaching colored students who were not residents of the state. In June 1833 Miss Crandall was arrested. Her supporters refused to give bond in order to saddle the town with the shame of her imprisonment, and the Tappans provided funds for excellent lawyers to carry the case through the courts. The case was fought on constitutional grounds, the defense declaring the law a violation of the provision that the citizens of one state are entitled to equal rights in all states. The first jury divided seven to five, but at the second trial, before the superior court, a verdict was returned against Miss Crandall, since a "Negro was not a citizen." On appeal to the supreme court of errors the decision was reversed on a technicality, so that the issue of constitutional rights was not settled.

The school remained in session during the trial and for a few months afterward, but public pressure was too great, and even the abolitionists could not advise Miss Crandall to continue. Samuel May said, "I felt ashamed of Connecticut, ashamed of my state, ashamed of myself, ashamed of my color." Within a few months Miss Crandall married and left the town, which tried to justify its intolerance in a resolution that is to posterity an admission of its guilt:

Resolved, that the Government of the United States, the nation with all its institutions, of right belong to the white men who now possess them. . . . that our appeal to the Legislature of our own State, in a case of such peculiar mischief, was not only due to ourselves, but to the obligations devolving on us under the Constitution. To have been silent would have been participating in the wrongs intended.[47]

The state legislature showed its approval of the extreme anti-Negro feeling evidenced in the Crandall case by commenting favorably on a memorial that stated, "Whether bond or free, the negro and 'his kind' have ever been blots on the fair face of civilized society, and corroding cancers to a free State." [48]

THE FEDERAL GOVERNMENT AND SLAVERY

In 1835 trouble in regard to the right of the abolitionists to make themselves heard cropped up in another quarter. Southern legislatures and executive authorities had relieved their overwrought feelings by outlawing prominent abolitionists, by trying them *in absentia,* by demanding their extradition, and by offering bounties for them dead or alive. But these gestures produced little comfort, for the condemned abolitionists stayed in their own territory.

Some of the flood of antislavery literature flowed into the South through the United States post offices, and in Charleston the post office was forcibly entered, and tracts and papers bearing the imprint of the American Anti-Slavery Society were seized and burned with derisive ceremony. Much to the distress and anger of the abolitionists, the United States government refused to force the society's literature upon the South. Amos Kendall, the postmaster general, wrote to the Charleston postmaster that, although he had no authority to bar such literature from the mails, he could not order local postmasters to deliver it. Asserting that the post office department was created to serve the people and not to injure them, he said:

By no act or direction of mine, official or private, could I be induced to aid knowingly in giving circulation to papers of this description directly or indirectly. We owe our obligation to the laws, but a higher one to the community in which we live; and if the former be perverted to destroy the latter, it is patriotism to disregard them. Entertaining these views, I cannot sanction and will not condemn the step you have taken. [49]

President Jackson fully agreed with Kendall in this policy, calling abolition literature a "wicked plan of inciting the negroes to insurrection and massacre," and in his message to Congress in December 1835 he roundly condemned the antislavery men and asked for a law that would prohibit, with severe penalties, the circulation in the South of incendiary publications. Such a law was not passed, nor was it necessary, for the *modus vivendi* of the postmaster general was adequate in ending the distribution of abolition tracts in the South. [50]

THE RIGHT OF PETITION

Of greater significance even than the question of free speech in the North was the Southern challenge in Congress of the right of petition. From the first antislavery petition in 1790 down to the days of the American Anti-Slavery Society there were occasional appeals to Congress but no concerted action. The organizers of the antislavery movement, however, were quick to see the specific points at which Congress might take action, and the petition flood started. Slavery was protected in the states where it existed, and there only persuasion and moral pressure might be used; but Congress ruled in the District of Columbia and in the territories, and Congress must act in the acquisition of new areas for expansion.

In 1828 came the first nationwide movement to petition Congress for the abolition of slavery in the District of Columbia, and from that date to the Civil War the antislavery forces never forgot the symbolic significance of such an action by the Congress of the United States. And Congress after 1830 furnished an incomparable arena for the struggle. These were the years of Webster and Calhoun, of Clay and Benton, of John Quincy Adams and Joshua Giddings and Henry Wise of Virginia. By 1836 the petitions were pouring in in such quantities that they would disrupt the agenda if time were taken for their consideration. Calhoun, the watchdog of Southern interests, set himself to stop the flood, or at least to render it innocuous.

In the Senate Southern forces were strong enough to make a mere tabling of the question sufficient, but in the House it was a different matter. The procedure provided that on specified days each state, beginning with Maine, should present any petitions sent to its representatives. As the number of such appeals grew, all business was blocked on petition days as some representative of each Northern state slowly unloaded the mass of papers that had been sent in since the last such occasion. Southern opposition aside, it was necessary to devise some plan to expedite this business. Would not the constitutional right of petition be satisfied if the petitions were received and then were automatically laid on the table, without being either printed or referred?

This was the origin of the "gag rule" of 1836. The issue was not entirely clear. Such "gags" had been used before to expedite business and had been unquestioned, but this was not a temporary expedient; it was designed to operate throughout the session. The rule was fought by the Whigs in order that the flood of petitions might obstruct the business of the Democratic administration they so abhorred. Southern representatives, of course, were determined to prevent full discussion of slavery in Congress, but the antislavery forces, for their part, were only too eager to make the gag rule the occasion for a hue and cry over all constitutional guarantees. The nuisance value of the issue was great, but even greater was its influence in bringing converts to the cause of abolition. It furnished the strongest of all links between the antislavery movement and American democracy.

John Quincy Adams, who had, as he said, "an abhorrence of slavery" that was "absorbing all my faculties," led the fight against the gag rule, and year after year presented his petitions, at times by the hundreds, finding opportunities legitimate and illegitimate to make speeches in their behalf. Andrew Jackson said Adams was as "fierce as ten furies, terrible as hell"; certainly, to the rage of the Southern members of Congress, he broke up whatever was left of their conspiracy of silence. When the gag rule was adopted again for the session beginning in December 1837, Adams answered to his name in the roll call with the statement, "I hold the resolution to be a violation of the Constitution of the United States, of the right of petition of my constituents, and of the people of the United States and of my rights to freedom of speech as a member of this House." In 1840 the gag rule was made a standing rule of the House, but this did not end the battle. Adams was joined by Slade of Vermont, Giddings of Ohio, and a group of other antislavery congressmen.

The greatest of all the petition debates was that of the winter and spring of 1842, when the House dared to attempt the censure of Adams, and later of Giddings, for violation of the gag rule. Adams was magnificent in combat, fully justifying his nickname of "Old Man Eloquent." Threatened with lynching if he ventured South, the recipient of anonymous letters, called "babbler" and "buffoon," he defended himself to the edification of the country and the despair of his opponents. In February he made the caustic comment in his diary that there were one hundred members of the House from the slave states and

Four fifths of them would crucify me, if their votes could erect the cross; forty members, representative of the free, in the league of slavery and mock Democracy, would break me on the wheel, if their votes or wishes could turn it round; and four fifths of the other hundred and twenty are either so cold or so lukewarm that they are ready to desert me at the very first scintillation of indiscretion on my part. The only formidable danger with which I am beset is that of my own temper.[51]

Unable to conquer the old statesman, his opponents finally permitted the resolution to censure to be tabled by a vote of one hundred and six to ninety-three. Joshua Giddings, however, did not escape their fury but was censured in March 1842. He resigned from the House at once and carried the fight back to Ohio, where he was triumphantly re-elected in May.

With constant pressure from these doughty fighters in the House, and with the aid of the antislavery lobby in Washington and their cohorts who engineered the petition campaign throughout the North, the majorities for the gag rule were reduced. In 1843 the measure was passed by a majority of only three, and in 1845 Adams won out with a vote of one hundred and eight to eighty. In his diary appears the comment, "Blessed, forever blessed, be the name of God."

Thus the fire-bell whose note Jefferson feared had been heard throughout the land before 1840. The humanitarian had joined the revivalist in calling the democrats of the North to aid in preserving the liberties of white men as well as in securing freedom for the slaves. When William Jay resigned his position as head of the New York Anti-Slavery Society, he summed up the position of the antislavery North in explaining why societies were no longer necessary in a movement that had burst such bonds:

We commenced the present struggle to obtain the freedom of the slave; we are compelled to continue it to preserve our own. We are now contending, not so much with the slaveholders of the South about human rights, as with the political and commercial aristocracy of the North for the liberty of speech, of the press, and of conscience. And politicians are selling our Constitution and laws for Southern votes. Our great capitalists are speculating, not merely in lands and banks, but in the liberties of the people. We are called to contemplate a spectacle never, I believe, before witnessed — the wealthy portion of the country striving to introduce anarchy and violence on a calculation of profit; making merchandise of peace and good order![52]

And across the Ohio in Kentucky Cassius Clay, a last representative of antislavery opinion in the South, agreed:

The most lamentable evil of slavery is the practical loss of the liberty of speech and of the press. The timid are overawed by the threatening array of physical force; the conscientious, who are naturally lovers of peace and good will, sink under bitter hate, and increasing persecution; the ambitious and spirited are overwhelmed by the unsupportable anticipation of sudden proscription, certain obscurity, and eternal oblivion. Thus truth ceases to be a virtue, and hypocrisy a crime; most severe of retribution of the violation of nature's laws; the limbs of the apparent slave are fettered with iron, but the living and immortal spirit of the master wears heavier and more insufferable chains! [53]

CHAPTER 18

A House Divided

Southern defenders of slavery were at first unable to realize either the extent or the strength of the antislavery movement. It seemed to them that Northern reformers, with true Yankee shrewdness, were directing the humanitarian movement into channels where the expense and responsibility would be borne by someone else. Without attempting to solve their own economic and social problems, Northerners were presuming to urge impractical reforms upon the South. "To preach distant reform," said one Southern writer, "is very cheap philanthropy — the cheaper in proportion to the distance. The feeling of self-satisfaction exists without the necessity of personal sacrifice." [1] This statement was, in itself, an easy means of dodging the issue and represented the Southern tendency to search for a sectional basis for the antislavery argument. Closer analysis of Northern opinion would have led the Southern writer to recognize the presence of both a passionate interest in the welfare of the Negro and a clear conviction that abolition of slavery and the continuance of American democracy were irrevocably connected.

The most widely read novel of the pre-Civil War period was *Uncle Tom's Cabin* by Harriet Beecher Stowe, a book that still, despite its melodrama and sentimentality, wrings the reader's heart. It is impossible to overestimate the effect of the book in its own day. Literally millions of Northerners and Europeans read it. The boys and girls who wept over Eliza and the tragic death of Uncle Tom were men and women when the Irrepressible Conflict broke out. It is probable that *Uncle Tom's Cabin* had more effect in shaping public opinion than had all the abolition tracts and societies together. In the South the book was anathema, and it was a penal offense to buy or sell it.

THE PROSLAVERY ARGUMENT

The problem of the protagonists of slavery was so to direct Southern thought that the five sixths of the Southern population unbenefited by the institution would accept the opinions of the one sixth for whom slavery was profitable. Slavery must be shown to be desirable in itself and its continuance as essential to the poor men of the South as to the plantation owner. The ideas of racial solidarity and identity of interest must be inculcated, Southern isolation stressed, and Northern condemnation made to seem the intervention of an outside and alien agency.

This idea that a self-conscious South must protect itself from foreign aggression was expressed by a governor of South Carolina when he recommended a "firm determination to resist, at the threshold, every invasion of our sovereignty and independence." [2] It was again emphasized by a Georgia editor in 1833:

We firmly believe that if the Southern States do not quickly unite and declare to the North, if the question of slavery be longer *discussed*, in any shape, they will instantly secede from the Union, that the question must be settled, and very soon, by the Sword, as the only possible means of self-preservation.[3]

The same feeling that the Union had already been undermined if not destroyed appeared in the writings of Thomas Cooper in the late 1830's. In a letter to the editor of the *National Gazette*, Cooper undertook to prove that the prosperity of the South was independent of the North, but that the converse was not true. A South freed from the Northern states could find economic and cultural contacts with Europe and could force Northern businessmen into dire straits by the severance of trade relations. It behooved the North, therefore, to walk circumspectly lest the South withdraw from a compact no longer to its advantage. Later, feeling that his warning had been in vain, Cooper sent this toast to a Fourth of July dinner he could not attend: "The Memory of the Constitution of the United States." [4]

No new proslavery arguments were found, but the old ones were vigorously restated, and intensive propaganda was undertaken to induce general acceptance of ideas that had heretofore been somewhat academic. Between 1835 and 1860 all the threads of Southern thought came to their culmination and were woven into a cloak designed to be impenetrable to the heat of Northern argument. Governor Hayne of South Carolina stated that he was convinced that slavery was indispensable to any "unmixed representative republic," and that Southerners had a sacred obligation to preserve for posterity the means of "*defending* and *preserving* an institution as essential to their existence and to their liberty as it is obnoxious to the *prejudices* of those who have the greatest possible facilities for assailing it." [5] If slavery was to be considered of such positive value to the South, the old theories of natural rights and of the equality of men must be sacrificed, and after 1830 the South was urged to repudiate Jeffersonian democracy and to accept a class structure already worked out by the supporters of slavery.

Perhaps the most important, and certainly one of the most aggressive, of Southern theorists was George Fitzhugh, who declared in the preface to his *Sociology for the South, or the Failure of Free Society* that it was now time to "act on the offensive, transfer the seat of war, and invade the enemy's territory." In this work, one of the first in English to use the new term *sociology*, he asserted that a slave society was the normal form, free society the aberration, and he called upon the free states to admit the failure of their social order and come back to the only practical and ethical social bases. According to Fitzhugh, paternalism and class rigidity were necessary for successful social organization; society must be organized for positive purposes, must be restrained and subjected to discipline; and each member of society must fit into his proper place, but once there he must be given due consideration and support. In Fitzhugh's world order there should be no freedom of trade or industry; laissez faire and free competition should be discarded and controls from above substituted for individual initiative; and the lowest elements in society could be best provided for in slavery. He thought that exploitation, the evils of child labor, and the neglect of the unfortunate were the ills of free society, and that the English and Northern factory owner should own his laborers and be held responsible for their welfare. In America, according to Fitzhugh, the boundless West should be a domain of great landowners cultivated by serfs from Europe's downtrodden millions, and for such a society the Southern planters would furnish leadership to make the United States the social model of the world.

In his second work, *Cannibals All! or Slaves without Masters*, Fitzhugh advanced to a further attack upon free institutions and an outright condemnation of democracy, liberty, and free will. Again and again he claimed the superiority of a feudalistic social order with an aristocracy protected by entail, primogeniture, and the perpetual enslavement of the workers. Free Negroes should be brought back into bondage and the African slave trade be reopened. The South should develop self-sufficiency: manufacture its own goods, train its own professional men, produce its own artists and men of letters. Then if the North refused to accord it the place that was its due, secession and war should follow, for "war elevates the sentiments and aims of men, makes them love honor, and appreciate each other according to each one's moral worth."

One of Fitzhugh's strangest notions was a concept of socialism that made the South a socialistic state. He believed that in the South Fourierism was perfectly worked out, with the plantation owner furnishing the direction and leadership without which so many socialistic and communistic experiments had failed. "Add a Virginia overseer to Mr. Greeley's phalansteries," he said, "and Mr. Greeley and we would have little to quarrel about." Slavery did away with labor competition and gave the worker security and support at all times. According to Fitzhugh, association of labor and a certain qualified community of property were characteristic of the plantation system:

A Southern farm is a sort of joint stock concern or social phalanstery, in which the master furnishes the capital and skill, and the slaves the labor, and divide the profits, not according to each one's in-put, but according to each one's wants and necessities.[6]

In many respects Fitzhugh's social philosophy was a statement of fascist ideology a century before its day. Fitzhugh was not, however, an isolated thinker, born too early to be appreciated. Every one of his ideas was accepted and restated by many of his contemporaries in the South. The idea that a class society is true socialism was reiterated by the poet, William J. Grayson, who claimed that slave labor was the only really organized labor and that in a slave society labor and capital were associated and not in conflict, forming "a phalanstery . . . where all work, where each member gets subsistence and a home and the more industrious larger pay and profits to their own superior industry."[7] Other "sociologists" of the day agreed that only in a slave society could there be a civilization without poverty, crime, insanity, or wars, where Christianity would rule everywhere and prosperity and contentment be the lot of all.

Slavery in the Light of Social Ethics by Chancellor William

Harper of South Carolina and Albert Bledsoe's *Liberty and Slavery* carried the moral argument in favor of slavery still farther, but the economic justification was doubtless of more significance to the average Southerner. Edmund Ruffin, economist and promoter of scientific agriculture, claimed that slavery made the ignorant African economically profitable and solved the race problem. Cheap labor in the cotton fields was necessary for the South, he said, and under slave labor the interest of the master served as a limit to exploitation. After 1852 Ruffin made many speeches on the slavery question, wrote numerous articles, and published four very popular pamphlets developing the thesis that slavery was a positive good to both races.

In *Cotton Is King: Economical Relations of Slavery* David Christy coined a phrase that led his fellow Southerners to believe the cotton kingdom invincible, and S. A. Cartwright published a pamphlet entitled *Education, Labor and Wealth of the South*, extolling the prosperity of the South and the merits of slavery. The editor of *De Bow's Review* was tireless in his support of this economic argument and in his efforts to urge economic and cultural self-sufficiency for the South. He felt that only by encouraging diversified agriculture and expanding manufacturing could the full economic advantages of the slave system be realized. In an article in the *Review* in January 1850 he argued that the best interests of the South demanded the development of manufacturing to increase the prosperity of the poorer whites, since

The poor man has a vote, as well as the rich man; and in our State, the *number* of the first will largely overbalance the last. So long as these poor, but industrious people, could see no mode of living, except by a degrading operation of work with the negro upon the plantation they were content to endure life in its most discouraging forms, satisfied that they were *above* the slave, though faring often worse than he. But the progress of the world is "onward" . . . and the great mass of our poor white population begin to understand that they have rights, and that they, too, are entitled to some of the sympathy which falls upon the suffering. They are fast learning, that there is an almost infinite world of industry opening before them, by which they can elevate themselves and their families from wretchedness and ignorance to competence and intelligence. *It is this great upheaving of our masses that we are to fear so far as our institutions are concerned.*[8]

$1200
TO
1250 DOLLARS!
FOR NEGROES!!

THE undersigned wishes to purchase a large lot of NEGROES for the New Orleans market. I will pay $1200 to $1250 for No. 1 young men, and $850 to $1000 for No. 1 young women. In fact I will pay more for likely

NEGROES,

Than any other trader in Kentucky. My office is adjoining the Broadway Hotel, on Broadway, Lexington, Ky., where I or my Agent can always be found.

WM. F. TALBOTT.

LEXINGTON, JULY 2, 1853.

A slave trader's advertisement. The figure of the running Negro was often used in advertisements for runaways and also as a heading for abolition tracts.

All proslavery argument after 1835 was directed toward the exposition of one or another of these premises. Chancellor Harper wrote: "It is as much in the order of nature that men should enslave each other as that animals should prey upon each other." [9] Matthew Estes in 1846 went still farther, saying he would not hesitate for a moment to maintain that the slave trade itself "had been the source of incalculable blessing to mankind." [10] The slave, it was claimed, did not suffer as the property of his master, for he was assured *"peace, plenty, and security*, and the proper indulgence of his social propensities — freed from all care for the present, or anxiety for the future with regard either to himself or his family." [11] The Bible and historical antiquity were searched to establish the origins of slavery and to make it respectable because it could be proved to be venerable. The conscience of the South, wounded by the attack of the abolitionist, was soothed by building up the idea that the slave was happy in his bondage. In an essay on the morals of slavery published in the *Southern Literary Messenger* in 1837, the novelist William Gilmore Simms came to the conclusion that "Providence has placed him [the slave] in our hands for his good, and has paid us from his labor for our guardianship."

If all these ideas were to be accepted as truths, false notions must be guarded against. Besides the additions to the slave codes that restricted the movements and prohibited the education of the slaves, the free expression of opinion on the part of the white population was slowly circumscribed, and by 1840 social pressures of every variety were applied to any who showed independence of thought and divergence of opinion.

DIVISION IN THE CHURCHES

The ministry became acquiescent if not outspokenly proslavery. All skepticism was stifled, and the ideal Christian was one who was completely subservient in opinion. The Episcopal church avoided all slavery controversy and was, in the South, representative of planter opinion. Bishop Chase of Illinois, in a letter to a group of English bishops, said the clergy could "tolerate the evil because of the good they could do for the souls of the slaves."

The General Assembly of the Presbyterian Church had in 1818 condemned slavery in no uncertain terms and had recommended to all Christians every possible effort to abolish it, but the clergy of the lower South gradually acquired control of the national assemblies, and Dr. Thornwell, president of a Southern college and editor of the *Southern Presbyterian Review,* became the real leader of American Presbyterianism. Southern Presbyterians refused to agree with their Northern brethren on either doctrine or the slavery issue, and finally, shortly before the Civil War, the two groups became estranged, the Southern faction issuing a declaration in favor of slavery. It was Dr. Thornwell who linked abolitionism with atheism and all else that was anathema to the orthodox:

The parties in this conflict are not merely abolitionists and slaveholders — they are atheists, socialists, communists, red Republicans, Jacobins on the one side, and the friends of order and regulated freedom on the other. In one word, the world is a battle-ground, Christianity and Atheism the combatants, and the progress of humanity the stake.[12]

Throughout the period of the great revivals the Methodists were strongly antislavery, but the increase of pressure in the South put an end to all unanimity of opinion in the councils of the church. In 1836 advocates of slavery declared in the General Conference that slavery was a blessing and not a curse. This challenge was accepted by the abolitionist delegates, and a vigorous fight was staged which resulted in the passage of a gag rule by a vote of one hundred and twenty-two to eleven. This conference provided, also, for the circulation of a Pastoral Letter suggesting that the clergy abstain from discussion of slavery and deploring the abolitionist activities of certain Northern ministers. By 1844 the conference was faced with the question of slaveowning in the episcopacy, when it was found that the wife of a Southern bishop had fallen heir to slaves which he refused to emancipate. Over this issue the church was split, and as a result the Methodist Episcopal Church South was organized.

The Baptists, as strong as the Methodists in the South, went through much the same experiences. In the conference of 1841, the Southern delegates attacked the Reverend Ebon Galusha for attending an antislavery convention in London and for supporting there a resolution condemning slavery as a sin. In 1845 the Southern Baptists formed separate organizations for both home and foreign missions and thus ended one of the few joint activities of the Baptist churches.

The Campbellites, strong among the poorer whites in the South, were generally antislavery in opinion. The Congregational church had no Southern branches and was brought into the controversy only indirectly, but it was condemned by the abolitionists when its missionary board took no stand against slavery in its work with the Indians of Georgia.

There were a few brave members of the Southern clergy who defied the taboos accepted by the majority. Robert J. Breckinridge of Kentucky continued to express antislavery opinions despite the pressure of his colleagues. John G. Fee, also of Kentucky but one of the Lane rebels, was disowned by his family, was mobbed twenty-two times, and was finally driven out of the state in 1859. His efforts to start a college similar to Oberlin produced Berea College, from the first open to both Negro and white students. Monecure Conway of Virginia, first a Methodist and then a Unitarian preacher, early became interested in the illiteracy of the poorer white people in his own district and was struck by Horace Greeley's comment that "Virginia's white children will never be educated till its coloured children are free." Conway was a man grown before he ever heard anyone say a word against slavery, but when his attention was at last fixed upon the hopeless position of the Negro, he went over to the antislavery cause even though it meant a separation from his family and withdrawal from Virginia.

FREEDOM OF PRESS AND SPEECH IN THE SOUTH

Constant pressure was exerted by the vested interests to prevent any criticism of slavery in the Southern press, and economic reasons alone were sufficient to deter most editors. William Swaim, North Carolina Quaker and editor of the Greensboro *Patriot*, was one of the few who refused to conform. He persistently discussed slavery in his editorials, and without molestation, for he lived in the center of the Southern Quaker area and he died in 1834 before the slavery cohorts had attained their full control of the press. Swaim said:

Before we will relinquish our right to think, speak, print, and publish our own deliberate opinions in relation to *public* men and *public* measures, we will renounce existence itself. Take away our rights as a free man and life has no charms for us! We shall deal plainly with the people, not caring who may be affected by our course. We would rather bask for one hour in the approving smiles of an intelligent and undeceived people, than to spend a whole eternity amidst the damning grins of a motley crew of office-hunters, despots, demagogues, tyrants, fools, and hypocrites.[13]

In communities where antislavery sentiment was frowned upon editors soon discovered that condemning slavery resulted in the cancellation of subscriptions, and one Virginia editor was killed in a duel fought because of his "abolition sympathies." Birney was prevented from establishing an antislavery press in Kentucky on the ground that such an enterprise would put the whole community in danger. Cassius Clay faced increasing difficulties in publishing his *True American* in Lexington, and it was finally suppressed altogether in 1845. The Vicksburg *Journal* had five editors in thirteen years, owing to its effort to eliminate all those whose opinions diverged from those of the subscribers. Buckingham concluded a list of the publications of South Carolina in 1842 with the remark:

Among all these publications, whether quarterly, monthly, weekly, or daily, there is not one that ever ventures to speak of slavery as an institution to be condemned or even regretted. They are all either indulgent towards, or openly advocates of, this state of bondage; and the higher the rank or character of the publication the more boldly it speaks out on this subject, and the more popular it becomes in the South by so speaking.[14]

Academic freedom suffered the same fate as freedom of the press. It was one of the boasts of the South that the enrollment in its colleges greatly exceeded that in Northern colleges, but probably most Southern institutions of higher learning, although called colleges, were in reality more like academies. In *The Mind of the South* William Cash says the claim to a superior culture was the least well founded of all the claims made by the Old South. He states that of all its colleges listed in 1860 the University of Virginia was the only one worthy to be named with a dozen or more Northern institutions of that day, and he calls attention to the fact that the percentage of illiteracy among the white people of the South was far higher than that of the North, despite the latter's heavy immigrant population. Moreover, the colleges of the South declined in number of students after 1840. There were only seventy-nine students in the University of Georgia in 1856; the faculty of William and Mary reported that the college was "moribund" in 1848; Transylvania went into a long decline after 1830; and South Carolina College dropped from about two hundred and fifty students in 1849 to one hundred and seventy in 1860.

In no Southern college after 1840 could a member of the faculty express with impunity any sentiment in opposition to slavery. The president of Georgetown College in Kentucky was forced to resign his position because of the excitement aroused when he voted for an emancipation candidate for the state constitutional convention. When Professor Hedrick of the University of North Carolina said he would vote for Frémont in 1856 if a Republican ballot were provided him, he was attacked in the press, was burnt in effigy by the students, was censured by the faculty, and was eventually dismissed from the university. A friend of Hedrick's, Professor Harrisse, met a similar fate for his outspoken defense of his colleague's conduct and of academic freedom:

You may eliminate all the suspicious men from your institutions of learning, you may establish any number of new colleges which will relieve you of sending your sons to free institutions. But as long as people study, and read, and think among you, the absurdity of your system will be discovered and there will always be found some courageous intelligence to protest against your hateful tyranny. Close your schools, suppress learning and thought, you have nothing else to do in order to be faithful to your principles, and it is the only means which remains to you of continuing the struggle with some chance of success.[15]

Augustus Longstreet, president of various Southern colleges and a fundamentalist in religion and a fire-eater in politics, early encouraged secession sentiment among his students. Most college authorities probably agreed with the president of the University of North Carolina, who said that no student in his institution was ever permitted to discuss a political issue in public and that all sermons before student audiences were confined to the doctrines of the Christian faith. That tireless traveler, Fredrika Bremer, commented on the parrotlike proslavery pronouncements of the students she met. She heard some graduating addresses at the University of Virginia and reported one young Southerner as declaiming in complicated metaphor:

Abolitionism! It was this scorpion, this *hydra* in the social life of the United States, which ought to be crushed (and the speaker stamped vehemently and angrily on the floor) and annihilated! Then first only would the United States, like two mighty rivers, be united, and side by side start forth toward the same grand honorable goal.[16]

SOUTHERN CULTURE AS DICTATED BY PROSLAVERY SENTIMENT

Southern defenders of slavery grew alarmed in the later pre-Civil War years over the dependence on the North for textbooks and for the printing of books written by Southerners. They also resented the practice of Southern parents of sending their children North to be educated. *De Bow's Review* printed an article on "Southern Thought" in October 1857, congratulating the South on its cultural leadership, its freedom from crime and from radicalism of every variety. The South was, the author said, the only really conservative area, because it was the only really satisfied section of the country, and its protection from the noxious ideas prevalent elsewhere could only be secured by emphasis upon its own schools, texts, and literature. *The Elements of Moral Science* by Francis Wayland was condemned because it deplored slavery, but there was no Southern text to take its place. The works of the popular Peter Parley were considered dangerous, but their use was continued for the same reason. Books on geography and history that were thought to misrepresent the interests of the South had to serve in the absence of any others. Southerners were alarmed, also, that young men preparing for the ministry, for the law, and for the teaching profession found it necessary to study in the North, and there was much agitation for Southern theological schools, law schools, and normal schools. Bishop Polk of Tennessee, for instance, proposed a university for the training of ministers and actually procured a grant of ten thousand acres and an endowment of half a million dollars for such an institution at Sewanee.

There were few lyceums in the South and almost no public libraries. Charleston boasted its St. Cecelia Society and a library hoary with tradition, but even in that city there was little record of creative art. Native men of letters were few and with little honor in their own country; the South preferred the novels of Scott and the English romantic poets for its literary diet. Modern Southern commentators have remarked on the fact that the South repudiated Jefferson, its greatest original philosopher, snubbed William Gilmore Simms, its best novelist, and so neglected Allston, its most famous painter, that he spent his last years in Boston. Le Conte and Audubon, it is true, were great scientists, but it is only by a considerable stretch of the imagination that they can be called products of the South.

Southern writers responded to the demand of the proslavery protagonists for a Southern literature with a flood of propaganda in the form of novels and poems. From the days of William Alexander Caruthers, whose *Kentuckian in New York, or The Adventures of Three Southerns* set the pattern, to J. Thornton Randolph's *Cabin and Parlor, or Slaves and Masters* twenty years later, the favorite theme was the beauties of the Southern way of life and the contrasts between Northern and Southern standards. The idea of Negro inferiority was tacitly accepted, and writers did not depict the Negro as a man with a personality and character of his own. The stories of Uncle Remus and the old family servants are modern, and there are few counterparts from the period before 1860.[17]

It was not because of unorthodox opinions that the South snubbed William Gilmore Simms, its most important novelist. He accepted without question the theories that a free Negro would not work and that Negro and white races could exist together only if the Negro continued to be a slave. In 1853 in the *Southern Quarterly* Simms asserted with extreme naïveté:

If it be admitted that the institution of negro slavery is a wrong done to the negro, the question is at an end. No people can be justified for continuance in error and injustice. Once admit that there is a wrong and a crime, and it must be followed by expiation and atonement. In the South we think otherwise. We hold the African under moral and just titles, founded upon his characteristics, his nature, his necessities and our own; and our accountability is to the God of both races. We, alone, are in possession of the facts in the case, and our consciences are in no way troubled in relation to our rights to hold the negro in bondage. . . . We shall never submit the case to the judgment of another people, until they show themselves of superior virtue and intellect.[18]

The best known and most pretentious example of proslavery poetry was William J. Grayson's *The Hireling and the Slave*, first published in 1854. Slavery was a positive good, said Grayson, and the lot of the Southern slave was infinitely above that of the Northern or English laborer.

Taught by the master's efforts, by his care
Fed, clothed, protected many a patient year,
From trivial numbers now to millions grown,
With all the white man's useful arts their own,
Industrious, docile, skilled in wood and field,
To guide the plow, the sturdy are to wield,
The Negroes schooled by slavery embrace
The highest portion of the Negro race;
And none the savage native will compare,
Of barbarous Guinea, with its offspring here.

If bound to daily labor while he lives,
His is the daily bread that labor gives;
Guarded from want, from beggary secure,
He never feels what hireling crowds endure,
Nor knows, like them, in hopeless want to crave,
For wife and child, the comforts of a slave,
Or the sad thought that, when about to die,
He leaves them to the cold world's charity,
And sees them slowly seek the poor-house door —
That last, vile, hated refuge of the poor.

Southern writers laid all the seething discontent and radicalism of the North at the door of abolition and congratulated the South upon its freedom from "movements" of every sort. There was general opposition to any sort of social experimentation and a rejection of spiritualism, socialism, women's rights, and every other "ism." Temperance and the peace movement alone gained a following in the South, and there was much self-congratulation that immigrants were not attracted to the region and that their subversive doctrines were foreign to Southern thought. George Fitzhugh summed up the contempt for Northern social ferment in an open letter to Northern abolitionists:

Why have you Bloomer's and Woman's Rights men, and strong-minded women, and Mormons, and anti-renters, and "vote myself a farm" men, Millerites, and Spiritual Rappers, and Shakers, and Widow Wakeman-ites, and agrarians, and Grahamites, and a thousand other superstitious and infidel isms at the North? Why is their faith in nothing, speculation about everything? . . . Why is Western Europe now starving? and why has it been starving for seventy years? Why is all this, except that free society is a failure? [19]

Southern authors were not entirely unanimous, however, in praise of slavery. An occasional voice was heard from the ranks of the non-elite. The most bitter and yet the most statistical and factual of these was *The Impending Crisis and How to Meet It* by Hinton Rowan Helper. The curse of slavery to the white Southerner was the main thesis of the author, who had himself been a middle-class nonslaveholder of North Carolina. It is difficult for the modern reader to realize that this dry tome was once a political firebrand, an antislavery tract as potent as *Uncle Tom's Cabin*. Helper hated the Negro and believed slavery to be the cause of the South's poverty and backwardness. He listed the economic assets of the North — its railroads, industries, growing population, and resources — and contrasted them with the retarded economic development of his own class in the South.

Economically Helper's work was a denial of the cherished prosperity argument for slavery; politically it was a challenge by a "poor white" of the supremacy of the planter aristocracy. Helper said, "The stupid and sequacious masses, the white victims of slavery . . . believe whatever the slaveholders tell them, and thus are cajoled into the notion that they are the freest, happiest and most intelligent people in the world." The book is of importance, therefore, as a refutation from the South itself of Southern economic theory and as an attempt to break the political solidarity of the South.

THE UNDERGROUND RAILROAD — NORTH

Among the many irritations that led Southerners to feel the North was united in a conspiracy against them was the constant escape of slaves across the line into the free states. The fugitive slave was a persistent and unanswerable denial of the claim that the slave was a happy and contented laborer. If the mulatto was undeniable proof of miscegenation and a refutation of the Southern claim to race purity, the fugitive proclaimed with equal force that the slave preferred freedom to bondage.

It was obvious that the Negro could not reach a safe haven in the North or in Canada without assistance. The Constitution provided for the return of fugitives, and the Fugitive Slave Law of 1793 implemented that provision. The assistance given the slave, therefore, was in contempt of the Constitution and in violation of the statute. It was, in short, the expression of allegiance to the "higher law" and another evidence to the South of hearty disapproval of its peculiar institution. It was obvious, also, that those who gave assistance did not act as separate entities but were linked in a subversive conspiracy in behalf of the fugitive. Whether or not there was any formal organization, the aid given was systematic, deliberate, and well planned. Southerners familiar with the American genius for accomplishing common ends by voluntary association soon recognized the nature of the agency that about 1830, probably first in Ohio, came to be called the Underground Railroad.

Before the end of the eighteenth century there were little colonies of free Negroes in Philadelphia and other Northern cities, some of them Northern freedmen but many others ex-slaves escaped from the Southern states. These groups extended aid to later fugitives and furnished leadership for the movements to better the conditions of Northern free Negroes. In the South itself there were groups of escaped slaves in the swamps and forests from Florida to Virginia — groups of desolate, homeless men and women called maroons, desperate people, Ishmaels against whom every hand was turned, hunted from time to time with dogs and guns, but, wise in wilderness ways, usually able to evade capture. Only to the despairing whose fate upon capture was death could the life of the maroon seem desirable; usually the slave who sought freedom set his feet upon a path that led northward.[20]

It was among the Quakers of the seaboard states that the first extensive effort was made to aid these fugitives to reach their goal and to establish themselves in the North. Naturally Pennsylvania was the center for the operations of those who acted as "conductors" on routes that could be called underground only because they were secret. And in Philadelphia lived Isaac Tatem Hopper, Hicksite Quaker, philanthropist, and friend of the Negro. For more than fifty years, until his death in 1852, Hopper was friend and counselor for innumerable black fugitives, and his wisdom and experience furnished them such protection that their pursuers often reported that when their quarry reached Philadelphia they disappeared as though the grave had closed over them.[21]

In many southern Pennsylvania towns men like Hopper opened their houses and their pocketbooks to ensure fugitives safe passage to safety farther North. Across the line in Delaware, Thomas Garrett defied slaveowners so often that his reputation equaled that of Isaac Hopper. When in 1848 Garrett was brought before Judge Taney on the charge of aiding slaves to escape, the intrepid man said to the judge, who had imposed fines sufficient to ruin him financially: "Judge, thou hast not left me a dollar, but I wish to say to thee, and to all in this court room, that if any knows of a fugitive who wants a shelter and a friend, send him to Thomas Garrett and he will befriend him." [22] In 1861 when the need for his efforts came to an end, old Thomas Garrett publicly lamented that he had hoped to be the means of three thousand slaves' reaching freedom, but that he had been stopped short of his goal at twenty-seven hundred.

By 1819 North Carolina Quakers were well organized in the work of aiding fugitives along the first stages of their journey. Men willing to help soon became known, safe routes were determined, and responsible and devoted conductors or agents were established for each part of the journey. Routes and conductors were in existence in Ohio by 1815, and a map of the later Underground Railroad would show Ohio the most crisscrossed of all the states with routes of transit. To Ohio from the region across the river and from the lower South by the route up the Mississippi came many fugitives to make the short journey across the state to Lake Erie and on by boat to Canada and safety. John Rankin, a Southerner by birth and a Presbyterian minister, was for many years one of the mainstays of the Ohio organization.

Indiana and Illinois vied with Ohio in numbers of routes and agents. In Newport, Indiana, Levi Coffin, a North Carolina Quaker, owned a mill and a store but made the freeing of slaves his main business. Coffin is reputed to have aided more than three thousand fugitives and was known as the president of the Underground Railroad. His house was on three routes, and he was seldom without some dusky-hued visitor, whose needs for food, clothing, and care he and his equally devoted wife supplied. Coffin helped in the escape of Eliza Harris, whose flight across the Ohio on the ice was made famous by Harriet Beecher Stowe.

The colleges of the Middle West were centers of the movement to aid fugitives just as they were hotbeds of abolitionism. Oberlin College was a busy station where five converging routes met, and it was said that wherever an Oberlin graduate lived there was a sta-

An antislavery cartoon entitled "The Resurrection of Henry 'Box'
Brown." Brown was a Negro who escaped to freedom by being
shipped out of the South as freight.

tion on the Underground Railroad. Western Reserve College near
the shores of Lake Erie also gave aid. Edward Beecher made Illinois
College a center of abolitionist effort, and at Knox College in Galesburg was located the principal Illinois station of the Underground
Railroad.

Pennsylvania and the Old Northwest were organized earlier than
New England, where the distance to be traversed from slavery to
freedom was greater, and where there were few free Negroes and
at first less interest and less reason for help. Boston, however, soon
became the center for fugitives escaping from Southern seaports on
Yankee boats, and the New England Underground Railroad was
provided with some sort of organization before 1830. It was the
coast towns chiefly that furnished asylum, but there were demands
upon western New England, also, when pursuit grew hot around
Philadelphia and New York. There was some transit to Canada by
way of the valley of the Connecticut, and Jonathan Edwards' old
town, Northampton, was an abolition center. There are living to-

day in the village of Amherst a few Negro families whose ancestors settled there in the pre-Civil War years when the college faculty furnished aid to the Underground Railroad.

The stations on the Railroad throughout the country were of many varieties. In the cellar of someone's barn, the attic of another's house, a church tower, an old mill, a cave in the woods, or the storeroom of a merchant — wherever safety could be secured, there the fugitive rested and waited for conveyance to the next station. Hidden in a false-bottomed wagon under a load of hay, grain, or wood, disguised as the servant of his conductor, occasionally passing as a white person, sometimes traveling as a mourner in a funeral cortege, even, perhaps, as the corpse in the crepe bedecked hearse, the slave used all his native art of mimicry in his flight. Passwords, special calls, the hoot of a night owl were all used at times to elude capture.

Illegal and working in secrecy, the Underground Railroad could not assume the usual form of voluntary associations and could not as openly or as successfully appeal for contributions as could other philanthropic agencies. The responsibility for procuring funds devolved upon the conductors and agents, and the inhabitants of friendly local communities in which the stations were located or through which routes ran contributed money, clothes, and food, asking no questions as to their destination. One agent told with amusement how he had persuaded a Southerner pursuing his fugitive slave to contribute to local charities and had then used the dollar to aid the fugitive. Abolitionists often contributed as individuals, and a little money came in from abolition societies, but, in general, those who did the work paid for it and sometimes ruined themselves by their devotion. Prosecutions and fines were the consequence of discovery, and Thomas Garrett was not the only man to lose his property when convicted of violation of the law. The life of a conductor was full of adventure and danger, and the risks of the enterprise were borne by him. He must have sung with fervor and conviction the old antislavery hymn:

> 'Tis the law of God in the human soul.
> 'Tis the law in the Word Divine;
> It shall live while the earth in its course shall roll,
> It shall live in this soul of mine.

Let the law of the land forge its bonds of wrong,
  I shall help when the self-freed crave;
For the law in my soul, bright, beaming, and strong,
  Bids me succor the fleeing slave.[23]

THE UNDERGROUND RAILROAD — SOUTH

The accounts of the Underground Railroad and its agents deal largely with the work of aiding fugitives in the passage across the free states to Canada. As antislavery men were gradually forced to leave the South — many of them to become leaders of the movement in their new homes — the routes in slave states were left almost entirely to the Negroes themselves. Fugitives came to know the plantations or farms where their own people would aid them, and they found shelter in the woods and swamps when it was unsafe to travel openly.

Northern men who had no compunctions about helping those who came to their doors were reluctant to go South to interfere with slavery there. There was a very real feeling that in the American system each state must be permitted control of its own institutions and that aid to slaves in their first steps toward freedom was of the nature of kidnaping. Once the fugitive had crossed into a free state, the pursuing master became the kidnaper as far as the abolitionist was concerned, and any law of state or nation to the contrary was in contravention of a higher law. A few brave souls refused to pay attention to this quirk in abolition logic and carried the war on slavery into the enemy's camp. Although there was little of underground organization in the slave states, there were conductors who took the risks involved and brought terror to the slaveowners at their own thresholds. Rage and demands for vengeance were unbridled when one of these men was arrested, and the penalties imposed were severe.

Levi Coffin, who in his youthful days in North Carolina had done the same thing, wrote about the adventures of John Fairfield of Virginia, who enticed hundreds of slaves away from their masters and led them in bands to Canada. Fairfield refused to take men he could not trust. He told the Negroes he would kill any coward or deserter, and he often shot his way out of difficulty. Several times arrested, he was never convicted, but was finally killed in Tennessee in 1860.[24] Calvin Fairbanks, an Oberlin graduate, went

South again and again and brought many Negroes to freedom. He was arrested and convicted more than once and spent, in all, seventeen years in prison, but he proudly asserted that no one of those he befriended was ever recaptured.

A New England minister, Charles Torrey, left his quiet parish in 1838 to aid the slaves. In the five years before his arrest and conviction in a Virginia court he aided in the escape of nearly four hundred slaves. He died in prison in 1846 and was hailed as a martyr in the abolition cause. Jonathan Walker, captain of a New England merchant ship, attempted to ferry seven slaves from Florida to the Bahama Islands but was captured and sentenced to stand in the pillory and to be branded on the hand with the letters *S. S.* (slave stealer). Northern friends paid his fines and greeted him with loud approval when he returned. Whittier welcomed him with a poem, "The Branded Hand," which was long declaimed as a schoolroom classic of antislavery literature. Laura Haviland, a Michigan schoolteacher, went down into Kentucky in an effort to bring out the wife and children of a Negro who had himself been a fugitive. She failed in that effort but remained active in aid of the race and established a school for Negroes in Windsor, Ontario. William Chaplin, an Albany editor who spent much of his time in Washington reporting the proceedings of Congress, in 1850 took part in an attempt to free two slaves, one belonging to Alexander H. Stephens, the other to Robert Toombs. The plot was betrayed and Chaplin was arrested. Wealthy abolitionists provided the twenty thousand dollars bond required, and on their advice Chaplin forfeited the bond and left town, since conviction seemed sure if he stood trial.

One of the most famous and dramatic of these adventures of Northerners in slave states was John Brown's exploit in Missouri in the winter of 1858–59. Brown had often aided fugitives to escape, but this was his first expedition into Southern territory for the purpose. Appealed to by a Missouri slave who feared that he was to be sold south, Brown and a handful of men dashed across the border and came back with twelve slaves and some horses and other property. Then Brown and a few of his company escorted these fugitives in the dead of winter on a wild journey of twenty-five hundred miles through Kansas, Iowa, and Illinois to Detroit, and then across the river to Canadian soil. The exploit roused both fear and fury in the South and made the name of John Brown of Osawatomie widely known there. Six months later occurred the raid on Harpers Ferry that resulted in his capture and death. It was John Brown who convinced the South that the abolitionists intended to interfere with slavery in the states where it legally existed.[25]

Some of those who made their way deep into the South to aid the Negro in his flight to freedom were Negroes who had themselves been fugitive slaves — men and women who were willing, after attaining safety for themselves, to risk all they had gained and their very lives in an effort to lead others out of slavery. They knew the truth of the statement, "The desire for freedom was in the mind of every enslaved negro." Love for their families, ignorance of the route to be taken and of the means to be used, fear of the consequences of failure, kept hundreds of restless, discontented slaves in a bondage from which they would have gladly escaped. From the more venturesome or the most mistreated of this group came those who succeeded in making their way to the Northern states or to Canada, and from this successful few came a half dozen or more who went back to aid their fellows.

In many of the Canadian towns between Detroit and Niagara there were little colonies of fugitives who had been made welcome by a government that refused to surrender them and placed no restriction upon them other than those common to all settlers. In a careful case study of many of these ex-slaves with whom he talked in 1856 Benjamin Drew recorded their reasons for flight and their experiences as fugitives. Some of them told him stories of terrible mistreatment and of desperate danger, but again and again the main motive for escape was an irresistible desire for freedom.[26]

Among these residents of Canada was Josiah Henson, who had been born a slave but had escaped with his wife and children in 1830. Henson was a man of intelligence. He had been superintendent, or overseer, for his master and a plantation preacher, and had learned to read and write when his children went to school in Canada. In his own story of his life he left a record of several journeys into Southern states to bring out relatives and friends of those in the Canadian settlement. From his first trip he returned with thirty fugitives. On his next expedition he guided about a half dozen to Canada and recorded that when the boat reached land they sprang forward "to touch the soil of the freeman" and that they "danced and wept for joy, and kissed the earth on which they first stepped, no longer the SLAVE — but the FREE." In all Henson was instrumental in conveying one hundred and eighteen to Canadian soil.[27]

Most famous of all the Negro conductors on the Southern extension of the Railroad was Harriet Tubman, called Moses by her own people and General Tubman by Northern abolitionists. This remarkable woman told Benjamin Drew that she had never been happy or contented in slavery and that she had seen "hundreds of escaped slaves, but I never saw one who was willing to go back and be a slave." From her own safe haven in Canada she went South nineteen times and rescued more than three hundred slaves. She knew many routes and many methods of escape, and her guile and bravery were fabulous. She knew abolitionists of all walks of life, from the New England intelligentsia to the humble farmers who would shelter her destitute companions. Strong and disciplined herself, she would tolerate no cowardice and assured the faint-hearted that she would not hesitate to use her revolver if necessary; "Dead niggers tell no tales, you go on or die." Her messages to those who awaited her in the slave quarters of a Southern plantation were conveyed by song, for no one noticed a Negro woman singing as she passed. When she sang the song that ended,

> Dark and thorny is the desert,
>   Through de pilgrim makes his ways,
> Yet beyon' dis vale of sorrow,
>   Lies the fiel's of endless days.

those who had made up their minds to escape slipped away and followed her; but they knew the time had not yet come if she sang,

> Moses go down in Egypt,
>   Till ole Pharo' let me go;
> Hadn't been for Adam's fall,
>   Shouldn't hab to died at all.

And when she had brought them safely across the bridge at Niagara, they all raised their voices in the triumphant

> Glory to God and Jesus too,
>   One more soul is safe!
> O, go and carry de news,
>   One more soul got safe! [28]

Whether in the North or in the South, the operations of the Underground Railroad, employing as it did the efforts of both Negro and white agents, were a constant irritation and danger to the owners of slaves. But the feeling aroused in both free and slave states was, perhaps, out of proportion to the total number of successful fugitives. If one slave escaped from a Southern plantation, the security of all those left in the neighborhood was endangered; if one poor fugitive was kept safe from his pursuers in a Northern community, it was a triumph for the Railroad and won adherents to the antislavery cause.

Wilbur H. Siebert, whose study of the movement is conclusive, states that it is impossible to determine the exact number who were aided by the agents of the Underground Railroad. The very essence of its success was its secrecy, for in both North and South its activities were illegal and discovery would be not only disastrous to its passengers but expensive, if not dangerous, to its agents. Official reports such as the United States census appear to show that the number of fugitive slaves was inconsiderable, averaging probably not more than five hundred a year. These figures fail to justify the losses claimed by Southern spokesmen. Governor Quitman of Mississippi, for example, stated that from 1810 to 1850 the South lost by "abduction" one hundred thousand slaves worth thirty million dollars. But it is Siebert's opinion that the Southern estimates were nearer the truth than those of the official reports. From a consideration of all material available on the operations of the Underground Railroad in Ohio, he infers that as many as forty thousand fugitives traveled through that state alone. There is evidence, also, that over nine thousand received aid in Philadelphia in the same period, 1830–60, and many other centers of activity are known to have done as well. More than fifteen hundred agents and conductors lived in Ohio, and a somewhat larger number worked in the other Northern states. As Siebert concludes, "it is safe to say that the Underground Railroad was one of the greatest forces which brought on the Civil War, and thus destroyed slavery." [29]

THE FUGITIVE SLAVE LAW

In the early 1840's began that series of problems that made of the slavery question a political issue of paramount importance, involving almost every aspect of domestic and foreign affairs. There is something of the inevitability of Greek tragedy in the succession of events from the annexation of Texas to the Mexican War; from the settlement of 1850 to the Kansas question and to Brook's attack upon Sumner; from the creation of the Republican party in 1854 to the disruption of the Democratic party in 1860; from the Dred Scott decision through the Lincoln-Douglas debates to the raid at Harpers Ferry; and from the election of 1860 to secession and war a few months later. This progress is too well known to need retelling here.

It was in the debate over the Compromise of 1850 that Seward spoke of a "higher law than the Constitution," and it was in the same debate that Calhoun made his last tragic appeal for recognition of the rights of minorities. In both North and South the cleavage between the sections was recognized as fundamental. Webster joined with Clay in support of the Compromise, declaring that since nature had already determined that slavery could not go into the new territories, he would not "take pains uselessly to reaffirm an ordinance of nature, nor to reenact the will of God." By this Webster won the opprobrium of the antislavery forces and the bitterness of Whittier's "Ichabod," whose lines

> Of all we loved and honored, naught
>   Save power remains —
> A fallen angel's pride of thought,
>   Still strong in chains.
>
> All else is gone, from those great eyes,
>   The soul is fled;
> When faith is lost, when honor dies,
>   The man is dead!

will ever be connected with Webster's name.

The part of the Compromise hardest for the opponents of slavery to bear was the stringent Fugitive Slave Law, upon the enforcement of which the South staked its future allegiance to the Union. From the beginning it was evident that many people in the Northern states had not the slightest intention of submitting to the enforcement of the act or of permitting the activities of the Underground Railroad to be restricted. Charles Sumner tauntingly compared the law to the Stamp Act, which was "disowned and discredited" within a year of its passage, and stated that it violated the Constitution and so shocked the public conscience that all honest men were bound to disobey it.[30]

Joshua Giddings of Ohio expressed the sentiment of his antislavery constituency in a speech in 1852:

Let me say to Southern men: it is your privilege to catch your own slaves, if anyone catches them. . . . When you ask us to pay the expenses of arresting your slaves, or to give the President authority to appoint officers to do that dirty work, give them power to compel our people to give chase to the panting bondman, you overstep the bounds of the Constitution.[31]

It was always Giddings' idea that a slave who reached a free state lost his property status and was legally a man with the same right to defend himself as a white man. The new law, therefore, was in contradiction to all his theories and was to be considered unconstitutional. It could best be nullified, he thought, by state legislation preventing the use of state facilities and agencies for its enforcement.[32]

Occasion for resistance to the new law was not long delayed; between 1851 and 1854 captures were made in many Northern states. The most famous cases were probably those that came up in Boston. Conservative citizens of that city had long been opposed to Garrisonianism and had heartily disapproved agitation of the slavery question by Boston writers and clergymen. They now applauded the Fugitive Slave Law and endorsed Webster for his support of the Compromise of 1850. Boston antislavery men, however, were strengthened in their conviction that slavery was a menace to the freedom of all men and determined to do everything in their power to render the law ineffective.

Best known of all the Boston preachers, after the death of Dr. Channing, was Theodore Parker. He had not joined the abolition ranks until well into the 1840's, but he now led the attack upon the Fugitive Slave Law and upon the institution of slavery. He was a leading figure on the executive committee of the Boston Committee of Vigilance — an organization of two hundred citizens and a formidable group in brains, family, and renown.[33] Samuel Gridley Howe, Wendell Phillips, Edmund Jackson, Charles Ellis, and Lewis Hayden — one of the most famous of the fugitive slaves — joined

Parker on the executive committee, and upon them rested the burden of the care of Boston refugees and of the rescue of any who might be recaptured. Richard Henry Dana acted as counsel for members of the committee accused of having aided fugitives to escape; Thomas Wentworth Higginson played an active part in attempts at jail delivery; and Horace Mann attended meetings to discuss plans for the lawbreaking.[34] Old Boston was shaken to its very center by the conflict; many men whose philanthropies and reforms the city had delighted to honor were in the ranks of the lawless.

Parker knew all the Negroes of Boston and counted many of them as his parishioners. It was as the friend and pastor of William and Ellen Craft that he took them into his own home when they were sought by slave-hunters, and he wrote his sermons that week with a loaded pistol on his desk.[35] And it was Parker who went with the eminent lawyer, Ellis Loring, to the hotel where the slave-hunters lodged to warn them that their chase was futile and that it would be well for them to leave Boston before they were forced to do so by an angry mob.

Early in 1851 the fugitive Shadrach was seized and lodged in the courthouse pending a hearing before the federal commissioner, for the use of the jail was forbidden by Massachusetts law. He was rescued by the Negro preacher, Lewis Hayden, and twenty of his friends from Nigger Hill and was spirited off to Canada with the help of many of Massachusetts' white citizens. Parker proclaimed it "the noblest deed done in Boston since the destruction of the tea in 1773." Several of those concerned in the rescue were tried in accord with the terms of the Fugitive Slave Law. Their guilt was undeniable, but the jury was hung because one man held out for acquittal. Long afterward he told Parker that he himself had driven Shadrach from Concord to Leominster after the rescue!

All such attempts were not successful, however, and more men probably came over to the antislavery cause after the tragic failures than after such rescues as Shadrach's. Two dramatic cases in Boston that resulted in the return of the fugitives to their Southern masters were those of William Simms in 1851 and Anthony Burns in 1854. On both occasions military protection was given the court, and military escorts guarded the prisoners as they were taken to the wharf for embarkation.[36] After the departure of Simms the Boston antislavery people held a huge mass meeting on the Common at which Phillips and Parker spoke, and a year later at a meeting of the Committee of Vigilance called in recognition of the first anniversary of that event, Parker delivered one of his greatest addresses on slavery, in which he condemned Webster and Boston in scathing terms. And after the failure of the attempt to rescue Anthony Burns, Parker's sermon, "The Law of God and the Statutes," was a challenging call to the support of the higher law.

Other Transcendentalists also advised against compliance with the law. Speaking in Concord in 1851, Emerson declared that every liberal study was discredited and the value of life was reduced when such a law could be enforced and when Boston became, for the fugitive, "his master's hound." [37] Thoreau, too, spoke on the subject:

I have heard a good deal said about trampling this law under foot. Why, one need not go out of his way to do that. This law rises not to the level of the head or the reason; its natural habitat is in the dirt. It was born and bred, and has its life, only in the dust and mire, on a level with the feet; and he who walks with freedom . . . will inevitably tread on it, and trample it under foot.[38]

Outside Massachusetts the law was administered with even less success. When asked what he would take for evidence of the identity of a fugitive slave, a Vermont judge said he would be satisfied with "nothing less than a Bill of Sale from the Almighty!" In Syracuse, New York, when the fugitive Jerry McHenry broke away at his first examination, the crowd opened its ranks to let him through, only to see him recaptured by the officers of the court. An alarm bell summoned the local vigilance committee, and Gerrit Smith and Samuel May planned the rescue, which was effected by a mob that broke into the courthouse and carried Jerry off in triumph. Eighteen persons were indicted, but, in a community so hostile toward the law, no other action was taken. The United States marshal was then put on trial for kidnaping before a local judge who stoutly declared the Fugitive Slave Law unconstitutional. In Oberlin, Ohio, college students and town residents rescued the Negro John Rice, and in Christina, Pennsylvania, a slave-hunter, Edward Gorsuch, was killed and several fugitives living in the town were rushed to safety. One man was arrested and tried for treason but was acquitted; others were held for "riot and murder," but the grand jury ignored the bill. Obviously, it was difficult to administer a law in regions growing steadily more hostile to its enforcement.

Mass meetings were held in many Northern states to express the approval of the people for the rescuers and their sympathy for the captured. State after state passed laws designed to obstruct the operation of the federal statute, and under these "personal liberty laws" slave-catchers were indicted as kidnapers, local jails and other facilities were denied them, and local militia refused the summons of federal authorities. The supreme court of Wisconsin upheld the rescuers of a fugitive, Joshua Glover of Racine, declared the Fugitive Slave Law unconstitutional, and virtually nullified the law for the state of Wisconsin by refusing to honor federal writs issued for those who violated it.

This increase of interest in the fugitive and of willingness to assist him in his flight from bondage led to a great increase in activity on the Underground Railroad. The years between 1850 and the beginning of the Civil War found every route crowded and conductors operating with an impunity they had not known before.

It is only against this background that the complicity of such men as Gerrit Smith, F. B. Sanborn, T. W. Higginson, and Theodore Parker in an adventure so violent and so illegal as John Brown's exploit at Harpers Ferry can be understood. Some of those who aided Brown may have thought with Higginson that his sole intention was to gather together bands of slaves whom he could guide to freedom or establish permanently in the mountain regions of the South.[39] Others like Sanborn, who admitted knowing that violence was inevitable in carrying out the plot, were ever afterward proud of the part they had played in it and were convinced that the martyrdom of John Brown had aided the cause of freedom.[40] Only one, Gerrit Smith, lost his nerve when the adventure ended in disaster and those who had aided Brown were faced with the possibility of being made to share the responsibility with him. Smith's repudiation of Brown and denial of knowledge of the plot was due to a combination of lack of courage and of genuine shock at the terrible results of the failure.[41] In no case was there any rejection of the idea that a higher law than those of state or nation justified illegality and violence.

When John Brown died the death of murderer and traitor, Northern bells were tolled and crepe fluttered in the Northern breeze. Emerson said that all people, "in proportion to their sensibility and self-respect," sympathized with John Brown,[42] and Thoreau made one of America's greatest public addresses in his "Plea for Captain John Brown."

Is it not possible [he asked] that an individual may be right and a government wrong? Are laws to be enforced simply because they are made? or declared by any number of men to be good, if they are *not* good? Is there any necessity for a man's being a tool to perform a deed of which his better nature disapproves? Is it the intention of lawmakers that *good* men shall be hung ever? . . . Some eighteen hundred years ago Christ was crucified; this morning perhaps, Captain Brown was hung. These are the two ends of a chain which is not without its links. He is not Old Brown any longer; he is an angel of light.[43]

The ideological cleavage between the antislavery North and the South was complete. The two positions were as far apart as the poles, and the South had ample proof that in respect to the Fugitive Slave Law the Compromise of 1850 was null and void.

THE TREND TOWARD SECESSION

The refusal of the North to accept Southern dictation in the matter of fugitive slaves was met by the elaboration and open expression of ideas inherent in the teachings of the great Southern political leader, John C. Calhoun. The Constitution, said Calhoun, is a compact between the states by which certain functions have been given by consent to an agent, the federal government. The rights of that agent are strictly circumscribed, and any trespass may be met with action by the aggrieved member of the compact. The states have never delegated control over their domestic institutions, and meddling on the part of the federal government, another state, or a combination of the citizens of other states, is not warranted by the Constitution and may weaken or destroy the Union itself.

Following such ideas to their logical conclusion, and Calhoun was nothing if not logical, he maintained that Congress could not interfere with slavery in the District of Columbia or in the territories, that any attack upon slavery in a free state was unconstitutional, that the people of a territory could not impair the right of property in slaves, and that slave property in free states or territories was entitled to the protection of the United States government by armed force if necessary. Any violation of these rights was to be considered an insult to the South and a step toward the destruction of the Union.

Calhoun's friends and disciples were not slow to accept his ideas, and they quickly cut through some of his involved logic to bring into the open the conclusion that Calhoun, in his love for the Union, had been reluctant to disclose. As early as 1833 the South Carolina fire-eater, Barnwell Rhett, had advised secession:

Sir, if a Confederacy of the Southern States could now be obtained, should we not deem it a happy termination — happy beyond expectation, of our long struggle for our rights against oppression? . . . a people owning slaves are mad, or worse than mad, who do not hold their destinies in their own hands.[44]

Few joined Rhett in this demand for secession in 1833, but as the years went on the idea grew more popular with Southern political leaders. Rhett of South Carolina, Yancey of Alabama, Edmund Ruffin of Virginia, Louis Wigfall of Texas, John Quitman and Albert Gallatin Brown of Mississippi, and many others, in the Nashville Convention of 1850 and later in their respective states, kept the idea before the Southern people, and repetition accustomed the public to it so that there was no general shock when these leaders piloted the respective states along the "course of the South to secession."[45] By 1850 there was widespread approval of the idea of secession, and Southern leaders were only awaiting a sufficiently dramatic crisis to win Southern consent to the creation of a new confederacy.

In the meantime other political leaders of the South added contributions to the proslavery literature. Howell Cobb of Georgia published *A Scriptural Examination of Slavery* in 1856. In 1853 Robert Toombs of the same state delivered an address at Emory College extolling the benefits of slavery which had made "unions, mobs, and strikes unknown." And Alexander H. Stephens slowly evolved the elaborate justification of both slavery and secession that he stated many years later in his *Constitutional View of the War Between the States*. The signs of the times were evident farther

North in the border states, also. As early as 1840 Professor George Tucker of the University of Virginia wrote:

The question of *separation* will always be the question of *war*. The *constitutional question* will be drowned in the din and tumult of arms and finally decided by the issue of the war. *Victory* is the great arbiter of right in national disputes, and the scale of justice on which she happens to light is almost sure to preponderate.[46]

The younger generation of Southern politicians were secessionists proudly and without apology. One of them, Preston Brooks, whom the assault upon Sumner had just made notorious, stated in 1856 that he had been a disunionist "from the time he first could think."

The bitterness of the South is expressed as well in the words of those who were not political leaders. In an editorial in *De Bow's Review* in May 1847 appeared the statement:

We have not been listened to while we spoke; they would not listen were one to speak from the dead. Even patience becomes a vice. What others think is nothing; for us there has come to be but one sentiment now, — as Southerners, as *Americans*, as *men*, we deny the right of being *called to account* for our institutions, our policy, our laws, or our government. For these there is no *explanation* to be made, no apology; it is sufficient that we, we the people of a State, we the people of half the States of this Union, in our sovereign capacity, in our sovereign right, in our sovereign independence of all other people or peoples upon earth, of all mortal men, have decreed our institutions as they are, *and so will dare to maintain them!* [47]

POLITICS AND ECONOMICS OF THE ROAD TO WAR

It was only with the issues arising from the thrust of settlement to the west of the Mississippi River that the slavery question came to be of great political importance. When Birney first ran for president on the Liberty party ticket in 1840, he polled but seven thousand votes. In 1848 in the midst of the controversy over the status of slavery in the area acquired from Mexico the Free Soil party received three hundred thousand votes. The change in both name and numbers is significant. In 1839 the Liberty Association of Knox County, Illinois, pledged its members to vote only for candidates who made "the protection of the inalienable rights of man" their first duty, but in the 1840 election only one of those who signed the pledge voted for Birney.[48] Within a decade the antislavery men of

Illinois knew that their interests as men of principle and as Western farmers were identical. This shift in position was characteristic of other Midwestern communities, where men had become convinced that it was essential to their interests that slavery be kept out of the territories. The Kansas question brought to the fore in opposition to slavery many men whose antislavery sentiments had not been urgent until that time.

This fundamental sectionalism has been the favorite theme of modern Southern writers, but in their assertion that it was the basic if not the sole cause of the Civil War they forget the moral issue, which was of far more importance than economics or sectionalism to countless Northerners. In the light of the seventy-five years of conflict over the ethics of slavery, the Southern emphasis on an "egocentric sectionalism" [49] by which Northern industrialists endeavored to force their will upon the South through the domination of a numerical majority seems altogether inadequate. That sectional interests were of importance in deepening the abyss between North and South cannot, of course, be denied.

The strength of the abolition movement had not been in Eastern urban areas but among the small farmers and merchants of the Middle West, and in the same area, among those who hoped to find new homes for themselves or for their sons in the trans-Mississippi area, the Free Soil doctrine took root. It was no coincidence that the Republican party was organized in that same Midwest when its Free Soil–antislavery position was assailed in the Kansas-Nebraska Bill. The spirit of the West was democratic and popular sovereignty was its natural expression, but only so long as the will of the people should be permitted free control in the territories. The attempt to make Kansas a slave state and the federal protection for slavery in the territories, implicit in the Dred Scott decision, made the Western Democrats almost as firm opponents of Southern demands as were the Free Soil Republicans. At last the agrarian region of the country was divided into hostile camps — Southern planters and their satellites against the farmer population of the Northwest. When the Republican party polled more than a million votes in its first presidential election of 1856, it was evidence of the strength of Western Free Soil sentiment as well as of Northern antislavery opinion.

With the threat of a split in the agrarian bloc that had been strong enough to prevent high tariffs and other aids to the industrial regions inimical to its interests, the South became increasingly conscious of its minority position and more and more inclined toward secession. In the 1850's the trend was all too apparent; the slave states had less than forty per cent of the nation's population, and a third of that was made up of slaves. The free states now had almost double the number of representatives in the House and, since the admission of California, a majority in the Senate. If an antislavery third party should elect a president or dominate a Congress, there would remain no obstacle to the rule of the majority. The South, therefore, demanded guarantees for its institutions and asked for equality in power even though it was outnumbered and though the slavery on which it staked its all was uneconomic and outmoded.

The Northwest wanted security for its penetration of the territories and its exploitation of their resources, a homestead act, and railroads. Those things the Northeast was willing to grant in return for protective tariffs, banking and currency reforms, and cheap labor. In the 1850's the union between the West and industrial capitalism was cemented, and that economic sectionalism of which the South had so long been apprehensive became a reality. Big business, which had for so long supported the proslavery position because of commercial ties, now became antislavery, and its entry into the Republican party was signalized by a protective tariff plank in the 1856 platform. When the one adversary was personified as the "Slave Power" and the other as "Black Republicanism," the political machinery of the country broke down and war instead of a peaceful solution of the problem was the result. A complex of emotions and motives drove men on to what seemed, in the words of Senator Seward in 1858:

. . . an irrepressible conflict between opposing and enduring forces. . . . it means that the United States must and will, sooner or later, become either entirely a slaveholding nation or a free nation. It is the failure to apprehend this great truth that induces so many unsuccessful attempts at final compromise between the slave and the free states; and it is the existence of this great fact that renders all such pretended compromises when made, vain and ephemeral.[50]

In the progress toward Armageddon animosities were stirred up that could not be calmed. The controversy had gradually invaded every phase of the life of both sections. The theory of a higher law rendered valueless all guarantees of the "peculiar institution" which the South persisted in considering a positive good, and the bitterness of the South was made unbearable by a realization that its way of life depended upon an institution condemned by the rest of the civilized world. It was illustrative of this bitterness that the old radical, Edmund Ruffin, should plead to be allowed to fire the first shot of a war for Southern independence, and that, when defeat came in that war, Ruffin should end his own life, leaving a message of "unmitigated hate to Yankee rule — to all political, social, and business connections with the Yankees, and to the Yankee race." There were few in the South in 1861, and perhaps few in the North, who heeded the sad conclusion of Lincoln's first inaugural address:

We are not enemies, but friends. We must not be enemies. Though passion may have strained, it must not break our bonds of affection. The mystic chords of memory, stretching from every battlefield and patriot grave to every living heart and hearth-stone all over this broad land, will yet swell the chorus of the Union when again touched, as surely they will be, by the better angels of our nature.

Epilogue

That is the story of how Americans, sometimes with high courage and deliberate design and sometimes by accident or through indifference, fulfilled the destiny decreed by their inheritance from the past, by the circumstances of space and resources, and by the spirit of the century in which they lived. There was room in America for seemingly limitless growth in population and an opportunity for incredible expansion of national wealth. There was room, also, for social experimentation; there was asylum for the oppressed of other lands; and there was an honest recognition of the worth of the individual and of his right to develop his capacities and take advantage of the rich opportunities offered him in the young republic.

In a time when the liberal and the humanitarian were accorded almost universal hearing and when men of many nations were asking a share in the democratization of institutions, Americans were superbly conscious of the fact that it was their duty and their privilege to lead the way in reforms that brought better care to the unfortunate, hope to the poor and downtrodden, and realization of their highest ambitions to the aspiring. Men of that day were more than a little touched with transcendentalism; the religious faith of the fathers was mingled with the perfectionism of the revival; and the rationalism of Jefferson merged with the democracy of the frontier. The result was a period of social ferment, sometimes a little mad, a little confused about directions, but always full of optimism, of growth, and of positive affirmation. The men and women who lived and worked in it were filled with confidence and joy in the present and with faith that the future would be what they and their children wished to make it.

America was the land of the free, and Americans were free men, willing and proud to share in its building. They were still imbued with the spirit of high adventure that had sent men forth in the sixteenth century to explore the far corners of the earth. But the day of the merchant adventurer and the pioneer was drawing to a close. The desperate perplexities of a nation divided into two economic systems and subscribing to opposing systems of social theory were to be resolved by a great Civil War, and the acceleration of all lines of development caused by that war was to change the entire American scene. The earlier humanitarian causes were swallowed up in the crusade against slavery. After the war industrial capitalism, greatly increased population, and growing urbanization so marked American life that when the later years of the century called forth a new wave of humanitarianism and aroused a dynamic civic conscience, both the times and the movements were different.

But the fundamentals of the American faith and the American way of life had been set by the pioneers and the crusaders of the early years: men to whom the life of the perfect Christ gave hope that their lives and their institutions might be perfected, men who saw no limits for the advancement of the individual or of the nation, men who were proud to fight in the cause of democracy and freedom.

Bibliography and Notes

This is a selective bibliography. It makes no claim to completeness. It comprises the works actually used in preparing this book and may be considered a rather wide sampling of a mass of similar material. The General Bibliography is made up of various categories of material applicable to more than two chapters of the text. These titles are not repeated under specific chapters unless they appear in footnotes. Following the notes for each chapter are listed additional books and articles used in its preparation but not included in the General Bibliography. The dates of publication, given with the first reference to each work, are those of the editions used by the author — the most convenient therefore, not necessarily the earliest.

GENERAL BIBLIOGRAPHY
Contemporary Descriptions of the American Scene: European and American Commentators

ABDY, EDWARD STRUTT. *Journal of a Residence and Tour in the United States of North America from April, 1833, to October, 1834.* 1835.

BAIRD, ROBERT. *Religion in America.* 1856.

BARTLETT, DAVID V. G. *Modern Agitators; or Pen Portraits of Living American Reformers.* 1855.

BIRKBECK, MORRIS. *Letters from Illinois.* 1818.

———. *Notes on a Journey in America, from the Coast of Virginia to the Territory of Illinois.* 3rd ed. 1818.

BOARDMAN, JAMES. *America and the Americans. By a Citizen of the World.* 1833.

BRADBURY, JOHN. *Travels in the Interior of North America, in the years 1809, 1810, and 1811.* Vol. V in Thwaites, *Early Western Travels* (1904).

BREMER, FREDRIKA. *The Homes of the New World; Impressions of America.* 2 vols. 1835.

BROTHERS, THOMAS. *The United States of North America as They Are; Not as They Are Generally Described: Being a Cure for Radicalism.* 1840.

BUCKINGHAM, JAMES SILK. *America — Historical, Statistic, and Descriptive.* 3 vols. 1841.

———. *The Slave States of America.* 2 vols. 1842.

CHAMBERS, WILLIAM. *Things as They Are in America.* 1854.

CHEVALIER, MICHEL. *Society, Manners, and Politics in the United States; Being a Series of Letters on North America.* 1839.

COBBETT, WILLIAM. *A Year's Residence in the United States of America.* 3rd ed. 1828. (First published in 1818.)

COLTON, CALVIN. *The Americans. By an American in London.* 1833.

COOPER, JAMES FENIMORE. *America and the Americans: Notions Picked up by a Travelling Bachelor.* 2nd ed. 2 vols. 1836.

———. *The American Democrat.* 1838. Mencken edition, 1931.

CRÈVECOEUR, MICHEL GUILLAUME ST. JEAN DE. *Letters from an American Farmer.* By J. Hector St. John de Crèvecoeur. 1926. (First published in 1782.)

DAVIS, EMERSON. *The Half Century: or, a History of Changes That Have Taken*

Place, and Events that Have Transpired, Chiefly in the United States, between 1800 and 1850. 1851.

DICKENS, CHARLES. *American Notes for General Circulation.* 4th ed. 2 vols. 1842.

DIXON, WILLIAM HEPWORTH. *New America.* 1867.

DWIGHT, TIMOTHY. *Travels in New England and New York.* 4 vols. 1821.

FAUX, WILLIAM. *Faux's Memorable Days in America, November 27, 1818–July 21, 1820.* 1823. Vols. XI and XII in Thwaites, *Early Western Travels* (1905).

FEATHERSTONHAUGH, GEORGE WILLIAM. *Excursion through the Slave States, from Washington on the Potomac to the Frontier of Mexico.* 1844.

FERRALL, S. A. *A Ramble of Six Thousand Miles through the United States of America.* 1832.

FIDLER, ISAAC. *Observations on Professions, Literature, Manners, and Emigration, in the United States and Canada. Made during a Residence there in 1832.* 1833.

FLOWER, GEORGE. *History of the English Settlement in Edwards County, Illinois, Founded in 1817 and 1818, by Morris Birkbeck and George Flower.* 1882.

FORD, THOMAS. *History of Illinois.* 1854.

GODLEY, JOHN ROBERT. *Letters from America.* 2 vols. 1844.

GRUND, FRANCIS J. *The Americans, in their Moral, Social, and Political Relations.* 1837.

————. *Aristocracy in America. From the Sketch-book of a German Nobleman.* 1839.

HALIBURTON, THOMAS CHANDLER. *The Americans at Home; or Byeways, Backwoods, and Prairies.* Edited by the author of "Sam Slick." 3 vols. 1854.

HALL, CAPTAIN BASIL. *Travels in North America, in the Years 1827 and 1828.* 2 vols. 1829.

HALL, MRS. BASIL. *The Aristocratic Journey.* Una Pope-Hennessey, ed. 1931.

HAMILTON, THOMAS. *Men and Manners in America.* 2 vols. 1833.

HULME, THOMAS. *Journal made during a Tour of the Western Countries of America.* Part III of William Cobbett, *A Year's Residence in the United States of America.*

JANSON, CHARLES WILLIAM. *The Stranger in America, 1793–1806.* 1935. (Reprinted from the edition of 1807.)

JOHNSTON, L. W. A. *Notes on North America.* 2 vols. 1851.

LATROBE, CHARLES JOSEPH. *The Rambler in North America, 1832–1833.* 2 vols. 1835.

LEVINGE, CAPT. R. G. A. *Echoes from the Backwoods; or Scenes of Transatlantic Life.* 1849.

LIEBER, FRANCIS. *The Stranger in America; or, Letters to a Gentleman in Germany: Comprising Sketches of the Manners, Society, and National Peculiarities of the United States.* 1835.

LYELL, CHARLES. *Travels in North America in the Years 1841 and 1842.* 2 vols. 1845.

————. *A Second Visit to the United States of North America.* 2 vols. 1849.

MACKAY, ALEXANDER. *The Western World; or, Travels in the United States in 1846–1847.* 3rd ed. 3 vols. 1850.

MACKAY, CHARLES. *Life and Liberty in America.* 1859.

MARRYAT, CAPT. FREDERICK (C. B.). *A Diary in America.* 3 vols. 1839.

MARTINEAU, HARRIET. *Retrospect of Western Travel.* 3 vols. 1838.

————. *Society in America.* 3 vols. 1837.

MELISH, JOHN. *Travels in the United States of America, in the Years 1806–1811 . . .* 1812.

MURAT, ACHILLE. *A Moral and Political Sketch of the United States of North America.* 1833.

NICHOLS, THOMAS LOW. *Forty Years of American Life, 1821–1861.* 1937. (First published in 1864.)

PECK, JOHN MASON. *Forty Years of Pioneer Life.* Rufus Babcock, ed. 1864.

POWER, TYRONE. *Impressions of America; during the Years, 1833, 1834, and 1835.* 2 vols. 1836.

REESE, DAVID MEREDITH. *Humbugs of New York: being a Remonstrance against Popular Delusion; whether in Science, Philosophy, or Religion.* 1838.

ROCHEFOUCAULD LIANCOURT, DUC DE LA. *Travels through the United States of North America, the Country of the Iroquois, and Upper Canada, in the Years 1795, 1796 and 1797.* 1799.

RUPP, I. DANIEL, comp. *An Original History of the Religious Denominations at Present Existing in the United States.* 1844.

SAXE-WEIMAR EISENACH, KARL BERNHARD, DUKE OF. *Travels through North America during the Years 1825 and 1826.* 2 vols. 1828.

SMITH, MARGARET BAYARD. *The First Forty Years of Washington Society.* Gaillard Hunt, ed. 1906.

STUART, JAMES. *Three Years in North America.* 2 vols. 1833.

STURGE, JOSEPH. *A Visit to the United States in 1841.* 1842.

THWAITES, REUBEN GOLD. *Early Western Travels, 1748–1846.* 32 vols. 1904–7.

TOCQUEVILLE, ALEXIS DE. *Democracy in America.* 2 vols. 1835.

TROLLOPE, FRANCES. *Domestic Manners of the Americans.* 1927. (Reprinted from 5th ed., 1839. First published in 1832.)

TUDOR, HENRY. *Narrative of a Tour in North America . . .* 2 vols. 1834.

VIGNE, GODFREY THOMAS. *Six Months in America.* 2 vols. 1832.

WOODS, JOHN. *Two Years' Residence in the Settlement on the English Prairie — June 25, 1820–July 3, 1821.* 1822. Reprinted as Vol. X in Thwaites. *Early Western Travels* (1904).

Published Works, Memoirs, and Biographies

ADAMS, JOHN QUINCY. *Diary.* Allan Nevins, ed. 1928.

ALCOTT, A (MOS) BRONSON. *Journals of Bronson Alcott.* Odell Shepard, ed. 1938.

ALCOTT, LOUISA MAY. *Louisa May Alcott; Her Life, Letters and Journals.* Ednah D. Cheney, ed. 1928.

AUSTIN, GEORGE LOWELL. *The Life and Times of Wendell Phillips.* 1901.

BANCROFT, FREDERIC. *The Life of William H. Seward.* 2 vols. 1900.

BARNES, GILBERT H., and DWIGHT L. DUMOND, eds. *Letters of Theodore Dwight Weld, Angelina Grimké Weld, and Sarah Grimké, 1822–1844.* 2 vols. 1934.

BASSETT, JOHN SPENCER, ed. *The Correspondence of Andrew Jackson.* 7 vols. 1926–35.

BEECHER, LYMAN. *Autobiography, Correspondence . . .* Charles Beecher, ed. 2 vols. 1865.

BEVERIDGE, ALBERT. *Abraham Lincoln, 1809–1858.* 2 vols. 1928.

BROOKES, GEORGE S. *Friend Anthony Benezet.* 1937.

BROWNSON, ORESTES. *Works.* Henry B. Brownson, ed. 20 vols. 1882–87.

CHANNING, W. E. *Memoirs of William Ellery Channing.* 6th ed. 3 vols. 1854.

————. *Works.* 6 vols. 1846.

COMMAGER, HENRY STEELE. *Theodore Parker.* 1936.

COULTER, E. MERTON. *William G. Brownlow, Fighting Parson of the Southern Highlands.* 1937.

CUNNINGHAM, CHARLES E. *Timothy Dwight, 1752–1817: A Biography.* 1942.

EMERSON, RALPH WALDO. *The Complete Works of Ralph Waldo Emerson with a Biographical Introduction by E. W. Emerson.* 12 vols. Centenary edition, 1903–4. (First published, 1883–94.)

————. *Journals of Ralph Waldo Emerson, with Annotations.* E. W. Emerson and W. E. Forbes, eds. 10 vols. 1909–14.

FUESS, CLAUDE M. *Daniel Webster.* 2 vols. 1930.

GARRISON, F. J. and W. P. *Life of William Lloyd Garrison.* 3 vols. 1894.

GOODMAN, NATHAN GERSON. *Benjamin Rush, Physician and Citizen, 1746–1813.* 1934.

GREELEY, HORACE. *Recollections of a Busy Life.* 1868.

GUMMERE, AMELIA M. *Journals and Essays of John Woolman.* 1922.

HARLOW, RALPH. *Gerrit Smith*. 1939.
HIGGINSON, THOMAS WENTWORTH. *Cheerful Yesterdays*. 1900.
HONE, PHILIP. *The Diary of Philip Hone, 1828–1851*. Allan Nevins, ed. 1927.
LOWELL, JAMES RUSSELL. *Letters*. C. E. Norton, ed. 2 vols. 1893.
LYMAN, GEORGE D. *John Marsh Pioneer*. 1930.
MACLAY, WILLIAM. *The Journal of William Maclay, United States Senator from Pennsylvania, 1789–1791*. 1890.
MAGUIRE, JOHN FRANCIS. *Father Mathew: a Biography*. 1898.
MALONE, DUMAS. *The Public Life of Thomas Cooper, 1783–1839*. 1926.
MARTINEAU, HARRIET. *Autobiography*. Maria Weston Chapman, ed. 3 vols. 1877.
MAYER, J. P. *Alexis de Tocqueville; a Biographical Essay in Political Science*. 1940.
MORSE, JOHN T. *Life and Letters of Oliver Wendell Holmes*. 2 vols. 1897.
MORTON, S. G. *A Memoir of William Maclure, Esq.* 1844.
OSSOLI, MARGARET FULLER. *Memoirs of Margaret Fuller Ossoli*. With biographical sketches by J. F. Clarke, R. W. Emerson, and W. H. Channing. 2 vols. 1852.
PADOVER, SAUL K. *Jefferson*. 1942.
PIERCE, EDWARD L. *Memoir and Letters of Charles Sumner*. 4 vols. 1877–93.
PIERSON, GEORGE WILSON. *Tocqueville and Beaumont in America*. 1938.
POPE-HENNESSY, UNA. *Three English Women in America*. 1929.
QUINCY, JOSIAH. *Figures of the Past from the Leaves of Old Journals*. 1883.
RICHARDSON, ROBERT. *Memoirs of Alexander Campbell*. 2 vols. 1868–70.
ROURKE, CONSTANCE M. *Trumpets of Jubilee*. 1927.
SCHLESINGER, ARTHUR MEIER, JR. *Orestes Brownson; a Pilgrim's Progress*. 1939.
SHEPARD, ODELL. *Pedlar's Progress; the Life of Bronson Alcott*. 1937.
STICKNEY, WILLIAM, ed. *Autobiography of Amos Kendall*. 1872.
STOWE, LYMAN BEECHER. *Saints, Sinners and Beechers*. 1934.
SUMNER, CHARLES. *Works*. 20 vols. 1900.
THOREAU, HENRY DAVID. *Works*. Riverside edition. 11 vols. 1884–93.
TURNER, RALPH E. *James Silk Buckingham, a Social Biography, 1786–1855*. 1934.
VAN DOREN, CARL C. *Benjamin Franklin*. 1938.
WADE, JOHN DONALD. *Augustus Baldwin Longstreet; a Study of the Development of Culture in the South*. 1924.
WEISS, JOHN. *Life and Correspondence of Theodore Parker*. 2 vols. 1864.
WHITE, ANDREW DICKSON. *Autobiography of Andrew Dickson White*. 2 vols. 1905.
WHITNEY, JANET. *John Woolman, American Quaker*. 1942.
WHITTIER, JOHN GREENLEAF. *Complete Poetical Works*. 1881.
WOODLEY, THOMAS FREDERICK. *Thaddeus Stevens*. 1934.

General Accounts, Standard Historical Works, and Monographs

ADAMS, EPHRAIM D. *The Power of Ideals in American History*. 1913.
ADAMS, HENRY. *The History of the United States of America, 1801–1817*. 9 vols. 1889–91.
ADAMS, JAMES TRUSLOW. *The Epic of America*. 1931.
BATES, ERNEST SUTHERLAND. *The American Faith; Its Religious, Political, and Economic Foundation*. 1940.
BEARD, CHARLES A. and MARY R. *The American Spirit*. 1942.
———. *The Rise of American Civilization*. 1927.
BOWDEN, WITT. *The Industrial History of the United States*. 1930.
BRANCH, EDWARD DOUGLAS. *The Sentimental Years, 1836–1860*. 1934.
CALVERTON, VICTOR F. *The Awakening of America*. 1939.
———. *Where Angels Dared to Tread*. 1941.
CARLTON, FRANK TRACY. *Organized Labor in American History*. 1920.
CHALFANT, HARRY MALCOLM. *These Agitators and Their Idea*. 1931.
CHANNING, EDWARD. *History of the United States*. 6 vols. 1905.

CHILDS, FRANCIS SERGEANT. *French Refugee Life in the United States, 1790–1800; An American Chapter of the French Revolution.* 1940.

COHEN, MORRIS R. *Reason and Nature, An Essay on the Meaning of the Scientific Method.* 1931.

COMMONS, JOHN R., and others. *History of Labour in the United States.* 4 vols. 1918–35.

CURTI, MERLE. *The Growth of American Thought.* 1943.

DABNEY, VIRGINIUS. *Liberalism in the South.* 1932.

DE VOTO, BERNARD A. *Mark Twain's America.* 1932.

FISH, CARL RUSSELL. *The Rise of the Common Man.* 1927.

GABRIEL, RALPH HENRY. *The Course of American Democratic Thought.* 1940.

GIDE, CHARLES. *Communist and Co-Operative Colonies.* 1930.

HACKER, LOUIS M. *The Triumph of American Capitalism.* 1940.

HARLOW, RALPH. *The Growth of the United States.* 1932.

HILLQUIT, MORRIS. *History of Socialism in the United States.* 1903.

HINDS, WILLIAM ALFRED. *American Communities and Co-operative Colonies.* 1908. (First published in 1878.)

JONES, HOWARD MUMFORD. *American and French Culture, 1750–1848.* 1927.

KIRKLAND, EDWARD C. *A History of American Economic Life.* 1939.

KITTREDGE, GEORGE LYMAN. *The Old Farmer and His Almanack.* 1904.

LUDLUM, DAVID M. *Social Ferment in Vermont, 1791–1850.* 1939.

McMASTER, JOHN BACH. *The History of the People of the United States.* 8 vols. 1915.

MESICK, JANE LOUISE. *The English Traveller in America, 1785–1835.* 1922.

MINNIGERODE, MEADE. *The Fabulous Forties, 1840–1850, a Presentation of Private Life.* 1924.

MORSE, JARVIS M. *A Neglected Period in Connecticut's History, 1818–1850.* 1933.

MYERS, GUSTAVUS. *The History of American Idealism.* 1925.

————. *History of Bigotry in the United States.* 1943.

NORDHOFF, CHARLES. *The Communistic Societies of the United States . . .* 1875.

NOYES, JOHN HUMPHREY. *History of American Socialisms.* 1870.

OSGOOD, H. L. *The American Colonies in the Seventeenth Century.* 3 vols. 1904–7.

————. *The American Colonies in the Eighteenth Century.* 4 vols. 1924.

PARRINGTON, VERNON LOUIS. *Main Currents in American Thought* (Vol. I: *The Colonial Mind.* Vol. II: *The Romantic Revolution in America, 1800–1860*). 1927.

PATTEE, FRED LEWIS. *The Feminine Fifties.* 1940.

POST, ALBERT. *Popular Freethought in America, 1825–1850.* 1943.

RHODES, JAMES FORD. *History of the United States from the Compromise of 1850.* 7 vols. 1893.

ROURKE, CONSTANCE M. *American Humor; a Study of the National Character.* 1931.

————. *The Roots of American Culture and Other Essays.* 1942.

ROWE, K. W. *Mathew Carey, a Study in American Economic Development.* 1933.

RUSK, RALPH LESLIE. *The Literature of the Middle Western Frontier.* 2 vols. 1925.

SCHLESINGER, ARTHUR MEIER. *New Viewpoints in American History.* 1934.

SELDES, GILBERT V. *The Stammering Century.* 1928.

SHRYOCK, RICHARD HARRISON. *The Development of Modern Medicine.* 1936.

————. "Sylvester Graham and the Health Reform Movement, 1830–1870," *Mississippi Valley Historical Review,* XVIII:172ff. (September 1931).

SIMONS, A. M. *Class Struggles in America.* 1907.

SMITH, BERNARD. *Forces in American Criticism; a Study in the History of American Literary Thought.* 1939.

SYMES, LILLIAN, and TRAVERS CLEMENT. *Rebel America; the Story of Social Revolt in the United States.* 1934.

TRAIN, ARTHUR C. *Puritan's Progress.* 1931.

TUCKERMAN, HENRY T. *America and Her Commentators. With a Critical Sketch of Travel in the United States.* 1864.

TURNER, FREDERICK JACKSON. *The Frontier in American History*. 1920.
————. *The Significance of Sections in American History*. 1932.
————. *The United States, 1830–1850*. 1935.
WECTER, DIXON. *The Hero in America*. 1941.
————. *The Saga of American Society; a Record of Social Aspiration, 1607–1937*. 1937.
WRIGHT, RICHARDSON. *Grandfather Was Queer*. 1939.

NOTES

Part One. The Faith of the Young Republic

[1] Quoted in Rourke, *Trumpets of Jubilee*, p. 31.

[2] Paulina Bates, *The Divine Book of Holy and Eternal Wisdom* (2 vols., 1849), preface.

[3] Henry Brown, *Narrative of the Anti-Masonick Excitement* (1829), preface.

CHAPTER 1. DYNAMIC DEMOCRACY

[1] Chevalier, *Society, Manners, and Politics in the United States*, p. 187.

[2] See Osgood, *American Colonies in the Seventeenth Century*, 1:202–3, for a discussion of the democratic implications of Calvinism.

[3] Adams, *Epic of America*, p. 102.

[4] Joseph Parker, "The Confederation and the Shays's Rebellion," *American Historical Review*, XI:42 (October 1905). See also the Washington letters quoted in J. C. Fitzpatrick, "Some Sayings of Washington Which Apply Today," *Daughters of the American Revolution Magazine*, LV:61.

[5] Quoted in C. E. Merriam, *History of American Political Theories* (1920), p. 99.

[6] Quoted in Schlesinger, *New Viewpoints*, p. 80, and in Beard, *Rise of American Civilization*, I:316–17.

[7] Fisher Ames, *Works* (2 vols., 1854), I:328. For Dwight's opinions see Schlesinger, *New Viewpoints*, p. 84.

[8] There was a light vote in all elections in those days. Means of communication were few, population scattered, and transportation facilities poor. Even in urban districts there was much indifference. In Philadelphia only about five per cent of the population voted for delegates, and in Boston only 760 out of 2,700 who were qualified. And yet the newspapers and pamphlets exhibited much excitement. See Charles A. Beard, *Economic Interpretation of the Constitution* (1923), pp. 246ff; and J. F. Jameson, "Did the Fathers Vote?" *New England Magazine*, n.s., I:484ff (January 1890).

[9] Jefferson's theory, as expressed by his friend John Taylor of Caroline, is summarized in Charles A. Beard, *The Economic Origins of Jeffersonian Democracy* (1915), Chap. 12, "The Politics of Agrarianism." See also Eugene Tenbroeck Mudge, *The Social Philosophy of John Taylor of Caroline* (1939).

[10] Dwight, *Travels*, II:461.

[11] Quoted in Turner, *The Frontier in American History*, p. 348.

[12] Samuel Crabtree to his brother from Wheeling, Virginia, 1818, quoted in Edith Abbott, *Historical Aspects of the Immigration Problem: Select Documents* (1926), p. 40.

[13] Thirty thousand immigrants were believed to have arrived in 1817, about one half of them Irish.

[14] Crèvecoeur, *Letters from an American Farmer*, p. 24.

[15] Flower, *History of the English Settlement*, p. 29.

[16] All the travelers mention the sensitiveness of the Americans, especially of the Westerners. See Mackay, *The Western World*, Vol. III, Chap. XI; Trollope, *Domestic Manners of the Americans*, p. 313; Marryat, *Diary in America*, I:87; Buckingham,

America, III:422; and Dickens, *American Notes*, Vol. II, Chap. X. See also Mesick, *English Traveller in America*, Chap. XI.

[17] Flower, *History of the English Settlement*, p. 276.

[18] *English Magazine*, quoted in Harlow, *Growth of the United States*, p. 311.

[19] Grund, *The Americans*, p. 151.

[20] Mackay, *The Western World*, II:205.

[21] For extremely critical opinions see especially Hamilton, *Men and Manners in America;* Fidler, *Observations on . . . the United States and Canada;* and Trollope, *Domestic Manners of the Americans.*

[22] The letter is really a brief essay on American government and is extensively quoted in Pierson, *Tocqueville and Beaumont in America*, pp. 152ff.

[23] De Tocqueville, *Democracy in America*, I:65. This opinion was shared by an English visitor who wrote ten years later: "The American Republic . . . is not a republic in simply not being a monarchy; it is a Democratic Republic in the broadest sense of the term. If it is not a monarchy, neither is it an oligarchy. It is the people in reality that rule; it is not a mere fraction of them that usurps authority." (Mackay, *The Western World*, III:330.)

[24] From the Washington's birthday toast of a frontiersman, quoted in Thomas D. Clark, *Rampaging Frontier* (1939), p. 120.

[25] Quoted in Ford, *History of Illinois*, p. 61.

[26] See Smith, *First Forty Years of Washington Society*, pp. 270ff, for an account of the effect of Jackson's election. Her story (pp. 290ff) of the inauguration of Jackson and the democratic orgy of the inaugural reception has been a wellspring for the social historian.

[27] Quoted in Wecter, *Saga of American Society*, p. 100.

SEE ALSO:

ADAMS, JAMES TRUSLOW. *New England in the Republic, 1776–1850*. 1926.

BECKER, CARL LOTUS. *The Declaration of Independence, a Study in the History of Political Ideas.* 1922.

BOND, BEVERLEY WAUGH. *The Civilization of the Old North West; a Study of Political, Social, and Economic Development, 1788–1812.* 1934.

COTTERILL, R. S. *History of Pioneer Kentucky.* 1917.

DRAKE, DANIEL. *Pioneer Life in Kentucky, a Series of Reminiscential Letters, from Daniel Drake to His Children.* 1870.

ERNST, MORRIS L. *Ultimate Power.* 1937.

GOODRICH, CARTER, and SOL DAVISON. "The Frontier as a Safety Valve: A Rejoinder," *Political Science Quarterly*, LIII:268 (June 1938).

———. "The Wage Earner in the Westward Movement," *Political Science Quarterly*, L:161 and LI:61 (June 1935 and March 1936).

HARDING, SAMUEL B. *The Contest over the Ratification of the Federal Constitution in the State of Massachusetts.* 1896.

JAMESON, JOHN FRANKLIN. *The American Revolution Considered as a Social Movement.* 1926.

KANE, MURRAY. "Some Considerations of the Safety Valve Doctrine," *Mississippi Valley Historical Review*, XXIII:169 (September 1936).

MATHEWS, LOIS KIMBALL. *The Expansion of New England.* 1909.

McLAUGHLIN, ANDREW C. *Steps in the Development of American Democracy.* 1920.

McMASTER, JOHN BACH. *The Acquisition of Political, Social and Industrial Rights of Man in America.* 1903.

MILL, JOHN STUART. *Dissertation and Discussions: Political, Philosophical, and Historical.* 2 vols. 1874. (First published in 1859.)

NEVINS, ALLAN. *The American States During and After the Revolution, 1775–1789.* 1924.

PAXON, FREDERIC L. *History of the American Frontier, 1763–1893.* 1924.

SAKOLSKI, AARON M. *The Great American Land Bubble*. 1932.
SCHAFER, JOSEPH. "Concerning the Frontier as a Safety Valve," *Political Science Quarterly*, LII:407 (September 1937).
————. "Was the West a Safety Valve for Labor?" *Mississippi Valley Historical Review*, XXIV:299 (December 1937).
SHUGG, ROGER W. *Origins of Class Struggle in Louisiana*. 1939.
SONNE, NIELS HENRY. *Liberal Kentucky, 1780–1828*. 1939.
TAYLOR, JOHN. *Construction Construed and Constitution Vindicated*. 1820.
TURNER, FREDERICK JACKSON. *Early Writings*. 1938.
VAN TYNE, CLAUDE H. *The Causes of the War of Independence, Being the First Volume of a History of the Founding of the American Revolution*. 1922.
————. *The Loyalists in the American Revolution*. 1902.
WERTENBAKER, THOMAS J. *Patrician and Plebeian in Virginia*. 1910.
————. *The Planters of Colonial Virginia*. 1922.

CHAPTER 2. EVANGELICAL RELIGION

[1] Parrington, *Main Currents in American Thought*, I:151.

[2] Hamilton, *Men and Manners in America*, I:167–68.

[3] W. S. Tyler, *A History of Amherst College* (1895), p. 266. For deism in other colleges see Post, *Popular Freethought in America*, pp. 20–21.

[4] Tyler, *History of Amherst College*, p. 267.

[5] From an account by Noah Porter, quoted in Robert Baird, *Religion in America* (1856), p. 403. See also Cunningham, *Timothy Dwight*.

[6] See James K. Morse, *Jedidiah Morse: a Champion of New England Orthodoxy* (1939), Chaps. 7 and 8, for the controversy in regard to Harvard and Andover. The quotation from Morse is given in Parrington, *Main Currents in American Thought*, II:321.

[7] Quoted in Lyman, *John Marsh Pioneer*, p. 30.

[8] Quoted in Earnest Elmo Calkins, *They Broke the Prairie* (1937), p. 166.

[9] All data on missions were taken from Davis, *Half Century*.

[10] Rusk, *Literature of the Middle Western Frontier*, I:46.

[11] Quoted in F. M. Davenport, *The Primitive Traits in Religious Revivals* (1905), p. 70. This book and Catherine Cleveland, *The Great Revival in the West, 1797–1805* (1916), contain many excerpts from diaries, letters, and other contemporary material.

[12] *Autobiography of the Rev. James B. Finley* (W. P. Strickland, ed., 1856), pp. 166–67. *The Autobiography of Peter Cartwright* (W. P. Strickland, ed., 1858) contains a long account of the Cane Ridge meeting.

[13] Cartwright, *Autobiography*, p. 21.

[14] Quoted in Clark, *Rampaging Frontier*, p. 142.

[15] Cooper, *America and the Americans*, II:318.

[16] Davis, *Half Century*, p. 415.

[17] See Post, *Popular Freethought in America*, for a full account of the movement.

[18] Smith, *First Forty Years of Washington Society*, pp. 158ff.

[19] Marryat, *Diary in America*, III:130.

[20] Hamilton, *Men and Manners in America*, II:394.

[21] Mackay, *The Western World*, III:251.

[22] Quoted in Davis, *Half Century*, introduction by Mark Hopkins, p. 2.

SEE ALSO:

ADAMS, CHARLES. *Evangelism in the Middle of the Nineteenth Century*. 1851.
ALLEN, ETHAN. *Reason the Only Oracle of Man . . .* 1940. (Reprint with introduction by John Pell. First published in 1784.)
ASBURY, HERBERT. *A Methodist Saint; the Life of Bishop Asbury*. 1927.
BRIGGS, CHARLES A. *American Presbyterianism*. 1885.

CLARK, ELMER T. *The Small Sects in America.* 1937.

COLTON, CALVIN. *History and Character of American Revivals of Religion.* 1832.

CORNELISEN, ISAAC A. *The Relation of Religion to Civil Government in the United States of America, a State without a Church, but Not without a Religion.* 1895.

DRAKE, DANIEL. *Pioneer Life in Kentucky.* 1870.

DUBOSE, HORACE M. *Francis Asbury.* 1916.

FINLEY, JAMES B. *Sketches of Western Methodism; Biographical, Historical, and Miscellaneous, Illustrative of Pioneer Life.* 1854.

FLINT, TIMOTHY. *Recollections of the Last Ten Years.* C. Hartley Grattan, ed. 1932. (First published in 1826.)

FOSTER, F. H. *A Genetic History of New England Theology.* 1907.

FUESS, CLAUDE. *An Old New England School, a History of Phillips Academy at Andover.* 1917.

GRANT, HELEN HARDIE. *Peter Cartwright: Pioneer.* 1931.   ·

HALL, THOMAS CUMING. *The Religious Background of American Culture.* 1930.

HOLBROOK, STEWART H. *Ethan Allen.* 1940.

JONES, ADAM LEROY. "Early American Philosophers," *Columbia University Contributions in Philosophy, Psychology, and Education,* Vol. II, No. 4.

KIRKPATRICK, JOHN ERVIN. *Timothy Flint, Pioneer, Missionary, Author, Editor, 1780–1840.* 1911.

LOUD, GROVER C. *Evangelized America.* 1928.

MODE, PETER G. *The Frontier Spirit in American Christianity.* 1923.

NOTTINGHAM, ELIZABETH K. *Methodism on the Frontier.* 1941.

PELL, JOHN. *Ethan Allen.* 1929.

SELLERS, CHARLES COLEMAN. *Lorenzo Dow, the Bearer of the Word.* 1928.

STRICKLAND, ARTHUR B. *The Great American Revival.* 1934.

SWEET, WILLIAM WARREN. *Methodism in American History.* 1933.

————. *Religion in Colonial America.* 1942.

————. *Religion on the American Frontier.* 3 vols.: *The Baptists, 1783–1830,* 1931; *The Presbyterians, 1783–1840,* 1936; *The Congregationalists,* 1939.

————. *The Story of Religions in America.* 1930.

TYSON, W. A. *The Revival.* 1925.

WINSLOW, OLA ELIZABETH. *Jonathan Edwards, 1703–1758.* 1940.

Part Two. Cults and Utopias

[1] *Dial,* July 1843; also found in Emerson, *Works,* X:352.

CHAPTER 3. TRANSCENDENTALISM

[1] W. H. Channing in *Memoirs of Margaret Fuller Ossoli,* II:12ff.

[2] Emerson, *Works,* I:317.

[3] *Memoirs of Margaret Fuller Ossoli,* II:13.

[4] Smith, *Forces in American Criticism,* p. 79.

[5] Clarence L. F. Gohdes, *The Periodicals of American Transcendentalism* (1931), lists nine such magazines in the period 1835–60.

[6] Emerson, *Journals,* VI:171.

[7] O. B. Frothingham, *Transcendentalism in New England* (1876), p. 283.

[8] Bremer, *Homes of the New World,* I:147.

[9] John Townsend Trowbridge, *My Own Story: With Reflections of Noted Persons* (1903), p. 358.

[10] *Memoirs of Margaret Fuller Ossoli,* Vol. I, section on "Temperament."

[11] Quoted in H. C. Goddard, *Studies in New England Transcendentalism* (1908), pp. 103–4.

[12] *Memoirs of Margaret Fuller Ossoli,* II:37.

[13] Greeley, *Recollections,* p. 178.

[14] Emerson, *Journals*, V:288.

[15] Frothingham, *Transcendentalism in New England*, and Van Wyck Brooks, *Flowering of New England* (1936).

[16] Emerson, *Works*, III:206.

[17] Thoreau, *Works*, II:9–11 *passim*.

[18] *Ibid.*, pp. 499–514 *passim*.

[19] *Ibid.*, X:131–70 *passim*.

[20] *Ibid.*, p. 233.

[21] Quoted in Goddard, *New England Transcendentalism*, p. 85.

[22] Frothingham, *Transcendentalism in New England*, p. 310.

[23] Quoted in Commager, *Theodore Parker*, p. 301. The estimate of Parker's influence is based on Commager and is borne out by Parker's writings.

[24] The essay, which was originally a letter to Dr. Channing, may be found in Orestes Brownson, *Works*, IV:140–72. The quotation is from p. 149.

[25] Quoted in Gohdes, *Periodicals of American Transcendentalism*, p. 81.

[26] Martineau, *Retrospect of Western Travel*, II:124–25.

[27] Quoted in C. E. Macartney and G. Dorrance, *The Bonapartes in America* (1939), p. 138.

[28] Channing, *Works*, I:xxiii.

[29] *Ibid.*, II:161.

SEE ALSO:

BROOKS, VAN WYCK. *The Life of Emerson*. 1932.

BURTON, KATHERINE. *Celestial Homespun: The Life of Isaac Thomas Hecker*. 1943.

CANBY, HENRY SEIDEL. *Thoreau*. 1939.

CARPENTER, FREDERIC IVES. *Emerson and Asia*. 1930.

CHADWICK, JOHN WHITE. *Theodore Parker: Preacher and Reformer*. 1900.

CHRISTY, ARTHUR. *The Orient in American Transcendentalism; a Study of Emerson, Thoreau, and Alcott*. 1932.

ELLIOTT, WALTER. *The Life of Father Hecker*. 1891.

FIRKINS, OSCAR. *The Life of Emerson*. 1915.

FOSTER, FRANK HUGH. *A Genetic History of New England Theology*. 1907.

HIGGINSON, THOMAS WENTWORTH. *Margaret Fuller Ossoli*. 1884.

HOLDEN, VINCENT F. *The Early Years of Isaac Thomas Hecker (1819–1844)*. 1939.

McQUISTON, RAYMER. *The Relation of Ralph Waldo Emerson to Public Affairs*. 1923.

OSSOLI, MARGARET FULLER. *Woman in the Nineteenth Century, and Kindred Papers Relating to the Sphere, Condition, and Duties of Woman*. 1855.

SEDGWICK, HENRY D., JR. *Father Hecker*. 1900.

WADE, MASON. *Margaret Fuller, Whetstone of Genius*. 1940.

CHAPTER 4. MILLENNIALISM AND SPIRITUALISM

[1] Thoreau, *Works*, I:97.

[2] *Ibid.*, pp. 91–92.

[3] This and other details of the personal life of Miller are from the *Memoir of William Miller* (1853) by Sylvester Bliss, a friend and coworker.

[4] Quoted in Clara Endicott Sears, *Days of Delusion* (1924), pp. 35–36.

[5] Davis, *Half Century*, p. 413.

[6] The examples of millennial frenzy are taken from McMaster, *People of the United States*, VII:135ff, which quotes from numerous local newspapers of the day.

[7] Letter to Himes, quoted in Bliss, *Memoir of William Miller*, p. 255.

[8] *Ibid.*, p. 256.

[9] Andrew Jackson Davis, *The Philosophy of Spiritual Intercourse, Being an Explanation of Modern Mysteries* (1854), p. 176.

[10] Emma Hardinge, *Modern American Spiritualism* (1870), p. 22.

[11] Bates, *Divine Book of Holy and Eternal Wisdom*, preface.

[12] See Hardinge, *Modern American Spiritualism*, Chaps. 29–33, for a description of the excitement in Ohio, where, she says, 1,200 mediums were operating in some sixty organized "circles."

[13] Quoted in W. G. Langworthy Taylor, *Katie Fox, Epoch Making Medium* (1933), p. 59.

[14] Greeley, *Recollections*, p. 239.

[15] Taylor, *Katie Fox*, p. 67.

[16] Orestes Brownson, *The Spirit Rapper, an Autobiography* (1854), p. 138.

[17] Nichols, *Forty Years of American Life*, pp. 251–52.

SEE ALSO:

DAVIS, ANDREW JACKSON. *The Magic Staff; an Autobiography.* 1859.

DOYLE, ARTHUR CONAN. *The History of Spiritualism.* 1926.

EDMONDS, JOHN W., and GEORGE T. DEXTER. *Spiritualism.* 1853.

FAUSET, ARTHUR HUFF. *Sojourner Truth, God's Faithful Pilgrim.* 1938.

MATTHEWS, ROBERT. *Matthias and His Impostures.* 1835.

McCABE, JOSEPH. *Spiritualism; a Popular History from 1847.* 1920.

OWEN, ROBERT DALE. *Footfalls on the Boundary of Another World.* 1860.

PODMORE, FRANK. *Modern Spiritualism.* 1902.

STONE, WILLIAM L. *Matthias and His Impostures: or, The Progress of Fanaticism. Illustrated in the Extraordinary Case of Robert Matthews . . .* 1835.

CHAPTER 5. THE STAKE IN ZION

[1] Quoted in W. A. Linn, *The Story of the Mormons* (1901), p. 13.

[2] *Ibid.*, p. 78.

[3] Harry M. Beardsley, *Joseph Smith and His Mormon Empire* (1931), Chap. 7. See also Linn, *Story of the Mormons*, Chap. 5, and M. R. Werner, *Brigham Young* (1925), Chap. 2.

[4] Beardsley, *Joseph Smith*, p. 85.

[5] Quoted in Linn, *Story of the Mormons*, p. 98.

[6] Rev. Jesse Townsend, December 24, 1833, quoted *ibid.*, p. 106.

[7] Werner, *Brigham Young*, p. 12.

[8] Both Mormon and non-Mormon historians should be consulted for the difficulties of the Saints in Missouri. Brigham Roberts, *The Missouri Persecutions* (1900), is the official Mormon version.

[9] Quoted in Linn, *Story of the Mormons*, p. 197.

[10] Copies of this correspondence may be found in Roberts, *The Missouri Persecutions*.

[11] Ford, *History of Illinois*, p. 323. The quotation is from a detailed account of the Mormons in Illinois, which is an apologia for a governor who made little effort to prevent the final debacle.

[12] Milo M. Quaife, *The Kingdom of St. James; A Narrative of the Mormons* (1930), gives a full and interesting account of this schismatic minority.

SEE ALSO:

EVANS, JOHN HENRY. *Joseph Smith, an American Prophet.* 1933.

————. *One Hundred Years of Mormonism.* 1909.

GREENE, SAMUEL D. *The Broken Seal; or, Personal Reminiscences of the Mormon Abduction and Murder.* 1873.

HOWE, EBER D. *Mormonism Unveiled . . .* 1834.

————. *Story of Mormonism.* 1840.

KAUFFMAN, RUTH, and REGINALD WRIGHT. *The Latter Day Saints; a Study of the Mormons in the Light of Economic Conditions.* 1912.

MACK, SOLOMON. *A Narrative of the Life of Solomon Mack.* 1810.

RIEGEL, OSCAR W. *Crown of Glory, the Life of James J. Strang, Moses of the Mormons.* 1935.

SMITH, LUCY MACK. *History of the Prophet Joseph, and Biographical Sketches of Joseph Smith, Jr., the Prophet and His Progenitors for Many Generations.* 1853.

CHAPTER 6. RELIGIOUS COMMUNISM IN AMERICA

[1] Noyes, *American Socialisms*, Chap. 3. Other standard texts are: Nordhoff, *Communistic Societies;* Hinds, *American Communities;* Hillquit, *History of Socialism in the United States.*

[2] Various dates may be found for the arrival of Beissel. Noyes, *American Socialisms*, gives the date 1713, obtained from a synopsis of religious communities made by A. Jacobi in 1858. Redmond Conyngham, *An Account of the Settlement of the Dunkers at Ephrata, in Lancaster County, Pennsylvania* (Pennsylvania Historical Society Memoirs, Vol. II, Part I, 1826), states that the community was founded in 1730. The *Souvenir of the Ephrata Cloister* (1921) by Samuel G. Zerfass, son of the secretary of the community in the days of its decline, dates Beissel's flight from Germany in 1720 and places the founding of the new order in the early 1730's. A. M. Aurand, *An Historical Account of the Ephrata Cloister* (1940), mentions 1728, as does *Chronicon Ephratense: A History of the Community of Seventh Day Baptists at Ephrata, Lancaster County, Pennsylvania* (1889; first published, in German, in 1786), by the two lay brothers, Lamech and Agrippa.

[3] It is very difficult to obtain full details about the life of Jemima Wilkinson. Contemporary accounts, largely from the pens of those passionately concerned with exposing what they believed to be an imposture, are bitterly prejudiced, citing as fact every innuendo. The standard exposure is Daniel Hudson, *Memoir of Jemima Wilkinson, a Preacheress of the Eighteenth Century; Containing an Authentic Narrative of Her Life and Character and the Rise, Progress and Conclusion of Her Ministry* (1844). An excellent brief and less biased account is Rev. John Quincy Adams, "Jemima Wilkinson, the Universal Friend," *Journal of American History*, 9:249–63 (April–July 1915). See also Colonel Johnson, "Jemima Wilkinson, American Prophetess," *Eclectic Magazine*, V:546ff (August 1845).

[4] Quoted in Hinds, *American Communities*, p. 22.

[5] Rochefoucauld Liancourt, *Travels in North America*, pp. 110–18.

[6] Reprinted in *Eclectic Magazine*, August 1845.

[7] Aaron Williams, *The Harmony Society at Economy, Pennsylvania* (1866), appendix, p. 182. John Duss, *The Harmonists: A Personal History* (1943), is a full account of the Rapp settlement written by the last trustee of the society.

[8] Quoted in George Lockwood, *The New Harmony Movement* (1907), p. 13.

[9] John Woods, *Two Years' Residence in the Settlement on the English Prairie in the Illinois Country* (London, 1822), reprinted in Thwaites, *Early Western Travels*, X:324ff. See also John Bradbury, *Travels in the Interior of North America*, reprinted ibid., V:314ff; and W. Faux, *Memorable Days in America*, reprinted *ibid.*, XI:248ff.

[10] Flower, *History of the English Settlement*, pp. 279ff.

[11] Birkbeck, *Notes on a Journey in America*, p. 140.

[12] Williams, *The Harmony Society*, p. 40.

[13] Much has been written about this sect in the state of Iowa, where its settlements still endure. Two of the best accounts are Bertha Shambaugh, *Amana That Was and Amana That Is* (1932), and Charles Fred Moe, "A Brief History of the Amana Society," *Iowa Journal of History and Politics*, II:162ff (April 1904).

[14] This story of Janson's conversion is told in Sivert Erdahl, "Eric Janson and the Bishop Hill Colony," *Journal of the Illinois State Historical Society*, Vol. 18, No. 3 (1925). Erdahl and Michael Mikkelsen, in "The Bishop Hill Colony, A Religious Communistic Settlement in Henry County, Illinois," *Johns Hopkins University Studies*, Series 10, No. 1 (1892), used much the same Swedish sources, chief among which was Emil Herlenius, *Erik-Jansismens Historia* (Jönköping, 1900).

[15] Quoted in Mikkelsen, p. 21.
[16] Quoted from Herlenius in Erdahl, p. 546.

SEE ALSO:

ARNDT, KARL J. "George Rapp's Petition to Thomas Jefferson," *American-German Review*, October 1940.

————. "Life and Mission of Count Leon," *American-German Review*, June, October 1940.

FAHNESTOCK, WILLIAM. "An Historical Sketch of Ephrata," *Hazard's Register of Pennsylvania*, XV:161 (March 1835). Reprinted in I. D. Rupp, *An Original History of the Religious Denominations at Present Existing in the United States* (1844).

HENDRICKS, ROBERT J. *Bethel and Aurora, an Experiment in Communism as Practical Christianity.* 1933.

KLEIN, WALTER C. *Johann Conrad Beissel, 1690–1768.* 1942.

LANDIS, GEORGE B. *The Society of Separatists of Zoar, Ohio.* 1898.

LOCKRIDGE, ROSS F. *The Labyrinth: A History of the New Harmony Labyrinth, Including Some Special Study of the Spiritual and Mystical Life of Its Builders, the Rappites, and a Brief Survey of Labyrinths Generally.* 1941.

LOCKWOOD, GEORGE. *New Harmony Communities.* 1902.

RANDALL, EMILIUS O. *The History of the Zoar Society.* 3rd ed. 1904.

SACHSE, JULIUS FRIEDRICH. *The Music of the Ephrata Cloister; also Conrad Beissel's Treatise on Music . . .* 1903.

SCHULZ-BEHREND, G. "The Amana Colony," *American-German Review*, December 1940.

STEPHENSON, GEORGE M. *Religious Aspects of Swedish Immigration.* 1932.

CHAPTER 7. THE SHAKER COMMUNITIES

[1] Calvin Green and Seth Y. Wells, eds., *A Summary View of the Millennial Church, or the United Society of Believers, Commonly Called Shakers* (1823), p. 6. There is a vast literature on the Shakers. Almost every traveler in America in the period 1820–50 visited at least one Shaker settlement, and the Shakers themselves wrote extensively on their history and doctrine both for their own people and for the outside world. Among the first of these expositions was *The Testimony of Christ's Second Appearing; Containing a General Statement of All Things Pertaining to the Faith and Practice of the Church of God in This Latter Day* by Benjamin Seth Youngs, published in Union Village, Ohio, in 1808. (The edition here cited is that of 1823). Another and perhaps the main source book for Shakerism is *The Testimonies of the Life, Character, Revelations and Doctrines of Our Ever-blessed Mother Ann Lee and the Elders with Her*, published by order of the church in 1816. In 1858 the church published a *Compendium of the Origin, History, Rules and Regulations, Government and Doctrine of the United Society of Believers in Christ's Second Appearing* (edited by Frederick W. Evans, Calvin Green, and Giles Avery), which contains brief biographies of all the early ministry. All other books about the doctrine and early history of the Shakers are in large part variations or extracts of these works. For no other American communistic sect is there such elaborately detailed information.

[2] Youngs, *Testimony of Christ's Second Appearing*, p. 376.

[3] Green and Wells, *Summary View of the Millennial Church*, p. 8.

[4] There are numerous affidavits as to these miracles in Youngs, *Testimony of Christ's Second Appearing*, pp. 441ff. They deal for the most part with miracles of healing. The Shakers were credited with such achievements as the cure of cancer, the restoration of a withered leg, and the recovery of several children at death's door from a variety of illnesses.

[5] Green and Wells, *Summary View of the Millennial Church*, p. 23.

⁶ *Ibid.*, Chap. 3.

⁷ See the *Autobiography of Peter Cartwright* for the effect on the circuit riders of the Methodist and other churches. The standard account of the founding of the Western societies is Richard McNemer, *The Kentucky Revival . . . with a Brief Account of Shakerism . . . in Ohio and Kentucky* (1846; first published in 1807).

⁸ From *The Roll and Book from the Lord God in Heaven* (published in 1843 by the society at Canterbury, New Hampshire), quoted in E. F. Dow, *Portrait of the Millennial Church of Shakers* (1931), p. 9.

⁹ Hervey Elkins, *Fifteen Years in the Senior Order of the Shakers: A Narration of Facts Concerning that Singular People* (1853).

¹⁰ Green and Wells, *Summary View of the Millennial Church*, pp. 259ff. See also a "Short but Comprehensive Definition of Shakerism," published in a collection called *Shaker Broadsides and Pamphlets*. Another pamphlet, called *A Brief Exposition of the Established Principles and Regulations of the United Society of Believers called Shakers* (1831), lists innocence, temperance, virginity, love, peace, justice, holiness, goodness, and truth as the cardinal principles of Shakerism. Philemon Stewart, *A Holy, Sacred and Divine Roll and Book; From the Lord God of Heaven to the Inhabitants of the Earth* (1843), is a long explanation of Shaker theology.

¹¹ This summary is compiled from Frederick W. Evans, *Autobiography of a Shaker, and Revelation of the Apocalypse* (1869); Green and Wells, *Summary View of the Millennial Church*; George Lomas, *Plain Talks upon Practical Religion* (1873); and Frederick W. Evans, *The Shaker Compendium* (1858). Shaker doctrine seems to have changed little after the first publications by the church about 1800.

¹² One of the fullest descriptions of this Shaker organization may be found in David Lamson, *Two Years' Experience Among the Shakers, a View of Shakerism as It Is* (1848). Lamson had been a Baptist minister, had lost his pastorate because of radical views, and tried life in several socialistic communities. He found Shakerism uncongenial and became a bitter critic. His facts seem accurate, but other writers differ from his conclusions. *The Autobiography of Antoinette Doolittle Prior to Becoming a Member of the Shaker Community at New Lebanon, New York, in the Year 1824* (1880) contains a detailed account of her novitiate and of the Shakers' lack of proselyting zeal.

¹³ These standards for admission have been taken from Shaker sources and have been compared with the statements of contemporary non-Shakers. *A Brief Exposition of the Established Principles and Regulations of the United Society of Believers Called Shakers* contains an excellent summary. Elkins, *Fifteen Years in the Senior Order of the Shakers*, and Anna White and Leila Taylor, *Shakerism; Its Meaning and Message* (1904), both emphasize the voluntary nature of admission of members. The two Shaker eldresses state that although one who withdrew from the society had no legal claim to any property, "enough is always given to smooth his way in the world to which he persists in going and, as far as possible, the principal that he brought is returned." (*Shakerism*, p. 305.) Disappointed and angry seceders were not always of the same opinion, but the courts of several states decided that valid title belonged to the Shaker trustees and that any restitution was a matter for their decision.

¹⁴ Quoted in Edward Deming Andrews and Faith Andrews, *Shaker Furniture: the Craftsmanship of an American Communal Sect* (1937), p. 111.

¹⁵ E. D. Andrews is again the authority. His own collection of Shaker furniture is unique and extensive.

¹⁶ Nordhoff, *Communistic Societies*, p. 168.

¹⁷ *Ibid.*, p. 169.

¹⁸ White and Taylor, *Shakerism*, states that the family relationship causes competition and that the logical end of the protection of dependents has come to be the destruction of others. "Communistic attempts admitting family relationships have

inevitably proved failures, from the excess of private family feeling. . . . Virgin purity is successful, happy and a blessing to man and woman, where the ripened condition has been reached, and the true brother and sister relation in Christ is found; and that is possible only in a pure and sustained Christian Communism." (P. 299.)

[19] E. D. Andrews, *The Gift to Be Simple; Songs, Dances and Rituals of the American Shakers* (1940), pp. 9ff. See also *A Collection of Hymns and Anthems Adapted to Public Worship and Published by the Shakers* (1892).

[20] Quoted in Pierson, *Tocqueville and Beaumont in America*, p. 179.

[21] Hall, *Aristocratic Journey*, p. 44.

[22] Marryat, *Diary in America*, I:116ff.

[23] Hamilton, *Men and Manners in America*, II:295.

[24] Cooper, *America and the Americans*, II:330.

[25] Horace Greeley, "A Sabbath with the Shakers," *Knickerbocker Magazine*, June 1838, pp. 532ff.

[26] Buckingham, *America*, II:353ff. Buckingham devoted three chapters (Vol. II Chaps. 18–21) to Shakerism.

[27] Dickens, *American Notes*, II:214.

[28] Benson Lossing, "The Shakers," *Harper's Monthly*, July 1857.

[29] See Bates, *Divine Book of Holy and Eternal Wisdom*. The inspired songs were legion. Many of them are given in Lamson, *Two Years Among the Shakers*, and in Andrews, *The Gift to Be Simple*. "These inspired writers were released from all secular duties, and, in order to be prepared for the complete absorption of the bodily powers in the work of the spirit, they lived on a simple diet, largely bread and water, abstained from unnecessary conversation, and, withdrawn into a room alone in silence received the messages imparted." (White and Taylor, *Shakerism*, p. 238.)

[30] Quoted among many others in Andrews, *The Gift to Be Simple*, p. 69. "Modder" was Mother Ann Lee, "Whity" was a white man, "shiny children" were the Shakers.

[31] The one at Hancock was called Mount Sinai; that at New Lebanon, Holy Mount; that at Enfield, Mount of Olives; and so on. Records were kept of the meetings at these holy spots. See Lamson, *Two Years Among the Shakers*, for a description of the Hancock meetings.

[32] Noyes, *American Socialisms*, pp. 596ff, quotes extensively from a manuscript, "Four Months among the Shakers," which was written in the period of spiritualism. The author describes some of these gifts; White and Taylor, *Shakerism*, pp. 233ff, gives others.

[33] From Evans, *Autobiography of a Shaker*, p. 61.

[34] From a conversation with Elder Evans quoted in Nordhoff, *Communistic Societies*, p. 160.

[35] E. D. Andrews, *The Community Industries of the Shakers* (New York Museum Handbook 15, 1932), quotes from a Shaker manuscript of 1845 called "Millennial Laws," which contains a code of some thirty or forty regulations for the conduct of deacons and trustees. This code covers every detail of Shaker business contacts and of the relations between the trustees and the ministry. It is invaluable for an understanding of Shaker economic life. Andrews' book is by far the best account of Shaker industries and is based on firsthand knowledge and manuscript sources.

[36] Dixon, *New America*, pp. 321–22.

[37] Andrews, *Community Industries of the Shakers*, pp. 40ff, gives a list of thirty-nine inventions for which he thinks the Shaker claims are valid. See also Daniel Mac-Hir Hutton, *Industries in Kentucky — Old Shakertown and the Shakers* (1936).

[38] Martineau, *Society in America*, I:310ff.

[39] Lossing, "The Shakers," *Harper's Monthly*, July 1857, p. 177.

SEE ALSO:

ALLEN, CATHERINE. *Biographical Sketch of Daniel Fraser of the Shaker Community of Mt. Lebanon, Columbia County, N.Y.* 1890.

BROWN, THOMAS. *An Account of the People Called Shakers: Their Faith, Doctrines, and Practices . . .* 1812.

MELCHER, MARGUERITE FELLOWS. *The Shaker Adventure.* 1941.

SEARS, CLARA ENDICOTT. *Gleanings from Old Shaker Journals.* 1916.

TAYLOR, LEILA S. *A Memorial to Eldress Anna White, and Elder Daniel Afford.* 1912.

CHAPTER 8. AMERICAN UTOPIAS OF RELIGIOUS ORIGIN

[1] Adin Ballou, *The History of the Hopedale Community* (1897), p. 2.

[2] This constitution is printed in full *ibid.*, pp. 27ff. It contains thirty-two signatures, most of them names of English origin and well known in New England history.

[3] Channing, *Memoirs*, III:119ff.

[4] Ballou, *History of the Hopedale Community*, p. 45.

[5] Adin Ballou, *Autobiography* (1896), pp. 346–48; and *History of the Hopedale Community*, pp. 98ff.

[6] *Ibid.*, pp. 361–67 *passim.*

[7] Bronson Alcott himself humbly accepted the stigma of insanity as the result if not the cause of the failure at Fruitlands. See F. B. Sanborn, *Bronson Alcott at Alcott House, England, and Fruitlands, New England, 1842–1844* (1908), p. 68. Alcott's biographer, Odell Shepard, says that Charles Lane "was temporarily ridden, to the verge of insanity, by an idea. While in America, at any rate, he showed the humorless, live-or-die, neck-or-nothing intensity and concentration of the uncompromising zealot. He believed that he had just one task to perform; and that was, to save the world." (*Pedlar's Progress*, p. 345.)

[8] Quoted in Sanborn, *Bronson Alcott*, p. 65.

[9] Louisa Alcott, "Transcendental Wild Oats," in *Silver Pitchers* (1876), and reprinted in Clara Endicott Sears, *Bronson Alcott's Fruitlands* (1915), pp. 173–74.

[10] Quoted in Zoltán Haraszti, *The Idyll of Brook Farm: As Revealed by Unpublished Letters in the Boston Public Library* (1937), p. 14.

[11] Quoted in Lindsay Swift, *Brook Farm, Its Members, Scholars, and Visitors* (1900), p. 15.

[12] Nathaniel Hawthorne, *American Notebooks, 1841–1852* (1932), pp. 75ff.

[13] See the numerous letters in the appendix to John Thomas Codman, *Brook Farm, Historic and Personal Memoirs* (1894).

[14] Emerson, *Works*, X:342–43.

[15] Georgiana Bruce Kirby, *Years of Experience, An Autobiographical Narrative* (1887), pp. 98–100 *passim.*

[16] Higginson, *Cheerful Yesterdays*, pp. 83–84.

[17] Hawthorne, *American Notebooks*, p. 81.

[18] This comment on Brook Farm was a part of an Easy Chair essay on Hawthorne's *American Notebooks* in *Harper's Monthly* in 1869. It was quoted extensively in Edward Cary, *George William Curtis* (1894), and in George W. Cooke's introductory chapter to the *Early Letters of George William Curtis to John S. Dwight, Brook Farm and Concord* (1898).

[19] Letters of January 26 and 27, 1845.

[20] Brisbane's own account of the failure of Brook Farm is a somewhat cold theorist's analysis of a situation the responsibility for which he seemed unable to acknowledge. See Redelia Brisbane, *Albert Brisbane: A Mental Biography, with a Character Study by His Wife* (1893), p. 218.

[21] Allan Estlake, *The Oneida Community* (1900), p. 21.

[22] Noyes, *American Socialisms*, p. 28.

[23] Quoted in G. W. Noyes, *The Religious Experience of John Humphrey Noyes*

(1923), pp. 306–9. This letter was later, without Noyes's consent, sent to T. R. Gates, a Perfectionist who was publishing the *Battle-Axe and Weapons of War* to launch his own theories on marriage. Published in this paper in 1837, the letter called attention to Noyes and won him both opprobrium and converts.

²⁴ The huge building, still called the Mansion House, was erected in 1860.

²⁵ In *My Father's House; An Oneida Boyhood* (1937) Pierrepont Noyes gives a charming picture of his boyhood in the Oneida Community.

²⁶ Estlake, *Oneida Community*, pp. 66–68.

²⁷ Excerpts from a long letter quoted in William Hepworth Dixon, *Spiritual Wives* (1868), pp. 347–53.

²⁸ Quoted in Pierrepont Noyes, *My Father's House*, pp. 17–18.

²⁹ See Noyes, *American Socialisms*, pp. 617–37, for a summary. See also G. W. Noyes, *John Humphrey Noyes, the Putney Community* (1931), pp. 116–22.

³⁰ Until 1867 few children were born into the community. Economic as well as social reasons had caused a carefully regulated birth control. But as the community grew more prosperous, Noyes felt that the time was ripe for an experiment in eugenics, and between 1868 and 1881 fifty-eight children were born to couples chosen for that purpose.

SEE ALSO:

BURTON, KATHERINE. *Paradise Planters, The Story of Brook Farm.* 1939.

DWIGHT, MARIANNE. *Letters from Brook Farm, 1844–1847.* Amy L. Reed, ed. 1928.

EASTMAN, HUBBARD. *Noyesism Unveiled: A History of the Sect Self-styled Perfectionists.* 1849.

O'BRIEN, HARRIET E. *Lost Utopias* . . . 1929.

PARKER, ROBERT ALLERTON. *A Yankee Saint; John Humphrey Noyes and the Oneida Community.* 1935.

CHAPTER 9. UTOPIAN SOCIALISM IN AMERICA

¹ *The Life of Robert Owen by Himself* (1920; first published in 1857), p. 22.

² Robert Dale Owen, *Twenty-seven Years of Autobiography, Threading My Way* (1874), p. 245.

³ *Ibid.*, pp. 240–41.

⁴ "First Discourse," p. 11.

⁵ Smith, *First Forty Years of Washington Society*, p. 196.

⁶ Robert Dale Owen, *Threading My Way*, p. 286.

⁷ Quoted in Frank Podmore, *Robert Owen, a Biography* (2 vols., 1908), I:292.

⁸ This constitution may be found in full in the *New Harmony Gazette*, and in extensive excerpts in George Lockwood, *The New Harmony Movement* (1905), pp. 105ff, and in Noyes, *American Socialisms*, Chap. IV.

⁹ G. D. H. Cole, *The Life of Robert Owen* (1930), p. 246.

¹⁰ *New Harmony Gazette*, III:204, quoted both in Podmore, *Robert Owen*, I:322–23, and in Cole, *Robert Owen*, p. 248.

¹¹ Duke of Saxe-Weimar Eisenach, *Travels Through North America*, II:106–20. The quotation is from p. 117.

¹² R. W. Leopold, *Robert Dale Owen* (1940), p. 42, calls the lack of careful planning and regulation "inexcusable" and states that the haste in initiating full communism was fatal.

¹³ Quoted in A. J. G. Perkins and Theresa Wolfson, *Frances Wright: Free Enquirer* (1939), p. 24.

¹⁴ *Ibid.*, p. 160.

¹⁵ Trollope, *Domestic Manners of the Americans*, pp. 22ff.

¹⁶ Dickens, *American Notes*, I:145ff.

¹⁷ Martineau, *Society in America*, II:53ff.

¹⁸ Chevalier, *Society, Manners, and Politics in the United States*, pp. 128ff.

[19] Quoted in Adams, *Epic of America*, p. 178.

[20] See Carter Goodrich and Sol Davison, "The Wage Earner in the Westward Movement," *Political Science Quarterly*, June 1935 and March 1936, and "The Frontier as a Safety Valve," *Political Science Quarterly*, June 1938; Murray Kane, "Some Consideration of the Safety-Valve Theory," *Mississippi Valley Historical Review*, September 1936; Joseph Schafer, "Concerning the Frontier as a Safety Valve," *Political Science Quarterly*, September 1937, and "Was the West a Safety Valve?" *Mississippi Valley Historical Review*, December 1937.

[21] For a consideration of this and other cases see Commons, *History of Labour in the United States*, Vol. I.

[22] *Ibid.*, p. 169.

[23] *Ibid.*, p. 285.

[24] Greeley, *Recollections*, p. 145.

[25] Redelia Brisbane, *Albert Brisbane: A Mental Biography*, p. 209.

[26] Greeley, *Recollections*, pp. 147ff.

[27] Many of them are discussed in detail in Noyes, *American Socialisms*, and are more concisely summarized in Hillquit, *History of Socialism in the United States*.

[28] Bremer, *Homes of the New World*, I:83.

[29] Quoted in Albert Shaw, *Icaria, a Chapter in the History of Communism* (1884), p. 24.

[30] See the editorials from *Populaire* for 1848 quoted extensively in Shaw, *Icaria*, pp. 40ff.

[31] See Cabet's "History of the Colony or Republic of Icaria in the United States of America," as translated in Thomas Teakle, "History and Constitution of the Icarian Community," *Iowa Journal of History and Politics*, XV:214ff (April 1917).

SEE ALSO:

BROWN, PAUL. *Twelve Months in New Harmony.* 1827.
CABET, ETIENNE. *Colonie Icarienne aux Etats-Unis d'Amérique.* 1856.
EVERETT, L. S. *An Exposure of the Principles of the "Free Inquirers."* 1831.
GALLAHER, RUTH. "Icaria and Icarians," *Palimpsest*, Vol. II (April 1921).
HEBERT, WILLIAM. *A Visit to the Colony of Harmony in Indiana.* 1825.
LOCKWOOD, GEORGE B. *The New Harmony Communities.* 1902.
MILLER, MRS. I. G. "The Icarian Community of Nauvoo, Illinois," *Publications of the Historical Library of Illinois*, No. 11 (1906), pp. 23, 103–7.
MORTON, S. G. *A Memoir of William Maclure, Esq.* 1844.
PRUDHOMMEAUX, JULES. *Icarie et son Fondateur, Etienne Cabet.* 1907.
WATERMAN, WILLIAM RANDALL. *Frances Wright.* 1924.
WEISS, HARRY B., and GRACE M. ZIEGLER. *Thomas Say: Early American Naturalist.* 1931.

Part Three. Humanitarian Crusades

[1] F. J. and W. P. Garrison, *The Life of William Lloyd Garrison*, I:200.

CHAPTER 10. EDUCATION AND THE AMERICAN FAITH

[1] There were legislative acts in Massachusetts making provision for common schools in 1647, 1692, 1701, and 1789.

[2] Quoted in Kittredge, *The Old Farmer and His Almanack*, p. 229.

[3] Quoted in Merle Curti, *The Social Ideas of American Educators* (1935), p. 3.

[4] Quoted in Padover, *Jefferson*, pp. 75–76.

[5] W. C. Ford, ed., *The Writings of George Washington* (14 vols., 1889–93), XIV:227.

[6] The three appeared as Parts I, II, and III of *A Grammatical Institute of the English Language*.

[7] Quoted in Henry Warfel, *Noah Webster* (1936), p. 304.

[8] From "American Social Elevation," signed H. J. G., in the *Southern Literary Messenger*, May 1, 1836, p. 386.

[9] *Ohio State Journal*, January 13, 1836, quoted in Myers, *History of American Idealism*, p. 100.

[10] Grund, *The Americans*, pp. 26–27, 124, 133–34, *passim*.

[11] Samuel G. Goodrich (Peter Parley), *Fireside Education* (1838), pp. 338–39.

[12] *Autobiography of Amos Kendall*, p. 59.

[13] Quoted in E. E. Slosson, *American Spirit in Education* (1921), p. 126.

[14] Horace Mann's seventh report, in Mary Peabody Mann, *Life of Horace Mann* (5 vols., 1891; Centennial edition, 1937), III:417.

[15] The eighth report, *ibid.*, p. 466.

[16] Quoted in E. P. Cubberley, *Public Education in the United States* (1934), p. 201, footnote.

[17] Two books published about 1850 give excellent summaries of the progress of education from a decidedly clerical point of view: Baird, *Religion in America*, pp. 296ff, and Davis, *Half Century*, pp. 50ff.

[18] Quoted in Slosson, *American Spirit in Education*, p. 153.

[19] Quoted in Shepard, *Pedlar's Progress*, p. 101.

[20] Jacob Abbott, *The Teacher; or Moral Influences Employed in the Instruction and Government of the Young* (1834), p. 239.

[21] Slosson, *American Spirit in Education*, p. 149.

[22] See Pauline Holmes, *A Tercentenary History of the Boston Public Latin School, 1635–1935* (1935), for a full account of this historic institution and of its English offshoot.

[23] A full "Quarter Card of Discipline and Studies for Mr. Alcott's School" is reproduced in Elizabeth Peabody, *Record of Mr. Alcott's School* (3rd ed., 1874; first published in 1835).

[24] Quoted in Shepard, *Pedlar's Progress*, p. 173.

[25] Listed in George E. Haefner, *A Critical Estimate of the Educational Theories and Practices of A. Bronson Alcott* (1937), p. 338.

[26] From an article in the *United States Literary Gazette* for February 15, 1825, quoted in M. A. De Wolfe Howe, *Life and Letters of George Bancroft* (2 vols., 1908), I:174.

[27] *The Life of Joseph Green Cogswell as Sketched in His Letters* (1874), pp. 143–44 *passim*.

[28] *Ibid.*, p. 151.

[29] A society was formed in Boston in 1846 to place teachers trained in New England in schools in the West. See Mae E. Harveson, *Catherine Esther Beecher, Pioneer Educator* (1932), Chap. 6. The chief difficulty was that the girls no sooner reached the West than they married and left the teaching profession.

[30] Quoted in M. A. De Wolfe Howe, *Classic Shades: Five Leaders of Learning and Their Colleges* (1928), p. 69.

[31] Quoted in Gamaliel Bradford, *Portraits of American Women* (1919), p. 74.

[32] Alonzo Potter and George Emerson, *The School and the School Master* (1842), p. 52.

[33] Quincy, *Figures of the Past*, pp. 23ff, and Higginson, *Cheerful Yesterdays*, pp. 43ff.

[34] Lyman, *John Marsh Pioneer*, pp. 40ff.

[35] Niels Sonne, *Liberal Kentucky, 1780–1828* (1939), p. 260.

[36] Quoted in Slosson, *American Spirit in Education*, p. 177. Charles M. Perry, *Henry Philip Tappan, Philosopher and University President* (1933), gives an account of the early years of the university.

[37] Walter R. Johnson, *A Concise View of the General State of Education in the United States* (1825), p. 4. A recent study of the monitorial system is Claude Eggert-

sen, "The Monitorial System in the United States," a manuscript thesis (1939) in the University of Minnesota library. The conclusions given in the text agree with Dr. Eggertsen's, pp. 394ff.

[38] There is ample material on the American Lyceum. Articles by William Russell in the *American Journal of Education*, II:188ff (1827), and Henry Barnard *ibid.*, XIV:535ff (1864), are histories of the movement by participants. A list of the objectives made in 1829 is given in *Old South Leaflets*, Vol. VI, No. 139 (1904). J. S. Noffsinger, *Correspondence Schools, Lyceums, and Chautauquas* (1926), and Cecil B. Hayes, *The American Lyceum* (1932), are recent secondary accounts.

[39] Quoted in Noffsinger, *Correspondence Schools, Lyceums, and Chautauquas*, p. 104.

[40] Manuscript diary of Elizabeth Stearns of Jaffrey, New Hampshire, in the possession of the author.

[41] Noah Webster, *Collection of Papers on Political, Literary, and Moral Subjects* (1843), pp. 299–300 *passim*.

SEE ALSO:

ANDERSON, L. F. "The Manual Labor School Movement," *Educational Review*, 46:369 (November 1913).

BURNS, JAMES A., and BERNARD J. KOHLBRENNER. *A History of Catholic Education in the United States.* 1937.

CALKINS, EARNEST ELMO. *They Broke the Prairie.* 1937.

CARTER, JAMES GORDON. *Essays upon Popular Education, Containing a Particular Examination of the Schools of Massachusetts, and an Outline of an Institution for the Education of Teachers.* 1826.

————. *Letters to the Honorable William Prescott, L.L.D., on the Free Schools of New England, with Remarks upon the Principles of Instruction.* 1824.

COLE, ARTHUR C. *A Hundred Years of Mount Holyoke College.* 1940.

EMERSON, GEORGE B. *Reminiscences of an Old Teacher.* 1878.

FAIRCHILD, JAMES HARRIS. *Oberlin: The Colony and the College, 1833–1883.* 1883.

FLETCHER, ROBERT SAMUEL. *A History of Oberlin College.* 2 vols. 1943.

FUESS, CLAUDE M. *An Old New England School; A History of Phillips Academy, Andover.* 1917.

GILCHRIST, BETH BRADFORD. *The Life of Mary Lyon.* 1910.

HALL, SAMUEL READ. *Lectures on School-Keeping.* 1929. (First published in 1829.)

HAYES, CECIL B. *The American Lyceum; Its History and Contribution to Education.* 1932.

JOHNSON, CLIFTON. *Old-Time Schools and School-Books.* 1904.

KNIGHT, EDGAR W. *Education in the United States.* 1929.

LYON, MARY. *Prospectus for Mount Holyoke Female Seminary.* 1835. Reprinted in *Old South Leaflets*, Vol. VI, No. 145 (1903).

McCADDEN, JOSEPH J. *Education in Pennsylvania, 1801–1835, and Its Debt to Roberts Vaux.* 1937.

MONROE, WILL SEYMOUR. *History of the Pestalozzi Movement in the United States.* 1907.

MORGAN, JOY ELMER. *Horace Mann: His Ideas and Ideals.* 1936.

MORISON, SAMUEL E. *Three Centuries of Harvard, 1636–1936.* 1936.

PALMER, A. EMERSON. *The New York Public Schools.* 1905.

PHILLIPS, WILBUR H. *Oberlin Colony: the Story of a Century.* 1933.

POND, JEAN SARAH. *Bradford, A New England Academy.* 1930.

REISNER, E. H. *Nationalism and Education since 1789.* 1922.

SHOEMAKER, ERVIN C. *Noah Webster, Pioneer of Learning.* 1936.

SMALL, WALTER HERBERT. *Early New England Schools.* 1914.

STEINER, BERNARD C. *Life of Henry Barnard, the First United States Commissioner of Education, 1867–1870.* 1919.

Stowe, Sarah D. (Locke). *History of Mount Holyoke Seminary . . .* 1881.

Tewksbury, D. G. *The Founding of American Colleges and Universities before the Civil War.* 1932.

Tolman, Frank L. *Libraries and Lyceums.* 1937.

Tyler, William Seymour. *History of Amherst College.* 1895.

Williams, E. I. F. *Horace Mann, Educational Statesman.* 1937.

Woody, Thomas. *A History of Women's Education in the United States.* 1929.

CHAPTER 11. REFORM FOR THE CRIMINAL

[1] Martineau, *Society in America,* II:281–82.

[2] Grund, *The Americans,* p. 165.

[3] Quoted in Harry Elmer Barnes, *The Evolution of Penology in Pennsylvania* (1927), p. 82.

[4] From the Papers of Louis Dwight, quoted in O. F. Lewis, *The Development of American Prisons and Prison Customs* (1922), p. 290.

[5] The Philadelphia society was founded in 1787, the Boston Prison Discipline Society in 1825, and the New York Prison Association in 1845.

[6] Barnes, *Evolution of Penology in Pennsylvania,* p. 85.

[7] Blake McKelvey, *American Prisons: A Study in American Social History* (1936), pp. 12ff.

[8] The work of Roberts Vaux and the Philadelphia society was summarized in Vaux's *Notices of the Original and Successive Attempts to Improve the Discipline of the Prison at Philadelphia and to Reform the Criminal Code of Pennsylvania* (1826). The work of the society is discussed in Barnes, *Evolution of Penology in Pennsylvania,* pp. 80ff, which is based largely on Vaux's *Notices.*

[9] *The Memoirs of the Notorious Stephen Burroughs of New Hampshire* (Albany edition, 1811; latest edition, 1924).

[10] A phrase used in a letter written by De Beaumont.

[11] Quoted in Pierson, *Tocqueville and Beaumont in America,* p. 102.

[12] Stuart, *Three Years in North America,* I:101.

[13] Tudor, *Narrative of a Tour in North America,* I:206.

[14] Gustave A. de Beaumont and Alexis de Tocqueville, *On the Penitentiary System in the United States, and Its Application in France* (Francis Lieber, trans., 1833), pp. 81 and 103.

[15] The gross earnings of the Charlestown prison, 1832–46, were $515,422.46, with 283 the average number of prisoners. The gross earnings of the Philadelphia prison for four years in the same period were $58,538.34, with 317 prisoners working. Charlestown produced $10 per month per prisoner; Philadelphia $4. (Francis C. Gray, *Prison Discipline in America,* 1847, p. 77.)

[16] Quoted in Frederick H. Wines, *Punishment and Reformation* (1919; first published in 1895), p. 158.

[17] Pillsbury had been the head of the prison at Concord, New Hampshire. Some accounts give the name as Pilsbury.

[18] De Beaumont and De Tocqueville, *On the Penitentiary System in the United States,* p. 59.

[19] *Ibid.,* p. 47.

[20] Quoted in Marryat, *Diary in America,* II:296–97.

[21] McKelvey, *American Prisons,* Chaps. 1 and 2.

[22] De Beaumont and De Tocqueville, *On the Penitentiary System in the United States,* Lieber's introduction, p. vii.

[23] Quoted from a report to the House of Representatives in Myers, *History of American Idealism,* p. 75.

SEE ALSO:

Adshead, Joseph. *Prisons and Prisoners.* 1845.

Annual Report of the Board of Managers of the Prison Discipline Society. Boston. 1826–36.

BARNES, HARRY ELMER. *A History of the Penal, Reformatory and Correctional Institutions of the State of New Jersey.* 1918.

————. *The Repression of Crime; Studies in Historical Penology.* 1926.

————. *The Story of Punishment; A Record of Man's Inhumanity to Man.* 1930.

CRAWFORD, WILLIAM. *Report of William Crawford, Esq., on the Penitentiaries of the United States.* 1834.

LIVINGSTONE, EDWARD. *A System of Penal Law for the State of Louisiana . . .* 1835.

QUINBY, G. W. *The Gallows, the Prison, and the Poor-house.* 1856.

ROSCOE, WILLIAM. *Observations on Penal Jurisprudence, and the Reformation of Criminals.* 1819.

VAUX, RICHARD. *Brief Sketch of the Origin and History of the State Penitentiary for the Eastern District of Pennsylvania.* 1872.

WILSON, HELEN. *The Treatment of the Misdemeanant in Indiana, 1816–1836.* 1938.

WINES, FREDERICK H. *The State of Prisons and of Child-Saving Institutions in the Civilized World.* 1880.

CHAPTER 12. WARDS OF THE STATE

[1] Duke of Saxe-Weimar Eisenach, *Travels Through North America*, I: 131, II: 199.

[2] Hamilton, *Men and Manners in America*, I: 183.

[3] Buckingham, *America*, I: 130.

[4] Crawford, *Report on the Penitentiaries of the United States*, pp. 44–45.

[5] Duke of Saxe-Weimar Eisenach, *Travels Through North America*, I: 167.

[6] Robert Kelso, *History of Public Poor Relief in Massachusetts* (1922), p. 109.

[7] Quoted in F. B. Sanborn, *Dr. S. G. Howe, the Philanthropist* (1891), p. 118.

[8] *Ibid.*, pp. 293–94.

[9] Quoted in Lowell S. Selling, *Men Against Madness* (1940), p. 74.

[10] Quoted in Francis Tiffany, *Dorothea Dix* (1890), p. 62.

[11] For brief summaries see Charles Folsom, *Diseases of the Mind, and Notes on the Early Management, European and American Progress . . . in the Treatment of the Insane* (1877), and Albert Deutsch, *The Mentally Ill in America; A History of Their Care and Treatment from Colonial Times* (1937).

[12] Quoted in Edward Jarvis, "What Shall We Do with the Insane?" *North American Review*, January 1843, pp. 171ff. The quotation is from pp. 175–76.

[13] Hall, *Travels in North America*, II: 192ff.

[14] Deutsch, *The Mentally Ill in America*, pp. 137 and 155.

[15] There was no provision in the states of Alabama, Mississippi, Illinois, Arkansas, Indiana, and Michigan, or in Florida, Wisconsin, and Iowa territories. In 1843 there were in the United States only fourteen hospitals exclusively for the mentally ill, and their joint capacity was 2,547 beds. In 1840 there were 17,434 insane in the United States. (Helen E. Marshall, *Dorothea Dix: Forgotten Samaritan*, 1937, Chap. 4.)

[16] From the second page of the report, reprinted in *Old South Leaflets*, Vol. VI, No. 148 (1904).

[17] Quoted in Tiffany, *Dorothea Dix*, p. 375.

SEE ALSO:

ALLEN, EDWARD ELLIS. *Education of Defectives.* Monographs on Education in the United States, No. 15. 1900.

BARNARD, HENRY. *Tribute to Gallaudet. A Discourse in Commemoration of the Life, Character and Services, of the Rev. Thomas H. Gallaudet, LLD.* 1852.

BROMBERG, WALTER. *The Mind of Man: The Story of Man's Conquest of Mental Illness.* 1937.

DAY, MARY L. *Incidents in the Life of a Blind Girl.* 1859.

DIX, DOROTHEA LYNDE. "Memorial to the Legislature of Massachusetts, 1843," *Old South Leaflets*, Vol. VI, No. 148 (1904).

GOLDBERG, JACOB A. *Social Aspects of the Treatment of the Insane.* 1921.

PENROSE, LIONEL S. *Mental Defect.* 1934.

RICHARDS, LAURA E., ed. *Letters and Journals of Samuel Gridley Howe.* 2 vols. 1909.

TUKE, D. HACK. *The Insane in the United States and Canada.* 1885.

WINES, FREDERICK H. *The State of Prisons and of Child-Saving Institutions in the Civilized World.* 1880.

CHAPTER 13. THE TEMPERANCE CRUSADE

[1] Quoted in Daniel Dorchester, *The Liquor Problem in All Ages* (1888), p. 110. This work is a mine of information on the history of the temperance movement.

[2] Quoted in H. K. Carroll, "Total Abstinence During the Century," in *One Hundred Years of Temperance, a Memorial Volume of the Centennial Temperance Conference held in Philadelphia, Pa. Sept., 1885* (1886). The quotation is from p. 124.

[3] Mason L. Weems, *The Drunkard's Looking Glass* (1813), as republished in *Three Discourses* (1929), p. 112.

[4] Greeley, *Recollections*, pp. 99–100.

[5] Finley, *Autobiography*, p. 248.

[6] Quoted in H. A. Scomp, *King Alcohol in the Realm of King Cotton* (1888), p. 205.

[7] Quoted in Richardson Wright, *Grandfather Was Queer* (1939), pp. 252ff.

[8] Arthur Train, *Puritan's Progress* (1931), p. 128.

[9] Quoted in John Allen Krout, *The Origins of Prohibition* (1925), p. 67. This monograph by Krout is one of the best treatises on the early temperance movement.

[10] See Dorchester, *The Liquor Problem in All Ages*, pp. 162ff, for a mass of illustrative material.

[11] Quoted in Ernest H. Cherrington, *The Evolution of Prohibition in the United States of America* (1920), pp. 52–53. Cherrington gives a good chronology of the temperance movement.

[12] David Ramsay, *History of South Carolina* (2 vols., 1858), II:391ff.

[13] These rules preface the 1813 edition of *The Drunkard's Looking Glass*.

[14] Quoted in J. E. Stebbins and T. A. H. Brown, *Fifty Years' History of the Temperance Cause* (1878), p. 227.

[15] Excerpts from this address may be found in *One Hundred Years of Temperance*, pp. 117ff.

[16] Dorchester, *The Liquor Problem in All Ages*, p. 229.

[17] Tudor, *Narrative of a Tour in North America*, I:229.

[18] Quoted in Ludlum, *Social Ferment in Vermont*, p. 69.

[19] *Ibid.*, p. 70.

[20] Quoted in *One Hundred Years of Temperance*, p. 116.

[21] Lyman Beecher, *Autobiography*, I:245.

[22] *Ibid.*, I:248–49.

[23] Cartwright, *Autobiography*, pp. 102–3.

[24] *One Hundred Years of Temperance*, p. 126.

[25] Martineau, *Society in America*, II:296.

[26] Stuart, *Three Years in North America*, II:499ff.

[27] Lyman Beecher, *Autobiography*, II:34ff *passim*.

[28] See Dr. Channing's temperance address of 1837 in his *Works*, II:299ff. Parker's views are analyzed in Commager, *Theodore Parker*, pp. 189–91.

[29] See Krout, *Origins of Prohibition*, p. 309, for a list of twenty or more weekly, monthly, quarterly, or annual publications.

[30] In 1835 four of these reports were published in one volume under the title of *Permanent Temperance Documents of the American Temperance Society*. The col-

lection is invaluable. The ninth annual report of the American Temperance Society (pp. 515ff), for instance, lists twenty-three reasons for temperance and supports them by quotations from numerous prominent men.

[31] See George Faber Clark, *History of the Temperance Reform in Massachusetts, 1831–1883* (1888), for a discussion of a typical legislative society.

[32] *Proceedings and Speeches at a Meeting for a Promotion of the Cause of Temperance in the United States, Held at the Capitol in Washington City, February 24, 1833* (1833), p. 47.

[33] Krout, *Origins of Prohibition*, pp. 143ff.

[34] For thirty years this secretary was the Rev. John Marsh, whose *Temperance Recollections: Labours, Defeats, Triumphs, an Autobiography* (1866) is an important source for the activities of the Union.

[35] Scomp, *King Alcohol in the Realm of King Cotton*, p. 305, says that when the Northern temperance groups became identified with the abolition cause, "the blight of the slavery question was to hinder, even when it did not wholly prevent, all active cooperation between the two sections in active temperance work."

[36] *An Address to the Citizens of the United States on the Subject of Ardent Spirits* (anonymous), 1822.

[37] Dickens in *Bleak House* and Charles Brockden Brown in *Wieland*.

[38] The ninth annual report of the American Temperance Society (*Permanent Temperance Documents*, pp. 515ff) contains numerous letters from such eminent Americans as Gerrit Smith, William Ladd of the American Peace Society, Professor Edward Hitchcock of Amherst College, and Lewis Cass, describing the beneficial effects of their own abstinence. An enthusiastic letter from Gerrit Smith on the subject of health and temperance is reprinted in Ralph Harlow, *Gerrit Smith* (1939), p. 76. In this epistle Smith combined a plea for abstinence from all intoxicants with advice to give up tobacco, coffee, tea, and all elaborate foods.

[39] Charles T. Woodman, *Narrative of C. T. Woodman, a Reformed Inebriate* (1843), pp. 30ff.

[40] Alonzo Potter, *Drinking Usages of Society* (1852), pp. 10–12 passim.

[41] Dorchester, *The Liquor Problem in All Ages*, p. 281.

[42] Martineau, *Society in America*, II:296ff passim.

[43] J. H. Hopkins, *The Primitive Church Compared with the Protestant Episcopal Church of the Present Day* (2nd ed., 1836), p. 387.

[44] *Ibid.*, p. 152.

[45] Reese, *Humbugs of New York*, Chap. 6.

[46] Leonard Withington, *Review of the Late Temperance Movements in Massachusetts* (1840), p. 13.

[47] *Ibid.*, p. 26.

[48] Thomas Hunt, *The Cold Water Army* (1840), p. 16.

[49] Quoted in Marsh, *Temperance Recollections*, p. 62.

[50] C. B. Porter, ed., *The Silver Cup of Sparkling Drops, from Many Fountains for the Friends of Temperance* (1852), pp. 102–3.

[51] See *T. S. Arthur: His Life and Works, By One Who Knows Him* (1873) for a brief account of his highly respectable life.

[52] See W. G. Hawkins, *Life of John H. W. Hawkins*, 1859.

[53] Quoted in Harry Malcolm Chalfont, *These Agitators and Their Idea* (1931), p. 102.

[54] Quoted in Stebbins and Brown, *Fifty Years' History of the Temperance Cause*, p. 235.

[55] See Krout, *Origins of Prohibition*, pp. 205ff, for quotations from Washingtonian lectures opposing legislative action.

[56] A history of the Sons of Temperance written by Frederick Fickardt may be found in T. S. Arthur, *The Sons of Temperance Offering* (1851), pp. 261ff.

[57] John Francis Maguire, *Father Mathew; a Biography* (1898), pp. 481ff.

⁵⁸ Ralph E. Turner, *James Silk Buckingham, 1786–1855: A Social Biography* (1934), p. 359.

⁵⁹ See Dorchester, *The Liquor Problem in All Ages*, pp. 284ff, for a full account of such legislation.

⁶⁰ *Reminiscences of Neal Dow, Recollections of Eighty Years* (1898), p. 200.

⁶¹ There is a mass of source material on this act in Henry S. Clubb, *The Maine Liquor Law: Its Origin, History, and Results* (1856), and in the biographies and reminiscences of Neal Dow.

⁶² Quoted in Commager, *Theodore Parker*, p. 190.

⁶³ Edward Payson, *The Maine Law in the Balance* (1855), p. 56.

⁶⁴ *The Ramrod Broken; or The Bible, History, and Common Sense, in Favor of the Moderate Use of Good Spirituous Liquors, Showing the Advantage of a License System in Preference to Prohibition, and Moral in Preference to "Legal" Suasion* (anonymous, 1859), p. 288.

SEE ALSO:

ARTHUR, TIMOTHY SHAY. *The Lights and Shadows of Real Life* . . . 1859.
————. *Six Nights with the Washingtonians; and Other Temperance Tales.* 1871.
————. *Strong Drink; the Curse and the Cure.* 1877.
————. *Ten Nights in a Bar Room, and What I Saw There.* 1855.
BEECHER, LYMAN. *Lectures on Political Atheism and Kindred Subjects, together with Six Lectures on Intemperance.* 1852. Also in Beecher, *Works*, Vol. I.
BENEZET, ANTHONY. *The Mighty Destroyer Displayed, in Some Account of the Havock Made by the Mistaken Use as Well as Abuse of Distilled Spirituous Liquors.* 1774.
BLAIR, HENRY WILLIAM. *The Temperance Movement, or, The Conflict between Man and Alcohol.* 1888.
CHEEVER, GEORGE BARRELL. *The True History of Deacon Giles' Distillery. Reported for the Benefit of Posterity.* 1844. (First published in 1838.)
CLARK, REV. T. M. *Annual Address, before the Massachusetts Temperance Society.* 1838.
CRAMPTON, R. S. *The Wine of the Bible and The Bible Use of Wine.* 1859.
DELAVAN, EDWARD C. *Temperance Essays.* 1869.
EDWARDS, JUSTIN. *The Well-Conducted Farm.* 1825.
FEHLANDT, AUGUST F. *A Century of Drink Reform in the United States.* 1904.
GOODRICH, SAMUEL GRISWOLD (Peter Parley). *Five Letters to My Neighbor Smith Touching the Fifteen Gallon Jug.* 1838.
GOUGH, JOHN B. *Autobiography and Personal Recollections.* 1869.
————. *Sunlight and Shadow; or, Gleanings from My Life Work.* 1882.
GRIMKÉ, THOMAS S. *The Temperance Reformation the Cause of Christian Morals. An Address Delivered before the Charleston Temperance Society.* 1834.
HOWE, M. A. DE WOLFE. *Memoirs of the Life and Services of the Rt. Rev. Alonzo Potter, Bishop of Pennsylvania.* 1871.
HUMPHREY, HEMAN, D. D. *The Parallel between Intemperance and the Slave Trade. Address Delivered at Amherst College, July 4, 1828.* 1828.
HUNT, RIDGELY, and GEORGE S. CHAPPELL. *The Saloon in the Home; or, a Garland of Rumblossoms.* 1930.
Journal of the Proceedings of the Massachusetts Temperance Convention. 1833.
KITCHEL, H. D. *An Appeal to the People for the Suppression of the Liquor Traffic. A Prize Essay.* 1848.
KITTREDGE, JONATHAN. *Address on the Effects of Ardent Spirits.* 1828.
MOEHLMAN, CONRAD HENRY. *When All Drank and Thereafter* . . . 1930.
MORRIS, CHARLES. *Broken Fetters; The Light of Ages on Intoxication.* 1888.
MORROW, HONORÉ W. *Tiger! Tiger! The Life Story of John B. Gough.* 1930.
NOTT, ELIPHALET. *Lectures on Bible Temperance.* 1857.

NOTT, SAMUEL, JR. *An Appeal to the Temperate, on the Vice of Intemperance.* 1828.

PARSONS, REV. B. *Anti-Bacchus; an Essay on the Crimes, Disasters, and Other Evils Connected with the Use of Intoxicating Drinks.* 1840.

A Primitive Washingtonian. A Resurrection of the Blue Laws; or, Maine Reform in Temperance Doses. 1852.

RUSH, BENJAMIN. *An Inquiry into the Effects of Ardent Spirits upon the Human Body and Mind, with an Account of the Means of Preventing, and of the Remedies for Curing them.* 8th ed., 1814.

RYDER, WILLIAM H., ed. *Our Country: or, the American Parlor Keepsake.* 1854.

SMITH, HENRY. *The Life and Adventures of Henry Smith: The Celebrated Razor-Strop Man.* 1848.

SPRAGUE, PELEG. *Argument of Peleg Sprague, Esq., before the Committee of the Legislature of Massachusetts upon the Memorial of Harrison Gray Otis and Others.* 1839.

SPRINGWATER, D. *The Cold-Water Man; or, a Pocket Companion for the Temperate.* 1832.

The Temperance Text-book; a Collection of Facts and Interesting Anecdotes, Illustrating the Evils of Intoxicating Drinks. 1836.

WAKELEY, JOSEPH B. *The American Temperance Cyclopaedia of History, Biography, Anecdote, and Illustrations.* 1879.

The Washingtonian Teetotaler's Minstrel. 1845.

WINSKILL, P. T. *The Temperance Movement and Its Workers.* 4 vols. 1892.

CHAPTER 14. DENIALS OF DEMOCRATIC PRINCIPLES

[1] Quoted in Harriet Weed, ed., *The Life of Thurlow Weed, including His Autobiography and a Memoir* (2 vols., 1883), I:216. This work (I:210–392) contains one of the most complete accounts of Antimasonry.

[2] Charles McCarthy, "Antimasonic Party, A Study of Political Antimasonry in the United States, 1827–1840," *Annual Reports of the American Historical Association*, I:367ff (1902), is, within the limits set, the best work available on Antimasonry in politics. The quotation is from p. 375.

[3] See *William Henry Seward: An Autobiography, 1801–1834* (1891), pp. 69ff; Andrew Estrem, *The Statesmanship of William Henry Seward as Seen in His Political Career Prior to 1861* (1892), p. 5; and Bancroft, *Life of William Henry Seward*, Vol. I, Chap. 3.

[4] Quoted in Childs, *French Refugee Life in the United States*, p. 199.

[5] The figures are approximations from W. E. Garrison, *Catholicism and the American Mind* (1928), based for the early years on Catholic estimates, for the later period on census returns.

[6] Nichols, *Forty Years of American Life*, p. 263.

[7] *Ibid.*, p. 276.

[8] Gabriel, *The Course of American Democratic Thought*, p. 52.

[9] Peter K. Guilday, *The Life and Times of John England, First Bishop of Charleston, 1786–1842* (1927), II:329–94.

[10] For an account of the Catholic defense in both press and debate, 1829–39, see Robert Gorman, *Catholic Apologetical Literature in the United States, 1784–1858* (1939), pp. 62ff.

[11] Quoted in Ray A. Billington, *The Protestant Crusade, 1800–1860* (1938), p. 84. This book is invaluable for any study of American nativism.

[12] Alexander Campbell and the Rt. Rev. John B. Purcell, *A Debate on the Roman Catholic Religion: Held in the Sycamore Street Meeting House, Cincinnati, from the 13th to the 21st of January, 1837* (1837).

[13] Ray A. Billington, "The Burning of the Charlestown Convent," *New England Quarterly*, X:3 (March 1937). See also Billington, *The Protestant Crusade*, pp. 68ff;

James Hunnewell, *A Century of Town Life: A History of Charlestown, Mass.,* *1715–1887* (1888); and the *Report of the Committee Relating to the Destruction of the Ursuline Convent, August 11, 1834* (1834).

[14] "Anti-Catholic Movements in the United States," *Catholic World*, March 1876, pp. 810ff.

[15] Reese, *Humbugs of New York*, pp. 212–17 *passim.*

[16] M. L. Hansen, *The Atlantic Migration, 1607–1860* (1940), p. 163.

[17] Edith Abbott, *Historical Aspects of the Immigration Problem: Select Documents* (1926), pp. 572 and 580ff.

[18] See J. R. G. Hassard, *Life of the Most Reverend John Hughes, D.D., First Archbishop of New York* (1866), pp. 351ff, for an account of the bankruptcy and sale of St. Peter's Church. The matter was of concern from 1838 to 1852.

[19] *Ibid.,* p. 260.

[20] Quoted in Estrem, *Statesmanship of William Henry Seward*, p. 19. A. Emerson Palmer, *The New York Public Schools* (1905), has a brief account of the Catholic school question. It is extensively treated in Hassard, *Life of John Hughes*, pp. 223–51.

[21] Louise Dow Scisco, *Political Nativism in New York State* (1901), p. 35.

[22] Quoted in Billington, *The Protestant Crusade*, p. 231.

[23] Nicholas Murray, *Letters to the Right Reverend John Hughes, Roman Catholic Bishop of New York* (1904; first published in 1849), pp. 89–92 *passim.*

[24] From *Brownson's Quarterly Review* for 1849, quoted in Arthur M. Schlesinger, Jr., *Orestes Brownson: A Pilgrim's Progress* (1939), p. 204.

[25] Quoted in Carl Wittke, *We Who Built America* (1939), p. 487.

[26] Listed in J. W. Laurens, *The Crisis, or the Enemies of America Unmasked* (1855), pp. 59ff.

[27] Quoted in E. M. Coulter, *William G. Brownlow, Fighting Parson of the Southern Highlands* (1937), p. 124.

[28] Quoted in Abbott, *Historical Aspects of the Immigration Problem*, p. 807.

[29] Benedict Webb, *The Catholic Question in Politics* (1856), p. 34.

[30] Quoted in Avery Craven, "Coming of the War Between the States: an Interpretation," *Journal of Southern History*, August 1936, p. 315.

[31] Henry Wise, *Seven Decades of the Union* (1881), p. 245.

[32] See W. E. Dodd, "The Fight for the North West, 1860," *American Historical Review*, XVI:774–88 (July 1911), and Joseph Schafer, "Who Elected Lincoln?" *American Historical Review*, XLVII:51–64 (October 1941), for two conflicting analyses of the vote of the foreign-born in the Northwest in 1860.

[33] G. F. Hoar, *Autobiography of Seventy Years* (2 vols., 1903), I:188.

[34] E. L. Morse, ed., *Samuel F. B. Morse, His Letters and Journals* (2 vols., 1914), II:338.

SEE ALSO:

Address of the Board of Managers of the American Protestant Association; with the Constitution and Organization of the Association . . . 1843.

ASBURY, HERBERT. *The Gangs of New York; An Informal History of the Underworld.* 1928.

BEAN, W. G. "An Aspect of Know Nothingism — The Immigrant and Slavery," *South Atlantic Quarterly*, October 1924, pp. 319ff.

BEECHER, LYMAN. *A Plea for the West.* 3rd ed. 1836.

BLEGEN, THEODORE C. *Norwegian Migration to America, 1825–1860.* 1931.

————. *Norwegian Migration to America: The American Transition.* 1940.

————. tr. and ed. (*Ole Rynning's*) *True Account of America, 1838.* 1926.

BRAND, CARL FREMONT. "The Know-Nothing Party in Indiana," *Indiana Magazine of History*, XVIII:266 (September 1922).

BROWN, HENRY. *A Narrative of the Anti-Masonick Excitement in the Western Part of the State of New York, during the Years 1826, '7, '8, and a part of 1829.* 1829.

BURTON, KATHERINE. *Celestial Homespun. The Life of Isaac Thomas Hecker.* 1943.
————. *His Dear Persuasion: The Life of Elizabeth Ann Seton.* 1942.
CARROLL, ANNA ELLA. *The Great American Battle; or, The Contests between Christianity and Political Romanism.* 1859.
COLE, ARTHUR C. "Nativism in the Lower Mississippi Valley," *Mississippi Valley Historical Association Proceedings, 1912–1913* (Vol. VI).
COLTON, CALVIN. *Protestant Jesuitism.* 1836.
CROSS, IRA. "The Origin, Principles, and History of the American Party," *Iowa Journal of History and Political Science,* 1906, pp. 526ff.
GAVAZZI, FATHER ALESSANDRO. *The Lectures Complete of Father Gavazzi, as Delivered in New York . . . To Which Is Prefixed . . . a Life of Gavazzi by G. B. Niccolini.* 1854.
GOLDMARK, JOSEPHINE. *Pilgrims of '48.* 1930.
GUILDAY, PETER K. *The Life and Times of John Carroll, Archbishop of Baltimore (1735–1815).* 1922.
HARRINGTON, FRED HARVEY. "Frémont and the North Americans," *American Historical Review,* XLIV:842 (July 1939).
HAYNES, GEORGE H. "The Causes of Know-Nothing Success in Massachusetts," *American Historical Review,* III:67 (October 1897).
KELLY, MARY GILBERT. *Catholic Immigrant Colonization Projects, 1815–1860.* 1939.
KENNEDY, JOHN P. *Memoirs of the Life of William Wirt.* 2 vols. 1872.
KINSMAN, FREDERICK JOSEPH. *Americanism and Catholicism.* 1924.
LEE, JOHN HANCOCK. *The Origins and Progress of the American Party in Politics . . .* 1855.
LORETTE. *The History of Louise, Daughter of a Canadian Nun: Exhibiting the Interior of Female Convents.* 1833.
MAURY, REUBEN. *The Wars of the Godly.* 1928.
MAYNARD, THEODORE. *The Story of American Catholicism.* 1941.
McCONVILLE, SISTER MARY ST. PATRICK. *Political Nativism in the State of Maryland, 1830–1860.* 1928.
McMASTER, JOHN BACH. *With the Fathers.* 1896.
MOCK, STANLEY UPTON. *The Morgan Episode in American Free Masonry.* 1930.
MONK, MARIA. *Awful Disclosures by Maria Monk, of the Hôtel Dieu Nunnery of Montreal; or, the Secrets of Black Nunnery Revealed.* 1st ed. 1836.
————. *Further Disclosures . . . Concerning the Hôtel Dieu Nunnery of Montreal.* 1837.
MORSE, S. F. B. *Foreign Conspiracy against the Liberties of the United States.* 1835.
NEVINS, ALLAN. *Frémont, the West's Greatest Adventurer.* 2 vols. 1928.
NORTON, REV. HERMAN. *The Life of the Rev. Herman Norton, to Which Are Added Startling Facts, and Signs of Danger and of Promise, from His Pen While Corresponding Secretary of the American Protestant Association.* 1853.
————. *Startling Facts for American Protestants! Progress of Romanism since the Revolutionary War; Its Present Position and Future Prospects.* 1852.
O'DANIEL, V. F. *The Father of the Church in Tennessee; or, the Life, Times, and Character of the Right Reverend Pius Miles, O.P. . . .* 1926.
O'DONNELL, JOHN HUGH. *Catholic Hierarchy of the United States, 1790–1922.* 1922.
O'GORMAN, EDITH. *Trials and Persecutions of Miss Edith O'Gorman, Otherwise Sister Teresa de Chantal of St. Joseph's Convent.* 1881.
O'GORMAN, THOMAS. *A History of the Roman Catholic Church in the United States.* 1895.
OWEN, ROBERT DALE. *Native Americanism.* 1844.
Rosamond, or a Narrative of the Captivity and Sufferings of an American Female under the Popish Priests in the Island of Cuba. 1836.
SANDERSON, JOHN P. *Republican Landmarks. The Views and Opinions of American*

*Statesmen on Foreign Immigration. Being a Collection of Statistics on Popula-
tion, Pauperism, Crime, etc.* 1856.
————. *Startling Facts for Native Americans Called "Know-Nothings," or a Vivid
Presentation of the Dangers to American Liberty, to Be Apprehended from For-
eign Influence.* 1855.
SCHAFER, JOSEPH. "Know-Nothingism in Wisconsin," *Wisconsin Magazine of His-
tory,* VIII:3 (June 1925).
SCHMECKEBIER, LAURENCE F. *History of the Know-Nothing Party in Maryland.* 1899.
SEDGWICK, HENRY D., JR. *Father Hecker.* 1900.
*Sons of the Sires; A History of the Rise, Progress, and Destiny of the American
Party . . . to Which Is Added a Review of the Letter of the Hon. Henry A.
Wise against the Know-Nothings.* 1855.
STEPHENSON, GEORGE M. *History of American Immigration, 1820–1924.* 1926.
————. "Nativism in the Forties and Fifties, with Special Reference to the Mis-
sissippi Valley," *Mississippi Valley Historical Review,* IX:185 (December 1922).
————. "When America Was the Land of Canaan," *Minnesota History,* X:237
(September 1929).
STICKNEY, CHARLES. *Know-Nothingism in Rhode Island.* 1893–94.
THOMPSON, RALPH. "The Maria Monk Affair," *Colophon,* Part XVII, 1934.
TUSKA, BENJAMIN. *Know-Nothingism in Baltimore, 1854–1860.* 1930.
WERNER, MORRIS R. *Tammany Hall.* 1928.
WHITNEY, THOMAS R. *A Defense of the American Policy, as Opposed to the En-
croachments of Foreign Influence, and Especially to the Interference of the
Papacy in the Political Interests and Affairs of the United States.* 1856.
The Wide-Awake Gift: a Know-Nothing Token for 1855, edited by "One of 'em."
1855.
WILLIAMS, MICHAEL. *The Shadow of the Pope.* 1932.
WISE, BARTON H. *The Life of Henry A. Wise of Virginia, 1806–1876.* 1899.

CHAPTER 15. THE CRUSADE FOR PEACE

[1] Quoted in Brookes, *Friend Anthony Benezet,* p. 125.
[2] Quoted in Rufus Jones, *The Faith and Practice of the Quakers* (1927), p. 110.
[3] From a collection of Franklin's statements on peace in *Old South Leaflets,* Vol.
VII, No. 162 (1905).
[4] *Memoirs of William Ellery Channing,* I:328–35 passim.
[5] Stated in a letter from Dodge to William Ladd, published in the *Advocate of
Peace,* September 1838, and quoted in Merle Curti, *The American Peace Crusade,
1813–1860* (1929), p. 9. Curti's monograph is the most complete account of the movement.
[6] Henry Ware, *Memoirs of the Rev. Noah Worcester* (1844), p. 67.
[7] Quoted in Edson Whitney, *American Peace Society: a Centennial History*
(1928), p. 14.
[8] Quoted in Channing's tribute to Worcester in Ware, *Memoirs of Noah Worcester,* pp. 139–40.
[9] Quoted in John Hemmenway, *Memoir of William Ladd, Apostle of Peace*
(1872), p. 143.
[10] Quoted in Whitney, *American Peace Society,* p. 17.
[11] The circular is printed in full in the first number of the *Harbinger of Peace,*
May 1828. The quotation is from p. 10.
[12] William Ladd, *An Essay on the Congress of Nations* . . . (1916), p. 72. This
essay was originally published in 1840 with a collection of the prize essays entitled
*Prize Essays on a Congress of Nations for the Adjustment of International Disputes,
and for the Promotion of Universal Peace without Resort to Arms, together with a
Sixth Essay, Comprising the Substance of the Rejected Essays.*

[13] The last three pamphlets may be found in a collection entitled *American Peace Society Documents: Peace Principles Safe and Right.*

[14] Emerson, *Works*, XI:176.

[15] Emerson, *Journals*, IX:362.

[16] This essay was first published in 1842 and was reprinted in 1919 with an introduction by Judge James Brown Scott. The quotation is from the 1919 edition, pp. 51–53.

[17] Thomas Grimké, *An Address on the Truth, Dignity, and Beauty of the Principles of Peace* (1832), p. 29.

[18] F. J. and W. P. Garrison, *Life of William Lloyd Garrison*, II:52.

[19] *Ibid.*, p. 149.

[20] *Ibid.*, pp. 201–2.

[21] Barnes and Dumond, *The Weld-Grimké Letters*, II:521–22.

[22] *Ibid.*, I:408.

[23] The best account of the convention of 1838 is F. J. and W. P. Garrison, *Life of William Lloyd Garrison*, II:225ff. The Declaration is reprinted in full pp. 230–34. In the following pages may be found the correspondence of the leaders of the movement elaborating their interpretations of the principles.

[24] Parrington, *Main Currents of American Thought*, II:357.

[25] Charles Sumner, *Works*, I:5–130.

[26] Quoted in Commager, *Theodore Parker*, p. 192.

[27] James Russell Lowell, "Biglow Papers, No. I," *Poetical Works* (Riverside edition, 1894), II:46, 53.

[28] Thoreau, *Works*, X:131–34 *passim.*

[29] See Charles Northend, *Elihu Burritt: His Life and Letters* (1879).

[30] Quoted in Curti, *American Peace Crusade*, p. 143.

[31] Elihu Burritt, ed., *Bond of Brotherhood*, No. 1 (August 1846).

[32] Horace Greeley, *Glances at Europe in a Series of Letters from Great Britain, France, Italy, Switzerland . . .* (1851), p. 281.

[33] Commager, *Theodore Parker*, pp. 192–93.

SEE ALSO:

ALLEN, DEVERE. *The Fight for Peace.* 1930.

BANNEKER, BENJAMIN. *Banneker's Almanack.* 1793.

BEALES, ARTHUR C. F. *The History of Peace; A Short Account of the Organized Movements for International Peace.* 1931.

BECKWITH, GEORGE C. *The Peace Manual; or, War and Its Remedies.* 1847.

BURRITT, ELIHU. "A Congress of Nations," *Old South Leaflets*, Vol. VI, No. 146 (1904).

———. *Thoughts and Notes at Home and Abroad.* 1868.

CHANNING, WILLIAM ELLERY. "A Sermon on War, 1816," *American Historical Pamphlets, 1812–1845*, Vol. 5, No. 16. Also in Channing, *Works*, III:29ff.

CURTI, MERLE. *The Learned Blacksmith.* 1937.

DODGE, DAVID LOW. *Memorial of David Low Dodge.* 1854.

———. *War Inconsistent with the Religion of Jesus Christ.* 1905. (First published in 1815.)

FRANKLIN, BENJAMIN. "On War and Peace," *Old South Leaflets*, Vol. VII, No. 162 (1905).

GALPIN, WILLIAM FREEMAN. *Pioneering for Peace; a Study of American Peace Efforts to 1846.* 1933.

HIRST, MARGARET E. *The Quakers in Peace and War; an Account of Their Peace Principles and Practice.* 1923.

LIVERMORE, ABIEL ABBOTT. *The War with Mexico Reviewed.* 1850.

MASSACHUSETTS PEACE SOCIETY. "A Circular Letter, 1816," *American Historical Pamphlets*, Vol. 5, No. 11.

MORITZEN, JULIUS. *The Peace Movement in America.* 1912.

SULLIVAN, GEORGE. *Speech at a Meeting of the Friends of Peace in 1812, Containing also a Memorial Signed by Daniel Webster, George Sullivan and Others Protesting against the Foreign Policy of the United States since 1807.*

CHAPTER 16. THE RIGHTS OF WOMEN

[1] Quoted in E. C. Stanton, S. B. Anthony, and M. J. Gage, *The History of Woman Suffrage* (6 vols., 1881–1922), I:32.

[2] Quoted in Ida Husted Harper, *Life and Work of Susan B. Anthony* (3 vols., 1898–1908), I:185–86.

[3] Hall, *Travels in North America*, II:153.

[4] Martineau, *Society in America*, II:125.

[5] Quoted from the *Free Enquirer* in William R. Waterman, *Frances Wright* (1924), p. 157.

[6] Quoted in Augusta G. Violette, *Economic Feminism in American Literature Prior to 1848* (1925), p. 54.

[7] Margaret Fuller Ossoli, *Woman in the Nineteenth Century, and Kindred Papers Relating to the Sphere, Conditions and Duties of Woman* (1855), p. 38.

[8] Quoted in *The History of Woman Suffrage*, I:514.

[9] Quoted in full *ibid.*, I:260–61.

[10] Alice Stone Blackwell, *Lucy Stone, Pioneer of Women's Rights* (1930), p. 161.

[11] Quoted in Pattee, *Feminine Fifties*, p. 104.

[12] Jane Grey Swisshelm, *Half a Century* (3rd ed., 1880), p. 49.

[13] *Ibid.*, p. 114.

[14] Theodore Stanton and Harriot Stanton Blatch, *Elizabeth Cady Stanton as Revealed in Her Letters, Diary and Reminiscences* (2 vols., 1922), I:170.

[15] Quoted from the *Carpet Bag* for 1851 in Alma Lutz, *Created Equal: A Biography of Elizabeth Cady Stanton, 1815–1902* (1940), pp. 65–66.

[16] Barnes and Dumond, *The Weld-Grimké Letters*, I:427. See I:452ff, for another long letter urging the sisters to avoid the question of women's rights and concentrate on the slavery issue.

[17] Written by the Rev. Nehemiah Adams, author of *The South-side View of Slavery*, and quoted in *The History of Woman Suffrage*, I:81.

[18] Both poems are quoted in full *ibid.*, I:82–86.

[19] A full account of the proceedings may be found *ibid.*, I:53ff; in Anna Davis Hallowell, *James and Lucretia Mott, Life and Letters* (1884), pp. 140ff; and in Stanton and Blatch, *Elizabeth Cady Stanton*, I:69ff.

[20] *The History of Woman Suffrage*, I:495.

[21] Quoted *ibid.*, p. 125.

[22] Quoted in Barnes and Dumond, *The Weld-Grimké Letters*, II:920.

[23] *The History of Woman Suffrage*, I:67.

[24] Quoted in full in *The History of Woman Suffrage*, I:368ff. The fragment quoted is from p. 372.

[25] Quoted from Matilda J. Gage's report of the convention in *The History of Woman Suffrage*, I:116. Arthur H. Fauset, *Sojourner Truth, God's Faithful Pilgrim* (1938), gives an account of the Negress' long and interesting life.

[26] Quoted in Rheta Childe Dorr, *Susan B. Anthony, the Woman Who Changed the Mind of a Nation* (1928), p. 140.

[27] *Harper's New Monthly Magazine*, November 1853, pp. 838ff.

[28] *Southern Literary Messenger*, July–August 1862.

[29] Stanton and Blatch, *Elizabeth Cady Stanton*, I:156.

SEE ALSO:

ARMSTRONG, MARGARET NEILSON. *Fanny Kemble, A Passionate Victorian.* 1938.

BEECHER, CATHERINE ESTHER. *The Evils Suffered by American Women and American*

Children: the Causes and the Remedy. Also An Address to the Protestant Clergy of the United States. 1846.

BLATCH, HARRIOT STANTON, and ALMA LUTZ. *Challenging Years: the Memoirs of Harriot Stanton Blatch.* 1940.

BRADFORD, GAMALIEL. *Portraits of American Women.* 1919.

BRANCH, E. DOUGLAS. "The *Lily* and the Bloomer," *Colophon*, Part XII, 1932.

FURNESS, CLIFTON JOSEPH, ed. *The Genteel Female; an Anthology.* 1931.

GOODSELL, WILLYSTIME. *Pioneers of Women's Education in the United States: Emma Willard, Catherine Beecher, Mary Lyon.* 1931.

GREENBIE, MARJORIE BARSTOW. *My Dear Lady; The Story of Anna Ella Carroll, the "Great Unrecognized Member of Lincoln's Cabinet."* 1940.

HAIGHT, GORDON S. *Mrs. Sigourney, the Sweet Singer of Hartford.* 1930.

HARE, LLOYD C. M. *The Greatest American Woman, Lucretia Mott.* 1937.

HECKER, EUGENE A. *A Short History of Woman's Rights from the Days of Augustus to the Present Time.* 1910.

JACKSON, GEORGE STUYVESANT. *Uncommon Scold, The Story of Anne Royall.* 1937.

OSTROGORSKII, MOISEI I. *The Rights of Woman; a Comparative Study in History and Legislation.* 1893.

PERKINS, A. J. G., and THERESA WOLFSON. *Frances Wright: Free Enquirer.* 1939.

SIGOURNEY, LYDIA HOWARD HUNTLEY. *Poems.* 1827.

SQUIRE, BELLE. *The Woman Movement in America.* 1911.

SWISSHELM, JANE GREY. *Crusader and Feminist; Letters of Jane Grey Swisshelm, 1858–1865.* Arthur Larsen, ed. 1934.

WRIGHT, RICHARDSON L. *Forgotten Ladies.* 1928.

CHAPTER 17. LIKE A FIRE-BELL IN THE NIGHT

[1] Quoted in Brookes, *Friend Anthony Benezet*, p. 78.

[2] Quoted in Whitney, *John Woolman, American Quaker*, pp. 188–89.

[3] *A Serious Address to the Rulers of America, on the Inconsistency of Their Conduct Respecting Slavery* (1783), p. 14.

[4] Quoted in Clement Eaton, *Freedom of Thought in the Old South* (1940), p. 19.

[5] Quoted in William Sumner Jenkins, *Pro-Slavery Thought in the Old South* (1935), p. 54.

[6] *Annals of Congress*, 1st Cong., 2nd Sess., p. 1200.

[7] *Ibid.*, p. 1198.

[8] One of the best of recent books on Southern society is William Joseph Cash, *The Mind of the South* (1941). Other useful analyses of the mentality and social background of the Old South include Benjamin Burks Kendrick and Alex Mathews Arnett, *The South Looks at Its Past* (1935); Francis Pendleton Gaines, *The Southern Plantation, A Study in the Development and Accuracy of a Tradition* (1925); Eaton, *Freedom of Thought in the Old South;* and Virginius Dabney, *Liberalism in the South* (1932).

[9] Cash, *Mind of the South*, p. 60.

[10] John Taylor, *Construction Construed and Constitution Vindicated* (1820), p. 314.

[11] Quoted in Jenkins, *Pro-Slavery Thought in the Old South*, p. 69.

[12] *The Diary of John Quincy Adams*, pp. 231–32.

[13] Quoted in Jenkins, *Pro-Slavery Thought in the Old South*, p. 73.

[14] Quoted in Malone, *The Public Life of Thomas Cooper*, p. 287.

[15] Quoted from *The Crisis*, p. 132, in U. B. Phillips, *The Course of the South to Secession* (1939), p. 104.

[16] Quoted in Jenkins, *Pro-Slavery Thought in the Old South*, pp. 76–77.

[17] Dwight L. Dumond, *Antislavery Origins of the Civil War in the United States* (1939), p. 8, says that this migration "deprived the South of men and women whose combined intelligence, moral courage, and Christian benevolence would have gone

far toward modifying the harsher features of slavery, toward preventing so great a unanimity of opinion in that section in support of slavery as a positive good, and toward keeping alive the spirit of free discussion."

[18] Quoted in Lewis Tappan, *Life of Arthur Tappan* (1870), p. 135.

[19] The figures for the transportation of freedmen are from Early Lee Fox, *The American Colonization Society, 1817–1840* (1919), p. 211.

[20] Quoted in Alice Adams, *The Neglected Period of Anti-Slavery in America, 1808–1831* (1908), p. 19.

[21] Quoted from the *African Repository* for 1839 in Fox, *American Colonization Society*, p. 29.

[22] Quoted in Theodore Davenport Bacon, *Leonard Bacon, a Statesman in the Church* (1931), p. 182.

[23] This correspondence is in Dwight L. Dumond, ed., *Letters of James Gillespie Birney, 1831–1857* (2 vols., 1938), I:59–100. The quotation is from p. 82.

[24] *The Life, Travels and Opinions of Benjamin Lundy . . . Compiled under the Direction and on Behalf of His Children* (1847), p. 213.

[25] Garrison and the founding of the *Liberator* are fully dealt with in the biography by his sons, Vol. I, Chap. 8. The first issue of the *Liberator* has been reprinted in *Old South Leaflets*, Vol. IV, No. 78.

[26] Quoted in Herbert Aptheker, *Negro Slave Revolts in the United States, 1526–1860* (1939), p. 30. Aptheker lists about 120 authenticated revolts, some seventy-five of them after the Revolution.

[27] Thomas R. Dew, *Review of the Debate in the Virginia Legislature of 1831 and 1832*, published in 1832 but best available in *The Pro-Slavery Argument: as Maintained by the Most Distinguished Writers of the Southern States, Containing the Several Essays on the Subject of Chancellor William Harper, Governor Hammond, Dr. Simms, and Professor Dew* (1852).

[28] William E. B. Du Bois, *Black Reconstruction, 1860–1880* (1935), p. 13.

[29] Charles Grandison Finney, *Lectures on Revivals of Religion* (1835), p. 375.

[30] Gilbert Barnes, *The Antislavery Impulses, 1830–1844* (1933), contains the most complete account of Weld and his activities. Barnes has rescued Weld from the comparative obscurity to which his own hatred of publicity consigned him and has given him a place far ahead of Garrison's in the abolition movement.

[31] Quoted in Albert Mordell, *Quaker Militant, John Greenleaf Whittier* (1933), p. 67.

[32] Lydia Maria Child, *An Appeal in Favor of That Class of Americans Called Africans* (1833), p. 222.

[33] W. E. Channing, *Slavery* (1835), p. 107. Also in Channing, *Works*, II:5–155.

[34] William Jay, *Slavery in America, an Inquiry into the Character and Tendency of the American Colonization and American Anti-Slavery Societies* (1835), introduction by S. H. Cox, p. xvi.

[35] Barnes and Dumond, *The Weld-Grimké Letters*, I:295ff.

[36] *Ibid.*, p. 341.

[37] 1886 edition, p. 223. The first edition was published in 1851.

[38] Greeley, *Recollections*, p. 285.

[39] *Dr. Daniel Drake's Letters on Slavery to Dr. John C. Warren of Boston* (1940), reprinted from the Washington *National Intelligencer* of April 3, 5, and 7, 1851.

[40] *Letters of James Russell Lowell*, I:158.

[41] Quoted in Bayard Tuckerman, *William Jay and the Constitutional Movement for the Abolition of Slavery* (1893), p. 74.

[42] Dumond, *The Birney Letters*, I:243.

[43] F. J. and W. P. Garrison, *Life of William Lloyd Garrison*, II:28.

[44] Quoted in Edward Beecher, *Narrative of the Riots at Alton; in Connection with the Death of Rev. Elijah P. Lovejoy* (1838), pp. 88–90. This book is an excellent source from the abolition viewpoint, for Beecher was in Alton working with Love-

joy up to the last hours before the riot. Joseph and Owen Lovejoy, brothers of the martyr, published in 1838 *A Memoir of the Rev. Elijah P. Lovejoy; Who Was Murdered in Defence of the Liberty of the Press, at Alton, Illinois, Nov. 7, 1837, with an introduction by John Quincy Adams.* This contains not only the biography but newspaper comment, letters, and sermons of the period.

[45] Quoted in Don C. Seitz, *Horace Greeley* (1926), p. 137.

[46] Wendell Phillips' speech may be found in *Old South Leaflets*, Vol. IV, No. 79.

[47] Quoted in Bernard Steiner, *Slavery in Connecticut* (1893), p. 52. See also F. J. and W. P. Garrison, *Life of William Lloyd Garrison*, Vol. I, Chap. 10.

[48] Morse, *A Neglected Period in Connecticut's History, 1818–1850*, p. 195.

[49] Quoted in William Birney, *James G. Birney and His Times* (1890), p. 188.

[50] See William S. Savage, *The Controversy Over the Distribution of Abolition Literature, 1830–1850* (1938), and Clement Eaton, "Censorship of the Southern Mails," *American Historical Review*, XLVIII:266–80 (January 1943).

[51] *Diary of John Quincy Adams*, pp. 537–38.

[52] Tuckerman, *William Jay*, p. 80.

[53] *Writings of Cassius Marcellus Clay* (1848), p. 129.

SEE ALSO the additional bibliography for Chapter 18.

CHAPTER 18. A HOUSE DIVIDED

[1] Quoted in Dumond, *Antislavery Origins of the Civil War*, p. 51.

[2] Quoted in Hilary Herbert, *Abolition Crusade and Its Consequences* (1912), p. 43.

[3] Quoted from the Augusta, Georgia, *Chronicle* in Jay, *Slavery in America*, p. 78.

[4] Quoted at length in Marryat, *Diary in America*, III:82ff. Cooper's toast is quoted in Malone, *The Public Life of Thomas Cooper*, p. 336.

[5] Quoted in Jay, *Slavery in America*, pp. 77–78.

[6] George Fitzhugh, *Sociology for the South, or the Failure of Free Society* (1854), p. 45.

[7] Quoted in Jenkins, *Pro-Slavery Thought in the Old South*, p. 303.

[8] "Manufacturing in South Carolina," *De Bow's Review*, January 1850, p. 25.

[9] Harper's "Memoir on Slavery," as well as the proslavery opinions of Hammond, Dew, and Simms, may be found in *The Pro-Slavery Argument: as Maintained by the Most Distinguished Writers of the Southern States* (1852). Other essays were published by E. N. Elliott under the title *Cotton Is King, and Pro-Slavery Arguments; Comprising the Writings of Hammond, Harper, Christy, Stringfellow, Hodge, Bledsoe, and Cartwright, on this Important Subject* (1860).

[10] Quoted in Jenkins, *Pro-Slavery Thought in the Old South*, p. 95.

[11] From a letter from Governor Hammond to Lewis Tappan in 1843, *ibid.*, p. 112.

[12] Quoted in Post, *Popular Freethought in America*, pp. 208–9.

[13] Quoted in Eaton, *Freedom of Thought in the Old South*, p. 165.

[14] Buckingham, *The Slave States*, I:55.

[15] Quoted in Eaton, *Freedom of Thought in the Old South*, p. 205.

[16] Bremer, *Homes of the New World*, II:528.

[17] For a discussion of pre-Civil War fiction in the South see Jeannette Reid Tandy, "Pro-Slavery Propaganda in American Fiction in the 1850's," *South Atlantic Quarterly*, January–March 1922.

[18] Quoted in William P. Trent, *William Gilmore Simms* (1892), p. 174.

[19] Quoted in Harvey Wish, *George Fitzhugh, Conservative of the Old South* (1938), p. 15.

[20] The classic and indispensable work on the fugitive slave is Wilbur H. Siebert, *The Underground Railroad from Slavery to Freedom* (1898). Siebert gathered his material while it was still possible to talk with many who had been connected with the Underground Railroad.

[21] See Lydia M. Child, *Isaac T. Hopper: A True Life* (1853).

[22] Quoted in Siebert, *Underground Railroad*, p. 110.

[23] *Ibid.*, p. 90.

[24] *The Reminiscences of Levi Coffin, the Reputed President of the Underground Railroad, Being a Brief History of the Labors of a Lifetime in Behalf of the Slave* . . . (1876), pp. 430ff.

[25] The material on John Brown is extensive. F. B. Sanborn, *The Life and Letters of John Brown* (1855), is the account of a friend who participated in all the preliminary stages of the Harpers Ferry raid. Oswald Garrison Villard, *John Brown, 1800–1859* (1910), is a more recent biography of almost equal interest.

[26] Benjamin Drew, *A North-Side View of Slavery; The Refugee; or, the Narrative of Fugitive Slaves in Canada, Related by Themselves* (1856), pp. 29, 33, and 43.

[27] *Truth Stranger than Fiction: Father Henson's Story of His Own Life* (1858), pp. 149ff.

[28] Sarah H. Bradford, *Scenes in the Life of Harriet Tubman, The Moses of Her People* (1886), pp. 26, 27, and 34.

[29] See Siebert, *Underground Railroad*, Chap. 11, for all estimates.

[30] Pierce, *Memoir and Letters of Charles Sumner*, III:296.

[31] Quoted in Siebert, *Underground Railroad*, p. 105.

[32] George Julian, *Life of Joshua R. Giddings* (1892), p. 415ff.

[33] Austin Bearse, *Reminiscences of Fugitive-Slave Days in Boston* (1880), lists the entire committee. Bearse was a Yankee captain whose vessel was often used to carry fugitives to safety.

[34] See Higginson, *Cheerful Yesterdays*, pp. 124ff, for an interesting account of the committee's activities.

[35] Parker's part in this and other rescues is told in Commager, *Theodore Parker*, Chap. 11.

[36] Marion G. McDougall, *Fugitive Slaves, 1619–1865* (1891), Chap. 3, is a compendium of cases of fugitives taken under the law of 1850. The *New England Magazine* for May, June, and July 1890, contains articles by Nina Moore Tiffany on the Shadrach, Simms, and Burns cases.

[37] Emerson, *Works*, XI:185.

[38] Thoreau, *Works*, X:179.

[39] Higginson, *Cheerful Yesterdays*, p. 220.

[40] F. B. Sanborn, *Recollections of Seventy Years* (2 vols., 1909), I:221.

[41] Harlow, *Gerrit Smith*, pp. 336ff.

[42] Emerson, *Works*, XI:280.

[43] Thoreau, *Works*, X:232–34.

[44] Laura A. White, *Robert Barnwell Rhett, Father of Secession* (1931), p. 27.

[45] The title of an excellent work by U. B. Phillips, published posthumously in 1939.

[46] George Tucker, "Discourse on the Progress of Philosophy . . ." *Southern Literary Messenger*, April 1835, p. 415.

[47] *De Bow's Review*, May 1847, p. 421.

[48] Calkins, *They Broke the Prairie*, p. 274.

[49] This is a term used by Frank Owsley in "The Fundamental Cause of the Civil War: Egocentric Sectionalism," *Journal of Southern History*, VII:3 (February 1941). In a book entitled *I'll Take My Stand* (1930), to which twelve Southerners contributed, Owsley developed the same thesis (pp. 61ff).

[50] See Bancroft, *Life of William Henry Seward*, Vol. I, Chap. 21, for an account of Seward's part in the period just before the war.

SEE ALSO:

ABEL, ANNIE HELOISE, and FRANK J. KLINGBERG, eds. *A Side-Light on Anglo-Ameri-*

can Relations, 1839–1858, furnished by the Correspondence of Lewis Tappan and Others with the British and Foreign Anti-Slavery Society. 1927.

ABERNETHY, THOMAS PERKINS. "Democracy and the Southern Frontier," *Journal of Southern History,* IV:3 (February 1938).

————. *From Frontier to Plantationism in Tennessee; a Study in Frontier Democracy.* 1932.

————. *Three Virginia Frontiers.* 1940.

An Account of the Imprisonment and Sufferings of Robert Fuller, of Cambridge. 1833.

ADAMS, NEHEMIAH. *A South-side View of Slavery.* 4th ed. 1860. (First published in 1854.)

American and Foreign Anti-Slavery Society, an Address to the Anti-Slavery Christians of the United States. Probably 1852.

The American Anti-Slavery Almanac for 1838. N. Southard, ed.

The Anti-Slavery Alphabet. 1847.

The Anti-Slavery History of the John Brown Year; being the Twenty-seventh Annual Report of the American Anti-Slavery Society. 1861.

BALLAGH, JAMES CURTIS. *A History of Slavery in Virginia.* 1902.

BANCROFT, FREDERIC. *Slave-trading in the Old South.* 1931.

BASSETT, JOHN SPENCER. *Slavery in the State of North Carolina.* 1899.

————. *The Southern Plantation Overseer as Revealed in His Letters.* 1925.

BIRNEY, JAMES G. *The American Churches the Bulwarks of American Slavery.* 3rd ed. 1885.

————. *A Collection of Valuable Documents, being Birney's Vindication of Abolitionists . . .* 1836.

BOURNE, GEORGE. *The Book and Slavery Irreconcilable.* 1816.

BREWTON, WILLIAM W. *The Son of Thunder; an Epic of the South.* 1936.

BROWN, WILLIAM W. *A Lecture Delivered Before the Female Anti-Slavery Society of Salem, at Lyceum Hall, Nov. 14, 1847.* 1847.

BUCKMASTER, HENRIETTA. *Let My People Go; The Story of the Underground Railroad and the Growth of the Abolition Movement.* 1941.

CALHOUN, JOHN C. *The Works of John C. Calhoun.* Richard K. Crallé, ed. 6 vols. 1854–57.

CARPENTER, JESSE T. *The South as a Conscious Minority, 1789–1861.* 1930.

CARR, CLARK E. *The Illini, A Story of the Prairies.* 1904.

CARROLL, JOSEPH CEPHAS. *Slave Insurrections in the United States, 1800–1865.* 1938.

CARSEL, WILFRED. "The Slave-holders' Indictment of Northern Wage Slavery," *Journal of Southern History,* VI:504 (November 1940).

CARUTHERS, WILLIAM ALEXANDER. *The Cavaliers of Virginia, or, the Recluse of Jamestown.* 2 vols. 1834–35.

————. *The Kentuckian In New York. Or the Adventures of Three Southerns.* 2 vols. 1834.

CATTERALL, HELEN TUNNICLIFF. *Judicial Cases Concerning American Slavery and the Negro.* 5 vols. 1926.

CHAMBERS, W. *American Slavery and Colour.* 1857.

CHANNING, WILLIAM ELLERY. *Remarks on the Slavery Question in a Letter to Jonathan Phillips Esq.* 1839.

CHILD, LYDIA MARIA. *Anti-Slavery Catechism.* 2nd ed. 1839.

————. *The Evils of Slavery, and the Cure of Slavery, The First Proved by the Opinions of Slaves Themselves, the Last Shown by Historical Evolution.* 1836.

————, ed. *The Patriarchal Institution, as Described by Members of Its Own Family.* 1860.

————. *The Right Way the Safe Way, Proved by Emancipation in the British West Indies, and Elsewhere.* 1862.

CLARKE, JAMES FREEMAN. *Anti-Slavery Days; a Sketch of the Struggle Which Ended in the Abolition of Slavery in the United States.* 1884.

COLE, ARTHUR C. *The Irrepressible Conflict, 1850–1865.* 1934.

CONWAY, MONCURE DANIEL. *Autobiography, Memories and Experiences.* 2 vols. 1904.

COOPER, THOMAS. *Negro Slavery; or, A View of Some of the More Prominent Features of That State of Society, as It Exists in the United States of America and the Colonies of the West Indies, Especially in Jamaica.* 4th ed. 1824.

COULTER, ELLIS MERTON. *Thomas Spalding of Sapelo.* 1940.

CRAVEN, AVERY O. "The Agricultural Reformers of the Ante-Bellum South," *American Historical Review,* January 1928.

————. *The Coming of the Civil War.* 1942.

————. "Coming of the War between the States: An Interpretation," *Journal of Southern History,* II:303 (August 1936).

————. *Edmund Ruffin, Southerner; a Study in Secession.* 1932.

————. *The Repressible Conflict, 1830–1861.* 1939.

————. "The 'Turner Theories' and the South," *Journal of Southern History,* V:291 (August 1939).

DAVIES, EBENEZER. *American Scenes and Christian Slavery; a Recent Tour of Four Thousand Miles in the United States.* 1849.

DODD, WILLIAM E. "The Fight for the North West, 1860," *American Historical Review,* XVI:774–88 (July 1911).

————. "The Social Philosophy of the Old South," *American Journal of Sociology,* 23:735 (May 1918).

————. *Statesman of the Old South; or, From Radicalism to Conservative Revolt.* 1911.

DOUGLASS, FREDERICK. *Life and Times of Frederick Douglass, Written by Himself: His Early Life as a Slave, His Escape from Bondage, and His Complete History to the Present Time.* Rev. ed. 1895.

EATON, CLEMENT. "A Dangerous Pamphlet in the Old South," *Journal of Southern History,* II:323 (August 1936).

————. "Henry Wise, a Liberal of the Old South," *Journal of Southern History,* VII:482 (November 1941).

FAUSET, ARTHUR HUFF. *Sojourner Truth, God's Faithful Pilgrim.* 1938.

FINNEY, CHARLES GRANDISON. *Memoirs of Rev. Charles Grandison Finney.* 1876.

FITZHUGH, GEORGE. *Cannibals All! Or, Slaves Without Masters.* 1857.

FRIENDS, SOCIETY OF. *An Exposition of the African Slave Trade from the Year 1840 to 1850.* 1851.

FROTHINGHAM, OCTAVIUS BROOKS. *Gerrit Smith; a Biography.* 1878.

GIDDINGS, JOSHUA R. *Speeches in Congress.* 1853.

GRAY, LEWIS CECIL. *History of Agriculture in the Southern United States to 1860.* 2 vols. 1933.

GRAYSON, WILLIAM J. *The Hireling and the Slave, Chicora and Other Poems.* 1856.

GREELEY, HORACE. *The American Conflict: A History of the Great Rebellion in the United States of America, 1860–1864.* 2 vols. 1865–66.

GRIMKÉ, ARCHIBALD H. *William Lloyd Garrison, the Abolitionist.* 1891.

HARRISON, JESSE BURTON. *Review of the Slavery Question . . . By a Virginian.* 1833.

HEARON, CLEO CARSON. *Mississippi and the Compromise of 1850.* 1913.

HELDEMAN, L. C. "A Social Scientist of the Old South," *Journal of Southern History,* II:148 (May 1936).

HELPER, HINTON R. *The Impending Crisis of the South: How to Meet It.* 1857.

HENSON, JOSIAH. *Life of Josiah Henson, Formerly a Slave, Now an Inhabitant of Canada, as Narrated by Himself.* 1849.

HEYRICH, MRS. ELIZABETH (COLTMAN). *Immediate, Not Gradual Abolition, or, An Inquiry into the Shortest, Safest, and Most Effectual Means of Getting Rid of West Indian Slavery.* 1838.

HOPKINS, JOHN HENRY. *The American Citizen: His Rights and Duties, According to the Spirit of the Constitution of the United States.* 1857.

————. *A Scriptural, Ecclesiastical, and Historical View of Slavery . . .* 1864.

HUME, JOHN F. *The Abolitionists; together with Personal Memories of the Struggle for Human Rights, 1830–1864.* 1905.

HUNT, GAILLARD. *John C. Calhoun.* 1908.

JAMES, HENRY FIELD. *Abolitionism Unveiled; or, Its Origin, Progress, and Pernicious Tendency Fully Developed.* 1856.

JAY, WILLIAM. *Miscellaneous Writings on Slavery.* 1853.

JULIAN, GEORGE W. *Political Recollections, 1840–1872.* 1884.

KEMBLE, FRANCES ANNE. *Journal of a Residence on a Georgia Plantation in 1838–1839.* 1863.

LAURENS, J. WAYNE. *The Crisis; or, the Enemies of America Unmasked.* 1855.

LEFLER, HUGH TALMAGE. *Hinton Rowan Helper, Advocate of "White America."* 1935.

The Liberty Bell. Maria Weston Chapman, ed. 1839–46.

LLOYD, ARTHUR YOUNG. *The Slavery Controversy, 1831–1860.* 1939.

MARTIN, ASA E. *The Anti-Slavery Movement in Kentucky Prior to 1830.* 1918.

MELLEN, G. W. F. *An Argument on the Unconstitutionality of Slavery, Embracing an Abstract of the Proceedings of the National and State Committees on This Subject.* 1841.

MERRIAM, GEORGE S. *The Life and Times of Samuel Bowles.* 2 vols. 1885.

MILTON, GEORGE FORT. *The Eve of Conflict: Stephen A. Douglas and the Needless War.* 1934.

MITCHELL, BROADUS. *Frederick Law Olmsted, a Critic of the Old South.* 1924.

NORWOOD, JOHN N. *The Schism in the Methodist Episcopal Church, 1844: A Study of Slavery and Ecclesiastical Politics.* 1923.

OLMSTED, FREDERICK LAW. *The Cotton Kingdom.* 2 vols. 1861.

————. *A Journey in the Back Country in the Winter of 1853–1854.* 2 vols. 1907. (First published in 1860.)

————. *A Journey in the Seaboard Slave States.* 1858.

OWSLEY, FRANK L. and HARRIET C. "The Economic Basis of Society in the Late Ante-Bellum South," *Journal of Southern History,* VI:24 (February 1940).

PARKER, THEODORE. *Discourses on Slavery.* 2 vols. 1863. (Vols. V and VI in Parker, *Works*).

PENDLETON, LOUIS B. *Alexander H. Stephens.* 1908.

PHILLIPS, ULRICH BONNELL. *American Negro Slavery.* 1918.

————. *Life and Labor in the Old South.* 1929.

PILLSBURY, PARKER. *Acts of the Anti-Slavery Apostles.* 1883.

PUTNAM, MARY B. *The Baptists and Slavery, 1840–1845.* 1913.

RAINWATER, P. L. "Economic Benefits of Secession. Opinions in Mississippi in the 1850's," *Journal of Southern History,* I:459 (November 1935).

RANCK, JAMES BYRNE. *Albert Gallatin Brown, Radical Southern Nationalist.* 1937.

RANDALL, JAMES G. *The Civil War and Reconstruction.* 1937.

RANKIN, JOHN. *Letters on American Slavery, Addressed to Mr. Thomas Rankin, Merchant at Middlebrook, Augusta Co., Va.* 5th ed. 1838. (First published in 1826.)

REESE, DAVID MEREDITH. *Letters to the Hon. William Jay, being a Reply to His "Inquiry into the American Colonization and American Anti-Slavery Society."* 1835.

RUFFIN, EDMUND. *The Political Economy of Slavery.* 1857.

RUSSELL, ROBERT R. *Economic Aspects of Southern Sectionalism, 1840–1861.* 1924.

SEARS, LORENZO. *Wendell Phillips, Orator and Agitator.* 1909.

SEITZ, DON C. *Horace Greeley, Founder of the New York Tribune.* 1926.

SHRYOCK, RICHARD H. *Georgia and the Union in 1850.* 1926.

SMEDES, SUSAN DABNEY. *Memorials of a Southern Planter.* 1906. (First published in 1886.)

STEINER, BERNARD C. *History of Slavery in Connecticut.* 1893.

STEPHENSON, WENDELL HOLMES. *Isaac Franklin, Slave Trader and Planter of the Old South.* 1938.

STYRON, ARTHUR. *The Cast-Iron Man; John C. Calhoun and American Democracy.* 1935.

SUNDERLAND, LA ROY. *Anti-Slavery Manual, Containing a Collection of Facts and Arguments on American Slavery.* 1837.

SYDNOR, CHARLES S. *A Gentleman of the Old Natchez Region.* 1938.

————. *Slavery in Mississippi.* 1933.

————. "The Southerner and the Laws," *Journal of Southern History,* VI:3 (February 1940).

TAYLOR, JOHN. *The Arator.* 1813.

THOREAU, HENRY DAVID. *A Yankee in Canada, with Anti-Slavery and Reform Papers.* 1866.

The Views of Judge Woodward and Bishop Hopkins on Negro Slavery at the South, Illustrated for the Journal of Residence on a Georgian Plantation by Mrs. Frances Anne Kemble. 1863.

WALKER, DAVID. *Walker's Appeal, in Four Articles: Together with a Preamble to the Colored Citizens of the World, But in Particular, and Very Expressly to Those of the United States of America.* 1829.

WARREN, ROBERT PENN. *John Brown; The Making of a Martyr.* 1929.

WEEKS, STEPHEN B. *Southern Quakers and Slavery.* 1896.

WELD, THEODORE DWIGHT. *American Slavery as It Is: Testimony of a Thousand Witnesses.* 1839.

WHITFIELD, THEODORE M. *Slavery Agitation in Virginia, 1829–1832.* 1930.

WILSON, FORREST. *Crusader in Crinoline, Biography of Harriet Beecher Stowe.* 1941.

WOODSON, C. G. *Education of the Negro Prior to 1861.* 1919.

————. *The Mind of the Negro as Reflected in Letters Written during the Crisis, 1800–1860.* 1926.

Index